INFANTRY ACES

INFANTRY ACES

The German Soldier in Combat in World War II

Franz Kurowski

STACKPOLE
BOOKS
Guilford, Connecticut

Published by Stackpole Books
An imprint of The Rowman & Littlefield Publishing Group, Inc.
4501 Forbes Blvd., Ste. 200
Lanham, MD 20706
www.rowman.com

Distributed by NATIONAL BOOK NETWORK
800-462-6420

Stackpole Military History Series paperback published 2005 by Stackpole Books
First Stackpole Books standalone paperback edition published 2020

British Library Cataloguing in Publication Information available

Library of Congress Cataloging-in-Publication Data available

ISBN 978-0-8117-3926-9 (paperback)
ISBN 978-0-8117-6920-4 (e-book)

♾™ The paper used in this publication meets the minimum requirements of
American National Standard for Information Sciences—Permanence of Paper for
Printed Library Materials, ANSI/NISO Z39.48-1992.

Table of Contents

Introduction

This work is a collection of soldiers from the ranks who made a name for themselves in the Second World War. They performed deeds—either alone or with a number of comrades—which decided the outcome of a battle or performed other acts of bravery or leadership that lived up to the best of German military tradition. Although the term "aces" is usually reserved for fighter pilots, it seemed appropriate in this context to refer to these extraordinary soldiers as "aces" of their trade as well.

The stories of these few men, chosen from among thousands of others, are representative of their fellow soldiers and provide a fitting memorial to them. These men stand for all those who returned wounded and broken, ashamed and beaten, bringing the horror of their war experiences home with them. But these chapters are also a memorial to others: Those who came to grief in the vast steppes of Russia, in the ice storms of the Murmansk Front, in southeastern Russia, in Africa or in the final struggle for the Reich.

This is an authentic account of infantry aces, common soldiers who were tossed into the maelstrom of death that was combat and who rose to the occasion and frequently offered up their lives for their comrades. A kind fate allowed most of the soldiers in this book to return home. They survived a long odyssey of death and destruction that claimed so many friends and comrades. After a walk through hell and purgatory, there and back, there was for them a new day in Germany, something denied millions of other German soldiers.

They took on enemy units alone, battled the steel giants that were enemy tanks and carried wounded comrades hundreds of meters under fire to safety. They fought alone behind enemy lines. They took out bunkers and carried out patrols. They served as machine gunners in a thousand dangerous actions. They tackled an enemy vastly superior in numbers with antitank rifles, *Panzerfäuste* (the German poor-man's equivalent of the bazooka), hand grenades, machine guns and submachine guns. They closed gaps in the front, defended their own lines, held river crossings open for their own troops to retreat over and drove out enemy forces that had broken into their own main line of resistance.

Through their actions they saved the lives of many thousands of their comrades. They guarded the front and stood fast in hopeless situations against an enemy one hundred times as strong as they. In this way they felt the inhuman grimace of war on their own bodies and survived, bleeding from many wounds. Here is their story: A perpetual road of horror and desperation, a road filled with blood and tears, at whose end, if they were lucky, stood a return home. Their experience taught them that war leaves behind neither victors nor vanquished, only victims.

Infantry Aces is a cross-section from the world of the common soldier in wartime, in which cruelty and toughness, but also comradeship and willingness to help, became perpetual assets. They were cast into the world of combat and death, playthings of world events, and only rarely did they emerge unscathed. Often reviled and scorned, humiliated and derided, they gave years of their lives in the service of their country, without knowing that they were nothing more than playthings in the hands of the powerful. But this in no way diminishes their accomplishments. They fought, were victorious and, in the end, were defeated.

Rudi Brasche as an Unteroffizier with the Knight's Cross.

Rudi Brasche

"Mount up!"

Unteroffizier Laupert, squad leader of the regimental pioneer platoon's 1st Squad, came rushing out of the makeshift battalion command post and toward the truck around which his squad had gathered. Feldwebel Wegener, the platoon leader, followed him on foot. Behind him came the other two squad leaders. "What's up, Unteroffizier?" called Kneisel, leader of the first machine-gun team.

"We're leaving at once. The bridge at Homyly must be taken before it is blown by the enemy."

The four Opel Blitz trucks that were parked in a wood at the side of the road moved out moments later. They left the main road and rolled along a country road. Rudi Brasche hung on tightly as the truck pitched and rolled. The first houses appeared in front of the trucks. That had to be Homyly. Soon the first rounds were fired in their direction from the outskirts to the village. "Ready the machine guns. Polle and Gambietz take over the antiaircraft machine gun." Machine-gun bullets chewed pieces of wood and metal from the trucks. Soon they could hear the shots. Kneisel and Nehring, the two machine-gunners, ripped their machine guns from the racks and placed them on the side of the truck.

"Faster, Grothe!" The Opel Blitz leapt forward. The village houses rushed closer. Rudolf Brasche saw the first smoking tracer rounds streaking toward the leading truck. Then the first burst of fire whipped from the MG 34 mounted on the truck in front of them. The second machine gun joined in and then the tripod-mounted MG 15, which was actually intended for antiaircraft purposes, began to fire as well.

Seconds later the three machine guns in Brasche's truck opened fire. The noise of the three guns nearly deafened him. As Brasche watched, Ecklebe, the second member of the gun crew, loaded a fresh belt of ammunition. Then a burst of fire struck the truck. Heierberg cried out. He let his rifle drop and half fell on Märtens, the second member of Kneisel's gun crew. The truck veered hard to the right. A house flew past on the left. They were then safe from the enemy machine gun. The truck came to a small patch of woods and jerked to a stop.

1

"Get out and follow me!" shouted Unteroffizier Laupert.

Brasche grabbed the two ammunition boxes. He jumped down and ran after Nehring, the leader of his machine-gun team. They reached the woods together with the 2nd and 3rd Squads. Feldwebel Wegener appeared from the fourth truck. Holtsteger's squad followed with explosive charges.

"Move along here! This dirt road leads right to the bridge."

Breathing heavily, Brasche ran along behind his leader. They had gone no more than 400 meters when they came under fire from machine guns and fast-firing cannon from ahead and to the right. Glowing steel whipped toward the German soldiers. Brasche and the others hurried on, following their squad leader, who ran into a stand of tall ferns.

In front of Brasche, Nehring fell to the ground heavily. The machine gun flew through the air in a high arc and fell into the ferns. Cursing, Nehring got to his feet, shook himself off and kept going. The forest thinned out before them. Then they saw the bright band of the road, and finally, the bridge appeared in front of them.

Four figures were visible. First Squad fired at them on the run. Three of the men returned fire, while the fourth ran back across the bridge.

"Stop, stop! He's going to blow the bridge."

Two bursts were fired at the fourth French soldier. One caught him before he was halfway across the bridge and knocked the man face down.

"Move across the bridge and dig in on the other side!"

Rudolf Brasche felt himself getting short of breath, but he kept on running, always following his squad leader. They reached the approach to the bridge. Machine-gun fire whistled in from the far end of the span. Kneisel threw himself down in the middle of the bridge and opened fire with his machine gun. The enemy troops quickly turned their machine gun on Kneisel. But the Obergefreiter was quicker. His burst struck the enemy position before the French could open fire and silenced the machine gun.

"Platoon, across the bridge in one rush. Let's go!"

Feldwebel Wegener jumped to his feet. Noticing movement behind the main pillar, he opened fire with his submachine gun while on the run. Rifle shots cracked from the riverbank. A man running behind Brasche cried out and fell to the ground. Then they were on the other side, and the fear that the bridge might blow up under them at any moment vanished.

An enemy soldier appeared ten meters to one side of Laupert's squad. He raised his weapon, but Nehring was quicker, firing his machine gun on the run. The Germans threw themselves down into the cover of the French position. A pair of figures emerged from the bunker, their hands raised.

Shouts drifted over from the woods that flanked the far end of the bridge. Then two armored cars appeared and opened fire on the bridge with cannon and machine guns. Bullets bounced off the steel buttresses and whizzed off in all directions.

"Infantry behind the armored cars, Feldwebel!"

By running and dodging, Feldwebel Wegener safely reached the hole occupied by Laupert's squad. Out of breath, he let himself tumble in.

"Machine guns: Open fire on the infantry!" he ordered.

The two machine guns opened up simultaneously. The enemy infantry that had emerged from the woods quickly pulled back again. However, two of the seven armored cars then turned and rolled toward the squad's foxhole. The two vehicles turned their guns on the machine-gun position. For an instant Brasche saw a red-yellow lance of flame; it seemed to be heading straight for him. He pressed himself against the ground and heard the ringing impacts of bullets striking the steel of the bridge behind him.

"Pass a belt here, Rudi!"

Brasche roused himself and passed along a fresh belt of ammunition. Bullets clattered against the frontal steel of the armored cars. Nehring aimed somewhat higher. He saw the flash of the impacting bullets. All at once the enemy machine gun stopped firing. The armored car then turned its cannon on the German position. It was soon joined by the second vehicle. "Damn, what's Holtsteger's squad doing, Feldwebel?"

"They're on the other side. They should have put their antitank rifle to use long ago . . ." The voice of the Feldwebel was drowned out by a sharp crack.

"That was the antitank rifle."

They saw the armor-piercing round strike the lead armored car. Smoke began to curl into the air above the vehicle. The armored car's ammunition supply blew up and the crew bailed out. On the far side of the bridge the 20-mm cannon opened fire. The roar of machine guns and the crackle of rifle fire added to the din.

Richard Gambietz crawled forward to Feldwebel Wegener. Rudolf Brasche, whom everyone called Rudi, followed. Nehring and Ecklebe joined them. "Kneisel, you hold here and keep their heads down while we work our way along those blackberry bushes—understood? When we're in the woods shift your fire to the right so you don't hit us."

Kneisel fired, sweeping the edge of the treed area. Feldwebel Wegener left cover and crept as fast as he could to the left, where he disappeared into the bushes. Brasche followed along behind Gambietz. He saw Nehring appear beside the Feldwebel and then disappear again almost immediately.

Brasche felt his hands gripping the handles of the ammunition boxes. They were becoming wet with sweat. He was afraid, but he knew that he would have to overcome his fear to be effective. The pace quickened.

Brasche had to keep pace in case Nehring should need ammunition. Gambietz paused and turned toward Brasche. His young friend with the slightly pointed face tried to smile but only managed a grimace. Brasche caught up with him and moments later they joined Nehring. Just then they heard the roar of an engine and the pointed nose of a French armored car pushed its way through the thicket. They all saw the machine gun and the 20-mm cannon.

Feldwebel Wegener signaled silently. He raised one of the four hand grenades he had stuck in his belt. Gambietz nudged Rudi Brasche and pulled out a grenade. Brasche put down the two ammunition boxes. He screwed off the metal caps of two hand grenades and crouched lower in the shadows of the bushes as the armored car rolled directly toward him.

The vehicle came nearer and nearer. Then Brasche spotted movement behind it: Enemy infantry trying to approach the bridge from the flank under the protection of the armored car. The French vehicle was then 30 meters away. Glancing to the side, Brasche saw that Nehring had aimed his machine gun at the enemy troops.

"Go!" shouted the Feldwebel. Rudi Brasche jumped up and threw one of the grenades. Gambietz and the Feldwebel did likewise. The enemy was already firing back when the grenades fell on the armored car. Nehring opened fire with his machine gun. The three hand grenades exploded. Brasche jumped to his feet. A bullet whizzed past his head. Behind him Nehring's machine gun roared again. Three figures appeared in front of him. He ripped the porcelain knob from the grenade and tossed it toward the group of three. At the same time he threw himself headfirst to the ground. Brasche landed hard on a stump. The burst of fire meant for him passed overhead. The blast from the hand grenade silenced the three enemy soldiers.

On the other side, Feldwebel Wegener reached the enemy armored car and threw two hand grenades inside. Gambietz overcame a second group of enemy troops. Then it was quiet, except for the sound of breaking branches as the enemy fled through the woods. There was a fresh outburst of firing to the right and then from the far side of the bridge, where a squad had been left behind.

"Back to the bridge!" the Feldwebel ordered. They hurried back, running at a crouch. They reached the foxholes and jumped inside. His lungs pumping hard, Rudi Brasche lay still for a few moments beside the machine gun. Nehring had already moved it into position again. Slowly his cramped body relaxed. He raised his head. Gambietz nudged him and Brasche turned towards him.

"Rudi, you were scared shitless, weren't you?"

"You can say that again!" Brasche wiped the back of his hand across his forehead, which was soaked in sweat. For three hours the small group of German soldiers held the bridge against repeated French attacks. The enemy was trying to reach the explosive charges, but they had already been rendered useless. Three armored cars made another attempt to reach the bridge but were forced to turn away. Then Oberstleutnant Radwan, the commander of the 2nd Battalion of the 93rd Infantry Regiment, arrived at the head of the relief forces. He was the first to roll across the bridge and into the enemy. As had often been the case before, this bold move succeeded, and the area in front of the bridge was swept clear. They had captured the Seine River crossing undamaged. The road lay open before them.

On 19 July 1940 Oberstleutnant Oskar Radwan was awarded the Knight's Cross in recognition of the conscientious and exemplary manner in which he had led his battalion and demonstrated his own personal bravery.

Standing beside his friend Richard Gambietz, Rudi Brasche received the Iron Cross, Second Class. Neither could know that they would both later be awarded the Knight's Cross.

THE RUSSIAN FRONT

"Looks suspicious to me, Rudi. I wouldn't be surprised if we get caught here east of the Mius after our eighty-kilometer retreat."

Richard Gambietz pointed to the wall of the brickworks, beside which Kumm's company had dug in. The remaining companies of 93rd Infantry Regiment were strung out to the east, where an extended low ridge stretched toward the east, forming the southern boundary of the Kamyenka Valley.

"But if Ivan attacks, he'll have to climb the ridge first, and that will give us a chance to stop him. What do you think, Wilhelm?"

The man in question and his two companions only grunted. "Some answer," grinned Brasche.

"Pioneer platoon leader: Report to the battalion!"

Feldwebel Wegener got up and walked back in the direction of Pokrovskoye, where the battalion command post had been set up behind the ridge.

"They're cooking something up, Rudi."

"About time. We've marched back eighty kilometers. It's damned cold and this brickworks would be the ideal spot to spend the winter."

"We could light the kiln," enjoined Wilhelm Grunge.

"If we had something to burn."

"We'll look for something. Want to bet there's fuel hidden in those buildings?"

The pioneer platoon had taken up position at the edge of the brickworks. The cable squad was already in the administrator's house at the south end. The thermometer was showing minus 22 degrees Celsius.

"Hopefully, Wegener will come back soon, Heinz."

Unteroffizier Laupert, the squad leader, came over to the men. He squatted in the corner between the low brick wall and the carefully layered pile of unbaked bricks, which had been laid out to dry the summer before.

"He should be back any minute, I imagine. Has anyone still got a little something to warm the stomach?"

"Here, Heinz. Left over from the whore houses of Rostov."

Märtens passed his canteen. The Unteroffizier gave it a shake. "Great . . . it's not even frozen." He unscrewed the cap and took a small swig, then he passed back the canteen.

"The Feldwebel's coming!"

Feldwebel Wegener walked along the footpath that ran through the snow like a dark line.

"He's got the company headquarters squad with him. Something's up."

"Squad leaders: Report to me!"

The three noncommissioned officers hurried over to the Feldwebel, who had squatted in the shelter of the wall among the men of Laupert's squad.

"Listen up. We're to check out the limekiln and see if it's suitable as a flanking position. If it is, then our line will run along the Mius to the left. From the limekiln the line would run precisely due east along the ridge. Ivan will attack from the direction of Kryekaya, or from the northeast." Feldwebel Wegener returned to his men and gave them their instructions. Holtsteger's squad stayed behind to clear a path to the rear, should it become necessary, while the remaining squads moved into the brickworks.

"Careful, Rudi. There's a house behind the shed."

Rudi Brasche pressed on, his machine gun at the ready at his hip. Gambietz stayed close beside him, while Grunge followed with the two ammunition boxes. Twilight had fallen on this first day of December 1941. The men could see nothing but the sharp outlines of the buildings, the kiln and the extended drying shed, which were silhouetted against the lighter background of the sky.

Here, where the roof had kept out the snow, they made good progress. Pieces of brick and red brick dust crunched beneath Brasche's boots.

Something stirred to his right, and he froze as if rooted to the spot. He suddenly felt his heart in his throat. Cautiously he raised his weapon. Gambietz and Grunge had frozen as well. Then a small shadow leapt out of the shadows and disappeared meowing in the direction of the huge circular kiln.

"Where there are cats, there are people, Heinz."

Unteroffizier Laupert nodded. He thought that it might be the Russians who had withdrawn toward the north in front of them the day before when they had crossed the road to Pokrovskoye.

"Follow me!" he whispered. He then crept onward. For a fraction of a second, Brasche saw his shadow cast against the wall by the falling moonlight. He walked around a pile of bricks and saw the circular kiln at the end of the roofed hall. He saw something else as well, something which caused him to freeze as if rooted to the spot. He slowly dropped to the floor.

He crawled backward a meter to reach the cover of the pile of bricks. Then he placed his machine gun on its bipod to make it more stabile. His companions joined him. They all pressed together behind the pile of bricks. Kneisel positioned himself on the other side of the pile with the second machine gun.

Obergefreiter Brasche saw a pair of figures in the typical padded jackets worn by the Russians. One of the figures lit a match and in its light he saw a bearded, haggard face.

"Ivan is in the brickworks."

Farther to the right one of the artfully stacked piles of bricks collapsed. Curses rang out through the night. The three Russians immediately disappeared into the kiln, only to reappear again an instant later. They came out in a long line. When their number had reached ten, Kneisel opened fire. Rudi Brasche saw the Russians go to ground. Bursts of flame from their seventy-round submachine guns flickered in the hall, which was open at the sides. Then he pressed the trigger.

The tracer flew into the center of the source of the enemy fire, causing it to cease abruptly, but only for a second. A cluster of glowing tracer came their way, a deadly spear of bullets from a Maxim machine gun. Rudi Brasche saw the tracers veer in his direction. He rolled over once to the right, and when the bullets smacked into the pile he was safely behind the bricks.

Pulling the machine gun behind him by the stock, he crawled back ten meters and reached a passageway leading off to the side. Pressed close to the ground, he crawled inside. The enemy fire intensified. Kneisel answered with his machine gun.

"Are we going to outflank them, Rudi?"

"Yes . . . first we move to the left, then we go behind the kiln and take out that machine gun."

"Hey, Grunge, come here!"

Several grenades exploded with a mighty crash where the neighboring platoon had knocked over the rack holding the bricks. They sounded like Russian egg-shaped hand grenades. There was already fighting going on in the area of the kiln.

The three men of the machine-gun team reached the end of the hall. A narrow path was visible in the white snow. They followed it and fifty meters on found a wider intersecting path, which led directly to the kiln. Brasche was about to enter the main path, which was flanked by meter-high snow, when he heard the sound of a large number of men running from the direction of the chimney and the house. The three Germans dropped to the ground at once. Brasche pointed his machine gun at the exact spot where the large path crossed their smaller one.

Shadows appeared. Wild shouts rang out through the darkness. Then he opened fire. The men storming down the path crumpled and fell. The sound of footsteps died away. Dark objects flew toward the three German soldiers. The first salvo of grenades fell in the snow beside the narrow path. The three pressed themselves tight against the icy surface of the foot-path. Their ears rang loudly as the grenades exploded. Again the Russians stormed forward, on their way to help the men at the kiln.

Rudi Brasche fired at the gap. When the Russians again took cover he fired a long burst back through the snow bank. Cries rang out through the night. Then more hand grenades flew through the air. One rolled across the hard snow and stopped right in front of Grunge's face. His hand shot forward, grasped the grenade and threw it back. It exploded in midair. Grunge ducked instinctively. A few fragments clanged against his steel helmet.

"Hand grenade, Richard!"

Gambietz screwed off the cap. He counted to three and threw the grenade into the main path. The grenade exploded on impact. There were wild shouts and the sound of men running away. Grunge and Gambietz threw two more grenades. Then they reached the main path and turned north. A burst of fire knocked the last of the retreating Russians into the snow.

Just as Brasche was about to start walking, he was struck a heavy blow in the back. He fell forward against the wall of snow, the sharp crack of a pistol shot from behind ringing in his ears. Then Gambietz's submachine gun roared.

"An Ivan was about to shoot you with his pistol, Rudi."

A patrol from the 4th Company of the 93rd Panzer Grenadier Regiment prepares to set off from the limekiln at the brickworks.

Before Brasche could thank him, Gambietz ran off in the direction of the kiln. He set out after him. Brasche's feet felt as if they were made of rubber. What would have happened if Gambietz hadn't been there?

A determined Brasche caught up with his companions and took the lead again. Then, suddenly, he spotted the Russian Maxim machine gun. He squeezed the trigger and fired a short burst. Then he fired another. Suddenly his machine gun fell silent.

"The extractor is broken!"

"Damn!" swore Grunge. He reached for the submachine gun slung over his back. His first burst caught a Russian just as he was about to throw a grenade. As Gambietz watched, the last two men scurried through a hole in the rear of the kiln. Unteroffizier Laupert and his three machine gunners came running from the other side. They reached the hiding place in the rear of the kiln. Laupert took off his helmet and stuck it through the opening on the end of his submachine gun. A rattling burst of fire from a submachine gun caused the helmet to dance and fall to the ground. Unteroffizier Laupert took two grenades from his belt. He armed the grenades and threw them into the hole from the side.

There was a dull rumble as the grenades exploded. Then the Unteroffizier threw in two more. From inside the kiln came cries in Russian:

"Pan, pan, pan!" Three Russians stumbled into the open, their hands raised. All were wounded. In spite of the darkness Brasche could see their bewildered expressions.

"Anyone left inside?" asked Kneisel, who spoke excellent Russian.

"Only dead! Only dead!" stammered one of the wounded men. The wounded were tended to and sent back to the battalion command post. Feldwebel Wegener appeared and assembled the squad leaders at the circular kiln. "What's happening, Feldwebel?"

"The company is going to occupy the southern part of the limekiln. Hauptmann Kumm will be here any minute." The tall figure of the company commander came into view. When the Feldwebel had made his report the Hauptmann cleared his throat and began to speak:

"The company is going into position here and will disperse itself as far as the snow-covered field in front of the big chimney."

"What about the narrow-gauge railway, sir?"

"The pioneer platoon is moving forward as far as the railway shed and will take up position there. They will fire two red flares at the first sign of an enemy attack."

Hauptmann Kumm waved to the company headquarters squad. The signals section had already set up in the cleaned-out kiln and established communications with the battalion command post. The four men and the Hauptmann disappeared into the kiln. Feldwebel Wegener turned to his men.

"Follow me!"

They walked about thirty meters to a shed off to the right. It contained the small narrow-gauge locomotive for the factory yards and several ore cars.

"We'll position ourselves here. The two machine guns to the left and right on the flanks with field of fire toward the north. Demolition squad in the center."

"Well, it doesn't look too rosy, but at least we have a roof over our heads and a pair of brick walls."

Rudi Brasche positioned his machine gun in a corner of the shed. He broke away a few more stones around the existing hole. When he was done enlarging the hole he had an eighty-meter-wide field of fire which extended to the large house with the chimney in front.

"Damned cold up here."

"Yes, but we only need one man on watch. The other two can go back to the trucks. If we can find some straw somewhere, we can make ourselves quite comfortable."

"I'll go have a look," said Grunge, the huge East Prussian. He stepped out of the shed. He returned five minutes later carrying a heavy bale of pressed straw.

"Man, that's great. Where did you get it?"

"Farther back in an underground structure where they have their machines." They hauled three of the ore carts off their undercarriages and positioned them so that they intercepted the wind blowing in from the northeast. Then they lined them with straw.

"Get my bed ready," called Richard from his position by the machine gun.

"Don't worry, it's just about finished. And if we . . ."

Flames sprang up into the night sky in the north, three- or perhaps four-hundred meters in front of the limekiln. A few moments later there were explosions in the brick works.

"Ivan is firing mortars!"

The heavy mortar rounds fell all around. Three rounds blew part of the shed roof high into the air, where the pieces were caught by the northeast wind and blown toward the Mius.

"What's with our Flak? They're back on Hill 189."

"They've knocked off for the day," joked Gambietz.

A mortar round fell into the snow twenty meters in front of them. The explosion left a black circle in the snow. Fragments whizzed through the air and struck the brick wall. Instinctively Gambietz ducked down behind his machine gun. Immediately afterward the mortar fire shifted to the east onto the other companies of the regiment.

"What do you think, Rudi? Will we stay here for a while or will we withdraw as quickly as we came?"

Brasche stared at his companion in surprise. It was unusual for the taciturn East Prussian to speak so many words at one time.

"It looks as if this will be our winter position, Wilhelm."

"I think so, too. Anyway, it's time to relieve Gambietz so he can get some sleep."

Grunge stood up. He towered above Brasche, radiating power and security. Brasche was very fond of the lumbering fellow.

"Thank God. It's damned windy up front!"

Gambietz sighed as he lay down in the straw resting place. He rubbed his hands until his knuckles cracked, then handed the spare bolt back to Rudi Brasche.

"Here, Rudi, our emergency brake in case the other two bolts should fail." Brasche took the bolt and placed it in his pants pocket. There it would stay warm and wouldn't freeze, as bolts sometimes did in the weapon or the spares box. Two minutes later Gambietz was asleep.

Rudi Brasche lay wide-awake, replaying the day's events over in his mind. The dark-haired, medium-sized man thought back to the previous noon, when he had first seen the snow-covered hills as they marched past them to this position. For a moment he was back in the Harz Mountains. He had not had a leave since the summer of 1940, before he and the regiment went to Rumania. When would he be able to go home again? When would he be able to sleep through the night without worrying about being overrun by the Russians?

When Grunge shook him by the shoulder he was already wide awake. "Anything special, Wilhelm?"

"Didn't see a thing . . . good luck . . . Make sure you wake us if Ivan comes. Don't try and do everything yourself."

Brasche picked up his submachine gun and slung it over his shoulder. Then he felt his pocket with his left hand. The machine gun bolt assembly, which had already become something of a talisman to the three, was still there. He sat down on the pile of straw and peered through the hole in the wall, straining to see something. The blanket of snow shone and glittered in the moonlight. Brasche felt the bite of the cold and pulled down his woolen ear warmer. His eyes began to tear, and his breath hung in front of his mouth like a cloud of ice. Off to the right, where Kneisel's machine gun was positioned, he heard the sound of metal scraping against metal. A muffled voice swore.

Then all was quiet except for the occasional mortar round fired by the enemy and the subsequent explosion farther to the right near the neighboring company. The house was eighty meters in front of him. The chimney stood in the way of one side of the building, blocking it from sight. If the Russians made a move, they would come from behind the chimney.

Carefully Brasche turned the machine gun so that he could sweep the chimney. Minutes passed, one merging into the next. Then he heard a grating noise from the left flank. Holding his breath, Rudi Brasche listened intently. He talked to himself, trying to stay calm. The wind whistled in his face as he left cover to check out the noise. He felt something resembling panic rising in him. Where was the enemy? Were they approaching from behind the trees on the broad hill? Would they leap out from all sides at any minute and storm the German positions?

Brasche was unable to find anything. But then he heard a noise from the other side. He thought it must be Kneisel again. As he listened he heard whispering from the machine-gun position and then silence.

Suddenly, the night was torn apart in front of him in a wide semi-circle. Bursts of fire whipped toward the position from four or five directions. Figures jumped up not thirty meters in front of Brasche and raced toward him. Wearing their white snow smocks, the Russians had succeeded in working their way close to the chain of German outposts. Brasche fired a long burst at the approaching forms. Kneisel's machine gun likewise opened fire. At the chimney a screen of bricks fell away and an enemy semi-automatic cannon began to fire. The 20-mm rounds punched holes in the brick walls.

Behind Brasche things had come to life. The sleeping soldiers had been awakened and then rushed forward. One man cried out as he was hit in the chest by a round and knocked onto his back.

Rudi Brasche swung his weapon around in a rapid movement. His burst struck near the enemy gun at the chimney. Then he took a sight picture at a position ten centimeters above the muzzle flash from the enemy weapon and fired again. A Russian emerged from behind the gun's steel protective shield. He took three or four steps and fell as if he had been struck by lightning.

Gambietz saw the onrushing Red Army soldiers. He also saw how Brasche swung his machine gun around to engage the enemy gun. He reached for the hand grenades he had placed beside him, their caps already screwed off. He armed them one after the other and hurled them toward the approaching enemy.

The grenades went off in rapid succession. To his right the gunfire rose to a crescendo. The enemy troops who had survived the hail of fire ran back in grotesque leaps and bounds. They disappeared into the snow as if the earth had swallowed them up. A wounded Russian crawled away on all fours, leaving a dark trail of blood behind him. He died before he could reach the safety of the trench the enemy had dug in the snow, his hands stretched out in front of him.

Then it was quiet. A moment later the silence was shattered by impacting rounds from Russian "potato throwers." The small mortars coughed all along a front of about 400 meters, and a rain of the dark objects fell and exploded, scattering fragments of steel that struck the brick walls.

"They're closer. It looks like an entire mortar battalion, Feldwebel."

"Looks that way. We've gone from the frying pan in Rostov into the fire here, and . . ."

A terrible scream rang out behind them and the hacking sound of a Russian submachine gun caused the men to drop to the ground. Brasche was the first to speak:

"What was that?"

"The Russians have penetrated!" shouted a voice from the direction of the machinery house.

"Laupert's squad follow me. Leave the machine gun manned!"

"Stay here, Richard!" Brasche shouted to Gambietz, who was about to set out after the others. Grunge crawled up next to his friend behind the machine gun. He readied a fresh belt of ammunition, however, no more enemy troops approached. The others returned an hour later.

"What happened, Richard?"

Gambietz threw himself down on the straw beside his two friends. With a tired movement he wiped his hand across his face, which was covered in sweat in spite of the cold.

"They stabbed Bungertz and Köhler. Killed them with their bayonets. They took the machine gun and Siebelhoff with them."

"But you caught them?"

"They disappeared from the face of the earth without a trace. No sign of them."

"Damn! They couldn't have run away, old man. They must be around here. Perhaps they're hiding somewhere."

"We've looked everywhere. Nothing."

"This could become uncomfortable."

And things did become "uncomfortable." They became more than that. The next four nights saw whole machine-gun teams disappear. Men vanished without a trace. While gunfire from attacking Russian assault groups and the German defenders split the night, other Russian patrols entered the German-occupied brick works. Where they came from was a mystery. They had to be coming from somewhere, but from where?

"If we could smoke out that hovel over there, we'd be able to advance as far as the slope, Rudi."

"I agree, Wilhelm, but how are we supposed to get to it? How could we get across the open terrain?"

"I know how we can do it. Listen: During the night we will move up to the chimney and place charges so that it falls right on the house. When that happens, we can take it."

"Man, Rudi, we'll never make it to the chimney," Grunge called out.

"It won't be so simple to do as that, Richard."

"If our mortars keep their heads down over there we can do it. We would dig a narrow path through the snow. The cannon in the chimney has been destroyed. I'm going to see Feldwebel Wegener. He'll see to it that the old man gives us supporting fire and not just on the bunker on the forward flank."

✠

"How did it go, Richard?" Brasche asked when his friend returned an hour later. The latter let himself fall into the straw beside them. He reached into his pack and produced several packs of cigarettes.

"From the old man. One pack for each of us as a special reward for our clever idea."

"Then we're going to do it?"

"At 2345 the division's artillery will open fire on the Russian positions on the hill on the far side of the brick works. The 50- and 80-mm mortars are moving up right now and will plaster the northern part of the brick works. The boundary line is the chimney. We'll use the ammunition sled to haul a few Teller mines, which we'll place right at the chimney. Then we'll pull back and up she goes."

It was 2340. The three men were lying behind the brick wall, the last piece of cover. They were wearing snow smocks sent up by the battalion. Beside Gambietz was Feldwebel Wegener.

"It's time. Good luck, comrades."

Rudi Brasche took the Feldwebel's hand and squeezed it firmly. Then he reached for the handle with which he was to pull the sled. Gambietz and Grunge were carrying entrenching tools.

There was an ear-shattering roar behind them as the field artillery opened fire. The first rounds whistled overhead and hammered into the northern part of the brick works.

"Go, Richard!"

Gambietz began to shovel and throw the snow to the side. They had sought out a shallow depression where they would be less noticeable. Nevertheless Rudi Brasche expected to hear an enemy machine gun open up at any second. But the only sound was the noise of the impacting rounds. When they had gone twenty meters the German mortars also began to fire. The mortar rounds fell close together. Fragments of steel crashed into the chimney. Steel also fell on the Russian-held building beyond the chimney.

Soon they were within four meters of the chimney. A pair of 80-mm mortar rounds fell in their direction with a wild howl. Rudi Brasche pressed himself to the ground. He thought his eardrums would break when the rounds burst not five meters away, hurling fragments of steel in all directions. More mortar rounds landed nearby, but the men soon reached the

chimney. Gambietz dug a trench halfway around the chimney. A glance at
the illuminated face of his watch showed Brasche that they had exactly ten
minutes left.

"Get going, Richard!" he whispered.

"I'm working on it."

They worked feverishly. Rounds impacted nearby, repeatedly forcing
them to take cover in their snow trench. Four rounds struck the forty-
meter-high chimney, but it did not move. Shattering blasts near the house
made it clear that the enemy was under heavy fire. Finally all the Teller
mines were in place.

"Let's go, but watch your ass!"

They left the sled where it was and crept back the way they had come.
When they reached their own positions they lay there for a few moments,
lungs pumping.

"The firing has stopped, Feldwebel."

"All right then, now it's our turn."

Feldwebel Wegener pressed the electrical detonator. There was a flash
at the base of the chimney. For a few seconds it looked as if the mighty
chimney wasn't going to move at all. But then it tilted forward, precisely in
the planned direction. A loud rumble drowned out the echo of the explosion of the eleven Teller mines. The chimney fell on the two buildings,
crushing them. Dense clouds of dust rose into the air. Flames appeared
through the dust and, on the right flank, the previously coordinated two
red flares shot into the sky. The mortars ceased firing.

Rudi Brasche grasped his machine gun and ran forward beside
Grunge and Gambietz. He saw men running forward on a broad front
before disappearing into the dust. Two machine guns opened fire from
the side of the second building, which had not been totally destroyed by
the falling chimney. The 4th Platoon, the company's heavy platoon,
opened fire on the enemy pocket of resistance with mortars.

Then they reached the shattered front wall of the house and rushed in
through the thick dust. Rudi Brasche felt the biting dust in his nose;
breathing was difficult.

Cries rang out above the noise of the crackling flames. Submachine
gun fire whipped out in the background. Brasche stumbled over a figure
lying in the center of the room. He tried to catch his fall with his left hand,
but it landed on the bearded face of a Russian. He felt hot breath and
pulled back his hand as if he'd burned it. A burst of fire flashed through
the wafting smoke not a meter from his face. He felt the rush of air as the
bullets whizzed past. Then Gambietz's submachine gun rattled. Rudi
clasped his weapon, pulled it close and fired at the source of the enemy

Rudi Brasche after assignment to the Panzer Demonstration Division, where he continued to distinguish himself. He destroyed five enemy tanks with the *Panzerschreck* and disabled a further two.

fire in the background. The firing stopped and they pushed on into the house, the center of which had been completely destroyed by the falling chimney. Ten minutes later they had eliminated all resistance.

The company spread out into the house and the shed beside it. Brasche and his companions hurried into the front room of the house, which faced north. They saw the slope that fell away from the house and, on the far side of the next slope, the tongues of flame from the Russian artillery. It was firing on the German positions at the limekiln.

✠

"The Russians used these tunnels to penetrate our positions, sir."

Leutnant Horst Heinrich nodded. He shone his powerful flashlight into the tunnel that began beneath the house. There were apparently side tunnels leading in all directions.

"It looks that way. Laupert's squad will come with me. The two flamethrowers as well. Don't do anything else here until you hear from me by runner, understood?"

The men of *Jagdkommando Heinrich*—Leutnant Heinrich's raiding party—nodded. The *Jagdkommando* had been formed just that morning after the destruction of the chimney. The Leutnant turned to the pioneer squad.

"Any questions?"

"No questions, sir."

"Good, follow me!"

They stepped into the walled tunnel that began in the cellar of the captured house. The underground passage led straight south. It was damp and smelled of mold.

It seemed to Rudi Brasche as if the low ceiling would have to fall on their heads at any moment. Who could say whether the Russians had placed demolition charges? It was likely that there were Russians in the tunnel, as they had spotted some when they entered the cellar after clearing the house.

Steel rattled loudly against steel in the narrow tunnel and the sound echoed back from the end of the passage. The Leutnant stopped. His flashlight flashed on for a brief instant and was immediately extinguished again.

"Are they going to blow it up, Rudi?"

"If they do, we've all had it, Richard."

They talked in whispers after they reached the end of the tunnel. The Leutnant felt a half-open door. He stepped outside and threw himself to the ground.

Not a second too soon. A burst of fire cut through the darkness. In the same instant, two thirty-meter-long streams of fire shot from the muzzles of the flamethrowers and struck the Russian gunner. Screaming loudly, the Russian turned around and disappeared. Shots rang out over the heads of the men. Then they reached the tunnel exit.

A narrow shaft of light fell down on them. Several voices called something in German.

"It's us! The *Jagdkommando*!"

A steel cover was thrown back and the men climbed up the steel steps that had been placed in the wall at the end of the tunnel. When they emerged they realized that they were at the foot of the machinery garage, in the large drainage canal.

The two Russians who had fled must have been sentries. But they had come back at the wrong time. Their bodies lay a few meters away where the neighboring company had cut them down. The air stank of burning cloth. Rudi Brasche felt ill. Unable to bear the horrible scene any longer, he had to turn away.

"We're going back. We have to inspect the other three tunnels."

Leutnant Heinrich turned round. The flamethrower squad followed. The men of the pioneer squad brought up the rear. The air stank of burned flamethrower fuel.

Under the administrator's house they entered the eastward-leading tunnel. After a few meters it branched off. The Leutnant ordered the two men with the flamethrowers to stay behind and not take their eyes off the two tunnel branches. The others advanced cautiously. They reached the outer edge of the kiln, where there was another drainage canal. Then they inspected the tunnel that led from there. After 200 meters they came to a set of stairs made of unbaked brick.

"That's the valley where they got the clay, sir."

"Stay alert! All weapons ready!"

The nearer they came to the exit the more cautious they became. Rudi Brasche heard Grunge's strained breath beside him. The tall East Prussian had to bend down as the tunnel had become lower. They were fifty meters from the end, then thirty. One of the men bumped into a supporting beam; suddenly, a machine gun began to fire. They threw themselves to the ground. Brasche saw tracers flit past above them. He pressed the butt of his weapon into his shoulder and pressed the trigger. The burst caused a loud crashing and smashing from the enemy side. But when the machine gun stopped there were still several submachine guns firing.

It was Gambietz who turned the situation around in the Germans' favor. He crawled forward as fast as he could. When he reached a niche in the wall of the tunnel he threw his hand grenades. They exploded among the enemy soldiers. The firing ceased.

Brasche and Grunge got to their feet. As they did so they saw the shadowy figure of Gambietz disappear in front of them. They heard the rattle of his submachine gun and the answering fire from Russian automatic weapons. The two reached the end of the tunnel together. They jumped into the low pump room and opened fire. Those Russians still alive surrendered.

"Get going, Grunge. Hurry back and send some explosives, understood?" The East Prussian ran back along the tunnel, while the rest of the men scanned the floor of the valley through the iron door of the pumphouse. They knew the Russians who had entered the brick works nightly through the tunnels and shot their comrades or dragged them away to captivity must be dug-in and hiding somewhere out there.

"There, sir!"

Brasche had spotted the glinting of the weak winter sun off steel. The flash had come from halfway up the slope on the far side of the valley.

"Damn, they've got a machine gun over there. Go ahead Brasche, let them have it!"

The MG 34 began to rattle. The enemy machine gun on the far side of the valley opened fire. Bullets slammed into the pump house. The first machine gun fell silent. Then Rudi Brasche realized that the enemy had them in their sights. He hauled down the machine gun and positioned it at the second side window.

☩

Wilhelm Grunge hurried back through the dark tunnel. He knew that he had to stay to the right where the tunnel branched off. The left tunnel would definitely not lead to the administrator's house. He had gone only 100 meters when he heard his squad's machine gun open fire. Instinctively, he quickened his pace.

Something hard struck his left shoulder, then something hit him in the back and knocked him to the ground. Grunge heard a wild Russian curse and felt hands clutch his neck and begin to squeeze. Instinctively, he tensed his neck muscles and tried to throw himself around. He half landed on his adversary before his turn was stopped abruptly by the wall of the tunnel.

Grunge felt a stabbing pain in his shoulder where the Russian had struck him. He slid his hand back over his head. He felt a bearded face and grabbed hold. Grunge pulled on the beard with all his strength. His opponent let out a painful cry. The hands released their grip. Grunge pulled again with all his strength. The enemy soldier sagged. His head fell back hard, then he lay still.

With shaking hands Grunge lit a match. He saw the flame reflected in the eyes of his dead enemy. As if seized by a wild fury, he ran on. Machine-gun fire rang out behind him.

☩

"They've got the range on this window too, Rudi. We must get out before they hit one of us."

"But where, Richard?"

"Here, through the drain."

One of the men had raised the wire lid. A pale light shone from the concrete tube. Gambietz slipped inside and disappeared. He reappeared three minutes later. He waved. Rudi followed him and landed on the muddy floor of the pit.

"Around here. They're coming from the side through the ravine."

Brasche was terrified when he saw the approaching enemy. They were moving forward through the overgrown ravine and had just reached a small lake. But then he threw the machine gun onto the rim of the pit and began to fire methodically. The Russian troops immediately took cover. Minutes passed.

"Gambietz, Brasche, come back!"

They ran back a few paces and Brasche passed the machine gun up. The two climbed up hand over hand.

"Get in. Get out of sight, if you don't want to get blown away."

"I'm going as fast as I can, Wilhelm. . . . Man, what happened to you? You look like shit!"

"A little run-in with an Ivan," Unteroffizier Laupert said, "but he told us all about this place. Get out of here; this place is about to be blown up."

They ran back behind the others, who were already about fifty meters ahead. The Leutnant appeared from a side tunnel. Two pioneers followed him. They had placed charges at the end of the tunnel.

"How's it look, Brasche?"

"They've just come through the ravine and should just about be at the pump house, sir."

"They must be preparing to counterattack through the tunnel."

Leutnant Heinrich turned to Unteroffizier Laupert, who had just come up from the pump house with the other two pioneers.

"All set?" he asked.

"All set, Herr Leutnant!"

The Leutnant turned to the Feldwebel holding the detonator. Then he waved to his men. Brasche took cover in a niche in the wall beside Gambietz.

"Detonate!"

The charges at the end of the tunnel went up with a roar. A powerful shock wave raced through the tunnel, but the German soldiers in the side tunnels were unscathed.

"Now the others."

All the tunnels linking the limekiln and the brick works were blown up. All through the afternoon explosions rang out over the sound of artillery fire. The catacombs had become useless to the enemy.

✠

"Careful, Richard. There's something up ahead."

In their snow smocks the two Obergefreite blended into the floor of the valley. Holding his breath, Rudi Brasche strained to hear something. Then Gambietz, too, heard the noises. They were coming from the opposite slope. It sounded as if a man walking down the slope had fallen and slid a distance. Brasche gave a hand signal and crawled to the right, where a snow-shrouded thicket offered cover. Gambietz followed. The snow crunched lightly under their hands and boot tips. They reached the hiding place unseen and unnoticed.

Two or three minutes passed. There was a dull rumble from the German artillery positions behind the limekiln. Rounds raced overhead and smashed into the Russian positions far beyond on the opposite slope. A Russian battery ahead and to their right answered the artillery fire. It concentrated its fire on the foremost German bunker. The Flak on Hill 189, directly behind the main German bunker, answered. The 88-mm rounds flitted straight at the enemy bunker on the far side of the valley—actually located in no-man's-land—and exploded. This was the usual nocturnal concert played out during the bitterly cold January days of 1942.

Rudi Brasche felt the cold in spite of the captured Russian fur-lined boots he was wearing. He flexed his right hand. A noise nearby caused him to freeze. Suddenly, they appeared. They were bent low and moved noiselessly, like figures from another world: Russians, eight of them. All were carrying submachine guns. In their white suits they blended into the snow. The eight were walking in single file. There was not even the crunching of snow beneath their feet. They crept past about three meters from the thicket. Brasche felt his palms becoming sweaty as they clutched the submachine gun. Then the shadowy figures were gone.

"Hurry! We have to get out of here before they come back!"

The pair took the same path as the Russians. Above them flashed the fire of several "Ratschbum" all-purpose field guns. Immediately afterward, the 76.2-mm rounds from the high-velocity guns burst on the opposite slope in the midst the German positions. Rudi Brasche saw that the tracks led into an area of brush. He slowed his pace. Beyond the bushes must be the Maxim machine gun they had spotted earlier. Their mission was to pay a visit to the position and capture one of the Russians.

Brasche brushed against a bush. A clump of snow fell. A grunting noise came from the other side of the bushes and the two Germans dropped to the ground. A figure emerged from the thicket, moving towards them. Brasche's submachine gun barked. His companion jumped to his feet. They charged through the bushes, saw three or four men of the

Russian outpost, and fired again. They spared the Russian on the far left, as they had agreed upon earlier.

Brasche reached the man, who was in the act of raising his weapon. But the sight of the barrel of the German submachine gun pointing straight at him caused him to raise both arms.

"That way, quickly!" said Brasche in broken Russian. He pointed towards the German lines. Bent low, they hurried back into the valley. Brasche veered east when several machine guns opened up from atop the slope. High above them several illumination flares ignited with dull thumps. They hung over the valley, casting an eerie light over the snow.

Rudi Brasche dragged the prisoner down to the ground. They remained motionless like bushes. The enemy fire raced into the night. One machine gun sprayed bullets in their direction. Just as Brasche had made up his mind to get up and run, the firing stopped.

The machine gun fire woke up the Russian "potato throwers." The light mortars began to cough. Then the Russian 76.2-mm high-velocity guns joined in and both sides were soon pounding both lines.

"Keep going, Richard!"

The two Germans and their Russian captive crept over the ground. There was still no sign of the Russian patrol. Had the Russian patrol already reached the German lines? Were they on their way back, thinking they might be threatened?

What they had feared then happened. The first Russian appeared about ten meters in front of Gambietz. The Russians had also made a wide arc and in the same direction. Instead of staying out of their way, they then ran straight into each other in the middle of no-man's-land.

Gambietz fired first. His short burst chased the Russians into cover behind the trees. Brasche glanced at the Russian captive lying two meters in front of him and made sure he was staying put. He scanned the bushes from which had come the first burst of Russian fire. He spotted an enemy soldier when the man moved. Then he saw the outline of his head, on which was perched a thick fur cap. His index finger curled over the trigger. The enemy soldier, who also wanted to fire first, jumped up. Three or four Russian sub-machine guns cracked, then the Russians dropped to the ground again. The bullets missed Brasche, who had dived into a shallow depression.

He saw the Russian prisoner move. "Stoi (stop)!" he shouted. The man froze. There were two pops as the Russians fired illumination flares. Gambietz immediately opened fire on the two men who had tired the flares. But these were equally clever, dodging to the side immediately. Both members of the German patrol heard the bushes rustling and a burst of fire sprayed from the shrubbery. Gambietz let out a painful scream.

Icy fear gripped Brasche. What had happened to his friend? Had he been hit? But then he saw Gambietz crawl to one side.

There were three coughs on the hill behind them. Even before the mortar rounds fell, the two Germans knew that the Russian patrol leader had requested them by firing the two flares. The earth seemed to fly to pieces. Mortar rounds fell in a circle around them. One Russian jumped up and started to run away. He was caught by an exploding round in mid-stride.

Brasche crawled forward. The cleft in the ground was deeper there. He waved to the prisoner, who crawled up to join him. Breathing heavily

A *Panzerschreck* team on the Ourthe River.

the Russian fell into the hole. Brasche saw the man make the sign of the cross. A man, he thought to himself. A man like any other, who knows fear and believes in God.

They waited five minutes. The firing gradually died down. There was not a trace of the Russians. Gambietz had crawled farther forward. When he stood up and raised his arm, Brasche knew that the enemy had withdrawn during the mortar barrage. Right then they were probably making their way back to their own lines in a wide arc. His supposition was confirmed when a German machine gun at the edge of the limekiln opened fire.

"Let's go!" said Brasche, prodding the Russian. Obediently the man began to walk. Just as they reached Gambietz a Maxim machine gun began to fire and they dropped to the ground. Then a German machine gun fired. The bullets were uncomfortably close.

"Damn, are they crazy?" cried Gambietz. "Rudi, the flare pistol!"

Brasche pulled out the heavy pistol, inserted a white flare and fired the pre-arranged signal. The German machine gun stopped firing immediately. The Russian gun then began firing wildly at the Germans' suspected position, but they had moved immediately after firing the flare. The Russian captive ran as if his life depended on being the first to reach the German position.

Gambietz heard a voice: "Up here!" He ran up the slope, came to a pathway in the snow and jumped in. Ten seconds later he stumbled into a bunker, out of breath. Rudi Brasche followed with the prisoner.

"You've caught a rare bird. Man, he's bleeding. There, on his arm."

Brasche looked and saw the jagged tear in the Russian's snow smock and the padded jacket beneath.

"Come here. Take this off, old friend!"

They stripped the clothing off the Russian and began to dress his wound. Gambietz stuck a cigarette between the Russian's teeth. The prisoner tried to smile as a gesture of thanks. He puffed energetically.

"We've got to get to the battalion command post. The old man will be waiting."

In his broken Russian, Brasche said to the captive: "You come with me. We'll talk there. For you the war is over!"

The Russian stood up and they set out through the trench toward the rear. When they reached the approach road they were met by a *Kübelwagen*. They climbed in and a few moments later were standing in the battalion command post.

"Brasche's patrol back with two men. One prisoner brought in. Firefight with a Russian patrol."

"Thank you, Brasche."

Oberstleutnant Oskar Radwan shook hands with both men. Then he looked at the prisoner.

"Wounded?" he asked in Russian.

The prisoner nodded.

The Oberstleutnant dismissed the two soldiers: "See Kraubler. He'll issue you special rations, Brasche."

Once again they had survived. Brasche and his friends sat safe and sound in their fortified bunker. But for how long? Until the next night? The day after? It was always the same: The fear, the tension, the same concentration of resources in order to survive this demonic war.

"Get some sleep. Tomorrow before dawn we're moving up to the Radau Bunker (Racket Bunker). We're going to relieve the Second." Rudi Brasche jumped to his feet. He stared at the speaker in disbelief.

"The Radau Bunker?" he asked, as if he hadn't heard correctly.

"Yes, that's a pleasant surprise," added Gambietz sarcastically. "The Russians will be glad to see such old friends again."

Rudi Brasche lay back and closed his eyes. The Radau Bunker appeared in his memory. They had celebrated Christmas there. The Russians had come down from the opposite hill during the night and tried to take the bunker. He again heard the rumble of exploding rounds and the roar of hand grenades, the rattle of submachine-gun fire and the cries of the wounded. They had been relieved there on 3 January. Now, on 12 January, they were to go back into the mousetrap—the Radau Bunker was a deathtrap. The Russians were only a hundred meters away. They had a bunker on the commanding heights and behind it a blocking position.

He was half asleep when Leutnant Heinrich came in, accompanied by Feldwebel Wegener. He heard the words of the two men as if through a thick fog.

"Two infantry squads, a squad of pioneers, a heavy squad. Don't forget the flamethrowers."

This could only mean that the entire *Jagdkommando* was being sent into the Radau Bunker. It also meant that they were going to assault the Russian bunker, as they had in December. They had managed to take the bunker then, but had lost it again after a four-hour barrage. The Russians subsequently attacked the German bunker but had failed to take it.

What would happen this time? Would they succeed? Would they occupy the Russian position and finally be able to guard the commanding heights from the Radau Bunker?

✠

The telephone rang. In a niche at the bunker's rear exit Unteroffizier Klingner picked up the receiver.

"Radau Bunker," he reported.

"Chow," came back the other voice. "The food's coming, request an escort."

"Understood. Out." The Unteroffizier replaced the receiver and stood up. He walked forward to where Rudi Brasche and the two members of his heavy machine-gun team were observing the Russian bunker through the scissors telescope that had been installed there.

"Rudi, the food detail is coming. It is requesting an escort."

"OK, Jupp. I'll look after it."

Brasche picked up his mess kit. He hammered against it with the reserve barrel, raised it through the embrasure on a broomstick and waved it back and forth. A signal flare was fired from the other side, and Rudi turned to the radio operator.

"Everything's fine, they can come."

Five minutes later the two men arrived with the containers of food— hot pea soup.

"Good trick, eh, Richard?"

"If you had told me about this a week ago, I'd have said you were crazy. Ivan leaving our rations bearers alone."

"We also leave theirs in peace. We scratch their back, they scratch ours."

The first time they had raised a mess kit as a joke and received no fire they assumed it was a Russian trick. But then the Ivans gave the same signal that same day, and the Germans held their fire. This went on for almost a week. Whenever the mess kit appeared, the firing stopped immediately.

During the night, however, there was no quarter offered. German pioneers went out after dark and mined the approaches to their positions. Russian patrols and assault groups ran into combat teams, or task forces, composed of elements from several different types of units (*Kampfgruppen*). Bitter night engagements alternated with futile Russian attacks on the Radau Bunker. They had just finished eating when Leutnant Heinrich, who had been summoned by Oberst Ritter von Weber, came back from the regimental command post.

The Leutnant sat down. Those men not on watch behind the machine guns gathered round him.

"Men, things are going to heat up tonight. The Third will relieve us and provide covering fire. We're going to move on the Russian bunker, take it out and then take the Russian trenches behind it."

"Damn tricky business, sir. If Ivan sees us in time he'll have us cold. It's only 100 meters to his bunker."

"The Flak is going to lay down a curtain of fire. They're in position on Hill 189 and on the two neighboring hills. Two batteries of 88s and two quad 20-mm guns. They'll be shitting their pants when they let them have it over there."

"And then?"

"Then we form the 'Heinrich Position' over there."

"Sounds mighty clever, sir."

"Yes, too much glory for me. But what would you have me do, Wegener? The old man has worked it out this way," said the Leutnant with a wry grin. "In any case we're going to make things very hot for them over there."

With this the discussion was over. The afternoon passed as if nothing special was up. Once Rudi Brasche tried to outwit a Russian sniper who was firing accurately at the bunker's embrasures. He had fetched his rifle and bored a hole next to the machine gun about a meter to one side.

"Fire a short burst, Richard," he instructed Gambietz. The gunner loosed off a few rounds. At once there was a flash from the enemy position, at least five meters to one side of the bunker. The bullet whizzed over the machine gun and struck the bunker wall. Gambietz fired back while keeping himself under cover.

The sniper fired again. This time Brasche had him in his sights. He squeezed the trigger. The crack of his rifle rang through the bunker. There was movement on the other side.

Grunge, who was observing through the scissors telescope, reported: "You've hit him, Rudi."

The rifle shot was answered by furious machine-gun fire. It soon died down, however, when the mess kit was waved; it was time for the evening rations to arrive.

Fifteen minutes later the Russians waved a mess kit. The weapons fell silent in the sector of the *Jagdkommando*. Not a shot was fired for half an hour.

"Get ready."

"Did you wash up, children?" joked Kneisel, as he assembled his machine gun. No one answered. The men of the Third had just arrived. They had brought their flamethrowers with them. Calls and greetings flew back and forth. Rudi nodded to Sepp Jäckl, who had been in his squad in France. With an ear-splitting crash, the 88s began to fire from Hill 189 behind them. They saw the red, blue and yellow trails of flame from the tracers as they hissed toward the enemy. Shells burst all around the bunker and machine-gun positions.

"Move out as ordered."

Oberleutnant Münzer called goodbye to his friend: "Good luck, Horst!"

Leutnant Heinrich nodded, then disappeared into the darkness.

Rudi Brasche ran down the hill behind his squad leader. They reached the floor of the small valley. A machine gun fired in their direction until it was blasted by four streams of fire from a quad 20-mm Flak.

Looking like fantastic, prehistoric creatures, the two pioneers with the flamethrowers moved in from the right. The men of the *Jagdkommando* raced forward through the valley. Each step brought them nearer to the main Russian bunker. With each step Rudi Brasche also felt the resistance growing in him. It was urging him to throw himself down and take cover. Then they were at the foot of the gentle slope leading up to the enemy bunker. Mines exploded to the right, where an infantry platoon was advancing. Up above a few Russian mortars opened fire. Positioned farther back, they could not be seen by the advancing Germans. Their shells became visible at the apex of their trajectory, before falling among the onrushing soldiers, spraying shrapnel through their ranks.

"Faster!" shouted the Leutnant. Brasche climbed up the slope. He saw an overgrown trench and headed towards it. Close behind him were Gambietz and Grunge. A few submachine guns fired thirty meters above them.

Suddenly, a dark red flash of fire shot into the heavens to their right and then a second one. Above the hammering of the rapid-firing weapons and the dull thud of hand grenades Brasche heard the roar of the two flamethrowers as the pioneers took out the enemy on the intervening hill. The two flamethrower squads ran on. As they advanced, Brasche jumped up and headed up the slope. Grunge slipped on a patch of ice and fell. One of the ammunition boxes tumbled down the hill.

As they reached the crest of the hill, the advancing Germans were met by machine-gun fire. Yellow tracers flitted past Brasche. He fired on the run, spraying the enemy gun position with bullets. Soviet submachine guns opened up, forcing Brasche and his men to take cover. Streams of fire sprayed the bunker. The white mantel of snow became blackened. Figures came stumbling out of the bunker, shrouded in flame. They screamed and tumbled to the ground. Others stood in front of the bunker with raised hands. The firing died down. Leutnant Heinrich and three men entered the bunker. He had his men turn the Maxim machine guns around and face them in the Russian direction.

"Two men take the prisoners back!" he ordered as he stepped outside.

The Flak guns had stopped firing. The group of about twenty Russian prisoners headed down the slope. The two men escorting them held their weapons at the ready, however, the horrible effects of the flamethrowers and the direct fire from the Flak had demoralized them. They were not about to offer any resistance.

"Here through the trenches! Flamethrowers: Move forward!"

They pushed ahead along the two communications trenches and, after advancing twenty paces, came under fire from Russian earth dugouts. Once again the flamethrowers went to work. Machine-gun fire rang out. Brasche spotted the figures that had raced forward across the snow-covered plain, dragging their machine guns on small sleighs. He threw his weapon down on the icy rim of the trench and opened fire. Gambietz fed in a fresh belt of ammunition as soon as the first was expended.

The enemy troops stopped, pinned down by Brasche's fire. Meanwhile, the pioneer squad moved forward. Wherever it met opposition the flamethrowers went into action, and more burning forms tumbled into the open and toppled into the snow.

An hour later the enemy positions to the left and right of the main bunker were in German hands. Under Soviet artillery fire, the pioneers began mining the approaches in anticipation of a counterattack.

✠

"Over there as far as that bush, Rudi."

Rudi Brasche nodded as he recognized the face of Gambietz beside him. He crawled onward, dragging the trip wire behind him. When he reached the bush he secured the pyrotechnic flare and fuse to it. He wound thin wire around it and pulled the trip wire to a fallen tree, where he attached the other end. "There'll be fireworks when Ivan comes. First the trip flares and then the mines."

The Soviets had tried four times in the past few days to capture the "Heinrich Position." Each time the attack had faltered in the face of defensive fire from German and captured Russian weapons. The 80-mm mortars of the heavy-weapons squad had also played an important role.

"Let's get back. Go, go, before Ivan comes and we're caught out here."

Rudi Brasche crawled to the shallow pathway in the snow, then walked to the smallest earth bunker on the left flank of the Heinrich Position, which projected some distance toward the north. They had enlarged the bunker to hold three men, but it was a tight squeeze. Leutnant Heinrich appeared through the communications trench and looked at the three men. He didn't have to say a thing; the men knew what he wanted to know. "All clear, sir. We have enough ammunition and the explosives are ready."

"Stay alert. This afternoon a reconnaissance aircraft spotted movements that suggest a tank assembly area. Sound the alarm at once if you see anything, understood?"

Bent low, the Leutnant went back the way he had come. Rudi Brasche peered into the inky blackness. The sky was obscured by low clouds. If it hadn't been so cold it would probably have been snowing again. Grunge broke the silence: "It looks like they're not coming, Rudi. It's already 0215."

"Just the right time and . . . listen!"

At that moment about a dozen tank engines began to rumble and the noise was moving in their direction.

A voice rang out from a neighboring hole: "Tank alert!"

The first tanks appeared in front of them—gray forms on the field of snow. Red flashes hissed from their guns. Rounds howled toward the Germans and smashed into the bunkers, followed by the booming crashes of gunfire. The tanks then again set themselves in motion again. They rolled nearer. The men in the trenches and holes could already hear the rattling of their tracks, when the Flak behind them on Hill 189 opened fire. One tank reared up as it took a direct hit. A red flame shot from its turret hatch. But the rest of the tanks continued to roll forward, and suddenly a brown wave of bodies appeared behind the armored giants.

"Urray—urray—urray!"

The Russian battle cry could be heard above the crack of tank cannon and the crash of impacting 88-mm rounds. In spite of the icy cold, the men in the trenches broke out in a sweat. Four or five tanks reached the first belt of mines. There were several explosions and the leading Russian vehicle ground to a halt. The other tanks stopped abruptly and opened fire with their cannon and machine guns on the German positions. The Germans had held their fire up to that point so as not to betray their location.

Then the infantry stormed forward past the tanks. They reached the mine belt. Individual mines exploded, hurling bodies into the air. Suddenly, a harsh flash of light lit up the right side. Blue and white illumination flares sprang up farther left and in the center. The harsh light of the pyrotechnics transformed the snow into a mirror, and on this mirror were the attacking Russians. With an ear-shattering crash all the German machine guns and captured Maxims began to fire.

The Russians immediately went to ground. Some crawled toward the German positions. They reached the tripwires and set off the explosive charges. Bright flashes ripped away the dark mantle of the night. Machine

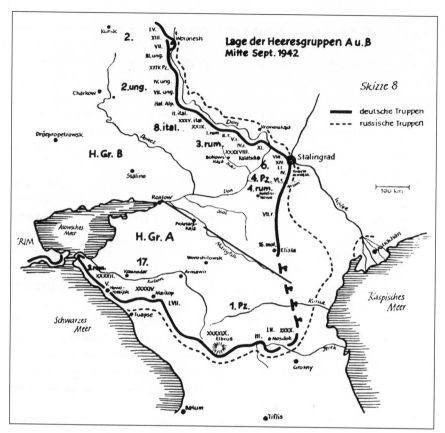

Advance into the Caucasus.

guns, submachine guns and rifles fired mercilessly on the attacking Russians. Mines detonated with mighty explosions. The Russian attack was halted in front of the Heinrich Position.

The Russian tanks were firing back at the Flak. Muzzle flashes lit the night. Then reinforcements arrived. Twenty tanks appeared, widely dispersed. They rolled forward, firing on the move. More infantry followed the tanks. Tanks by themselves were senseless. Only if the infantry followed could they hope to win back their old position.

The tanks rolled nearer and nearer. It was obvious that they had been given precise instructions this time. They didn't allow themselves to be deterred by the fire of the Flak. They simply rolled forward.

The tanks rumbled over the mines. Three were disabled, their tracks tom apart. Nevertheless, they continued to fire their cannon and machine guns. The flanking Russian tank was heading straight toward Brasche's bunker. As he watched, Brasche saw Russian infantry appear behind the tank. He swung the machine gun around and fired. The burst knocked the Russians off their feet. The tank's main gun swung around. Flames shot from its muzzle and, at the same time, the tank's machine gun opened fire. Grunge pulled Brasche back into cover. The burst of fire struck the machine gun and flipped it upside down. Then the tank began to move forward again. Brasche and his men could smell the choking diesel fumes. The bow of the tank rose higher and higher before them, then it reached their earth bunker.

The three pressed themselves to the ground. Noise assailed their eardrums. Exhaust gases blew into their hole. Clumps of frozen earth from the bunker walls sprinkled down on them. Creaking loudly, the T-34 began to turn. The earth trembled. A side wall collapsed, pinning Brasche's arm against his body. He felt it trembling. A single thought went through his mind: Don't let me be buried alive! For a fraction of a second he saw his mother's face before him. But suddenly he realized he was still alive; the frozen earth had stood the strain.

"Get out!" shouted Gambietz into his ear, "Before we're overcome by fumes." They scrambled out from beneath the tank. Just as Brasche was about to crawl out between the two rear roadwheels he felt the tracks begin to tremble and heard the engine, which had been at idle, begin to rev up. Frozen with fear, Brasche lay still. Then, suddenly, the engine returned to idle. The tank shook from the recoil of its main gun.

All at once life returned to Brasche. He crawled on and found himself looking right into the face of a Russian coming up the hill. They stared at each other for half a second, eye to eye. Then both reached for their weapons. But Gambietz's submachine gun roared from the other side of the tank, killing the Russian and two others lying behind him.

Brasche called out to Grunge, having noticed that the huge East Prussian was missing. The tank rolled on. Twenty meters farther it turned left and approached the second flanking position. In the same moment that it halted and lowered the long barrel of its main gun, a round from a Flak gun smashed into its flank and left it a blazing torch in the middle of the Heinrich Position.

"Back men, back!" Leutnant Heinrich appeared beside them. He pointed to the Russian tanks rolling over the German position, trying to extinguish all life beneath their rattling tracks. Farther to the rear another wave of infantry appeared. Every second they hesitated in this exposed position would result in the death of more of their comrades.

They ran down the slope. Brasche zigzagged as bullets whizzed past him. The burst struck a bush beside him. Two red flares shot into the sky, indicating to the Flak that they were free to fire on the German position. The two quad Flak guns opened fire. They were soon joined by all the 88's. The enemy troops firing on the Germans fleeing down the hill were forced to withdraw to the cover of the recaptured trenches.

The majority of *Jagdkommando Heinrich* managed to reach the Radau Bunker, where the 3rd Company of the 93rd Infantry Regiment had opened fire with its machine guns and mortars, adding its weight to the barrage.

As Rudi Brasche let himself fall to the floor of the bunker he knew that this time they had taken a beating. It had only been the Flak guns that had saved the operation from coming to a bad end.

The Russians launched no further attacks that night. They also refrained from attacking the following four nights, giving the defenders of the Radau Bunker a chance to complete their preparations. This mistake was to cost the enemy dearly.

✠

"Everyone listen to me! We're going to continue mining tonight and at this location."

Leutnant Heinrich had assembled the men of the pioneer platoon around him. He stood at the rough-hewn table, on which lay a map with part of the battlefield pencilled in. About 100 black dots on the white grease-proof paper showed where mines had been laid. The table was pushed against the wall and above it a multitude of wires hung down from a rack. From the loops of wire hung round markers with numbers. The same numbers were pencilled in on the map, showing where the mines had been laid. Red numbers indicated that three mines had been placed together. The Leutnant pointed toward the left flank, where a part of the semi-circular defensive area was still empty.

"The pioneer squad is going to mine this section, Brasche. Install your patented illumination at this spot, clear?" Rudi Brasche nodded. He looked at the sketch map. He, Gambietz and Grunge had been busy the past few nights.

"All right, move out. The artillery will put down harassing fire. But watch out for patrols so you don't get captured."

✠

"You take the pyrotechnics, Wilhelm. Richard, take the machine gun. I'll take the wires and fuses."

Obergefreiter Brasche was the first to leave the large bunker, whose powerful armament was probably capable of repulsing smaller Russian attacks. They reached the forward slope and crawled down toward the floor of the valley through the narrow trenches. Then they reached the area where the flares were to be set up.

"I'll go forward to the one-man hole," whispered Gambietz. He then disappeared into no-man's-land. Rudi Brasche began to work. He placed the pyrotechnics around the roots of bushes and the stumps of shattered trees and joined them with trip-wires, which he stretched here and there in the tangled undergrowth. If one of the wires were cut by the enemy, the pyrotechnic could still be set off by another wire. It took Brasche half an hour to place all his pyrotechnics. All the while shells fired by the divisional artillery boomed overhead. He placed one last large pyrotechnic on the extreme flank of the attack zone before crawling over to Grunge.

"Ready, Wilhelm?"

"My zone is clear. Those people back there are making noise as if they're all alone here." With a move of his head Grunge gestured toward the pioneers, who were busy emplacing their mines. The sound of shoveling was clearly audible. During pauses in the firing the sound of steel against steel was doubly loud.

"He's not coming, Rudi! Richard isn't answering."

"It's probably nothing. I'll go have a look."

"I'm coming with you!"

✠

Richard Gambietz had worked his way forward to the one-man hole they had dug the first night. It lay in a shell-hole where the ground was soft enough for digging. Breathing heavily, he wiped the sweat from his brow as he positioned his machine gun in the same place it had been the previous night and the night before.

Less than ten minutes had passed when he spotted movement. It was coming from some bushes directly in front of him. Snow fell from the bushes and then he heard a low moan. He felt the sharp cold. If only his machine gun hadn't frozen up. But he dared not move it.

Once again there was a rustling sound in the bushes, then more moans. He left the machine gun and reached for the submachine gun slung across his back. Cautiously he moved the weapon in front of him. He slid the safety to off with a soft click. Then he slithered out of the hole. He approached the bushes, his nerves strained to breaking. Again he heard a low moan. Gambietz swung out to one side and circled the bushes. Suddenly something hard struck him on the head. He felt his head swell, growing larger and larger until it seemed his steel helmet would burst. Then he submerged into fiery-red unconsciousness.

Gambietz came to. He felt himself moving and heard voices. He opened his eyes to slits and closed them immediately when he saw faces beside and in front of him. There were at least twenty Russians, all wearing snow smocks and armed with submachine guns. Four men grabbed his arms and legs and dragged him about 100 meters to the rear. A low voice said something to the one who had stayed behind and then his footsteps, too, disappeared in the direction of Brasche and Grunge.

Gambietz opened his eyes again. He saw a haggard face. Dark eyes flashed, and he could see that they were peering in the direction where the others had disappeared. Those heavily armed men were heading toward where his two companions were working and depending on him. He thought everyone outside the bunker was going to be killed.

Gambietz moaned loudly and rolled onto his side. His arm brushed against something hard. His fingers closed around a stone—or was it a piece of shrapnel? The icy cold was creeping through him and threatened to paralyze him.

Only the awareness that he had just moments caused him to act. Barely half recovered from the heavy blow, he saw that his captor had turned his head toward him. Cursing, the Russian got up and came over. He bent low, his submachine gun hanging directly over Gambietz's face.

Summoning all his strength, Gambietz swung his left arm upwards. At the same time, he knocked away the Russian's gun with his right. The stone struck the Russian in the face. He let out a cry of pain. The weapon fell from his hand and dropped into the snow. Stars swirled before Gambietz's eyes. Nevertheless, he picked up the Russian's automatic weapon. The flashes of gunfire from Hill 189 showed him where to run. Then he found the tracks the Russians had left in the snow. Gasping, he reached his old observation position. A figure stood up. A voice said: *"Ruki verkh!"* ("Hands up!") Gambietz fired. The figure collapsed and disappeared into the hole. His comrades must have heard that. That would have warned them; they would have recognized it as a Russian submachine gun.

The enemy troops appeared from the bushes ahead. Gambietz fired at the first one. A burst of fire reached out, forcing him to leap into the cover of the bushes. The bullets had missed by inches. Gambietz fired back immediately. As soon as he had fired he rolled onto his side and thus escaped the rain of bullets that poured into the bushes. Gambietz fired again. The weapon bucked in his hands. He wriggled into the snow and saw tracer passing overhead. One of the Red Army soldiers came running towards him.

Richard Gambietz raised his weapon. He saw the enemy soldier do the same. Then he fired. His attacker froze in mid-stride, stumbled backwards a few steps and collapsed into the snow. Three or four men followed. The first entered his field of fire. Gambietz pressed the trigger. Two shots rang out, then nothing but a sharp clicking noise. He had no more ammunition for the Russian gun and the enemy was approaching fast.

✠

Brasche and Grunge had moved forward about twenty meters. But they didn't go far. Brasche heard a noise from the direction of the one-man hole. Where was Gambietz? Brasche hesitated. Something was wrong here. Gambietz should have been back long ago.

A burst of fire from a Russian submachine gun caused him to drop to the ground. The submachine gun fire again, then a second weapon opened up. Figures emerged from the bushes to the left and right. Russians! Brasche fired at the closest figure. Then he heard Grunge's weapon roar.

"Forward, Wilhelm!" cried Brasche, trying to shout over the din. He saw Grunge run forward. Then he too began to run toward the source of the gunfire. Gambietz must be in trouble.

The snow crunched beneath his feet. Once he broke through and sank up to his knees. Then he spotted two men running towards the bushes. Two shots were fired from the bushes, then all was quiet. Brasche emptied his magazine and immediately rammed the next one home. Grunge was still firing. Two enemy soldiers dropped to the ground, the others disappeared into the night. Brasche fired after them. Then he ran at a crouch toward the bushes. A figure stumbled towards him: It was Gambietz.

"Thank God, Richard!"

"I was finished if you hadn't come."

They made their way back carefully, as the Russians might still be hiding nearby, waiting to ambush them. Leutnant Heinrich came running toward the three from the central sector.

"What happened out there?"

Speaking rapidly, Gambietz described the large Russian patrol, his capture and how he had managed to overcome the enemy soldier and warn his comrades in time.

"Gambietz, you'll get the Knight's Cross for this. After all the patrols and special missions this tops it all."

✠

"They're really hammering away. That means a Russian attack, Rudi."

"It looks that way," replied Brasche. He peered through the machine gun's snow shield. Brasche was the gunner, while beside him Grunge was ready to load fresh ammunition belts. It was as if the huge East Prussian were deaf to the rumbling of the Russian artillery, as if the bursting shells which were shaking the Radau Bunker to its foundations left him cold. Inside the bunker it was warm. The meters-thick earth shelter, which they had laboriously blasted out of the ground the previous autumn, was impervious to the cold and shrapnel. Even direct fire by the much-feared *Ratschbum* could not pierce the walls of the bunker.

The previous night small Russian combat patrols had tried to approach the bunker. However, they ran into German patrols in the valley and bitter night fighting broke out. By day the appearance of the mess kit was still the signal for a brief cease-fire. As Brasche watched, rounds hammered into the slope in front of them. One of the exploding rounds set off a Teller mine, which went up in a harsh rosette of flame.

"Number 71 is gone, sir!" reported Brasche. The Leutnant reached for one of the tagged strips of wire and removed it. Suddenly, the Russian artillery shifted its fire to the German rear.

"Stay alert, everyone. They'll be coming soon."

All of a sudden the far side of the valley came alive at the bunker and the dugouts that had been blasted out of the ground. In their white snow smocks the enemy soldiers looked like wisps of fog that, by chance, had assumed the shapes of men.

"Here they come!"

The Leutnant had hurried over to the middle lookout. He saw the attackers through his binoculars. Rudi Brasche aimed his machine gun at the spot he had selected. As soon as the enemy reached the edge of the valley he would open fire. There was something fascinating about the attacking enemy that had an effect on Brasche. They were running straight into the bullets. They knew that many would be killed, but they listened to their leaders and ran and ran, until they were cut down.

"Attention, Rudi! They've reached the fire point!"

Brasche pulled the trigger, as did Kneisel and Wiegmann on the right flank. Rudi Brasche moved his machine gun from left to right. Then it fell silent. "It's jammed!" he cried.

Grunge was on the spot and, in seconds, he had cleared the stoppage. But the enemy had then gone to ground. There was nothing to be seen of them. For an instant Brasche thought he was having a hallucination. Then he saw the second wave rush forward. Kneisel opened fire with his heavy machine gun. He allowed the weapon to glide to the side on the guide rails. All the while the bolt chewed up the ammunition belt and spat out the empty shell casings to one side.

"Replacement barrel!"

Grunge passed the new barrel and the asbestos cloth. With practiced motions Brasche changed barrels. In front of them the first wave got to its feet and stormed toward the position.

On the far slope the Russians opened up with mortars and field guns. Shells smashed into the bunker and fell among the mortar positions. The platoon's attached heavy mortars answered. The six tubes fired 80-mm rounds into the valley. The mortar rounds exploded with bright flashes, throwing the soldiers of the second wave into the snow.

"There, the two machine guns on carts. They're approaching Point 34, Rudi."

Brasche stopped firing. He saw the group of enemy soldiers with the two machine guns. They were running toward an uprooted tree. He realized that the Russians would be in cover in a matter of moments.

"Thirty-four!" he shouted.

Leutnant Heinrich heard the call. He grasped the wire with the number 34 between his fingers and pulled. There was a flash of fire as two Teller mines exploded and the two machine gun carts disappeared. It was like the explosion of a heavy round. Pieces of weapons and men flew through the air. Explosion followed explosion. The first wave of Russians, who had worked their way close to the German position, were then in the killing zone. Pyrotechnic flares hissed into the sky, ripping away the protective veil of darkness. Suddenly, the enemy troops were exposed and in the open. Automatic weapons fire cut down the Russians. Shells burst and mines exploded. Whenever a group of Russian troops approached a point designated on the large control panel, the man watching that sector called out the appropriate number to the Leutnant, who detonated the mines emplaced there. Brasche was a witness to the deadly effectiveness of the Teller mines. Nevertheless, small groups and lone Russian soldiers penetrated the cordon of fire and came nearer and nearer.

The illumination flares bathed the area in front of the bunker in a harsh light. Every movement was visible. The chain of pyrotechnics ignited one after another. Richard Gambietz opened fire with his rifle on a group of Russians who had approached to within thirty meters of the bunker. He

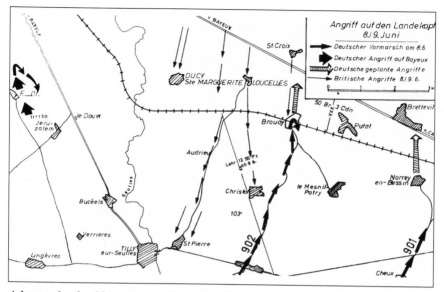

Advance by the 901st Panzer Grenadier Demonstration Regiment from Cheux to Bretteville.

called a warning to Brasche. The Russians were aiming at the muzzle flashes from his machine gun. Brasche swung his weapon toward the enemy. A bullet came through the embrasure and creased his helmet. Then he had the enemy in his sights and cut them down with a long burst of fire.

The second wave reached the mine belt. More Teller mines went up. It looked as if German heavy batteries were firing in the valley. Leutnant Heinrich detonated several mines that lay outside the attack area, reinforcing the deception that artillery was wreaking the havoc among the enemy. The sound of explosions rang out through the night. The men inside the bunker felt the shock waves from mines exploding nearby. The Radau Bunker—the racket bunker—was living up to its name this night.

The advancing enemy troops ignited the concealed pyrotechnic flares. They struck the tripwires that Brasche and his companions had set up, turning night into day for the defenders. The last wave collapsed ten meters from the bunker. The attackers streamed back. When they reached the top of the far slope they ran into heavy fire from the German Flak guns that were shelling the enemy bunkers and trenches. German mortars joined in and this terrible night ended in a final orgy of steel and fire. Leutnant Heinrich's voice rang out through the bunker: "Pioneer platoon, get ready!" The interior of the bunker was heavy with powder smoke, which made breathing difficult. The pioneers reached for their mines, ready to prepare the battlefield for the next attack.

February 1942 passed. The terrible cold, which had taken its toll on the men of the 93rd Infantry Regiment, eased a little. Temperatures were still minus 20 degrees Celsius, but what was that compared to the minus 40 to 45 degree temperatures of December and January.

The Russians made repeated efforts to capture the Radau Bunker. Six times they drove out the bunker personnel, but each time it was retaken by a German counterattack. As often as it changed hands, neither side considered blowing up or rendering unusable this vitally important bunker on the hill overlooking the broad valley. For friend and foe it was an oasis of warmth and safety in the midst of the killing zone.

The Russians also kept up their attacks on the limekiln, but their strongest efforts were reserved for the Radau Bunker. They were well aware that observers were directing the fire of the German Flak and artillery from inside the bunker. This small, bitter war in the Kamyenka Valley demanded the utmost of every soldier. Each night Russian artillery pounded the German positions and patrols from both sides clashed in no-man's-land.

Richard Gambietz was the subject of much comment. It was he who set out alone into no-man's-land when a prisoner was needed. All alone, he repeatedly went forth into the lion's den, this young man with the narrow face and cheerful eyes. When he needed one or two men to accompany him it was always Rudi Brasche and Wilhelm Grunge. These three men were the backbone of *Jagdkommando Heinrich*.

The Russians launched one last attack on the Radau Bunker at the end of February. They committed three infantry battalions. Again the night was torn apart by igniting illumination flares and exploding mines. Russian artillery added to the din. One of the older men who had participated in the Battle of Verdun in 1917 compared the fighting to that First World War battle.

A handful of stubborn men held the bunker. Brasche fired his machine gun; Grunge fed in fresh ammunition belts. Gambietz called out which mines to detonate as groups of enemy troops approached. The attack by the three Russian battalions collapsed within hand-grenade range of the bunker. The enemy didn't recover from this blow. They did not return. The Radau Bunker seemed to have become an impregnable fortress.

"Raise the mess kit, the food is coming!"

It was Unteroffizier Klingner who called out. Brasche reached for his mess kit. Instead of the expected quiet, a hail of bullets whizzed about the raised metal container.

"What's going on? They seemed to have forgotten our agreement." Brasche lowered the mess kit.

"They've been relieved. That explains the noise we heard during the night, sir."

"You might be right. But if Ivan's been relieved, then something's up. They've probably brought in fresh forces for another attack." Leutnant Heinrich went over to the telephone. "Get me headquarters, Klingner."

Jupp Klingner called the regimental headquarters. The adjutant who answered called Oberst Radwan to the phone. Radwan had simultaneously been promoted to Oberst and named regimental commander following the transfer of Oberst von Weber to the Army Procurement Office, where he was to participate in the development of new weapons. Von Weber had earlier played a part in the construction of the MG 34 machine gun.

"What's up, Heinrich?"

"Yesterday's report that the Russians were being relieved seems to have been proved correct, sir. The Russians are firing at the mess kit."

"That's rather meager proof, Heinrich," smiled the regimental commander. "Can't you get anything more substantial?"

"Patrol, sir?"

"Exactly, Heinrich! But only for the purpose of capturing one of the new Russians."

"We'll do it tonight, sir."

"Good, Heinrich. Out."

"Listen everyone. We need a small patrol to bring back a prisoner."

"Here, sir!"

Rudi Brasche stepped forward. He grinned when he saw the surprised look on the face of Richard Gambietz. Gambietz was usually the first to volunteer for such missions.

"Very well. Select two men to accompany you."

"I guess we'll be coming along to the party," said Gambietz, slapping Grunge on the shoulder.

Three hours later they were hurrying down the slope. Ivan had begun his nightly fireworks, and mortar rounds were falling on the snow-covered slope, blackening the fresh snow that had fallen that afternoon. They reached the valley floor and Rudi Brasche turned to the left. Moving in a wide arc they came to the hill with the Russian bunker.

They swung out farther to the west when a Russian machine gun began to fire on the left flank, not thirty meters from the bunker. Then they reached the slope and crawled toward the top. Thirty meters below the machine-gun position the three men stopped to rest.

"Wilhelm to the left. Richard to the right of the hole. I'll take the center." Brasche's two companions crawled to the sides. Rudi Brasche remained behind. Suddenly he was the loneliest man on earth. He had to force himself to begin crawling again. He covered meter after meter, stopping about eight meters from the machine gun. He heard the muffled voices of the Russians. Three clouds of mist rose from the hole, indicating to him that there were three men inside who would have to be overpowered.

Brasche heard a muffled laugh. All of a sudden two of the men stood up. Their heads were projected onto the snow as long shadows by the moonlight. Then there was the sound of footsteps crunching in the snow. The footsteps were moving away in the direction of the Russian bunker.

Relief, thought Brasche. It was time to act before the enemy returned. He crawled forward and reached the pile of dirt in which a notch had been cut for the machine gun. Brasche jumped to his feet. The enemy soldier, who was looking in the direction in which his two companions had disappeared, swung around. The Russian reached for a submachine gun, but before he could reach it Brasche swung his weapon and struck the man on the skull. The Russian collapsed without a sound.

"Have you got him?" asked Gambietz, who had appeared from the side.

"Yes. Hurry up and place the charge, thirty-second delay on the fuse."

Rudi Brasche reached for the unconscious Russian. But Grunge brushed his arm away. The powerful East Prussian took the Russian under his arm like a doll and disappeared down the hill.

"Ready, Rudi!"

"Let's go then!"

They ran down the hill. Once Brasche tripped over a root and slid a few meters down the slope. Loud shouts rang out from the Russian bunker. Men raced to the machine-gun position. They had not quite reached it when the explosives went up in a flash of red flame. Brasche caught up with Grunge, who had swung the captive over his back.

"Over there to the left, Wilhelm!"

They ran to the left, reached the narrow trench that ended there and hurried along toward the German positions. German mortars and infantry guns then opened fire to prevent any Russians from pursuing the patrol.

With Gambietz covering the rear, the three reached the hill in one piece and handed over their prisoner.

Interrogation of the prisoner and papers found on him revealed without a doubt that the Russians had regrouped and that the trenches and bunkers opposite the Radau Bunker were then manned by Caucasian troops. A new Russian offensive was imminent!

✠

"What's the date, Richard?"

"The seventh of March."

"Well, it looks as if winter's just about over, even if there's still snow lying about."

"In a month at most we'll be stuck in mud, I can tell you that."

"Perhaps we'll move before then" interjected Grunge. He looked into the smiling faces of his two comrades. Then he, too, cracked a smile.

All of a sudden the Russian artillery fire intensified. The heavy guns, which had begun adjustment fire at first light, reduced the interval between salvoes.

The men listened attentively. They looked at each other and Kneisel said what they were all thinking:

"Ivan's coming today. Today, for sure. Judging by the assembly area that air reconnaissance spotted he's got at least 100 tanks parked over there on the reverse slope."

"That should be enough to make things hot for us."

"Let's wait and see what happens," said Grunge in his sonorous voice.

"I'd like to know where you get your optimism, Wilhelm."

"What's that got to do with optimism? We must stop them so they don't cut off our comrades," was the simple answer from the Obergefreiter. Everyone knew that they all felt the same way. Warmth rose in Rudi Brasche. Warmth and his affection for the huge man, who radiated trust and confidence.

The Russian mortars stepped up their barrage. From the lightest to the heaviest they all poured shells into the German positions. The mortar rounds fell in rows. Their howling mingled with the first explosions, and soon the men could hear nothing but the crash of exploding shells and the chirping of shell fragments.

"Take cover!" yelled Feldwebel Wegener. They disappeared into the holes they had dug on either side of the Radau Bunker. Brasche pressed himself against the bricks he had laboriously dragged from the brickworks and installed over the previous weeks. He felt the earth tremble as shells burst nearby. All he could think of was that this firing must stop soon or he would go mad. But the firing did not stop. Shells of all calibers poured down. The heavier rounds seemed to be concentrating on the area of the limekiln. Towering columns of smoke rose into the air. Red flames spurted up. An ammunition dump was hit and yellow, green and red flashes filled the air. Suddenly, the Russian artillery shifted its fire onto positions in the German rear. A signal flare rose into the sky from the left, where the forward flanking position was located. Tank attack!

"Tanks?" asked Kneisel in disbelief. "Tanks?"

Then they heard the roar of many engines and the rumbling sound of tracks.

"There they are!" shouted Ecklebe.

The first tanks appeared on the hill on the far side of the valley. They were KV tanks. To the left and right of the first group of five steel giants appeared T-34s. They raced onto the top of the hill and joined the KVs. They halted and opened fire. Then came the second wave of at least twenty tanks. They reached the hill, nosed forward and rolled down the hill toward the limekiln.

"My God!" stuttered Ecklebe. Brasche, too, was speechless. The enemy had never before attacked with such massive forces. Behind them the two Flak batteries began to fire. They were soon joined by the three guns on the two flanks and in the center of the northern edge of the limekiln.

The new morning was torn apart by harsh flames as the tank-versus-Flak duel was played out. The tanks waiting on the hill fired on the tongues of flame from the Flak. The first enemy tank was hit and burst into flames. A second, immobilized with track damage, continued to fire until it was hit beneath the turret by an 88-mm round. The round blew the turret off the Russian tank. Flames shot into the air, enveloping the crew as it tried to escape.

"Infantry, Feldwebel!"

Behind the tanks that had reached the floor of the valley appeared Russians in earth-brown uniforms and white snow smocks. They were running after the tanks. Their objective was the limekiln, the left flank of the German defense. If they had that, they could roll up the German lines from the flank. The two quad 20-mm Flak opened fire, sweeping the field behind the tanks clear.

The 88s were then firing in salvoes. A dozen enemy tanks were burning in the valley. Then the leading tanks rolled into the belt of mines around the limekiln. Three were disabled, their tracks shattered. The others turned and headed back. They had not yet reached the bottom of the far slope, when the tanks firing from the hill began to move and rolled down the slope. Three of them took direct hits from the Flak and blew apart. But the rest kept rolling toward the limekiln.

"The pioneer platoon will create a barrier in front of the attacking tanks. Follow me!" Leutnant Heinrich left cover. He reached the communications trench to the limekiln and the Leutnant.ran along it to the west. Brasche saw the men from the forward flanking position join

"Grab your things!" he called, pulling his machine gun from its position. Rudi Brasche ran through the narrow trench, its sides already crumbling in places. In front of him rounds fired by the Russian tanks hammered into the limekiln. Machine guns fired on the Germans still holding out there. Then he spotted the onrushing enemy in the valley below him to his right. A quick look told Brasche that his companions were close behind. He vaulted out of the trench. A burst of fire flitted toward him. He zigzagged, saw a circular crater three meters below him and jumped inside. Gambietz landed hard on his shoulder, and Grunge tumbled into the hole right behind him.

Brasche dug a small pit with his spade and placed his machine gun in it on its bipod. For an instant he saw a group of enemy soldiers. They were running under cover behind a T-34 but were vulnerable from the flank. Brasche fired a long burst. The tank turned, its tracks rattling. The long-barreled gun spat flames and the round struck the slope two meters above their position. An avalanche of earth and small stones rained down on the three men crouching in the crater. Then a Russian machine gun began to rattle. To the left and right Russian troops swelled out from behind the cover of the tank and headed toward the shell hole containing the three members of the pioneer platoon. Brasche fired again. The Russians were caught in mid-stride and dropped into the snow. The enemy soldiers fired back with submachine guns and a Maxim gun they had dragged with them.

Rudi Brasche heard firing from above on the slope. Some of his comrades had installed themselves there and had opened fire on the advancing Russians. The tanks had halted below in the valley. The duel between tanks and Flak continued. Flames continued to flash from the guns of the tanks, and the sound of rounds striking home rang out through the morning of 7 March.

Brasche coughed as he felt the biting powder smoke in his lungs. He watched Gambietz load a fresh belt of ammunition into the gun, cradling it in his hands to ensure a smooth feed. Brasche took aim at a burning tank, behind which he had spotted movement. Then the enemy stormed forward again. Brasche pulled the trigger and swung the barrel of the machine gun around. His burst of fire took the impetus out of the attack.

All of the German machine guns joined in and the Russian attack was halted in the valley. The Russians who had still been visible quickly disappeared into the snow, trenches and holes. It was as if the earth had swallowed them up.

"Watch out, Rudi. There—on the right. There's some just to the right of the shot-up tree."

Rudi Brasche took aim at that spot. He searched for his target with cool determination, ready to fire before the enemy did. He saw a flash and fired, but it was already too late. He felt a heavy blow against his helmet. As he rolled over he heard the crack of a sniper's rifle through the noise of battle. Then he lost consciousness for a few moments.

When he came to Grunge had bedded him down at the bottom of the crater, which he had lined with his coat. The worried face of his friend looked down at him.

"What happened, Wilhelm?"

"Your steel helmet saved you. The bullet pierced the helmet. It was deflected upward, nicked your skull and must have skipped along the back of the helmet. Then it entered your shoulder. The bullet's still in there somewhere. Look at this button."

Grunge gave Brasche the button that had held his shoulder strap. It had been flattened like a postage stamp.

The Russians attacked again while Brasche was on his way to hospital. They came during the night of 7–8 March. Gambietz and Grunge again played a leading role in the successful German defense. Grunge ran through enemy fire to keep the machine gun supplied with ammunition. Gambietz fired until his index finger was shot off. Grunge bandaged his friend's wound and took over the machine gun. The Russian attack was repulsed. The line in the Kamyenka Valley had held.

On 3 June 1942, while still in hospital, Richard Gambietz was presented the Knight's Cross for his heroic actions in the defense of the positions in the Kamyenka Valley.

✠

"Here we are, and the neighboring hill is still not occupied, Rudi."

Wilhelm Grunge gestured to the right, where Hill 419 projected against the sky. It was to be occupied that day, because the regiment's left flank would be the first objective of the Russian counterattack.

"It's a pity that Gambietz isn't here with us, Wilhelm. The it would be like old times."

"You call that the old times? Exactly six men and an artillery observer on his rickety wooden tower—that's the entire defensive line. If Ivan knew that perhaps he'd make things hot for us."

"Just let them come, Rudi," said Kneisel, the only original member of the squad—apart from Grunge—who had been at the limekiln. The three newcomers grinned. Bent low, Brasche went over to where the second machine gun was positioned. He clapped Madel on the shoulder.

"How's it going, Siegfried?"

"Nothing to be seen. All quiet."

Brasche stepped up to the machine gun and looked down. The slope dropped away vertically for twenty meters then ran into a brush-covered area. One man was enough here.

In the west the sky was blood red as the sun went down on 14 September. Brasche arrived at the center of the weak defensive position. Below he could see the men occupying Hill 419. He called something down to them. The platoon leader looked up and waved back. Just then Russian mortars opened up again and Brasche was forced to take cover.

From his lofty perch Leutnant Köhler passed on information to the artillery, which was ranging in on the enemy's main firing position.

"How are we fixed for hand grenades, Wilhelm?"

"Back there in the cellar—eighteen crates full. We won't need any more here. By the time we've thrown all those either the Ivans will be finished or we'll have received fresh supplies.

"Let's hope so! In any case we still have plenty of explosives."

The Russian attack began an hour after midnight on 15 September. The Russian attackers—two infantry battalions—stormed the two neighboring hills with the courage of desperation. They reached the foot of Hill 419, where they were pinned down by fire from the MG 42s—a new weapon which had just reached the front. Waves of attackers then appeared in front of Hill 489.

"Open fire!" shouted Brasche to his squad.

Kneisel, who was manning the machine gun, began to fire on the onrushing waves of enemy troops. His weapon tore wide gaps in their ranks. Nevertheless, many reached the cover of the vegetation that covered the flanks of the hill. The two flanking machine guns were firing too. There was only one man behind each gun. Only Kneisel, who was manning the heavy machine gun, had a second man standing by to feed in fresh belts of ammunition. Abusch and Madel had to look after themselves, because Rudi Brasche had reserved the most difficult task for himself and Grunge: To drive the Russians out of the bushes and back down the precipice.

Kneisel lost sight of the enemy: "Damn, they've gone into cover. I can't see them, Rudi!"

Brasche stood up. He peered down over the steep slope and fired an illumination round. The flare arced downward, bathing the slope in light for a few seconds. Figures emerged from the darkness, and the three machine guns opened fire as one on the suddenly visible enemy.

"Over here, Wilhelm!"

Grunge crawled over to the rocky projection, dragging two boxes of grenades with him. They had earlier scooped out several shallow holes there, knowing they might be needed later on. It had become time to occupy them. Rudi Brasche worked his way over to the crag. He reached his hole and, peering through the narrow slit he had bored through the earth, scanned the terrain below. He saw the flash of submachine guns. From the flank one of the machine guns of the four squads on Hill 419 opened fire, adding its weight to the three on Hill 489. Nevertheless, the enemy reached the saddle between the two hills and continued clambering upwards.

"Ready, Wilhelm?"

"All set, Rudi."

The pair threw their hand grenades almost simultaneously. They sailed through the air in a high arc, landed at the feet of the leading Russians and rolled down the hill. There were two loud explosions as the grenades went off. The two men hurled grenade after grenade. Bullets whistled past them. The Russians kept climbing. The wave of attackers grew denser as the second wave caught up with the first. Hand grenades burst almost without letup. Brasche and Grunge were throwing from a prone position. Only their arms were visible for a brief instant as they hurled the grenades. The Russian attack ground to a halt. The survivors, including the wounded, crawled into holes and crevices with a skill seemingly unique to the Russians.

"All clear?" Brasche asked. "Anyone hurt?"

His six companions checked in one after another. Brasche breathed a sigh of relief. An hour passed, during which the Russian mortars kept up a steady fire on the hill. The Russians concentrated their next attack on the neighboring hill, which was flatter and easier to reach.

The night rang with the thunder of weaponry. The six men on the hill were forced to watch helplessly as the Russians literally flooded the other hill. They fired as long as they could without threatening their own people. But then the Russians broke into the trenches on the neighboring hill. Flashes lit the night. Hand grenades and Teller mines detonated, killing friend and foe. Then all was quiet, and the mortars that had been firing on Hill 419 prior to the Russian attack then turned their attention to Hill 489.

"We're alone now, Rudi."

"Yeah, Wilhelm. And I'll bet all my money that they'll come across the saddle before the night's over."

"Then we'll make things hot for them when they come."

"Right. I think we can take Madel from the cliff and position him at the saddle. He can cover us while we lay the Teller mines."

Grunge ran off and came back through the mortar fire two minutes later. Madel and Toppolczan took four Teller mines and ran into the deep gully that led eastward toward the saddle between the two hills.

"Stay in this hole, Madel. Make sure the Ivans don't bother us while we work."

Grunge followed his two companions. He carried two Teller mines in each fist, holding them by their metal grips. He ran even faster than Brasche and the Hungarian. They reached the lowest point of the saddle and began to emplace their mines.

Five minutes passed. From Hill 419 they could hear the hooting of the victory-drunk Russians. Then Madel opened fire, a sign the Russians were moving forward through the gully.

"One mine left, Rudi!"

"Go, go! Back, before they see us!"

"Here they come, Rudi."

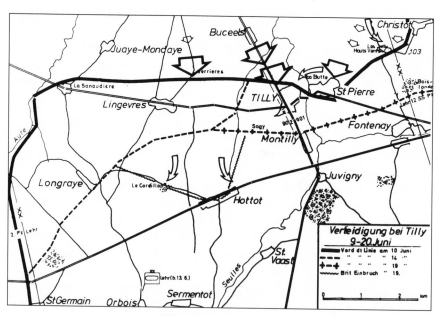

The defense of Tilly.

"Damn, I can't see them!" Brasche raised his flare pistol and fired. The slope stood out as clear as day. The machine gun rattled. The deadly new MG 42 could fire 1,200 rounds per minute, making it a fearsome weapon.

"Left, Rudi."

Brasche pulled the left wire. The Teller mine detonated with a thunderous explosion. The enemy soldiers stopped, then felt their way forward cautiously until they determined that the way above was clear.

Once again the Russians stormed forward. Again Brasche raised the flare pistol. There was a crack and the illumination flare arced into the night sky. Two hours later, as the sun began to appear in the eastern sky, they were certain they had done it—they had prevented the enemy from reaching the hill. Three hours after sunrise contact was finally reestablished with battalion, and Brasche was on the line with the battalion command post.

"Brasche's squad here. Sir, we urgently need reinforcements."

"How many men have you got left up there, Brasche? Did you rescue anyone from Hill 419 or did any get through to you?"

"None, sir. There are just six of us. None wounded. But we need help if we're to hold."

"Brasche, the way to your position has been under observation by the enemy since early this morning. Anyone we tried to send would be killed. But we'll try to get through during the night. Hold on until then. Your hill has become the pivotal point of the whole front. Everything depends on you and your squad."

"What shit!" swore Brasche as he threw down the receiver.

"What is it, Rudi?"

"No reinforcements, Wilhelm. The Ivans are shooting anyone who tries to reach us."

"Then we'll have to hold out alone."

✠

The second night had fallen. The six men lay in their holes, their faces haggard, dirty and unshaven. They allowed the Russian barrage to pass over them. Brasche crawled from one man to the next. Making his way through the shells, which fell from the heavens and ploughed up the hill, he reached the slope leading down to the saddle.

"Rudi, here they come again!"

Brasche reached for his binoculars. Adjusting them, he caught sight of the enemy soldiers, who were creeping single file through the night towards the hill.

"Wilhelm, let's move a few meters towards them. Then we'll be able to get them with our hand grenades again."

Brasche left cover. He was pressed close to the ground. He crawled down the slope and reached the steep bank that had stopped the enemy the previous night. There was already a box of grenades in the hole, as there was in the one occupied by Grunge. They had placed them there right after dark.

Rudi Brasche screwed off the caps of all the grenades. He reached for the lines leading to the pyrotechnics hanging from bushes and tree stumps sixty meters below.

The Russians came nearer. There were perhaps thirty men, trying to take the hill in a surprise attack. When they reached the area of trees and bushes Brasche ignited the first pyrotechnic and threw his grenades. The grenades sailed downwards toward the startled group of Russians; by then, they were fully illuminated by the pyrotechnics. Two machine guns opened up on the exposed enemy troops. The Russians charged forward. Teller mines went off and the two Germans threw hand grenades until the last enemy soldier had gone to ground.

The Russian mortars began to fire again. A moment later Kneisel reported a Russian attack from the north.

As Brasche and the others reached the crest of the hill they could hear the shouts of the attacking Russians.

"Get the hand grenades ready!"

Suddenly Jozef Toppolczan cried out. His outstretched arm pointed towards the left, in the direction of the steep slope. Figures had appeared there and were running toward them. Brasche swung round and threw his hand grenades. Then he seized his submachine gun and emptied the magazine at the enemy.

Wilhelm Grunge followed the actions of his squad leader. Finally, the enemy soldiers who had managed to negotiate the steep bank were overcome. But a short time later more Red Army soldiers appeared over the rocky crest. Hand grenades flung them backwards down the precipice. Their horrible cries rang out above the noise of battle.

Suddenly Grunge jumped to his feet. He raced toward the steep slope. A mortar round exploded not ten meters from him, knocking him to the ground. But then he reappeared from the thick dust. Hands flying, he threw grenades down onto the rocky crag, which had been reached by a Russian element advancing from the west through the field of rocks.

Fifteen hand grenades took all the life out of the Russian advance. Grunge sent a burst from his submachine gun after the fleeing enemy.

Then he crawled back to the hole from which Kneisel was firing on more approaching enemy troops.

Brasche was horrified to see that the Russians were within 100 meters. The heavy machine gun could no longer reach them.

"Hand grenades everyone."

Again they rained death down the slope. Grenades burst below. The Russian mortars shifted their fire onto the battalion's sector. Fighting broke out below, from where the reinforcements should have come.

Kneisel's voice rang out over the din: "No more hand grenades!"

"I've only got one left!" shouted Grunge.

"Explosive charges!"

Brasche reached for a satchel charge. He could already hear the panting enemy soldiers and their leaders shouting orders. Then the defenders heard the sneering, confident cry of death ringing in their ears: "Urray—urray—urray!"

Brasche flung the explosive charge down the hill. Then another. A third followed. Grunge was throwing as well. All of a sudden the figure of Toppolczan rose from cover. He was holding his machine gun at his hip and, standing erect, he fired into the inferno caused by the charges. A burst of tracer reached out for the Gefreiter from below. The bullets knocked him backward. He fell heavily to the ground next to Brasche's foxhole. Brasche hauled his comrade into the hole. Then he heard the thunderclap of one of the last charges going off and the footsteps of the enemy as they retreated. The three-kilo explosive charges had put them to flight. Gefreiter Toppolczan was dead.

The Russian battle cry rang out three more times that night. Brasche was everywhere at once, directing the defense of the hill. He ran through enemy fire to threatened positions. Contact was lost with battalion. A direct hit blasted the artillery observer out of his observation post. Hill 489 became Hell on earth. The night of the hand grenades had become the night of the explosive charges.

All of the following day was spent by the five survivors laying mines and lowering pyrotechnics and explosive charges on wires over the slope under the direction of their squad leader.

Darkness fell and Brasche organized the defense once again. When the enemy attacked for the fourteenth time. They suffered the same fate they had met the first time. Rudi Brasche was a tower of strength. The other three men positioned themselves around him and the towering East Prussian. In this way the five men defeated the Russian battalion trying to take the hill.

Finally, about an hour later, reinforcements arrived. The five could scarcely believe they had been saved. Brasche and his small group of men had held the rocky hill for three days and nights. A little later the five survivors were standing before the regiment's commanding officer. He personally pinned the Iron Cross, First Class, on each of them.

"Brasche," said the regimental commander, "I hereby promote you to Unteroffizier for bravery in the face of the enemy. At the same time I would like to inform you that I am going to recommend you for the Knight's Cross."

✠

On 30 September Rudi Brasche received written confirmation that he had been awarded the Iron Cross, First Class. The fighting went on. Brasche was wounded for the fourth time during the fighting at Ordshonikidze in the Caucasus while repulsing an enemy attack. That was during the night of 2 November 1942. Brasche lost consciousness and awoke to find himself in Kislovodsk hospital.

Once again he had escaped death. His face had become narrow. His wounded leg worried him. But six days later he was able to stand again. He queried every new arrival at hospital about his regiment. Then it was 9 November 1942. Listening to the midday news, Brasche learned of the battles in the southern sector of the Eastern Front. He was about to switch off the set when the announcer declared: "The Führer and Supreme Commander of the Wehrmacht has awarded the Knight's Cross of the Iron Cross to Obergefreiter Rudolf Brasche, squad leader in a panzer grenadier regiment (by this time the 93rd Infantry Regiment had been redesignated as the 93rd Panzer Grenadier Regiment). During three days and nights he and his squad, completely on its own, repelled fourteen battalion-level Russian attacks and held a position vital to the division."

The men in the ward were beside themselves. Their Rudi, the dark, quiet youth, who had helped them selflessly since getting out of his sickbed, had won the Knight's Cross.

Finally, after his wounds had healed, Brasche was given convalescent leave. He was able to go home. Halberstadt gave him a hero's welcome. During the subsequent, brief recovery period he had a joyous reunion with Richard Gambietz. Then he was sent to Magdeburg, to the replacement and training unit of the 13th Panzer Division. However his wounded leg was still giving him trouble. Not until October 1943 was he transferred to the 1st Company of the 901st Panzer Grenadier Training Regiment, which had been sent to Italy to combat partisans.

The regiment, which was later to form the panzer grenadier core of the panzer training division, remained in Fiume until January 1944. Then it was transferred to Nancy, where the division was formed.

NORMANDY AND THE END OF THE WAR

Rudi Brasche took part in the occupation of Hungary with the panzer training division. In May 1944 his regiment was transferred back to France. The division was placed on alert early one morning. The Allies had landed in the Bay of the Seine. The invasion had begun. It fell to the division, one of the best-equipped divisions in the German Army, to drive the enemy back into the sea.

Unteroffizier Rudi Brasche and the 1st Company reached Norrey early on the morning of 8 June. (Norrey was the designated regimental assembly area; the regiment was commanded by Oberst Scholze. Brasche was a squad leader in the 2nd Platoon.) The entire panzer training division was regrouped in the Tilly area. From there it was to attack and take Bayeux. On 9 June, when the attack was already rolling, the division received orders to call off the attack and fall back toward Tilly. Never before had Rudi Brasche seen such confusion in command.

When 10 June began the division was holding a seventeen-kilometer-wide sector of the front, extending from Christot-Tilly to St. Germain-d'Extot. Elements of the British 7th Armoured Division attempted to break through this front. Deployed in wedge formation, the 1st Company worked its way forward. Leading the way, the 3rd Platoon advanced along the road and reached the edge of an area of fields and scrub pines, beyond which was visible a hedgerow, so typical for this region.

While the 2nd Platoon advanced to the right of the road, the 3rd Platoon remained concealed in bushes behind it and to the left. Perhaps 100 meters farther to the rear, behind the 1st Platoon, was the 4th Platoon. The latter was armed with heavy machine guns and 80-mm mortars. Oberleutnant Monz, the company commander, was up front with the 3rd Platoon.

Unteroffizier Rudi Brasche, whose squad had received two *Panzerschreck* bazooka-type weapons, stopped for half a minute. Visible to his left was a sunken road that opened onto the main road. He could only see about 100 meters, as the defile curved away toward the north. He had taken three steps when the voice of Jasper Lagemann stopped him.

"Tanks from the left, Rudi."

"Becker, report to the company commander: Tanks from the left rolling straight toward the company's flank." Obergefreiter Becker raced forward to the 3rd Platoon. Brasche ran across to the right side of the sunken road and threw himself into the ditch.

Rudi Brasche took aim at the first tank and fired. A streak of flame shot from the *Panzerschreck*. The projectile flitted toward the tank and struck the base of the turret. As if raised by a ghost's hand, it was tossed twenty meters through the air and landed on the second tank with a crash. Flames spurted from the second vehicle. In the same instant the third tank opened fire. The battle for Tilly had begun.

"Follow me. We must knock out the last tank in the column, then they'll be trapped in the defile and we can take them out one at a time."

They ran forward at a crouch and were met by hectic machine-gun fire. Then they were through the danger zone. A muzzle flash revealed the location of the last tank. Rudi Brasche worked his way through the scrub pines to the sunken road. Suddenly, the turret of the Sherman appeared through the bushes, and the *Panzerschreck* was moved into position. Once again one of the deadly projectiles bored into an enemy tank. There was a mighty explosion as the tank's reserve ammunition went up. Everyone in the area of the fire-spewing volcano pulled back.

"Hill and Lagemann follow me. The rest of you remain here and stay alert."

Brasche ran through the bushes. Branches whipped his face. Thorns bloodied his hands. He reached the wall of the defile. A tank's main gun bellowed nearby. They jumped down near the tank, and Brasche spotted a group of British soldiers. He turned his submachine gun and fired three short bursts. After the British had gone into cover, Hans Hill raced toward the Sherman. With a bound he leapt onto the tank. He pulled open the hatch, tossed in his hand grenades, slammed the hatch shut and jumped down from the tank. Shots whipped through the semi-darkness of the defile. Lagemann and Brasche fired on the enemy troops, allowing Hill to reach the safety of the wall.

"Give me covering fire!" ordered Rudi Brasche. Before his companions could answer he had disappeared into the undergrowth which stretched along the defile.

There he crawled into a thick hazel bush, stood up in the shadow of the wall and saw that he had guessed correctly. There was another Sherman not five meters away. As Brasche watched, the tank fired its main gun. Rudi Brasche hesitated for a second. He knew his life wouldn't be worth a penny if he left cover. The sunken road was crawling with enemy soldiers looking for the Germans who had inflicted this carnage on them.

Brasche took the hand grenades from his belt. He unscrewed the cap from the middle grenade and crawled forward. Luckily, the inner side of the defile was overgrown with blackberry bushes. A pair of men wearing flat steel helmets appeared diagonally in front of him. Firing flared up from the direction where Lagemann and the other members of the squad were waiting. The enemy troops disappeared behind the second tank, which was still smoldering. Moving quickly, Brasche reached the rear of the British tank. For an instant he heard voices, then a clinking sound as a fresh round was shoved into the breach of the tank's main gun.

Brasche forced his hand grenades under the overhanging part of the turret, pulled the fuses and raced away to the rear. As he ran he stumbled over a root and fell flat on his face. The four hand grenades detonated with a thunderous roar. Flames shot from the tank's engine compartment. Hatches flipped open up front. Again, submachine guns began to fire.

Running at a crouch, Unteroffizier Brasche disappeared into the bushes. It was not a moment too soon, for just then a group of enemy infantry appeared behind the last tank. They fired blindly into the bushes. Brasche crawled up the embankment. When he reached the top his back was soaked in sweat.

"Rudi, the platoon has arrived. We're all ready."

"Brasche's squad: Move forward along the edge of the defile!" ordered Oberleutnant Monz, who had returned to the main body of the company from the 3rd Platoon. The other squads closed up from the right. Staying out of sight in the bushes and hedges, they reached the end of the defile.

"Damn, it's a whole infantry battalion!" called Lagemann on spying the assembly of enemy infantry at the edge of a small wood.

"We'll let them have it with the *Panzerschreck*."

The round from the rocket launcher flitted towards the enemy and exploded in the midst of a dense group of soldiers. It had a devastating effect. The enemy immediately withdrew into the woods.

The enemy forces trying to break through the wide-meshed net of the panzer training division had been repulsed. Brasche's Squad had destroyed five Sherman tanks with its *Panzerschreck* antitank weapons and hand grenades. This success was mentioned in the division's order of the day.

The company moved out during the afternoon of 12 June. The 2nd Platoon followed behind the 1st Platoon as it worked its way forward along a road on the right flank. On the left flank was 3rd Platoon. Behind the 3rd—as always—was the 4th (Heavy) Platoon.

Dusk fell. The men could hear the sound of bursting rounds from Tilly. The British were pounding the wrecked city with artillery and naval guns. The darker it got, the brighter the flashes became in the sky in front of the advancing company.

"We'll move forward to the meadow and halt there. The 2nd and 3rd Platoons at the southern edge of the meadow. The 1st Platoon on the eastern edge. The 4th Platoon behind the 3rd."

The men stumbled over the scrub-covered terrain. The squad's *Panzerschrecks* seemed to weigh several hundred pounds. Brasche identified the outline of the large meadow and its many low bushes. The 2nd Platoon reached a hedgerow that surrounded the field.

"Great trench, Rudi. We'll have enough cover here."

Brasche jumped into the trench. He tried to scan the field through a hole in the hedgerow but in vain.

"Dig in a little deeper, men. The deeper the better."

Grumbling, the men of the squad set to work, while Brasche dug a hole in the hedgerow, through which he inserted the *Panzerschreck.* He could see nothing but the dark shadows of the bushes, which were scattered about the meadow.

"Hannes, cut a hole in the hedgerow for the second *Panzerschreck.*" Soon afterward Oberleutnant Monz arrived.

"One hundred percent readiness, Brasche."

"*Jawohl,* sir!"

A tank motor roared to life not forty meters in front of the hedge. Flames flickered from its exhausts and the broad shadow, which looked like a clump of bushes, set itself in motion and rolled past 2nd Platoon in the direction of the eastern hedge. Rudi Brasche felt paralyzed as he stared at the steel monster through his hole in the hedge. As he watched, more of the shadows in the meadow began to move. Four tanks were nearing the eastern hedge. If they drove over the hedgerow they would be able to overrun the entire 1st Platoon in its shallow trench.

Rudi Brasche snapped up a *Panzerfaust,* a man-portable individual anti-tank rocket launcher. Lagemann jumped up to help. They ran along the trench to the corner of the hedge, and managed to overtake the slow-moving tank. Brasche saw a gap in the hedge at the corner. The tank appeared through the gap. It approached almost head on, then turned. Brasche fired.

The roar as Brasche fired the *Panzerfaust* and the hard, metallic crash made by the impacting projectile merged into one. A harsh, red flame shot from the enemy tank. Red flashes from the guns of the British tanks pierced the night. The tanks, which had just about reached the eastern hedge, halted. Rudi Brasche managed to get off another round. The second tank was also hit and began to burn. The tanks rolled back into the meadow. The two that had been hit remained near the hedgerow, enveloped in flames.

The two men ran back to their platoon and took cover in the trench. It was not a moment too soon. Muzzle flashes from thirty or forty tank cannon lit the night as bright as day. Machine guns sent streams of tracer through the night. The 4th Platoon's mortars began to fire. The shells burst in the center of the meadow. In the light of the exploding rounds Brasche and his men saw infantry appear in the background and join the bailed-out tank crews.

The MG 42s began to fire, laying down a pattern of fire half a meter above the ground. They mowed down everything in their path. The rounds of *Panzerschrecks* and *Panzerfäuste* crackled through the air. Rounds from the British tanks ripped the hedgerow apart. Steel fragments whizzed through the air. The night had become frenzied.

"Take cover!"

Brasche's men disappeared into the trench. Only he stayed in view, trying to spot the approaching enemy. As he watched, one of the enemy tanks rolled forward at the southeast corner of the meadow. For a fraction of a second he saw several figures in the flashes of gunfire. He thought he recognized Oberleutnant Monz. The man who jumped onto the tank was caught by a burst of fire and knocked to the ground.

Brasche raised his submachine gun and fired on the position where the enemy had to be. His fire was answered immediately. Three or four bursts forced him to take cover. He disappeared into the trench and crawled a few meters to one side. Then he tried again.

Brasche burrowed through the shattered hedge. He pushed himself forward and saw the muzzle flash of a machine gun and a spurt of flame from the main gun of a tank. He raised his submachine gun and fired. He saw a muzzle flash from a rifle and turned. At the same instant, a burst of tracer rounds hissed past. Something struck his upper left arm and threw him backwards.

For a second Brasche lay pressed against the ground. Then he crawled back and let himself fall into the trench.

"Man, you've been wounded! You're bleeding!" shouted Hagemann. Hannes Hill jumped up to help. Together they ripped off Brasche's tunic and bandaged his upper arm.

"The bullet's still in there, Rudi. It's a mess."

"Damn!" swore Brasche. He bit his lip as the wound began to hurt.

The small-arms fire, which had begun hesitantly, intensified from second to second. News arrived that Oberleutnant Monz had been wounded while attacking an enemy tank. Orders came to withdraw.

The platoons fell back. Brasche was evacuated to the rear in the next ambulance. While the company secured the regiment's assembly area, Brasche began a journey that would take him through Falaise to Paris, and from Gare du Nord back to Germany, where he was sent to Tuttlingen hospital. Once again he was mentioned in the division's order of the day.

✠

By mid-August Brasche's wounds had healed sufficiently for him to be sent to Küstrin to the replacement battalion of the 901st Panzer Grenadier Training Regiment. There he received shocking news. His friend Richard Gambietz had been killed on 24 April 1944 while defending against a Russian attack on Tiphina on the Dnestr.

Even the news that Wilhelm Grunge, who was still with his old unit, had become the third Obergefreiter of Brasche's machine-gun squad to receive the Knight's Cross, could not console him. One of the finest men he had ever known was gone.

Brasche was assigned to the flamethrower platoon of the Headquarters Company of the panzer training division. The unit was dispatched to Kochern on the Moselle River. There Brasche was given the job of training Luftwaffe noncommissioned officers in infantry warfare.

When the Ardennes offensive began on 16 December 1944 the four flamethrower armored personnel carriers rolled westward with the rest of the panzer training division. Travelling by night, the division had reached the Kyllburg area by 16 December. The tanks had been sent by rail to conserve fuel. They were unloaded in Bensborn and Birresborn.

Unteroffizier Brasche and the four other members of the crew rolled across the Our early on the morning of 17 December. The same day the division took Draufeld. The following day, Oberwampach and Niederwampach were reached. The flamethrower vehicles saw their first operations in the west when the division's forces approached an enemy-occupied patch of woods. Brasche was on the forward machine gun. The two men manning the flamethrowers sent sixty-meter-long streams of fire pouring into the nests of resistance. The smaller, portable flamethrower stowed in the rear was not required.

Enemy resistance was quickly broken. The flamethrower platoon was on the advance. It moved south past Bastogne and toward Rochefort, which was reached on the afternoon of 22 December and taken that night.

The entire German offensive soon lost momentum, however, and the period from 5–11 January saw the panzer training division on the retreat. The four SPW of the flamethrower platoon could move only by night. The weather had cleared and enemy fighter-bombers attacked everything that moved. There were no German fighters in the air. It was at this point that Generalleutnant Bayerlein, the divisional commander, was forced to abandon no less than fifty-three tanks at the side of the road for lack of fuel. The tank crews were forced to walk back over snow-covered roads. When Hochschneid was lost on 23 January 1945, the division was forced to pull back to the Westwall. The Battle of the Ardennes was over.

The panzer training division had ten tanks and six tank-destroyers left. Seventy tanks had been lost. The fighting elements had 400 men left. 200 wheeled vehicles had also been lost. The division had virtually ceased to exist. Generalleutnant Bayerlein left the division and took over the LIII Panzer Corps. Known as Corps Bayerlein, it was given the task of stopping the American advance in the Jülich-Dürken area.

On 1 February 1945 Rudi Brasche was promoted to Feldwebel.

Then came his final action. It was in the marshes at Udem. The Headquarters Company had set up positions in a patch of woods. Nearby were two self-propelled *Nebelwerfer* rocket launchers. The enemy fire, the full weight of which had been falling on the woods, shifted farther to the rear beyond the marshes. At the same moment, the two multiple-rocket launchers, which had pulled back 600 meters into the trees, moved forward. They stopped at the edge of the woods and opened fire. After three salvoes, the two vehicles rolled back into the cover of the woods. It was just in time, because the enemy then opened up on the marshes with everything it had.

"Those bastards know what they're doing," said Feldwebel Brasche, appreciation in his voice.

"Headquarters Company: Move forward to the right edge of the woods."

The men picked up their weapons and equipment and left the part of the woods the enemy was softening up for his breakthrough to the Rhine.

The Allies launched "Operation Veritable" to take the Reichswald. The operation was carried out by a British corps under General Horrocks. It had five infantry divisions, three armored brigades and six special-purpose regiments. Facing the onslaught was a single German division, and a 5-1/2 hour artillery barrage shattered it. Enemy aircraft would attack, followed by another round of artillery fire. It was then that Brasche felt a hard blow on his shoulder and toppled forward. Two members of his platoon raced to his aid. They bandaged the shrapnel wound, which was bleeding heavily.

Two hours later Brasche was on his way to the rear in an ambulance. As his friends put him inside, Obergefreiter Bocholtz said to him: "Good luck, Rudi! The war's over for you. Get home if you can. All the best!"

In fact, the end was not far away. From Waldbreitbach Hospital Feldwebel Brasche was sent to Elspe and from there to Burg Altena. There he remained and there he heard the news of the end of the war.

Feldwebel Franz Juschkat after receiving the Knight's Cross.

Franz Juschkat

"Have the platoon leaders report to me, Juschkat!" ordered Oberleutnant Neumann-Corrina. The officer had just returned from the regimental headquarters, where he had received orders for the second day of the attack.

Obergefreiter Juschkat ran through the pale twilight of morning to the company, which was camped in a patch of woods beside the road. A moment later he returned with the platoon leaders. They lined up expectantly in front of their company commander.

"Men, we have been the reserve for some time. Strong Polish forces are nearing the route of advance on the division's left flank. We are to stop them. Our company will assume the lead in the flanking group. Direction of advance is this railway embankment and the woods beside it. The enemy occupies the embankment and woods. Our job will be completed when we have the railway embankment."

The platoon leaders stared at the map in the light of a shielded flashlight. Unteroffizier Matuzat, section leader of the company headquarters section in which Juschkat served as bugler, winked at the Obergefreiter Juschkat forced himself to smile back.

It was 2 September and the sun was not yet above the horizon when the company moved out across the area of bushes and heath. From the right Juschkat heard the rattle of a Polish heavy machine gun. The Poles were trying to halt the division spearhead. Rounds howled toward them from the enemy side and fell in a field behind the company.

Juschkat saw the railway embankment through some vegetation. Seconds later gunfire flashed from the camouflaged greenery. The first salvo whistled by about a meter over Juschkat's head and struck the bushes behind him. A member of the 3rd Platoon cried out. He fell to the ground and lay still. Medics tended to him while the others worked their way forward. Two enemy heavy machine guns were firing directly in front of Juschkat. They were well emplaced in the embankment and were difficult to pick out. The bursts of fire forced the company to take cover.

Juschkat strained to pick out the guns. All he could see was occasional flashes of gunfire. He shouldered his rifle and, when the next muzzle flashes became visible, he fired. One of the enemy guns fell silent, but the second was now firing directly at the leading group of German soldiers around the company commander. That group, too, suffered its first casualties. Juschkat crawled deeper into the trench as the machine gun turned its fire in his direction.

Farther left he could hear Paul swearing. More than two meters tall, it was difficult for him to find suitable cover. Then a German machine gun opened fire. Obergefreiter König sprayed the railway embankment.

"We can't go any farther, sir," gasped the platoon leader.

"We must advance, otherwise the division's left flank will be unprotected. Bring me my horse!"

The Feldwebel went back and soon returned through a ravine on the horse.

Oberleutnant Neumann-Corrina turned to the Obergefreiter, who was carrying his trumpet slung over his shoulder, and said: "All right, Juschkat. Blow the signal to attack and then on to the embankment."

Franz Juschkat looked at the Oberleutnant. This small man, with his typical East Prussian features, was his role model. But what he had in mind now seemed a hopeless undertaking.

With the first signal blast the Oberleutnant swung into the saddle. He held his "zero-eight" pistol in one fist and the reins in the other. Then he set out towards the embankment at a wild gallop.

"Get up!—Move out!" roared Unteroffizier Matuzat. The men of the company headquarters section ran after their commander. The company rose in unison and ran toward the railway embankment. From an intermediate position Obergefreiter König, the leader of the machine-gun team, opened fire on the enemy machine gun directly in front of him and silenced it. Bullets whistled over the heads of the advancing troops, who had reached the blind zone below the embankment.

As he crawled up the embankment on all fours, Juschkat could hear the shouts of the fleeing Poles. When he reached the tracks, bullets whistled past his ears from a dense patch of woods on the far side of the embankment. König and Paul, the second member of his machine-gun team, threw themselves down between the tracks.

The company commander's horse was hit and fell to the ground. Oberleutnant Neumann-Corrina fell off and rolled down the embankment. He caught himself behind a bush and crawled quickly into cover.

"Over the embankment individually!" ordered Matuzat. The first was Obergefreiter Palke. While König provided covering fire, the company headquarters section caught up with its commander.

"Company: Move out from here on a broad front and clear the woods."

The two runners dashed to the left and right. They took cover in the bushes at the foot of the embankment. Rifle and machine-gun fire forced both men to repeatedly halt and take cover as they tried to reach the platoons. The woods echoed with the crack of rifles and the rattle of machine guns. The company worked its way forward methodically. Groups of enemy soldiers were taken prisoner. The German infantry continued to advance. Suddenly, machine gun fire whipped towards them from a tangle of blackberry bushes.

"Hand grenades!"

Juschkat pulled out the grenades stuck in his belt. He pulled the porcelain knobs to ignite the fuses and lobbed the grenades toward the enemy position. Then he threw himself flat on the ground. The pursuit continued. Rifle fire whipped toward the soldiers from the left. A member of 3rd Platoon's 3rd Squad was hit and killed. Juschkat heard the whistle of bullets.

"Forward!" shouted the company commander. Veering right, Juschkat tried to catch up with him. A branch whipped back and struck his helmet a hard blow. Finally, he caught up with his section. Juschkat and the others ran on and came to the gently sloping edge of a depression. Suddenly, they heard machine-gun fire and rifle shots from below. Close in front of Juschkat, Oberleutnant Neumann-Corrina pitched forward.

"Sir . . ." A hard blow on the right knee knocked Juschkat to the ground. He tried to hold on to some bushes but was unable to keep his balance and rolled down the slope into the enemy-occupied ravine. As he fell, Juschkat could hear the noise of battle and the rattle of machine guns. There was also machine-gun fire behind him. One final tumble and he landed in a Polish machine gun nest whose crew had not yet fired.

He saw faces before him, frozen in terror. One of the Poles reached for his pistol. Juschkat pointed his rifle at the man. Fortunately, he had managed to hang on to it as he had fallen. The enemy soldier raised his arms. Then he heard a familiar voice:

"Juschkat! Where are you?"

"Here, Matuzat!" Juschkat stood up for a second. There was a rustling above the machine-gun nest. Branches snapped and stones tumbled down the slope as Matuzat rushed into the hole. Not a moment too soon, because the enemy suddenly rushed out of the bushes on the far side of the ravine. They fired on the run at the Germans who had invaded the depression.

"Stop them!" shouted Matuzat. He turned the Polish machine gun around and opened fire. By then the enemy soldiers were only about thirty meters away. Obergefreiter König and his tall helper reached the floor of the depression. Soon they were firing on the Poles. The tide of battle had turned in the Germans' favor. The loud voice of Leutnant Zumbrock rang out: "I'm assuming command!"

The enemy was on the run. Half an hour later the German infantry reached the far side of the woods. The division's flank had been secured. Juschkat's wound began to hurt. Until now he had felt little, due to the shock. Three men helped him up the slope. There he saw his company commander. Oberleutnant Neumann-Corrina would never issue another order. The Polish bullet had pierced his heart. Juschkat had known the officer for two years. The man had been more than a superior to him, and he was unable to hold back his tears.

Franz Juschkat soon found himself aboard one of the first hospital trains bound for Germany. In hospital in Wismar he received the Iron Cross, Second Class for his actions and the capture of the Polish machine gun, one of the first members of the company to receive the decoration.

"It was just by chance," he told his comrades. "I don't know who was more scared, the Poles or me. In any case, they raised their arms and I had won."

✠

After recovering from his wounds, Juschkat returned to his unit's replacement battalion at Insterburg. He tried to get transferred back to his company, but his knee was not yet completely healed. Instead, he became an instructor. Soon afterward he and the replacement battalion were moved into the "Reich Protectorate of Bohemia and Moravia."

On 15 May 1940, five days after the beginning of the Western Campaign, Juschkat was promoted to Unteroffizier. Further attempts to get sent back to his former unit were unsuccessful.

The war against the Soviet Union began on 22 June 1941. Finally, his replacement company was sent to Russia. At the Neva River the 1st Infantry Division was in action against attacking Soviet forces. The replacement company was assigned to the badly weakened 1st Battalion of the 43rd Infantry Regiment. Together with Gefreiter Mertens, Unteroffizier Juschkat rejoined his old company, the 43rd Infantry Regiment's 1st Company. And what shape he found it in! More than half the unit's personnel had been killed at the Neva. The company had only sixty-eight men fit for combat.

One of his old comrades was still there: The former Unteroffizier Matuzat, since promoted to Oberfeldwebel. Unteroffizier Juschkat now began a period of operations which was to last until June 1942 without a break.

✠

Born on 13 February 1917, Franz Juschkat spent his early childhood in his father's small hotel in Groß-Warkau in the Insterburg District. This carefree childhood was followed by years of hard work. In the winter he worked in the forest with his father felling trees. The hard work hardened Juschkat and inured him to adverse weather. These were qualities that later stood him in good stead in the pitiless Russian winter landscape, especially in the snow-covered forests on the Neva.

Now and then Juschkat traveled to Insterburg. The city was the garrison of the East Prussian 1st Infantry Division. He talked with the soldiers and felt a growing desire to become a soldier himself.

On 3 November 1937 he joined the 43rd Infantry Regiment of the division. The regiment with which he saw action in Poland and where he remained assigned for the entire war. Juschkat became a Gefreiter and, in 1939, an Obergefreiter. The summer of 1939 arrived and there were increasing rumors that war with Poland was imminent. On 1 September 1939 the rumors became fact.

✠

"Welcome to the Neva. We never thought we'd see you again." Juschkat reported to the Leutnant. When he had received his instructions he stepped outside. Oberfeldwebel Matuzat clapped his friend from the Insterburg days soundly on the shoulder.

"Are you familiar with the wasp's nest?"

"Good bunker. Except that it's very close to Ivan. I'll take you there."

Gefreiter Mertens also left the company orderly room at the same time. W hen he saw the Oberfeldwebel he came to attention.

"Oberfeldwebel, I am supposed to go to the 'wasp's nest' with you," he reported.

"There's no need for formalities here. I am Jakob Matuzat from Insterburg."

"Hello, Mertens, welcome to the group and good luck here."

The three men first went to the quarters of the Oberfeldwebel. He wanted to give his comrades a welcoming drink. W hen they were ready to leave Juschkat turned to his friend: "Can you tell me what the situation is here, Jakob?"

"We're in position along the Neva road on the east bank of the Neva. During the past few months the Russians have made repeated attempts to cross the river and cut the road. At first all that was here were elements of the 126th Infantry Division and the 30th Motorcycle Battalion of the 20th Infantry Division. Then a few weeks ago the 1st Airborne Regiment and our division were thrown in because it was determined that the Russians were preparing an offensive."

The three men walked out of the command post through a shell-shattered patch of woods where the vegetation had thick snowcaps and offered goad concealment. Narrow footpaths led through hollows and bushes. Now and then a shell howled over the heads of the men and impacted far behind them.

"The usual Russian harassing fire, Franz. Nothing much to speak of."

They reached a path through the snow to the bunker and were soon standing before the entrance, which was fitted with a narrow wooden door over which tarpaper had been nailed.

The sentry in the ice trench in front of the bunker came around to the back. The Oberfeldwebel waved him away and the sentry returned to the front of the bunker. The three men stepped inside.

"Close the door!" called a deep, bass voice that Juschkat recognized all too well. Warmth surrounded the three men who had just stepped inside from the frosty evening darkness. Tears began to run from Juschkat's eyes.

"Comrades, allow me to introduce you to your new strongpoint commander, Unteroffizier Juschkat. He comes from the replacement battalion and is a soldier of long standing from within the division."

"Mercy!" rumbled the bass voice, and a figure sitting on a low bench rose to its full imposing size, its head almost touching the roof of the bunker.

"Paul!"

"Franz Juschkat, so it is you." The tall soldier welcomed his friend. The attitude of camaraderie was heightened by the bottles of vodka the Oberfeldwebel had brought with him. The Oberfeldwebel left shortly before midnight to inspect the battalion's remaining bunkers.

"Franz, make sure that the men are relieved on time. Hourly! Otherwise they'll return to the bunker with frozen noses. And if someone has a white nose: Rub, rub, rub!"

"Thanks for the advice, Jakob."

Juschkat stepped into the open with his friend. He watched the Oberfeldwebel as he walked through the communications trench to the next strongpoint, only fifty meters away. Then he turned to the sentry outpost.

"Obergefreiter Ochtrop on watch. Nothing unusual to report, Unteroffizier."

"Fine, Ochtrop. Are you from East Prussia, too?"

"That's correct, Unteroffizier!" was the snappy reply of the Obergefreiter, as yet unsure what type of man the new strongpoint commander was.

"No need to make a fuss. My name's Franz."

"Herbert."

Ochtrop pulled off a glove and rubbed his left earlobe. A sharp frost hung in the air. On the far side of the Neva there were several flashes. It was a few seconds before the howling of the approaching rounds became audible. Ochtrop stared tensely at his new superior. What would he do now? Franz Juschkat did nothing, because he heard the rounds were passing high overhead.

Suddenly there were muzzle flashes from their side of the Neva as well.

"Is that the Russians who have established a bridgehead on this side of the river?" asked Juschkat.

The Obergefreiter nodded. "They crossed the river somewhat farther south, near Dubrovka and near Petroshino. Three days ago the paratroops reduced the bridgehead near Petroshino. You should have seen it. A terrific display of fireworks. The paratroops did it. They attacked in battalion strength and took the bridgehead held by a Russian regiment. The commander is said to have died of his wounds from that night yesterday."

"Is Ivan trying to get across at other places?" asked Juschkat.

"Everywhere. From Schlüsselburg to south of Kolpino and, starting yesterday, from Leningrad itself."

"Then we can count on a visit from the other side tonight, or do you think that . . ." Franz Juschkat was unable to complete the sentence, because a Russian Maxim machine gun began to rattle from about 200 meters away. The fire was coming from a hill that was about two meters higher than Juschkat's bunker. The streams of tracer snaked across to the neighboring bunker. A German machine gun opened fire from the next position. The tracer seemed to be trying to pierce the hill.

"The Russians are able to observe part our trenches from that bunker over there. For three days they've been sniping at us from there."

"The Russian bunker should be smoked out. If we could capture it . . . ," Juschkat thought.

"Some of our people were there. The Ivans threw them out during the night and have been there ever since. The terrain around the bunker is mined. There's nothing we can do, Franz." The sound of steps from the communications trench caused the pair to fall silent. It was Paul, come to relieve the sentry.

"Make sure you get inside where it's warm. Your ear lobes are already completely white."

"Very well! Good night!"

The tall soldier took the field glasses, pointed them at the hill with the Russian bunker and adjusted the focus. Then he let them dangle at his breast.

"It's good to see you again, Franz. But you won't have things quite as easy in this hellhole."

"Perhaps you have it easy, Paul."

"You're damned right, and if I . . ."

"Quiet!" hissed Juschkat. Somewhere behind them a twig snapped under the weight of its load of snow. But suddenly the sound was there again: a buzzing, half-grinding noise.

"Sleds, Franz! The Ivans are coming!"

Juschkat reached the bunker entrance after a few quick strides and stepped inside. Within seconds he had awakened his men. Moments later the heavy machine gun, which could sweep the battlefield as far as the enemy-held hill, was manned. Pietsch and Groß, the two machine gunners, peered through the embrasures, but there was nothing to be seen.

"Where is the light machine gun?"

"Here, Unteroffizier!"

"Come with me!" Bichlap and Ochtrop, the two members of the light machine-gun team, followed the strongpoint commander outside. They went to the left end of the trench in front of the bunker. Juschkat set up the machine gun there, where it could cover the blind spot on the left.

"See anything, Paul?"

"Nothing. Nothing at all. But I've heard several more sleds."

"Stay alert! I still think Ivan's coming."

Paul had placed his rifle in a notch in the trench's parapet. He held the field glasses pressed to his eyes and scanned the area in front of the bunker, where scattered bushes and uprooted trees offered ideal cover. He spotted the first Russians when they were about 100 meters from the German trench. Their white snow smocks had emerged from the gray-white of the hollow.

"There they are, Franz!"

Juschkat suddenly saw several clouds of white mist: It was the breath of the Russian soldiers. In the cold it gave away the locations of the enemy soldiers who had so skillfully approached the German position. Quickly, and without a sound, Juschkat crept over to Bichlap.

"Got them!" he said, even before the Unteroffizier could speak.

"Open fire!"

As the machine gun began to rattle, Juschkat opened fire with his rifle. He took aim at a Russian who had come into the hollow on skis. Exactly three seconds after the action began the heavy machine gun opened fire; at the same time, one of the Maxim machine guns the Russians had hauled into the depression also began to fire. Clusters of tracers from the Russian weapon hissed over the rim of the trench. The bullets struck the ice-covered bunker with a smacking sound. Finally, the two neighboring strongpoints opened fire as well. The entire snow-covered plain in front of the 1st Battalion of the 43rd Infantry Regiment came to life. The Russians jumped up and came running toward the German positions.

Three or four Maxims were firing at that point, and they were joined by other automatic weapons from the hill and two field positions on the left and right. The Soviets drew nearer and nearer. They were scarcely forty meters from the bunker when the flanking machine gun fell silent.

"What is it, Bichlap?"

"Jammed!" answered the Obergefreiter, while he desperately tried to clear the stoppage. Juschkat dropped his rifle and pulled his "zero-eight" pistol from its holster. He released the safety with his thumb. With loud shouts of "Urray!" the Russians charged the German lines on a broad front. The bursts of fire from the heavy machine gun passed harmlessly over the heads of the attackers.

"Take the ones on the left!" roared Paul. The light crack of pistol shots was drowned out by the crash of exploding hand grenades, which Paul had lobbed toward the attackers. At the last minute the light machine gun opened fire again and halted the onrushing Soviets. Franz Juschkat was amazed at how quickly the Russians could disappear. They were like ghosts. They concealed themselves behind snowdrifts and bushes and in depressions. They were still there, though, and the enemy soldiers fired on any German who allowed himself to be seen.

It was quiet for two minutes. Then the Soviet artillery opened fire. Rounds fell in front of the German main line of resistance and some among the bunkers and trenches. Geysers of snow shot into the air. Chunks of ice rained down on the defenders, forcing them to keep their heads down. While the artillery was pinning down the defenders, the second Soviet attack wave worked its way forward. They also dragged their heavy weapons with them on sleds. Other groups of enemy soldiers brought mines, which they intended to lay close to the German positions to prevent any attempt to retake the bunker on the hill.

The men in the "Wasp's Nest" repeatedly tried to spy over the parapets. Paul crawled over to Juschkat, dragging a metal hand grenade box behind him.

"Here, Franz, in case they should get within hand-grenade range."

They took out the grenades, unscrewed the caps and placed them in a niche in the frozen wall of the trench within easy reach. A dull, rumbling sound caused them to wince in fear. The two men instinctively ducked down against the wall of the trench. There was a thunderous explosion as the satchel charge that had landed a meter in front of the trench went off. The shock wave forced the air from their lungs.

"Get up, get up!" shouted Paul.

Acting on instinct, Juschkat seized two hand grenades as he got to his feet. He saw the onrushing enemy troops about twenty meters in front of him. He threw the two grenades and then drew his pistol. The grenades tore gaps in the enemy ranks, but they were not enough to halt the assault. A dozen white-clad figures leapt into the trench. Juschkat saw a tall, bearded Siberian right in front of him. He fired as quickly as he could. A blow on the left side of his helmet dropped him to his knees. In doing so he avoided a burst of submachine-gun fire, which smacked into the wall of the trench.

Obergefreiter Paul grabbed his rifle and swung it at the enemy soldiers. The men of the heavy machine-gun crew fired on the following

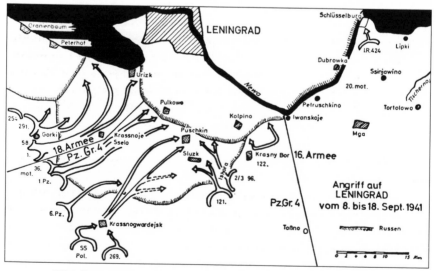

The German assault on Leningrad, 8 to 18 September 1941.

Russian troops farther back in the assault wave. They were soon joined by the flanking machine gun. Juschkat inserted a fresh magazine into his "zero-eight" and eliminated the last of the intruders. Paul was still throwing grenades. The enemy attack bogged down in front of the "Wasp's Nest."

In Feldwebel Körting's strongpoint to the left, however, the roaring of the Soviets could be heard. Above the noise of the enemy troops shots rang out and hand grenades crashed.

"Mertens, Paul, Jagst, follow me!"

They reached for their hand grenades and ran along the trench at a crouch. Three times they had to step over dead or wounded Soviets before they began to take fire. Juschkat saw the Soviets who had reached Feldwebel Körting's bunker. He threw two hand grenades in rapid succession and ran forward in long strides. His upper body was fully exposed to the Russian riflemen, but there was no firing from the forward Russian trench, perhaps out of fear of hitting their own people.

The Russian infiltrators, who had just taken out the machine-gun crew, were cut down before they could turn around. Juschkat made contact with the battalion by telephone. He alerted battalion headquarters to the situation and requested relief for the surviving members of the strongpoint's crew. Juschkat and the three men of the small relief force dressed the wounds of the injured men; the two machine gunners were beyond help. Their bodies were completely riddled with bullets.

✠

The Soviets attacked all along the Neva front. They crossed the river in fast assault boats and broke out of the encircling ring around Leningrad. Finally, the ice became thick enough for them to cross on foot. But the strongpoints of the East Prussian 1st Infantry Division held.

✠

"Careful, Franz. This is where the area under enemy observation begins."

The two men, who were trying to make their way to the 43rd Infantry Regiment's 2nd Battalion, were forced to creep through this section of trench. Unteroffizier Juschkat crawled along close behind Oberfeldwebel Matuzat. He spotted two German soldiers in a cleverly camouflaged machine-gun nest. One was trying to pinpoint the location of a Russian sniper using binoculars in hopes of taking him out with a surprise burst of fire. As soon as he raised himself up from behind the armored shield there was a curious smacking noise, and immediately afterward Juschkat heard the crack of the sniper's rifle. Struck in the forehead, the machine gunner collapsed. Juschkat and Matuzat crawled into the position, but there was nothing they could do. Moments later they arrived at the battalion headquarters. They were welcomed by Hauptmann Dörner. His face became livid when he heard of the death of the machine gunner. He looked at the two men in silence for a moment, then cleared his throat and said: "We've got to smoke out that bunker. I've lost eleven of my best men in the past six days, all to snipers lurking in the bunker on the hill and the two flanking positions."

"But how, sir? We've tried four times and been repulsed with heavy losses each time."

"I think I could do it," interjected Juschkat.

The Hauptmann looked at him skeptically. "You've only been here a week, Juschkat. You don't know the Russians."

"I'm from East Prussia and I know how to sneak up on them. We will only need a handful of men."

"The enemy has at least four machine guns and thirty men up there, Juschkat."

"Nevertheless, it could be done with four men. Do you think, sir, I can get permission for an assault on the bunker?"

"I'm warning you. It could turn out badly for all of you."

"It's been bad enough already for our comrades here for days now, sir."

"Very well, Juschkat, if you want to try it. I'll speak with the regiment at once. Come back in half an hour."

The pair left the command post and went back into the trench. Several snipers from division were there, trying to pick off the Russian sharpshooters, but so far they had met with little success. They had managed to hit two enemy snipers, while the Russians had shot four of their number. Juschkat went over to one of the snipers, who was squatting in a well-camouflaged foxhole watching the flanking sector of the hill with the enemy bunker: "May I try your rifle, comrade?"

"Here, knock yourself out! It shoots very accurately if you squeeze the trigger smoothly. Aim at the lower edge of the target."

"Jakob, hold your helmet over the rim of the trench. My father told me they surprised the enemy this way in the last war. But only leave it up for a second, understood?"

The Oberfeldwebel called for an entrenching tool. He placed his helmet over the end and raised it for perhaps three seconds. Three seconds were enough for the Russian. A bullet hissed past the helmet, just missing. Franz Juschkat took aim at the spot where he had seen the muzzle flash.

"Once again, quickly, before he can change positions!" Again the steel helmet appeared above the parapet. Peering through the telescopic sight Juschkat saw a movement. He squeezed the trigger. On the enemy side a figure stood up from cover and fell forward heavily. Wordlessly, Juschkat handed the rifle back to the sniper.

"Let's go back to Hauptmann Dörner," suggested Matuzat. Silently they returned to the command post. Hauptmann Dörner greeted them with a bottle of captured vodka. He poured each man a drink, then turned to Juschkat:

"You've got your assault team, Juschkat. Four men. I've already spoken with the battalion commander. He'll see you after I'm done and brief you.

✠

"This is how it's going to go, Juschkat: You will take four volunteers from your bunker and advance on the bunker hill. As soon as you're up there fire a green signal flare and the division's artillery will lay down barrage fire west of the hill, so the Soviets can't reach it from the bridgehead. At the same time, a battalion assault group will set out for the hill and relieve you. The attack begins at 0215. That will be all."

The battalion commander stood up and walked over to the Unteroffizier, who was likewise standing. "Good luck, Juschkat. And if you see that something's going wrong turn back before it's too late. Don't try to succeed at any price, understood?"

"Understood, sir."

The comfortable warmth of the bunker enveloped the five men when they returned from the battalion command post. They sat at their usual places and inspected the two new submachine guns they had received.

✠

"Here, boys, we've made you something to eat."

The unit "glutton," Gefreiter Mertens, was happy at the thought of something extra to eat: "Great, my stomach's empty, too. Bring on the food."

They had managed to obtain a roast from the supply sergeant. The aroma wafted seductively past Juschkat's nose. Nevertheless, he took only a small piece. Juschkat was thinking of the four men he had chosen from among those who had volunteered. In fact, everyone had volunteered.

There was Mertens, who had come with him from the replacement unit. He was a clever fellow, skilled in the use of explosives. Then there were Ochtrop and Bichlap. Both were dependable men who had been in action since the beginning of the war and had already been awarded the Iron Cross, First Class. And finally there was Paul, who had a hard time squeezing his 2.02 meters through the bunker entrance. He was responsible for these men. If anything happened to them he would have to ask himself if it could have been avoided. Juschkat field stripped and inspected the submachine guns. Then he reassembled them and checked the magazine springs.

Mertens completed the explosive charges, which he planned to detonate simultaneously using det cord. There were six explosive blocks; each weighed six kilograms.

The sentry was relieved. The man came into the bunker and shed his thick winter jacket, which had come from captured stocks. He rubbed his ears and nose until color returned to them: "Damned cold outside. At least thirty degrees below."

"In the shade?" asked Jagst.

"In the sun, naturally."

"Notice anything, Groß?"

"All quiet around here. The only fighting seems to be farther north in the sector held by the parachute troops. The Ivans are doing plenty of firing there."

"That's good for us. Real good!"

Juschkat glanced at his watch. Five minutes to go. "Get ready! Don't forget anything!"

"Good luck! Perhaps you can bring us back something to eat and drink."

The five left the bunker. Franz Juschkat led the way, followed closely by Paul, Mertens and Ochtrop. Bichlap brought up the rear carrying his light machine gun. Moving through the communications trench to the next strongpoint on the left, they reached the spot Juschkat had found the day before. From there an ice-covered brook ran westward, directly toward the Neva. The brook flowed about 100 meters south of the bunker hill.

"Be careful!" whispered the Unteroffizier. From there they had to crawl to the brook, where they would be concealed by the dense vegetation along its banks. In their white parkas they blended into the snow, whose surface was frozen hard. Juschkat crept to the bushes. He reached a concealed position and lay on the ice of the frozen brook. The ice surface was about $\frac{1}{4}$ of a meter lower than the surrounding terrain and had a light covering of snow. He crawled forward cautiously. He didn't bother to look around, because he could hear the sound of his comrades behind him. Meter by meter they crawled along the ice. Juschkat stopped once to judge their position; they were at most halfway there.

Just then they heard a muffled Russian curse from in front of them. They immediately disappeared into the vegetation. The clicking of a safety catch from where Ochtrop was lying rang loudly through the stillness of the night. The only other sounds were the occasional howl of an artillery round passing overhead and the constant rumble from the north. Juschkat carefully slipped off the safety. Then he saw the first figures. They were difficult to see in their white parkas and only became visible when they stopped in front of the darker wall of vegetation: Three men.

"Don't fire!" whispered Juschkat. The three Russians came nearer and nearer. They were carrying submachine guns and talking softly among themselves. Then they were even with Juschkat's assault team. The Russian leading the party stopped as if rooted to the spot and bent down. Then he turned round. All three Russians dropped to the ground and blended into the uneven snow-covered surface of the ice. Then one of them jumped up and ran into the bushes. He crashed hard into Paul, who knocked him out with several blows. The other two heard the racket and raised their weapons.

A burst from Bichlap's machine gun bowled over the two Russians. The five Germans lay breathless. Two machine guns fired from the bunker hill. Tracer flitted over the rows of bushes, then the guns fell silent.

"What will we do with this Russian, Franz?"

"He's unconscious. Leave him here until we return. We can't drag him with us and we can't leave anyone behind."

They crept onward and ten minutes later reached the spot where they would be forced to leave the good cover afforded by the streambed.

"Across to the ravine one at a time!"

Paul was the first to go. It took him five minutes to reach the ravine. After he had disappeared, Ochtrop set out. Fifteen minutes later they had all assembled in the hollow. From there to the southern flank of bunker hill was only about forty meters. The area of level terrain was virtually devoid of cover. At the base of the hill there were low bushes, also covered with snow.

"Spread out. We'll all start out at the same time. Reassemble at the extreme southwestern point."

Juschkat crawled off in a northwesterly direction. He wanted to get as far into the rear of the troops manning the hill as possible. He had gone about twenty meters when a sound nearby caused him to freeze. Two Red Army soldiers appeared from a ravine. They were looking in his direction. He closed his eyes, wishing he had a camouflage cap. For two minutes he lay still while the icy cold crept slowly through his clothing. Finally, the Russians moved off toward the west and disappeared.

The Unteroffizier crawled onward. He reached the edge of the hill and the bushes, which formed a thick, compact wall in the snow. He lay there under cover until he heard the sound of his companions crawling over the snow. Paul was first to appear. Juschkat raised his arm to show him where he was. The others arrived within three minutes.

"We're going to try and reach the top along the Russian trench. Understood? I'll lead. No talking!"

Juschkat crawled forward until he came to a narrow footpath that zig-zagged up the hill. He turned into the path and headed up the hill at a crouch. Even before he reached the small plateau he heard behind him— about 300 meters away—voices and steel knocking against steel.

"There comes the relief force, Franz!"

"Faster, faster!"

They reached the upper edge of the plateau. According to the aerial photos, they would be in a flanking position if they turned right into the tangle of trenches.

"Block this trench with explosive charges, Mertens!"

Ochtrop stayed behind with his automatic weapon to cover Mertens while he placed the charges and covered them with snow. The remaining three continued on. A heavily muffled figure appeared at a bend in the trench.

"Hands up!" The Russian said, raising his weapon. Paul ran toward him and knocked him to the ground. The other two heard the sound of muffled blows.

"Quickly, follow me!" They ran east through a side trench and found themselves twenty paces from the hill's southern machine-gun nest. Bich-lap fired a burst into the position. As if this had been a signal, all Hell broke loose on the hill. Figures poured out of the bunker, firing wildly into the darkness. Juschkat fired a green signal flare. The flare hissed into the sky and exploded in a momentary flash of brilliance.

The German artillery opened fire. Gunfire flashed along a width of about 2,000 meters and rounds of every caliber howled over the hill and crashed into the Russian bridgehead on the east bank of the Neva. At the western foot of the hill orders echoed through the night. It was the relief force, and it was charging up the hill.

"Where are Mertens and Ochtrop?"

The two came hurrying towards them. Mertens had the unrolled the det cord in his fist, while Ochtrop was firing on the run at the enemy troops hurrying west along the trench to summon help.

"Watch out! Here they come!—Blow it!" The Russian troops were in the first trench when the six explosive charges went up with an ear-splitting roar. The Russians in the trench were killed instantly.

Bichlap fired at the bunker entrance, through which the bunker guards were hurrying into the open. Juschkat ran along the trench toward the bunker. He had not yet reached it when a burst of fire from the side embrasure caught him. Juschkat felt a heavy blow on his right side and fell to the ground. His only thought was that he had been hit. However, as he crawled forward to escape the machine-gun fire that was spraying blindly from the bunker, Juschkat realized that he was having no difficulty moving. He crawled until he was beneath the machine-gun fire and then ran toward the machine-gun embrasure at a crouch. Juschkat reached the bunker, stuck the barrel of his submachine gun through the embrasure and fired a long burst, sweeping the interior of the structure.

Paul came running with long strides. He threw a hand grenade through the entrance and then entered the bunker. Bichlap was still firing at the enemy soldiers running down the hill. Soon the last resistance on the hill was broken.

The men of the relief force left the German positions. They ran through the enemy fire that had just begun, reached the foot of the hill and began to climb. One of the men leading the relief force was the commander of the 1st Company.

A relieved Franz Juschkat watched the relief force occupy the Russian trenches and machine-gun nests. He reported to his company commander: "Assault team Juschkat: Mission completed!"

"Thank you, Juschkat. I won't forget you." The officer shook hands with the medium-sized Unteroffizier. "Get to the rear. How're your men?"

"Ochtrop slightly wounded, and I . . ." Just then Juschkat recalled the heavy blow on his side. He looked around in the pale light and continued: "Knapsack and canteen are gone, sir."

The four men left the hill. Not until they reached the foot of the hill did Juschkat notice that Mertens and Paul were carrying what seemed to be a lot of weight. The Russian artillery began firing on the German main line of resistance, and the small group was forced to take cover in a crater.

"What have you brought with you then?" asked Juschkat.

"Preserves and vodka, Franz!"

They reached the "Wasp's Nest" in one piece, and they received an enthusiastic welcome from the men who had stayed behind. "It's good you've made it back. When we heard the firing up there we thought the Russians might have got you."

"That could have happened. But moving while the Russians were being relieved worked like a charm. They were all in the bunker collecting their things. In fact, we nearly had the relief down on our necks."

"Franz, the unconscious Russian at the brook!"

"We'll have to go get him, otherwise he'll freeze to death for sure."

"That's crazy! He must be awake and gone by now."

"It doesn't matter! I'm going to have a look."

"Have you gone crazy? What if he shoots at you?"

"Guys, he's been lying out there in the cold for more than an hour now. If he stays out there another hour he'll be finished."

Franz Juschkat could not be swayed. He inspected his submachine gun, inserted a fresh magazine and left the bunker.

He heard steps behind him and turned round. It was Paul. "Stay here, Paul."

"I'm going with you, Franz. We'll get him out of there. After all I'm the one who knocked him out. He's a man like us, Franz."

"So be it."

They found the Russian, who had just come to and was rubbing his face. When he saw the two Germans coming, he hastily raised both arms. "Don't be afraid! We're going to take you to the aid station," said Juschkat in broken Russian.

The two Germans handed over the Russian and made for their beds. The rumble of explosions and the hectic rattle of automatic weapons from the hill interrupted their sleep.

Next morning the sense of relief among the men in the trenches was apparent. No longer was their section of trench under direct enemy observation. During the next fourteen days they repulsed three Russian attacks on the main line of resistance, one of them a major assault. The forward hill's fortifications were expanded. Belts of mines protected it to the west and eight additional machine-gun positions kept the Soviet positions in the bridgehead under constant fire.

✠

The cold became worse. Temperatures dropped as low as minus 50 degrees centigrade. Quite surprisingly the 43rd Infantry Regiment was withdrawn from the front and transferred by forced march to Konduja, where the Soviets had attacked with nine fresh divisions in an effort to crack the German ring around Leningrad from the northwest.

The Soviet divisions charged across the ice-covered Neva River. Dubrovka fell into their hands. The enemy advance gained ground in the snow-covered forests. Elements of the 96th Infantry Division were surrounded. Their supply route through the forests had been cut by the Soviets.

The night was clear and cold as the 1st Company of the 43rd Infantry Regiment marched toward the main supply route. The men in the slow-moving column could hear the sound of engines and the rattling of tracks from the position where the Soviets had punched through the German lines with tank support. High above, shells howled over the heads of the infantry. One salvo would come from the east, the next from the west.

Farther forward, machine-gun fire whipped through the night, then all was silent again. Then there was the sound of an engine in the air above them. "The 'sewing machine,' sir!"

"Take cover in the ditches!" The company ran to both sides of the road and within seconds had disappeared from view. The "sewing machine"—German soldier slang for a Russian biplane engaged in harassment missions-buzzed overhead and a little later the soldiers heard it circling farther behind them. Flak began to fire. The "sewing machine," which appeared almost nightly, went into a dive and, trailing a banner of smoke, smashed into the ground and exploded.

A messenger arrived in a motorcycle-sidecar. The machine stopped and Oberleutnant Beinke hurried over to it. "Sir, the liaison officer is waiting two kilometers ahead. He has a tank for your use"

"Thank you."

Twenty minutes later they reached their destination. The men saw the shadow of the tank in the bushes beside the road. Oberleutnant Beinke conversed with the liaison officer, while the men slipped into the vegetation behind the tank.

"Platoon leaders: Report to me!" called the company commander on his return. Paul nudged his companion: "Get going, Franz, he means you too."

Juschkat was temporarily in charge while Matuzat was at regiment. Juschkat joined the other platoon leaders. They gathered around the Oberleutnant, who began to speak:

"To make things brief: The Russian-occupied area begins about 500 meters ahead. There are also burnt-out vehicles that were stopped and set on fire last night. We will advance in the following formation: 1st Platoon will take the road and push through as quickly as possible behind the tank. 2nd and 3rd Platoons left and right through the woods, 300 meters from

A machine-gunner of 1st Battalion, 45th Infantry Regiment.

the road. As soon as we reach our main line of resistance, both wings will turn toward the center, meaning the road."

The platoon leaders returned to their units. Franz Juschkat assembled his thirty men behind the tank. The tank commander was standing in the turret hatch. Obergefreiter Pietsch called up to the tank commander: "Just don't pull ahead of us!"

"Just keep up and everything will be alright. There'll be no stopping, understood? Then we'll climb right up the Russian's ass. Let's go! Stay close!"

The Skoda tank's engine revved and the vehicle began to roll forward like a huge beetle, crushing the frozen branches of a downed tree. Flames flickered from its exhausts. Then the tank reached the road, and the men around Franz Juschkat set themselves in motion. The Unteroffizier waited until everyone had passed before hurrying forward, where Paul willingly made room for him. Its engine roaring, the tank rolled along the main supply route. The men stamped along in the ruts in the snow left by its two caterpillar tracks.

Five minutes later they passed the first burnt-out vehicles. The entire column had been shot up and Juschkat could well imagine what had happened to the soldiers escorting the supply trucks. There was already firing from about 300 meters behind and to the left. It appeared that the Soviets had advanced somewhat farther there. As the platoon advanced Juschkat scanned the area to the left, where the forest ended to reveal a clearing perhaps eighty meters wide.

White-clad figures emerged from the upper end of the clearing. They glided downhill, picking up speed as they headed straight toward the road. "*Achtung!* Ahead and to the left: A Russian ski squad!"

At that moment the Russians began to fire on both sides of the road. The tank halted and all hatches clanged shut. Soon afterward the turret machine gun opened fire and then the 37-mm main gun. High-explosive rounds struck the ground and exploded. Juschkat ran to the ditch at the side of the road and threw himself down. There was scarcely room, as the ditch was almost drifted over with snow. Bichlap sought cover beside him. He fired his machine gun at the rapidly approaching ski troops. His long burst knocked several of the white figures into the snow.

By now the tank was firing to its left and right. When the enemy fire died down it once again began to move. "Follow, follow!" The troops jumped up and hurried after the tank. Obergefreiter Koralewski had not yet reached the protection of the tank when he was hit and fell. Heintze and Zünkley suffered the same fate. The others fired on the run at the muzzle flashes that betrayed the enemy's position.

To the left and right the woods echoed with the sound of rifle fire and exploding grenades. The main force of Russians was engaged there by the two platoons led by Feldwebel Sauermann and Feldwebel Schwelske. The Soviet survivors turned and fled. They raced after their ski troops, pursued by gunfire from the lone German tank.

Ten minutes later Juschkat and his platoon reached the main line of resistance and reported the main supply route clear. The tank remained up front with the company. Attached armored vehicles were dug in as steel pillboxes.

"We're going to turn south and make for Schwelske's Platoon. The situation seems to be poor there."

Twenty-three men followed the Unteroffizier. Seven had become casualties, killed or wounded in the meantime. Juschkat was the first to enter the forest. He slipped into a clearing that led straight toward the sound of the fighting. The noise of exploding hand grenades filled the air.

"Each squad form a skirmish line! Ten meters interval!"

Obergefreiter Pietsch led his squad to the left, while Unteroffizier Bielitz went over to the right. Juschkat positioned himself in the center, at the head of Palke's squad. Right behind him was Unteroffizier Palke. Juschkat hoped to sneak up silently on the Russians, who were still firing wildly. The characteristic rattle of Russian submachine guns echoed through the woods.

Juschkat and his men still had twenty meters of clearing to cross when a group of four or five Russians, crouched low, came running straight towards them. Juschkat took cover. He had hurried on about thirty meters ahead of the rest and, when Palke saw him drop, he gave a hand signal which instantly caused the entire group to disappear into the snow. Juschkat fired at the first Russian and wounded him. Then he and his men got to their feet and charged across the clearing into some spruce woods. The Soviets were lying behind a small hillock on which every tree seemed to sparkle. From there they were firing at the men of Schwelske's platoon.

All three of Juschkat's squads opened fire on the Russians virtually simultaneously. The enemy troops turned around. Bursts of automatic weapons fire whipped toward the Germans, forcing them to take cover. A member of Bielitz's squad fell to the ground, fatally wounded. Hemmed in from two sides, the Russians surrendered. The prisoners were disarmed. They and their conquerors then carried the dead and wounded back to the main line of resistance. When they arrived, Feldwebel Sauermann had combed the woods and brought in about twenty prisoners.

The Soviet forces that had tried to block the sole supply route had been eliminated. Juschkat's platoon lost eight men in the fighting.

The Soviets had made several penetrations against the German front around Leningrad, and they kept up the pressure in an effort to force a decisive breakthrough. When they committed their new T-34 tanks the situation took a turn for the worse. The German defenders fought desperately to hold off and drive back the Russian spearheads.

✠

There was a new moon. When Juschkat's assault team entered the forest it took several minutes for the men to get used to the prevailing darkness. Finally they were able to make out the outlines of the trees and bushes. Their exhalations hung above the men like white clouds as they trudged through the woods. They were heading towards the Russian armored spearhead. Late that evening it had overrun the trenches of the flanking battalion and taken its men prisoner.

Paul was dragging two Teller mines. Juschkat offered to take one of the heavy mines, but the tall soldier only replied: "It's easier to drag two, they both weigh the same." They had still not reached the former German main line of resistance when they heard the sound of tanks approaching along a forest road. Wordlessly they disappeared into the bushes, while Paul buried one of the Teller mines in the snow. Tension mounted as the moments passed. Then the first tank appeared. Juschkat recognized it as a T-34 by the sloping silhouette of its turret. Close behind followed two more tanks. Soviet infantry were riding on the tanks, and more followed behind them on foot. Juschkat had received some replacements two days earlier. He now had twenty-six men. They were well armed and equipped with explosive devices.

By now the first T-34 had almost reached the spot where Paul had buried the Teller mine. Twenty-six pairs of eyes intently followed the tank's progress. There was a loud boom as the mine exploded beneath the tank's right track. There was a flash of flame and the soldiers crouched on the tank's rear deck were tossed to the ground.

The tank stopped and turned on the remaining intact track until its main gun was facing at right angles to the road. A yellow flame shot from the long barrel and the round sawed off one of the spruce trees. The two following tanks turned off the road to the left and right. One landed in front of a tree. The engine roared and the spruce tree crashed to the ground, its flat roots torn from the earth.

A small-arms engagement broke out between the Red infantry and Juschkat's assault team.

"Mertens, give me covering fire! Paul get over here!" Juschkat reached for an explosive charge and crawled toward the rear in the direction of the second tank, which had disappeared into a ravine. The tank had turned back toward the German troops and was firing into their positions from behind. The roar of tank engines echoed through the night. The sound of tank guns firing at close range almost deafened the men. The disabled tank sitting on the road also opened fire.

When Juschkat, who had been joined by Mertens, had crawled far enough to the side he turned to look for Paul. The tall soldier was creeping behind a snowdrift. Only his head was visible. Russians appeared behind Juschkat's tank. The leader of the assault team dropped the three-kilo charge and reached for the submachine gun slung over his shoulder. But before he could fire Bichlap loosed off a burst with his machine gun. The Russians threw themselves to the ground.

Suddenly, there was an explosion. Turning his head, Juschkat saw flames coming from the rear of the disabled enemy tank. Spilling diesel fuel ignited, briefly enveloping a tree before dying down again.

"Stay alert!"

The explosive charge in his left hand, Juschkat moved forward toward the enemy tank in the forest. As he began to move the tank fired its main gun. As he ran, Juschkat saw two Russians running away behind the tank. Mertens' machine gun sent a long burst after them. Then he was at the Russian tank. Juschkat heaved the three-kilogram charge onto the deck beneath the overhanging part of the turret and pulled the fuse cord. A few bullets whizzed past him and struck the tank before howling away to the side. Juschkat hurried into the undergrowth and threw himself into a snow-filled depression.

The explosion and shock wave struck the Unteroffizier and pressed him deeper into the snow. He heard the crackle of flames and an unusually high roaring sound. Then the snow began to crunch with the footsteps of a large number of men. He thought it must be his men, but when he raised his head he heard Russian voices, not ten meters away. If he moved at that point they would see him for sure and shoot him. He lay motionless, his face pressed into the snow. The murmuring voices remained close to the edge of the depression. Suddenly a Russian submachine gun opened up with an ear-shattering roar. Juschkat expected to feel bullets striking his body, but the Russians were firing at his comrades, who returned fire.

Cautiously, millimeter by millimeter, Juschkat raised his head. He opened his eyes a fraction and saw a Russian soldier barely two meters away. The man had just fired a long burst and was inserting a fresh magazine. Juschkat could hear wounded crying from the German positions. Juschkat reached for his submachine gun. He pressed the trigger and immediately turned his gun on the main body of Russians, who were working their way forward. The first Russian to be hit turned slowly. His weapon swung towards Juschkat, but he had no chance to fire.

There was another mighty explosion, this time from the far side of the road. A tongue of flame shot from the turret hatch of the third tank, filling the night with flickering brightness.

"That was the third tank, Franz."

Suddenly, Paul was lying next to the Unteroffizier.

"Assault team assemble! We're going after them as far as their lines!"

Mertens and Jagst ran off to pull together the assault team. Four minutes later everyone was in place. Two men had sustained minor wounds and had been evacuated, while a third, Gefreiter Hermanns, was dead. He had been killed by a burst of machine-gun fire while trying to approach the last Russian tank.

"We're going through the forest. As little noise as possible. Form up into squad columns."

Juschkat led his men in an arc toward the south. Not until they reached a forest lane 500 meters south of the road did they turn right again toward the west. The soldiers moved almost silently through the frosty night. The only sound was the snow crunching beneath their feet. After ten minutes they left the path, which led straight to the Russian main line of resistance, and entered the undergrowth, which was covered with a heavy layer of snow. Juschkat felt certain that the path would be mined from that point. Two days earlier a patrol from the 22nd Infantry Regiment had run afoul of Russian box-mines; three men had been badly wounded. Juschkat wanted to eliminate this risk. A solid wall barred the way. Moving along its edge, Juschkat and his men looked for a way through. Finally they came to a sort of tunnel, about one meter high.

"A Russian crawlway, Franz," whispered Unteroffizier Bielitz, whose squad was walking point.

"That's what it looks like. I don't want to risk running into them in there. Wait here, I'm going through. Mertens, come with me."

The two men disappeared, while the rest of the assault team ducked down among the bushes. Two minutes later Mertens returned. "It's clear. Follow me!" The men crawled through the approximately forty-meter tunnel, which was the sole passageway through this wide area of overgrown wilderness.

"The Russian main line of resistance is about 200 meters farther. If I'm not wrong, there's a bunker at this projecting position. We'll snap up a couple of men who relieved the old bunker crew yesterday," said Juschkat. This was their actual mission: Take prisoners in order to determine whether new Russian units had arrived. The operation was a success, and Juschkat and his men returned with the prisoners.

The pot-bellied stove roared. The stovepipe glowed cherry red and the men in the bunker had removed their jackets. Juschkat was reading a letter he had just received from home. He learned that his brother had just been called up. All the men of his family, including his father, were now at the front. From the main line of resistance could be heard the sound of impacting rounds. Juschkat and his men were in a bunker about 100 meters behind the front.

"What do you think, Franz? Will the Russians come tonight?"

"What do I know? In any case another new division has been identified in front of us and that would indicate that Ivan hasn't given up on breaking the encirclement of Leningrad."

"Tomorrow's Christmas. But I fear we'll be outside in the cold," interjected Mertens.

"There'll be no roast goose and gingerbread for us."

"You greedy shit. Aren't you satisfied with what we've got? Army bread and nigger sweat (ersatz coffee) and, in the evening, if the hot food arrives, a hearty all-in-one meal?"

"Sure! Anything's better than nothing. But you know, goose breast in aspic. Pity! That would be something."

"The main thing is that at least we've got a few days rest. Life will begin again if we finally get pulled out of here, I can tell you that."

"Pulled out of here? Man, are you nuts? Who's supposed to relieve us?"

"Quiet!" said Paul. Suddenly they all heard it. A dull rumble pierced the din of the shellfire. Moments later they were certain. There was no mistaking the sound.

"Russian tanks!"

At that moment someone began to ring the alarm which had been fashioned from a number of empty shell casings. Before the ringing and clanging had subsided, Juschkat had pulled on his jacket and was reaching for his submachine gun. He was the first one outside. He ran toward the section of trench that had been assigned to the 1st Company of the 43rd Infantry Regiment. To the left and right the bunkers spewed forth men who had been warming themselves inside.

As they ran toward the trenches they could see the enemy tanks approaching across the snow-covered fields. Some stood out as dark shapes, while others, in white camouflage finish, were only outlines. The latter were only visible when flashes of gunfire silhouetted them against the black night sky. Juschkat and the others reached the trench line. The heavy machine gun on the flank began to rattle, halting the Russian infantry advancing behind the tanks.

At that moment the German divisional artillery opened fire. Shells smashed into no-man's land. One of the tanks was hit. The steel giant rolled into a crater and remained there nose down. Four or five tanks turned straight toward Juschkat's platoon. They were moving at high speed and firing their machine guns as they came. German antitank guns opened fire. The infantry could see clearly how the 37-mm rounds bounced off the armor of the T-34s. The first T-34 reached the trenches sixty meters to the left of Juschkat's position. The nose of the tank pushed into the trench, then the T-34 turned parallel to the trench line, tilted at a steep angle.

The long-barreled gun spat a red-orange tongue of flame. Juschkat pressed himself into the ground. Three or four men panicked and fled the trench in front of the tank. They were caught by Russian machine-gun fire and mown down. Juschkat saw the steel nose of the tank thirty meters in front of him. The rattling of the tank's tracks swelled to an ear-shattering inferno. The engine roared loudly and the air stank of cordite and diesel fumes.

Twenty meters! The tank filled the entire trench. Its right track was grinding along the floor of the trench, while the left rolled along the forward parapet. Juschkat jumped to the left. The tank track was now rolling straight towards him. He would have to crawl higher up the somewhat sloping wall of the trench to avoid being ground to a pulp.

The tank was now ten meters away. Once again the long gun spat flame and the round howled away over the trench. Tank motors likewise roared to the right. Two T-34s had rolled over the trench and were heading for the bunker, followed by infantry. Juschkat scrambled quickly up the icy side of the trench. The right track of the T-34 rolled through the ice and frozen ground not five centimeters from his boot, throwing fragments of ice into his face. Then a clump of ice gave way beneath him and he fell against the track. This was the end!

Just then the tank stopped. The turret hatch opened and a head with a fur cap emerged. Instinctively, Juschkat jumped up, raised his submachine gun and fired upward at a sharp angle. The tank commander fell back inside the tank. A tall figure appeared behind Juschkat. It was Paul. He raced toward the tank, jumped onto the rear deck and tossed a bundle of hand grenades inside before the crew could close the turret hatch. The grenades went off inside the tank with a dull thump. The tank seemed to rear up from the force of the explosion. Then flames shot into the air.

"Franz, over here! Are you injured?"

"Everything's all right."

Juschkat moved past the disabled tank. Suddenly there were several explosions from inside the vehicle. He hurried on after Paul. A tall officer appeared to the right. From that direction the sound of exploding grenades rang out through the night.

In the Cholm Pocket in early 1942.

"Juschkat, seal off this area! We're going to counterattack with the reserve platoon."

The officer, Hauptmann Dörner of the 43rd Infantry Regiment's 2nd Battalion, disappeared the way he had come. The heavy machine gun began to fire. The Russians got to within hand-grenade range before they were stopped. The Russian artillery opened fire, an indication that they had called off their attack. Behind them the men could still hear the two Russian tanks firing. As Juschkat watched, one of the tanks turned back and headed toward the trench again.

"Satchel charge!" he called to Mertens. The tank rumbled closer and closer. It drove two German soldiers in front of it into a narrow communications trench. The tank halted and, straddling the trench, began to emit dense black smoke.

"It's trying to run over those two men!"

The Russian assault groups poured back past the tank. Now the men manning the trenches had to fire to the east and west at the same time. Bichlap heaved his machine gun around and opened fire on the Russians.

"Cover me!"

Franz Juschkat knew that the narrow trench was only about a meter wide and completely covered by the tank. If those men didn't get out soon, they would be lost. They were members of his platoon. He got up from the ground and ran towards the tank. A machine gun opened fire, forcing him to take cover. He fell forward, landing hard on his right side, where he was holding the hand grenade bundle. Finally, he reached the tank. Juschkat hammered against the side of the turret with his pistol. The hatch opened; he fired into the tank before tossing the bundle of grenades inside. He then let himself roll to the side. There was a dull thud. The tank jerked around, ending up across the trench. Smoke began to pour from inside the T-34.

Juschkat jumped down into the trench beside the tank's right track. He found the first man and began pulling him out. Just as he dragged the man free, Paul came running up to him. Bichlap and the others kept on firing at the retreating Russians as they emerged from the trenches and foxholes.

"Pull him out, Paul!" The mighty East Prussian lifted the unconscious man from the trench as flames began to lick from the tank.

"It's about to go up, Franz, get out!"

For fractions of a second Juschkat thought about jumping out of the trench, but he knew there was another man under the tank. He would surely be lost to the fire. He crawled back in. A frozen clump of earth barred the way. Behind him he could see the flickering flames. Desperately he struggled to move the lump of earth to the side, but in vain. Instead, he crawled over the obstruction and reached the second man, who was likewise unconscious. A shadow fell over the trench. It was Paul. He reached down, seized the limp figure, pulled him forward and lifted him out.

Juschkat could feel his strength leaving him when a tongue of flame moved toward him. With a desperate leap he reached the firm frozen earth of the upper edge of the trench. A second leap brought him out of the immediate danger zone. The firing behind the main line of resistance had ceased. The only firing now was from the west as Juschkat, assisted by Paul, dragged the two unconscious men to the bunker. The company medic, Feldwebel Loboschitz, a druggist by profession, took charge of the two men. He administered warm milk and within a few minutes the two had regained consciousness.

✠

The following days brought no peace. The Soviets made repeated efforts to break through the German main line of resistance. Fresh Russian divisions continued to appear at this part of the front. Soviet tanks made repeated efforts to smash a path through the thin German lines for the infantry in hopes of achieving a decisive breakthrough. For the Soviets it was of vital importance to break the ring around Leningrad at this spot. If they succeeded, the German divisions defending towards the east would find themselves under attack from the rear.

An overwhelmingly superior Russian force surrounded the few German divisions in the bottleneck, which extended along the Neva as far as Schlüsselburg and, in the east, from Lipki through Pogostye to a point north of Kirischi on the Volkhov. The Soviets had placed a clamp around the German encircling front, so to speak.

Defending between Schlüsselburg and Kolpino, the 1st, 96th, and 121st Infantry Divisions were attacked by nine Russian divisions and several brigade-sized armored units. Holding the east side of the corridor were the 227th and 223rd Infantry Divisions, part of the XXVIII Army Corps under General der Infanterie Loch. Between Kolpino and Oritzk on the southern front of the ring around Leningrad was the L Army Corps under General der Infanterie Lindemann. That corps had the 121st, 122nd, 269th, and 58th Infantry Divisions and the 4th SS-Police Division.

The Soviets attempted to break through between the 4th SS-Police Division and the 121st Infantry Division at Kolpino. The front was stalemated. A mood of desperation had seized Leningrad. If the encircling ring around the city were not broken, hundreds of thousands would be condemned to death by starvation. Aware of this single alternative, the Soviet divisions repeatedly attacked with everything they had. The German troops defending against their attacks soon learned what this meant.

In early January Stalin ordered the formation of a new army group, which he named the "Volkhov Front." Between his 52nd and 59th Armies he inserted the Second Shock Army under Lieutenant General Vlasov, who had participated in the successful defense of Moscow. The army was composed of elite mobile units. No fewer than eight rifle divisions and eight shock brigades, each consisting of two battalions of infantry as well as an artillery and a mortar battalion, and ten ski battalions arrived at the front. Facing the Second Shock Army were only two German infantry divisions, the 126th Infantry Division on the right and the 215th Infantry Division on the left.

✠

The company had been placed on alert. Unteroffizier Juschkat had just left the command post and was hurrying back to his platoon. As he entered the platoon bunker, which housed his platoon headquarters section and part of the 1st Squad, he could hear the rumble of shells falling on the neighboring sector.

"Get ready!"

The men pulled on the thick parkas they had captured from the Russians. The alarm went off, and they rushed out into the trenches.

"Franz! Over there to the right!"

Numerous figures were hurrying across the shell-torn fields of snow. They were travelling on skis and were approaching rapidly. The weapons remained silent. Suddenly, the mortars began to fire and, seconds later, the heavy machine guns in the strongpoints opened up. The skiers were thrown to the ground as if they had been caught by a whirlwind. Several nevertheless continued to try and reach the German positions, but they also fell in the rapidly intensifying rifle fire.

Juschkat felt as if a hand were around his throat, choking him. What he was witnessing was so indescribably horrible that he didn't want to believe it. But it was true. The Soviets were simply moving their ski battalions forward across the open terrain. The Soviets tried again at the same spot. This time, however, they changed their tactics. Tanks rolled toward the German main line of resistance in a wide formation. The 37-mm anti-tank guns were next to useless against the Russian heavy tanks. Their only chance was to score a direct hit on the turret ring.

The "88" battery that had gone into position with the 3rd Battalion of the 43rd Infantry Regiment opened fire when the Soviets tanks were 800 meters from the German line. The soldiers in the trenches could follow the paths of the rounds from the "88s" as they streaked westwards. The first tank was hit and ground to a halt, pouring smoke. The remaining Russian tanks increased speed. They closed formation and altered course, giving the appearance that they were going to attack another sector. Then the enemy tanks split into two groups. While one headed in the direction of the 22nd Infantry Regiment, the other came straight toward the 43rd Infantry Regiment.

"There, Franz!"

Russian infantry appeared in dense waves. Several dragged sled-mounted machine guns behind them, others had mortars in tow.

"Open fire!"

The heavy machine gun began to rattle. One of the tanks stopped. It fired two rounds at the machine gun in rapid succession from a range of 400 meters. The second was a direct hit which put the machine gun out of action. A wave of white-clad figures raced toward the trench. Almost every man of the 1st Company trained his weapon on the onrushing infantry. The only one not firing was the man on the field telephone, who made repeated requests for artillery support. The guns didn't begin firing until the enemy was within eighty meters. By then some of them had run under the artillery fire.

The Soviets reached the tripwires. Flames shot from the ground as explosive charges and Teller mines went up. The Soviet soldiers threw grenades at the trenches. A "pineapple" hand grenade clattered across the frozen ground not five paces in front of Juschkat and rolled to a stop in front of the trench. He ducked and fragments whistled over his head. When he stood up the Soviets were only meters away.

Juschkat emptied the entire magazine of his submachine gun in one long burst. Then he reached for hand grenades. Paul had already lobbed several toward the advancing Russians. The Soviets were stopped in front of the company's positions. However, they had broken into the trenches of the 2nd Company and were threatening to roll up the position.

"Platoon: Follow me!"

Juschkat hurried along the trench. They came upon the Russians, who turned their backs on them and ran along the trench towards the north. The firefight lasted ten minutes. No one was sure who was friend or foe. Russians fired on the platoon from a German machine-gun position. Heinemann and Rolfs were fatally wounded. A round tore a hole in Juschkat's sleeve. He paid it no mind, as more Russian troops were appearing every minute. They were fought off with hand grenades, spades and bayonets. Finally, the penetration was sealed off. But the cost of the nocturnal attack had been heavy. Attacker and defender alike sought to recover their wounded.

It was beginning to get light as Unteroffizier Juschkat returned to the bunker. He pulled off his jacket and looked at the flesh wound that had torn a centimeter-wide strip across his upper arm. The battalion commander stepped inside. Juschkat got up to report, but the officer motioned to him to stay where he was.

"Come, Juschkat. We're to report to the regimental command post immediately."

"What have I done now, sir?"

"I don't know, Juschkat."

They set out in the direction of the village where the command post was located. The pair stepped into the anteroom. A few men were sitting beside a stove on a bench.

"Wait here, Juschkat," said the Major.

Juschkat said hello to the others and leaned against the wall. Messengers came in and quickly disappeared again. The telephone rang continuously. A Feldwebel stepped into the room.

"You're here too, Juschkat. What's up?"

"No idea."

"I could tell you something," interjected an Obergefreiter sitting behind a typewriter. "How about a bottle of vodka?"

"We'd rather wait, Hitzel!" growled Feldwebel Schwelske.

Oberfeldwebel Matuzat stumbled into the room. He wore no helmet; instead, a dressing half covered his haggard, bearded face. He went over to the stove and warmed his cold-stiffened hands. Then he recognized his old friend.

"Hello, Franz. Congratulations!"

"Congratulations?" echoed Juschkat in astonishment.

"Congratulations for what?"

"Perhaps you've become a father," quipped one of the men. Laughter filled the room. Then the door opened.

"Unteroffizier Juschkat, the Oberst wishes to speak to you."

"Good luck, old man!"

Franz Juschkat stepped into the dimly lit room and came to attention.

"Unteroffizier Juschkat, effective immediately you are being promoted to Feldwebel for bravery in the face of the enemy. At the same time I award you the Iron Cross, First Class. You cleared a major enemy penetration and prevented the enemy from breaking through the front in several places."

The Oberst stepped up and pinned the Iron Cross on his tunic. Then he extended his hand. "All the best, Juschkat! Continued good luck!"

"Thank you, sir!"

Juschkat shook hands with the "old man," who was feared for his sternness but held in high respect for his courage. Afterward Juschkat left the office and was met by the grinning Feldwebel, who passed him his Feldwebel shoulder boards on a plate.

The 1st Infantry Division remained in the same sector until January 1942. The division was withdrawn from the front and transferred back to Mga to rest and refit. It had lost nearly sixty percent of its authorized strength. Many wounded had been sent to hospitals in Germany. Others, who had suffered severe frostbite, had been discharged. Juschkat's company was one of the last to be relieved. Juschkat arrived in Mga with the rest of his platoon. First they went to the sauna. Then they were issued new uniforms; their old things were almost falling off their bodies.

The troops were able to rest for the first time after long weeks of combat. In spite of this, Juschkat had difficulty sleeping. The bearded faces of the Siberians he had faced frequently appeared in his dreams. Within a week the "bloodhounds," as Soviet propaganda had dubbed the East Prussian 1st Infantry Division, had demonstrated their willingness to help the population in Mga and surrounding villages. The actions of the troops flew in the face of the propaganda image of the German soldier as a "criminal." The civilian population received food and medical care. There was no war here. Where the civilian population was concerned, the tough East Prussians were just people ready to help where they could.

During the division's rest period it was called upon to carry out several operations against infiltrating partisan bands. The Russian offensive against the 18th Army on the Volkhov had not been very successful. Although the German army was at the end of its strength, the front on the Volkhov continued to hold. This was the result of the efforts of every one of the army's soldiers, from General Lindemann, who was later hanged on Hitler's orders, to the last infantryman, radio operator and even cook.

Units were shuffled back and forth between sectors as the situation demanded, plugging gaps in the front. Formations in quiet sectors were withdrawn from the front and sent to sectors under attack. There were regimental headquarters on the Neva whose troops were in action on the Volkhov or near Pogostye.

In March 1942 it was the time for the 1st Infantry Division again. The formation marched in several march groups in the direction of Volkhov, where the Soviet Second Shock Army under Vlasov was already partially surrounded. By the end of January, the Soviets had pushed forward to the Novgorod-Leningrad railway line. In February, they managed to expand their penetration as far as the Oredesch, where they were halted by the 285th Security Division.

The Soviet advance toward Lyuban was stopped by elements of the 212th Infantry Division. As a result, the supply line to the Kirischi bridgehead remained in German hands. By 8 March the Soviets had been pushed back as far as Chudovo.

Nevertheless, the Soviets had captured an area seventy kilometers deep, resulting in a salient of approximately 200 kilometers. Lieutenant General Vlasov took command in the pocket that was forming after the original Russian commander had been recalled by Stalin. During this phase of the fighting powerful elements of the Soviet 52nd and 59th Armies were sent in to guard the flanks of the penetration. Fighting began at Pogostye on 9 March. It lasted three weeks. The German defenders included the 96th and 223rd Infantry Divisions and the 5th Mountain Infantry Division.

The battle for the Volkhov pocket was decided at the road between Podbyeresye and Spaskaya Polist. This was the only place where the enemy's communications with the rear could be cut and the pocket closed. On 15 March 1942, during the fighting west of Spaskaya Polist in the Pogostye area, the 4th SS-Police Division attacked south. Formations in the south— the 58th Infantry Division as well as elements of the 126th and 250th Infantry Divisions (the latter being the Spanish "Blue Division")—drove northwards. After four days of fighting in deep snow the two formations linked up at the notorious Erika forest lane. The ring around the Volkhov area had been closed, resulting in a huge pocket.

The Soviets fought desperately. By the end of the month they succeeded in opening another supply road. The corridor extended no more than three kilometers on either side of the Erika lane. And although the Soviets built two field railways through this narrow corridor they were unable to bring in sufficient supplies for their 18,000 soldiers inside the pocket. The 1st Infantry Division was sent toward this corridor, which ran south from Tregubovo about twenty kilometers to Mostki. The division's mission was to close the Soviets' last exit from the pocket. When the division arrived, a Russian force of seven regiments and two tank brigades was attacking westwards in an attempt to break into the pocket. At the same time four divisions inside the pocket were attacking towards the east. It was the beginning of a dangerous situation.

✠

The shaky log road under the boots of the soldiers imparted a feeling of threatening uncertainty. The 1st Company of the 43rd Infantry Regiment was on its way to the front at Spaskaya Polist. The 1st Infantry Division was to attack from the north with the 4th SS-Police Division and seal off the Russian corridor. Juschkat was walking along the left side beside Paul. The latter had just taken Bichlap's machine gun and was carrying it over his shoulder like a fence slat.

A huge sign appeared on the left side of the path, which led into the deepening marshland. Juschkat tried to decipher the black letters. Finally, he read aloud: "The ass of the world starts here." A laugh went through the lines of men, and they slowed their pace to read the sign as they passed.

"It couldn't be any worse than at the Neva, could it, Franz?"

"We'll see. Don't say anything, maybe we'll be lucky."

Feldwebel Juschkat passed the sign. As he turned, he saw there was writing on the back as well.

Printed in large letters was: "If you're leaving this place, you can kiss my ass!

"I think," said Paul softly, "that we're walking into a lovely mess." He was soon to be proved correct.

✠

The Volkhov night drew to an end. The men in the bunker on the island in the marshland awoke when artillery began firing from within the pocket. At first the Russians employed field guns and *Ratschbum* multipurpose guns. Then the heavy 150-mm guns joined in. Finally, the shrieking and howling of Stalin Organs added to the din. Juschkat raised his open hand to his forehead.

"Got him!" he said as he saw the squashed mosquito in his open hand. The whole bunker seemed to be buzzing. The men, who had only been there a few days, had already learned that the mosquitoes were a formidable enemy. But the plague had not yet reached its climax; it was only April 29 and the mosquitoes were far worse in summer.

Howling and shrieking, the rocket salvo fell into the marsh. Geysers spurted into the pale morning sky, dumping mud and water on the men cowering in the trenches.

A shout went up from outside the bunker: "Alarm!"

Juschkat had anticipated this and he and his men tumbled outside. Juschkat ran to his sector, struggling through the ankle-deep mud that had formed on the floor of the trench. Then he reached the combat trench with its trench boards of logs and branches.

The attackers emerged from the first greenery sprouting from the puny trees that blocked the defenders' view of no-man's-land. As far as the eye could see there were brown-clad figures. They ran forward, hurried across the log road and then disappeared into the swamp. A machine gun began to rattle from a forward listening post. At the same time other weapons opened up all along the strongpoint-style main line of resistance. There was a small lake about 400 meters in front of the main line of resistance. The listening post was on a wooded island in the middle of the lake. Juschkat saw a group of enemy soldiers crossing the lake in two or three inflatable boats.

"Fire at the inflatable boats!"

The platoon's two machine gunners trained their weapons on the lake. Bullets smacked into the water and walked their way towards the

A German soldier assists his wounded comrade, both are equipped with full winter clothing of padded parkas and trousers plus felt boots.

boats. The Russians jumped overboard. Riddled, the inflatable boats collapsed. Several heads bobbed in the water. To the right of the lake the Soviets broke through the swamp, using the narrow, slippery footbridges that were also used by German patrols. As soon as they came into view they were fired on by the defenders, who were safe in their almost impregnable swamp positions.

There were two thunderous explosions as the Soviets reached the middle of two of the footbridges. The defenders had booby-trapped both with mines. Logs and men were tossed into the air. The Russians were halted along the entire width of the sector. There would be no breakthrough in that sector.

Suddenly, Paul shouted and pointed to the end of the lake. How the Russians had done it was a mystery, but two assault boats were gliding towards the island. One of the boats was hit by machine gun fire and began to burn, but the other reached the island. There was an outburst of firing from submachine guns, pistols and rifles and the dull thud of hand grenades. Suddenly all was quiet.

Two minutes later the first Russian Maxim machine gun began firing from the island. The bullets chirped off the steel shields and tore the last branches off the birch trees nearby.

"They have the island!"

"Those poor bastards in the 2nd Company" said Mertens softly.

While the firing died down, the defenders on the west side of the corridor heard the sound of tanks from the east. The Soviets were continuing to attack there, as the ground was firmer. But that sector was held by the 22nd Infantry Division and a Waffen-SS unit. They would soon halt the enemy. The sound of fighting from the east grew ever louder. It seemed to be getting closer. Repeated calls went out in effort to find out what was going on in the eastern sector.

At about 0815 the Soviets launched a second attack in the west. They came through the marshland in dense formations. How they managed it, heaven knows, but they came. The first Russians appeared, camouflaged with greenery from birch trees.

"Fire, fire!" roared Ochtrop.

The Germans opened fire. The Russians had meanwhile moved up a mortar unit and this began firing on the defenders. The 5-cm mortar rounds, known to the German troops as "potatoes," flew across the marsh in dense clusters, exploding as they struck the ground. Heavier mortars joined the barrage. The regiment's sector was blanketed by steel fragments. Finally a salvo of rockets came screaming in.

Juschkat ducked as the rockets began falling about eighty meters away. The last fell just in front of the position. The explosions sprayed mud over the trenches. A mortar round struck the heavy platoon's ammunition bunker. There was a terrific explosion that collapsed the structure.

"Watch out! The Ivans will be here soon if we don't get our noses out of the mud, Franz!"

Paul had to shout to make himself heard. Juschkat nodded. He crawled forward and raised his head. A glowing mortar fragment howled past his head and struck the slab behind him. The fragment stuck in the mud, hissing as it cooled. Juschkat felt as if he had been shaved with a dull razor, but what he saw caused him to open fire immediately.

The Soviets had reached the wire not sixty meters from the trench. Explosive charges detonated. Russian assault rifles and submachine guns opened fire on the Germans as they emerged from cover. The mortars shifted their fire onto the German rear. The magazine of Juschkat's submachine gun was empty. It took only seconds to duck down, eject the empty magazine and insert a fresh one. Paul, Bichlap, Mertens and Ochtrop were already firing their captured Russian submachine guns. Three others lobbed hand grenades. Once again the Russian attack collapsed just in front of the German lines. The enemy artillery began firing again.

"If they keep this up, there'll soon be no ammunition left in the pocket," said Mertens, lighting a cigarette.

The sun hung over the swamp. Its warmth brought forth a myriad of mosquitoes. Juschkat raised his field glass and scanned his sector as far as the lake. He saw the three sleds on which the Soviets had dragged their heavy machine guns across the marshy ground. "We'll go get them tonight," he said, pointing to the machine guns.

"But Ivan will want to get them back too, sir," replied one of the younger members of the platoon.

"Then we'll get there before he does. We can make good use of the Russian Maxims, especially if we can find enough ammunition."

The mess detail arrived with the food at twelve o'clock. They brought with them the latest news. The Soviets had attacked from the east with large numbers of tanks, but most of them had become stuck in the mud. The thin German lines on the east side of the corridor had held. The men in the strongpoint began to eat, while the mess detail personnel took off their boots and poured out the marsh water that had seeped in.

After Juschkat had emptied his mess kit he lit a cigarette. He wondered if any of their comrades on the island were still alive. Perhaps the Russians were planning to take them back for interrogation after dark. They wouldn't dare attempt it at that point on account of the German harassing fire. If he took out a small patrol after dark he might get lucky.

"Why so quiet, Franz?" asked Obergefreiter Pietsch of the platoon headquarters section.

"You know, Helmut, I was thinking of our comrades on the island. We should get them out of there."

"And how to you intend to do that?"

"We'll simply go over."

"And how are we supposed to approach without being noticed?"

"After we're relieved we'll go around the island and come from the west."

"I'm with you, Franz."

Paul had just emptied his mess kit. Grinning, he gestured towards Mertens, who was scraping out one of the food containers: "Look at the glutton. I'd like to know where he puts it all."

"We're planning to go through the swamp tonight, Paul."

"No need to tell me. I've been with you long enough to know what we're in for."

"I want to go to battalion first. Coming with me, Paul? We can see if there's any mail."

"It's already arrived at battalion," interjected one of the mess detail soldiers.

The pair left the position through a trench that ended in a thicket eighty meters to the rear. The water in the trench was knee deep. A log road led from the thicket to the Russian cottage that housed the battalion command post. As they reached the log road another salvo of rockets howled over their heads. The forest in front of them, which already looked bare enough, was stripped once again as the rockets struck, sending trees and bushes whirling through the air.

"Let's go, before the next one hits."

They began to run. The slippery logs rocked beneath their boots. Paul stumbled, sailed a few meters across the logs and just caught himself before he slid off the side. Cursing, he got up. As the pair reached the tall stands of trees, the next salvo fell behind them.

"Exactly one minute apart. You can set your watch by them."

"Go ahead to the mailroom. I'll come as soon as I'm finished at battalion."

"Understood. But don't promise the Major too much. We can't clear the entire pocket tonight, Franz!"

Juschkat looked wryly at his tall companion: "Get lost!"

Moments later Juschkat was in front of the battalion commander outlining his plan. When he had ended the Major walked over to the map that hung on the front wall of the cottage.

"There's the lake and the bunker next to it. If the Soviets stay on the island—and there's no doubt of that—you'll have to attack from the western shore and move quickly. But there are probably Russians on the western shore too, waiting to cross to the island."

"I know a way across the lake. It leads over the brush-covered islands and the reed bank to the island from the northwest. There was a log road there more than two weeks ago. It should still be there, sir."

"Very well then! Take a patrol with five men. Smoke out bunkers, remove mines and, if possible, bring back our captured comrades. . . . One more thing, Juschkat. Tomorrow morning the new division commander will be inspecting the main line of resistance. I am assigning you to accompany him, as he is coming alone. No formalities, understood?"

"When is he supposed to be here?"

"Be here by eight, that's early enough."

An hour later Paul and Juschkat returned to their strongpoint with the mail. To the east the Soviets continued to attack with tanks in an effort to break through and widen their exit from the pocket. The mail was quickly handed out. After everyone had read their letters Juschkat cleared his throat and began to speak.

"Patrol. I need five men."

Mertens, Pietsch, Bichlap and Ochtrop were already standing beside him before he began to speak. Bielitz joined them but he was pushed away by Paul.

Juschkat and his patrol set out just as dusk was falling. They left the main line of resistance near the thick stand of bushes that gave them the best chance of approaching through a water-filled ravine. Three logs bound together formed a bridge over a brook. When Juschkat reached the middle the logs sagged almost to the surface of the bubbly swamp water. He raised his arm in warning and the next man, Paul, waited until the Feldwebel was across before he followed.

They pressed on into the tangled growth that sprouted from both sides of the log road. The bushes, the bottoms of which were under water, provided good cover. Once Juschkat sank up to his knees. He took hold of a bush and hauled himself out of the hole, finally reaching firm ground. It took half an hour to cover the 200 meters to the lake's northern outlet. Suddenly, Juschkat stopped and ducked down. The men behind him blended into the bushes as irregular shadows. In front of them a group of Russians wearing their typical fur hats were struggling with a curious-looking support base. Then they put the barrel in place. A line of bearers came through the swamp, carrying longish boxes between them. Their weapons were slung.

"Look at that! A new mortar position. At least fifteen centimeters."

"Let's get them! Mertens take the right mortar and crew. Ochtrop the one beside it. Bichlap and Pietsch the ones farther to the rear. . . . Ready, fire!"

The submachine guns hammered. Standing by—"in reserve"—Paul stood half erect and tossed hand grenades. The ammunition bearers dropped their loads and ran back through the swamp.

"After them!"

They charged through the bushes. Branches whipped their faces. Juschkat led the way. He ran, leaping over narrow channels, and fired at the fleeing Russians. When he saw a bunker projecting from the island group to his right, he ceased firing.

"This way!"

The group kept moving. The smell of decay was in the air. From the bunker a heavy machine gun fired in the direction of the mortars. The bursts were far away. Then they reached the shore of the lake. Up to their chests in water, they waded step by step, weapons held at eye level. Splashes from the west side of the lake betrayed the presence of Russians in the bushes along the shore, where there was a narrow footbridge. Juschkat recognized an inflatable boat that was being rowed to the island. In it were eight Russian soldiers.

"Let's go!"

One behind the other they tramped through the reeds and rushes. The marsh plants rustled, but the noise was drowned out by the Russians, who had just reached the island and were now carrying their supplies through the bushes. Even more noise was created by the salvoes which repeatedly flew from the pocket into the German corridor and tore up the ground there. At one point the patrol members reached a spot where the water was up to their chins. Juschkat cursed under his breath. The water stank, and the mud gripped their boots. Soon, however, the water became shallower and finally they were within thirty meters of the island. There now remained only an open, shallow stretch to cross. Just in time they spotted a sentry as he approached along a footpath from the east side of the island.

"Let him pass!" whispered Juschkat. But the sentry stopped behind a bush and lit a cigarette.

"Damn! He won't move from that spot, and I'll bet the Ivans are about to take the prisoners back in the boat."

"I'll go get him."

Pietsch gave Paul his weapon and disappeared up to his nose in the water. Within seconds he was gone from sight. The seconds dragged on forever. The sentry seemed to be rooted in one place. All at once his knees sagged and he fell forward. There was a cracking and rustling in the bushes. Pietsch stood up from the bushes and waved, then disappeared again at once.

"Let's go!"

Juschkat reached the shore. Pietsch had taken the Russian sentry's submachine gun and pulled his fur hat down over his ears. The patrol moved on, no longer worrying about noise. From inside the bunker they could hear a few Russians shouting. Others came out, loaded down, followed by five or six men. Juschkat felt a surge of emotion. They were the captured German soldiers—there was no doubt about it. Even in the darkness their uniforms were unmistakable.

"Both of us will go to the bunker. The rest will take the Russians heading for the shore. . . . Go!"

The six men jumped to their feet as one and opened fire as they began to run.

"Get down, comrades!" shouted Paul.

Juschkat was the first to reach the bunker entrance, which was wide open. He fired at a Russian shooting blindly into the open. Paul tossed a hand grenade into the bunker. One last burst of fire at the Russians escorting the prisoners and then the surprise night attack was over.

"Over here!" Ochtrop and Mertens called to the prisoners. The men came hurrying over. Almost all of them were wounded. "Here, take these!"

The former captives were given the Russians' weapons. Soot-black figures emerged from the bunker with raised hands and surrendered.

"We'll take them with us! You go ahead, Mertens will lead the way. Go back the same way we came. We still have to destroy the mortars."

They were turning to go, when suddenly one of the freed prisoners stopped.

"What is it? Get going, we have to get out of here quickly. The Russians will be here soon."

"Beerwald is still in the bunker!"

"Get going, quickly! Paul, come with me."

They ran back to the bunker. When Juschkat stepped inside he was met by a burst of fire which almost knocked the helmet off his head. He fired as he fell, and the wounded Russian who had stayed behind dropped to the ground. They found the other prisoner. He was badly wounded and his eyes were wide and fever-glazed.

"Take me with you, comrades, don't let me die here."

"The two shelter halves Paul!" They pulled the two shelter halves down from the bunks and tied them together.

"Clench your teeth, comrade!"

They heaved the man onto the shelter halves and grasped both sides firmly. As they left the bunker they saw the fiery tails of a rocket salvo as it howled towards them from out of the pocket. The rockets were going to fall on the island! The two placed the wounded man in a trench and threw themselves to the ground. The firestorm smashed into the swamp at the west side of the lake and into the water as well. The shock wave passed over them like a hurricane. Ripped-up birch saplings rained down on the surface of the lake. Then all was quiet again.

They tramped after their companions, who had ducked under water when the rockets fell and were now hurrying towards the shore. Juschkat had to hold the shelter half at chest level. Within minutes their burden seemed to weigh a ton.

"On your shoulders, Franz! On your shoulders!" said Paul.

They heaved their groaning comrade onto their shoulders and, when they reached the spot where the deep ravine began, Paul reached for the man's head and held it above water. The others reached the shore ahead of them. Juschkat and Paul crossed the ravine without being spotted by the Russians.

A nocturnal fight then began against a numerically far-superior enemy force. Juschkat was able to eliminate two mortar teams and halt an enemy squad that was coming through the swamp as reinforcements. After destroying the two remaining mortars with explosives they found, Juschkat ordered Paul and Ochtrop to head back with the severely wounded man and the freed prisoners, while he and the rest covered the rear. Bichlap had the machine gun. They held off the pursuing Russians and when they disappeared into the bush-covered ravine, the following enemy troops ran into machine gun and mortar fire from the strongpoint.

Not until the patrol had reached safety did Juschkat breathe easier. The patrol had not lost a man. The wounded man was tended to and sent back to the rear with his liberated companions. Once again Juschkat had used luck and experience to lead a patrol with good results.

✠

"Feldwebel Juschkat reports as ordered, sir."

"It's about time, Juschkat, the General should be here any second." The command post door opened and the lookout stepped inside.

"Sir, the General is here!"

"Come, Juschkat."

They stepped outside. The thump of artillery and crack of tank cannon, which had only been a dull rumble inside, grew louder. It was coming from the east. Generalmajor Ernst-Anton von Krosigk came roaring up in a motorcycle-sidecar. In the motorcycle coat he looked like a Feldwebel or Leutnant. The General had only taken command of the division a few weeks ago. The unit's former commander, Generalleutnant Phillip Kleffel, had been promoted to corps commander. The Major stepped up and came to attention. The General waved him away: "Do not report!"

A second motorcycle was close behind the first. Accompanying the General were his executive officer and a messenger.

"Well then, Ziegler, have you found someone to guide me around?"

"This is Feldwebel Juschkat, sir. I've told you of his patrols."

"Aha! Good day, Juschkat! Lead the way, just keep us out of trouble, understood?"

"*Jawohl*, sir!"

Juschkat grinned when he saw the officers' shiny boots and clean trousers.

"Start with the 1st Company of the 43rd Infantry Regiment and, from there, the entire sector as far as the 2nd Battalion of the 43rd Infantry Regiment, Juschkat."

The party started on its way. A walk of several hundred meters along the log road brought them to the company command post. The company commander made his report. From there Juschkat led the party to the company's bunkers. Now and then shells whined overhead. Then they reached Juschkat's own bunker. The executive officer passed out lozenges and cigarettes. After a brief visit the party continued on its way.

"Duck down here, General. The next fifty meters is under Soviet observation. That's the reason for the steel screens."

"Good, Juschkat. Lead the way."

The Feldwebel ducked low and set out at a good pace. He could hear the officers panting behind him. One of the party hadn't bent low enough, and a shot rang out from the swamp. The bullet hissed over the steel screen and struck a crippled spruce tree. The ground sank somewhat deeper and the men disappeared behind the marsh bushes. A narrow log road led to the next, larger bunker.

Juschkat and the others were about to step inside when a Soviet "Katyusha" (Stalin Organ) fired a salvo of rockets. It seemed as if the projectiles were homing in on the General, because they were heading straight for his position. In seconds the rockets were on their way down.

"Take cover, General!" warned Juschkat. He jumped forward to make room for the division commander.

Juschkat heard splashing in the swamp behind him to the left and right. At the same time the rockets impacted to their right and showered everyone with a thick, stinking brew. When the din had died down and Juschkat could hear again, he heard swearing that would have done drunkest sailor proud. It was coming from the mouth of the General. The exec-

A photograph of Juschkat from
his hometown newspaper.

utive officer, who had likewise thrown himself down in the swamp, was
cursing as well. Only the messenger had dropped onto the log road, like
Juschkat.

Juschkat and the messenger pulled the General from the viscous brew.
Then it was the executive officer's turn. Grinning, the two soldiers set
about trying to scrape the muck from the General's uniform with their
bayonets.

"Stinks like a wild boar!" proclaimed the General. When the messenger chuckled out loud he abruptly turned to the men. "You find this funny,
do you? If you breathe a word of this, you'll be locked up so long you'll
think you're back in the Stone Age, understood?"

Juschkat found it impossible to remain serious. And if they did lock
him up, could it have been any worse than where he was then? He grinned
more and more until he could no longer control himself and finally
laughed out loud. He laughed so hard that he was in danger of falling off
the log road. The laughter proved infectious, however, and the General
also began to laugh. Following that, things went well.

The inspection ended and the General was finally able to go back to
the division headquarters and change his uniform. Several days later
Juschkat was again overcome with laughter while thinking of the incident.

His companions in the bunker stared at him and shook their heads. Juschkat refused, however, to tell them what was so funny.

The fighting for the corridor approached its dramatic climax, with the Soviets making repeated efforts to smash it. The Germans were forced to make repeated counterattacks to recapture areas of swamp taken by the Russians. Franz Juschkat and his small band of men made repeated forays into the swamps. The sprouts growing from the ends of the log roads were now as tall as a man. The mosquito plague had reached levels beyond description. If the men ate a piece of bread and butter they could be certain that they would be eating a half-dozen mosquitoes with every bite. The troops in the swamp dubbed the area the "Green Hell." Even mosquito nets and face nets could not save the troops. Stinking mud brewed myriads of germs. At the end of May 1942 the swamp steamed beneath a glowing sun. Swarms of mosquitoes, looking like gray smoke clouds, danced above the swamp.

Each day demanded sacrifices. Men became casualties through Russian mortar or sniper fire, but also from malaria and swamp fever. Jaundice and foot rot also claimed their share of victims. The German troops lay apathetically in their bunkers and in the open. The *Organisation Todt* (a paramilitary force that was assigned to construct field fortifications and military-construction projects) had built a network of log roads, but these were in the rear. The men in the front lines had none; they were in the middle of a moor.

With the strength of desperation the Soviets made repeated efforts to break through. However, by 13 May the Soviet units, which had been attacking since 29 April, had been driven back. The Volkhov pocket had been closed again. The Soviet command ordered the evacuation of the pocket with all means available. The first ones to try to get through the Erika lane were the supply troops.

The 18th Army ordered a counterattack to block these movements. As many enemy troops within the pocket as possible were to be captured. The battle to reduce the pocket began on 22 May. In the north, the 20th Motorized Infantry Division and the bulk of the 1st Infantry Division attacked southwards, while at the same time the 58th Infantry Division in the south struck northwards. The objective was the Erica forest lane. An opening of the pocket had to be prevented.

Franz Juschkat and his platoon led the regiment's attack force. He knew that his fellow soldiers were moving forward on his left and right. They advanced southwards through the swamp in an attack sector of 2,000 meters. They had gone scarcely 100 meters when the first Russians appeared.

Rolling straight towards them were a T-34 and a T-26, followed by infantry in battalion strength. The men of the 1st Platoon, who had camouflaged themselves with birch branches, let the two tanks roll over their lines. Then they waited until the Soviet infantry were completely in the open before opening fire.

"Satchel charge!" Juschkat called softly, extending his arm to the rear. He felt the handle of the middle grenade, which was pushed into his fist. The T-26 had stopped not twenty meters away and was firing its cannon and machine guns. The Feldwebel began to run. He saw muzzle flashes and felt the bullets as they whistled past. Amid the racket of gunfire and the idling tank engine he reached the tank and pushed the bundle of grenades onto the rear deck. Then he ran a few meters to one side and dropped into the bushes. He landed right on a Russian, who was about to fire. Juschkat swung the barrel of his machine gun and knocked the enemy soldier down. The thunderous roar of the explosion rang in his ears. There was another, louder explosion farther to the right; the T-34 had been put out of action as well. Hauptmann Beinke appeared at the location of the 1st Platoon.

"Keep moving, Juschkat! We must not stop, even if the flanking units get bogged down."

They advanced deeper into the primeval, forested swamp. Now and then they sunk in the mud. Finally, Juschkat and his men reached a patch of woods on a section of higher ground and the pace quickened.

Russian snipers fired from perches high in the trees, and many German soldiers were fatally wounded. On one occasion the advancing troops encountered a Russian assault group. The Soviets had four machine guns and held up the company until Juschkat and a few men outflanked the enemy and attacked from the rear. Juschkat's move cleared the way for the company. The advance resumed. They could begin to hear the rattle of German machine guns to the south, and headed towards the sound. Juschkat and his men came to the Russian improvised railway that was built on a platform of logs. These had sprouted considerable vegetation and offered good concealment. As they were preparing to cross the railway, an armored train came steaming out of the pocket.

"Blow it up!"

Four Teller mines blasted the track before the train arrived. The Russians aboard the train jumped down and tried to break through to the east on foot.

"Don't get decisively engaged. Keep moving."

But they were halted again in the midst of an unbelievably dense forest when Russian machine-gun fire began to spray the attack area. Once again Feldwebel Juschkat took a party forward and, in conjunction with the rest of his platoon, silenced the machine guns. Half an hour later a group of Russians came running towards them. They were obviously fleeing, as they had almost no weapons. When met by machine-gun fire from the northern group, they raised their hands and surrendered.

German soldiers emerged from the swamp on the heels of the Russians. They, too, had adorned their helmets with greenery. Paul's deep, bass voice rumbled through the evening mist: "Don't fire! We're from the northern group!"

The firing ceased and the two groups met in the center of the cleared forest lane. Juschkat shook hands with his opposite number. The man was Oberfeldwebel Anton Hermann of the 3rd Battalion of the 158th Infantry Regiment (58th Infantry Division).

"Man, am I glad to see you!" sighed the Oberfeldwebel. The exhausted man took off his helmet, revealing a gray-white bandage.

"Same here . . . I guess we've closed the pocket."

"It's closed now, but will it stay closed?"

"We'll see."

✠

The pocket remained closed in spite of determined Soviet attempts to break through the narrow German ring, only two kilometers wide. Juschkat fought every night at the Erika forest lane against powerful Soviet groups attempting to break out. Although he was suffering from a fever, he remained in the lines. It was non-stop, close-quarters fighting. The German soldiers faced constant, deadly danger. As many as eight Russian regiments sought to break through in the sector held by the 1st Infantry Division. Taking advantage of strong artillery and mortar support, several Russian groups almost made a breakthrough, but only a few scattered elements managed to slip through the German ring of steel.

On 10 June Franz Juschkat received the Close Combat Clasp in Silver and the Wound Badge in Silver from the hand of the battalion commander. Trembling with fever, Juschkat led his troops as they fought off yet another Russian breakthrough attempt. Finally he was also evacuated from the ring of forces around the pocket. Out of the danger zone, the Feldwebel was taken to a field hospital.

Juschkat recovered and was given home leave. But before he could depart a telegram arrived ordering him back to the front. In mid-September he rejoined his division. It had exhausted itself during the fighting for the corridor and, by the time it left the "Green Hell," its strength was equivalent to that of a regiment.

Following the costly fighting on the Volkhov, the division took part in the First Battle of Lake Ladoga, which lasted until 2 October. It fought at Grusino with the 61st Infantry Division as part of the I Army Corps. At the end of September the division was withdrawn to Chudovo to rest and refit. When Juschkat arrived there, preparations were under way for the division's next operation.

✠

"Glad to have you back with us, Juschkat."

With these words Major Ziegler greeted the Feldwebel, who had just been brought to the battalion command post.

"Something special, sir?"

"Tomorrow morning we're going to cross the Volkhov and relieve the Saxons in the strongpoint at Svanka monastery."

"Things are going to get hot again, sir?"

"For sure. The Russians are preparing to launch the Second Battle of Lake Ladoga. Now listen: The regiment has received orders to form an attack reserve consisting of two platoons—one infantry platoon and a heavy-weapons platoon. Leutnant Koop will command the heavy platoon. I have recommended you for the infantry platoon, because I know you have the greatest experience, Juschkat."

"Thanks, sir," Juschkat replied dryly.

"You can select the personnel from your old platoon for this mission, Juschkat. Maximum strength twenty-five men."

Juschkat went back to the company, which was in a small village, and reported to Hauptmann Beinke. Then he walked over to the cottage containing his comrades of the company headquarters section. He closed the cottage door and crossed the dark floor to the large living room. Inside, there was a roaring fire in the cottage's tiled stove. Juschkat announced his arrival:

"Good evening, everyone."

Speechless, Paul dropped his razor. Then he strode over to his friend and shook him back and forth. Within minutes the others had arrived from the neighboring cottages. König had become an Unteroffizier. Ochtrop and Bichlap, both from Insterburg, were daydreaming about their home leave, which was to begin soon. But it looked as if they were going to be disappointed. After the welcome had died down, Juschkat described his discussion with the Major. The entire platoon volunteered for the attack reserve.

"I hope this works out," said Paul, realizing that virtually the entire noncommissioned officer corps was standing behind Juschkat.

"Time will tell, Paul, you should know that."

On 2 October 1942 the 1st Infantry Division crossed the Volkhov and occupied the strongpoint-style lines along the flooded river. The center of the line and the division command post were at the monastery.

Juschkat's assault platoon remained in reserve. He and several of his men carried out orientation patrols to check the terrain in which they might be called upon to fight. The weather turned colder and the swollen river was soon covered with a shining sheet of ice. Runner Jagst, originally from Memel, built a boat out of ice. From then on Juschkat and his "flying patrol" were able to hurry from strongpoint to strongpoint at speeds of up to eighty kilometers per hour.

More than once envious comrades reproached him:

"You have it pretty good. Warm your rear end by night and play all day." But Juschkat didn't let it bother him. He seemed to know that his time was coming. Juschkat and Leutnant Koop, known as "Bubi" because of his youth, made frequent forays beyond the front, often far behind Russian lines. They always stuck to the dense, snow-shrouded forests. The pair usually brought back fresh fish for the men from their patrols. But the platoon soon became bored. In an effort to keep them from getting rusty, Juschkat obtained permission for a night patrol to a porcelain factory that was 400 meters beyond the Russian lines and near a clay pit.

The eight-man patrol set out on the night of 3 November 1942. Its task was to bring back several prisoners. The men crept silently eastward along a tributary of the Volkhov under a moonless sky. Frozen into the water, the birch trees stood like brooms on the undulating plain. Franz Juschkat led the way. Close behind him was Ochtrop, who would turn twenty in a few weeks. Unteroffizier König was on his first patrol. Bichlap, Groß and Palke brought up the rear. Groß pulled a flat sled, whose runners swished softly through the snow. Shells howled overhead from the east, before falling far to the rear near the division command post, adding to the wasteland of shell craters. For the first time, the men had received their own winter clothing. They perfectly matched the white winter landscape. Juschkat looked for the best route. Keeping an eye out for Russian patrols, he and his men worked their way cautiously through no-man's-land.

The eight men entered a forest clearing with tall ferns. They crept on silently, until they spotted the clay pit ahead of them at the forest's edge. On the far side of the pit was the factory.

"We'll have to detour to the left. We must get to the fence."

The eight men crawled the last few meters. The wire cutters were passed forward. Juschkat snipped the barbed wire, creating a hole through which they could pass.

"Bichlap, stay here and cover our rear."

Creeping along the side of a low shed, they reached the first kiln and the first storage shed immediately behind it. The door opened. Before them the interior of the long structure lay in darkness. Gradually, their eyes became accustomed to the twilight.

"Here, Franz, great dishes!" called Ochtrop from one of the stands.

"Give me the sack." They packed a batch of plates inside. One fell and shattered on the concrete floor. Everyone froze. There was a rustling sound. Juschkat raised his submachine gun, then realized that it was only rats.

Juschkat and his men were about to move on when the sound of footsteps rang out through the hall. Squatting near the door, Unteroffizier König watched tensely. The door to the next room swung back. A Russian, who had obviously been sleeping, came in. He was holding up a thick candle on a plate.

König leapt at him. The plate crashed to the floor. Groß also jumped at the Russian and together they wrestled him to the floor. Juschkat heard a deep voice from the next room ask in Russian: "Are you all right?" He mumbled an unintelligible reply, while König and Groß dragged the captured Russian soldier into the shadow of the stand. The second Russian came in. He had also just woken up. He was overpowered like his companion.

"How many of you here?"

"We're the radio section. Only four."

"Where is the radio room?" The Russian gestured upwards.

"Ochtrop and Palke come with me! The rest of you stay here and watch the Russians. Collect two dozen cups and saucers and a few other things."

Juschkat walked through the hot, sticky room where the Russians had been sleeping. From the four bunks he saw that the captive had been telling the truth. Cautiously, he climbed the stairs. Fortunately, they were made of concrete and did not squeak. Juschkat saw a light from beneath a door and heard the chirping of an incoming radio message. He raised his hand, signaling his men to wait until the message was completed.

Then all was quiet, until the clicking of the sender key began. Finally, they heard the voices of the two Russians. The three Germans approached the door on tiptoe. Then Juschkat threw open the door and jumped into the room, followed closely by Palke and Ochtrop. The completely surprised radio operators made no attempt to resist. They raised their arms and let themselves be led downstairs. Juschkat screwed a ten-minute, delayed-action fuse into the demolition charge hanging from his belt and placed it near the radio equipment.

"Let's get out of here! This place is going to go up in ten minutes!"

They took the prisoners with them. While Juschkat and Ochtrop watched the Russians, König, Groß and Palke carried the sacks of porcelain on their backs. They left the porcelain factory the same way they had come. Bichlap, who had been guarding the rear, joined them. Ten minutes later they heard a dull boom. Seconds later, flames shot from the roof of the factory.

"Nothing left to do now but get out of here."

With two men pushing the sled, they hurried back toward the German lines. Behind them the night was lit by the flash of illumination flares. The blaze in the factory was spreading. Russian mortars began to fire and there were irregular bursts of machine-gun fire. Juschkat and his patrol reached their strongpoint with the prisoners and porcelain without incident. They received a warm welcome. From that day on the Juschkat assault platoon ate from the best Russian porcelain.

✠

One night later the Russians tried to turn the tables. They crept up on the German positions completely unnoticed. But then they gave away their presence when they stumbled onto the concealed tripwires and set off a fireworks display. The defenders spotted the Russian troops and drove them off. On 11 November the men of the assault platoon were waiting for the field kitchen. Just before the wagon was to arrive, the Russians plastered the road leading to the monastery with mortar fire. The horses bolted, and the wagon raced past the strongpoint in the direction of the enemy.

"Jump!" the men shouted to the two drivers. The two men jumped off the wagon and escaped with bruises. That night the Russian loudspeakers thanked the Germans for the excellent food they had sent. Their only complaint was that it had been somewhat too cold, and they hoped the Germans would exercise proper care next time. This was one of the few occasions where the Russians displayed a sense of humor.

Several days later Feldwebel Juschkat was ordered to division head-quarters. The division commander informed him that he and another member of his platoon might go on leave. Juschkat negotiated with the General and, when he left the office, he had leave passes in his pocket for himself, Ochtrop, Bichlap and Unteroffizier König, whose homes were all in the Insterburg area. This was to be his first leave since the war began.

Partisans stopped the train on the way. Juschkat and his men stormed after the partisans and drove them back into the woods. When he arrived in Groß-Warkau he was met by his brother in his Panzer uniform. His father was also at home. As a result of this fortunate coincidence, the entire family was together for Christmas.

Soon, however, it was time to say farewell again. Juschkat met his companions at the Insterburg station. Their rucksacks were full of sausages and ham for their comrades at the front.

On 28 December 1942 they rejoined their platoon. The division had moved in the meantime. It was now south of Lake Ladoga, in the bottle-neck south of Schlüsselburg. This sector was under the command of the XXVI Army Corps. Deployed there in addition to the 1st Infantry Division were the 223rd, 227th, and 170th Infantry Divisions. The Soviets were preparing to launch the Second Battle of Lake Ladoga.

✠

"Listen to that. The Russians are up to something with their tanks!"

The track and motor noises could be heard clearly even in the assault platoon's reserve position. Juschkat carved the last piece of ham and passed the slices along. News of an alert raced through the night. Everyone waited for the great event, but all remained deathly quiet in the front lines. The only interruptions were occasional illumination flares fired by nervous sentries. Now and then someone fired a burst into the night.

"I'm going out to check on the right. Don't bother getting undressed, boys."

Juschkat went from one dugout to the next. The men were as nervous as he.

"Is it going to start, Franz?" asked Obergefreiter Groß.

"It looks that way. Stay alert, so we can move quickly if we're needed."

"Here, have a cigarette."

Franz Juschkat smoked the cigarette offered by Palke, then walked on. Thirty minutes later he reached the most distant outpost. Illumination flares climbed above the shell-torn forest and lit the darkness. Juschkat slowly made his way back. He crawled into his straw bed fully clothed.

Juschkat was awakened by sand sprinkling into his mouth. The bunker was rocking so badly that his first impression was that he was on a ship at sea. Then he jumped to his feet.

"This is it. Ivan has begun his attack."

Juschkat's men, usually quick with a wisecrack, sat silently on their bunks. Franz Juschkat went outside. Scanning the main line of resistance through his field glasses, he saw that it was shrouded in a towering wall of smoke that was punctuated by bright flashes of flame. The flashes increased in number until the whole front seemed to be flickering. The divisional artillery was still silent. Only a few heavy rounds howled overhead on their way to the enemy.

The Soviet guns pounded the German main line of resistance for two hours, before finally shifting to the rear. Rounds landed closer and closer to the reserve position. The divisional artillery opened fire at that point. The reserve platoon had not yet received any reports or orders. Feldwebel Juschkat and his men felt the tension growing. What was going on up front in the main line of resistance? Had the Russians broken through? Were they going to arrive soon?

"Feldwebel: Report from regiment!"

The runner, who had slipped into the bunker, handed Juschkat the report.

"Ochtrop, we're going to regiment."

Russian rounds were falling closer now. The two men left the bunker and ran back to the regimental command post, which was farther to the rear. The commander was outside with the troops, but the adjutant knew what was going on.

"Juschkat, get your platoon ready. Here are a few bottles of schnapps. It would be a shame if they were broken by the bombardment. Assemble your people in the bunker and wait for further orders."

The two men hurried back. Ochtrop brought all the men of the platoon to the large combat bunker. Their time had come. Artillery rounds crashed into the frozen earth. The roaring and crashing went on for thirty minutes before the Russian guns shifted their fire farther to the rear onto the divisional artillery positions. The men crawled out of the bunker. Eight meters away a position belonging to the 1st Platoon had been reduced to a pile of smoking rubble. There had been twelve men in the position, among them Unteroffizier König. None survived. The sound of fighting rang out from the main line of resistance. They could hear tank guns firing and mines exploding.

"Prepare to move out!"

Juschkat saw the tense faces of his young comrades. Now it was up to him to say a few words to encourage them and relieve their fear, without revealing that he was just as afraid himself. With iron self-discipline Juschkat gained control over the men. The regimental runner came hurrying, as the telephone lines had been cut by the artillery bombardment. He brought Juschkat the platoon's orders. Juschkat read the message to his twenty-five men: "The Russians have broken through the neighboring division and have torn a gap in the main line of resistance four kilometers wide. The division's left flank is open."

Leutnant Koop came running. He had also received the order.

"Listen up, Franz. My people and I are going to try to halt the advancing Russians. You and your men screen the open flank. You must dig in about one kilometer in front of the regimental command post."

"Very well, Koop. We'll move out right away. Bichlap and Ochtrop forward. Everyone else follow in a skirmish line."

They ran towards the firing. Widely dispersed, the men covered meter after meter. Suddenly they came under fire. Red Army soldiers came running through the smoke. The platoon took cover.

"Open fire!"

The heavy machine gun began to rattle. The Soviets likewise threw themselves down. They had advanced 600 meters past the German main line of resistance.

"Heavy machine gun and 3rd Squad give covering fire. 1st and 2nd Squads attack with me! Up—Move out!"

Juschkat got up from the ground and ran towards the enemy, who immediately began to fire. The platoon's heavy machine gun, which had been positioned somewhat off to one side, hammered away in long bursts. Bullets hissed past Juschkat's head. He immediately began to duck and dodge. Someone began to shout and the others joined in, releasing their pent-up emotion. Juschkat fired on the run at a group of Soviets trying to set up a machine gun.

The first Russians came out of their holes with their hands raised. "Back, back!" They simply sent the Russians to the rear. There was no time to worry about prisoners; the Russians were on the run. The 3rd squad followed with the machine gun. They pursued the Soviets, who were falling back toward the former German main line of resistance. Juschkat stormed onward. He heard snatches of a Russian song and shouting from the company bunker behind the main line of resistance. The Soviets had found schnapps inside the bunker. Juschkat ducked low and crept toward the bunker. Ochtrop joined him. He ran to the side of the bunker and tossed a pineapple hand grenade into the stovepipe.

After the explosion, the Russians stumbled outside, their clothes blackened and smoldering. When they saw the submachine gun pointing at them they raised their arms. The prisoners had just disappeared when the first T-34s appeared and began shooting up anything that moved. One of the tanks moved straight towards the bunker, forcing the men of the assault platoon to take cover.

"Aim at the vision slits, Künzmann!"

The heavy machine gun fired two belts of ammunition at the tank's vision slit with no apparent effect. The tank concentrated its fire on the bunker. Juschkat realized that his immediate counterattack had bogged down:

"Take cover!" he shouted. He ran across in front of the tank to Pietsch, who had his squad grouped round him. "Make me a satchel charge!"

Moving from crater to crater, they worked their way closer to the T-34, which had shot up half the bunker. Then the tank moved nose-down into a crater. It appeared to be stuck.

"Give me covering fire from here, Ochtrop!"

Juschkat got up and ran towards the tank. He dashed past the vehicle's right flank and jumped onto the rear deck from behind to stay clear of the tank's machine gun. He felt his heart in his throat. Just then the tank moved with a mighty jolt. The motion caused Juschkat's right arm to swing against the turret. The satchel charge—several grenades bound together with wire—fell apart, and he was left with only the grenade in the center in his hand.

Juschkat hung on as the tank began to move, rolling away from Ochtrop, who shouted something. Ochtrop then opened fire on the Russian soldiers who had appeared from their holes in the ground. For a moment Juschkat though about jumping, but instead remained crouched behind the turret. After about 100 meters the tank halted. Suddenly the turret hatch began to move. Juschkat was terrified. It was the decisive moment. He grasped the trigger button between his index and middle fingers.

The hatch cover flipped back and the bearded face of the tank commander appeared. Juschkat pulled the button and dropped the grenade past the Russian's head into the tank. For perhaps a second he stared into the wide, disbelieving eyes of the Russian tanker, then jumped down to the ground and rolled away, striking his head so hard that he lay stunned for a few moments. Still semiconscious, he heard the dull thump of the explosion. The wild shouts of the platoon, which was charging toward the smoking tank, finally brought him back to consciousness.

"Get away from here, keep going!" he shouted. He began to move, and not a moment too soon, because the T-34 was suddenly transformed into a fire-spewing volcano. The tank's ammunition exploded in a whirlwind of fire. Suddenly, there was a howling noise from the sky to the left. Salvoes from Stalin Organs were preparing the way for fresh Russian attack groups. The Russians in front of the assault platoon also opened fire. Off in the distance, figures in camouflage uniforms were running straight toward Juschkat's platoon. Behind them were others. Suddenly, Juschkat recognized the first squad from the heavy-assault platoon under Leutnant Koop among the pursuers.

"Watch out, those are our people."

Caught in a trap, the Russians surrendered.

"Listen, Juschkat! We must advance farther and seal off the penetration. We're the only forces available."

"Very well, Koop. I'll go left and you go right."

The troops formed up and moved forward. Meter by meter they retook the terrain captured by the Russians. Finally, they reached the former main line of resistance and came under fire from the left.

Rounds from a deadly Russian high-velocity gun smashed into the trenches and foxholes. Bichlap, who was trying to reach his platoon leader, was hit and fell to the ground.

"Give me covering fire!"

Under fire, Juschkat ran over to Bichlap and dragged him into the nearest crater. Bichlap had lost his left leg. Juschkat applied a dressing to the stump. The platoon dug in, manning the bunkers, dugouts and trenches. Of the original fifty men, there were only thirty-eight left who had not been wounded.

The next day Leutnant Koop was called away to take command of the 1st Company of the 43rd Infantry Regiment, whose commander had been killed. Juschkat became the reserve commander. A few men, stragglers from other units, were placed under his command.

On the evening of the third day the Soviets fought their way into the trenches. They were driven out again in close-quarters fighting. A Russian attack had just been repulsed when Ochtrop, who was fighting beside his platoon leader, was hit and killed instantly. Juschkat and exactly thirty-eight men held out against attacks from two sides for eight days. There was little opportunity for the defenders to rest. Juschkat himself went virtually without sleep. Not a day passed that the Russians didn't attack at least twice.

The accomplishments of Juschkat and his small band of men bordered on the impossible. Finally, a pioneer company moved forward to beef up the line and Juschkat was able to breathe a little easier.

Franz Juschkat was awakened by Unteroffizier Palke during the night of 11–12 January 1943.

"Listen to that! Something's up!"

A terrific din was coming from the Russian lines. Engines roared, probably tanks and self-propelled guns.

"Highest state of readiness!" ordered the Feldwebel. The lookouts were doubled. Juschkat went out to check the positions. Sensing that his comrades needed him, he was on his feet all night. Morale improved noticeably when he appeared at a position. Juschkat, who had sealed off the enemy penetration, had become something of a symbol to his men. The way he accepted hardships that would have overwhelmed others impressed the men and spurred them to give their utmost. The sentries fell asleep on their feet. Juschkat himself shook them awake. There was no talk of courts martial or similar threats, only a gentle admonishment:

"We're the pillar. If we break, then everything else will collapse."

Juschkat went back to the bunker to try and catch a few hours sleep. However, unknown to him, the Soviets were about to attack in a fashion quite unlike their usual style. Juschkat was awakened by the alarm shouts of the sentries. The Soviets were already in the trenches. He reached for his submachine gun and ran outside. A towering Russian appeared in front of him. The enemy soldier swung his rifle butt down at Juschkat. The blow struck Juschkat's helmet, knocking him to the ground. As if through a thick blanket he heard a ringing Russian victory cry. Suddenly he recognized Paul's East Prussian dialect. The big man cut down the Russian and several of his companions and dragged his platoon leader out of danger.

A close-quarters fight broke out behind the parapets and dugouts, the likes of which the assault platoon had seldom experienced. Having regained his senses, Juschkat got to his feet and fired into a group of attackers. Paul whirled a captured Russian rifle about him. Ten minutes after the alarm had been sounded the Russians had been thrown back. The medic and his four men worked as quickly as they could. Meanwhile, Russian mortars had opened fire. The medics soon ran out of dressings and, while Paul ran back for more medical supplies, Juschkat instructed some of his men to man the abandoned machine-gun position. He organized everything to defend against the expected new attack.

When he finally found time to look through the scissors telescope in the direction of the Russian lines, Juschkat was terrified by what he saw. The enemy position was swarming with figures. Suddenly, the horde jumped up. Russian troops in long coats raced across the open field. It seemed to Juschkat as if they were shoulder to shoulder.

"Everyone out who can hold a rifle!"

Even the wounded had to help. A voice called out from behind: "Juschkat! Feldwebel Juschkat!" An artillery Oberleutnant appeared.

"Here, over here!"

"Juschkat, fill me in, I'm to direct the artillery fire."

"You can see them coming, sir. Request fire in front of the positions."

His two men with the radio equipment followed the Oberleutnant into the dugout. In a calm voice he passed the information on to the artillery. By now the leading Soviet troops were within 100 meters. The machine guns opened fire. More and more Soviet troops worked their way forward across the crater-filled landscape.

Three minutes after the Oberleutnant's arrival the first German rounds roared over the front lines and smashed into the ground at the exact spot where the Russians had assembled for the final charge. Suddenly, the Soviet troops got to their feet and, with loud shouts of "Urray!", stormed toward the German lines. Hand grenades exploded.

"Fire, fire!"

The Oberleutnant directed the artillery to place its rounds right in front of the German positions. The advancing enemy was felled by the exploding shells. As each group was wiped out another appeared to take its place.

"Juschkat, let your people know that a heavy rocket battalion is going to fire in two minutes. Take cover as soon as you hear the sound of the rockets."

"Stay alert, men, *Nebelwerfer!*"

The Feldwebel went from man to man. Then they heard a swelling noise behind them. Everyone took cover. The howling intensified and then the rockets struck and exploded. All was still. Even the rifle fire had died away. From the area in front of his position Juschkat could hear crying and moaning.

Cautiously, he raised himself and peered over the parapet. The terrain had been transformed into a broad field of craters. As far as he could see there was nothing standing. Juschkat wiped his eyes. His breathing was cramped. Then Paul's voice broke the silence.

"There, Franz! Our own men!"

Feldwebel Juschkat ran over to Unteroffizier Bielitz. A heavy rocket had fallen close to his position. Bielitz was dead and Unteroffizier Gruber badly wounded, as was Obergefreiter Pietsch. Unteroffizier Beer had lost his right arm. Almost the entire headquarters section was wounded in some way, with the exception of Paul. Gefreiter Kühn crawled from the shattered machine-gun position. His face was ghostly pale, but apart from a scratch on his nose he was unhurt.

The terrible effects of the rocket salvo had halted the Russian attack. When the casualty reports from the squads reached Juschkat he simply couldn't believe his eyes. He stared mutely at the piece of paper. But the figures were there. Of the thirty-eight men, there were sixteen left; all the others had been killed or wounded.

Something in him broke that day; something he couldn't name. When a few men from the rear-echelon units appeared that evening to fill the gaps he briefed them apathetically. The survivors fell into their beds, dead tired. Only Juschkat got no rest. He stayed up front in the dugouts, and it was not until Paul fetched him for supper that he returned to the main bunker. Finally the Feldwebel fell into a restless sleep. Even this was interrupted when the stovepipe came crashing down across the entrance to the bunker. Everyone jumped up and reached for their weapons. Kühn banged his head on the low bunker ceiling.

Soon afterwards the bunker door flew open with a crash. A Russian slid down the steep, icy slope and ended up sitting somewhat bemused in the center of the floor.

"Don't shoot!" he cried and held up a photo of his children. The man got up and with trembling fingers offered the Germans some of his tobacco. He told them he had been lying in front of the palisades for twenty-four hours waiting for an opportunity to defect. He was half starved. The soldiers gave him some bread and a cup of coffee and the Russian related how he had crept up to the bunker and then slid on the ice.

✠

The next few days remained quiet. Night after night Juschkat and Paul went into no-man's-land to collect Russian weapons, which lay about everywhere. At headquarters he could trade a Russian submachine gun or two automatic rifles for a bottle of schnapps.

Juschkat's assault platoon was relieved on 16 February 1943. The exhausted soldiers trudged back to the division trains, where they received new uniforms. Late in the evening—the new uniforms were still being issued—a messenger came from the division.

"Feldwebel Juschkat, Unteroffizier Palke, Obergefreiter Groß and Unteroffizier Heinemann are to report to division headquarters at once."

"We must be in for it," Paul observed dryly in his East-Prussian dialect. The next morning the four men set out on a horsedrawn sleigh. At division they found themselves being stared at by everyone, and gradually Franz Juschkat found himself becoming uneasy. Feverishly he tried to figure out what he might have done. A stubborn East Prussian always ready to argue, he was already well known for "mutinies" of all sorts. His men, all born in 1920 and 1921, called him "Papa Juschkat," even though he was only 26 years old. However, his beard made him look much older.

"Form up here, comrades," ordered the senior noncommissioned officer, acting very formal. They lined up in front of the division headquarters. A group of men from the trains formed a cordon, and suddenly General von Krosigk came out the door followed by his staff. The General, who had proved an exemplary officer during his year with the division, presented Juschkat's three comrades with the German Cross in Gold. Then he stopped in front of Juschkat.

"Feldwebel Franz Juschkat: The commander-in-chief has awarded you the Knight's Cross of the Iron Cross for your heroic action in defending against a major Russian attack and the successful counterattack that you carried out on your own initiative. I feel especially honored to be allowed to present it to you today."

The executive officer held the Knight's Cross on a red cushion and, while the General placed it around Franz Juschkat's neck, the adjutant stepped behind him and tied the ends of the red, white and black ribbon.

This was the greatest moment in the life of a simple soldier, who had merely done his duty and never thought that he might be awarded such a high decoration for his efforts.

✠

The fighting went on. Juschkat had been asked to go back to Germany and train replacements on account of his wounds, but he stayed with his unit. When the front on Lake Ladoga was retaken, Juschkat succeeded in destroying two Russian tanks that were attempting to complete the encirclement of a group of German troops. During a subsequent action Unteroffizier Muschkat was killed at his side. Juschkat was once again wounded, but not seriously.

Near Krivoy Rog he was captured by the Russians and held prisoner for three days. He was able to free himself and returned with the Russian who had been guarding him. He then took over the division's reconnaissance platoon, which was nominally under the leadership of an Oberleutnant. In reality, however, it was led by the experienced Juschkat. He and the platoon operated for four weeks as far as 100 kilometers behind the Russian lines, receiving assistance from Ukrainians.

Juschkat was badly wounded near Velikiye Luki. A Russian Rata fighter strafed the trenches with cannon and machine guns. Juschkat fired back with his rifle, but was hit twice by shell fragments in the calf and thigh. Juschkat enjoyed a period of light duties as a courier between Munich and Rome before returning to his unit.

The final months of the war saw him in action again in East Prussia and, finally, Berlin. At the end of December 1944 he was awarded the Close Combat Clasp in Gold and was promoted to Oberfeldwebel.

During fighting in the Berlin area he destroyed two Soviet tanks with a *Panzerfaust*. As leader of a tank-killing detachment, he succeeded in halting the Soviet advance for a time near Friesack. Badly wounded once again, he was taken to a hospital in Wolfenbüttel.

The war was over for Franz Juschkat and a few days later for all of Germany as well.

Josef "Sepp" Lainer after having received the Knight's Cross on 8 October 1943. At the time he was a SS-Oberscharführer with the 1st Company of the 4th SS-Panzer Grenadier Regiment *"Der Führer."*

Sepp Lainer

THE PREWAR YEARS

In late March 1938 the German entry into Austria had been bloodless and was welcomed enthusiastically by the population. To the troops involved it was a *Blumenkrieg* ("war of flowers").

SS-Oberführer Keppler was given the job of forming the third regiment of the *SS-Verfügungstruppe*, the armed branch of the SS. The formation was to be comprised primarily from Austrians, who were then eligible to join the *SS-Verfügungstruppe* as a result of the annexation. The result was *SS-Standarte "Der Führer."*

The *Leibstandarte SS "Adolf Hitler" (mot.)* in Berlin provided a cadre of capable noncommissioned officers and officers for the new regiment. Additional personnel were provided by the two existing regiments of the *SS-Verfügungstruppe, SS-Standarte "Deutschland,"* and *SS-Standarte "Germania."*

The headquarters of *SS-Standarte "Der Führer,"* together with its regimental units and the 1st Battalion of *SS-Standarte "Der Führer,"* established themselves in Vienna. The 2nd Battalion was stationed at Graz, while the 3rd Battalion moved into quarters in Klagenfurt.

The new regiment's commanding officer, SS-Standartenführer Georg Keppler, was a veteran of the First World War, where he had won the Iron Crosses, First and Second Class. Following the reduction of the Reichswehr to 100,000 men on 31 January 1920, he had become a police officer in Hanover. Keppler was promoted to Major in the reserves on 1 July 1931. In early 1935 there was a need for officers following the implementation of the first phase of a general expansion of the army and Keppler reentered active duty.

Major Keppler initially spent several months with the 32nd Infantry Regiment. On 10 October 1935 he took over the 1st Battalion of *SS-Standarte 1 "Deutschland"* at Königsberg Training Area, however. As a result of Ministry of War declaring service in the *SS-Verfügungstruppe* as equivalent to general military service in September 1933, such transfers were not uncommon, especially since the *SS-Verfügungstruppe* needed leadership with prior military experience.

127

With his new command came the equivalent SS rank of SS-Sturmban-nführer. By the time he assumed command of *SS-Standarte "Der Führer,"* Keppler had risen to the rank of SS-Standartenführer

For the benefit of the reader there now follows additional information on the *SS-Verfügungsdivision,* the forerunner of the formation that ultimately became the 2nd SS-Panzer Division *"Das Reich."*

FORMATION OF THE THREE WAFFEN-SS REGIMENTS

On 13 November 1934 the Army General Office issued a secret command document (Number 10.470/34): The tables of organization and equipment for SS units. The document called for the creation of formations equivalent to army regiments in size. This decision was implemented by a revised version of the document issued on 13 February 1935 (AHA Ia B 364/35).

The result was the formation of the following elements:

The *Leibstandarte SS "Adolf Hitler"* (mot.) at Berlin-Lichterfelde.
SS-Standarte 1 (minus the regimental headquarters) at Munich.
SS-Standarte 2 (minus the regimental headquarters) at Hamburg, Arolsen, Soltau and Wismar.
SS-Pioniersturmbann (combat engineer battalion) at Dresden.
SS-Nachrichtensturmbann (signals battalion) at Dresden.

The "Inspectorate of the *SS-Verfügungstruppe*" was formed after Himmler was named to the post of Chief of German Police on 17 June 1936. The inspectorate was officially created by an order issued on 1 October 1936. In charge of the inspectorate was SS-Gruppenführer Paul Hausser. A highly-decorated First World War officer, Hausser had retired from the regular army on 31 January 1932 with the rank of Generalleutnant.

The creation of *SS-Standarte "Der Führer,"* the third SS regiment, completed the formation of the core formations of the *SS-Verfügungsdivision.*

The 1st Battalion of *SS-Standarte "Der Führer"* was activated in early April at the Radetzki Barracks in Vienna. The regimental headquarters occupied a house in the Kopfgasse. The subordinate units of the new regiment were stationed in various parts of Austria:

1st Battalion (SS-Sturmbannführer Bittrich) at Vienna
2nd Battalion (SS-Hauptsturmführer von Scholz) at Graz-Tobelbad
3rd Battalion (SS-Sturmbannführer Wäckerle) at Klagenfurt

The first cadre personnel were ordered to report for service at their new bases. Among these were the first Austrian volunteers. One was the eighteen-year-old Josef Lainer from Brixen im Thale in North Tirol. He soon became known to his comrades as "Sepp" and was to remain so until the end of the war and beyond.

Lainer was born on 13 March 1920 in Brixen, the son of a railroad switchman. In May 1938, after graduating from high school, he volunteered for service in the *SS-Verfügungstruppe*. Lainer ended up in the 1st Battalion of *SS-Standarte "Der Führer"* under SS-Sturmbannführer Wilhelm Bittrich, a highly-decorated World War I pilot and a veteran of the *Freikorps*, non-governmental military organizations that saw a lot of fighting in the disputed border regions of the post-war years. The battalion's 2nd Company was to become Lainer's home for some years.

Josef Lainer and his comrades endured the tough SS training under the watchful eyes of the veteran officers. He later recalled:

> It was a difficult time for all of us newcomers. But we had one thing in common: The homeland from which we came and the iron will to serve as "soldiers of the Führer," as we then thought of ourselves. We also wanted to ensure that Austria, as an essential part of the Reich, survived and could be defended at any time. We were young, eighteen-year-old recruits, used to hard work, full of ideals and not pampered; after only a few weeks in uniform we were acting like grizzled veterans.

Volunteers continued to stream in from all over Austria. Soon the regiment was forced to implement strict selection procedures to ensure only the best personnel were admitted. The young soldiers were well received everywhere and were treated as welcome guests in their garrison cities. The regiment's replacement training center, which was located in Vienna under SS-Hauptsturmführer Stickdorn, was always full. Sepp Lainer described the initial training: "The parade march—the so-called 'goose step'—was practiced first, then other types of drill and ceremonies. Very soon the parade-ground drills were replaced by combat training."

Lainer and his comrades in the 2nd Company participated in the 10th Reich Party Day—the so-called *Großdeutschland* party day—which was held from 5–12 September 1938. The regiment had been selected to represent the *SS-Verfügungstruppe* at the event and was given its standard there. It also became the first Austrian regiment to march past the residents of Nuremberg in the Reich proper.

What followed was hard combat training by day and night, with plenty of alerts. Every member of the regiment knew that this was not unfair treatment, but survival training. Their leaders preached: "Sweat saves blood!"

Hausser, Keppler and Bittrich, all battle-tested First World War officers, had experienced this first-hand and knew what they were talking about.

On 1 October 1938 Lainer had been a soldier just five months. *SS-Standarte "Der Führer"* left its assembly area around Zwettl in Lower Austria on that day and moved out in the direction of Zanin. The regiment was taking part in the German occupation of the Sudetenland, the border region of Czechoslovakia where ethic Germans predominated. Patrols had scouted the frontier and beyond several days earlier.

SS-Mann Lainer and his companions of the company advanced towards the Czech border. However, before there were any hostilities, the regiment's soldiers learned that the Czech government had ordered a peaceful withdrawal of Czech forces from the Sudetenland. Lainer:

> In our eyes the reuniting of the Sudetenland with the Reich was a foregone conclusion, because the area had been populated by Germans for many centuries. Furthermore, during a plebiscite in the area on 14 June 1938, the population of the Sudetenland had voted 91.4% for annexation by Germany. The new Reich Commissar of the Sudetenland, Konrad Henlein, was a man who enjoyed the trust of the people living there. But we were happy that it had come off without any fighting, because our training was not yet complete and any hostile contact would certainly have cost many lives. We were housed in private quarters in Znaim and soon afterwards returned to our garrisons.
>
> What followed was a period of reorganization in which the units still dependant on horses became fully motorized. It had been our experience during cross-country exercises and field training that horse-drawn units were significantly slower than those that were already motorized.
>
> During the next few weeks the companies, battalions and regiment all enthusiastically practiced the techniques involved in the use of motor vehicles. This resulted in a number of accidents but, fortunately, no one was killed.

By the end of March 1939 SS-Standartenführer Keppler was able to report that *SS-Standarte "Der Führer"* was ready for motorized operations. Consequently, the unit was one of those selected to participate in the occupation of the remainder of Czechoslovakia. The regiment was given the job of seizing Preßburg (Bratislava) in a rapid advance from the south.

The first part of the regiment was already on the road when SS-Standartenführer Keppler was ordered to report to the corps headquarters in

Vienna. There the Commanding General of the XVII Army Corps, General of Infantry Werner Kienitz, informed Keppler that his regiment was now to cross the Czech frontier east of Gänserdorf (northeast of Vienna) at dawn on 15 March. It was then to move through the Lesser Carpathians to Bösing (Peczinok). There it was to veer south through the Waag Valley toward Preßburg, while sending part of its forces north into the Jablonica area. Moreover, he had to release one battalion to an infantry division advancing farther to the north.

The march toward Bruck on the Leitha River, which was fully under way, had to be stopped. After regrouping, the regiment set out for its new destination. At dawn on 15 March the first elements of *SS-Standarte "Der Führer"* advanced out of the Gänserdorf area and crossed the border. Sepp Lainer recalled:

> We moved through dense blowing snow, which had begun to fall at the feet of the Lesser Carpathians. The regimental commander had driven ahead to Bösing. A short time later he received a report there that the regiment had lost only one vehicle during its difficult march. At midday on 15 March our radio net control station sent a message that we had reached our objective. Once again not a shot had been fired. On 17 March the Commander-in-Chief of the Army, Generaloberst von Brauchitsch, paid us a visit. We learned that we were the only ones to have met the march target set by corps.

PRELUDE TO THE POLISH CAMPAIGN
Guard Regiment in Vienna—The Watch in the West
In May 1939 the *SS-Standarte "Der Führer"* was transferred to the Groß-Born Training Area. The unit made the journey by road, travelling through Silesia and the Warthe District. Lainer:

> For us young soldiers, who had never left the area where we had grown up, it was a unique experience to roll through the broad German countryside and experience the warm reception we got everywhere. We were impressed by the breadth of the landscape without mountains. When the first windmills came into sight and we saw the stork nests on the houses in the north, it was a completely new world to us. As the son of a railroad switchman, this trip was unimaginably interesting for me.
>
> In the Groß-Born Training Area we learned more about the use of weapons and battle tactics. Coordination between the infantry

and the heavy weapons, assaults with machine-gun squads, and mortar rounds howling over our heads from the rear gave it all an air of reality, especially since we often used live ammunition.

The regiment's commanding officer, Georg Keppler, later said:

It was there that the foundation was laid for the later success of this regiment. During the course of the Second World War it produced no less than seventeen recipients of the Knight's Cross, five recipients of the Knight's Cross with Oak Leaves and three of the Knight's Cross with Oak Leaves and Swords.

At the end of June the now fully equipped and trained regiment was transferred into the Reich Protectorate of Bohemia and Moravia, where it was to serve as a guard regiment under the Reich Protector, Konstantin Freiherr von Neurath. Lainer:

Standing guard at Hradschin Palace in Prague and in front of the other buildings housing the seat of government of the Reich Protectorate was another great experience for us all. When it was time to relieve the guard we left our barracks and marched through Prague with the band playing.

The Polish Campaign began on 1 September 1939. Germany was at war. On 3 September England and France declared war. For the soldiers of SS-Standarte "Der Führer," guard duty was not the role they had hoped for. But orders were orders, and the regiment was assigned additional security duties at railroad stations, important rail installations and government buildings.

Not until mid-September, when the Blitz campaign against Poland was nearing its end, did the regiment receive orders to transfer to the West. It was assembled as the motorized reserve of the 7th Army under General of Artillery Friedrich Dollmann. The regiment stood ready in case the "Phony War" being waged by the French in the west—known as the Sitzkrieg, or "sit-down war" on the German side—should escalate. England and France had promised Poland they would help their ally by attacking in the west, which would force Germany to withdraw forces from the east. However, nothing of the sort took place.

The SS-Standarte "Der Führer" moved into the Waldkirch area in the Black Forest. Deployed in the southern part of the Westwall, its mission was limited to small-scale raids and nocturnal patrols. Every soldier was admonished not to be the first to open fire. In early October the regiment was moved again, this time to the Brdywald Training Area near Pilsen. There, together with the other regiments of the *SS-Verfügungstruppe*, which had participated in the Polish Campaign (albeit attached to various infantry divisions), it was incorporated into the newly formed *SS-Verfügungsdivision* on 19 October.

Commanding the division was SS-Gruppenführer Paul Hausser, who had participated in the Polish Campaign attached to Panzer Division Kempf. A First World War officer, Paul Hausser created from the *SS-Standarten "Deutschland," "Germania,"* and *"Der Führer"* the fully motorized *SS-Verfügungsdivision*. When finished with its division-level training, SS-Gruppenführer Hausser had under his command one of the best-equipped and most well-trained divisions in Germany. The final division-level exercises were carried out at Brdywald.

Paul Hausser created a new type of soldier in his division, one capable of passing the most severe tests of endurance. His maxim was: "The object is not to pursue vague possibilities which a far-seeing eye might be able to perceive, but to live in the present and carefully prepare the way today for an action that might be required tomorrow."

The Campaign in the West

In December 1939 SS-Gruppenführer Hausser received orders to detach one of his division's regiments to the army. Following a discussion with his regimental commanders, *SS-Standarte "Der Führer"* was chosen. The regiment was given an artillery battalion under SS-Hauptsturmführer Erspenmüller, a combat-engineer company and a logistics section.

The now reinforced *SS-Standarte "Der Führer"* moved into the Datteln area, where it was billeted. The regiment was attached to the 207th Infantry Division under the command of Generalleutnant Karl von Tiedemann. Sepp Lainer, who had been promoted to SS-Sturmmann in November, remarked of this time:

> That winter we learned to dig in and how to conduct a river crossing. We carried out joint exercises with the 207th Infantry Division, which was part of the X Army Corps under Generalleutnant Christian Hansen and earmarked for operations in northern Holland. The first groups of replacements arrived, and once again several friends from Tirol were among them. One brought greetings from my parents, including some of the nourishing variety.

The Western Campaign began on 10 May. Like the fighting in Poland, it was a Blitz campaign. Several days earlier *SS-Standarte "Der Führer"* had been moved forward from the Datteln area to Bocholt.

The Battle in Fortress Holland

As part of the 18th Army, the reinforced *SS-Standarte "Der Führer"* advanced into northern Holland. Its objective was to drive across the Ijssel and through the Grebbe Line to Amsterdam and Haarlem. The order to attack reached the regiment on 9 May.

The 2nd Battalion of *SS-Standarte "Der Führer,"* reinforced by a platoon each from the 13th and 14th Companies, was attached to the 368th Infantry Regiment (of the 207th Infantry Division) as the attack's motorized spearhead. The infantry task force, known as Battle Group Zugspitze, was commanded by Generalmajor Österreicher, sixty years old at the time and a recipient of the *Pour le Merite* during the First World War. Otto Weidinger, an officer in the *Standarte* and later the divisional historian, described the initial phase of the attack:

> Early on the morning of 10 May the first assault detachments stormed forward, overran the Dutch border posts and quickly reached Babberich, our initial objective. The 3rd Battalion, which was spearheading the assault, met little resistance from the Dutch border troops. The battalion was instructed to requisition every available bicycle and advance as quickly as possible toward the Arnhem Bridge to prevent its destruction by the Dutch.

Battle Group Zugspitze of the 207th Infantry Division rolled towards Arnhem. The following description is taken from the war diary of the X Army Corps:

> In accordance with the corps order of 25 March 1940, the elements of the X Army Corps went into the attack early on the morning of 10 May. They had begun moving forward into their assembly areas at 0235. While moving up, the 207th Infantry Division started reporting a series of loud explosions and the glow of fires from the Elten area to the west and southwest at 0200. Battle Group Zugspitze went as far as the Westervoort railway station and the Ijssel Bridge without contact, but found the latter barricaded by Dutch troops. (War Diary, X Army Corps, 10–20 May 1940)

The reinforced 374th Infantry Regiment's 1st Battalion and the regiment's 10th Company detrained under covering fire from Armored Train Number 7 and were ordered to support the elements of *SS-Standarte "Der Führer"* as they attempted to cross. Both units were temporarily placed under the command of the SS formation.

The *SS-Standarte* had crossed the border on the Elten-Babberich-Zevenaar road but then had to detour around barricades of concrete and fallen trees. The commander of the 2nd Battalion was ordered to requisition every available bicycle and send part of the advance guard ahead to the bridge at Westervoort. The bridge and the river were reached at 0720, however, before Armored Train Number 7 could reach the Ijssel Bridge, it was blown up by the enemy.

The bridge at Westervoort was defended by a company of the Dutch 35th Infantry Regiment and twenty-five men of a police unit. The Dutch commander was Captain Heijnen, who had had his men occupy the fortifications on both sides of the river. It was from these that the first shots were fired against the advancing 2nd Battalion. The German side immediately replied. A direct hit on one of the embrasures knocked out a 50-mm gun positioned there. But the armored train was hit as well. The locomotive and several cars caught fire. When the defenders saw several German pioneers running toward the bridge, they immediately blew it up. The first German attempt to cross was repulsed by Dutch machine-gun and mortar fire.

Ten minutes after H-hour the leading elements of the 207th Infantry Division took the monastery at Heerenberg. The 332nd Infantry Regiment, also part of Battle Group Zugspitze, advanced into the village against weak resistance. This success allowed the 2nd Battalion to advance through Doetinchin at 0830. At 0930 the battalion reached the Ijssel near Doesberg, but found that the bridge there had also been destroyed. An attack across the Ijssel north of the bridge by Battle Group Scholz led to the capture of the crossing by midday.

At 0830 the regiment's commander ordered the 3rd Battalion under SS-Sturmbannführer Wäckerle to stand ready to cross the Ijssel. The 2nd Battalion, the divisional artillery and the heavy weapons of *SS-Standarte "Der Führer"* opened fire on the enemy fortifications on the north bank of the river, finally concentrating on the fort at Westervoort. Several antitank guns and heavy machine guns were deployed to fire at the fort's embrasures. Under covering artillery fire several crossing sites were scouted and the inflatable rafts were brought forward and made ready.

The attack began at 1100. By now some of the enemy guns had been silenced. Assault groups and pioneers stormed forward. Hintze's pioneer

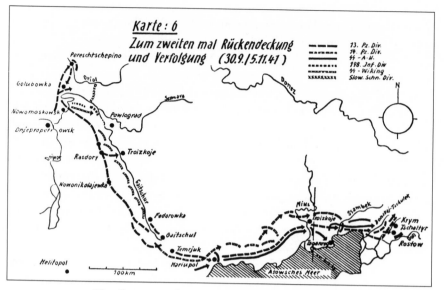

The German advance to Taganrog and Rostov.

section, which had been attached to the *SS-Standarte* for this attack, led the men safely to the water. Nevertheless, the crossing attempt failed in the face of heavy flanking fire. Not until 1115 did the first squad get across; it immediately began cutting its way through the barbed-wire obstacles. Wave after wave followed across the river and, by 1230, all of the 3rd Battalion was across.

Even before the main body was across, SS-Hauptscharführer Ludwig Kepplinger of the 11th Company and his assault group were fighting their way through the rubble of the fort. Employing hand grenades and explosives, he and his men forced the garrison to surrender. Dutch troops tried to retake the fort, but were driven off with hand grenades and pistols. Ludwig Kepplinger had "created a situation that permitted the rapid capture of Westervoort and a subsequent rapid advance by the regiment." SS-Oberführer Keppler recommended him for the Knight's Cross. The recommendation was endorsed by SS-Gruppenführer Hausser and, on 4 September 1940, Kepplinger received the coveted decoration, the second member of the regiment to be so decorated.

SS-Oberführer Keppler allowed the Dutch commander of the Westervoort to retain his sidearm "for his brave defense" and to show "respect for him and his brave soldiers." In Keppler's words this was "just the soldierly thing to do." With Westervoort in German hands, the Commanding General of the X Army Corps, General Hansen, and his Chief of Staff, Oberst i.G. (i.G. = *im Generallstab* = general-staff officer) Gause, came to the Ijssel to congratulate SS-Oberführer Keppler on his success.

From there the 3rd Battalion set out in the direction of Arnhem. SS-Sturmbannführer Wäckerle took possession of the city without fighting and immediately moved his forces forward to the city's western boundary. Near Renkum Wäckerle's forces came under fire from a unit of the 5th Squadron of Hussars under Captain Nijhoff. The cavalry unit had scouted the area between the Ijssel and the Grebbe Line and now defended itself east of Wageningen with antitank guns and light machine guns. The battalion suffered heavy casualties here. Not until 1800, when Captain Nijhoff was ordered to withdraw toward the Grebbe Line, was the battalion able to take Wageningen. All the elements of the regiment that had crossed the military bridge at Arnhem were assembled in the Renkum area for the night. Heavy security was posted.

The regiment had reached its objective on the first day of the Western Campaign and was now only a few kilometers from the main Dutch fortification: The Grebbe Line. Patrols sent out the next morning found the Dutch positions around Lenkum empty. The enemy had withdrawn to the Grebbe Line.

Josef Lainer Sees His First Combat

At first light on 11 May the *SS-Standarte "Der Führer"* deployed and moved forward. In the lead was its reinforced 15th Company. Advancing on the right was the 1st Battalion and, on the left, the 3rd Battalion. Behind the two forward units was the 2nd Battalion. Barricades of fallen trees and minefields blocked the entrances to Wageningen. Step by step the SS men fought their way through the town. Sepp Lainer described the part played by his company (the 2nd):

> We began taking fire from the left from several single-story houses. "Advance along the hedge!" came the order from our company commander.
>
> My platoon turned, ran beneath the enemy fire, ducked into the cover of the hedge and kept running. Leading the way was the platoon leader, followed by the machine-gun team. I was carrying two boxes of ammunition. The third man of the machine-gun team had been wounded and I took his place. In front of me I saw the back of Siebert, the leader of the machine-gun team, as he reached the end of the hedge and the white-painted single-story house next to it. At that moment a machine gun opened up on us from a multi-story building directly to our right. We took cover. I

watched as the loader fed in a fresh belt of ammunition and SS-Unterscharführer Schnell pointed to the new threat. The first belt was gone in no time and another was loaded.

"Hey, Sepp! Bring a fresh box!" called the loader.

Pushing one of the boxes of ammunition in front of me, I crawled over to the loader. I then went back and got the second box. The firing from the tall building stopped abruptly.

In the midst of this confusion, the company commander shouted: "Get up! Move forward!"

The company roused itself and advanced. Bent low, the men waited for the next burst of fire, ready to jump into cover. Relieved of his burden of ammunition boxes, Lainer spurted ahead to the SS-Unterscharführer. The outlines of figures in Dutch uniforms appeared behind trees and bushes. The machine gunner fired from the hip as he advanced. The forms quickly disappeared.

"Sepp, get over here!" shouted Schnell. "Get hand grenades ready!"

As soon as Lainer arrived he saw what was happening. A machine gun was firing from behind a low wall from which several stones had been knocked out and, farther to the right, there was rifle fire coming from a house.

Lainer screwed the safety caps off three hand grenades. He held them in his left hand by their wooden handles and waited for the squad leader's signal.

"Now!" shouted Schnell.

Together they threw their hand grenades at the machine-gun position, then repeated the toss a second and a third time. After the grenades had exploded the squad got to its feet. Schnell raised his arm and they all ran towards the house. Someone kicked the door open. His pistol at the ready, Lainer found himself facing several unarmed Dutch soldiers coming down from the upper story, their hands raised. Two of the men were bleeding from shrapnel wounds. The prisoners were led out of the house; a soldier with minor wounds was escorted to the rear, where the medics were waiting with two ambulances.

Lainer and the others combed the row of houses. They occasionally took fire, which they returned until the enemy fell silent. As he walked up to a house on a corner, Lainer suddenly came face to face with a group of enemy soldiers about to enter the house. One of the Dutchmen turned and raised his weapon. Lainer shot first and saw the man fall and roll onto his side. He then threw a hand grenade through the open door. The grenade exploded in the hall, apparently with good effect. At first three figures, then four came out with hands raised. Several of the Dutch soldiers had been wounded by grenade fragments.

Moving from house to house, the company reached the town limits. Just then Dutch artillery opened fire.

"Take cover!" ordered one of the platoon leaders.

The soldiers threw themselves down behind a low wall. Lainer pressed himself close to the bricks. A round struck the ground about fifteen meters away. Fragments whizzed through the air. Farther to the right a member of the company was hit and cried out. Seconds later a call for a medic rang out and Lainer saw his friend Saininger running toward the wounded man with the first-aid kit.

Bursting rounds started several fires, especially where they had fallen on houses. Here, as at other scenes of fighting in Holland—especially in Rotterdam—the Dutch were not squeamish, even when it was their own houses. They engaged the enemy regardless of the damage that resulted. They later reproached the Germans for bombing Rotterdam and sending the houses of civilians up in flames. That remains the perplexing illogic of the battle for Fortress Holland. The Germans knew that Rotterdam could not claim to be an open city. Dutch troops were still holding out in the city and had turned it into a battlefield.

Sepp Lainer described his feelings following his first taste of combat:

Not having seen action in Poland, we now learned for the first time what war really meant. We saw our own men: Killed, wounded, exhausted. And we also saw the enemy's dead. It all seemed horrible to us. But yet we could not and dared not stop fighting. He who gave up perished! In addition, we were firmly convinced that by being there we were defending our German fatherland. Not until later, in Russia, did we discover that our sacrifices in dead and wounded in Holland were only a minor prelude to the real struggle.

Later Lainer explained:

The war had shown us its devilish face for the first time, and we mourned the deaths of many old comrades while, at the same time, feeling relief that we had survived. However, we could see that our turn would also come if the war did not end soon.

✠

At noon on 11 May SS-Oberführer Keppler received orders to attack the Grebbe Line. The assault was to be made with the 1st Battalion (right) and the 3rd Battalion (left). The boundary between the two battalions was the Wageningen-Grebbe road. Elements of the divisional artillery went into position east of Wageningen. The forward observer set up his observation post at the southeast end of the town. SS-Oberführer Keppler requested and received additional artillery support from the 207th Infantry Division to support the attack. He kept the 2nd Battalion in reserve, to be committed if necessary.

Contrary to the information supplied by agents, the Grebbe Line was not a "field position, which can be occupied easily." It turned out to be an in-depth defensive line with trenches, bunkers, embrasures and artillery positions, whose guns were trained on precisely ranged targets and which were deadly accurate. Stands of trees and hedges provided additional cover for the defenders. This defensive line had its origins in the Eighteenth Century. In addition, the defenders could use a system of locks, dams and trenches to flood the approaches. In 1939 the Dutch built powerful strongpoints at the sites of the old De Aschgat and De Rotseiaar fieldworks, which served as forward outposts. Behind these strongpoints was the main defensive line.

There was a windmill under construction at the south end of the defensive position. It was near the Grebbe lock at the Rhine, but it had not been completed by 10 May. At Scherpenzeel and Amersfort, however, the necessary flooding measures had been taken. Under the command of General van der Bent, the Dutch IV Army Corps, comprising the 7th and 8th Infantry Divisions, was to hold the position against all attacks. The entire defensive system of the Ijssel, the Betuwe and the Grebbe Line, was under the command of Lieutenant General Baron van Voorst tot Voorst. Large parts of the area in front of the IV Army Corps were already under water.

The war diary of the X Army Corps contains the following entry concerning the attack that day on the Grebbe Line:

> The 207th Infantry Division and the reinforced *SS-Standarte "Der Führer"* carried out the attack on the Grebbe Heights. Following the capture of Aageningen and the forward Grebbe positions, the attack was continued against the Grebbe Heights at 1630.

Originally planned for the early morning, the attack on 12 May had to be postponed until afternoon. *SS-Standarte "Der Führer"* came under fire from the defenders even while regrouping for the attack. Works 26—the

Grebbe lock—kept the approaches under heavy fire. Artillery was called in to silence the enemy position. At 1400 hours four batteries of artillery opened fire and continued firing for twenty minutes. Following the bombardment, the 2nd Battalion attacked; at the same time, farther to the northwest, the 3rd Battalion also went into the attack. SS-Oberführer Keppler held back his 1st Battalion north of the road. It was to expand on any success by either of the committed battalions and force a breakthrough.

Assault detachments from the 9th and 12th Companies approached the fort at the foot of the Grebbe Heights on the Wageningen-Grebbe road and the fortifications on either side. A further assault detachment from the 16th Company followed close behind in inflatable boats. The attackers worked their way through the enemy positions and, at 1900, SS-Oberführer Keppler reported that he had taken the Grebbe Heights. This information was not completely accurate, however.

The Attack by the 1st Battalion of the *SS-Standarte "Der Führer"*
"When will it be our turn, Obersturmführer?" asked platoon leader Weickl.

He was lying beside the commander of the 2nd Company, who was waiting for the order to attack.

"It'll be our turn soon enough! Don't worry, the war won't end without us getting involved."

Sepp Lainer checked the hand grenades he had stuck in his belt. He looked to his right and saw the tense faces of his companions. They listened to the crash of exploding artillery rounds and the distant rumble of the guns in the rear. In the distance they saw fountains of dust and dirt as the rounds exploded among the Dutch positions. The 1st Battalion was to crack this important position in the Grebbe Line.

Sepp Lainer was part of an assault detachment under platoon leader Weickl. The attack signal was given. Lainer got to his feet and began to run, following the company commander. Before they had gone more than a few meters they began to take fire from the right. After a few bursts the enemy gun fell silent.

Suddenly, two machine guns opened fire from a concealed bunker right in front of them, causing Lainer and the others to take cover. When the firing stopped they got up, only to throw themselves down again as the two guns flickered to life once more. When he was close enough, Lainer threw several hand grenades towards the bunker's embrasure. Others did the same.

This served to draw the enemy's fire while SS-Oberscharführer Otten and his assault detachment advanced on the right flank. On seeing Otten's signal flare they held their fire and stopped throwing grenades. Eight to ten seconds later a heavy explosion shook the bunker. A hatch flew open and flames spurted forth. Otten's men stormed the bunker, but there was no fighting left to do. The wounded Dutch had already laid down their weapons.

"Forward, follow me!" ordered Otten.

He and his men moved on, while to the left Weickl's group kept pace. Lainer ran alongside the machine gunner. He heard him breathing heavily and only then noticed that he was out of breath himself. A short burst from a Dutch machine gun caused them to take cover. Seconds later Lainer and the others were on their feet again. Dutch soldiers appeared from out of the smoke and dust. Following a brief exchange of fire they gave themselves up.

"Send them back with the two who aren't wounded too badly!" ordered the company commander.

The attack went on. They stormed bunker after bunker. A rifle bullet screamed past Lainer's helmet. He felt a heavy blow and fell to the ground. Anxiously he reached up and felt the left half of his face. There was no blood, but he still felt somewhat stunned by the impact.

Lainer called out to a comrade. "Have a look," he said, pointing to his helmet.

"A long, shallow dent. If you're careful the supply sergeant won't notice," Stofels replied with a grin.

"You know what you can do, don't you?" called Lainer, half exuberant and half angry. If the bullet had been one or two centimeters farther to the right it would certainly have killed him.

"I know all too well. But I'm not going to put in for a decoration for exceptional bravery," joked Stofels, which caused Lainer to laugh.

The attack continued. All the bunkers were either taken out or abandoned by the enemy. But victory at the Grebbe Line was not yet complete, because the 2nd and 3rd Battalions were still fighting on the heights. They had fought their way through two enemy positions but were now pinned down by heavy fire from the third.

"The 3rd Battalion has broken into the enemy positions," the signals sergeant called out to the commander of the 2nd Company".

"Our company is to move up as reserve. We'll skirt around the flanking bunkers and then turn towards the center from behind the enemy bunker line," explained the company commander. "Then we'll to link up with the 2nd Battalion."

They moved out in single file through the outer communications trenches. When they saw the corner bunker off to the right, SS-Hauptsturmführer Harmel, the company commander, crept forward to the edge of the trench and peered over. He saw the hectic firing from the third Dutch position. As he watched, the Dutch launched a counterattack aimed at driving the Germans out of the second position and putting them to flight.

He waved to the leader of 1st Platoon, SS-Oberscharführer Otten: "Follow me! Quickly!"

Crouched low, they squeezed sideways along the narrow trench. The trench was littered with discarded items of equipment and the occasional weapon. When Sepp Lainer and the rest of his group reached the left flanking trench, the company commander and the men of the headquarters section had already gone into position there.

"Bring another machine gun over here!" ordered the company commander.

Lainer nudged the machine gunner. "Let's go, Franzel, this way!"

He ran toward the specified position: A protrusion which would allow the machine gunner to set up so that he had a good field of fire while offering a low silhouette. "Aim at the left flank!—Open fire!"

The three machine guns of the company opened fire. Lainer fed belts of ammunition into the nearest gun. The advancing enemy troops were mown down. Soon the field had been swept clear and the few Dutch troops who survived the machine guns crawled away towards the rear. They had smashed the first attack and would then repulse the two that followed as well. Finally, the requested mortars arrived. The commander of the 15th Company, the heavy weapons company, positioned the weapons according to SS-Hauptsturmführer Harmel's instructions. Three minutes later the mortars opened fire. Mortar rounds hammered into the trenches of the third Dutch line.

✠

Not until the pioneers had thrown a bridge across the Grebbe was SS-Oberführer Keppler able to send the other heavy weapons across. The 1st Company and the combat engineers of the 16th Company distinguished themselves in this action. They carried out their difficult task in record time, all while under enemy artillery tire.

Nevertheless the attack, which had began with such promise, had bogged down on the Grebbe Heights. The enemy was defending with great determination. Although the 1st Battalion had attacked the Dutch positions northeast of the Grebbe Heights and had broken through, allowing the battalion commander to reach the base of the heights at 2000. His report to the regimental commander that he would be on the heights in another two hours proved overly optimistic. SS-Oberführer Keppler ordered SS-Sturmbannführer Wäckerle to break through along the Grebbe-Rhenen road with his 3rd Battalion and establish a bridgehead due east of Rhenen at the railway embankment. General Tiedemann, the divisional commander of the 207th Infantry Division, inserted the 1st Battalion of the 322nd Infantry Regiment into the resulting gap between the 2nd and 3rd Battalions.

The 3rd Battalion under SS-Sturmbannführer Wäckerle attacked at 2300. By 2400 the railway line had been reached. During the night the battalion had to fight off several Dutch counterattacks. The Dutch discovered the gap between the two SS-battalions, because the 322nd Infantry Regiment's 1st Battalion had not yet moved into position. The battalion had become lost in the darkness and did not arrive until morning. During the night, General Tiedemann gave orders for all of 322nd Infantry Regiment to attack early on the morning of 13 May. The regiment was to set out from the area of the heights and advance west through Rhenen. He ordered the 1st and 2nd Battalions to advance toward the northwest and roll up the enemy positions on the Grebbe.

On 13 May SS-Oberführer Keppler committed the two battalions. The stubbornly defending Dutch were driven from the bunkers of the third line. By 1100 hours, 1,500 meters of the enemy position were in the regi-

The fourth battle of Kharkov, August 1943.

ment's hands. Nevertheless, SS-Oberführer Keppler had to call off a further advance, as the 322nd Infantry Regiment had not yet advanced westwards beyond the Grebbe Heights. As a result, the SS regimental flank—extending 1,500 meters—was undefended. Any Dutch attack there would have terrible consequences.

At the same time, at the viaduct at the railway line near Rhenen the forces under SS-Sturmbannführer Wäckerle were driven back by machine-gun fire from Dutch forces under Captain Gelderman. Gelderman had been positioned there with fourteen solders. His orders were: "No one, friend or foe, is to get through here to the west or withdraw to the west."

Wäckerle's battalion was driven back as far as the De Stohamer Factory, southeast of the viaduct, by fire from the two machine guns. Two further attacks against Gelderman's strongpoint were repulsed. The situation of the 3rd Battalion was precarious. The enemy positions behind it had closed up again after having been penetrated. The SS battalion was surrounded as a result. To make matter's worse, SS-Sturmbannführer Wäckerle had been wounded in the fighting and had to be evacuated to the main dressing station and then to a military hospital.

The requested air support arrived in the early afternoon. Six Stukas dove on the enemy positions, their sirens screaming. The dive-bombers hit and put out of action an important enemy position. The attack by the 322nd Infantry Regiment began to show signs of success and gained ground towards the west.

✠

SS-Oberführer Keppler had assembled his battalion commanders in his forward command post. "We're continuing the attack!" he informed them. The regiment's commander ordered the 1st and 2nd Battalions to lead the attack; he kept the remaining battalion in reserve. The Grebbe Line was to be rolled up as far as the flood plain. The individual battle groups moved forward.

Once again Sepp Lainer and his comrades of the 2nd Company advanced toward the fire-spitting sector that the enemy so desperately wished to hold. They reached the field of fire of the first bunker, which was flanked by two machine guns.

"I need two volunteers to take out those two machine guns," called out SS-Hauptsturmführer Harmel. To his own amazement, Sepp Lainer stepped forward. His friend Weickl did the same.

"All right, Lainer, go around to the left. When you are within no-miss hand-grenade range, take out the machine-gun nest with three grenades.

Weickl, you do the same on the bunker's right flank. Take the two communications trenches, left and right. Be careful, there might be a few Dutchmen hiding there." Harmel looked at his watch. "Throw your grenades in five minutes. Afterwards, we will attack and open fire, so keep your heads down."

Sepp Lainer slipped through the chest-high trench until it turned and led diagonally toward the machine gun. There he had to leave the trench, because there was nothing between him and the enemy troops in the machine-gun nest. If he made the slightest noise they would spot him and he wouldn't stand a chance. Lainer left the trench and moved forward through same low bushes. He only half listened to the firing of his comrades and the enemy as he concentrated on the machine-gun nest. He took cover briefly when a burst of machine-gun fire hissed close by, but it was obviously meant for his comrades farther back in the trench. He crawled another ten meters and saw one of the Dutch soldiers. The man was looking over the parapet, but not in his direction.

The shallow pit in which he was lying allowed Lainer to throw his grenades from a kneeling position. As a result, it was possible for him to toss the grenades a good thirty meters. He looked at his watch and saw that he still had thirty seconds. He placed two of the grenades in front of him on the edge of the pit, where they would be ready to throw. He screwed off the safety cap of the third, gripped the fuse's porcelain knob between his index and middle finger and waited.

When the time was up he pulled the cord, waited two seconds and threw the first grenade into the enemy machine-gun nest. Even before it detonated he had thrown the second. As he was throwing the third grenade, the first exploded. Through the noise of battle he heard hand grenades exploding to his right; that had to be Weickl. Lainer tossed his last grenade, which landed in the midst of the machine-gun nest. He immediately took cover. Behind him he heard his comrades open fire and, through the noise of the fighting, he could hear the tramping of their boots. A man landed beside him in his pit. It was the company commander.

"Well done, Lainer," he called to the young soldier. "Now let's get that bunker!"

They stormed into the enemy machine-gun position. Both machine guns near the bunker had fallen silent. Lainer and the others hurried on through a communications trench. One man blew open the door at the rear of the bunker with a Teller mine. The enemy surrendered.

When they reached the trench that made up the third line and jumped in, the enemy had already withdrawn. They gave chase by running through the supply trenches and overcoming pockets of resistance as they formed. They then stormed onward. By 1900 hours they had overcome the last bunker and had taken all the sector as far as the flood plain.

When it was finally over, Sepp Lainer found that his hands were shaking. He hid them behind his back, but a glance at the others was enough for him to see that they were experiencing the same thing. The battalion commander, who had been with the 3rd Company, came over to them.

"Well done, men! That's the kind of assault I like." He handed out several packs of cigarettes and informed the men that they could expect to rest that night and all they had to do was prepare for an eventual Dutch counterattack. As he left, the battalion commander said: "They are a tough bunch. They should have been on our side. After all, they're basically Germans."

✠

News came in that the 322nd Infantry Regiment had reached the railway line east of Rhenen but was stalled there. Strong patrols were sent into the Rhenen area to determine the enemy's strength and position. As all the motorized units of the 207th Infantry Division had already been committed, General Tiedemann tasked SS-Oberführer Keppler for an armored car platoon. The armored reconnaissance vehicles rolled into the night and helped the 322nd Infantry Regiment get its attack toward Rhenen moving.

Early on the morning of 13 May, The 2nd Battalion was moved into an area ten kilometers northwest of Rhenen to guard the left flank of the 207th Infantry Division. The infantry division was advancing through Amerongen toward Doom at that point. The Germans had broken through the three main zones of the Grebbe Line that morning.

At this point we will provide the reader with a brief look at the Dutch defenders, who fought so bravely.

THE DEFENDERS OF THE GREBBE HEIGHTS
The "Little Verdun" in Holland

When the units of *SS-Standarte "Der Führer"* advanced across the Grebbe River, they ran into the rear of the 2nd Company of the Dutch 8th Infantry Regiment in position beyond the Grebbe Bridge. The surviving soldiers from the northern sector of the Hoorn defensive fortification had withdrawn to this position. The retreat had succeeded thanks to covering fire from the machine gun of armored cupola G 19. Not until its ammunition was gone did the gun crew withdraw to G 16.

The 2nd Company's 1st Platoon fought until its men were exhausted and both heavy machine guns broke down in the afternoon. Lieutenant Slager withdrew his platoon to a trench line north of his former position when SS armored cars approached. He continued the fight from there. Soon afterward it was discovered that men of *SS-Standarte "Der Führer"* had occupied the Heimerstein House, an important part of the defensive system.

Several Dutch positions broke out white flags. Lieutenant Slager and the commander of the 11th Company of the 8th Infantry Regiment (which contained the regimental antitank platoon), which had arrived in the meantime, decided to attempt a breakout. First they moved to the north; later they headed west. The attack by *SS-Standarte "Der Führer"* and the 207th Infantry Division was halted by fire from Dutch armored cupolas G 20, G 21, and G 22. An antitank gun of the Dutch 8th Antitank Company also destroyed an armored car.

During the night of 13–14 May, the Dutch troops along the Grebbe withdrew unnoticed from the water line. Leading the Dutch forces in this area was Colonel van Loon, commander of the 4th Infantry Division, of which the 8th Infantry Regiment was a part.

Unable to assess the strength of the attacking German forces, Major General Harberts, who was the commanding general in this zone, labeled the men who retreated in the face of the onslaught "cowards." Parts of Harbert's communications network had been knocked out. It was not until Lieutenant General Baron Voorst tot Voorst, Commander-in-Chief of the Dutch Field Army, arrived at corps headquarters that Harbert received a relatively accurate overview of what was happening.

Task Force Jacometti (the 2nd Battalion of the 8th Infantry Regiment), which was attacked by SS forces, was hit by heavy machine-gun fire as it passed a patch of woods occupied by the Germans. Major Jacometti and many of his men were killed. Colonel Hennink, commander of the 8th Infantry Regiment, requested reinforcements from the divisional commander. He received one and a half companies from the 3rd Battalion of the 11th Infantry Regiment under Major Ploeg.

The Commander-in-Chief of the Field Army intervened at that point in an effort to instill order. Several small groups of forces were still fighting on the Grebbe Heights, and they needed support if they were to withdraw successfully. At the same time Colonel Van Loon received orders to set up a new defensive line at Elst with his 4th Infantry Division.

Rhenen was ablaze. In the command post of Major Landzaat the engagement was not decided until most of the defenders had been killed. In the end Major Landzaat was down to four officers and twelve men. A

Major operated a machine gun, while a Captain functioned as loader. The antitank guns of *SS-Standarte "Der Führer"* opened fire on this nest of resistance. The pavilion, in which the last of the defenders had holed up, was hit. Major Landzaat ordered his men to withdraw. Then he pulled his pistol and ran outside. He was struck by several bullets and killed.

The 8th Infantry Regiment's command post on the Grebbe Heights was also the scene of bitter fighting. There it was Lieutenant Hannink die Seele who led the defense. Both sides suffered heavy losses in machine-gun duels. A German attack on the command post on the morning of 14 May was barely repulsed. Hannink ordered the regiment's colors taken to 4th Infantry Division headquarters. Leaving behind the medical officer, six assistants and twenty-two wounded, Hannink managed to lead a breakout toward the southwest.

Sepp Lainer commented on the Dutch troops he faced in Holland:

They were men like us! They fought bravely and without dirty tricks. They kept fighting in hopeless situations, and I could only hope that if we were in such a situation we could muster the same courage.

The struggle for the Grebbe Line and the Grebbe Heights is one of the forgotten, dramatic battles in Holland that cost both sides heavy losses.

The End in Holland

The young Austrian volunteers distinguished themselves in the fighting for the Dutch bunker line and on the Grebbe Heights. Under fire, they coolly approached the enemy bunkers and put them out of action with hand grenades and explosives. The fourteenth of May was a quieter day for the regiment, with only sporadic fighting. When Utrecht surrendered that evening, everyone hoped for a quick end to the fighting. When the Dutch surrender did come the next day it took the members of *SS-Standarte "Der Führer"* by surprise. They had not expected such a move after the bitter fighting they had been through.

SS-Standarte "Der Führer" was placed on alert at 0500 hours on 15 May. The unit prepared for another long advance. The commanding general of the X Army Corps, General Hansen, halted the advance of the 207th Infantry Division. He decreed that the SS regiment should be the first formation to resume the advance through Holland, having been the first element to break through the Ijssel and Grebbe Lines.

Setting out from Amerongen at 1000 hours, the regiment moved through Utrecht and Amsterdam to Haarlem, where it took over coastal security duties near Ijmuiden and Zandvoort. It was there that the regiment learned of the Dutch surrender.

Three and a half hours after the German air attack on Rotterdam on the afternoon of 14 May, which General Student was unable to prevent, the Dutch Commander-in-Chief, General Winkelman, offered the surrender of all Dutch armed forces. The surrender document was signed in the Dutch headquarters in Den Haag on 15 May by General Winkelman and Generaloberst von Bock, the Commander-in-Chief of Army Group B. General of Artillery von Küchler was also present. In a radio broadcast, General Winkelman justified his decision:

> We had to lay down our arms, because there was no other choice. Everyone was firmly determined to defend his fatherland to the utmost. Left to our own devices, we were not in a position to protect the civilian population against this power. It is this hard fact that forced me to make my very serious decision. We have ceased fighting. There could be no other decision.

During only four days of fighting in Holland, *SS-Standarte "Der Führer"* had lost 118 men killed, including seven officers. Of the 231 wounded, seven were officers. In addition, there were fifteen missing. These figures represented a serious rate of loss for the regiment.

During his parting visit with General Hansen, SS-Oberführer Keppler received several Iron Crosses for awarding to his brave soldiers. The first to receive the Iron Cross, First Class, was SS-Obersturmbannführer Wäckerle, who had been wounded on 13 May. General Hansen expressed his special appreciation to SS-Oberführer Keppler for the efforts of his regiment. Keppler replied: "I'm proud of my soldiers. I would like all my replacements to come from Austria, because they're real fighters."

SS-STANDARTE "DER FÜHRER" IN THE FRENCH CAMPAIGN

On 17 May 1940 *SS-Standarte "Der Führer"* rejoined the *SS-Verfügungs* Division near Marienbourg. The regiment was given several days to reorganize and reequip. On 22 May the unit was brought to march readiness. Its objective was to capture the Kemmelberg, a hill that had been hotly contested during World War One. It was to clear the way for the following units. This order was subsequently cancelled as other units had already taken the Kemmelberg from the east.

The regiment was assigned a security zone along the Lys River and the Lys and La Basse Canals. There it was under the command of Generalleutnant Reinhardt's XXXXI Motorized Army Corps. Enemy forces encircled by Reinhardt's corps attempted to break out to the south during the night of 23–24 May. Strong armored forces led the enemy attacks.

About fifty tanks rolled towards the positions of the 9th Company. A French infantry battalion followed close behind. The infantry broke into the company's positions. SS-Hauptsturmführer Harmel, who had earlier distinguished himself at the Grebbe Heights, mastered the situation until SS-Hauptsturmführer Kumm, the new commander of the 3rd Battalion, arrived with hastily assembled reserves. A machine-gun platoon of the 1st Company and the regimental antitank platoon drove the French back before the main body of the regiment counterattacked.

In the village of Hilaire a handful of antitank guns engaged a large force of enemy tanks. Thirteen of these were knocked out and 500 French soldiers surrendered. The breakthrough attempt had failed at that location, however, the main body of French tanks bypassed this position and reached the outskirts of the city of Aire, where the 7th Company was in position. In the subsequent urban fighting, SS-Hauptsturmführer Lingner was able to halt the powerful enemy force. The struggle was man versus tank, and the SS soldiers prevailed using explosives and bundles of hand grenades. All of the French tanks that entered the town were destroyed.

On the morning of 24 May SS-Oberführer Keppler was able to report to the commanding general, who had hastened to the scene, that the enemy breakout attempt had failed. Generalleutnant Reinhardt expressed his admiration for the courage and coolness with which the regiment had dealt with this difficult situation.

The next day the entire regiment attacked across the Lys near Aire. A bridgehead was established on the north bank of the river. It was there that the regiment encountered British forces for the first time. The attack on the morning of 28 May across the Lys was initially unsuccessful. A second assault that afternoon achieved the desired success after antitank guns were sent across the river. Employing direct fire, they shot up nests of resistance. The British Expeditionary Force streamed back towards Dunkirk.

On 1 June 1940 Sepp Lainer was promoted to SS-Rottenführer and given command of a squad in recognition of his extraordinary performance. Although he had been promised the Iron Cross, he was not to receive that decoration until later in Russia.

During the second phase of the French Campaign Lainer and his squad saw continuous action. The division, attached to the XVI Army Corps of the 6th Army (Generaloberst von Reichenau), advanced across the Somme as the second wave. The advance began early on the morning of 7 June.

During the night of 7–8 June, *SS-Standarte "Der Führer"* moved past the enemy's open flank and into his rear. The enemy force was a colonial regiment. At this point, however, the regiment was withdrawn and moved west to take part in the attack across the Avre towards Montdidier-Compiegne with the rest of the *SS-Verfügungs* Division.

Advancing on the left flank, *SS-Standarte "Deutschland"* was unable to cross the Avre. Strong enemy forces had dug in on the other side in the area around Guerbigny. The second attack, in which *SS-Standarte "Der Führer"* was to have taken part, became unnecessary when Panzer Group Guderian broke through farther to the east.

The *SS-Verfügungs* Division was then withdrawn from that sector and moved to St. Quentin. From there, as part of the XIV Army Corps under General von Wietersheim, the division advanced through Soissons. It then crossed the Marne at Chateau Thierry and the Seine at Romilly. There was a brief engagement at Romilly. The next contact with French forces—units from the Maginot Line trying to escape to open country in the west—did not take place until 17 June. In a 380-kilometer advance that began on 21 June, the division rolled through Orleans, Tours and Pottiers to Bordeaux. On 26 June it was in the famous resort of Biarritz, near the Spanish border.

Sepp Lainer wrote in his personal diary:

> It was simply incredible when this wild advance was behind us. It was as if we had been transported into a completely new world. We moved past endless columns of enemy soldiers who had thrown down their weapons and then been directed to some camp. There were huge quantities of heavy weapons and equipment at the sides of the road and in the ditches. In addition, there were machine guns, rifles, guns, vehicles, tanks and masses of materiel. Now we knew for certain: The French Campaign was over. The French were defeated.

The period of rest and recuperation in Biarritz came to an end on 2 July. Outings to the beach, sightseeing through the city streets with their shops and the overhauling of weapons and equipment became a thing of the past.

Sepp Lainer had grown closer to the men in his squad and company. Many of these friendships had been forged under enemy fire and lasted beyond the end of the war. The men within the unit understood each other well. Sepp Lainer knew that he could depend on every man in the 2nd Company. He had become a member of the machine-gun squad, led by SS-Rottenführer Holzinger. The second and third members of his machine-gun team were SS-Sturmmann Winter and SS-Sturmmann Gries, both battle-tested soldiers.

When *SS-Standarte "Der Führer"* pulled out on 3 July 1940 every vehicle was in 100% working order. The unit's destination was Meppel in northern Holland. When they crossed the German border near Aachen, the troops received a jubilant reception from the population. Their welcome in the Meppel-Zwolle district was less warm, as the regiment had been sent to the area following an outbreak of unrest and strikes.

Training that incorporated the lessons learned in Holland and France was pushed forward and replacement personnel arrived. The regiment also made preparations for the planned invasion of England, Operation "Sea Lion." Embarkation and disembarkation exercises were carried out and the troops practiced assaulting an enemy-held coast. The preferred training area was Den Helder.

Departure orders arrived in mid-December. By this time the *SS-Verfügungs* Division had been redesignated. Initially it was called SS-Division *"Deutschland."* Because of possible confusion with *SS-Standarte "Deutschland,"* however, it was further redesignated as SS-Division *"Reich"* (January 1941–May 1942). About the same time, the infantry regiments of the division were redesignated as well, with *SS-Standarte "Der Führer"* becoming SS-Infantry Regiment *"Der Führer."* *SS-Standarte "Germania"* was detached from the division to help form SS-Division *"Wiking."* That left the division with two motorized infantry regiments.

The regiment was next moved to the Langres Plateau, west of Vesoul in the Vosges Mountains. From there Lainer and many of his comrades went home on leave. Lainer spent time with his parents and friends, although many of the latter had been called up for service in the armed forces. When he returned to his regiment in January 1941, Sepp Lainer was wearing the rank of SS-Unterscharführer. He had been notified of his promotion, which took effect 1 January 1941, by Teletype message.

The coup d'etat in Yugoslavia in early April 1941 brought about an unexpected turn in the situation in the Balkans. The result was the unplanned campaign against Yugoslavia. SS-Division *"Reich"* was transported from the Vesoul area to Ternesvar (Timisoara) via Munich, Salzburg, Vienna and Budapest. There it was placed under the command of Panzer Corps Reinhardt.

The Yugoslavian border was crossed on Good Friday 1941. The objective for SS-Infantry Regiment *"Der Führer"* was the city of Seleus. Resistance was light, although there was a flare-up at the Theresien Canal, where the bridges had been blown. The capture of Seleus ended the role of SS-Infantry Regiment *"Der Führer"* in the Yugoslavian Campaign. By that point,

German armored divisions were already advancing along the south bank of the Danube towards Belgrade.

During this phase of the campaign SS-Hauptsturmführer Klingenberg and ten soldiers of the division's motorcycle battalion (which had been created from the former 15th Company of SS-*Standarte "Der Führer"*) moved into Belgrade in a surprise move and forced the city to capitulate. On 14 May 1941 Fritz Klingenberg was awarded the Knight's Cross for this exploit. The campaign over, SS-Infantry Regiment *"Der Führer"* and the rest of the division road marched through Budapest and Vienna on their way to the Eferdingen area west of Linz. Once again the units took time to overhaul their weapons and equipment.

OPERATION BARBAROSSA: THE ASSAULT BEGINS

When the attack on the Soviet Union began, SS-Division *"Reich"* was designated as part of the reserve for Panzer Group 2, commanded by Guderian. It was attached to the XXXXVI Panzer Corps. Another notable unit in that armored corps was Motorized Infantry Regiment *"Großdeutschland"* under Generalmajor von Stockhausen. That formation went on to become the foundation of the Panzer Grenadier Division of the same name (and, by war's end, a Panzer Corps).

Once the bridges over the Bug had been freed up SS-Division *"Reich"* was to be sent in behind the left wing of *Panzer Group 2.* The division did not depart the Lublin area until 26 June, after the city of Brest Litovsk had fallen. The division moved out on the road to Baranovichi. In the middle of the march formation was SS-Infantry Regiment *"Der Führer."* Fighting still raged in the fortress of Brest Litovsk, where Soviet officer cadets were defending the officer school there.

The division was moved forward to provide flanking cover towards the south (in the direction of the Pripet Marshes). Sepp Lainer experienced the pitiless heat of the open country and the terrible plague of mosquitoes and biting insects. The division marched through Slutsk and reached Svisloch. There the division received orders to advance northeast along the east bank of the Beresina toward Mogilev. Crossing the Beresina proved difficult, however, as the bridge had been blown. SS-Infantry Regiment *"Der Führer"* initially advanced along the west bank, planning to cross the river at Beresino. The crossing took place during the night of 6–7 July.

The attack began early in the area east of Makoshin. Generaloberst Guderian made a surprise appearance at 1400 hours and ordered the regiment to attack at once, without waiting for the promised Stuka support. The regiment's motorcycle troops had successfully carried the attack into the enemy positions, when the Stukas suddenly appeared overhead.

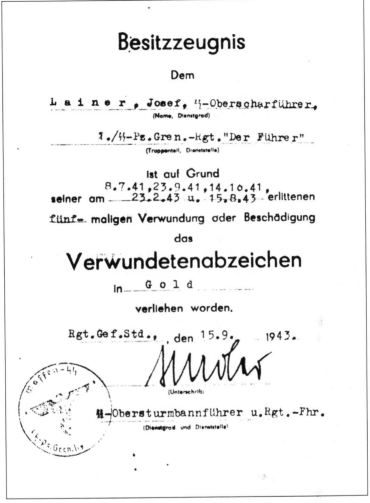

Award certificate for the Wound Badge in Gold to "Sepp" Lainer.

A total of twenty-seven dive-bombers in three waves dropped their bombs. Identification panels and star shells failed to prevent the attack on the position, which had already been taken by German troops. The motor-cycle troops suffered heavy casualties at the hand of their own aviators. During the same attack several Russian armored trains were destroyed and resistance in Makoshin was broken. The enemy withdrew. But the cost!

News reached the 1st Battalion of SS-Infantry Regiment *"Der Führer"* that SS-Untersturmführer Frank, the commander of the regiment's 14th Panzer Destroyer Company, and the commander of the antiaircraft machine-gun company, SS-Obersturmführer Rentrop, had bypassed the village and reached a bridge over the Desna, where they had defused the demolition charges.

The battalion immediately followed up so as to make use of the crossing site and expand the small, hastily formed bridgehead. Instead, however, SS-Sturmbannführer Kumm, the new regimental commander, decided to send the 1st and 3rd Battalions across the river west and east of the bridge during the night of 7–8 September. In doing so he hoped to avoid the enemy fire which had prevented a previous crossing attempt. The crossings by both battalions went smoothly, as the enemy had not reckoned with such a move. The 3rd Battalion captured the village of Slobotka. After crossing the river Infantry Regiment *"Deutschland"* continued to advance.

On 5 September 1941 the 1st Battalion was moved to the area of operations of the XXIV Panzer Corps (General of Armored Troops Geyr von Schweppenburg), where it became the corps reserve for several weeks. The rest of the regiment, particularly the 2nd Battalion under SS-Hauptsturmführer Stadler, had done quite well during the same time period. The 5th Company had killed 900 enemy soldiers and captured or destroyed 30 guns, 13 tanks and about 150 vehicles. The much-contested city of Priluki was captured by the regiment.

During the night of 18–19 September regiment was placed on alert and issued the following order:

> The enemy is moving in a recently formed corps to open the [Smolensk] pocket. It consists of an infantry division and a tank brigade. It is coming from the direction of Kharkov, and its objective is Romny. Our own forces are insufficient to deal with this additional threat. As a result, SS-Division *"Reich"* will be committed against it. SS-Infantry Regiment *"Der Führer"* will lead. It is to move toward Romny in a forced march, attack the above-named enemy forces in front of the friendly combat-outpost line and destroy them.

The regiment moved out in the early morning. Its commander had already moved ahead to establish contact with the security forces in the area of operations and reconnoiter the new sector. SS-Sturmbannführer Kumm arrived at the positions of a regiment of the 10th Infantry Division in a village. From the church tower he was able to view all of the potential battlefield. A ridge marked the boundary of the infantry division's bridgehead on the far side of the Romny. There was no sign of the enemy.

SS-Sturmbannführer Kumm breathed a sigh of relief when the 1st and 3rd Battalions arrived one after another that afternoon. They crossed the river and assembled for the attack. Attacking from the bridgehead, the two battalions were to take the Sidorovka Heights and the village of the same name. Several assault guns were attached to lend support. The 2nd Battalion, the last battalion to arrive, was still on the other side of the river. It was deployed five kilometers to the northeast for a flanking movement.

THE 1ST BATTALION ON THE DEFENSIVE

"Ivan is coming!" The call was passed from position to position. SS-Sturmbannführer Ehrath had already ordered a heightened state of readiness. At that point, he placed his troops on alert. A little later a dull roaring and rumbling became audible, which turned out to be the sound of approaching tanks.

"There they are, Sepp!" SS-Rottenführer Holzinger shouted to his squad leader.

The first enemy tanks had just emerged from the tangled growth on the nearest rise. They advanced hesitantly, then suddenly picked up speed and rolled towards the regiment's positions in an inverted wedge formation.

"There are at least twenty-five of them," cried SS-Hauptsturmführer Hahn, the new company commander. He was taken aback.

Sepp Lainer counted the tanks and corrected his commander: "There are exactly thirty, Hauptsturmführer!"

The first flashes appeared from the guns of the Russian tanks. Artillery rounds smashed into the bridgehead of the 10th Infantry Division. It was four seconds before the sound of firing was heard. Visible behind the tanks were brown-clad figures. They left the cover of the tanks and ran towards the next group of bushes. The muffled shouts of "Urray!" reached the German troops. The two assault guns—"Derfflinger" and "York"—rolled forward. They approached to within 800 meters of the leading enemy tank, halted and opened fire. Soon the first T-34 was smoking. The friendly attack began. The 1st Battalion left its trenches and positions and ran toward the enemy, whose tanks were now engaged with the assault guns. Two 88s joined the fray.

SS-Rottenführer Holzinger fired his machine gun from the hip as he ran. The approaching enemy soldiers took cover. Farther to the left another brown wave rose up. The 2nd Company took cover as well. When the German machine guns opened up, the wave of Soviet troops was almost upon the company.

SS-Hauptsturmführer Hahn stood up and shouted: "Get up! Move forward!"

SS-Mann Noedl was knocked down by a burst of machine-gun fire. Lainer raised his submachine gun, pointed it at the onrushing Russian soldiers and fired three bursts, emptying the magazine. Quickly he inserted a fresh magazine and, taking advantage of the momentary pause in the firing, ran forward over the crater-filled battlefield. When the Russians resumed firing, Lainer leaped into a crater, where he almost landed on the heads of several Russians. A bayonet flashed. Instinctively he pulled the trigger and turned as he fired. His attacker collapsed and the bayonet missed its target. The others had fallen to the bottom of the crater.

Lainer crawled up to the edge of the crater. He spied his men ten to twenty meters away and sprinted after them. SS-Sturmmann Winter was carrying a Teller mine and SS-Sturmmann Gries an explosive charge. They approached to within sixty meters of the closest Russian tank, which was firing at a target to its right. Russian soldiers appeared from behind the tank and fired at them. Holzinger had dropped to the ground; he fired back with his machine gun and eliminated the threat.

"Attack, I'll give you covering fire!" shouted Lainer.

He crept a few meters to the side so he could keep a check on the rear of the two closest tanks. Winter hauled his Teller mine over to the tank and heaved it under the right track. A Russian came out from behind the tank to kill Winter, but Lainer was fractions of a second quicker. His burst of fire struck the Russian in the chest, knocking him to the ground. Winter ran a few paces to the side and threw himself into a deep crater. The tank rolled forward and the Teller mine exploded with an ear-shattering roar. The explosion raised the nose of the tank off the ground and shattered its tracks. One of the tank's road wheels was dislodged and rolled a dozen meters before falling over. The Russian tank crew scrambled clear, but it was cut down by Holzinger's machine gun.

Still carrying his explosive charge—several hand grenades bound together with wire—Gries approached the second tank. The long barrel of the tank's main gun swung around slowly. Gries jumped onto a fender, scrambled up onto the tank's hull and hammered against the side of the turret. When the hatch cover flipped open, Gries tossed his explosive charge inside. He leapt clear of the tank, ran eight or nine paces and threw himself to the ground.

It was not a second too soon: Seconds later there was a mighty explosion inside the tank. The hatch cover was blown open and a towering column of fire shot into the sky, interspersed with metal and other items. With the two tanks out of action, the Russian infantry attempted to withdraw, but they were cut down by automatic weapons fire. The attempted breakout from the Smolensk pocket had failed. Twenty-eight knocked-out Russian tanks, some of them burning, littered the plain. Severed tracks lay behind some of them like giant saurian footprints. Only two tanks managed to escape destruction through flight.

While the fighting against the tanks was under way, the 2nd Battalion counterattacked across the river. Since it was several kilometers beyond the enemy's field of fire, the battalion was able to take the village of Sidorenkov in a surprise raid. The 1st and 3rd Battalions caught up with their sister battalion during the night of 19–20 September.

On the morning of 20 September it was time for the other divisional infantry regiment, SS-Infantry Regiment *"Deutschland"* to make its contribution. After bitter hand-to-hand fighting, it captured the village of Shuravli and advanced as far as the enemy-held Hill 91.55. SS-Infantry Regiment *"Der Führer"* was then committed to the right of SS-Infantry Regiment *"Deutschland"* in the afternoon and made good progress in the face of weak resistance.

The next morning both regiments attacked Hill 91.55 with assault-gun support. Sepp Lainer's squad took the point position in the company. It advanced quickly, but as it reached the top of the hill it was fired on by three Maxim machine guns.

SS-Hauptsturmführer Hahn summoned Lainer: "Swing out to the right and take out the machine-gun nests."

Lainer and his men crawled off to one side, taking advantage of the cover offered by bushes. In that way they worked their way to within attack range. Following a volley of hand grenades, they stormed the position. Lainer ran toward a Maxim machine gun. Two very tall Russians came to meet him. One reached for his assault rifle. Before he could fire, however, Lainer's burst of fire knocked him back over the machine gun. A hand grenade flew towards the Germans. Gries picked it up and threw it back. The grenade detonated over the soldier who had thrown it. A jagged fragment smacked against Lainer's steel helmet. He picked it up, but the piece of metal was so hot that it burned his fingers.

The first machine gun was eliminated and the second overrun by Winter. The two platoons that had provided covering fire moved up. The 2nd Company linked up with the 1st Company. The 1st Company had advanced farther on the right and was also in contact with the 3rd Company. The entire area of commanding high ground was taken from the enemy.

Patrols discovered enemy forces moving in from the south; the regiment was sent to stop them. The regiment made good progress and reached the village of Sakunovo, where it was met by heavy fire. The advance halted.

At the regimental command post SS-Sturmbannführer Kumm briefed his battalion commanders on the following morning's attack: "The regiment will attack at first light. This time there will be no artillery preparation. The enemy-held line of hills beyond the village is to be taken and held against all counterattacks."

WOUNDED A SECOND TIME

It was not yet light as the 1st Battalion got ready. The individual companies had been briefed. Two assault guns were attached to lend supporting fire. Weapons at the ready, the 2nd Company worked its way along the southern outskirts of the village. Its path led close past the houses. Suddenly, there was a burst of firing from a wooden shed to the right. A German machine gun fired a long burst into the structure. The engagement developed into a series of running fights. The attackers fired at enemy troops they spotted behind huts, woodpiles and hedges.

The crash of gunfire from the two assault guns could be heard from the main street. It was followed shortly by the sound of exploding rounds.

"I don't like the smell of this, Sepp!" declared SS-Sturmmann Kratzert. They had scarcely come under fire so far. "Yesterday we were fired on like crazy from this area. They surely haven't withdrawn yet."

Lainer warned his squad: "Stay alert and don't get caught napping!"

They passed through several gardens, came to a cornfield and advanced along one side. They had just passed the end of the field when they came under fire from behind from cottages and concealed positions.

"Jesus!" roared Kratzert. "We should have seen this coming!"

They threw themselves into cover. The company commander's order was passed from one soldier to another: "Turn around and pull back slowly. The enemy is hiding in the village and the cornfield."

The two assault guns had already turned and had began firing high-explosive rounds into the corn. They cleared two wide lanes. Both battalions then approached the village through which they had just passed.

Lainer's squad was about forty meters from a haystack when hand grenades came flying out. They immediately fired their weapons at the still unseen enemy. Then Lainer felt something strike him hard in the thigh. He examined his leg with his hand and felt blood. He crawled into a depression, where he could roll to one side and tend to the wound. Kratzert crawled over to him, while Holzinger fired short bursts at the Russian soldiers withdrawing from the haystack and at a low wall behind it.

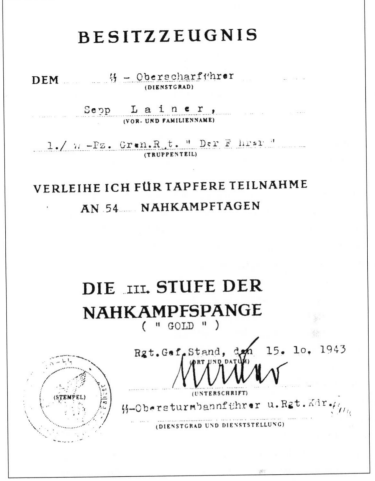

BESITZZEUGNIS

DEM ⅍ – Oberscharführer
(DIENSTGRAD)

Sepp L a i n e r ,
(VOR- UND FAMILIENNAME)

1./ ⅍-Pz. Gren.Rgt. " Der Führer "
(TRUPPENTEIL)

VERLEIHE ICH FÜR TAPFERE TEILNAHME

AN 54 NAHKAMPFTAGEN

DIE III. STUFE DER NAHKAMPFSPANGE
(" GOLD ")

Rgt.Gef.Stand, den 15. 1o. 1943
(ORT UND DATUM)

(UNTERSCHRIFT)

(STEMPEL)

⅍-Obersturmbannführer u.Rgt.Kdr.

(DIENSTGRAD UND DIENSTSTELLUNG)

Award certificate for the Close-Combat Clasp in Gold to "Sepp" Lainer for his participation in fifty-four close-combat engagements.

Kratzert bandaged the squad leader's wounded leg. "It's just a flesh wound," he said reassuringly.

"Keep moving. Don't let the enemy settle down," ordered the battalion commander, who ran past to take over the lead.

"Can you carry on, Sepp?" asked Kratzert.

"Of course. Let's get after them!"

They fought their way into the village. Each house was full of Russians. They had allowed the regiment to walk into a cleverly disguised ambush.

The fight lasted the whole day, and the cost was high. From the west the Russians fired rockets into the village.

Lainer and his men attacked a low building at the far end of the village and were met by rifle fire. Hand grenades exploded.

"We're taking that house. Everyone fire on the run," Lainer called to his men. As he ran, Lainer heard something strike the ground beside him with a dull thud. Instinctively he headed for the nearest cover, but before he reached safety he felt a stabbing pain like before, but his time in the other thigh. He managed to keep up with the others though, and helped clear the house. Afterwards, he lay down on a bench in one of the rooms. Once again it was Kratzert who saw to him.

When evening came, Lainer was taken to the dressing station by a dispatch rider. The medical officer saw to Lainer's two wounds between operations. He dressed the wounds and was filling in a card for the hospital when Lainer asked: "I can still walk, why should I go to the hospital?"

"Because it's better you do that," explained the doctor.

"But I want to stay with my comrades. I'll heal just as well in the rear area here as in the hospital."

"I'll not be responsible if anything goes wrong," the doctor decided. Once Lainer's wounds had been dressed, he was discharged. He made his own way back to the company, where there was another noisy reception.

WOUNDED THREE TIMES IN ONE DAY

After the clearing of the Smolensk pocket the Wehrmacht daily report announced the capture of 665,000 Russian soldiers. 884 enemy tanks and 3,718 guns had been destroyed or captured. The Commander-in-Chief of the Soviet army group, Marshall Budenny, had been relieved of command during the battle. His successor, General M. P. Kirponos, and his Chief of Staff, Lieutenant General Purkayev, were both killed while attempting to break out of the pocket. General Potapov, Commander-in-Chief of the Soviet Fifth Army, was taken prisoner. Five Soviet armies had been destroyed in this huge pocket. In total, the Red Army lost one million soldiers in this one battle of encirclement.

The *"Der Führer"* Regiment alone took 15,000 prisoners and destroyed a large number of tanks and guns. 200 enemy guns were captured. On 24 September SS-Division *"Reich"* marched northwards and, after passing through Chernigov and Gomel, arrived in the Roslavl area. There the division rested. Replacements arrived and were assigned to the units.

The scene of the division's next operation was to be the Vyazma-Briansk area. The powerful Soviet forces in the field there were to be split up, encircled and destroyed to clear the path to Moscow for Army Group Center. SS-Division *"Reich"* had been attached to the XXXX Panzer Corps under General of Armored Troops Stumme. Stumme's orders were to advance into the Yuchnov area, swing north after crossing the Oka and close the pocket around Vyazma at the Smolensk-Moscow highway at Gzhatsk. The division entered the new area of operations without making any enemy contact.

The first snow fell on 6 October. It was clear to everyone that winter had arrived early and that they were unprepared for it. On 9 October the bridge over the Oka near Yuchnov was crossed. Led by the assault guns, SS-Infantry Regiment *"Deutschland"* attacked north in order to cut off any enemy forces that might be trying to cross the division's route of advance to the east and escape the pocket. The enemy was driven back. SS-Hauptsturmführer Günster, commander of the divisional assault-gun battery, was killed in combat with Russian tanks.

On the morning of 10 October the 2nd Battalion of SS-Infantry Regiment *"Der Führer"* became involved in heavy fighting while assaulting the village of Molchanovo. Just when it seemed that the battalion might be pinned down on the open terrain, SS-Obersturmführer Holzer, commander of the 7th Company, rallied his men and stormed the village. They took the village house by house and sent ahead patrols as far as the main road. The regiment made preparations to defend Molchanovo. An attack by several KV-I and KV-II tanks was repulsed by the assault guns.

During the next few days the attack was resumed along and astride the main road. The 3rd Battalion was sent to the 1st Battalion of the 7th Panzer Regiment (of the 10th Panzer Division). On 13 October the battalion rolled to the attack aboard the tanks. The mobile battle group moved through two villages and, by evening, had reached one of the defensive positions ringing Moscow.

Aerial reconnaissance photos showed the position to be laid out to a depth of 2,000 meters. A zigzag antitank ditch followed the course of a stream. Behind this was a barrier of iron obstacles and fishbone trenches, all of which ran at sharp angles to the main trench. The trenches running through the position were all protected by barbed wire. Concrete bunkers and dugouts alternated with tanks dug in up to their turrets. In the intervals were flamethrower bunkers. Behind these positions tank battalions waited in staging areas at the edge of a patch of woods, while artillery observers sat perched in the tops of trees.

The regiment halted on a rise, protected by dense forest growing on both sides of the main road. The division commander arrived at the command post and ordered: "Carry out reconnaissance and make preparations to attack on 14 October."

✠

The attack began at first light. The 2nd and 3rd Battalions moved forward, while the 1st Battalion remained in reserve about 3,000 meters to the rear. Late in the evening it was moved up behind the 3rd Battalion, where a breakthrough seemed most likely.

The attack was made at first light. Leading the way for the 1st Battalion was SS-Unterscharführer Lainer's squad. The German troops fought their way into the first line of trenches. The 2nd Company breached the trench line. Assault detachments of both battalions stormed forward. Lainer and his squad eliminated three positions. The squad leader himself took out one of the dangerous flamethrower bunkers.

The squad then came to a fortified trench line, where heavy fire forced Lainer and his men to take cover. When they tried to dig in with their entrenching tools, they discovered that the ground was frozen hard. As they lay on the ground the cold bit through their totally inadequate summer uniforms. Winter clothing had been promised for weeks, but it had not yet arrived. The majority of the soldiers had nothing warmer than a pullover sweater.

(The winter clothing had already been sent, but was parked on sidings in the Königsberg area. This may have been a planned action by opponents to Hitler among the officer corps, who hoped to end the war without any active participation on their part by allowing the Russian winter to defeat the German Army).

While the cold ate through their clothing, Lainer tried to get his machine gun into the best position. They found a shallow trench and were able to scoop away a section of parapet to create a free field of fire. Three members of Lainer's squad had already been wounded. He was holding this part of the position with only five men. A group of Russians attacked but were driven back. Suddenly a machine gun opened fire from a camouflaged trench position about 200 meters away; they silenced the Maxim. Scanning the terrain through his binoculars, Lainer spotted another machine gun. Situated in a shallow depression in the ground, it was firing on the 3rd Platoon.

"Beitner and Aigner get over here. We have to smoke out that position!"

Together they moved toward the enemy position, crawling through a shallow ditch whose sides were somewhat overgrown. Meter by meter they neared the machine-gun position. The sound of fighting rang out to the left and right. Light artillery, antitank guns and tank cannon fired one after another; the main enemy trench had not yet been reached. Lainer and his men had to leave the ditch when they were almost even with the machine-gun nest. The trench veered away from the enemy position at that point. First to leave cover was Lainer. He saw the machine-gun nest directly to his right, about sixty meters away. He crawled back into the trench.

"We're outside the machine gun's field of fire. We must approach in one rush, toss grenades from thirty meters and take out the gun crew with our first volley of fire."

They screwed the caps off the hand grenade handles and, on signal from Lainer, jumped out of the ditch and ran towards the enemy. When in range they tossed their grenades into the position. The grenades exploded and Lainer jumped in with his submachine gun at the ready. He fired at a shadowy figure as it raised a weapon, knocking it to one side. At the same moment Aigner and Beitner jumped into the position. The enemy had been eliminated. The only German casualty was Beitner, who had been wounded in the arm.

Ten minutes later the men of the 1st Battalion tried again. They gained several dozen meters of ground before enemy fire forced them to take cover again. Holzinger landed in a crater beside Lainer. He swore softly as he moved his machine gun into position.

Holzinger had just fired his second burst when suddenly he reared up and fell backwards. Lainer grabbed hold of Holzinger and dragged him deeper into the hole, while Winter took his place at the machine gun. One look told Lainer that Holzinger was beyond help. A bullet had struck him just below the rim of his helmet, near the bridge of his nose. He was already dead.

"Move over," said Lainer. He slid over and took the gunner's place behind the machine gun. He fired at the muzzle flashes from the Maxims and silenced one of them. The next target was a group of Red Army soldiers moving from one bunker to another. Two long bursts mowed down the enemy troops.

The firefight had been going on for an hour already. Lainer spotted movement and fired. The Russians fired back. SS-Sturmmann Winter, who was serving as loader, suddenly cried out. He stopped feeding the ammunition and, when Lainer looked at him, he saw that he had been badly wounded.

"Reinecke, send me someone," Lainer called to platoon leader SS-Untersturmführer Reinecke. The latter raised his right arm to indicate

SS-Gruppenführer Walter Krüger, the commander of the 2nd SS-Panzer Grenadier Division *"Das Reich,"* presents Lainer with the Knight's Cross.

that he had understood. But before he could send a man forward Reinecke was hit and fell backwards.

"Kölbel, come here!" called Lainer to the runner.

The man was kneeling beside the SS-Untersturmführer, somewhat bewildered. He crawled over to Lainer.

"The Untersturmführer is dead," he said in a toneless voice.

"Load the belt," Lainer said to him.

Mechanically, Kölbel began to work. They got the machine gun working again just in time to help stop a Russian attack. Lainer fired at any Russian who showed himself. A burst of fire came in from the side. As Lainer swung around he saw a muzzle flash. The Ivans were firing from both sides. Lainer felt a blow on his upper arm; within seconds the arm was useless. Blood flowed from the wound.

"You must go back, Sepp," shouted Kölbel as SS-Sturmmann Gries bandaged Lainer's wounded arm.

"I'll carry on," said Lainer through clenched teeth. "The bullet went clean through. The bone is undamaged."

They gave Lainer a sip of coffee and, a few minutes later, he was behind his machine gun again, driving off a group of Russians trying to approach from the left. The platoon's other two machine guns, both of which were still firing, brought the next Russian attack to a standstill. The fighting went on.

Lainer's wounded arm had now started to hurt, but he stayed. Thirty minutes later a stronger force of Russians attacked from the left. Lainer fired into the mass of earth-brown forms. Suddenly, several snipers began shooting at him from the right, attempting to take out the German machine-gun positions. A rifle bullet pierced his left arm above the elbow. Lainer cried out in pain. He knew at once that this wound was more serious. His companions dragged him to cover and Beitner took over the machine gun. They dressed his wounds, but by now Lainer had lost a lot of blood. His vision began to blur.

"We're going to take you back, Sepp," said Beitner.

Lainer tried to protest, but he could only manage an unintelligible croak. Not wanting to take men from the firing line, Lainer waited until the shooting died down and the enemy attack had been repulsed. He then crawled out of the crater towards the rear.

Sepp Lainer recalled for the author:

When I reached our first trench I was safe. Several comrades met me and pulled me down into cover. At first I just lay there fighting for breath. They put fresh dressings on my wounds, as both bandages were blood-soaked. Then they helped me to my feet and took me to a Russian antitank ditch that was about 200 meters behind our main line of resistance.

As I stumbled back, I was fired on by several Russians who had hidden themselves somewhere between our main line of resistance and the antitank ditch. I felt a searing pain in my left side. It was a grazing wound, not too serious. I had been suffering from jaundice for three weeks and should have been hospitalized, but our company commander had kept me at the front as he needed every fighter. However, the illness had weakened me, and together with the first two wounds it almost finished me.

I staggered toward the antitank ditch. I was shot at several more times. Fortunately, I was not hit a fourth time. Crawling the last few meters on all fours, I reached the antitank ditch and took cover simply by allowing myself to slide down into the ditch feet first.

There I was met by four *Hiwis* (Russian volunteers who served with German rear-echelon units). They hastily fashioned a litter on which they carried me to the aid station, which was about 300 meters farther to the rear in a patch of woods. After initial treatment I was taken to the main dressing station. What happened there I do not know, as I had lost consciousness due to loss of blood.

Sepp Lainer received the best care available. The doctor was especially concerned about the second arm wound, which had broken the bone. Even with the excellent care he received, the chances that it would heal smoothly were small. From the main dressing station Lainer was passed on through several hospitals, finally ending up in Konstanz on Lake Constance. The doctors there told him that his career as a frontline soldier was probably over, as he was likely to have little movement in the arm. However Sepp Lainer knew better. Released as a convalescent, he told the head doctor: "I'm going back to my comrades."

IN GERMANY—LAINER IS DECORATED

At Konstanz it seemed as if Lainer's arm wound would never heal. His other wounds had long since healed. Finally, in April 1942, Lainer joined a convalescent company. He had just finished a period of leave and had recovered well in his Tirolean home.

On 15 June 1942, while with this company, Lainer received the long-overdue Infantry Assault Badge in Bronze. It was not until 15 October that he was awarded the Wound Badge in Silver; by then he had returned to his regiment's replacement and training unit.

In November 1942 Lainer was promoted to SS-Oberscharführer and was made a platoon leader in charge of training new recruits. Lainer was given home leave for Christmas 1942. He had maintained contact with his regiment and knew that he must return as soon as he was able. He learned that "Papa" Hausser, having recovered from serious wounds that left him blind in one eye, had been given the job of forming an SS corps, which was later to be named II SS-Panzer Corps.

It was with great pleasure that Lainer learned that Otto Kumm, his regimental commander, had received the Knight's Cross on 16 February 1942. He also learned that the commander of SS-Infantry Regiment *"Deutschland,"* SS-Brigadeführer Bittrich, had taken over command of the division, since redesignated first as SS-Division *"Das Reich"* and then as SS-Panzer Grenadier Division *"Das Reich"* (effective 9 November 1942). Lainer's regiment had also been redesignated as the 4th SS-Panzer Grenadier Regiment *"Der Führer."* SS-Sturmbannführer Harmel had taken over the newly redesignated 3rd SS-Panzer Grenadier Regiment *"Deutschland."*

As the result of a recommendation by Otto Kumm, the division was transferred to Germany on direct orders from Hitler. The surviving members of the division were sent on leave and told to report to Fallingbostel Training Area in the Lüneburg Heath by the end of March 1943.

IN ACTION IN 1943

During the summer and fall of 1942 new recruits and replacements began reaching the 4th SS-Panzer Grenadier Regiment *"Der Führer"*; among them was SS-Oberscharführer Lainer. He received an enthusiastic reception from the few original members of the unit still left. Lainer took over the 1st platoon of the regiment's 2nd Company. His company commander was SS-Obersturmführer Hans Hillig, a brother of Herbert Hillig, his former company commander, who had been killed during the winter of 1941.

In December 1942 the regiment was placed on alert at Rennes in preparation for a move to the Eastern Front. In late January 1943 the unit was sent into action near Kiev in the Bley-Volchansk-Velikiye Burluk area. The 2nd and 3rd Battalions engaged far superior enemy forces, which forced the regiment and the rest of SS-Panzer Grenadier Division *"Das Reich"* to give up the Oskol River line.

The 4th SS-Panzer Grenadier Regiment *"Der Führer"* was withdrawn and sent into the Merefa area, where it was placed under the command of SS-Panzer Grenadier Division *"Leibstandarte SS Adolf Hitler."* In its place SS-Panzer Grenadier Division *"Das Reich"* received a regiment from the *Leibstandarte* to help stabilize the situation east of Kharkov. There was much fighting and the replacements and new recruits who had been trained in France received their baptism of fire. In early February the cross-attachments were ended and the regiment returned to the division, with the exception of the 1st Battalion.

During the night of 13–14 February 1943 the regiment moved into Ryabushino. The next day's objective was Okotskaya, ten kilometers farther south. SS-Untersturmführer Nickmann of the 10th Company led a patrol out on a night reconnaissance. He took fire from Okotskaya and reported the village occupied by the enemy. All available forces took part in next morning's attack.

At the same time, the 1st Battalion, still with the *Leibstandarte*, was involved in heavy fighting. The battalion was attempting to throw the enemy out of the villages of Rakitnoye and Borki Station and break through toward the south between Borki and Vadola in order to relieve Kharkov.

In the ensuing fighting Sepp Lainer distinguished himself once again. On 14 February 1943 he finally received the Iron Cross, First Class, from the commander of Army Detachment Fretter-Pico, to which the *Leibstandarte* was temporarily attached.

On 23 February the 1st Battalion engaged enemy forces in the Voroshilov area south of Pavlograd. The attack began in the early morning.

✠

Lainer's Platoon moved into the lead position. SS-Obersturmführer Hillig ordered Lainer and his platoon to first take the enemy's flanking position, then turn left towards the main body of the company. Lainer warned his men to look out for Russian snipers concealed in trees. Sepp Lainer said of this mission: "The object was to get the attack moving forward as quickly as possible, cross the approaches in several massed dashes and drive the enemy out of their positions."

When the attack signal was given, Lainer's platoon was able to advance in the cover of a heavily overgrown streambank. On the right, the 3rd Company was already in a firefight with enemy troops. Two assault guns rolled forward between the two companies and engaged enemy machine-gun nests. Following the stream, Lainer and his men worked their way forward quickly. Ten minutes after the attack began they were within striking range. Lainer detailed two of his three machine guns to lay down flanking fire and protect his left and right.

When SS-Obersturmführer Hillig fired the designated signal flare, the platoon charged forward with Sepp Lainer in the lead and the company headquarters section behind and to the left. They ran towards the Soviets' right flanking position. Two machine guns opened fire and Lainer and the others took cover. Soon afterward the two guns fell silent and the advance was resumed. There was still fifty meters to go.

Suddenly, the Russians opened fire from two concealed positions. One of the platoon's squads was mown down. Sepp Lainer increased the tempo. Then he was hit in the left thigh and knocked to the ground. The leader of the company headquarters section took cover beside him. He saw the blood flowing from Lainer's thigh wound and watched in fascination as the platoon leader opened a packet dressing and pressed it tightly over the wound. Then he helped Lainer bind the wound.

"I'll send the medic. Stay here!"

Then he was gone, in pursuit of the others who were storming the enemy position.

Five minutes later two medics arrived and evacuated Lainer on a stretcher. An ambulance was waiting behind the woods in which the attack force had assembled. SS-Obersturmführer Hillig appeared as a medical officer was tending to the wound of the SS-Oberscharführer.

VORLÄUFIGES BESITZZEUGNIS

DER FÜHRER
HAT DEM

SS-Oberscharführer L a i n e r ,
Zgfhr.1./SS-Pz.Gr.Rgt."Der Führer"

DAS RITTERKREUZ
DES EISERNEN KREUZES
AM 8.10.1943 VERLIEHEN

HQu OKH, DEN 9. Oktober 1943

OBERKOMMANDO DES HEERES
I.A.

Preliminary award certificate for the Knight's Cross of the Iron Cross to
SS-Oberscharführer Lainer.

"How's it look, doctor?" he asked.

"Clean penetration. It should heal in four weeks."

"Then I can stay with the trains," suggested Lainer.

"Out of the question, Sepp. We want you back here healthy as soon as possible. That means you're going to hospital!"

Following three intermediate stops, Lainer arrived in Kiev military hospital. He followed events at the front from there and learned that "Papa"

Hausser and his SS-Panzer Corps had retaken the city of Kharkov, the city he had evacuated earlier. A short time later he heard the special bulletin: "After days of heavy fighting, units of the Waffen-SS, effectively supported by the Luftwaffe, have recaptured the city of Kharkov in an enveloping attack from north and west."

OPERATIONS LEADING UP TO THE FIGHTING AT KOROTICH

The fighting in the Voroshilov area had been some of the most difficult for Sepp Lainer. However, he had no way of knowing what lay ahead in the middle of the summer. At the end of March Lainer rejoined his battalion. On his return Lainer was transferred to the 1st Company, which had suffered heavy casualties in noncommissioned officers. He became a platoon leader.

His company commander was SS-Obersturmführer Pahnke, a veteran of the Eastern Front and a skilled leader. Pahnke had earlier been the regimental adjutant. He had been instrumental in getting the 1st Battalion back to the regiment after it had been detached to SS-Panzer Grenadier Division *"Leibstandarte SS Adolf Hitler."*

Due to the heavy fighting at Kharkov, the battalion had to be reorganized. Following its reorganization, it consisted of two companies. The battalion's 1st Company was led by SS-Obersturmführer Pahnke; the 2nd Company by SS-Hauptsturmführer Lex. In addition, there was a heavy weapons company under SS-Obersturmführer Rudolph. By this time, the regiment was under the command of SS-Obersturmbannführer Sylvester Stadler. Stadler wrote the following reply to the author's inquiry:

> The men whom I was now to lead had demonstrated courage and willingness to sacrifice, offensive spirit and steadfastness; they possessed a grim determination and had endured deprivation. In a constant cycle of attack and defense, immediate counterattacks and planned offensive operations beyond the Dniepr and into the Zhitomr combat zone, this operation demanded the greatest sacrifices from everyone. For all of us it was a great and bitter period in our lives.

On 6 April SS-Hauptsturmführer Vinzenz Kaiser, a friend of Lainer's from the Steiermark region in Austria and the commander of the regiment's 3rd (Armored) Battalion was awarded the Knight's Cross for his decisive role in the Battle of Kharkov. Sepp Lainer helped his friend celebrate his well-earned decoration. The same day the new regimental commander, Sylvester Stadler, also received the Knight's Cross for his feats during the Battle of Kharkov. It was a great day for the regiment.

Operation "Citadel", one of the largest offensive operations ever launched by the Germans in the Eastern Campaign, began at the beginning of July 1943. By 7 July 1943 SS-Panzer Grenadier Division *"Das Reich"* was involved in the fighting for Prokhorovka station. Both the 2nd and the 3rd Battalions were decisively engaged. Tanks, artillery and rocket launchers supported the 3rd Battalion, which reached the railway embankment and drove out the enemy forces entrenched there.

On 14 July SS-Unterscharführer Simon Grascher, a platoon leader in the 9th Company attacked a well-fortified Russian field position at the Belenichino railway embankment. Grascher, already a recipient of the Wound badge in Gold (five or more wounds), personally took out two bunkers and several machine-gun nests and finally destroyed a T-34 with a hollow charge. He attacked a second T-34 with hand grenades. It had been firing into his company's flank. He tossed the grenades through the open turret hatch. Grascher later took over the company after all the officers had been put out of action. Simon Grascher was killed in the subsequent fighting. Lainer:

> He was my age, came from my same region in Austria and had grown close to all our hearts on account of his modesty. SS-Gruppenführer Krüger sent the mother of this brave soldier his wound badge and the posthumous Knight's Cross awarded him on 14 August.

In the days that followed Operation Citadel, all the battalions of the regiment participated in the forest fighting at Gresnoye. The enemy fell back. SS-Hauptsturmführer Lex, now in command of the 3rd Company, gave pursuit and took a Russian corps headquarters by surprise. The Russian general and his officers were taken prisoner. In recognition of this exploit, Lex was awarded the Knight's Cross on 10 December. (Lex was killed near Shepetovka on 11 March 1944.)

On 12 July Generaloberst Hermann Hoth appeared at the regimental command post and handed SS-Obersturmbannführer Stadler a teletype message from Generalfeldmarschall von Manstein: "Special acknowledgement of the splendid effort by the regiment, its commanding officer and its brave men during the armored fighting east of Kalinin."

The fighting in the Kursk salient ended with the German retreat and the beginning of the Soviet counteroffensive. SS-Gruppenführer Krüger,

commander of SS-Panzer-Grenadier-Division "Das Reich", led the division
into the Mius area where the Red Army had also gone on the offensive.
Early on the morning of 31 July the division launched a surprise attack led
by SS-Obersturmbannführer Stadler.

Once again, Sepp Lainer and his platoon were in the first wave. As
mortar rounds began howling overhead, the German soldiers moved forward toward a hill position. Close-quarters fighting broke out. Sepp Lainer
had to fight off several Russian soldiers. His platoon stormed over the hill
and swarmed into the forward Russian trench, before reaching and overwhelming an enemy command post. SS-Obersturmführer Willi Grieme,
commander of the 4th Company, distinguished himself in this attack. He
led the decisive assault and captured the hill, which was vital to the continuation of the division's attack. Grieme was awarded the Knight's Cross on
17 September 1943.

SS-Panzer Grenadier Division *"Das Reich"* fought with undiminished
bravery on the Mius. Every attempt by the enemy to break through was
halted. On 4 August the 4th SS-Panzer Grenadier Regiment *"Der Führer"*
marched into its new cantonment area at Stalino. There were rumors that
the division was to be relieved and transferred to Italy. But dreams of a
"trip to Italy" vanished with the start of a new Russian offensive.

Powerful Soviet armored forces struck out at the 4th Panzer Division.
The objective of the attack was to force a breakthrough against the 167th
and 33rd Infantry Divisions. The two infantry divisions were unable to
withstand such an overpowering assault, and the Soviets broke through on
a twelve kilometer-wide front.

During the further course of the fighting the Germans had to give up
Belgorod. The Soviets drove from the north towards Kharkov. SS-Panzer
Grenadier Division *"Das Reich"* was hurriedly sent forward to parry the
Soviet thrust. The 4th SS-Panzer Grenadier Regiment *"Der Führer"* occupied a line from Solochev to Bogodukhov. The regiment was augment by
the 2nd SS-Panzer Reconnaissnace Battalion *"Das Reich"* under SS-Sturmbannführer Weidinger.

Its neighbor on the right was the 3rd Panzer Division. There was no
contact to the left. The SS reconnaissance battalion and several companies
from other divisions were fed into the gap. The 4th SS-Panzer Grenadier
Regiment *"Der Führer"* was sent west to straighten out an area of the front,
which it did successfully.

During the night of 9–10 August the regiment was withdrawn from the
front and transferred to Bogodukhov. On 15 August the regiment underwent another frontline reorganization. The commander of the regiment's
1st Company, SS-Hauptsturmführer Hesselmann, became regimental adju-

tant, while SS-Hauptsturmführer Schulze took over the 2nd Battalion. SS-Untersturmführer Joachim Krüger was killed on 14 August and SS-Hauptsturmführer Kämpfe was forced to take command of the 3rd Battalion. Krüger was awarded the Knight's Cross posthumously.

THE KNIGHT'S CROSS FOR SEPP LAINER

When the 4th SS-Panzer Grenadier Regiment *"Der Führer"* reached the northern edge of Korotich, the first enemy tanks with mounted infantry were already attacking. Sylvester Stadler and a few men reached the new position. Lainer's platoon was deployed with its three machine guns and stopped an attack by Soviet infantry. Artillery fire directed by a forward observer smashed the onrushing wave of enemy tanks. One T-34 reached the German trench, but it was put out of action by a direct hit and burned out.

Enemy infantry stormed the positions of the 1st Company. At this point, however, the remaining units arrived and moved into the front. Stadler's orders were: "Counterattack and close the gaps created by enemy penetrations. Reach and hold the railway embankment!"

The regiment worked its way forward as the enemy fire intensified. Fresh waves of Soviet tanks attacked, but these were destroyed by the small number of assault guns and artillery available and also by German infantry firing from close range. The entire Soviet Fifth Guards Army was attacking.

The men under Sepp Lainer neared the enemy position and the railway embankment. Under supporting fire from the artillery, they stormed up the embankment. A Russian appeared in front of Lainer and raised his submachine gun. Lainer shot him down. Another enemy soldier threw a hand grenade. Lainer dropped to the ground a fraction of a second too late and was hit by several splinters. One grazed his arm and two entered his leg, but he carried on. Lainer and his comrades reached the enemy positions at the embankment and silenced them with hand grenades and automatic-weapons fire. The Russians turned to flee but were cut down by machine-gun fire from Lainer's platoon.

"Everyone dig in. Man the enemy dugouts and turn the weapons around. Set up two machine guns in flanking positions, the third at my disposal." Lainer's instructions were brief, precise and fitted the situation. Every available heavy weapon was moved up. Two Maxim machine guns were moved into position. The regiment had to hold there to prevent the enemy from breaking through and outflanking the 4th Panzer Army.

Immediately following the storming of the Russian positions, the 1st Company and the remaining companies of the regiment, reached the railway embankment. The Russians attacked repeatedly and Sepp Lainer was a leading figure in the successful German defense of the position. He remained with his men in spite of his wounds.

During the night he accompanied a pioneer squad into no-man's-land that had been placed under his command. They laid Teller mines and a zigzag line of trip-wires connected to explosive charges. Should the Russians attack by night they would contact the trip-wires strung a few centimeters above the ground and detonate the explosives. They had been back scarcely an hour when the first explosions were heard.

In seconds the weapons were manned and ready. The Russians approached in company strength, thinking they had not been seen. When the leading enemy troops reached the lower end of the embankment, Lainer gave the order to fire. A barrage from three German machine guns and the captured Maxim guns and a flurry of hand grenades almost wiped out the Russian company. The few survivors dropped to the ground and crawled back the way they had come.

During the fighting of the next few days Lainer was a tower of strength. The following morning he and his platoon and the pioneers repulsed another Russian attack, this time in battalion strength. The other two platoons also helped fend off the attack. Immediate counterattacks dealt with any Soviets penetrations.

This was war at its most pitiless; it all came down to "him or me." During the second night an enemy patrol infiltrated the platoon's right flank. Sepp Lainer was on his way to one of the Maxim machine guns when he noticed the enemy. He emptied the entire magazine of his submachine gun at the shadowy figures, knocking them all to the ground.

Before sunrise the next morning the enemy came from the other flank and achieved a break-in against the 3rd Platoon. Lainer led an immediate counterattack which cut off and encircled the enemy force. The Russians were wiped out to the last man. Lainer took part in four actions that night, all fought at close quarters. He escaped with just a scratch on his right arm. He was a fearless trench fighter, armed only with his submachine gun and a 9-mm pistol.

The fighting raged on. The Soviets were trying to force a decision by breaking through the German front. The regiment's losses were crippling. Lainer's platoon had suffered 75% casualties. Hundreds of dead Russians littered the ground in front of its positions. The fifth night saw another Russian penetration. Dense waves of Red Army soldiers approached the embankment and rolled over it like a huge breaker.

SS-Obersturmführer Pahnke committed the reserve platoon. Lainer received reinforcements. Several Russians had hunkered down in a crater in the middle of the railway embankment. Lainer and his platoon headquarters section stormed the position and drove out the Russians. They then drove through the Russian troops preparing to enlarge the breakthrough, turned around behind them and drove them towards the embankment, where they were met by fire from the 2nd Company.

The leader of the platoon headquarters section was hit. Lainer grabbed the machine gun from his hands and ran after the retreating Russians. He dropped to one knee and emptied the entire belt. Then he reached for his submachine gun and fired off three magazines in quick succession, until the barrel was glowing hot. His platoon's two machine guns fired on the Russians withdrawing to the left and right. The attack was over ten minutes after it had begun. The attacking Soviets had suffered very heavy losses. An hour later SS-Obersturmführer Pahnke was able to report to the regiment's commander that the 1st Company had held again.

The sixth morning saw Lainer and his small band of grenadiers facing almost ceaseless counterattacks. He held the regiment's left flank against every Russian breakthrough attempt. The Russians launched a heavy attack on the evening of 25 August with thirty tanks and an entire rifle battalion.

The previous night a dozen mines had been placed in front of the position on Lainer's orders. He was now down to ten grenadiers. Three Russian tanks were disabled when they rolled through the cleverly- positioned mine belt. German artillery engaged the others as they rolled toward the embankment in a widely dispersed formation. Visible behind the tanks were the onrushing Red Army soldiers.

Lainer readied his machine guns. They opened fire from 100 meters. Rows of enemy soldiers were cut down. The rest of the 1st Company on the right opened fire as well. Nevertheless, about forty Russians reached the foot of the embankment. Hand grenades rained down on them. Led by a commissar, several Russian soldiers made it to the crest of the embankment, but were immediately cut down by a burst of machine-gun fire.

Four of Lainer's ten men were wounded in this attack, but the threat of a Soviet breakthrough was averted. Lainer and his men ran after the retreating Russians until enemy fire forced them to turn back.

That evening Sylvester Stadler wrote up the recommendation for the awarding of the Knight's Cross to Sepp Lainer. The decoration was long overdue and his six-day defensive success was simply the icing on the cake. Many other soldiers were awarded for their heroic actions during the intense fighting.

Things would not have turned out as well as they did for the defenders at the railway embankment had not the 1st and 2nd Battalions held the enemy tanks at bay. SS-Hauptsturmführer Kesten, commander of the 6th

Lainer strikes an informal
pose after his award of
the Knight's Cross.

Company of the 2nd SS-Panzer Regiment *"Das Reich,"* earned the Knight's Cross, at the same time. He received the award on 12 November 1943 for the actions of his company during the same fighting. His nine Panzer IVs destroyed twenty-nine Soviet tanks from a group of sixty T-34s and KV-Is. On 10 December SS-Sturmbannführer Christian Tychsen was awarded the Knight's Cross with Oak Leaves for the effective manner in which he had led the 2nd Battalion.

On 16 September 1943 SS-Obersturmbannführer Stadler became the 303rd soldier to receive the Knight's Cross with Oak Leaves. It was in recognition of his accomplishments in a defensive role.

On 8 October Sepp Lainer was awarded the Knight's Cross. On 10 October a radio message was received from the division: "On 8 October 1943 the Führer awarded the Knight's Cross to SS-Oberscharführer Josef Lainer. My special congratulations to the winner and the regiment.— Krüger."

A few days later, on 15 October, SS-Obersturmbannführer Stadler presented Sepp Lainer with the Close Combat Clasp in Gold. At that point Sepp Lainer had participated in close-combat engagements on fifty-four occasions. Earlier, on 15 September, he had been awarded the Wound Badge in Gold, but news of this did not reach him until 15 October. This award, the highest level of the wound badge, was in recognition of his being wounded on 8 July 1941, 23 September 1941, 14 October 1941, 23 February 1943 and 15 August 1943.

On 5 November 1943 the regiment was assembled for a double award ceremony. SS-Obersturmbannführer Stadler received the Knight's Cross with Oak Leaves from SS-Gruppenführer Walter Krüger. He then decorated Sepp Lainer with the Knight's Cross. Stadler and Lainer were photographed together, and the event remains one of Lainer's fondest and most impressive memories.

In January 1944 Lainer was promoted to the rank of SS-Hauptscharführer. At the same time, the division received its last redesignation. It had become the 2nd SS-Panzer Division *"Das Reich."*

ACTION IN THE WEST AND CAPTIVITY
Fighting Withdrawals—Southern France

During the further retreat of the German forces on the Eastern Front Sepp Lainer was constantly in action, which taxed him and his men to the utmost. At Christmas 1943 the 4th SS-Panzer Grenadier Regiment *"Der Führer"* was relieved and sent by train to Stablack Training Area in East Prussia, where the process of reorganizing and re-equipping the regiment began. The reorganization was completed in southern France. The regiment received a new commanding officer, SS-Obersturmbannführer Otto Weidinger, a man who had fought alongside the unit in a number of operations.

Commander of the reformed 1st Battalion was SS-Sturmbannführer Dieckmann, while the 2nd Battalion was led by the veteran SS-Sturmbannführer Schulze. The 3rd (Armored) Battalion remained under the command of SS-Sturmbannführer Kämpfe, a specialist in the use of armored personnel carriers.

The training period in southern France—up to the Allied invasion on 6 June 1944—saw an increase in the activities of *Maquisard* (French Resistance) snipers. Soldiers, railway personnel and, on one occasion, sixteen officer cadets of the Luftwaffe Ground Warfare School were shot to death and their bodies mutilated.

The countermeasures by the German armed forces were carried out ruthlessly. Such actions have been and are considered necessary by armies past and present in order to reduce casualties to snipers firing from ambush. They consider themselves soldiers but claim the right to be treated as civilians when caught.

With the beginning of the invasion, the 2nd SS-Panzer Division *"Das Reich"* was placed on alert. Preparations for departure were completed on 7

June. March orders arrived that afternoon and the motorized elements of the division rolled toward the front. The morning of 8 June found the division moving along National Highway Number 20 in the direction of Limoges. At the head of the division was the 4th SS-Panzer Grenadier Regiment *"Der Führer."* Its leading elements were the motorcycle troops of the 15th Company. They were followed by the 16th, 14th, and 13th Companies, the special-purpose companies of the regiment. Next in line was the 3rd Battalion, with the 1st Battalion bringing up the rear. The 2nd Battalion under SS-Obersturmbannführer Wisliceny was not yet ready to depart.

Limoges was reached on 9 June. The regimental headquarters moved into the Hotel Centra. SS-Sturmbannführer Weidinger took over command of the regiment on 14 June. The same day the unit moved out towards Le Ferriere. There the regiment was placed under the command of the army's 2nd Panzer Division. That same day SS-Standartenführer Stadler took over the 9th SS-Panzer Division *"Hohenstaufen."*

As the regimental elements had not yet been fully assembled, the regiment remained in the assembly area around St. Lo, a city that had been totally destroyed by American bombing. Sepp Lainer instructed his platoon in offensive tactics as well as those employed in close-in fighting. As army-group reserve, the 2nd Panzer Division and the 2nd SS-Panzer Division *"Das Reich"* saw no fighting in the period to 26 June. On 26 June orders were received for the 1st Battalion of the 3rd Panzer Regiment and the 4th SS-Panzer Grenadier Regiment *"Der Führer"* to move to Jurques by night.

Advancing along the road through Villers Bocage, the British 11th Armoured Division had crossed the Odon and, from there, driven deep into the area held by the 12th SS-Panzer Division *"Hitlerjugend."* Its aim was to capture the key terrain known as Hill 112.

The route of march of the 4th SS-Panzer Grenadier Regiment *"Der Führer"* led it through Jurques into the area south of Mons, where it arrived on the morning of 27 June. Also there was the Panzer Demonstration Division under Generalleutnant Fritz Bayerlein. Together with the Panzer Demonstration Division, the 4th SS-Panzer Grenadier Regiment *"Der Führer"* was to close a gap in the front and restore the situation east and northeast of Noyers while establishing contact with the 12th SS-Panzer Division *"Hitlerjugend"* on the right.

The attack outlined above did not take place as envisioned. Instead, the regiment was attached to the 10th SS-Panzer Division *"Frundsberg"* (SS-Brigadeführer Harmel). As part of the II SS-Panzer Corps under SS-Obergruppenführer Bittrich, that division and the other corps division, the 9th SS-Panzer Division *"Hohenstaufen,"* attacked from the area southeast of

Villers-Bocage. They were joined in this effort by the 1st SS-Panzer Division *"Leibstandarte SS Adolf Hitler,"* which was positioned somewhat farther to the east. The German counterattack was supposed to cut off and destroy the enemy forces that had broken through to the south. All three units were at less than full operational strength.

As the attack began the men of the regiment advanced toward the enemy in their armored personnel carriers. But they had not gone far when several hundred enemy guns opened fire.

LAINER'S FINAL OPERATIONS

The reconnaissance troops advancing in front of the 1st Company were blanketed by the enemy artillery fire. Sepp Lainer saw several armored personnel carriers blasted apart by direct hits. Others were disabled and pulled off to the side, while some became bogged down among the hedgerows. Soon afterward a halt was ordered. To continue would have been suicide.

"These damned hedgerows!" cursed Lainer, pointing to the meter-high, tangled rows of bushes and trees that divided the area into irregular squares. "Not even the tanks can get through there!"

A short time later the long-range guns of the British opened fire, hitting the building housing the regiment's command post. Ten members of the regimental staff were killed. SS-Standartenführer Stadler was wounded. SS-Sturmbannführer Müller took command of the division in his place.

An attempt to continue the attack on 30 June likewise failed. A crisis arose when SS-Obersturmbannführer Dieckmann was killed in the afternoon. Things grew even worse that night when the regiment's command post, which was near the front lines, was attacked by four British tanks with mounted infantry. The 16th Company under SS-Obersturmführer Eberstein engaged and knocked out the British tanks from close range.

The attack on 1 July initially made good progress. Sepp Lainer and his platoon advanced to the left of the 3rd Company, which was led by SS-Untersturmführer Klar. The 4th Company advanced too far and was outflanked and surrounded by the British, suffering extremely heavy casualties. SS-Obersturmführer Scholz, commander of the 1st Company, sent Lainer's Platoon to free the surrounded company. The 2nd Company under SS-Obersturmführer Schwarz, also took part in the effort.

Sepp Lainer led his platoon against the enemy. He ordered his machine gunners to give covering fire and dashed into the enemy position, firing his submachine gun. Miraculously, he came away unwounded. Two bullets tore his right sleeve, another cut the left leg of his pants, but "not a single drop of blood flowed."

The remnants of the 3rd Company were freed. SS-Untersturmführer Klar was posted missing and several badly wounded soldiers were captured by the British. On 29 June Generaloberst Dollmann, Commander-in-Chief of the 7th Army, died from a heart attack. SS-Obergruppenführer Paul Hausser took command of the decimated Army. During the afternoon, the regiment was relieved by elements of the 227th Infantry Division and with-drawn from the front. It was sent to the St. Lo area to regroup. SS-Ober-führer Lammerding, the new commander of the 2nd SS-Panzer Division *"Das Reich,"* met with SS-Obergruppenführer Hausser there and described to him the situation of his division.

The 1st Battalion had suffered 60% casualties in the recent fighting. Sepp Lainer's platoon had lost seven killed and ten wounded. In an effort to keep the regiment fit for action, it was sent assault guns, several batter-ies of artillery and the 2nd SS-Panzer Reconnaissance Battalion *"Das Reich."* The 1st Battalion remained close behind the front while the regrouping was under way.

On 10 July the regiment was returned to divisional control. Its 1st and 2nd Battalions were still not fit for combat, however. Lainer's Platoon remained in the rear until 17 July, when the regiment was ordered to relieve the 3rd Battalion of the 3rd SS-Panzer Grenadier Regiment *"Deutsch-land."* The next day the 2nd Battalion of the 4th SS-Panzer Grenadier Regi-ment *"Der Führer"* returned to the division as well.

On 19 July elements of the American 29th Infantry Division pene-trated as far as St. Lô. The next day saw tremendous thunderstorms and hail, which turned the roads into impassable morasses and paralyzed all movement on both sides. News of the attempt on Hitler's life reached the troops on the evening of 20 July. The fact that senior officers and com-manders had taken part in the assassination attempt filled the fighting troops with horror and disgust.

The fighting went on and the 2nd SS-Panzer Division *"Das Reich"* suf-fered heavy losses. The division commander, Lammerding, was wounded. SS-Obersturmbannführer Tychsen assumed command. He was killed dur-ing an attack by enemy armored forces on his command post at Trelly. Orders to withdraw arrived during the night of 28–29 July. A move through enemy-occupied territory to the new sector at Percy with the 6th Parachute Division turned out to be a disaster for the regiment and the whole divi-sion. SS-Sturmbannführer Baum, now commanding the division, reported heavy losses to enemy fighter-bombers. The march route had been speci-fied by the supreme command. Losses among tanks and artillery were heavy.

The division fell back from position to position. On 5 August it arrived in the St. Clement area, east of Mortain. On 6 August the remnants of the division formed up with the 1st SS-Panzer Division *"Leibstandarte SS Adolf Hitler"* for a joint counterattack. The *Leibstandarte* had received new tanks. Under the overall command of the XXXXVII Panzer Corps (General of Armored Troops Freiherr von Funck), it was to carry out Operation Lüttich, whose objective was Avranches.

The days that followed saw SS-Hauptscharführer Lainer and his men in continuous action, struggling against the overpowering enemy and his air armada. The 1st Battalion of the 4th SS-Panzer Grenadier Regiment *"Der Führer"* came under heavy fire among the houses of l'Abbaye Blanche and was forced to leave its armored personnel carriers and attack on foot. The well-entrenched defenders, the American 30th Infantry Division, repulsed the attack. Sepp Lainer succeeded in capturing a section of trench. He ran along it, firing at any American soldier who showed himself. As he ran around a bend in the trench, he found himself facing a group of men who were pointing their weapons at him. One of the Americans said: "Hands up!"

This was the end. Lainer had to surrender if he were to survive. For the first time in the war, Sepp Lainer dropped his weapon and raised his hands. He and several other members of his platoon were sent to the rear.

While under interrogation Lainer gave his name and rank, nothing more. The enemy accepted this and sent him to a temporary camp, where he was reunited with a number of men from his division. Three nights later Lainer escaped in hopes of rejoining his unit. He managed to flee into a patch of woods. The next night he made his way towards the front. He was spotted by a group of *Maquisards*, who chased him for some time. Had they caught him, his life wouldn't have been worth a dime.

Lainer evaded his pursuers by employing a simple trick. Instead of running deeper into the woods, he turned towards the main road and hid in a dense thicket. The next night he entered a house. An old woman gave him bread and some milk. Lainer thanked her and left. For seven nights he made his way ever closer to the front. By the eighth night he was only several hundred meters from his own people. He could even hear the unmistakable sound of MG 42s firing.

Lainer pressed on through a defile that led down to a stream. When he reached the bottom, he suddenly found himself encircled by a dozen enemy troops. He was taken prisoner again. From there Sepp Lainer was sent to England and then to the USA. He remained in captivity there until early 1946. Afterwards, he was shipped back to Europe as a free man. However, his release papers were not accepted by the French. They imprisoned a large number of the former soldiers arriving from the USA and forced them to work in their coal and lead mines.

Four months later Sepp Lainer was sent to Germany and, after a hearing, was again released by the Americans. This was at Babenhausen. Nevertheless, he remained a prisoner. The "custodial powers"—as they called themselves—cared little for the Red Cross convention. They wanted, in the words of one officer, to "break the Krauts of playing at war."

As an "internee," which he had never been, Sepp Lainer was locked up again. There were insufficient rations at the camp and thousands died from outbreaks of disease. Lainer decided that his only hope was to escape again.

"This time," Lainer told the author, "I wasn't about to allow myself to be captured, as it would have meant certain death for me."

In December 1946 he broke out of the camp. Despite an intensive manhunt his flight was a success, and Lainer managed to return to his home.

IMPORTANT DATES IN THE LIFE OF JOSEF "SEPP" LAINER

13 March 1920: Born in Brixen im Thale, Tyrol.

May 1938: Joins the SS-Verfügungstruppe in Vienna as a volunteer. Assigned to the 1st Battalion of *SS-Standarte "Der Führer"* in Vienna with the rank of SS-Mann.

November 1939: Promoted to SS-Sturmmann.

June 1940: Promoted to SS-Rottenführer and assigned as a squad leader.

22 June 1941: Participates in the German invasion of Russia.

8 July 1941: Wounded by shrapnel.

28 July 1941: Awarded the Iron Cross, Second Class.

23 September 1941: Wounded in both thighs by shrapnel.

14 October 1941: Wounded three times in the space of ninety minutes. Evacuated from the front to recuperate.

15 June 1942: Awarded the Infantry Assault badge in Bronze.

15 October 1942: Received the Wound badge in Silver for his previous three incidents of wounds.

1 November 1942: Promoted to SS-Oberscharführer and appointed as a platoon leader.

14 February 1943: Received the Iron Cross, First Class.

23 February 1943: Shot through the left thigh.

15 August 1943: Wounded by grenade shrapnel.

15 September 1943: Received the Wound Badge in Gold for previously suffered wounds.
10 October 1943: Notification of receipt of the Knight's Cross.
15 October 1943: Awarded the Close Combat Clasp in Gold.
1 January 1944: Promoted to SS-Hauptscharführer.

Erich Lepkowski prepared for combat in Normandy.

Erich Lepkowski

CORINTH AND CRETE

Erich Lepkowski was born in Giesen (East Prussia) on 17 September 1919. Of somewhat more than average height, with a strong "vulture's beak" for a nose, he was a wiry and fit youth when he reported to the *Reicharbeistdienst* (Reich Labor Service) in 1936.

When his father died he took over the family farm, even though he would have liked to have stayed longer with the labor service. When the war began Erich Lepkowski was called up by the Luftwaffe signals corps. He said of his activities at that time: "I had to copy routine weather reports and soon felt like a fish out of water."

He had a much different concept of the duties of a soldier. When he heard of the German parachute troops (*Fallschirmjäger*) for the first time, he knew: that was the place for him! Then came the Western Campaign and with it the first large-scale actions by German paratroops in Holland and against the Belgian fortress of Eben Emael.

There was no stopping the young Lepkowski. He volunteered for the paratroopers, and his training was influenced by Operation Sea Lion, the planned invasion of England. Lepkowski passed every course. He was trained as a combat engineer, skier, driver, radio operator and even as a locomotive engineer.

He was assigned to the 2nd Parachute Regiment, which had been formed by Oberst Alfred Sturm following the Western Campaign. His battalion commander was Hauptmann Kroh.

In 1941 the 2nd Parachute Regiment was unexpectedly moved to Bulgaria, beginning on 20 March. Gefreiter Lepkowski was the leader of the radio section of the regiment's 4th Company. When the paratroops arrived at Plovdiv rumors spread that the unit was to participate in a drop on one of the Greek islands.

Generalleutnant Süßmann, commander of the 7th Air Division, was given command of the battle group. He reported to General von Richthofen, the commanding general of the VIII Air Corps. Gefreiter Lep-

187

kowski and his comrades were staged at one of the four airfields designated for use by the parachute units.

The attack was originally to have taken place some time after the beginning of the Balkan Campaign. However, when British forces reached the canal at Corinth in the course of their rapid retreat through Greece and radio intelligence learned that they were planning to sink several ferries to block the canal, the old plan was tossed out the window.

Generaloberst Lohr, commander of the 4th Air Fleet, decided to foil the British plan through a quick airlanding operation. As a result, a typical paratroop operation came about. Battle Group Süßmann's mission: "Open the narrows leading to the Peloponnese, seize the lone bridge over the Corinth Canal and, at the same time, cut off all enemy forces staged in Attica."

The paratroops of the 2nd Parachute Regiment were flown to Larissa from Plovdiv, only 200 kilometers from the objective. The next morning, at about 0500 hours, Erich Lepkowski and his men boarded their aircraft, while his remaining comrades marched towards other Ju 52 transports.

Standing close to Lepkowski, Gefreiter Ehrlich whispered: "There's no going back now. I'm damned scared."

"It's no joy ride, Jupp," replied Lepkowski, squinting as he peered through the window of the Ju 52.

The first aircraft took off. The ground began to slide past Lepkowski's view. The Ju 52 picked up speed, reached takeoff velocity and lifted off. They climbed steeply. The machines leveled off at 2,600 meters, the altitude required to cross the peaks of the Pindus Mountains.

Someone began to sing a song—their song. Erich Lepkowski joined in:

> The sun shines red, get ready!
> Who knows whether it will smile on us tomorrow.
> Start up the engines, forward the throttle!
> Take off, on course! Today we head for the enemy!
> To the machines! To the machines!
> Comrades, there's no going back!
> There are dark clouds far to the east.
> Come along and don't waver! Come along!

For a while Lepkowski thought of the men leading the battle group in gliders. Leutnant Teusen was leading the platoon. They were to make a surprise landing and seize the bridge. Lepkowski saw jagged rocks below them. Then they were across.

"Water, Erich!" called Jupp Ehrlich.

"The Gulf of Corinth. We're there already!"

The aircraft turned onto a southerly course and descended. Soon the waves looked near enough to touch. The practiced voice of the jumpmaster rang out:

"Get ready! Prepare to jump!"

The realization went through Lepkowski like a shock. This was no training jump. This time the enemy was waiting for them. This time there would be firing.

The men stood up and made their way towards the open door in the side of the aircraft.

"Good luck, Erich!" said Jupp Ehrlich.

"Stay close!" Lepkowski reminded his comrades.

There were bright flashes below them. Enemy antiaircraft fire! Grey puffs of smoke appeared among the leading formation. One aircraft was hit. Lepkowski saw parachutes hanging in the sky like white puffs of cotton. Then the horn sounded.

The first men jumped. One after another they left the aircraft. The man in front of Lepkowski looked around. He smiled and pointed in front of him, where the ground was sweeping past 120 meters below. Then he jumped, followed one second later by Lepkowski.

He sailed through the air, felt the jolt as the canopy deployed and floated downwards. Everywhere he looked the sky was filled with parachutes; there were hundreds, and more every minute.

Smoking tracers filled the sky. There was a thunderous explosion as the canal bridge was blown to pieces. As he descended, Lepkowski was caught in the rising wall of fire and smoke.

What had happened? Had Leutnant Teusen failed to reach the bridge?

✠

The transport glider carrying Teusen's platoon had come down close to the bridge. Hans Teusen and the members of his platoon stormed forwards. Bursts of machine-gun fire flitted towards them. A few British soldiers appeared. Bursts of machine-gun fire pinned the enemy down. Hand grenades exploded and bullets whizzed close past Teusen. Then they were upon the closest enemy antiaircraft battery. Resistance by the gun crews was quickly broken.

"On to the next battery. Everyone follow me!" ordered the young Leutnant.

Firing from the hip as they ran, the paratroops overran the next anti-aircraft battery as well.

Above their heads the sky was filled with hundreds of parachutes. A Ju 52 was hit by antiaircraft fire. The aircraft blew apart in a tremendous fireball, spreading wreckage for half a kilometer.

The first group of attackers stormed towards the south end of the bridge. The accompanying pioneers scrambled up the superstructure and ripped out the cables leading to the explosive charges. At that moment, a single British heavy antiaircraft gun began firing from the north end of the bridge. The rounds streaked across the bridge like glowing comets and struck the ground far to the south.

Machine-gun fire forced Teusen behind a boulder. He had just written down a report for transmission when he saw war correspondent Ernst von der Heyden race across the bridge with a small number of paratroops. They were trying to reach the charges on the far side of the bridge and disarm them. The British antiaircraft gun fired again.

Suddenly, there was tremendous explosion on the bridge. Dismayed, Hans Teusen saw how the long, narrow bridge collapsed in the middle and plunged into the canal. The small party of men from his platoon and *Sonderführer* (Civilian Official) von der Heyden, who were on the bridge, were blown to pieces.

✠

Parachutes came down everywhere. The regiment's 6th Company under Hauptmann Schirmer landed in a valley at the south end of the canal and very near the enemy.

"Attack!" shouted Hauptmann Schirmer.

He led his men forward through the British positions in the direction of the canal. It was at that moment that the explosion at the bridge took place and, soon afterward, Schirmer learned what had caused it. A round from the enemy antiaircraft gun had struck the already disarmed demolition charges and caused them to explode.

"Move on to Corinth airfield!" called the Hauptmann. He and his men stormed onwards.

✠

Gefreiter Lepkowski hit the ground hard. He rolled once and released his harness. From the right he heard Ehrlich's voice: "Over here!" The company commander appeared.

"Here, sir!" reported Oberjäger Klose. He was waving as Hauptmann Morawetz, quick in spite of his size, came running. A machine gun began to rattle.

"Damn it! A 13-millimeter twin machine gun!"

Erich Lepkowski saw the strings of tracer. They flew past him far to the right.

"Let's go! Call the platoon, Lepkowski," ordered the company commander. Lepkowski had already warmed up the radio. The 2nd Platoon reported in, but he was unable to raise the other two.

"We're moving forward!"

The paratroops stormed toward the bank of the canal in one rush. A rifle bullet whistled about a centimeter past Lepkowski's helmet. Then they were under the cover of an overgrown streambed. Soon afterward the British position was in front of them. Hauptmann Morawetz fired on the run at the flat steel helmets visible above the parapet. Erich Lepkowski ran as fast as he could. Then they reached the first trench and jumped inside.

A British soldier wheeled about and started to raise his weapon.

"Hands up!" screamed Lepkowski. The Tommy surrendered. Within minutes the Germans had taken the position. Lepkowski got on the radio again, and the 4th Comapny assembled for the assault on Corinth. The advance went quickly. Lepkowski and the others were picked up by a captured British truck.

The sun shone down hot on the paratroops as they reached Corinth airfield. It had already been captured by the 6th Company.

"The enemy is giving ground, Schirmer!" said Oberst Sturm to the Hauptmann, who had taken command of the 2nd Parachute Regiment's 2nd Battalion in place of its wounded commander.

"We need to follow up, sir!"

"Absolutely. After them! Head towards Argos and Nauplia."

Erich Lepkowski and his comrades rolled through the chaos left behind by the British. Completely disorganized, they ran and drove away from the few Germans who had taken them completely by surprise by falling from the sky.

The paratroops stormed on, staying close to the enemy's heels. Argos and Nauplia were seized. The Commander-in-Chief of the Greek Peloponnesian Army was captured. All troops on the peninsula under Greek command lay down their weapons. During this operation Erich Lepkowski saw first hand the value of such surprise blows. The jump from the skies had demoralized the enemy.

On 14 June 1941 Hauptmann Schirmer was awarded the Knight's Cross for this success.

✠

Leutnant Teusen, who had moved from Naupalia in the direction of Tolon on his own initiative, caught and overwhelmed the British rear-guard. Enemy fire rained down from the heights. He assaulted the next rise, but he and his men were halted halfway up and Teusen was wounded. Teusen sent an English-speaking Feldwebel as emissary. The British were told that an entire parachute division was on the way and that Stukas and bombers were going to arrive any minute to pound the British troops into the ground.

The trick worked. 1,400 British troops surrendered to Teusen's platoon. When the 2nd Battalion approached, it encountered the disarmed British heading the other way. Hans Teusen was also decorated with the Knight's Cross for his actions on 14 June. Erich Lepkowski and the men of his radio section received the Iron Cross, Second Class.

✠

The legendary Crete operation began on 20 May 1941. For Erich Lepkowski the ten-day struggle was to be the high point of his career as a soldier.

Lepkowski and his comrades of the 4th Company waited nervously for news as noon approached on 20 May. How had things gone for the first wave of paratroops? What was the situation on the island? Various rumors made the rounds. According to one, the paratroops had been wiped out. Another said that they had landed and had suffered casualties.

Late that morning Oberstleutnant Snowadzki had taken off in a Ju 52 for Maleme airfield to coordinate the arrival of air-landed troops from the 5th Mountain Infantry Division. Snowadzki returned from Crete at about noon. The news he brought was shattering.

Maleme airfield was still in enemy hands. A landing by the mountain troops to relieve the paratroops was impossible. The second wave, which was scheduled to take off at 1300, had to stay on the ground. The bombing attacks to prepare the way for the scheduled landing had taken place. The Stukas dove towards the stony soil of Crete, their sirens wailing. Towering pillars of smoke rose into the air above the island.

But the paratroops, who should have been jumping at that point to take advantage of the shock effect, were not there. They were still waiting, like Gefreiter Lepkowski at Magara airfield. The first radio message from the island was sent by Oberst Heidrich's 3rd Parachute Regiment. Heidrich and his men had taken the hill fort near Khania, but were not strong enough to assault the town itself. He requested that the 2nd Parachute Regiment under Oberst Sturm be sent in, so as to be able to take the town, which was also the enemy's command center. However, the regiment could not be redirected. The pilots of the transport aircraft had no means of navigating to Khania.

The objective of the 2nd Parachute Regiment was the city of Rethimnon and its airfield. The regiment had to do without its 2nd Battalion, which, under the command of Hauptmann Schirmer, had been attached to the eastern group (Heraklion).

First to take off was Kroh's group, consisting of the 1st Battalion of the 2nd Parachute Regiment; the 2nd Company of the 7th Parachute Machine Gun Battalion; a platoon each from the 2nd Company of the 2nd Parachute Machine Gun Battalion; and the 13th and 14th Companies of the 2nd Parachute Regiment, the regiment's heavy companies. The mission of Battle Group Kroh: "Jump on both sides of the airfield, capture the runway and secure same for the landing of reinforcements."

At 1300 Erich Lepkowski marched to his Ju 52. This would be his second combat jump. Once again Lepkowski had been seized by a feeling of excitement that would not let go.

An hour earlier Hauptmann Morawetz had told them: "We're leading the way, men! We'll be jumping with the battalion headquarters staff, the first company to go in."

Soon they were in the air again. The aircraft were bathed in brilliant sunlight. Clouds of dust stirred up by the propellers of the first transports delayed the departure of the following companies but, squatting in the aircraft staring at the neck of the man in front of him, Lepkowski was unaware of this.

The target area appeared below them. The Bosch horn sounded and they jumped. Immediately after leaving the aircraft Lepkowski could hear the sound of exploding antiaircraft rounds. He saw the smoke trails left by machine gun bullets and saw figures suddenly go limp and hang lifeless in their chutes. The ground came up quickly. At that point Lepkowski could see the airfield, at most a kilometer to the west. The defensive fire from the ground grew even heavier. He heard a ripping sound as bullets tore through his parachute. Hauptmann Morawetz and his adjutant, who had jumped just before him, swung towards the ground. The adjutant swung lifelessly beneath his parachute. Then he struck the ground, rolled and released his harness. Lepkowski ran five paces and took cover behind a boulder. Nearby was a paratrooper with a broken ankle. The man moaned. Another paratrooper was tending to his injury.

The Gefreiter heard Feldwebel Brenninger call to him from behind. Then Keller let out a piercing cry. Lepkowski crawled over to his friend. He looked into the white face; Keller's eyes were fixed and staring. He was dead. Two bullets had ripped through his chest.

Samkohl crawled nearer. Feldwebel Brenninger also reached the boulder. Paratroops were still falling from the sky, and the British defenders continued to fire. Cries rang out as men were wounded. Lepkowski felt as if a giant fist were pressing on his chest; breathing was difficult.

"I'm taking command!" shouted the Feldwebel. Then again: "Everyone follow the orders of Feldwebel Brenninger! We're going to attack the airfield!"

The paratroops got up and ran perhaps a dozen meters before being forced to take cover by the massed fire from the Australian troops defending there. More paratroops joined the small group, but there were still only forty men under Feldwebel Brenninger's command.

"Get up! Forward!"

Once again Gefreiter Lepkowski got up and began to run. He covered perhaps fifty meters before the enemy fire once again forced him to take cover. For ten seconds he lay on the ground, his pulse pounding. He felt the heat emanating from the rock. Then he saw the Feldwebel jump up; he again stormed forward. A machine gun that had previously been silent then began to fire. Erich Lepkowski saw the glimmering tracer and was about to dodge out of the way when he was hit. A heavy blow against his left leg knocked him to the ground. Cautiously he put weight on the leg; to his surprise, it held.

Cries for medics sounded from the left and right. Then another voice said: "Hands up!" Lepkowski saw flat steel helmets as the Australian soldiers appeared. Two men ran up to him and held their submachine guns under his nose. One man motioned for him to stand up. Lepkowski shrugged his shoulders and pointed to his leg. The two Australians grabbed hold of him and took him to the vineyard heights. A medic who had been tending to the wounded Feldwebel Brenninger came over to them.

"Help the Feldwebel first," said Lepkowski.

"Sorry," said the medic sympathetically, "he's already dead."

The Australian looked at Lepkowski's leg. "There's a bullet in there," he said in broken German. "We'll cut the thing out and you can take it with you into captivity as a memento."

"It's a long way from being decided who takes whom along," replied Lepkowski bitterly.

"You mean that your people will try and get you out of here?" asked the medic, who, as it later turned out, had studied medicine in Germany for a year.

"You can count on it!" nodded the Gefreiter.

"You buggers!" replied the Australian, grudging admiration reflected in his voice. "You pull off the damnedest tricks! But you won't succeed in tossing us into the brook here!"

"Wait and see, wait and see!" murmured Lepkowski.

What had happened? What had awaited the other companies on the ground? The 4th Company, which had come down precisely in the target area, had lost all its officers except Hauptmann Morawetz. The following 3rd Company was dropped about seven kilometers east of its target area. The paratroops landed in a rocky area west of Hill 217 and there were many injuries.

The 1st Company jumped near the 4th Company in the vicinity of the airfield. When the two companies tried to push through to the airfield they were met by heavy defensive fire and were badly battered even before the 1st Company had picked up the airdropped canisters containing its weapons. Nevertheless, the decimated companies continued to attack. They knew how important it was to have an airfield in their hands for the arrival of the mountain infantry.

The paratroops were halted in front of the vineyard hill where Gefreiter Lepkowski had been wounded, however. The two companies were still 600 meters from their objective. The headquarters staff and Major Kroh had come down with the 3rd Company. He immediately assembled the 3rd Company under Oberleutnant von Roon and the 2nd Company of the 7th Parachute Machine Gun Battalion, which had landed in and around an oil refinery. The Major also set out with his group towards the airfield.

It was about 1750 hours when this small battle group reached the road, 400 meters east of the vineyard hill. The heat made the going difficult for the paratroops, but Oberleutnant von Roon drove them on. Whenever a man faltered, it was he who shouldered his weapon and set an example for the others to follow. The Oberleutnant was determined to reach the day's objective, and the day's objective was Rethimnon airfield.

Finally the paratroops were on the north slope of the vineyard hill. "All right men, up the hill!"

The men shouted as they charged up the hill. Every bush and rock provided welcome cover and, finally, the paratroops reached the crest and dug in. They had succeeded where elements of 1st and 4th Companies of the 2nd Parachute Regiment, with the 7th Parachute Machine Gun Battalion's 2nd Company, had failed.

Ninety minutes later every paratrooper in this sector launched another attack. The way was led by Oberleutnant von Roon. He was first to reach the well-fortified enemy positions. A brief, bitter struggle began. The Australians were driven back.

"The Germans fought like Vikings," John Hall wrote in his book *The Battle for Crete.*

The surviving Australians fled in the direction of Rethimnon and, by 1900 hours, the entire vineyard hill was in German hands. The freed prisoners, among them Gefreiter Lepkowski, were greeted enthusiastically by their liberators.

✠

"It's about time!" said Lepkowski as he was ringed by his comrades of the 4th Company.

"You know, Erich, miracles take a little longer," remarked Gefreiter Samkohl with a grin.

"Who was up here, Lepkowski?" asked Oberleutnant von Roon.

"Elements of the 19th Australian Brigade under Lieutenant Colonel Campbell, sir."

"How were they? Their morale, I mean."

"I think, they were completely fed up!"

Erich Lepkowski was checked out by a German medic. When it was recommended he be taken to a dressing station in the rear, he categorically refused.

Lepkowski said to the German medic: "I would like to see your medical colleague from the other side again. I'd like to know what kind of face he's making now."

Hearing this, Oberleutnant von Roon relented: "Very well, Lepkowski," he said, "carry on if you're able."

✠

When darkness had fallen, the Germans advanced on the airfield. They began taking fire even before they reached the airfield perimeter.

The darkness provided adequate cover, however. Crawling and creeping and, finally, in one fast dash, they reached an enemy dugout.

Lepkowski, Samkohl and Willrich tossed hand grenades inside. Half a minute later the occupants came out with hands in the air. Most were wounded and all were unarmed. Major Kroh arrived and inspected the captured enemy machine gun.

"Turn the machine gun around immediately!" he ordered.

They fired on the visible muzzle flashes and silenced three more machine guns. The paratroops then stormed the airfield, while Lepkowski and several other wounded men provided flanking covering fire. The attack lost its impetus in the center of the airfield when Australian troops opened up on everything in sight from their positions among the hills at the south end.

"Dig in!" ordered Oberleutnant von Roon.

Major Kroh assembled his battle group. When the counting was over it turned out that a total of 400 men had been put out of action: Killed, wounded or missing. It was a shattering realization. But how had things gone for the second battle group and the regiment's commanding officer?

✠

Battle Group Wiedemann—the 3rd Battalion of the 2nd Parachute Regiment with the attached 1st Company of the 7th Parachute Machine Gun Battalion, the 2nd Company of the 7th Parachute Artillery Battalion, and the 2nd Company of the 7th Parachute Flak Battalion—did not take off from Megara airfield until 1400 hours.

The group came under heavy fire while in the air over the island. The enemy was now alerted and a concentration of defensive firepower awaited all further landings. At 1610 hours the Bosch horns sounded in the Ju 52s. By 1630 hours all the paratroops of Battle Group Wiedemann had jumped; they came down on either side of the bridge at Platanias. Not all the weapons containers could be recovered in the difficult terrain of the drop zone, however. Some ammunition containers had been blown up in mid-air by enemy ground fire.

Three Ju 52s badly damaged by antiaircraft fire came down on the island and made more or less successful forced landings. As soon as the units had assembled, Hauptmann Wiedemann led the 9th Company, reinforced by elements of the 11th Company and antitank and antiaircraft squads, towards Rethimnon.

The battle group managed to break through the Greek defensive positions and advance as far as the eastern limits of the city. There, however, it was pinned down by heavy defensive fire from the city itself. Artillery fire poured down on the paratroops from the flanking British positions on the southern hills, which commanded the area to the coast. The enemy launched a powerful counterattack at about 1800 hours. The battle group held out for an hour, but then Hauptmann Wiedemann was forced to give the order to pull back. By about 2000 hours the Germans had reached their original line of departure and formed a hedgehog position around the village of Peribolia. The British attacked after night had fallen but were repulsed.

Battle Group Schulz consisted of the regimental headquarters, the signals platoon, the headquarters of the 7th Parachute Machine Gun Battalion, the 2nd Company of the 2nd Parachute Regiment, and a platoon each from the 13th and 14th Companies of the 2nd Parachute Regiment. Its mission was to land west of Rethimnon airfield, clear the area and then stand by as the regimental reserve. Oberst Alfred Sturm, at 52 the oldest soldier in the paratrooper force, intended to commit this reserve at critical points himself.

But events were to turn out differently, much differently! The battle group took off from Tanagra airfield at about 1300 hours. As the leading aircraft approached the Rethimnon area it came under extremely heavy antiaircraft fire. A Ju 52 carrying men of the 13th Company crashed in flames. The remaining paratroops jumped around 1550 hours over the intended drop zone, just west of Rethimnon airfield, although the jump by the 2nd Company was apparently delayed by antiaircraft fire.

It was late when Major Schulz assembled the majority of his headquarters and the rest of his men. At about 2230 hours he reached the spot chosen for the regimental command post. There he found the regimental adjutant and the headquarters section of the 1st Company. The latter had become dispersed from the main body of the company. The adjutant reported that the headquarters had been dropped in the wrong place and had become separated. As it turned out the next day, the regimental signals platoon had come down eight kilometers too far to the east and had to find its way to the 1st Battalion.

In addition, part of the regimental headquarters had parachuted into the middle of enemy-occupied territory, suffering heavy casualties before the troops reached the ground. Oberst Sturm was missing and the worst was feared. It was later learned that he and ten men had been dropped far from the drop zone and, once on the ground, they were isolated. Sturm tried to make his way to the main force and fought throughout the day and coming night against groups of enemy troops he encountered. By the evening of the second day he and his surviving men had run out of ammunition following a firefight lasting several hours. Sturm was forced to surrender. (Oberst Sturm was freed by German forces after ten days in captivity.)

Major Schulz took over command of the regiment. He led his small battle group westwards and, during the night of 20–21 May, joined up with Battle Group Wiedemann, which was fighting at the bridge at Platanias.

✠

How had the situation developed with Battle Group Kroh?

"We're forming an assault detachment, men!" said Oberleutnant Rosenberg on his return from a headquarters briefing. "The entire 4th Company is going!" All that was left of the 4th prepared to move out.

"You should stay here, Lepkowski," said Oberleutnant Rosenberg, pointing to the Gefreiter's bandaged leg.

"It doesn't bother me, sir," countered Lepkowski.

"Very well then, you can go along! But don't expect us to wait for you!"

Ducking low, the paratroops crept through the shadows of an olive grove. Occasionally they heard the rattle of a machine gun or the cough of a mortar. The Australians, part of the 19th Brigade under Lieutenant Colonel Campbell, had defended well. It was obvious that they were not going to let themselves be dislodged as easily as the Greek units and the British at Corinth Canal.

"Watch out! Shadows ahead!"

Unteroffizier Beckmann had scarcely hissed his warning when an illumination flare shot into the air above the Germans. For one or two seconds the men froze. Suddenly, a machine gun began to fire.

"Take cover!"

The paratroops dropped to the ground, which was just as well, as a hail of gunfire was fired in their direction. The crash of fast-firing guns sounded between the bursts of machine-gun fire. Rounds hissed through the night leaving glowing trails; mortars coughed.

Steel fell all around Lepkowski. A mortar round struck the ground three meters away, but the hail of fragments passed over him. For five minutes they were showered with glowing steel, then there was a short pause in the firing.

"Crawl forward! We'll assemble up ahead there at the brook."

The order was passed from man to man. Erich Lepkowski crawled along after Samkohl. Occasionally there was a rustling sound. Stones rolled down the slope. The Australian machine guns opened up again. Erich Lepkowski felt a growing pain in his wounded leg. He cursed under his breath. Just don't fall behind now! He crawled on and laid down covering fire from an intermediate position, allowing the leading squad to rush across the stream bed.

The first squad reached the far side and opened fire, allowing the others to follow. They raced across the last thirty meters of open terrain. Lepkowski was halfway across the field when two illumination flares lit the night. the enemy machine guns began laying down simultaneous heavy fire. Five men were hit and fell to the ground. Erich Lepkowski ran for his life. A burst of fire was directed at him from the left. He saw the flitting glow of the tracers.

Only three meters to go! The Gefreiter dove headfirst over the edge of the bank. "Roll!" he told himself, "roll!"

Lepkowski landed on the stony streambed with a crash. Stunned, he lay there for a moment. Then he turned around and began searching for his submachine gun, which had fallen when he jumped. As he reached out his hands for his weapon all Hell was breaking loose in a semicircle around the paratroops. Rifles and machine guns fired, hand grenades exploded and the Australians pressed in from three sides.

"They've lured us into a trap!" cried Oberleutnant Rosenberg. "Fall back in stages. 3rd Squad first . . ."

The Australians were pressing ever closer to the Germans. The paratroops fired everything they had. Many of the attackers fell, but there were more and more of them—and then they were in the streambed.

Oberleutnant Rosenberg and a few men managed to pull back, but fifty-five men were cut off, among them Erich Lepkowski. Soon the ammunition was gone and the paratroops were forced to surrender. For a second time Erich Lepkowski was taken prisoner by the Australians, this time with fifty-four fellow soldiers.

"What happened, Rosenberg?" asked Major Kroh. The Oberleutnant had come running back, out of breath. He only had a handful of men with him.

"The Australians have captured the bulk of the company, sir. We ran into an ambush at the stream."

The Major thought for a minute. Then he raised his head.

"I need thirty men! Roon, pick the thirty paratroops. In five minutes we're going to counterattack and free our comrades!"

Major Hans Kroh had realized that only a lightning counterstroke could snatch his men back from the Australians. The small force moved out soon afterwards. They reached the streambed and ascertained it was occupied by an enemy machine-gun outpost. Noiselessly the paratroops crept forward and overpowered the soldiers manning the outpost. They then moved along the streambed to the Australian positions. The enemy were apparently convinced that the Germans had had enough for this night. The Australians appeared unconcerned as they chattered away in a loose circle around the prisoners. Only a few men were standing guard.

"We'll break through, free our men and get out as quickly as possible!" whispered the Major. The word was passed from man to man. The paratroops fell on the unsuspecting Australians, shouting loudly. Their attack was violent and surprise was complete. The Australians took cover. Soon Major Kroh and his men reached the prisoners.

Erich Lepkowski had watched the attack. He immediately dropped to the ground and crawled to one side where the Australians had piled the German weapons. He reached for a submachine gun and opened fire. His companions realized what was happening and likewise armed themselves. Together with Major Kroh and his men they put the Australians to flight.

"Everyone here? Then let's go back . . . go, go!" shouted the Major. The paratroops fired as they withdrew and reached the safety of the dry streambed. Back at the main body they were greeted by congratulatory shouts.

"Now then, Lepkowski," observed Oberleutnant Schindler, who had assembled a company from the remains of the 1st and 4th Companies, "you've been freed a second time."

"It's also happened to me for the last time, sir," promised Lepkowski.

"We hope so!" replied Schindler with a smile.

The paratroops of Battle Group Kroh took up positions in the defensive zone at the refinery. During the early morning hours of 22 May the Australian 1st Battalion began laying down preparatory fire.

"They'll attack soon, Erich," observed Oberjäger Beckmann.

"Looks that way," confirmed the Gefreiter. "But we're in a good position here. Just let them come."

"If they have tanks then it's all over for us," croaked Samkohl.

The sun rose quickly. It was going to be another very hot day. At that point the Australians attacked.

"*Achtung*, tanks!"

Enemy infantry appeared ten seconds after Samkohl sighted the two tanks of the 7th Tank Regiment. Widely dispersed, they advanced behind the two armored giants.

"Let them approach to within 100 meters!" shouted Oberleutnant Schindler. Get the captured gun ready!" ordered the Major. The tanks rolled closer, all the while firing on the German machine-gun positions.

Leutnant Lepkowski during the winter fighting on the Mius River.

Then the captured antiaircraft gun opened fire. After three rounds the first tank ground to a halt. The fourth round caused it to explode in flames. The gun commander, Oberfeldwebel Stache, shouted to his gunner: "Take aim at the next one!"

Moments later the second tank was on fire and the crew bailed out. The infantry—two Australian companies and a battalion of the 4th Greek Brigade—stormed on. They passed the two smoldering wrecks and ran into fire from the German machine guns. The machine gunners halted the Australians a hand-grenade's throw from the German positions.

Suddenly, the hammering of weapons died away and the only sound to be heard on the battlefield was the calls for help from the wounded lying in the blazing sun. Lepkowski and a few others tried to recover several wounded from a nearby foxhole but came under fire.

"Damned idiots!" cursed Samkohl. "It's their people we're trying to save."

"They couldn't imagine that," interjected Lepkowski. "Especially since we're always made out as criminals to them."

They lay under the hot sun. The uniforms stuck to their bodies; their tongues lay thick on the roofs of their mouths. Finally, there was some tea, and the paratroops drank it by the cupful.

Unteroffizier Beckmann was the first to see the emissary with the white flag being waved. Beckmann shouted for the Oberleutnant. Schindler came running.

"What is it, Beckmann?"

"There, sir! A white flag!"

Two Australians came across the open terrain. They were waving a handkerchief on a stick back and forth.

"Lenters, go fetch Major Kroh!" Oberleutnant Schindler spoke with the two emissaries until Major Kroh arrived.

"Sir, our commander requests a two-hour cease-fire to recover the wounded." Hans Kroh thought for a moment. "We agree to the cease-fire, gentlemen!"

During the next two hours German medics helped tend to wounded Australians. On the other hand, Australian medical teams found seventy German paratroops in an evacuated sector who had been wounded during the fighting and looked after them. The harsh and pitiless battle for Crete held its breath for a short while.

At 1400 Major Kroh ordered Oberleutnant Rosenberg to go to the British sector commander and demand his surrender. The enemy rejected the proposal. This was not unforeseen, but the commander of the parachute troops did not want to leave this possibility of avoiding further bloodshed untried.

The enemy artillery began firing again at 1400 hours. German antitank and antiaircraft guns fired back. An Australian mortar that had been found on the beach complete with ammunition was manned and employed against the enemy artillery with success. Throughout the day enemy snipers fired at the Germans from trees and other hiding places on Hill 254 southwest of the oil refinery. Battle Group Kroh held its positions.

✠

The 22nd of May was also a day of heavy fighting for Battle Group Wiedemann. Fortunately, six Ju 52s had arrived before noon and dropped ammunition and supplies. Stukas arrived on the scene just as enemy troops were forming up for an attack in this sector. German ground forces used visual signals and smoke to designate the targets for the dive-bombers. With arrows laid out on the ground showing them the way, the Stukas bombed and machine-gunned the assembled enemy forces. In spite of this setback, the enemy launched an attack against the Chapel Heights.

The 2nd Parachute Regiment's 11th Company, which was on the high ground, held fast.

An hour later an enemy force in battalion strength attacked towards Peribolia from the south and southeast. The fighting raged until precisely 1842 hours, when it ended in a bloody rebuff for the attackers. But the Australians were tough fighters. Twenty minutes later they were back. This time they employed several diversions in an effort to reach their objective.

For example they fired off German signal flares, which caused some confusion as dusk arrived. No one knew where friend and foe stood. It was at that point that the Australians broke into the German positions. The paratroops were forced to pull back to Peribolia and then even as far as the road which ran through the northern part of the village along the coast to the northeast. The paratroops dug in there and repeatedly struck out towards the south. The Australians were driven back in house-to-house fighting. Meter by meter the territory which had just been won by the hard-fighting enemy was taken back.

By 2140 hours the last enemy troops had been driven from Peribolia. During the night the German forces regained their entire former main line of resistance. However, on the Chapel Heights, where the 9th Company was defending, the situation became critical. The company lay under heavy artillery fire from east and west for hours. Casualties began to mount. The British then attacked under cover of the barrage.

They worked their way up the slope to within striking range of the 9th Company. As the front around Peribolia was being pulled back, they attacked the isolated position. The company carried out a fighting withdrawal from its outer bastion towards the cemetery, where it established a hedgehog position. The British then attacked the cemetery. The paratroops suffered casualties in a hand-grenade duel at the walls of the cemetery.

In this desperate situation Leutnant Kühl gathered a handful of his men together and launched a counterattack. The determined officer and his small force of paratroops succeeded, wiping out the enemy groups which had broken into the German positions. The counterattack was of such violence that the British scattered as if struck by a hurricane. The cemetery heights had been saved.

✠

The paratroops near Rethimnon were fighting an almost hopeless battle. But they had to hold on, because their steadfastness was tying down powerful enemy forces and thus preventing them from intervening at other points, especially near Maleme, where the airfield was finally in German hands and the first of General Ringel's mountain infantry had landed.

On the evening of 22 May Oberleutnant Rosenberg came to the positions manned by Lepkowski and his radio section.

"Men, I need twenty volunteers!"

"Another combat patrol, sir?"

Rosenberg nodded. Lepkowski joined the group of volunteers.

"Lepkowski, stay in constant contact with the battle group so that Major Kroh always knows what's going on."

That night they moved forward to the low hill over which the enemy had attacked that morning. They crept up the hill to the crest and suddenly found themselves face to face with an Australian patrol.

"Open fire!"

Machine guns began to rattle. Lepkowski saw a towering Australian spring towards the Oberleutnant. He loosed off a burst from his submachine gun and the enemy soldier dropped to the ground.

"Up the hill after them!"

The paratroops ran forward and came under fire. A hand grenade exploded almost at Lepkowski's feet. He felt a blow on his belt buckle, but kept running and blasted a way clear for himself and the others. Then all was silent on the hill. The relatively weak force of Australians holding it had been scattered.

"Keep moving! Lepkowski, report our location to the Major!" Erich Lepkowski sent the message while the others passed by to his left and right.

Lepkowski tried to hurry his men: "Let's go, let's go! Get ready!"

Samkohl had just heaved the heavy radio set onto his back when a group of Australians charged towards them from the right. Lepkowski and the two others dropped to the ground and crawled into a ravine. There they were able to hold out for five minutes. They fired wildly, but they were surrounded by a dozen Australians.

"Hands up!"

Erich Lepkowski had been captured for a third time. Lepkowski and his companions were taken to the rear, which placed them in danger of being hit by bullets from withdrawing German paratroops. In the Australian trench position Lepkowski again encountered the medic who had studied in Germany. The Australian greeted him with a grin:

"There you are again, old boy!"

"But not for long. It's just about over for you here on the island," Lepkowski said. He was bluffing, unaware of how the other landings were going. The medic became contemplative.

"You're a damned tough bunch," he said with grudging admiration. "You probably don't know what it means to give up"

"Give up? What's that?" asked Lepkowski. Both men grinned.

"Here, have a drink." Lepkowski drank the strong tea and shivered. "Taste all right?"

"Like rat poison!" observed the Gefreiter. The Germans were taken somewhat farther into the rear and led into an underground shelter.

"What's your unit? What is your commanding officer's name? How strong are you?" The questions were showered down on Lepkowski. He looked fixedly at the powerfully built Australian.

"I am Gefreiter Lepkowski," he answered. "I can tell you no more."

"We'll send you to Hell," grunted the Australian. "You're as good as finished."

"When it's over you'll learn everything you want to know."

"Get them out of here!" snapped the Captain furiously. Two-hundred meters to the rear the captives were penned up in a square which had been formed out of trucks.

Two hours later, while their guard snored peacefully, Lepkowski crawled over and reached for the submachine gun lying at the Australian's side. Then he crept back to the others.

"All ready?"

"Affirmative, Erich!" replied Willrich.

"Let's go! But keep low until we're out of the camp."

They crawled away until they reached some bushes, where they were able to stand up and run. A half-hour later the paratroops were challenged in German. They identified themselves. Erich Lepkowski had survived captivity and made his way back to his unit for a third time.

✠

In the days that followed, Erich Lepkowski took part in attacks from the villages of Kimari and Prinos. He distinguished himself on several occasions, and Major Kroh, who was to notice this determined and daring paratrooper several times, earmarked him for promotion. Completely on their own for ten days, the two battle groups near Rethimnon had nonetheless held out. On 30 May at 0600 hours they launched the final attack on the oil refinery. Erich Lepkowski and his radio team advanced toward a bend in the road, where they met German motorcycles. Sitting on the machines were soldiers in field-gray: mountain troops of the 55th Mountain Motorcycle Battalion of the 5th Mountain Division.

A few hours earlier the mountain troops had taken 1,200 Australians prisoner in the area of the oil refinery. The Australians had surrendered, convinced that Crete was in German hands. Erich Lepkowski shook the hands of the motorcycle troops vigorously.

"I'm happy that you're finally here," he said over and over again.

The Battle of Crete was over. It had been decided at other places on the island, but Battle Group Kroh had played an important role. All of Battle Group Kroh numbered nine officers and 448 men. There were also 34 wounded at the main dressing station.

The 1,380 German soldiers in the Rethimnon area had faced 6,730 Allied soldiers. Erich Lepkowski was awarded the Iron Cross, First Class for bravery in the face of the enemy and promoted to Oberjäger. Soon afterwards he had to enter hospital in Athens for treatment of jaundice. He subsequently traveled to Tangermünde, where he rejoined his regiment. There the unit was to be brought back up to strength for a new mission. But there were to be no more parachute jumps into combat.

On 19 July 1940, the day he reviewed the Knight's Cross recipients from the Crete operation, Adolf Hitler said: "Crete has proved that the days of the parachute troops are over! The parachute arm is a weapon of surprise; the surprise factor has by now been exhausted."

A few months later the parachute troops would be sent into action in Russia in penny packets. From then on they bled on the Eastern Front: On the Neva, at Petrushino, on the Mius and in the swampy Hell of the Volkhov.

OBERJÄGER LEPKOWSKI ON THE MIUS

The most vigorous opposition to further air landing operations came from the German Air Ministry, which had been dismayed at the high loss rate suffered by the transport units. But there were other voices speaking against airborne operations. Overly cautious advisors at Führer Headquarters at Rastenburg convinced Hitler that landing troops from the air always entailed great risk.

The airlifting of the 2nd Battalion into the bridgehead at Petrushino marked the beginning of a process that was to see the parachute units dispersed and used in roles far different from that for which they had been created. The Soviets had crossed the Neva near Petrushino, which posed a great threat to the 16th Army.

The 2nd Parachute Regiment under Generalmajor Sturm, who had received the Knight's Cross on 9 July 1941, was sent on its way to the right wing of the German Eastern Front in November 1941. Reinforced by the

Parachute troops on Hill 159.9 near Kirovograd. On the far left is Leutnant Lepkowski.

addition of antitank units and a company from the regiment's machine-gun battalion, the regiment was to fight the Soviets in the southern sector.

The paratroops reached Stalino in late November. During the weeks and months that followed, the focus of their operations was to be the villages of Voroshilovka, Ivanovka and Petropavlovka.

The regiment arrived in the middle of the worst Russian winter in fifty years, with temperatures as low as minus 40 degrees Celsius. For Erich Lepkowski the first six weeks in Russia were like a nightmare. This was Hell, and he and his radio team had been deposited right in its midst.

On 17 January 1942 Erich Lepkowski presented himself in front of his battalion commander: "Oberjäger Lepkowski reporting as ordered!"

Major Pietzonka stood up and shook hands with the young para-trooper.

"Listen, Lepkowski! You are to relieve Kohl's radio team in Voroshilovka and form a standing patrol there."

"With the blackshirts, sir?" asked the solidly built East Prussian, somewhat skeptically.

"Yes, the 63rd Blackshirt Battalion is there. But I want to know right away what is going on there. One other thing, the village is almost 1,000 meters in front of our main line of resistance."

"When shall I leave, sir?"

"Right after dark. Is your radio equipment serviceable?" asked the Major and, without waiting for a reply, continued: "Have supply issue you a new machine gun!"

For a few seconds the Major looked into the face of the Oberjäger with its hawk-like nose and bright, clear eyes and once again offered him his hand. "Good luck, Lepkowski!"

When Lepkowski stepped outside he could hear several guns firing and the sound of combat from the Russian main line of resistance, almost two kilometers away. He saw distant flashes and within seconds a salvo of mortar rounds came howling in and struck the ground several hundred meters to his right. More mortar rounds came in as he made his way to the bunker and trench positions of the 4th Company. The Oberjäger was forced to take cover once. Clumps of earth, ice and stones rained down on him. A rock struck him on the neck. He cursed softly, got up and seconds later reached the first trench. He came to the third bunker in the trench line and slipped inside.

The heat from the round iron stove nearly took his breath away. Outside it was bitterly cold on this late evening of 17 January 1942. Schmauder greeted him in his best Schwabian dialect:

"What's up, Erich?"

"We're moving to Voroshilovka."

"With the Italians?" asked Stock.

"The 63rd Blackshirt Battalion to be exact."

"That's all we need!" cursed Stock, throwing the playing cards onto the table.

"That's how it is. Get ready! We leave in an hour. Don't forget that we have to take along enough ammunition for the new machine gun I'll be getting from supply!"

When Erich Lepkowski returned with the machine gun his two comrades were ready.

"All right, let's go!"

Lepkowski put on his paratrooper's steel helmet and slipped the chin strap under his chin. Then he reached for the machine gun, which held a fresh belt of ammunition. As soon as they left the bunker they were seized by the icy cold, which was blown into their faces by the wind.

"Let's go through those woods; it will give us some cover from the wind."

The snow crunched under their boots. Off to the left a village was burning. Lepkowski and his men took a break in a small defile.

"The 2nd Battalion under Hauptmann Schirmer is over there," remarked Schmauder matter-of-factly. Stock, who was carrying the radio set on his back, was impatient to get going. Oberjäger Lepkowski led the way. But they had not yet cleared the small woods when Russian rounds began falling. Schmauder saw the Oberjäger disappear in a wall of smoke and flame. He threw himself to the ground and began to crawl. Stock appeared some distance to his right.

"Stay together!" roared Lepkowski between two shell bursts. They panted onward. Once all three sank into the chest-deep snow that lay over a shell crater. Cursing, they worked their way out. Lepkowski could feel Schmauder's breath on the back of his neck as they passed through a ravine that extended to the southern edge of Voroshilovka pressed close together. Finally they reached the village and the safety of a shell-proof dugout. A relieved Feldwebel Kohl greeted them.

"I was beginning to think that Ivan had stamped you into the snow," he said. "Now we can get out of here."

By the time the Feldwebel and his two radio operators were ready to leave, the sound of fighting had ebbed. The mortars had shifted their fire farther to the rear.

An hour later a Russian night harassment aircraft—known to the Germans as the "Iron Gustavs" or "Highway Crows"—arrived on the scene. The aircraft flew directly towards Voroshilovka. For seconds the night was torn by a bright flash. The earth shook as the shock waves from two bombs passed over the houses. The Russian aircraft disappeared into the distance. The rest of the night passed relatively quietly but, early the next morning, the Soviets attacked Voroshilovka from three sides.

Obergefreiter Stock was first to sound the alarm. It was their job to maintain a continuous watch on the enemy and report immediately any changes in the situation by radio. Erich Lepkowski peered through the observation slit of the stout bunker. Through his field glasses he could see the Russians clearly. They were wearing white snow smocks and dragging Maxim machine guns on sleds as they approached.

"Radio message to regiment: Enemy in grid square JD 3419."

One minute after the message had been sent the German artillery opened fire on the Russians. It was directed by Lepkowski. But the enemy did not give up. The Soviets opened fire on Voroshilovka with their heavy machine guns. Bursts of fire ripped into the earth bunkers and stitched lines of perforations in the walls of the wood-framed houses. However, the attackers were unable to withstand the concentrated defensive fire for long.

"They're pulling back!" Lepkowski reported to the rear.

When the Russian infantry was far enough away from the village, the Soviet artillery began to fire. The barrage became heavier and heavier. Heavy rounds exploded among the Italian positions, inflicting casualties. The Italians in Voroshilovka had twenty-six killed on this bloody Sunday. The Blackshirts were depressed, because it was clear they were facing an enemy several times more powerful and one who was prepared to fight to the death. Oberjäger Lepkowski made his way forward through the shell-fire several times to the eastern edge of the village, where he could better observe the enemy. Then he raced back to issue corrections to the artillery.

By midday the Red Army soldiers were pressing in on Voroshilovka. They raced forward until halted by machine-gun fire. They then disappeared into the snow and let their heavy Maxim machine guns answer. Bullets struck the walls of the observation bunker manned by the German paratroops. Once again Erich Lepkowski had to creep forward as much as 200 meters to direct artillery fire onto the Russian machine-gun positions. Crawling from hole to hole, he had helped the German artillery range in by evening. It was well that he had, because the Russian offensive began the next morning, 23 January 1942.

✠

Operation Collective Farm had failed the previous day. Oberleutnant Griesinger was to have led a combat patrol to mine a collective farm in front of the main line of resistance. The operation's point of departure was the positions manned by Lepkowski's section. Lepkowski had been sent a heavy mortar which, together with its machine gun, was to provide covering fire. The mortar opened fire. Meanwhile, the field telephone line had been extended to Lepkowski's location so that it could direct the fire of the Italian and German artillery located on the hills around Voroshilovka.

The combat patrol began. Oberleutnant Griesinger worked his way forward. Suddenly, the patrol came under heavy fire. Field guns, machine guns, automatic rifles and submachine guns fired from the collective farm. It was obvious that a lightly armed patrol was not going to take this forward Russian position. Leutnant Gleitzmann and a Gefreiter were killed. Several paratroops were wounded.

Operation "Collective Farm" had to be called off. Directed by Ober-jäger Lepkowski, the German and Italian artillery then opened fire, pouring 1,000 rounds into the Russian positions and farmhouses. The next morning, Russian rounds began falling on the German positions. The Soviet attack began several hours later.

✠

Erich Lepkowski sent a stream of reports to Major Pietzonka and Hauptmann Schirmer. Meanwhile, the Blackshirts had been replaced by Bersaglieri, Italian mountain infantry. It was the first time they had experienced a major attack by the Red Army.

"The Italians are starting to run away!" reported Lepkowski to his companions as he watched the Bersaglieri on the right flank pull back.

"Why aren't they firing?" cried Schmauder furiously. "They've got six antitank guns and plenty of heavy machine guns! They could hold off the Russians!"

The Red Army troops also stormed towards main line of resistance of the 1st Battalion.. Major Pietzonka let them come to within 100 meters before ordering his men to open fire. The machine guns and several mortars halted the enemy advance. At about midday Lepkowski sent back a report that the Russians had reoccupied the collective farm. Several heavy machine guns began firing into the Italian positions from the farm buildings. Half an hour later the Russians launched an attack from the collective farm. The sight of the onrushing wave of shouting soldiers put the Italian infantry to flight. When the Russians were within the machine gun's field of fire, Lepkowski ordered the gunner to open up.

The young man from Hamburg nodded. He expended the first belt of ammunition in three long bursts. Schmauder installed a fresh belt and the paratrooper opened fire again. To the right and left the Italians got up and ran, only to be cut down by automatic-weapons fire.

"What's with those macaronis?" cursed Lepkowski. "Two of their machine guns in flanking positions would be enough to stop the Russians...stay alert, I'm going over there."

Lepkowski left the bunker. A burst of machine-gun fire forced him to take cover. He came upon a group of Italians preparing to retreat.

"What's going on? Why aren't you firing?" screamed Lepkowski at the Italian Lieutenant, pointing to an antitank gun and a heavy machine gun. Mortar rounds exploded all around and the Italians ducked for cover. Lepkowski also threw himself to the ground.

"Fire! Fire!" he shouted angrily, gesticulating wildly with his arms. But the Italians took advantage of a pause in the firing to run towards the rear. Many were cut down by Russian machine-gun fire. The others threw themselves into the snow and tried to crawl away. Erich Lepkowski saw that the Russians were only 100 meters away. The only return fire at that point was from the machine gun in the radio bunker. He ran back to his people, zigzagging to avoid the enemy fire.

"The Italians are running away! They're abandoning their positions! We must blow up the bunker and withdraw if we don't want to find ourselves in Siberia." Erich Lepkowski hastily made the necessary preparations.

"Fire the last belt then let's get out of here!"

The last belt was expended in one long burst. The Red Army soldiers in front of the bunker disappeared.

"Ready?—Go!" Lepkowski lit the fuse and followed his two comrades out of the bunker. He took along the light machine gun and hurried along behind the last of the Italians. A burst of fire reached out after them. Lepkowski whirled around and fired from the hip, silencing the Russian machine gun. They reached the houses of Voroshilovka and dropped into the snow to take a breather. Soon, however, they were on their feet again and running for a barn that stood at the outskirts of the village.

The crack of rifle fire and the chattering bursts of fire from Russian submachine guns pursued them. Stock, who was running behind Lepkowski, let out a piercing scream. The Oberjäger heard a heavy thud and dropped to the ground. Schmauder came crawling over from the right. They reached Stock at almost the same instant.

"I'll give covering fire!" shouted Lepkowski. He fired short bursts at the Russian troops as they appeared between the houses, while Schmauder applied a dressing to Stock's chest wound. Schmauder reported that he was ready.

"Let's go then!" called Lepkowski.

Schmauder hoisted the wounded man onto his back and hurried back across the hard-packed snow. Erich Lepkowski continued to fire until Schmauder disappeared into a shallow defile about 200 meters away. Then he also sprinted away. Bullets whistled about him. He dropped to the ground and crawled ten meters to the side. Then he got up again and ran thirty meters before the Russians spotted him again.

Lepkowski had to repeat this maneuver several times, until he finally landed, shaking from exhaustion, in the defile with Schmauder and their wounded friend. A dozen Italian Bersaglieri had also taken cover in the defile.

"You take our wounded comrade with you, and we'll give you covering fire!" suggested Lepkowski. An Italian Lieutenant who spoke some German agreed. The Italians placed Stock on an improvised litter and left the defile, pursued by Russian mortar fire. Schmauder and Lepkowski lay at the edge of the defile and held off the Russians. Not until they were almost out of ammunition and the Russians were within sixty meters did the pair pull back. Lepkowski and Schmauder were unable to describe in detail how they finally managed to reach the battalion's lines. They received a joyous welcome from their comrades, and Lepkowski reported to Major Pietzonka.

When he had finished his report, he and Schmauder went over to the Italians to collect Stock. They were met by the Bersaglieri Lieutenant. Worry and guilt were reflected in his face as he spoke with Lepkowski. The four men who had been carrying Stock were missing and there was no sign of the wounded German.

Erich Lepkowski clenched his teeth; his mouth became a narrow slit. "Schmauder, let's go and look for them!"

The Schwabian nodded. They set out at dawn the next morning. It was possible that the Italians had been killed and Stock was lying in the open somewhere. Schmauder and Lepkowski searched for hours. The Russians fired grimly at the two Germans, and it was a miracle they were not hit. But they were unable to find Stock, even though they went back to within 200 meters of the position from where they had held off the pursuing Russians.

Depressed, the pair returned to the battalion's positions. Gefreiter Stock lies buried somewhere near Voroshilovka in the Stalino area.

✠

The Italians launched a counterattack on Voroshilovka on Sunday, 25 January 1942. Lepkowski led his radio section forward through enemy fire to Hill 331.7, where an observation post was established. When Lepkowski reached the hill he encountered Leutnant Schönicker.

"How does it look, sir?" he asked.

"The Italians have done it. They've retaken Voroshilovka. Over there their reserves are moving up." He pointed down to the left, where the Italians were advancing in dense groups.

"We'll move farther forward then, sir," said the Oberjäger.

"Good, Lepkowski. As soon as anything new happens report it by radio."

Together with Schmauder and Gefreiter Klingler, Lepkowski moved cautiously along the road in the direction of Voroshilovka. Two volleys of mortar rounds forced them to take cover. One round impacted two meters behind Lepkowski; it was a dud. A few seconds later the three paratroopers moved out again and soon came upon a wounded Italian. They tended to the Italian's wounds, but in so doing they exposed themselves to fire from the village. First it was a Maxim machine gun, but soon automatic rifles and submachine guns were firing at them too. The Italians, who were already in the western part of Voroshilovka, pulled back again. Several came running past Lepkowski.

"Here, take your wounded comrade with you!" he shouted to them, pointing to the wounded Italian. But they raced past the Germans, ignoring their countryman's appeals for help. The Italian attack had failed, and Erich Lepkowski made a report of the events to Hauptmann Schirmer.

Everyday life in Russia was difficult for the soldiers, with its bitter cold and plagues of lice. Every footpath and road was covered with deep snow. Casualties from freezing and illness increased. Fever, as well as stomach and intestinal disorders spread among the men.

On 30 January two platoons of the 2nd Battalion attacked Voroshilovka. The paratroops fought their way into the village. But the Soviet troops, masters of camouflage, held the upper hand in house-to-house fighting. Leutnant Kober was killed along with eleven other paratroopers. The survivors were forced to withdraw from Voroshilovka. This small Russian village had already claimed many victims and there was no indication when the battle for the warmth-giving, life-saving settlement would finally be over. Communications with the rear were very bad. Even worse were mail deliveries. Erich Lepkowski waited ten weeks for news from home. Only someone who has been in a similar situation can appreciate what mail from home means to the frontline soldier.

There was a general sigh of relief in the command post at Ivanovka when the first break in the weather occurred on 8 February. It was hoped the front would then freeze into immobility in the ensuing mud.

However, at 0300 hours on Saturday, 21 February 1942, the Soviets attacked Hill 292 following an intensive artillery bombardment. About twenty paratroopers with several machine guns defended the hill. Ten were wounded in the fight, but they held their positions. Later, no less than 140 dead Russians were counted around the hill. This appeared to be just the opening act. It was almost certain that "Red Army Day" would see further attacks on the German main line of resistance.

In an effort to head off the expected assault, the regiment ordered an attack on Russian bunkers on the heights in front of the main line of resistance by a strong combat patrol. Armed with submachine guns, machine guns and two mortars, a platoon-sized force of paratroops penetrated the Russian positions. Three bunkers were destroyed. A Russian combat patrol was badly shot up by the Germans during the night of 25–26 February. Surviving Russian soldiers stated that a Russian attack on the 2nd Battalion from the northwest was imminent.

The next morning, with fog lying over the landscape like a dense shroud, the Russians did in fact attack. Initially, however, the assault was directed solely against the 4th Company. Oberjäger Kuhn sighted the attackers. Schmauder, who was manning the machine gun, fired the first burst. Within a few seconds every German weapon had joined in the defensive fire. Nevertheless, the Russians reached the German positions. Ten to twelve ghostlike figures emerged from the white background in front of Kuhn. Kuhn raised his submachine gun and fired off all twenty rounds. Schmauder ripped the machine gun from its stand and sprayed the attacking Soviets. The attackers were halted barely five meters from the position. Soviet troops managed to break into 2nd Platoon's forward trench but were thrown out again in hand-to-hand fighting.

Feldwebel Piepenburg and a platoon from the 3rd Company continued to hold Hill 292. Erich Lepkowski had taken ill on 6 February and did not participate in these actions. He was sent back to the main dressing station with a temperature of nearly 104 degrees Fahrenheit. Lepkowski was suffering from advanced stomach and intestinal illness. By the time he returned to his unit, things had quieted down. He remained in Petropavlovka until 6 March. There he learned that Major Pietzonka had been recommended for the German Cross in Gold for his actions in the Voroshilovka area. The decoration was not forthcoming, however.

Back with his unit, Lepkowski heard that the entire regiment was to be withdrawn from this sector and sent to Germany to rest and refit. He breathed a sigh of relief. There was a steady flow of casualties from the frequent, punishing artillery barrages and the regular patrol-sized attacks. Sleep was out of the question. Moreover, his illness had seriously weakened him.

On 8 March Lepkowski and his radio team were relieved from their forward position and sent back to the regimental reserve in Ivanovka. For the first time in a long while they were able to get a good night's sleep, an unbelievable luxury.

On 18 March the regimental reserve drove in trucks through light snow flurries in the direction of Orlovo-Stalino. It had become cold again. The first day of spring, which Lepkowski experienced in Stalino, saw temperatures of nearly five degrees below zero Fahrenheit.

On 23 1942 March all of the 1st Battalion arrived in Stalino.

"Comrades, you're going home!" prophesied one of the clerks secretively. The soldiers in the orderly room listened skeptically. "Everyone who believes that can kiss my ass!" grunted Feldwebel Köpke.

On 28 March the unit did in fact entrain and was taken through Dniepropetrovsk and Fastov to Kiev. The morale of the troops sank on 2 April, however, when the train maintained its northwesterly direction past Gomel. They were not heading towards Germany. There was a great deal of speculation until the train turned west near Vitebsk.

On 4 April the huge transport train crossed the Lithuanian border. A day later—Easter Sunday 1942—the cars were stopped near Krasnogvardeysk. There was no room left for optimism now, and Erich Lepkowski summed up the situation with the laconic words: "Guys, we're staying with little mother Russia!"

However, it was not until they detrained in Tosno that the last of the paratroops were convinced of the correctness of the prognosis presented by Oberjäger Lepkowski.

On 15 April Erich Lepkowski was ordered to the regiment's signals platoon at Lipovik. Three days later he was wounded in the eye by shrapnel during a Russian bombardment. Lepkowski was taken to the main dressing station and then to a field hospital but, on 21 April, he reappeared at the front. This time he reported to Oberleutnant Ewald:

"Oberjäger Lepkowski reporting to the 5th Company as ordered!"

"Thank you, Lepkowski! Welcome to our company. Hopefully you will be with us for a long time."

Erich Lepkowski did stay with the 5th Company for a long time—until the last paratrooper laid down his weapons in Brest on 19 September 1944. This marked the beginning of Oberjäger Lepkowski's greatest test: Thirty days in which he led forty-eight patrols, weeks in which he faced death a hundred times—and survived.

PATROLS

When the paratroops arrived at the Volkhov, the great Easter fighting of 1942 had just ended. In mid-April a thaw had set in. The large encirclement attempt planned by the Germans had failed. As a scapegoat was needed, the commanding general of the XXXVIII Army Corps, General von Chappius, was relieved of his command, as was Generalleutnant Altrichter, the commander of the 58th Infantry Division. General Chappius took his own life later that same year.

With the thaw began what the German frontline soldiers termed the "Green Hell of Volkhov," something none of them would ever forget. It

Lepkowski discusses the raid on Braspart to free 130 fellow paratroopers.

was the beginning of a period of terrible hardship, with the soldiers lying in the mud and swamp of a fever-infected, mosquito-plagued landscape. They were fighting an enemy prepared to risk everything to get out of the pocket. Yet once again the German soldier demonstrated his steadfastness and willingness to sacrifice.

The 2nd Parachute Regiment joined the army divisions in trying to complete the encirclement and destruction of the Soviet Second Shock Army under General Vlasov. The Second Shock Army had almost been cut off completely from early January to late March. Inside the huge "pocket" were 180,000 Russian troops. The hardest fighting was at the notorious "corridor," which stretched from Tregubovo south into the Mostki area. It had a length of twenty kilometers and a width of up to four kilometers. The "corridor" was the Soviet lifeline.

When the regiment participated in the encirclement effort, it had been reinforced by an antitank company and additional elements. Indicative of the mood for the entire operation, however, was a sign put up by German soldiers at one of the narrowest points of the corridor: "Here begins the ass of the world."

✠

Oberjäger Lepkowski sought out the command post in the impenetrable jungle of the Volkhov region and reported to Oberleutnant Ewald. It was 21 April 1942.

"Your job is going to be to lead the company combat patrol," declared the Oberleutnant. "But get settled in first."

Erich Lepkowski went to the bunkers and positions, some of which were already under water. Soon he was ringed by old comrades. Obergefreiter Samkohl clapped him on the shoulder.

"Great to have you here, Erich. Now we're all back together again. Willrich and Keller are here too. Feldwebel Beckmann is over there with the Third."

"I'm glad to be back with you, too," said the Oberjäger. And he meant it, because nowhere does a soldier feel so secure, even in the uncertainty of war, then with old comrades-in-arms.

Occasionally heavy rounds roared over the positions and into the stands of birch to explode on or near the main supply route leading back through the marshes. The men paid them no attention whatsoever. That evening they toasted their reunion and, the next morning, Lepkowski went along to the forward command post.

The birch, ash and hazelnut trees seemed to acquire more greenery from day to day. It was only midday, but already Lepkowski was wiping the sweat from his brow.

"Damned hot springs in these latitudes," remarked Willrich laconically. "I estimate we'll have temperatures like those in Crete here soon."

Samkohl paused from spooning up his double helping of lentil soup. "Better than the damned cold," he said.

That evening the rations carriers stumbled over the railway embankment, the only access to this section of the marshes, for the second time that day. As well as food and tea, one of them brought a small sack of mail. Lepkowski had eaten and was about to settle down to read one of the books sent from home when Oberleutnant Ewald showed up.

"Patrol, Lepkowski! Select seven men from the 3rd Platoon. You are to reconnoiter the leading edge of the forward Russian position and bring back an Ivan from there. The regiment would like some information."

It took Lepkowski only five minutes. It was only natural that he would select his old comrades to accompany him on patrol. They left an hour after midnight. Samkohl, who knew the terrain, led the way. Erich Lepkowski was close behind him. The six others followed with submachine guns at the ready. The log road was already beginning to sprout, but no one could yet imagine that within a few weeks the growth would form a dense green wall. After a few hundred meters the men left the log road, which continued on in a wide arc, and slipped into a birch wood. The soles of their boots made a sucking noise as they walked over the swampy ground. Erich Lepkowski sank to his knees in the stinking brew once and was only able to extract himself with some difficulty.

They were just 200 meters into the woods when Samkohl suddenly dropped. Lepkowski automatically slid to the ground. At that instant the night was lit by muzzle flashes from twenty guns. Bullets whistled past the paratroopers, ripping branches from the trees. Lepkowski took aim at the muzzle flashes.

"Open fire!"

He fired and rolled to the side. Just in time! A burst of fire ripped into the ground where he had been lying seconds before.

"Strong Russian patrol, sir," whispered Rohloff into Lepkowski's ear.

The Oberjäger nodded and scanned the terrain. There was nothing to be seen. Or was there? He raised his weapon. A shadow came nearer and rose up suddenly, its arm cocked to throw something. Lepkowski fired. The burst struck the Russian in the chest and knocked him into the bushes. The Soviets stormed forward from the left and right. Willrich's light machine gun fired several bursts into the night. An illumination flare hissed into the sky above the paratroopers, leaving them exposed for a few seconds. One of the Germans was hit and cried out. From the left came the warning:

"Sir, they're outflanking us!"

It didn't take Lepkowski long to make his decision. They couldn't hold here. They had to withdraw.

"Fall back! Willrich and I will give covering fire!"

The two fired at the Russians while the others withdrew. Then Lepkowski and Willrich got up and ran back. A few shots were fired after them, then all was quiet. When the patrol reached its own positions Oberleutnant Ewald was waiting.

"What happened, Lepkowski?"

"Strong Russian patrol, sir. At least a platoon."

"Still, it was lucky you ran into them. If you hadn't noticed them, they would probably have killed our forward sentries."

Next evening Lepkowski was assigned to patrol the left flank of the 3rd Company, which was on the left wing. Several Russians had been observed in the marshes in front of the position. It was suspected that more and more Red Army soldiers would infiltrate there and turn up suddenly in the German lines some night.

Once again it was an hour past midnight when the patrol set out. The members of the patrol marched through the darkness one behind the other. Startled swamp birds fluttered into the air. The sky was a black canopy with dark blue sides. Stars twinkled brightly in the blackness. A grotesque concert of chirping frogs filled the night. Slowly the paratroopers made their way forward. There was an occasional flash in the distance as a gun fired from inside the pocket. But the quiet was deceptive. Somewhere, perhaps directly in front of them, were the Russians, just waiting for the German soldiers to drop their guard.

The men of the two surrounded Soviet armies were fighting for survival, for their very lives. Half-starved, inadequately and irregularly supplied from the air, they had to place everything on one card if they were to turn the page in their favor. No longer could they hold out in complete isolation.

Lepkowski and his men came to a flat, lake-like pool of water. Cautiously they made their way forward. The mud grabbed at their ankles. The high-pitched buzzing of mosquitoes made them nervous. The sound bored into the brain like a needle puncture. Willrich slipped and sank to his belt buckle in the stinking brew.

"Give me the machine gun!" Keller took the machine gun while the others pulled the Obergefreiter out.

"Stinks like a thousand baboons!" murmured Keller as he handed Willrich back his machine gun. Occasionally, metal brushed softly against metal, which brought an involuntarily hiss from Lepkowski. They came to a five-meter-wide stream. Tree trunks had been laid across it.

"Be careful! It might be mined!" warned Lepkowski.

He crawled forward and searched the trunks for tripwires and mines. Finally, he reached the other side and waved the patrol across. The others followed. Gefreiter Rohloff, the last to cross, slipped in the middle of the makeshift bridge and landed in the water with a splash. Instinctively he reached up and grasped a leg-thick tree trunk and swung hand over hand to the far side.

"Always showing off!" snorted Samkohl, poking fun at his friend, "can't you cross like a normal person?"

There was an outbreak of muffled laughter. It stopped as if cut by a knife when Lepkowski raised his arm. The men disappeared into the fresh greenery and waited. It almost seemed like a false alarm. Lepkowski was about to give the signal to move on when there was movement in front of them. In the pale moonlight he spotted three shadows moving towards the bridge.

"Russians!" whispered Willrich, raising his weapon. Lepkowski placed his hand on his comrade's forearm in warning. Willrich lowered his submachine gun. The Red Army soldiers came nearer, stopped at the stream not five meters away and began arguing. Apparently there was some disagreement as to whether they should cross the bridge or not. At Lepkowski's signal the paratroopers jumped up and stuck the barrels of their guns under the noses of the Russians.

"Hands up!" shouted Lepkowski in Russian. The three Russian infantrymen raised their arms, letting their weapons fall to the ground. Visibly shocked, they surrendered.

"Samkohl," ordered the Oberjäger, "tell them they'll be shot if they try to escape." Samkohl, the big Prussian from Dierschau, passed on the message in broken Russian. The three prisoners nodded vigorously that they understood.

"Ask them where their unit is and what lies directly in front of us in the jungle."

Once again Samkohl turned to the Russians, who answered eagerly. "They say they're from a forward camp, 200 meters farther to the rear. There are weapons and ammunition in the camp. Perhaps for a breakout attempt?" continued Samkohl.

Lepkowski sized up the situation at once. "Samsel, go back to the company! Oberleutnant Ewald needs to send us a radio team to direct the artillery."

Gefreiter Samsel headed back towards the German positions. In seconds he had disappeared into the darkness.

"Rohloff and Keller, stay with the Russians! The rest of us will go and have a closer look at that camp."

Lepkowski and his men set out in single file. It was a good 250 meters to the Russian camp. They had to crawl the last stretch. Lepkowski saw makeshift huts made from birch and ash logs and two sentries manning a Maxim heavy machine gun. It was more than an hour before Obergefreiter Lutz arrived with his radio team.

"Look at that, Lutz! A ripe target for our artillery!" The Obergefreiter established contact with the artillery unit and passed the position of the enemy camp.

"Everything's ready!" he said softly. "As soon as the rounds fall we'll go get the heavy machine gun. Get hand grenades ready!"

The patrol crawled to within hand-grenade range of the outpost and waited. It was perhaps several minutes until the first rounds came howling in and landed in the camp. As the rounds exploded they threw their grenades into the Russian outpost. One of the Russians tried to run, but a single shot cut him down. Lepkowski and his men ran back to the radio team.

"I'm getting out of here now. If things get too hot you come too, Lutz."

"Understood, Erich."

Lutz turned to his equipment and requested a minor correction in the artillery fire. Round after round fell on the enemy camp. Lepkowski and his men reached the spot where they had left the three Russian prisoners with Rohloff and Keller. But they were not there. Erich Lepkowski deliberated. Had the three Soviets somehow overpowered his two men and taken them off?

A call rang out from the far side of the bridge. It was Rohloff. They had hurried the prisoners across the bridge as a precaution and were waiting in the bushes on the other side. Breathing a sigh of relief, Lepkowski crossed the slippery log bridge. Rounds were still exploding in the Russian camp when they reached the company. Suddenly, there was a mighty explosion. A tremendous fireworks display of red, green, blue and white lit up the night as the tracer ammunition, flares and ammunition exploded.

"They're finished," Willrich said softly. A cold shiver went through Lepkowski when he thought of the 120 Russians the prisoners had said were in the camp. The patrol had been a complete success.

The next day Lepkowski and several paratroopers went forward to the Russian lines and made a surprise attack. They had taken along two machine guns, which provided flanking fire, while the main body attacked with submachine guns and hand grenades and drove the Russians from their forward positions. Three-kilogram explosive charges were used to destroy the dugouts and their machine guns. After that had been accomplished, the paratroopers headed back to their own lines.

The following day saw Lepkowski on a reconnaissance patrol, this time during evening twilight. He located numerous Russian patrols and forward positions. Everything pointed to a Russian attack in the coming days. The Soviet forward sentries were fired upon and driven back. Then Erich Lepkowski withdrew. A few minutes later rocket salvoes fell on the spot where the Germans had been. Throughout the night salvoes of sixteen rockets howled in and smashed into the swamps, shaking the ground.

✠

"Oberjäger Lepkowski, report to Major Pietzonka at once!"

Erich Lepkowski, who was preparing to shave, put away his razor and buckled his belt. He put on his steel helmet and stepped out of the wooden bunker. On the way he thought of 26 April a year earlier. Then he had jumped over Corinth. Now, a year later, he was in the Russian jungle. The Oberjäger reported to the battalion commander. Major Pietzonka cleared his throat. "Lepkowski, tonight you and Oberleutnant Fischer are to lead a strong patrol to determine the possibilities of an attack from the flank on the Russian camp you discovered. The enemy has already moved back into the same place."

"*Jawohl,* sir! May I take my old patrolling comrades once again?"

"You may. The rest will come from the 3rd Platoon." The Major outlined the operation on the map. When he finished he added: "Keep an eye on Oberleutnant Fischer. He's new here. Theoretically, he's in charge of the patrol, but for all practical purposes you're in charge, understood?"

"Understood, sir!"

The patrol departed at midnight. The new growth sprouting from the log road and felled trees was already half a meter tall and, in several places, provided a good shield from enemy eyes. Again they encountered a Russian patrol. A firefight broke out which lasted two hours. The Germans drove the Russians back to the camp and were able to complete their mission.

The events of this night provided more proof that the Russians were up to something. For the Germans it was vital to stay one step ahead of the enemy and discover his intentions. The result of this was an increase in patrol activity; during one twenty-four-hour period in early May Lepkowski led four patrols.

Erich Lepkowski came to know every path that led through the swamp and always managed to return with valuable information. He was in the Volkhov forests day and night, scouting out enemy positions. There were frequent clashes with Russian troops and Lepkowski soon developed a type of sixth sense that enabled him to see the enemy before they saw him. Often he returned with prisoners. He snatched them away from their weapons, from their comrades and in brief, surprising advances penetrated deep into the Russian defensive system. The regiment had complete confidence in his ability to lead patrols and get the required information. Lepkowski led his twentieth patrol on 6 May 1942.

A week later he was given a mission more befitting a paratroop unit. "You are to take ten men and two Oberjäger through the Russian lines to the artillery observation post which is marked here on the map and smoke it out. You are to bring back prisoners!"

The orders were clear. They left after dark and it was not until they were under way that Samkohl noticed that there were thirteen men.

"Erich, we must turn back!" he whispered. They had just stopped to rest and the men were crouched in a circle around several knocked-over trees.

"Why?" asked Lepkowski, aghast.

"Because there's thirteen of us!"

"You must be nuts if you're counting yourself as one of the men. There are twelve men here and one nervous Nelly!" Everyone laughed and Samkohl gritted his teeth. He was nervous at the thought of the unlucky number. They continued on. The swamp swallowed them up. The sprouts were now almost a meter tall; the green wildness virtually impenetrable. After another 300 meters they reached the forward Russian positions. A bunker on the right flank was taken by surprise and five Russians captured.

"Watch your step! No noise!"

"Fly if you can!" joked Willrich. The patrol slipped through the Russian positions undetected and came to the artillery observation post.

"Get hand grenades ready! Standby! Toss them!" Thirteen hand grenades flew toward the circular wall, fell and exploded.

"Get up! Move out!" Lepkowski screamed. The paratroopers stormed towards the wall, firing as they ran. Opposition was minimal and the position and its equipment were blown up. As they left through a communications trench, Russians appeared in front of them.

"Go back! I'll give covering fire!" Erich Lepkowski was carrying a captured Russian submachine gun and he opened up on the approaching group of Russians, who were on the way to relieve the crew of the observation post. He emptied the magazine, let the Russian weapon drop and reached for his own submachine gun. Four Russians came running from the right. Lepkowski caught them with a burst of fire, but one survived. The two soldiers lay about two meters apart. The Russian's eyes seemed to glow in the darkness.

"*Pardonnez moi!*" said the Russian in French.

Lepkowski fired another burst in the direction from which the enemy troops had come, rammed a fresh clip into the weapon and called encouragingly to the wounded Russian, "get moving!"

The Red Army soldier, an officer as it later turned out, got to his feet and ran ahead of Lepkowski, one hand pressed over a bleeding arm wound. They had gone sixty meters when a machine gun opened up behind them. Willrich's machine gun, which was quite close, answered. The enemy weapon fell silent.

Lepkowski and his patrol took a different path and soon were in no-man's-land. A half-hour later the Russian artillery officer was being interrogated by the Major. For the second time Major Pietzonka recommended Erich Lepkowski for the German Cross in Gold.

✠

On 1 June Oberjäger Lepkowski was promoted to the rank of Ober-feldwebel for bravery in the face of the enemy.

The fighting continued. The period of white nights began. There were only a few hours of darkness each night. The swarms of mosquitoes reached an unimaginable denseness, while the swamps discharged poison-ous vapors. Stukas roared past overhead and dropped their bombs on tar-gets within the pocket. The earth trembled and shook. Geysers of mud flew into the air. It was a monstrous and terrifying scene.

"The poor swine!" said Willrich, referring to the Russian soldiers within the pocket. But there was no pity during their nightly forays. Sym-pathy for the enemy meant certain death. The Russians fought with the courage of desperation, employing every weapon and every trick available in an effort to avert what seemed certain doom.

The heat became more oppressive day by day. One day Willrich observed wryly: "Anyone who goes to Hell from here will have to take him-self along a few warm blankets!"

The paratroopers continued to slip around and through the swamps, using rifles, automatic weapons and explosives to prevent the Russians from escaping the pocket, which had been reduced to twenty by twenty kilometers by 30 May. That same day German forces—the 20th Infantry Division (motorized) and elements of the 1st Infantry Division from the north and the 58th Infantry Division from the south—finally closed the last gap at the infamous Erica forest road. They established a blocking position two kilometers wide and 1.2 kilometers deep across the sole Russ-ian supply line into the pocket. The outcome had been decided, but the Russians refused to give up. It was another four weeks before the stubborn Russian resistance was overcome and the pocket cleared.

In the Erica road sector the Russians made daily attempts to break out with four to six regiments. At the same time, elements of the Soviet Fifty-Ninth Army attacked from the east in an effort to crack the German ring. But the battle was nearing its end. The 5th Company of the 2nd Parachute Regiment was withdrawn on 21 June. Oberfeldwebel Lepkowski and his platoon were pulled back to Chudovo. From there they were to be trans-ported back to Germany.

In Chudovo on 25 June 1942 Erich Lepkowski received the recently created Luftwaffe Ground Combat Badge. Finally, on 6 July, Lepkowski and the other paratroopers left for Germany. A significant chapter in Erich Lepkowski's career as a soldier had come to an end. At the Volkhov he had shown what he was capable of—enduring unbelievable hardships and achieving outstanding success as a patrol leader.

AFRICA—THE BATTLE FOR ROME—BACK TO RUSSIA

On 28 October 1942 the 2nd Parachute Division transferred to Mourmelon le Grand in France. The regiment was reorganized to provide a cadre of personnel for the division which was to be formed later in the Quequidan area, but that was in the future. Lepkowski was detached to the Luftwaffe ground warfare school as an instructor and later to the officer candidate school. His aim was to become an officer.

In late April 1943 he and the rear detachment of the battalion at Mourmelon departed for Africa, where the main body of the battalion was in action in the Tunis area. On 3 May the aircraft landed at Rome. A few hours later they took off for Capodichino airfield, south of Naples. Two days later they departed for Africa. During his two-day stay at Capodichino airfield Oberfeldwebel Lepkowski heard numerous rumors. If even half of them were true they were flying to Africa only to be killed or captured by the British or Americans within a few days. They were in the air over the Mediterranean when General der Flieger Student succeeded in obtaining permission to recall the paratroops. The aircraft returned to the mainland. The surrender of the *Deutsches Afrika Korps* was imminent.

With the 2nd Parachute Division in Normandy: The struggle for Bohars, a suburb of Brest. The soldier in the background has an *Ofenrohr* ("stove pipe") the German version of the "Bazooka" infantry antitank weapon.

The parachute troops returned to France to train replacements. At that point, the 2nd Parachute Division was formed. Elements of Brigade Ramcke, which had seen action in Africa, and the other paratroops formed the core of the three regiments: the 2nd Parachute Regiment (Oberstleutnant Kroh), the 6th Parachute Regiment (Major Liebach), and the 7th Parachute Regiment (Oberstleutnant Pietzonka) (Note: The 7th Parachute Regiment was not actually formed until December 1943.) Beginning on 26 July 1943, the 2nd Parachute Division was transported by air into the Rome area. King Victor Emanuel III had replaced Mussolini in Italy with Marshall Badoglio.

On 8 September 1943 the news broke that the Italians had betrayed their Axis brothers-in-arms and surrendered to the Allies. At once the Germans began disarming the Italian forces. Within two days the 5th and 6th Companies of the 2nd Parachute Regiment had rounded up 2,000 prisoners.

Following this operation, which lasted until 11 September 1943, the 2nd Battalion was moved to Santa Marinella. On 4 October Oberfeldwebel Lepkowski went to see General Student in Civitavecchia. The reason for the visit was Lepkowski's long overdue promotion to Leutnant following his successful visit to the officer candidate school. During their brief discussion General Student assured Lepkowski that he would review the case immediately and, a week later, Erich Lepkowski received his officer's shoulder boards. He was now a Leutnant of the parachute troops. He had thus achieved a goal of his: To become an officer.

In early November 1943 the Soviets struck their long-awaited blow near Kiev. On 3 November the First Ukrainian Front (Marshall Vatutin)—consisting of thirty infantry divisions, twenty-four armored brigades and ten motorized brigades—broke through the weak front held by the 3rd Panzer Army. Kiev fell two days later. Several Soviet armies, including a tank army, stormed towards the rail junction at Fastov. Other forces drove towards Zhitomir and Korosten. The German front had been tom apart. It appeared as though the Soviets were about to drive right through Army Group Middle. Capable reserve forces were desperately needed on the Eastern Front and the 2nd Parachute Division under Generalleutnant Ramcke received orders to transfer to Russia. The core of the division was the 2nd Parachute Regiment, which had left Russia in July 1942.

One of the first elements to arrive was the regiment's 5th Company, commanded by Hauptmann Schott. It arrived in Zhitomir on 26 November. The city had only recently been recaptured by the 7th Panzer Division. For a brief period Major Pietzonka took command of the regiment in place of Oberstleutnant Kroh. Major Ewald became commander of the 2nd Battalion during Pietzonka's absence.

On 30 November the company moved up through Maryevka to the main line of resistance, where it took over positions from a unit of the SS-Panzer Grenadier Division. Leutnant Lepkowski led a platoon in the 5th Company of the 2nd Parachute Regiment. They held the position for twelve days, easily fending off rather weak Soviet attacks. Meanwhile the rest of regiment and elements of the 6th Parachute Regiment had arrived. Under the command of Hauptmann Finzel, the 6th Parachute Regiment's 1st Battalion took part in an attack on Beresizy on 7 December and on Yelnyich-Radomyshl the following day.

On 12 December the paratroops were ordered back to Zhitomir by air transport. They were urgently needed in the Kirovograd area, where the 8th Army under General Wähler was being hard pressed. The Second Ukrainian Front under Marshall Konev had launched an attack with four armies and a cavalry corps.

On 13 December the paratroops arrived north of Pervomaysk and assembled in preparation for an assault on the enemy-held city and the surrounding hills.

THE FIGHTING FOR HILL 159.9

The attack on the hills near Pervomaysk began the next morning. The three combat-ready companies of the 2nd Parachute Regiment's 2nd Battalion advanced at first light on 18 December; the 5th Company was led by Hauptmann Schott, the 6th Company by Oberleutnant Beinhauer, and the 7th Company by Oberleutnant Nowarra. The paratroops fanned out as they advanced. Russian rocket batteries tried to smash the attack before the Germans reached the hills. The noise was deafening as salvoes of rockets howled in.

Lepkowski's platoon worked its way up the slope. Russian Maxim machine guns and mortars laid down barrage fire in front of the attackers, but the paratroops went on. When evening came on 18 December the 5th Company was on the hill in front of the Soviet positions. Hauptmann Schott ordered a charge against the Russian positions. He was felled by a bullet and Leutnant Lepkowski assumed command of the company.

The advancing paratroopers reached the first Russian foxholes. Bursts of automatic weapons fire cut down the defenders, while dugouts were taken out with hand grenades. Soon the Russian positions on the hill were in German hands. The three companies then made preparations to defend the hill. The Russian heavy weapons were turned around and manned by German gun crews. Leutnant Lepkowski went back through the beginning Russian artillery fire to the battalion command post to report on the situation. He remained there overnight.

The next morning an Obergefreiter brought a report that powerful Russian infantry forces supported by seven tanks had attacked and had already broken into the positions of the 6th Company.

"Get going, Lepkowski!" called Major Ewald. "Get up there and launch a counterattack!"

Leutnant Körner interrupted: "We've received three assault guns, sir."

"Thank you, Körner. We'll send them to you quickly, Lepkowski!" promised the Major. He dispatched two messengers at once to fetch the assault guns. Erich Lepkowski hurried back up the hill to his company.

"Prepare to counterattack!" he ordered. The paratroops were ready in three minutes. They waited for the Leutnant's signal. Then came the order: "Get up! Move forward!"

They charged across the snow-covered hilltop plateau. Several men were wounded, but most reached the enemy-occupied trench. The paratroops jumped in, firing their weapons and tossing hand grenades. The Russians gave ground.

"We'll wait here for the assault guns. Then we'll resume the advance!" decided Lepkowski.

Several minutes later the three armored vehicles came rolling up the hill. Under Russian fire, Lepkowski ran over to them and briefed their commanders. The three assault guns opened fire with their long-barreled 75-mm guns and engaged Russian machine-gun positions. One after another the Soviet weapons were silenced.

Suddenly, two T-34s rolled out of a hollow to engage the *Sturmgeschütze*. But the German commanders had recognized the new threat. Armor-piercing rounds struck the first Russian tank just below the turret. It was torn from the turret ring. Two more direct hits set the crippled T-34 ablaze. The second tank was hit in the right track. One of its roadwheels bounced across the snow. The Russian tank fired three rounds from its main gun, but it was soon silenced by a hail of fire from the three assault guns.

"Shellfire from the ravine, sir!" reported Oberjäger Müschenborn.

Flashes were visible from a deep depression. Soviet tanks were positioned there and were firing on the German positions. Also firing from the depression were heavy machine guns and 50-mm mortars, known to the Germans as "potato throwers."

"I'll get the assault guns!" Lepkowski called to Oberfeldwebel Fritz.

He then set out through the geysers of dirt and smoke from the impacting mortar rounds. A short time later he returned with the self-propelled guns and briefed their commanders on the new threat. Round after round flashed from the long gun barrels. Four enemy tanks were hit and set on fire. Undeterred by enemy fire, Lepkowski directed fire for the assault guns. The three gunners had never before worked with such an efficient fire-director. They blasted the Russians out of their assembly areas—individual defiles—before they could counterattack. They averted the threat of a breakthrough. The German front had been saved once again.

Leutnant Körner was wounded on 20 November and died soon afterward. Major Ewald summoned Leutnant Lepkowski.

"Lepkowski, you must fill in for Körner as battalion adjutant until replacements arrive."

"But not for too long please, sir," pleaded the Leutnant.

Next morning the 7th Company attacked a hill beside the main road near Novgorodka. The result was a bloodbath and this was to be the blackest day in the company's history. Oberleutnant Nowarra led the attack by the company. Leutnant Sachse was in charge of the 4th Platoon and Feldwebel Martin had the heavy machine-gun section.

Two assault guns supported the operation, which initially made good progress. Advancing through deep snow, the company reached the hill. Then, however, Russian tanks attacked from the flank. Their massed fire halted the 7th Company, and the men took cover in former Russian positions. One of the assault guns knocked out two T-34s. Russian infantry and antitank guns moved forward. The heavy machine gun of Obergefreiter Rudolf Müller took a direct hit. Two members of Müller's gun crew were killed and another badly wounded. Müller alone escaped uninjured. Casualties were high in the trench positions, but everyone who could hold a weapon fired back at the onrushing Red Army soldiers.

Among those killed in the trenches was Oberleutnant Nowarra. He was felled by a sniper's bullet. Oberjäger Heinz Bohn and a company medic were killed beside him. Unable to hold its positions on the hill, the 7th Company withdrew as darkness fell. It had been a grim day for the company. The parachute unit's medical officers saved many lives. Dr. Langemeyer, Dr. Schmieden, Dr. Coers and Dr. Möschel worked until they were ready to drop. The doctors went wherever there were wounded, even into the most forward foxholes. Elements of the 5th Company had attacked with the 7th Company. When the soldiers returned that evening Leutnant Lepkowski established a new defensive line to the right and left of the main road.

Early on the morning of 22 December Lepkowski received orders to once again attack Hill 167, which had been evacuated. The entire battalion or, more accurately, what was left of the 2nd Battalion, moved out. This time two Panther tanks were to support the attack. However, the antitank fire was too heavy and both tanks halted halfway to the main road. The soldiers of the 5th Company, led by Erich Lepkowski, approached to within striking distance of the first Russian trench. To the company's right the wheeled vehicles of the 7th Company under Oberfeldwebel Zausch stormed forward with great elan. Leutnant Lepkowski's men overran a Russian antitank battery, but that was as far as the attack got before bogging down.

As darkness fell the companies of the 2nd Battalion pulled back from Hill 167 for the second time. They assembled on the reverse slope. The 7th Company was down to thirty-five men. The 5th Company had also suffered considerable losses. The latter company was given a breather in Novgorodka. The following night it moved into rest positions at Novo Andreyevka, where it spent a somewhat melancholy Christmas.

On 25 December Leutnant Lepkowski was awarded the German Cross in Gold in recognition of his personal accomplishments and the success as a patrol leader at the Volkhov.

The rest period was brief. On 27 December the 5th Company, its strength now up to forty-five men, marched back to the front to relieve the 6th Company on Hill 159.9.

✠

"Take cover!" screamed Lepkowski.

The warning was unnecessary. The veteran troops had already heard the distant roaring, which intensified into a deafening shriek in seconds, and quickly dove for cover. Sixty rockets struck the frozen ground and exploded. The shock wave tore across the ground.

"Keep going! Follow me!" ordered the Leutnant.

Lepkowski hurried forward, followed closely by the company headquarters section with Oberfeldwebel Fritz, Oberjäger Müschenborn, Obergefreiter Albin and Gefreiter Nagel. All safely reached the reverse slope of Hill 159.9.

The company took a breather before climbing the slope in single file. Leutnant Lepkowski found the commander of the 6th Company a bit further on. He briefed his platoon leaders as the relieved company marched off. Then he followed the headquarters section into the command post. It was a roomy bunker, sunk deep into the earth. Two ledges ran left and right along the wall and could be used as seating places or beds.

A 75-mm antitank gun had been emplaced in each of the sector's flanking positions. Lying in the approaches to the position were several assault guns that had been knocked out by enemy fire. The next morning Lepkowski detached a platoon to assist in the recovery of the assault guns. The assault-gun battalion's prime movers successfully recovered the disabled vehicles in spite of heavy harassing fire from the Russians, who knew only too well that the assault guns would soon be put back to deadly use against their tanks. The Soviet high command had forbidden its tank crews from becoming involved in duels with the German assault guns. In spite of the enemy fire and the biting cold, the assault guns were recovered one after another and towed back to the battalion maintenance facilities.

"We'll be back tomorrow!" promised one of the assault-gun commanders.

✠

In the Kirovograd area was the XXXXVII Panzer Corps under General Nikolaus von Vormann. The corps possessed seven divisions, almost the strength of an army. However, on account of the unusual width of this sector, most of the German defensive lines were thinly manned.

The Soviets intended to attack from the east with four armies and a cavalry corps and from the north with three armies. Objective of the attack was Pervomaysk on the Bug. Had they succeeded, all German forces in the triangle between Kanev on the Dniepr, Kirovograd on the Ingul and Pervomaysk on the Bug would have been destroyed. The German troops were under orders to hold the area—one of the most significant industrial centers in the Soviet Union—at all costs.

The Russian attack on Hill 159.9 began on 5 January 1944. In the days leading up to the assault the Soviet artillery fire had increased steadily. Every weapon the Second Ukrainian Front had was committed.

✠

Lepkowski shouted a warning to the men in the middle sector of the trench as a new barrage of rounds howled towards them. The soldiers ducked into their trenches and pressed themselves against the frozen ground. The rounds exploded all around with mighty crashes.

From a forward outpost came a report that the Russians were attacking. Infantry forces of the Red Army stormed the hill from three sides. Lepkowski hurried to the command post and contacted division artillery. Luckily, the telephone lines had survived the initial barrage.

"Final protective fires at Anton, Dora and Cäsar!" he called.

As the first rounds from the German artillery began falling, Soviet heavy machine guns opened up on the hill position. The Soviets attacked five times that day, sometimes in regiment strength. Forty-five paratroopers repulsed them five times. Once again the Russian artillery opened up with a heavy barrage. Apart from the nerve-fraying noise, however, the bombardment had little effect, as the frozen ground over the bunkers was impervious to any shell.

On the morning of 6 January the equally hard-pressed 2nd Battalion fought its way up to Hill 159.9. It had also been encircled by the enemy, but had managed to force its way through. It took up position to the left of the hill.

It was about 0530 hours and still completely dark when the Soviets launched their first attack against the hill. Four T-34s rolled towards Lepkowski's company lines, followed by several waves of infantry. A few hundred meters from the main line of resistance one of the armored giants ran over one of the mines laid during the night. There was a tremendous explosion as the tank and its reserve ammunition blew up. The second T-34 tried to turn away, but it struck another mine. When the smoke cleared, the tank was ablaze. The two remaining T-34s halted and opened fire with their 76.2-mm guns. Soviet infantry streamed past the tanks toward the German positions.

"Open fire!" screamed Lepkowski.

The enemy infantry were within eighty meters of the tripwires and mines. Within seconds the MG 42 machine guns, which possessed an exceptionally high rate of fire, had forced the attackers to go to ground. The Russian assault collapsed. It was about 1100 hours, and Erich Lepkowski had just gone back to the command post to coordinate subsequent measures with battalion, when Oberjäger Klaus reported that the next Soviet attack had begun.

As Lepkowski jumped into the trench he saw five enemy tanks. They were moving almost one behind the other, probably in an effort to minimize the threat of mines. Within seconds, however, two more Teller mines exploded and two more Russian tanks were ablaze. The two antitank guns in concealed positions on the flanks now joined the fight. They fired quickly and accurately. The effects were deadly. One of the tanks was destroyed, another damaged. The damaged T-34 and the remaining intact vehicle were able to turn away and escape into a depression. The last armor-piercing round whistled past the damaged tank's turret.

The infantry attack was also stopped, largely due to the effects of the newly issued MG 42s. Darkness fell. Erich Lepkowski requested several volunteers for a patrol. Every one of the paratroopers wanted to go with the man who had gained such renown as a patrol leader at the Volkhov.

The patrol worked its way towards the knocked-out Russian tanks. Lepkowski had seen enemy soldiers around them and wanted to foil any attempt by the Russians to recover these T-34s. When they reached the first T-34 there were already Soviet soldiers inside. The paratroopers placed two explosive charges and lit the fuses. There was a loud boom and within seconds the Russian tank was in flames.

"On to the next one!" called Lepkowski.

Russian soldiers appeared from the remaining tanks and opened fire. At first Oberfeldwebel Fritz kept their heads down with his submachine gun. Then he got behind the MG 42 and systematically sprayed the hatches of the enemy tanks. Taking advantage of this covering fire, Lepkowski raced up to the nearest tank and stuck a hollow charge under the turret. He had barely reached cover when the charge exploded, blasting the T-34's turret from the turret ring. A Teller mine was placed under the hull of the third disabled tank; five minutes later it was also in flames. The Russians could have the tanks at that point; they were little more than scrap metal.

During the night of 6–7 January 1944 the Soviets launched a surprise attack on Hill 159.9, dispensing with the usual tank and artillery support. The Soviet troops, masters of stealth, crept up the hill and into the trenches. Lepkowski was awakened from a restless sleep by a piercing scream.

From outside the command post a paratrooper shouted, "Alarm! Alarm!" The Leutnant reached for his submachine gun. The men of the company headquarters section likewise grabbed their weapons. They ran out of the command post and right into the leading enemy troops.

"The Russians are in the trench!"

The main line of resistance had been lost, but Lepkowski acted without hesitation. He had to drive out the Russians before they could solidify their hold on the hill.

"Let's go! Counterattack!"

There were only six men, but they all had machine guns, and they cleared the trenches with a murderous hail of fire. It was a miracle, but they did it! The quick, decisive counterattack drove the Russians off the hill. Russian artillery opened fire, and Obergefreiter Albin was wounded in

Leutnant Erich Lepkowski after receiving the Knight's Cross.

the neck by shrapnel. He was carried into the company command post and cared for by Dr. Marquard, who had stayed behind on the hill with the paratroopers.

Driven on by their commissars, Russian troops launched another assault on the hill. This was the only obstacle in the way of a complete breakthrough. If the Soviet forces had rolled past on both sides of the positions they could have attacked from the rear.

The attack on 7 January 1944 was part of a major Soviet offensive in the Kirovograd area. The 7th and 8th Mechanized Corps attacked north and south of the city. The 67th Tank Brigade, the core unit of the Fifth Guards Tank Anny (General Rotmistrov), carried out daring armored thrusts in the Guderian style in an attempt to break through. By next day three of the seven divisions of the XXXXVII Panzer Corps had been encircled: the 10th Panzer Grenadier Division, the 14th Panzer Division, and the 376th Infantry Division.

The 2nd Parachute Division was facing a similar threat. Had Hill 159.9 not been held for two days and nights, the division would have been facing a catastrophe. The steadfast defense of the hill gave time for Panzer Grenadier Division *Großdeutschland* and SS-Panzer Division *Totenkopf* to arrive.

The Soviets attacked again with tanks. Leutnant Lepkowski and Stabsarzt Dr. Marquard rushed outside when the alarm was sounded. Fog hung over the hill. Glowing red lances of flame pierced this gray curtain. The roaring and howling of Katuschka salvoes forced the paratroopers to take cover. The impacts transformed the hill into a fire-spitting volcano. Suddenly, enemy tanks appeared; they were already halfway up the hill. High-explosive rounds destroyed two machine guns and killed their crews.

A close-range duel developed between the tanks and the Pak. Once again, the Soviet tanks ran into a mine belt in front of the German main line of resistance. But one enemy group broke into the lines. By throwing in the last available reserves, the defenders just succeeded in restoring the situation.

"They're retreating!" screamed Albin.

The others joined in his triumphant howling. They were giving vent to their relief at having fought off yet another attack. A short while later Lepkowski saw that the Russians were rolling past the hill to the north. Flames from the exhaust stacks of the Russian tanks lit the way as they rolled westwards. It looked like a flashing warning light: Watch out! Soon we'll have you in the bag!

The next infantry attack was also repelled. Then the Soviet infantry also bypassed the hill and streamed westward on both sides. The enemy had broken through the parachute division's main line of resistance and cut off the men of the 5th Company sitting on Hill 159.9. Lepkowski's attempt to make radio contact with battalion failed. Oberjäger Müschenborn was sent on foot. He returned with news that the Soviets had forced the battalion back, and that there was only a narrow gap left for the company to escape towards the west.

The Leutnant acted at once. He had the hill evacuated. When the men reached the former battalion command post below, they found a few members of the division who had become separated from their units. They had also fallen back to the command post. They also found the regiment's horses. They rode through the dark night in the direction of the main road. In doing so, the company ran straight into the midst of a Russian unit as it marched westwards. A wild firefight broke out. The paratroopers fired from horseback and cleared a path through the enemy unit.

The road was thick with the enemy; Russian tanks and vehicles were trying to stay on the heels of the retreating Germans to prevent them from setting up positions elsewhere. Germans and Russians alike were heading for the Ingul bridge. This single bridge was also Lepkowski's objective. There he would try to sneak through somehow. However, the retreating German forces blew the bridge before the Russians could reach it. Lepkowski saw the explosion.

"Well that's it. The bridge is gone," declared a dejected Müschenborn.

Trying to swim the ice-cold river would have been tantamount to suicide. Under cover of darkness the paratroopers crept up to the wrecked bridge.

"We can get across!" said Lepkowski confidently.

They crawled slowly and cautiously onto the approach to the bridge, which was still standing, and then over projecting crossbeams. There were some large gaps to cross. At that point the Russians spotted movement on the wrecked bridge and a machine gun began to fire. A second and a third joined in. A little later the night was shattered as several tanks and antitank guns opened up. Lepkowski urged his men on:

"Faster, men, faster!"

There was a scream as one of the paratroopers was hit and fell into the river. Filled with a powerless rage, Lepkowski fired off an entire magazine in the direction of the enemy. A machine gunner moved his weapon into position and opened fire on the muzzle flashes on the Russian side. Finally, the survivors were on the west bank. Lepkowski and the man with the machine gun followed. They had escaped dying hero's deaths by a whisker. Soon afterward the paratroops came upon German troops. The men of the rearguard unit stared at them as if they'd fallen from the moon. Leutnant Lepkowski reported to Major Ewald. Deeply moved, the battalion commander extended his hand.

"Lepkowski, you've saved the battalion, indeed the regiment," he said.

Ewald was speaking the truth. The 5th Company had prevented an early Soviet breakthrough. Oberstleutnant Kroh, the regiment's commander, arrived and requested a detailed report. He immediately recommended Leutnant Lepkowski for the Knight's Cross. Lepkowski had already been recommended once but, like his first recommendation for the German Cross in Gold, it had been ignored.

The 2nd Parachute Division was sent to another exposed position on the southern sector of the Eastern Front during a major counterattack at the loop in the Dnestr River. Oberst Kroh was in command of the division; General Ramcke had fallen ill in mid-March.

The paratroopers launched an energetic assault and drove back the enemy. The division took 10,000 Russian prisoners in a dramatic foot race. Oberst Kroh was awarded the Oak Leaves in recognition of his skilful leadership. General of Parachute Troops Ramcke, who died on 5 July 1968, once said of Kroh: "Of all the commanders to have worn the steel helmet of the parachute troops, Johannes Kroh was one of the bravest and most circumspect leaders in combat; and that's saying something. There was always calm and confidence wherever he went."

Following the hard and costly battles at the Dniepr the decimated division was withdrawn from the front and sent to Germany. After resting and training replacements at Köln-Wahn, the division was once again sent to France. The invasion had begun.

IN THE FORTRESS OF BREST

On 22 June 1944 the headquarters of the 2nd Parachute Division was located in Lampaul, twenty-five kilometers east of Brest. Lepkowski's company and the other units of the 2nd Parachute Division were manning positions in the countryside south of Chateaulin. Lepkowski had been appointed as the actual commander of the company as opposed to being its acting commander. That was something of an honor for a young Leutnant.

Lepkowski saw his first action in France during the night of 4–5 August. He was in a position between the Aulne and the Brest-Nantes Canal.

"Tanks approaching!" reported the combat outpost.

"Sherman tanks!" added Oberfeldwebel Fritz several seconds later. The paratroopers, who had paused for a brief rest, reached for their machine guns and *Panzerfäuste* (literally: "armored fist", these were rocket-propelled hollow-charge antitank grenade launchers).

"Second Battalion follow me!" ordered Major Ewald.

Müschenborn grabbed two boxes of machine-gun ammunition. With several belts over his shoulder, he followed Nagel, who was jogging along behind Leutnant Lepkowski.

The outlines of the enemy tanks appeared from out of the morning fog. Red muzzle flashes pierced the gloom. High-explosive rounds howled in, struck the ground and exploded with a poisonous crash. The paratroopers veered off to the right of the paved road. Behind them, the 1st Battalion turned away to the left. Several antitank guns rolled forward. The crews were briefed on the threat and the weapons disappeared into the bushes. Two minutes later the antitank guns opened fire on the enemy tanks.

"Lepkowski, over here!"

"Sir?" inquired a panting Lepkowski.

"Stay here with the Fifth Company!" ordered Major Ewald. "Deploy your men toward both bends. The Sixth will cover to the road and the Seventh to the canal."

Major Ewald ran to his *Kübelwagen* (staff car) and moved through the tank fire down to the canal, where the regimental command post was situated.

The leading enemy tank sat burning on the road. The antitank guns, concealed in bushes on both sides of the road, continued firing, and the tanks answered. Soldiers in olive-green uniforms then appeared. Two Shermans rumbled through the bushes. They had not been spotted by the antitank guns and, suddenly, they were in front of the positions of the 5th Company.

"*Panzerfaust* firing!" warned Oberfeldwebel Fritz.

One of the paratroopers, who was directly behind him, quickly crawled off to the side. The meter-long flame shot from the rear end of the launcher. The explosive head whipped towards the tank and struck the hull just above the bow machine gun. There was a hard crash. The hatch flipped back and a jet of flame shot out.

"A hit, Fritz!" shouted Lepkowski jubilantly.

The crash of gunfire and the roar of Panzerfaust rockets sounded along a 600-meter front. At least a dozen American machine guns fired. The sun was burning through the fog when Major Ewald came roaring up in a motorcycle-sidecar.

"Lepkowski, form a combat patrol! The enemy has cornered the pioneer platoon. The radio team reports they can't get out on their own!"

The 1st Platoon got ready. Lepkowski instructed the squad leaders and then they set out. The paratroopers worked their way forward through blackberry shrubs and other undergrowth. They came upon the Americans quite by surprise.

Nagel was first to fire. At the same instant a bright flash almost blinded the onrushing Germans. A camouflaged Sherman had fired its main gun. The round whipped past Lepkowski, who dropped to the ground. The tank suddenly began to move. It came nearer and nearer. Lepkowski rolled into a blackberry thicket. The tank's right track missed his leg by less than half a meter. Lepkowski jumped up, took a hand grenade from his belt and leapt onto the now stationary Sherman. He felt the armored vehicle rock as it fired its main gun. Lepkowski banged against the turret hatch and heard the latch being worked. He then hauled open the hatch with a jerk, tossed the live grenade inside and jumped down.

There was a dull boom from inside the tank. For a few seconds all was quiet, until the tank's reserve ammunition went up in a ball of fire. The paratroopers stormed on and freed the trapped members of the pioneer platoon.

✠

While the 2nd Parachute Regiment held due west of Carhaix, the fighting near Huelgoat raged back and forth. A battle group under Oberst Pietzonka—the reinforced 7th Parachute Regiment—was engaged with the main body of the enemy. Aiding the American armored units, which were seeking to break through to Brest via the shortest possible route, were the French resistance fighters. One of the largest *Maquisard* camps in Brittany was in the Huelgoat area. Major Becker and the 2nd Battalion of the 7th Parachute Regiment had run into a murderous crossfire from the *Maquis*. He was able to fight his way out towards the west with some of his men, but losses were high.

General Ramcke directed the division's defensive effort from the high ground at Commana. He was effectively supported by Oberst Pietzonka. For three days the American 3rd Armored Division stormed the Monts d'Arree, but was unable to take the line of hills. The German defenders destroyed thirty-two American tanks, several armored cars and troop trucks.

The 2nd Parachute Division received orders to pull back into the fortress of Brest and hold the city.

On 9 August the division reached the approaches to the seaport fortress, which until now had been defended by elements of the 334th Infantry Division on under the command of Oberst von Mosel.

On 12 August an German High Command order named Generalleutnant Ramcke as commander of the entire fortress area. Oberst von Mosel became his chief-of-staff and Oberst Johannes Kroh assumed command of the division. Both parachute regiments took up position outside of Brest. The 5th Company had been moved into the Bohars area several days earlier. The unit had been designated as the fortress reserve.

✠

The company had scarcely occupied quarters in a small chateau when a messenger arrived from battalion, summoning Lepkowski to report to Major Ewald. Before leaving, Lepkowski ordered the company to get ready for operations. He suspected that the Major had something special in mind for his unit. Sitting on the back of the motorcycle, the Leutnant learned on the way that Major Ewald was with the fortress commandant. That's where Lepkowski was being taken.

"Come over to the map, Lepkowski!" said General Ramcke.

Oberst Kroh began the briefing: "Lepkowski, the situation is as follows: Near Huelgoat about 130 paratroops have been captured by members of the FFI (*Force France Interieurs*). Today the French sent two of these prisoners to us with a demand that we surrender Brest. We have two days to think it over. When this deadline expires the prisoners will be shot as hostages."

Lepkowski knew what they wanted of him: "The Fifth will get them out, sir!" he answered.

"I expected that, Lepkowski, but I have to tell you it won't be easy."

"Being a paratrooper means no life insurance," replied the Leutnant. The General laughed softly.

"Very well then. The prisoners are in Braspart, a village that lies sixty kilometers behind the enemy's main line of resistance. You have to get through the enemy lines, then through partisan-infested villages. And—you must get back again!"

"Begin at 2400 hours, Lepkowski. We will start a feint attack in another place to divert the Americans. Good luck!"

The barrage by the fortress artillery began. The engines of the vehicles roared to life. In an armored car at the head of the column was Leutnant Lepkowski. He looked at his watch. The final seconds ticked away.

"Move out!"

The daring operation from the fortress of Brest was under way. The vehicles moved across the fields and through some woods and then along a dense hedge. The night was filled with the hammering of weapons as the diversionary attack got under way. Where they were, however, all was quiet. The column reached a simple road barricade and two military policemen stepped into view.

"Open fire!" ordered Lepkowski.

The armored car's machine gun roared to life and the German vehicles rolled through the barricade at high speed. They zigzagged wildly to avoid the bursts of machine-gun fire that were fired after them.

A village appeared. Outside were guards; they were partisans of *Les Diables Bleus*. The French recognized the crosses on the approaching vehicles and an antitank gun began to fire. It was silenced quickly by the two 20-mm cannon. The Germans moved to the center of the village to the mayor's office, which they recognized by the legend *Maire* in the light of the hooded headlights. The men stormed into the house, smashed the telephone switchboard and ripped the cables from the wall. Three *Maquisards* were taken prisoner. The vehicles rolled on.

The column bypassed the next two villages in case they had got wind of their approach. An antitank barricade halted the column at the fourth village, but a way through was soon found and the movement continued. Each of the paratroopers accompanying Lepkowski on this dangerous "outing" from the fortress was determined to carry out his mission successfully.

Braspart appeared ahead. Lepkowski issued his orders: "We'll move straight through to the school. That's where our comrades are supposed to be. The SPW will remain at the entrance, with the armored car to its right. The twin Flak will guard the door into the school."

A little later they reached the large square, at whose edge was the school. Several figures came running.

"Germans! Germans!" screamed one of the *Maquisards.*

Machine guns and automatic rifles began firing. The twin 20-mm Flak answered with a salvo of blue and yellow tracer. The automatic rifle fell silent under the hail of fire.

"Let's go, everyone follow me!"

The paratroopers raced into the schoolhouse behind the Leutnant. They ran through a dark hall and entered the classrooms. The French resistance fighters raised their hands and surrendered.

"Bring them all out!" ordered Lepkowski.

They took more than forty French prisoners, but the men they were seeking were not in this schoolhouse. Instead, they were in a second schoolhouse in the village. The paratroopers immediately hurried on. Along the way their vehicles were fired upon. Machine guns fired from windows and cellars. Lepkowski urged his men to hurry: "Don't stop! Keep moving!"

The second schoolhouse appeared in front of them. The paratroopers jumped out while the leading vehicle was still rolling. They raced into the building after Lepkowski. There was a brief skirmish; once again the French surrendered.

The Germans found their captured comrades, all 130 of them. There was a terrific outburst of joy when they recognized their old comrade-in-arms Lepkowski. The captives looked awful. They had been mistreated. Some were dressed only in their shirts and pants, and their valuables, as well as their boots, had been taken. This was not the work of regular French troops! Only bloodthirsty partisans acted this way.

The building was scoured for more captives. None were found.

"No time to lose! We have to get out of here!" ordered Lepkowski.

They climbed into the trucks. The vehicles drove away. The column raced past the first two villages at high speed. As they were coming from recently liberated territory the paratroopers were greeted jubilantly by several Frenchmen—they thought they were Americans. The Maquisards realized their mistake too late and fired a few ineffective shots at the disappearing vehicles.

"Everyone out! Advance along both sides of the road!"

The paratroopers jumped down from the vehicles, leaving four men to guard the prisoners, and fought their way forward in textbook fashion. Machine-gun fire, grenades and small-arms fire drove back the *Maquisards.*

Leutnant Lepkowski stood in the open hatch of the armored car and directed the vehicle toward barricades that the French had thrown across the road. The armored car pushed aside the obstructions while it and the twin Flak fired on muzzle flashes. The way was clear again and the partisans had paid for their fanatical resistance with heavy losses.

News of the successful raid spread through Brest like wildfire. The operation had taken the enemy completely by surprise and the only German casualties were two wounded. Lepkowski appeared before the fortress commandant and made his report. When he had finished Bernhard Hermann Ramcke was visibly moved.

"I knew you would do it—Oberleutnant Lepkowski," he said, and replaced the Leutnant shoulder boards with a pair bearing a single star. "I congratulate you on being promoted from the ranks for bravery in the face of the enemy."

Major Becker arrived. Erich Lepkowski saw him hug each of his men, one after another. With tears in his eyes this Knight's Cross recipient congratulated his men on their liberation. He had given them up for lost.

On 22 August 1944 Erich Lepkowski was once more summoned by General Ramcke. The fortress commandant handed him a radio message which had just come in from the German High Command: "In recognition of his heroic actions in the southern sector of the Eastern Front, Leutnant Erich Lepkowski is hereby awarded the Knight's Cross of the Iron Cross."

"Lepkowski, this decoration is well-deserved. But it's not for your special action here at Brest and your breakout. For that you have been recommended for the Oak Leaves."

The ring around the fortress grew ever tighter and deeper. Once again Oberleutnant Lepkowski and his 5th Company were in the thick of the fighting. During one of their numerous attacks the Americans employed flamethrower tanks and flamethrower squads. This was a weapon the paratroops hated like no other. Erich Lepkowski led a counterattack and his men wiped out the flamethrower squads. However, the enemy had gained a firm foothold in a complex of ruins between the lines.

A counterattack was made the following night to drive out the Americans. Lepkowski led his company as it charged into the ruins, weapons blazing. The enemy withdrew and the paratroopers chased them as far as the northern edge of St. Pierre. Here, however, they were caught in the open. A wall of flame and fire suddenly appeared before them. The Americans met them with an unbelievably dense hail of bullets.

"We have to move forward, men. Into the American main line of resistance. There's no going back!"

"Artillery support, sir?" asked Müschenborn.

"Certainly! Hecker, run back and request artillery fire. And bring back reinforcements!"

Hecker ran off. He was never seen again. One of the many rounds must have caught him.

The paratroopers waited an hour under the murderous barrage. Lepkowski sent two more soldiers back at brief intervals with a report to battalion that the 5th Company of the 2nd Parachute Regiment was advancing and it intended to attempt to penetrate the American positions. For this, however, it needed reinforcements. Again nothing happened. They couldn't stay where they were much longer. Lepkowski turned to an Obergefreiter lying nearby:

"Let's go! We've got to try it!"

The Obergefreiter nodded. Lepkowski handed command of the company over to one of his platoon leaders. They waited until the next salvo had landed, then he and the Obergefreiter ran into the storm of enemy fire. Erich Lepkowski heard a fresh salvo howling in.

"Take cover, Hermann!" he shouted.

The Oberleutnant dove into a shell crater. After the rounds had impacted he looked around. Scarcely five meters behind him was the Obergefreiter. He had been killed by a shell fragment. Lepkowski ran on alone. Shells and mortar rounds fell all around, spraying glowing steel in every direction. The Oberleutnant threw himself to the ground, then jumped up again and raced on. Suddenly, he felt a blow in his chest. He lost consciousness and collapsed to the ground.

✠

Erich Lepkowski has no memory of what took place during the next five days. He was found by a relief force that had moved forward with several antitank guns. He was 300 meters from the position where he had been wounded. How he got there remains a mystery. The crew of one of the antitank guns carried him to the main dressing station. Lepkowski was taken for dead and placed with the other fallen.

A shaken Oberstabsarzt Dr. Marquard bent over his friend and examined him. He unbuttoned his shirt and became suspicious. On closer inspection the doctor determined that Lepkowski was still alive. His upper lip was torn. A shell fragment had struck his left arm. On the left side of his chest was a harmless-looking wound about a centimeter long. These were not life-threatening wounds. Dr. Marquard concluded that Lepkowski must have suffered a severe concussion, resulting in deep unconsciousness.

All of this had taken place early on 13 September 1944. Erich Lepkowski had been unconscious for five days. On 16 September the doctor drained half a liter of bloody fluid from his lungs. General Ramcke looked in on Lepkowski a day before Brest surrendered. The last defenders withdrew toward Crozon Peninsula, where they held out until the evening of 20 September.

The seaport fortress of Brest surrendered at about 1900 hours on 20 September 1944. The many bombing raids and continuous heavy artillery fire had transformed the city into a pile of rubble. No Allied ships were able to use the port until well after the end of the war. The fortress had held out seven weeks against an entire American army corps.

✠

Oberleutnant Lepkowski was taken prisoner by the Americans. He was hovering between life and death. Barely a year after being wounded, an American surgeon opened up his chest cavity and discovered that a tiny shell fragment, which had caused the small wound on the left side of his chest, had passed between two ribs and was lodged in the left auricle of his heart. A risky and complicated operation saved Erich Lepkowski's life. In late 1945, classified as sixty-percent disabled, he was released from captivity.

Erich Lepkowski built a new life on Fehmarn Island. He took on his disability with incomparable energy and overcame it. The battle lasted years, but it was well worth the effort. Erich Lepkowski regained his life's ambition when he strapped on a parachute for his first jump as a sport jumper. In the following years he jumped sixty-eight times, earning the silver and gold parachuting badges.

During the winter of 1959 Erich Lepkowski joined the Bundeswehr, the new German armed forces. Several months later he was a soldier again and placed his knowledge and abilities in service of the defense of the Federal Republic of Germany.

He became a Hauptmann, passed staff officer testing and was eventually promoted to Major. Erich Lepkowski is not a man one could call a willing subordinate. Always looking for something new and better, he constantly bombarded his superiors with innovations and the latest novelties. His greatest achievement, however, was his recovery, which enabled him to parachute again and serve in the defense of his country. We leave the final words to Erich Lepkowski:

> It is my opinion that there is no other sport besides manual parachute jumping in its various competitive disciplines—with the exception of ski jumping and, possibly, tournament riding—that demands of the sportsman a comparable concentration of physical conditioning, quick decision making and the ability to react in fractions of a second. The educational value of this sport far surpasses all others. In the military field it can be a vent for the abundant thirst for action of our enthusiastic and idealistic young soldiers. This has been recognized and implemented by armies all over the world.

Feldwebel Franz Schmitz received the Knight's Cross while serving as a medic with the 3rd Company of the 279th Grenadier Regiment.

Franz Schmitz

Morning dawned on 22 June 1941. During the night the divisions of Army Group South had moved up into their jumping-off positions.

The battalion commanders read out to the troops the order from the Führer that was to lead them into Hell:

> . . . Soldiers of the Eastern Front, this moment marks the completion of a build-up which, in scope and extent, is the largest the world has ever seen.
>
> German soldiers! You are about to embark upon a hard and responsible and difficult struggle: The existence of our nation now rests in your hands!

At precisely 0315 hours thousands of guns opened fire along a 1,350-kilometer front. Three million soldiers went on the offensive from the Baltic to the Black Sea. It was the beginning of a struggle more terrible than anyone could imagine. It was to be a struggle that was to bring death to millions of people and lead to the total defeat of Germany.

In the sector of Army Group South the bombers, heavy fighters, dive-bombers and single-seat fighters of the Luftwaffe opened the campaign. The 1st Group of Fighter Squadron 3 under Hauptmann Hans Hahn raced toward Lvov and arrived over the Soviet airfield at first light. The Messerschmitts strafed the aircraft parked there, setting many of them alight. When the Bf 109s flew away they left behind twenty-one destroyed Russian aircraft.

Near Stanislau thirty-six Russian bombers were destroyed in a similar surprise attack. The 6th and 17th Armies moved forward. From Wlada on the River Bug to the Hungarian border, German troops rose up, ran to the river, crossed in inflatable rafts and assault boats and pressed ahead into the wooded and swampy terrain. The attackers were met by fire from cleverly camouflaged islands in the swamps, from fallen-down shacks, from behind blinds and from the trees. Nevertheless, the leading divisions of the 6th Army advanced as far as fourteen kilometers into enemy territory.

Seventy kilometers to the south was the army's other corps, whose two divisions took possession of the bridge over the Bug at Hrubaschow. At noon on the first day the 14th Panzer Division had rolled across the bridge and prepared to advance. Between the two army corps were the motorized units and infantry corps of Panzer Group 1 under Generaloberst von Kleist.

The Russians attempted to block the German thrust toward Lvov. There was bitter fighting in the area west of the city. However, the infantry of the "Cloverleaf Division" (the 71st Infantry Division) under Generalleutnant von Hartmann and the 1st Mountain Division under Generalmajor Lanz stormed into Lvov on 30 June. During this phase of the battle the XIX Army Corps, which was the Army high command reserve, was moved forward. One of the divisions of General of Infantry Obstfelder's corps was the 95th Infantry Division under the command of Generalleutnant Hans-Heinrich Sixt von Arnim.

✠

The division disembarked near Rovno. Within hours it was engaged in heavy fighting against an enemy that used the terrain to its advantage.

"Fist Company, follow me!"

Oberleutnant Roth, a massive officer from Lingen in the Emsland district, had assumed the lead. The company was advancing on the right wing of the attack group formed from the 279th Infantry Regiment. It was still dark, but the first light of the new day was already visible in the east.

"Don't hang back so far, Schmitz!" Hauptfeldwebel Max-Ernst Krause shouted to the Obergefreiter, who was in charge of the company's f-man medic section.

"Close up!" Schmitz called over his shoulder, at the same time looking at his comrade Horst Bolland.

They came to a patch of woods. Advancing along its right flank, the soldiers came to an area of open terrain. Ahead were a few fields. The two neighboring companies pressed on into these. Suddenly, there was an outburst of hectic rifle and machine-gun fire from four or five directions.

"Cover!" roared Oberleutnant Roth. He threw himself down in a shallow drainage ditch, which, fortunately, was dry. Directly in front of him the soldiers of the 2nd and 3rd Platoons returned fire. The cries of wounded soldiers rang out from the cornfield. Franz Schmitz, who had jumped into a trench, ducked low. Bullets whipped through the branches of a bush above him. Then he heard a cry: "Medic!—Medic!—Medic!"

"Ready?" he asked his companions.

"Ready!" cried Bolland and Zünkley together.

Schmitz rose up and ran in the direction of the wounded man while bullets chirped all about him. Behind him he heard a terrible cry. Men cried out like that when they had been hit by a fatal bullet. Schmitz hurried on, ducking and dodging. He saw fountains of dirt moving his way and dodged to one side, avoiding the burst of fire. Finally, he reached the cornfield and plunged inside.

There he found a group of five or more men, all wounded. He kneeled down beside a man whose thigh was spurting blood in rhythm with the beating of his heart. With trembling fingers he pulled a dressing from his bag and applied a pressure bandage to the wound. Bolland appeared beside him. He was dragging the litter by himself, his face distorted with terror.

"Where is Hennemann?" cried Schmitz.

"Hennemann is dead!" stammered the Gefreiter.

Zünkley appeared beside them, followed by Pötter. "Take this one back to the dressing station! Get a move on!"

The two men heaved the now unconscious man onto the litter and hurried away. Franz Schmitz and Horst Bolland dressed the wounds of the other wounded men. Then they placed one of them on the litter and headed back through the enemy fire, which was still coming from the far side of the field.

The pair reached the edge of the woods, out of breath. The burly Obergefreiter with the open, slightly full face and the brown eyes called something to his comrade. The latter shouted a reply, but Schmitz didn't hear it. He was already on his way back into the cornfield where the company's dead and wounded were. He reached the spot where he had earlier tended to the seriously wounded man. He heard men calling and several soldiers with minor wounds came walking towards him.

"The Russians have reached the edge of the cornfield; they'll be here any minute!"

"Stop, stop!" called Schmitz, more angry than frightened.

Five soldiers went into position. A squad from the heavy platoon moved forward to the edge of the cornfield, set up an 80-mm mortar and began lobbing shells at the far end of the field. Just then Schmitz saw the second pair of stretcher-bearers approaching on the run. As he watched, Paul Pätter threw his arms into the air and fell to the ground. Zünkley dragged the litter alone for a few paces before he, too, was knocked down into the dust by the same burst of fire.

"Horst, we'll have to carry them. We'll each take one."

Bolland nodded.

"Hang on, but don't snap your neck!" called the Obergefreiter to the man he had slung across his back.

"Bring me back!" pleaded the wounded man. Schmitz carried the man back to safety. Repeatedly he ran forward through the death zone, which was under enemy mortar fire at that point as well, to the broad field to recover more wounded. All the while fighting was going on on both sides of the field.

Calls for medics rang out above the noise, causing Schmitz to get up, leave his safe spot and run to where a wounded comrade was calling for help. Once he felt a hard blow against his back; Schmitz fell to the ground and lay there, momentarily paralyzed. He reached back with his left hand. There was no blood! A bullet had pierced his canteen, allowing the tea inside to run out. He jumped to his feet and ran on. Schmitz had just reached the near edge of the cornfield when he heard voices not twenty meters away. They were Russian voices, apparently giving orders.

Schmitz took cover, reached for his pistol and flipped off the safety. Four men came through the corn, bent low. They carried submachine guns at the ready—Red Army soldiers! Schmitz aimed and fired. Three times he pressed the trigger of the 9-mm pistol. One Russian cried out and fell. The others disappeared to the left and right and then bullets were flying toward the Obergefreiter.

The medic pressed himself to the ground. A burst of fire from a submachine gun hissed close overhead, snipping off a number of corn stalks, which fell on top of him. He looked for the enemy but saw nothing. Then he saw a muzzle flash and fired. There was a scream and a rustling sound as a rolling body knocked over the corn. Suddenly, a MG 34 opened fire to his right. The burst ripped through the corn. The two surviving enemy soldiers got up and ran for their lives. In seconds they had disappeared. Horst Bolland appeared next to Schmitz; he was gasping for breath. He was carrying the machine gun of a fallen comrade.

"Thanks Horst!" called Schmitz, who then crawled forward. He reached the second Russian. The man was still alive. The man's lips were pale, almost drained of blood. "Don't shoot!" he stammered in Russian. "War over."

Wordlessly Schmitz began dressing the Russian's wounds. Then, with Bolland's help, he dragged him to the far end of the field. There they laid him in a depression and hurried forward again.

Hours passed. High in the sky, the sun beat down on the men pinned down in the cornfield. Oberleutnant Roth appeared on the scene. "The Third Battalion is going to outflank and drive back the enemy, Schmitz," he explained.

"I hope . . ." replied the Obergefreiter. By late afternoon Franz Schmitz had brought back twenty-three wounded soldiers from the firing line.

The fighting took on an even deadlier aspect when the 3rd Battalion of the 279th Infantry Regiment ran into an enemy field position and was forced to take cover. The enemy fire grew steadily heavier. Volunteer stretcher-bearers took the wounded from the edge of the woods to the aid station.

It was getting dark when Schmitz once again went forward and dropped to the ground beside the company commander. "How's it look, sir?" he asked.

"Sixteen dead, Schmitz, and twenty-two wounded from our company alone. Sixteen dead!" Visibly shaken, the Oberleutnant turned away.

Suddenly, there were noises ahead and to the right. The men started. The forward machine gun swung around in the direction of the sounds. Oberleutnant Roth raised his submachine gun. When he saw the enemy, he fired off a long burst. The second machine gun joined in. Shots rang out from deep inside the field. Schmitz ducked deep into the depression. He heard the rattle of the weapons, then an unusual smacking sound beside him and, afterwards, a groan. Schmitz saw the company commander bend over and grasp his body with both hands.

"What is it, sir?" he asked.

"Belly wound!" gasped the officer.

The Obergefreiter was terrified. There was no way he could carry this heavy man alone. And besides, a man with a stomach wound had to be transported lying down. He crawled over to the company commander. He could see where the bullet had entered, but there was no exit wound. Then he pressed two first-aid packets over the wound and secured them with tape.

"I'll get a litter, sir. We'll get you out!"

"Good, Schmitz, good!" stammered the officer.

Schmitz ran as fast as he could. He reached the edge of the forest and the unit trains. Krause, the senior noncommissioned officer present, appeared. "Sir, I need at least two helpers. Oberleutnant Roth has a serious stomach wound. He's lying up forward in the cornfield!"

"I'll come with you myself, Schmitz," said Krause. Then he turned round. "I need two or three volunteers, the company commander has been wounded."

Moments later the five men ran forward. They reached the company commander unharmed, as their machine gun had just driven the enemy back. Leutnant Willrich, the platoon leader of the 1st Platoon, and his men had meanwhile moved forward and were now defending this sector.

"Careful, be very careful!" called Schmitz.

They placed the huge man on the litter. Four men picked up the litter and headed back. Once incoming artillery fire forced them to take cover but, finally, they reached the dressing station. There the company commander was given preliminary treatment before being packed into a Fieseler Storch aircraft and flown back to the main dressing station. By then it was dark. The enemy fire ebbed and died out. At last Schmitz was able to lie down and take a brief rest. Horst Bolland came over to him.

"How are Zünkley and Pötter?" asked Schmitz.

"They'll pull through."

The next morning the enemy had disappeared. The Soviets had pulled back toward the Stalin Line during the night. Oberst Siegfried Runge, commander of the 279th Infantry Regiment, went forward to visit his 1st Company. On his neck he wore the *Pour le Merite*, which had been awarded to him during the First World War. Runge was escorted by Hauptmann Hahne, the battalion commander.

"Obergefreiter Schmitz: Report to me!" ordered the Hauptmann.

Schmitz approached the two officers and came to attention a few paces in front of them.

"Obergefreiter Schmitz, for your brave conduct during yesterday's fighting and for rescuing twenty-two of your wounded comrades from no-man's-land, I present you, as the first member of my regiment in the Russian campaign, with the Iron Cross, Second Class."

Hauptmann Hahne pinned the decoration on the medic's tunic. Then the Oberst stepped up to Obergefreiter Schmitz and gave him his hand.

✠

On 9 July 1941 the 13th Panzer Division took Zhitomir. Troops of the 16th Infantry Division took the Lyubar bunker and captured the bridge over the Slutsk. The Stalin Line had been pierced. Kiev was the next objective. Panzer Group 1 received the following order: ". . . seize a deep bridgehead east of the Dniepr near Kiev as a base for the continuation of the campaign east of the river."

The armored divisions of Panzer Group 1 stormed ahead, eventually leaving the infantry trailing behind them by as much as 200 kilometers. The 95th Infantry Division reached Shepetovka. By 21 July it reached the Zhitomir area, which had withstood enemy attacks from the north and south. It finally arrived at the Dniepr, south of Kiev, and Hill 142, which was occupied by the enemy.

"We must take this hill," the division commander explained to the commanders of his regiments and battalions. "If we can take it the ring will be closed to the south. The 71th Infantry Division will be joining our attacks on the left."

✠

Dawn had just broken on 8 August when the 95th Infantry Division sent its two assault regiments forward. In reserve was the 280th Infantry Regiment. Oberst Runge made a forward gesture with his arm and gave the order to advance. He had come forward to personally accompany his 1st Battalion. Schmitz saw the massive figure of the Oberst to his right. At his side was the battalion commander. The soldiers moved forward at the run, reached the first bush-covered area and saw Hill 142 appear before them. Seconds later, rounds from Russian guns and bullets from enemy automatic weapons hissed through the early morning air.

"Ratschbum!" called Horst Bolland, throwing himself to the ground. ("Ratschbum" was soldier slang for the Soviet 76.2-mm general-purpose gun. The name derived from the fact that the sound of the weapon's report practically coincided with the sound of the impacting round, due to the tremendous muzzle-velocity of the weapon.)

The rounds fell among the vegetation and exploded, showering the area with mud and steel.

"Onward, men!" shouted the Oberst. "That hill is our objective!"

Again the soldiers got to their feet and hurried forward, only to be met by fire from the forward slope, which bristled with machine guns.

"Mortar platoon forward!"

The men of the mortar platoon hustled to the front, set up their weapons at the edge of the vegetation and opened fire on the Russian field positions.

"First Battalion to the right to the river and outflank the hill! Second and Third Battalions pin down the enemy!"

Oberleutnant Meuthe, acting commander of the 1st Company since the wounding of Oberleutnant Roth, waved his company forward.

"Move out, get the lead out!" called Leutnant Willrich to the 1st Platoon.

"Coming!" shouted Unteroffizier Grenzel.

They turned east, entered the vegetation and came to marshy ground on the west bank of the Dniepr, where they turned north. The soldiers cursed softly as they slogged through the sometimes waist-deep muck. One of the men called out: "There's the hill!" The crest of the hill appeared before them through the branches of the small patch of woods.

"Turn! Through the woods to the hill!" ordered the regimental commander, who had arrived with Hauptmann Hahne and his staff of runners.

The soldiers crept through the woods. To their left they could hear the plopping of Russian mortars. The hard crack of Russian 76.2-mm guns rang through the wood. All of a sudden, there was a roaring noise overhead. Rounds from the Russian fortress artillery raced westward and southwestward and smashed into the ground far behind the units spearheading the division's attack. Then a water-cooled Maxim machine gun opened fire from the edge of the woods.

The weapon was easily recognizable by its slow tack-tack-tack. Cries rang out from the battalion's left flank, where the 2nd Company was advancing. There was also the sound of faster-firing MG 34s.

"Keep moving, don't stop. The hill is also being assaulted from the front!" called Oberst Runge.

Leutnant Willrich fell to the ground right in front of Schmitz but, before the medic could reach him, he was back on his feet and running. Finally, they reached the edge of the forest. Flitting tracers and muzzle flashes pierced the morning twilight. To the right, the men of the 3rd Company shouted as they charged forward. They reached a shallow gully and began taking fire from the far side. Several men were hit and toppled forward. Schmitz hurried over to the nearest wounded man. He saw a jagged exit wound on the back of the man's neck and knew instantly that he was beyond help.

"Get up! Move forward!" Once again it was the Oberst who got the men moving. He got to his feet and ran up the slope. The 1st Company followed. Oberleutnant Meuthe fired from the hip at Soviet troops as they appeared on the crest. The enemy troops disappeared.

Schmitz ran up the slope, holding his 9-mm pistol in his fist. On reaching the top he was met by machine-gun fire. It came from Hill 142 and whistled high over his head. Nevertheless, he dropped to the ground. Crawling forward several meters, Schmitz spotted four Russian soldiers squatting in a dugout. The enemy troops raised their weapons. Schmitz fired twice, then ducked just in time as bullets were sprayed in his direction. Horst Bolland threw a grenade over his prostrate form into the Russian rifle pit.

The explosion silenced the position. When Schmitz jumped into the hole he saw blood spurting from a wound in the neck of one of the Russian soldiers. Acting quickly, he moved over to the man and applied a packet dressing to the dangerous wound. He saw a flicker of gratitude in the dying man's eyes, and felt his hand as it grasped his own, as if pleading for him to stay at his side. Then the man stiffened and fell backwards.

The Obergefreiter heard an order. He saw the company get up, cross the last depression and run up the hill. The sole enemy machine gun that had been raking the advancing troops could no longer reach them. They ran onward. The 3rd Company had also made it across the depression. Soon afterward, the advancing troops reached the heavily vegetated hill.

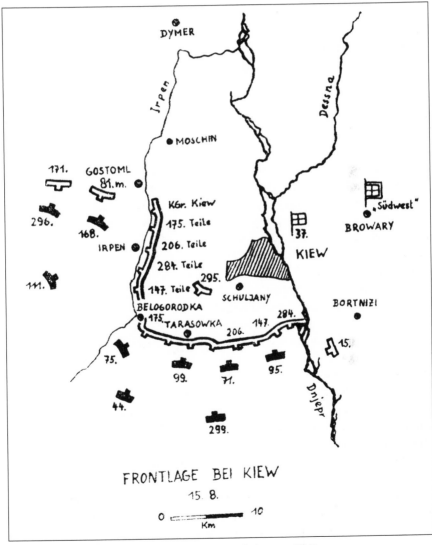

The front near Kiev, 15 August 1941.

Rushing forward, they came to the first dugout, jumped in and ran up the communications trench until they reached the position of the heavy Maxim machine gun. It was still firing at the pinned-down 2nd Company. Two hand grenades silenced the enemy machine gun. Unteroffizier Rothe and Gefreiter Schumacher were badly wounded while trying to knock out one of the main bunkers on the hill. The two men cried out for help. They lay about twenty meters from the bunker, from which machine guns and automatic rifles were still firing.

"I'll get them!" shouted Zürn.

He ran towards the two wounded men, zigzagging as he went. But he didn't get far. A burst of fire knocked him to the ground.

"Antitank rifle: Get over here!" called Oberleutnant Meuthe.

The two antitank riflemen came running. They had to crawl the last few meters, dragging their long, heavy weapons behind them. Finally, they reached the trench. The two men positioned their antitank rifles and opened fire. Three rounds from each weapon were enough to silence the bunker and its machine gun. Schmitz was the first to run over to the wounded men. Zürn's wounds were minor. Schmitz saw at once that he could look after himself. The other two had been badly wounded.

At that point the main body of the regiment reached the top of the hill. The enemy, who had been defending on the hill's south and west flanks, now ran down the far side of the hill in the direction of Michelovka. It was one of the small cities that made up Kiev's defensive perimeter.

German troops combed the hill. Schmitz and his helpers had their hands full recovering all the wounded and evacuating them to the main dressing station. Hill 142 had been taken. The Russians had built numerous field fortifications on the long hill. Four captured 76.2-mm guns were moved to the north face and emplaced there during the night. At first light they opened fire on the enemy in Michelovka and on the last line of hills outside of Kiev, the Lysa Gora.

Heavy guns spat fire in Kiev. Through his binoculars Oberleutnant Meuthe could see the tower that would come to symbolize this day to the soldiers of the XIX Army Corps: The tower of the famous Lavra Monastery. The main turret with its cross could be seen from a great distance in the bright light of morning.

"That's where we have to go, Schmitz!" said Meuthe.

"It doesn't look good, sir. What are the Russians doing?"

"The Russians are defending like lions, but the 71th Infantry Division broke through the outer ring of fortifications yesterday and its left wing has reached Shulyany."

"That's very close to Kiev's south railway station!" called Leutnant Willrich, joining the conversation.

"They have the south station too," confirmed the company commander. In fact, the men of the 3rd Battalion of the 530th Infanterie Regiment were already there. The battalion had found a gap and simply marched through it. They were approaching the airfield and the towers of the citadel were in sight to their right, when a heavy armored train forced them to stop and take cover. The fire from the armored train was so heavy that they were forced to dig in.

"What's going on on the left?"

"There is no contact with the elements which have broken through on the left. The 44th and 99th Infantry Divisions have so far failed to get through. They're bogged down in the outer ring of fortifications."

"And when do we move?" asked Leutnant Willrich.

"As soon as the 280th Infantry Regiment has moved up on the left flank."

"*Achtung!* Aircraft!" a voice shouted shrilly. The warning reached the men of the north side of the hill. Looking up, Schmitz saw that numerous flashing silver objects had appeared high in the sky.

"Take cover!" shouted Leutnant Willrich.

Schmitz threw himself into the observation trench and pressed himself to the ground. He heard the satanic howling of the falling bombs, then the world seemed to disappear. The shock waves from two exploding bombs squeezed the air out of Schmitz's lungs. He felt as if his eardrums must break. Cries rang out through the clouds of dust and smoke. More bombs fell, creating huge craters on Hill 142.

"Medic!—Medic!"

Schmitz heard the familiar cry for help.

"Krämer, Bolland: Get over here!"

The two men came crawling through the trench.

"That came from over there, Franz!" called Heinz Bolland. He was pointing to the right, where the 2nd Company was. The three medics got up and ran across the field. There were more explosions, creating fresh clouds of powder smoke and dust. The air was filled with the nerve-wracking howling and whistling of falling bombs. Schmitz and his companions sought cover in a trench. The exploding bombs drowned out the droning of aircraft engines and the barking of the two 37-mm anti aircraft guns that vainly tried to engage the enemy bombers. But the enemy aircraft were too high. Lumps of dirt sprinkled down on Schmitz. He got to his feet and hurried on. He saw that a bomb had covered over part of a nearby position. Four men were digging with spades in a pile of dirt. Schmitz was on the scene in minutes; he snatched away one of the spades and stuck it in the ground.

"Enemy aircraft!" roared Bolland.

Everyone took cover. Schmitz had just uncovered one of the men. As he threw himself across the man, he heard the bark of cannon and the rattle of machine guns. A stream of bullets stitched the ground, ending not five meters from him. Schmitz took a deep breath, threw the spade to the side and began digging with his hands. He pulled out one of the buried men and, helped by one of his companions, dragged him back to the safety of an intact trench. Schmitz cleared the man's mouth, ears and nose and began working to resuscitate him. He had just finished when a second survivor was brought in. He, too, was successfully revived. In all, seven men were rescued; however, the eighth and ninth were dead.

This was the beginning of the Russian counterblow. Batteries of long-range guns fired from the fortified area of Kiev, which for some weeks had been prepared for a fight to the end.

It was midday when the 279th received orders to advance through the woods on both sides of Hill 142 and drive the enemy back to Michelovka. It was to take the town and then drive into the city of Kiev itself. Oberst Runge made his way over to the left group, which consisted of the 1st Battalion and a company from the 3rd Battalion. The soldiers walked down through the tangle of bushes covering the hillside and began to advance through the woods. In the point position was the 3rd Company. Obergefreiter Schmitz was at the rear of the company. His three helpers followed and, directly in front of him, was the squad led by Unteroffizier Grenzel.

Suddenly, a sniper opened fire from his hiding place high in a tree. Ahead of them, the 3rd Company had run into a field position running through the woods. Hand grenades exploded, an indication that the 3rd was about to break into the Russian position. Shouts echoed through the forest. Schmitz and the others took cover. There was a flash from a pine tree not fifty meters ahead. Bolland loosed off a burst from his captured submachine gun in the direction of the muzzle flash. There was a snap and a crash, and then the sniper tumbled through the branches. He fell to the forest floor and lay still.

The voice of Leutnant Willrich rang out through the noise of battle: "Medics up front!"

"Let's go! Follow me!" cried Schmitz.

He got up and ran forward, past soldiers who had gone to ground and were firing back at the enemy. Schmitz came under fire from the left and began to evasive maneuvers. Then he reached the main body of the 1st

Company, which had moved up close behind the 3rd Company. Schmitz dropped down beside the Oberleutnant: "The Third's medic team has been put out of action, Schmitz!"

"Where are the wounded?" asked the Obergefreiter, wiping the sweat out of his eyes.

"Along that path," answered the Feldwebel who had passed on the call for help. He pointed to a path leading in the same direction from which the hammering of enemy machine guns could be heard.

"Horst, Gerhard: Follow me! Zürn: Stay here and look after the others," said Schmitz.

Shortly afterwards he crossed the path with several long strides. A burst of fire came his way and Schmitz leapt into a bush, which collapsed beneath his weight. He was slightly stunned, but was aware that Bolland and Krämer had also made it across.

Schmitz crawled on until he reached a freshly planted area, through which he worked his way toward the enemy, parallel to the path. After about 150 meters he came upon a group of Red Army soldiers, apparently attempting to outflank the German attack force.

"Krämer, go back to the old man! Report on the enemy movements and stay there!" whispered Schmitz into his companion's ear.

Bolland gestured at his weapon and then toward the enemy. Schmitz shook his head. He knew that if they fired the enemy would take up positions. They would then be unable to reach the wounded. Krämer crawled back. Schmitz let the Russians pass before moving on.

Finally, they had crawled far enough to see the muzzle flashes from the Russian machine gun. "From here we go right!" whispered the Obergefreiter to his companion. Bolland nodded in acknowledgement. They crawled for a distance, reached the periphery of the path and found the first of the wounded. Schmitz left him in Bolland's capable hands, while he glided on towards the path and discovered three members of the 3rd Company. One of the men was a man he knew from his home station at Lingen.

One after another he pulled the men away from the path and into a thicket. There he dressed their wounds.

"Is that all?" he asked one of the wounded.

"Up ahead are Nägele and Scheimann. The Russians let them get close. I think they're dead."

Once again Russian bombers roared overhead. A fresh hail of bombs fell on the hinterland. Then the Russian artillery opened up. Bolland returned and helped tend to the wounded. "I'll crawl forward and look for the other two," said Schmitz.

"Be careful, Franz!" warned Bolland, knowing that Schmitz, who was as strong as a bear, would do everything he could to recover the last of the wounded.

The Obergefreiter crawled forward, keeping to a narrow trail which ran alongside the footpath. Moments later he spotted the first one through the bushes. It was Scheimann. He was moaning softly. Schmitz crawled on. He found Nägele and crawled up close to him.

"Nägele?" he called softly, and then again: "Nägele?"

There was no answer. He was lying on the footpath, his head buried face-down in the grass. Cautiously, Schmitz tugged at the man's left boot. Nägele's body moved. Suddenly, there was a burst of fire from the Russian positions! The bullets struck Nägele's body, but he did not move. It was clear that Schmitz had been trying to rescue a dead man. Hastily the Obergefreiter crawled back to Scheimann, keeping a lookout to both sides. He hauled the wounded man into the bushes, then he took him by the arms and ran with him back to Bolland.

The two medics went forward four more times. Each time they returned with a wounded comrade. On returning to their position for the fourth time they heard a burst of firing from several machine guns far to the left. Russian automatic rifles and submachine guns could also be heard.

"The commander has sent in the rest of the Third," said Krämer, who had arrived immediately to take over care of the wounded. A short time later Hauptmann Niehaus, company commander of the 3rd Infantry Regiment, came back. When he saw the wounded men he silently extended his hand to the medics.

In the meantime the 3rd Battalion had advanced one kilometer. That afternoon both battalions launched a simultaneous assault on the Russian positions. Once again Schmitz followed behind the 1st Company. He saw the flashes from the Russian guns. Soon afterward, the German troops leapt into the first trenches. They threw hand grenades and smoked the bitterly defending Russians from their holes. Red Army soldiers had often been known to cower in their holes and let the advancing Germans pass, then fire on them from behind.

The Russian positions were taken and the advance continued through the forest. It had already become dark. Suddenly, the place was swarming with Russians. Bitter hand-to-hand fighting broke out. The enemy repeatedly threw themselves at the advancing Germans, using spades, hand grenades, pistols and submachine guns. The German attack ground to a halt.

"New enemy groups have appeared, sir!" reported Leutnant Guhlich, the regimental adjutant. He had come over from the 3rd Battalion to report that the battalion was bogged down in the forest.

"Everyone halt! Dig in!" was the next order.

The men began digging into the forest floor. They had scarcely started when a large number of tank engines suddenly roared to life. Ahead lay a depression with a deep ravine. It extended from in front of the town of Michelovka to the Dniepr.

"Tanks, tanks!"

The cry went up as the first Russian tanks were spotted in the twilight. They rumbled out of the ravine and rolled forward in a wide wedge formation. The Russian tanks, a dozen or more, stopped. Their long-barreled guns spat flame. High-explosive rounds fell at the edge of the woods, shaving off the crowns of trees, which fell on the German troops in cover below. Direct hits cut down whole squads as they advanced and, once again, the call for medics echoed through the forest. Schmitz heard the screams and followed them. He raced into the Hell of the battle, where everyone else was taking cover and trying to offer the smallest possible target. New orders were given:

"We're falling back to the jumping-off positions!"

Oberst Runge had no other choice. Advancing behind the tanks in dense waves were fresh attack groups of the Red Army. They would reach the edge of the woods for certain and, accustomed to the forest and equipped with infallible instincts, would probably destroy the German units during the night.

The German troops withdrew in stages. The Soviet tanks rattled through the forest and then ploughed through the tall field of corn.

"Form antitank teams and stop them!"

This order from the regiment's commanding officer had just been issued. It had become clear that the tanks would be capable of destroying the whole regiment, if they succeeded in overrunning the withdrawing companies. The antitank teams were formed. They slipped into the cornfield, approaching tanks that had halted to fire, and put them out of action with high-explosive charges.

Nearly exhausted, the men of the 1st Company also reached the hill from which Soviet heavy machine guns were firing on their mortars and infantry guns. They hurried up the sides of the hill and, on reaching the top, threw themselves down in the trenches and sucked the cool air into their burning lungs.

"There are still a number of wounded out there, Schmitz!" These were Oberleutnant Meuthe's first words to Schmitz when the Obergefreiter reported to him.

"Where are they, sir?" asked Schmitz, looking at his company commander. The two were standing in one of the Russian command posts on the northern edge of the hill. Schmitz had been summoned there by a messenger from the company headquarters personnel.

"Only one man from the antitank teams has returned. He will tell you where the others are—Kummernuß, fetch the Feldwebel."

The messenger disappeared. Schmitz gnawed on a sausage sandwich that the company commander had had prepared for him.

"Feldwebel Schütten reporting!" The Feldwebel was the leader of the 4th Platoon, which had provided the company's two antitank teams. Schmitz looked into the haggard face. The battle against the Soviet tanks and infantry had left its mark, as had the knowledge of the loss of his men.

"Schütten, where did you lose the two teams?" asked Oberleutnant Meuthe.

The Feldwebel had to clear his throat several times before he found his voice. Then he described the fighting: "The two teams were on the right side of the cornfield. Six T-34s were attacking there in single file. Gefreiter Bäumker and I were able to disable the first one. As we approached the second one, we were suddenly surrounded by Russians. Bäumker was shot down and Obergefreiter Luserke, who tried to create some breathing room and free the second team with his machine gun, was killed by a hand grenade."

"And then? What happened to the second team and your fourth man?"

"I don't know, sir," said the Feldwebel, sobbing. "I don't know! I ran away. I was wounded in the arm." He gestured to his torn sleeve, through which a bandage was visible. "And then I reached the hill."

"Very well, Schütten. Obergefreiter Schmitz is going to look for the men."

"Sir," asked the Feldwebel, "Let me go with him."

"Good, go with him!" said the commander after an inquiring sideways glance at Schmitz. "You leave in half an hour."

"Good luck, men!" With these words Leutnant Willrich bade farewell to the two men as they set out into no-man's-land in front of Hill 142 to look for the wounded.

"Thanks, sir," replied the medic Obergefreiter, looking at the officer.

Together the two men left the cover of the German positions. Bent low, they crept through the small patch of woods, expecting to be surprised any minute. After 300 meters they heard a noise: Voices giving orders in a foreign language. They skirted the area where they had heard the voices and entered the bush-covered terrain that extended inland from the bank of the Dniepr. After another 300 meters they came to the point where they had to leave the bushes.

The night sky was now clear. In front of them the two saw three rising columns of smoke. They marked the locations where the enemy tanks had been knocked out. The wrecks were still smoldering.

"To the right!" whispered Feldwebel Schütten. Cautiously, they moved onwards, came to the trampled field and slipped into the corn. The outline of the smoldering enemy tank grew higher in front of them. Suddenly, they were challenged in Russian:

"Hands up!"

Schmitz and Schütten dropped to the ground and rolled to the side. A submachine gun opened up, but the bullets went wide and to the right. Feldwebel Schütten replied with his captured Soviet submachine gun, then dodged to the side as quickly as he could. There was another burst of firing. Schmitz took aim at the muzzle flash and fired. The rattling ceased abruptly. It had become deathly still. Schmitz tried to breathe softly. Tensely he stared into the night.

Suddenly, a voice rang out through the night: "Comrades, over here! Help us!"

"That's Luserke!" gasped Schütten.

The two ran in the direction of the voice. Bullets whizzed towards them from ahead and to the right. They found Luserke and dropped to the ground beside him. Schütten reached for the machine gun, turned it around and fired a long burst through the corn. Schmitz kneeled beside the badly wounded man, who had bandaged his own wounds as best he could. He was about to properly dress the wounds when a Russian tank suddenly opened fire in front of them. Round after round cracked from the long barrel and hissed through the night. High-explosive rounds howled over the men in no-man's-land and smashed into the German positions on the hill.

"Do you know anything about the others?" Schmitz asked after he had dressed Luserke's wounds.

"A while ago one of them called out. Up ahead, almost to the Russian tank that's firing."

"You stay here! We'll come back as soon as we find out what's going on," promised Schmitz.

They crept forward. Schmitz was leading the way and had a machine gun at the ready. Soon they could recognize the outline of the enemy tank.

Schmitz (2nd from left) with members of his 2nd Company. On the far right is the company's senior NCO, Hauptfeldwebel Göttert.

A meter-long tongue of flame leapt from the long gun. The report of the gun firing deafened the two Germans for a few seconds.

"Comrades!—Comrades!"

"There he is!" called Schütten excitedly. He wanted to jump up and run over to the wounded man, and it took all of Schmitz' strength to restrain him.

"That's a Russian!" hissed Schmitz.

"Help, I'm hurt!" Again they heard the cry. Schmitz was almost moved to get up, run beneath the gunfire from the tank and rescue the man. But his instinct told him that something wasn't quite right. He concentrated his attention on the tank and the terrain in front of it. He saw a dark shadow, from whose direction a call rang out for the third time:

"Help me!"

Feldwebel Schütten jumped to his feet and ran toward the spot where the voice had just called out. A rifle shot rang out. The Feldwebel fell to the ground, fatally wounded. The Obergefreiter crawled off to one side. It was well that he did, because a burst of machine-gun fire from the tank tore up the ground where he had been lying before. Schmitz remained motionless for some time, listening to his own breathing. Then he cautiously crawled forward. About sixty meters to one side of the tank he stopped again and tried to peer through the darkness. Some time later he found two of the missing men. Both were dead. But there was still one missing. If he had been taken alive, he could only be inside the tank.

Meter by meter Obergefreiter Schmitz crawled eastward. The corn provided good cover, as this part of the field had not been crushed by the tanks. He crawled in an arc until he was several meters behind the T-34. He saw a Russian emerge from beneath the tank. The man stood up, began to climb onto the back of the tank and shouted something. A few strides and Schmitz was upon him. The tanker, who was in the process of climbing onto the tank, turned in surprise.

Schmitz saw the man open his mouth to shout a warning. He swung his fist, which was clutching his weapon, and struck the Russian a hard blow on the chin. Gurgling softly, the Russian dropped to his knees. Everything else happened quickly. Schmitz jumped up onto the fender. As he reached the hull of the tank, the commander's head appeared through the turret hatch. The Russian called out something. His voice rang out sharp and clear. Then he saw the German. He tried to close the hatch, but a shot from the 8-mm pistol caused him to freeze in mid-movement. His upper body fell across the rim of the hatch. Hans Schmitz stuck his pistol down into the tank and shouted in Russian: "Hands up!"

The pale light of an instrument panel lighted the interior. A Russian was crouched beside the tank's gun. He looked up and cried in broken German: "Don't shoot! Don't shoot!" The German survivor forced himself through the turret hatch.

"Jump down and go straight ahead!" said Schmitz.

"Luserke is over there. You must call to him, then he'll answer. But hurry, I'll be right behind you."

The man ran in the specified direction and disappeared into the corn. Glancing to his right, Schmitz saw soldiers running through the field. They were plainly visible in the light of the rising moon: Russians. They would cut off his escape route if they maintained their direction. Schmitz reached for a hand grenade. He armed the grenade, waited two seconds, threw it inside the tank and immediately closed the hatch. The grenade exploded as Schmitz hit the ground and rolled. At once he was on his feet and running after his comrade.

Commands were shouted through the night. Groups of Russian troops hurried to the scene. Suddenly, Schmitz heard Luserke's machine gun roar to life. It was being operated by the man he had rescued from the tank.

"Cover the rear!" Schmitz shouted to him. "Every fifty paces stop and fire a burst to keep their heads down!"

Then he heaved the wounded Luserke onto his back and began to move. Behind him, the machine gun roared, allowing him to run about fifty paces. Exhausted, he allowed himself and the wounded man to sink to the ground, where he lay gasping for breath. The rescued soldier came running up, threw himself to the ground and expended the rest of the belt of ammunition. Laboriously, Schmitz heaved the wounded machine gunner onto his shoulder and stumbled on.

Shots howled through the night. After twenty meters Schmitz felt as if he were breathing molten lead instead of air. Soon he was about to give up the ghost, but he refused to give up. They had covered about 400 meters when they were met by Leutnant Willrich and Grenzel's squad. Two men lifted the heavy burden from his shoulders.

A short time later they reached the German positions on the side of the hill. Standing in a trench was Oberleutnant Meuthe. He seemed to notice only Schmitz, who tagged along after the bearers. Apparently he couldn't fathom that once again the medic had returned and brought a wounded man with him.

"Where is Feldwebel Schütten?"

"He's dead, sir!" answered Schmitz.

"Schütten tried to rescue his comrades and, in so doing, ran into a Soviet trap."

"Schmitz!" said the Oberleutnant, as he extended his hand to the medic. "I'll never forget what you have done."

✠

Evening had come on 21 August 1941. The sun had shone down all day and, even after the onset of darkness, the ground was still warm. The men of the medic team squatted in front of their two earth bunkers on Hill 142. Schmitz was lying on a shelter half, his rolled up shirt under his head. He stared into the sky, across which the dark of night was gradually spreading. The first stars twinkled in the dark ball of the firmament. The moon rose on the far side of the Dniepr. Now and then there was a muzzle flash from the ring of fortifications around Kiev. The city was one corner of a triangle in which there were five Soviet armies.

Kiev, situated where the Desna flows into the Dniepr, was the pivot of the entire front. Kremenchug, the German bridgehead east of the Dniepr, was the most southeasterly point. In the east German armored units had advanced along the Desna and Seym as far as Konotop and south of Glukov. If the forces in the north moved simultaneously with the ones in the south holding the bridgehead at Kremenchug, they would trap entire Soviet armies.

Shells from the fortress roared overhead as the men talked. Suddenly, there was a shout from a forward sentry post: "Be quiet!" There was no doubt. Something was happening near the village of Myschelovka. The men on the hill could clearly hear the sound of tank engines warming up. Wordlessly they began to pull on their boots and reach for their weapons. They knew what was coming; they had experienced several surprise enemy attacks during the past few weeks.

Minutes passed and the sound of tank engines grew louder. At the foot of the slope down below a pair of illumination flares hissed into the night sky. Suddenly, the two Flak 88s on the flanks roared to life. The rounds released two parachute flares at an altitude of about 6,000 meters. The flares drifted down over the no-man's-land in front of Michelovka and bathed the area in light. Peering through his night glasses, Oberleutnant Meuthe, who had hurried to the forward trenches following the first report, saw the gray giants moving along the ravine towards the flank of Hill 142. Behind them appeared dense waves of Soviet infantry. Oberleutnant Meuthe reached behind him.

"Get me the regiment, Zischker!" The man immediately made contact with the regiment. The telephone operator handed him the receiver.

"This is Oberleutnant Meuthe. Russian attack with tanks on both flanks. Objective Hill 142. Request fire on the designated positions!"

"Understood, Meuthe: I'm coming up there myself!" replied Oberst Runge.

The two 8.8-cm Flak had spotted the enemy tanks and opened fire from a range of 1,800 meters. The heavy rounds left a visible trail in the darkness. The first round from the gun on the right hissed over a Russian tank and struck the ground behind it. The second was a direct hit. Smoke pouring from the turret hatch, the T-34 halted. Seconds later flames spewed from inside the tank. While at least twenty tanks halted and began firing on the hill, the first tank's reserve ammunition exploded, tearing the vehicle to pieces. Schmitz observed these happenings from his foxhole. He saw the flashes of gunfire and heard the howling of rounds.

Then the T-34s began to move again. Several veered westwards and disappeared into a patch of woods. The others came nearer. Behind them were swarms of infantry.

"Open fire!" ordered Oberleutnant Meuthe.

The heavy machine gun began to roar next to Schmitz. Mortars and infantry guns joined the barrage. A series of illumination flares lit the battlefield. A voice rang out above the noise of the fighting:

"There . . . one of them is trying to run over the outpost position."

They saw the T-34 as it turned toward the center and rolled at high speed toward the spot where tracer and bursts of machine-gun fire flitted through the night.

"Covering fire!" roared Grenzel.

"Will do, Hubert!" shouted Alfred Dickel, the number-one gunner in the heavy machine-gun team.

He fired at the Red Army troops attempting to follow the tanks. Grenzel, Trimhold and Kröger jumped out of their holes and began to run. They raced through machine-gun fire and past bursting rounds. Breathing heavily, they reached a communications trench and disappeared inside.

"They've done it, Franz!" shouted Bolland over the din. Schmitz nodded. He raised the binoculars he had obtained from battalion headquarters and scanned the parapet of the trench. That's where Grenzel would have to be if he was to be in position to catch the T-34. The Russian tank had stopped not fifty meters from the trench and was firing on the German positions with its main gun and machine gun. Grenzel then appeared, followed by Kröger and Trimhold. As Schmitz watched, Grenzel fired a burst from his submachine gun.

Seconds later Grenzel jumped to his feet and raced toward the tank. For a few seconds he stopped beside the rear of the tank. For an instant Schmitz saw the outline of a concentrated charge in his hands. Then Grenzel leapt to the side and disappeared into a hole. Soon afterwards a dense flame shot out from the T-34. There was considerable confusion. The Russians had overrun the forward outpost and turned its machine gun on the men in their foxholes on the ridge, forcing them to take cover.

Cries of "tanks, tanks, tanks!" rang out from the sector's left flank. Schmitz crawled down the hill through the communications trench. About ten meters behind him was Bolland, ready to give covering fire. They heard the creaking of tank tracks, the roaring of the engines and the crash of gunfire. At the foot of the hill they suddenly found themselves facing a group of Russians who were apparently about to climb the hill.

Obergefreiter Schmitz threw himself down on his stomach. Bolland raised his submachine gun and fired over his head. The enemy troops took cover. Schmitz took the hand grenades from his belt, unscrewed the caps and held them ready to throw. He spotted movement at a bend in the trench and threw the first grenade, followed immediately by the second, third and fourth, which he tossed over the dividing wall into the other section of trench. After the fourth one had detonated, Schmitz and Bolland got up and hurried onwards. Moments later they crawled into the crater into which Grenzel had disappeared.

They found him there, bleeding from numerous wounds.

"Call for Kröger and Trimhold. They must be hiding farther back!"

Bolland crawled back a few meters, until he could see into the main trench. Cowering inside were several enemy soldiers. He fired a long burst down the trench. Then he rammed in a fresh magazine and called to his two comrades.

Kröger came first. He was holding his shattered left hand tightly with his right and moaning softly. Trimhold had been wounded in the calf. Schmitz dressed their wounds, then turned to Trimhold.

"Can you go ahead and clear the way for us?"

Trimhold nodded, then asked: "How is Hubert?"

"He's unconscious. You can worry about him if we get back to the hill."

Trimhold led the way. Bolland followed with Kröger. Then came Schmitz with the unconscious Grenzel, whom he had slung over his shoulder. The night was filled with the sounds of fighting. The enemy tanks still had not reached the hill. The T-34s on the left flank were unable to fire; they had their hands full trying to negotiate the steep slope. Farther back on the flank of the ridge the two 3.7-cm antitank guns of the battalion antitank platoon were firing. The Russian infantry had been forced to take cover in front of the hill. Nevertheless, they fired at anything that moved on the hill. The small group of medics was repeatedly forced to seek cover in shell holes but, in the end, they made it back.

Grenzel, Trimhold and Kröger were taken to the main dressing station. The Russian assault seemed to have been repulsed. But that was not to be the case. An hour later the Red Army attacked again. This attack was also repelled. But then, at about 0325 hours, a third attack group with four T-34 tanks broke through and reached the hill.

The four tanks rolled over the trenches, collapsing them, and shot up the "88" on the right flank. A flood of Russian infantry poured across the ridge. The men of the 279th Infantry Regiment withdrew slowly. They were forced to give up the hill. Schmitz and his companions dragged several badly wounded men with them. Some time later Hill 142 was again in Russian hands.

"Immediate counterattack! We must drive the enemy back, before they can settle into the position, Runge!"

The division commander had driven forward. He and the commanders of the 278th and 279th Infantry Regiments were standing just behind the fall-back position. A steady flow of stragglers found their way in and rejoined their units.

The rested 278th led the attack. The regiment fanned out as it stormed forward through the early morning. At the same time, the 279th once again worked its way through the dense vegetation of the Dniepr Valley. The soldiers had to wade through several small streams, but they finally reached the edge of the bush-covered area. Russian fire poured down from the south side of the hill. At that point, the divisional artillery began ranging in on the ridge. It was directed by a forward observer.

"They're already going at it" observed Paul Zürn. Rounds of every caliber hammered down on the hill.

"Get up! Move out!" Oberst Runge rushed out of cover and ran toward the east flank of Hill 142.

The men followed. The 1st Battalion advanced behind the 2nd and 3rd Battalions as the attack reserve. The men moved forward toward the hill and began to climb the flank. They were in familiar territory as they prepared to storm the plateau atop the hill. This time they ran along the east side until they could see the north slope. There they went into position and overpowered the Russians defending to the east. From there they watched their sister regiment attack and drive the enemy back.

"Open fire!"

Every weapon opened fire on the right flank of the withdrawing enemy. A Russian tank rolled towards them. Several men jumped onto the tank and lit demolition charges. There was a loud explosion and flames sprang from the tank's engine compartment. The other regiment stormed onward. The Soviets, who had retaken the hill after three attacks, were driven off it again. They withdrew under heavy fire.

The medics spent the whole morning scouring the battlefield and recovering casualties. Those on the north slope had to be recovered as well. Every available Russian gun hammered the hill. Then close-support aircraft came and strafed the positions. The remaining 8.8-cm Flak engaged the attackers and shot one down. The battle for Hill 142 had reached a decisive stage. The Russians gathered their forces for a renewed assault, however, every attack was repulsed.

The last major assault on 12 September 1941 saw the Soviets again penetrate the German positions. Oberst Runge led the regiment's small reserve force in an immediate counterattack, which drove out the intruders. On 15 September Schmitz and his comrades on Hill 142 heard that the battle was about to be decided. Wild rumors circulated among the men.

"Do you think the stories are true, Franz?" Horst Bolland asked his friend. They had just recovered several wounded men from the area in front of the lines.

"We'll know soon. Come with me, we'll drop in on the commander."

The two medics walked over to the command post. There they learned that at noon on 15 September the southwards advancing elements of the

3rd Panzer Division had linked up with the leading tanks of the 9th Panzer Division from the southern group.

"The pocket is closed. In the next few days we'll attack and drive into Kiev!" Oberleutnant Meuthe assured them.

The course had been set. The Russian "Southwest Front" army group was facing destruction inside a giant triangle whose legs were formed by the Desna and Dniepr Rivers. Stalin had categorically ordered that Kiev was to be held no matter what the cost.

But then 750,000 soldiers had been surrounded. Still holding around Kiev were the divisions of the Soviet Thirty-Seventh Army. The two armies in the north of the pocket—the Fifth and Twenty-First—scattered in all directions. On the Dniepr front was the Twenty-Sixth Army. It had incorporated the remnants of the Thirty-Sixth Army, which had already been smashed near Kremenchug.

Marshall Timoshenko, who had taken command of the "Southwest Front," instructed two armies and two cavalry corps on 16 September to attempt to break into the pocket from the east. This desperate attempt came to nothing, however. German dive-bombers and close-support aircraft smashed the units spearheading the relief attack. And while the besieging divisions around Kiev were preparing to assault the city, the Soviet chief of operations, Major General Bagramyan, flew into the pocket and reported to Timoshenko's army group headquarters in Priluki. From there he telephoned General Kirponos and gave him the order to evacuate Kiev.

The General radioed Moscow requesting confirmation of the order, because Stalin had always said that Kiev was to be held no matter what the cost. But this time he received a very different order from STAVKA (Stalin's headquarters in Moscow).

Marshall Shaposhnikov, Stalin's left-hand man, answered in laconic brevity: "Break out to the east!" All of the army headquarters had to confirm receipt of the order. This they did and then set about putting the order into action. Only the Thirty-Seventh Army in and around Kiev was no longer reporting. Its Commander-in-Chief, General Vlasov, was out of contact with the army group. The Thirty-Seventh Army fought where it stood: In the Kiev area!

"On your feet! Move out!"

The soldiers of the 95th Infantry Division set out towards the north and Kiev. It was 17 September 1941 and the sun had not yet risen. However, the first rays were visible in the eastern sky beyond the great river, announcing that daybreak was imminent.

The 1st Battalion advanced in the middle of the attack sector. As usual, Schmitz walked at the rear of the company. His four litter bearers were close behind him. He could recognize the back of the regimental commander ahead. He was with the 3rd Battalion, which was spearheading the advance. The advancing troops were met by fire from Myschelovka and the wooded high ground south of the village. The heights extended almost to the belt of vegetation along the Dniepr. Russian field guns fired from every hill and small rise. Rounds hammered into the ground, tearing up the cornfields and bushes and blasting apart the forest.

Leutnant Willrich watched as the 3rd Battalion was repeatedly forced to take cover. "No one can get through there alive!" he shouted. 7.62-cm guns and 10-cm mortars fired from the village. The groups of attacking soldiers were repeatedly stopped and forced to seek cover. The fighting had been going on for seven hours already. The sun was now high in the sky, shining down hot on the men below as they were forced again and again to burrow into the ground in an effort to find cover. Finally, the 9th Company reached the school on the southern outskirts of the village. There it halted. Oberst Runge, who had accompanied the company, was forced to call off the attack. The last 800 meters to the village and the ridge beyond were pure Hell, which no one could have passed through alive.

An order came through: "Medics from all units move forward!"

While the others dug in as best they could, Schmitz and his four helpers ran forward. They reached the men of the 3rd Battalion and saw them lying in the field. Exploding mortar rounds made fresh black smudges in the earth.

"Quickly, everyone: Follow me!"

Schmitz got to his feet after shrapnel from a volley of mortar rounds had whizzed over the foxholes. They ran as fast as they could. A howling noise in the air announced that another volley was on its way. The Obergefreiter dropped to the ground. He heard an explosion not ten meters away and felt lumps of dirt striking his back. A fragment pinged off the side of his helmet. Schmitz got to his feet again but came under fire from a Maxim machine gun emplaced on the forward slope. He was forced to hit the ground again. Bolland came running up to him.

"Take cover!" shouted Schmitz. But it was too late. The second burst caught the medic in the chest and threw him several meters backwards. He lay there motionless. Then he disappeared in a cloud of dust and powder smoke from the next exploding mortar round. Schmitz ran over to his friend but, when he turned him over, he realized that the man was beyond help. The other two medics caught up with Schmitz. Together with Schmitz they crawled on through the field. They found the first seriously wounded soldiers and dressed their wounds. Then they came upon a man with a stomach wound. He was holding in his intestines with both hands. Schmitz felt nausea rising in him. He suppressed it, pushed Zürn to one side and went to work.

They left the man lying where he was, as they had to concentrate their efforts on those who could be saved. This was a situation Schmitz had always feared. Nevertheless, there was no other choice. Sänger was wounded. At that point he was left with only Zürn and Krämer. They carried the men Schmitz dragged back from the front lines to the main dressing station. Enemy machine guns frequently fired at the three soldiers. Oberst Runge watched from the school, which was under heavy fire, as Obergefreiter Schmitz continued to drag back wounded comrades. And each time he immediately went forward again to carry out another daring rescue operation.

"Look at that man," said the Oberst. "I have never seen anything like it. He has the strength of ten men!" Finally, Runge himself ran into the cornfield to help. Others followed. Bach was given a wounded man to carry as Schmitz brought them in from the terrain that was almost devoid of cover and concealment.

The divisional artillery began moving forward as it was getting dark. Throughout the night guns of every caliber were moved up. Mortar platoons set up and selected their targets, but did not fire. By early morning on 18 September the artillery had maneuvered into favorable positions all along the division's attack front. On command, the guns began laying down a destructive barrage.

For twenty minutes the earth shook, as rounds of every caliber pounded the Russian positions. Fires flared up. Russian batteries attempted to destroy the German guns; they were spotted by forward observers and eliminated with several salvoes. Huge clouds of dust and smoke and extensive fires were proof of the barrage's effectiveness. Following the bombardment the infantry received the order to attack. This time the regiment was to lead the way. The 1st Battalion moved through the positions of the 3rd Battalion and assumed the point position. Soon they reached the schoolhouse, from which two German machine guns and a 3.7-cm Pak were firing on the village. Schmitz saw the regimental commander take his place among the soldiers. They were met by machine-gun fire from the slope,

A formal portrait photo of
Franz Schmitz, with a personal
dedication to the author.

where the Russians had installed bunkers. In spite of this, the attack made good progress.

Up front they encountered the spearhead group from the 280th Infantry Regiment. Obergefreiter Schmitz learned that the division commander, Generalleutnant Sixt von Arnim, was likewise taking part in the attack. He led from the front, allowing him to make immediate decisions, as the constantly changing situation demanded. The presence of the two officers inspired the soldiers. Schmitz was also caught up in the euphoria that offensive operations can sometimes generate. They stormed ahead, reached the barbed wire and cut lanes through it. The soldiers began climbing up the far slope but were met by hand grenades and machine-gun bullets and forced back. A second attempt was successful and they reached the top of the hill. Hand grenades were stuck through the embrasures of the bunkers, and one nest of resistance after another was eliminated.

The enemy defended bitterly. A hand grenade exploded near Schmitz. One man lost a leg. Schmitz was on the scene in seconds, tending to the serious wound. The field positions in front of the village were taken, but the advance continued. Heavy fire spewed from the center of the village. Schmitz threw himself down in a Russian communications trench and landed beside the regimental commander. A few meters to the side was Generalleutnant von Arnim.

"There, the Stukas!"

The troops roared with excitement at the appearance of the dive-bombers. They flew overhead in tight formation. Schmitz counted eighteen machines. Seconds later the bombers went into a dive and plunged down towards the village, sirens howling. The sound of explosions reached the soldiers. The heavy bombs fell right in the midst of the enemy's last heavily fortified defensive position. Flames, towering clouds of smoke and fountains of earth from exploding bombs darkened the horizon.

"Attack with your regiment, Runge!"

The Oberst nodded. Three red flares were fired into the air and, as one, the infantry began to move. They reached the village and broke all resistance. Oberst Runge knew what he had to do in this moment of enemy weakness. His order followed immediately:

"The regiment is to continue attacking: Stay on the enemy heels, prevent him from regrouping and storm into Kiev!"

The advance continued. Ignoring an open right flank, the regiment stayed on the retreating enemy's heels. The Lysa Gora appeared ahead through the afternoon mist.

"The last fortified heights before Kiev!"

This call passed from mouth to mouth, encouraging the men. For a second time the Stukas appeared. They attacked the hill positions and put the heavy guns out of action. From the far bank of the Dniepr Russian antiaircraft guns opened fire on the dive-bombers. The formation was already turning away. One aircraft was shot down, but the crew managed to escape by parachute. In spite of the air attack, the assault companies were met by strong machine-gun and rifle fire.

"Dig in!"

Once again the soldiers began to dig; every centimeter meant more security. Schmitz and his men dug in too. When evening came there would be wounded to recover and treat. While the others rested, Schmitz and the others went into action. They saved the lives of men who might be caught again by the fury of the war. Also creeping through no-man's-land were groups of Russian stragglers. Bursts of gunfire were an indication that the enemy was nearby, perhaps waiting to shoot them in the next shell hole or bomb crater. Nevertheless, Schmitz and his men worked their way forward until the last of the wounded had been found.

The night of 19 September 1941 was lit by terrific fires burning on the reverse slope of the Lysa Gora. They also illuminated the battlefield for the searching medics. When morning came they caught a few hours sleep. The advance resumed as soon as it was light. Oberst Runge had issued the final, decisive order during the night: "The regiment will go around the Lysa Gora to the west and storm into Kiev!"

The regiment attacked at first light and went around the Lysa Gora, where it found itself facing Russian forces that were trying to halt and make a stand. Nevertheless, the outflanking maneuver resulted in a surprise victory. The 1st Battalion made the enemy's confusion complete when it overran this part of the Russian defense. Subsequently, the regiment neared the city. At the same time, far to the northwest, the 71st Infantry Division was storming toward the metropolis of the Ukraine. Schmitz saw the tower of the Lavra Monastery appear before him. He had been able to see it for weeks from atop Hill 142, but now it was near enough to touch.

The Russian troops pulled back. The sun, previously hidden behind morning clouds, broke through. Its light spread across the houses of the southern suburbs and bathed the dome of the monastery in gleaming brightness.

"Keep going, keep going, the battalion will continue the assault through to the citadel!" ordered Hauptmann Hahne.

The rows of soldiers set themselves in motion again. Bullets whistled toward them. Soviet resistance gradually weakened and was finally broken. Schmitz saw the first people emerge from houses, cellars and hiding places to welcome the German soldiers. The tremendous Lavra Monastery grew nearer and nearer.

"Turn to the right, to the right!" roared one of the regiment's staff officers from the point. The units turned. The troops advanced at the double, with the 1st Battalion leading the way. The companies had become intermixed. Led by Oberst Runge, they pushed on into the citadel. Several messengers and orderlies ringed the Oberst. Schmitz tended to the few men hit by the last rounds from the defenders.

Suddenly, a many-voiced shout of relief rang out through the late morning. Looking up, Schmitz saw the German war flag being raised from the highest tower of the citadel. Kiev, which had held out for six weeks, had fallen.

The next day the regiment's commanding officer presented Schmitz with the Iron Cross, First Class. In addition, he was promoted to a medical-corps Unteroffizier for bravery in the face of the enemy.

"Schmitz," said Oberst Runge to the young soldier. "More than anyone else, you have earned this decoration. Through you the regiment has saved at least 200 soldiers. You have also met the requirements for the

Infantry Assault Badge, which is also being awarded to you. I'm proud of you and your men."

The Battle of Kiev was over. For 650,000 soldiers of the Red Army the city had become a trap. All went into captivity. Eight hundred eighty-four tanks, 3,718 guns and huge amounts of other war materiel were captured or destroyed.

Following the Battle of Kiev the 95th Infantry Division was attached to the LV Army Corps which, as the western corps of Army Group South, was in contact with the XXXXVIII Panzer Corps, a formation of Army Group Middle.

Unteroffizier Schmitz and his medics took part in the advance that saw the regiment move along the Desna and Seym Rivers towards Kursk. There were always wounded to recover and it was always the burly Unteroffizier who risked his life by going out into no-man's-land to recover the wounded.

Such forays frequently led to encounters with the enemy at close quarters. Schmitz had to ward off prowling enemy troops as he sought out the wounded. There were many close shaves and more than once he thought his time had come. He saw the whites of the enemy's eyes and fought to keep from being killed.

The battle for Kursk was a bitter affair that resulted in high casualty figures. Once again the medical corps demonstrated its eagerness to assist in many rescue operations. The soldiers of the 95th Infantry Division finally went over to the defensive behind the Tim. The Oberst with the "Blue Max"—the soldier's term for the WW I decoration, the *Pour le Merite*—was a tower of strength. Oberst Runge spread calm and confidence wherever he went. The Russians had amassed powerful armored and cavalry forces against this sector of the front. The attacks were repulsed by the German troops in their winter position on the Tim. Schmitz experienced several cavalry attacks there. He saw the mounted Soviet units gallop across the snow-covered plain. When the horsemen came within range of the German heavy weapons they were killed one after another. The cries of men and horses merged in a horrible orgy of destruction.

Unteroffizier Schmitz also saved a number of Russian soldiers in this sector. He and his comrades were aware that their duties as medics superseded any differences in uniform.

In the meantime, it had grown bitterly cold. In addition to the wounded, Schmitz was called upon to treat increasing numbers of frostbite cases. This was one of the hardest things for a medic to deal with. They saw young men whose feet froze and quickly became black lumps. Or others, whose hands and feet simply rotted away, men without ears and noses! The winter days on the Tim were a terrible time for Unteroffizier Schmitz as well. Nevertheless, there was only one thing for him and his comrades: Out into a winter night or a howling snowstorm to search for and bring back the missing.

On one such search mission he ran into a Russian patrol. It had approached the German lines almost noiselessly on skis and suddenly appeared in front of him. On this occasion it was his old friend Paul Zürn who saved the day; he fired a quick burst before the enemy could open fire and thus averted the threat. They then looked after the survivors and later brought them to the village, where the main dressing station was located.

By then it was late December. Oberst Siegfried Runge had received the Knight's Cross on 20 December 1941. The next morning the Soviets attacked directly in front of the 95th Infantry Division.

"Here they come!"

White-clad figures were visible through the blowing snow as they rushed phantom-like over the snow on skis. Russian attack units had crossed the frozen Tim River and were approaching the German positions in open battle order.

"Open fire!" shouted Oberleutnant Meuthe.

The enemy was 200 meters from the position. Every machine gun opened fire. Bullets hissed over the snow-covered fields. In the first light of day Schmitz and his companions saw the Russians halt in front of their barbed wire barricade. Within seconds they had disappeared into the snow.

"They're out there at the wire somewhere and will try to crawl through. And then they'll be here in no time! One hundred percent readiness!"

Hardly had the battalion commander spoken these words, when the Teller mines in the wire went up. Bright pillars of flame shot up out of the ground. There was shouting, and the Russians jumped up and began to charge toward the position. Then they were caught in a hail of rifle and machine-gun fire. Some went to ground, others continued to run through the storm of bullets.

They reached the trench firing their rifles and stabbing with their four-cornered bayonets, but they were driven out by the defenders with spades, pistols, rifles and submachine guns. Schmitz saw three or four figures throwing themselves at Grenzel's squad's machine-gun position. He ran a few paces and came under fire. He was forced to take cover briefly and then fired up at a Russian about to fall upon Alfred Dickel. The man toppled over and fell across the machine gunner, where he was struck by a burst of fire from a second Russian soldier who had taken aim at Dickel.

Oberleutnant Meuthe and the company headquarters personnel came from the right. Firing on the run, he closed in on the group of enemy soldiers who had penetrated the position. Suddenly, a hand grenade exploded. The severely wounded Russian soldier who had armed the grenade was literally blown to pieces. Oberleutnant Meuthe took some of the shrapnel and fell to the ground. It was a critical moment. Several platoons were on the verge of pulling back.

"I'm taking command!" roared Leutnant Willrich. "1st Platoon: Counterattack to the right flank!"

The platoon leapt up. Schmitz followed. Firing on the run, they raced through the trench, stumbling over their own and enemy soldiers lying at the bottom. They reached the 3rd Platoon, whose bunkers had been overrun. Bitter hand-to-hand fighting broke out. The enemy were driven back and forced out of the trenches.

Finally, the firing died down. Silence settled over the company's sector of the front. Farther north the sound of fighting intensified. Unteroffizier Schmitz ran over to Oberleutnant Meuthe. He bent over his commander, examined the shrapnel wounds and bandaged his badly bleeding hand. Russian machine guns were still firing from no-man's-land. A mortar brigade fired light-caliber rounds into the German positions. The troops lay exhausted on the ground. But Schmitz and his helpers were on their feet, seeking out the wounded and tending their injuries.

Three hours later they learned the Russians had broken through at the boundary between two units and had already stormed several kilometers towards the west.

Nevertheless, the German defenders at the Tim didn't take flight. Once again, the situation was stabilized. Soon it was Christmas. The soldiers "celebrated" in their own way in their bunkers and holes as well as in huts farther to the rear.

✠

On New Year's morning Russian ski troops attacked the positions of the 95th Infantry Division. They were driven back by the 9th Panzer Division, under its outstanding commander Generalleutnant Dr. Alfred von Hubicki. The tanks, some without fuel and unable to move, were employed as "positional artillery". They were dug in up to their turrets. The 279th Infantry Regiment was attacked by KV-I and T-34 tanks, whose broad tracks allowed them to negotiate the deep snow. Oberst Runge organized the defense. The enemy was growing stronger daily, but the German positions held.

On 19 January 1942 the Red Army launched a new offensive against the German front on the Tim. This time they broke through at the boundary between the LV Army Corps and the XXXXVIII Panzer Corps. Russian cavalry and infantry divisions poured westward through the breach and, by the evening of the next day, had already reached the outskirts of Shchigry. The 95th Infantry Division pulled back. The individual regiments withdrew over the snow-covered fields on sleighs, in captured *panje* wagons and on foot. Schmitz had once thought that there could be nothing worse than the battle at the Tim. He was to find out there was.

The division literally died. Growing numbers of men fell by the wayside. The wounded were placed on requisitioned or homemade sleds. There were insufficient horses, so the men had to pull the sleds. It seemed like the beginning of the end.

At this critical moment the 3rd Panzer Division, which had been involved in heavy fighting at Wypolsowa and Shumakovo, was placed on alert. The first elements of the division—a motorized rifle battalion under Oberstleutnant Müller, an artillery battalion and a company of combat engineers—reached the area of operations of the 9th Panzer Division and were immediately employed. By the next day the entire division—with the exception of 3rd Motorcycle Battalion under Major Pape had been committed. The motorcycle battalion remained in its former positions.

The armor division fought a dramatic battle, in which it saved the retreating remnants of the 95th Infantry Division and prevented the loss of Kursk. Shchigry fell into enemy hands temporarily, but was retaken a few days later by elements of the 3rd Panzer Division.

On 27 January 1942 two battle groups from the 3rd Panzer Division stormed out of Shchigry and Poshidayewka. They advanced into Alexandrovka from two sides and smashed the enemy forces there. By evening they had reached Krivzovka. The enemy broke and fled in panic. These engagements gave the 95th Infantry Division, especially those elements trailing far behind, the opportunity to escape almost certain encirclement and destruction at the hands of the Red Army. In the days that followed the Russian 32nd Cavalry Division was smashed.

The 95th Infantry Division moved back into its old positions on the Tim. The winter battle for Kursk was over. The Red Army had failed to break through the German front at that location. Throughout the rest of the winter and into March 1942, the enemy launched no further major attacks. The 95th Infantry Division held its assigned positions.

During those weeks and months the number of frostbite casualties steadily increased. Schmitz found it simply impossible to believe that indifference or faith in a new Blitz campaign in Russia had kept the fighting troops from being supplied with winter clothing. Like everyone else, he also heard rumors about trainloads of winter clothing being shunted around the vast Russian railroad net, unable to reach their destinations.

One day, as he was escorting the latest sleigh-load of suffering to the field hospital, he heard one of the doctors observe bitterly: "Whoever is responsible for this suffering is a criminal."

But soon the first signs of spring began to appear. It became warmer. The muddy period set in. Combat operations came to a halt on both sides.

On 28 March 1942 Hitler summoned the senior commanders of the German Armed Forces to the Wolf's Lair, his forward headquarters in East Prussia. In the low, concrete bunkers Keitel, Jodl and Halder (Commander-in-Chief of the Army) squatted around Hitler on low wooden stools. Also present were several officers from the other branches of the Wehrmacht.

Hitler stood at a map table and gave the word for the Chief of the German Army General Staff to begin. Generaloberst Halder described the plan that bore the name "Case Blue." Three hours later those assembled were in agreement. Two army groups were to create a huge pincer. The northern arm of the pincer was to advance on Voronezh from the Kursk-Kharkov area and then push southeastwards along the middle Don. The southern arm was to advance eastward from the area around Taganrog. The two groups of forces were to meet west of Stalingrad and afterwards destroy all Soviet forces between the Don and Donets.

At the same time a third attack formation was to be formed. It was to set out from the Rostov area and advance into the Caucasus. Its final objective was the Caspian Sea and the Baku oil-producing region. Before implementing this far-reaching plan, the Germans would first have to capture several areas in the southern sector that might be a threat to their rear. Primarily this meant the Crimea and the peninsula's main fortress, Sevastopol, but also the Soviet salient near Izyum.

On the Soviet side, however, Marshall Timoshenko had his own plan against Army Group South. On 12 May 1942 he launched a major offensive aimed at destroying the 6th Army. The divisions of the Soviet army group attacked from the salient near Izyum. The Soviet Twenty-Eighth Army comprised the northern arm of the pincer, while the southern one consisted of the Sixth and Fifty-Seventh Armies.

Kharkov was in danger of being destroyed by the northern group of enemy forces. Advancing from the bend in the Izyum, the southern arm of the Soviet pincer reached the periphery of Poltava on 16 May 1942. Poltava was the site of Feldmarschall von Bock's headquarters.

In spite of this, the Germans launched Operation "Fredericus" on 18 May 1942. It was aimed at smashing the Soviet salient at Izyum. The double attack was now out of the question, as the 6th Army was being hard pressed. The operation had to be launched with only one arm of the pincer: Army Group Kleist.

Schmitz signs his name in the "Golden Book" of the city of Bonn.

Generaloberst von Kleist succeeded in advancing north from Barvenkovo to Bayrak with the III Panzer Corps. On 22 May the soldiers of the 14th Panzer Division and the 44th Infantry Division (of the 6th Army) joined hands near Bayrak. The Izyum salient had been pinched off. A pocket had closed around Timoshenko's attacking divisions. 239,000 Soviet soldiers went into captivity. 1,250 tanks and 2,026 guns were destroyed or captured. The prelude to the great summer offensive had been a success. The Russians had wanted to encircle the Germans but ended up suffering the same fate themselves.

On 28 June 1942 Army Group von Weichs, consisting of the 2nd Army, the Hungarian Second Army and the 4. Panzer-Armee, had attacked toward Voronezh. Leading the spearhead and heading straight for the city was the 24th Panzer Division. On 30 June, some 150 kilometers to the south, the divisions of the 6th Army began the attack towards the northeast, also toward Voronezh.

The planned pincer operation failed, however, because the Soviet forces carried out a fighting withdrawal instead of holding their positions. Hitler therefore decided that Voronezh would not be the first objective. In the headquarters of Army Group South he said to Feldmarschall von Bock: "I no longer insist on the capture of Voronezh. I no longer consider it necessary, and I leave you free to advance south immediately."

That had been on 3 July 1942. The following day reports reached Army Group headquarters that it might be possible to take the city quickly, as the 24th Panzer Division had captured an intact bridge over the Don.

Because of that information, it was intended for Voronezh to be taken in a lightning raid. Elements from the 24th Panzer Division and Panzer Grenadier Division *Großdeutschland* were in the city on 6 July, and Hitler authorized the capture of the city. But, at the same time, he ordered that the XXX Panzer Corps, which was to have struck the decisive blow at Voronezh, must set out south in the direction of the Caucasus.

As a result, the divisions of that corps were not available for the decisive battle for the city. Although the western part of the city was taken on 7 July and the Wehrmacht report that evening announced the fall of the city, there was still heavy fighting going on in the university quarter and the dense forests north of the city on 13 July. The 95th Infantry Division found itself engaged in heavy fighting against Russian forces in those forests.

✠

"The First Battalion is to advance on the village on the right flank and take it!"

The regimental commander's order reached Major Hahne after he crossed a cornfield following a brief engagement. The Major issued the necessary instructions to his companies: "1st Company: Take the point! The Third will follow, staggered to the right. The Second will secure the woodline on the left flank!"

Schmitz advanced with the others. It was 27 July 1942 and the division was deployed north of Voronezh. The sound of fighting rang out from the right, where the 3rd Company of the 279th Infantry Regiment was in contact with the 2nd Battalion.

"It's started over there!" called Oberleutnant Willrich, now in command of the 1st Company. Some time ago he had received the German Cross in Gold. A little later the 2nd Company, which was securing the woodline, came under fire from a field and a ravine.

"Now the shit will hit the fan!" murmured Zürn.

Kurt Zünkley, who had returned to the company a few weeks earlier, nodded. The forest swallowed them up. When the point squad of the Third Platoon reached the last trees, it was greeted by a wild hail of fire.

"Cover!" screamed the Oberleutnant.

The men threw themselves down and crawled behind trees and into depressions. Yellow tracer rounds flitted through the woods in front of them. Russian field guns cracked. Schmitz ducked behind a fallen tree trunk as a round burst in the treetops. Twigs and branches rained down on the men. The first wounded from the 2nd Platoon crawled back. The Unteroffizier gave the men of his section a wave. They moved out, ducking from cover to cover, until they reached the woodline. There they met Feldwebel Schnittger of the 3rd Platoon.

"Where are the wounded, Jupp?" Schmitz asked the Feldwebel.

"Over there in the field. But the Russians are in there too. I'll send a machine gun and Knörzer's squad to accompany you."

Knörzer's squad took command. Unteroffizier Schmitz and his four litter bearers followed. They traced an arc through the woods, reached a brook and waded in. The water was waist-deep and cold. Both banks were heavily overgrown, offering good concealment as Schmitz and the others waded through the brook. They heard orders being given in Russian farther to the left from above in the cornfield. Several Russian soldiers appeared. They crept towards the brook and disappeared into the bushes. Gefreiter Scholz, who was carrying the machine gun, sent a long burst after them. The others stood crouched in the water for a few moments. Someone fired in their direction from the field. Bullets mowed off the tops of the bushes.

"Move out, but be careful!" said Knörzer.

They climbed up the bank and slipped through the bushes. After what seemed like an eternity, they came to the field and halted there, breathing heavily. After a brief rest Schmitz and the others carried on. They found the first casualty about thirty meters into the field.

"Take up a position here and guard to the east, Jochen," said Schmitz to his comrade. Knörzer nodded and directed the machine-gunner into position using hand signals. The men formed a defensive screen while Schmitz and his men recovered the wounded and moved them to the western edge of the field. There they were picked up by litter bearers and evacuated to the rear. So far Schmitz and his men had not been fired upon. But suddenly their own machine gun opened up from the security screen. Immediately afterward a hail of mortar rounds fell on the cornfield.

Schmitz ran forward. Out of breath, he reached Jochen Knörzer and saw the last Russian running back through the field. Again there was the whistle of incoming. mortar rounds. The fresh volley forced the small group to take cover again.

"Shit!" growled Knörzer.

One of the mortar rounds landed in the shallow depression where the machine-gunner had positioned himself and his weapon. For a moment there was nothing to be seen of Scholz. But when the smoke and dust cleared they saw that he had been tom apart by the round. Schmitz ran over to the second member of the machine-gun team. The man opened his eyes and groaned. Schmitz inspected him carefully. Miraculously, the man had suffered only minor shrapnel wounds in his left leg. Schmitz cut off the pant leg and applied dressings to stop the bleeding.

"We've got them all!" reported Zünkley, who had just come back from the edge of the field.

After a brief delay, the medical-corps Unteroffizier lifted the wounded man onto his back. They hurried across the open area between the field and the forest and reached cover. Once again, Schmitz and his men had rescued a number of wounded from under the nose of the enemy.

After dark Schmitz lay in a hastily dug foxhole at the edge of the wood with his comrades of the 1st Company. They watched as a number of men from the 2nd Company prepared to go out on patrol. They were led by Feldwebel Corzilius.

"Your mission is to work your way to the far side of the field to the village and see if the Russians have left there too!" said Oberleutnant Willrich, who had just returned from a briefing in the battalion command post.

"And then?" asked Zürn.

"Then we move out. We are to get to Voronezh and then change direction."

A little later the rations detail came roaring up. There was mail as well. Schmitz buried himself in letters from his parents, his five brothers and four brothers-in-law, all of whom like him were in action in Russia. He saved one letter until last. It was from his fiancée. Reality disappeared from view, and his thoughts wandered home, thousands of kilometers away.

"Was that firing?" asked Zürn.

He had just dozed off. Seconds later the single round was followed by the hectic rattling of automatic weapons and the crash of exploding hand grenades.

"The patrol!" cried Oberleutnant Willrich, who had just arrived in the trench. The firefight lasted ten minutes, then all was silent again. Some time later a figure stumbled out of the cornfield, crossed the strip of open ground and fell into the trench.

"What happened, Haupt?" asked the Oberleutnant.

The Gefreiter, a member of Corzilius' patrol, stammered: "All dead, all dead!" Schmitz bent over him and bandaged a wound on the man's upper arm.

"I'll take my men out and look for them!" declared the Unteroffizier.

They set out five minutes later. Schmitz led the way, followed by Zürn and Zünkley carrying a litter. On the flanks were Krämer and Noll. They were armed with submachine guns and provided cover. The field in front of them was about 700 meters long. They passed through uneventfully and, when they reached the far side, the moon was rising over the Don. They saw something move in front of the village but soon lost sight of whatever it was.

"Watch out. Something's going on!" warned Schmitz.

The five men worked their way forward from one group of bushes to the next. Barely five minutes later they saw the four men from the patrol lying in the field. There was no movement from any of them. Franz Schmitz hurried towards the four forms, but was greeted by a burst of machine-gun fire. The Unteroffizier kept going and threw himself down beside Feldwebel Corzilius. One look told him that the Feldwebel was dead. He crawled over to the others, but they too were dead.

Suddenly, another burst of fire whipped towards him. It came from a weapon that had not fired before. The bullets tore up chunks of ground in front of the medic. Schmitz got to his feet and was about to run back, when he received a heavy blow on the side, then another against his thigh. He fell to the ground and lost consciousness.

"They got Franz!" cried Noll in dismay.

"Let's go! Give us covering fire!"

Noll and Krämer fired at the flickering muzzle flashes of the machine gun. They succeeded in temporarily silencing the enemy, allowing Zürn and Zünkley to reach their wounded comrade. They laid him on the litter and hurried back with the unconscious Unteroffizier. When they reached their own positions, Oberleutnant Willrich sent at once for an ambulance. They placed the badly wounded Schmitz and the other casualties inside, then the driver turned the vehicle in the direction of the main dressing station. Zürn and Zünkley went along in the ambulance. They wanted to do everything in their power to help their friend. Having helped save hundreds of wounded, Schmitz had now suffered the same fate himself.

Following initial treatment, Schmitz was taken to the field hospital, where he underwent surgery. As soon as he was well enough to move, he was transferred to the military hospital at Annaberg in Upper Silesia.

Schmitz survived his serious wounds and was given time to recuperate fully. He was sent to Italy for two months to aid his recovery, the only man in the entire hospital to be so favored. Finally, this respite came to an end. After spending a brief period with a replacement unit, Schmitz rejoined his unit in the Rzhev salient. Hitler had ordered this section of the front held at all costs.

Like Stalingrad and Rostov, Leningrad and Moscow, Rzhev was one of the key points in Germany's eastern strategy. It was located at the large bend in the Volga. The city was taken in 1941, and Soviet attacks in December 1941 and during 1942 failed to retake it.

In Hitler's view this city on the upper Volga was an ideal springboard for a possible second attack in the direction of Moscow. Holding this sector of the front was the 9th Army. It had withstood attacks by Soviet divisions under General Yeremenko during January and February 1942. It was exactly 180 kilometers from Rzhev to Red Square in Moscow. As long as German divisions held the city, the Soviet capital had to remain in a constant state of alert.

It was winter when Schmitz returned to his unit, and catastrophe was looming at Stalingrad. This was to be the second winter the Unteroffizier spent with the other members of the company in the cold of Russia. Hauptmann Meuthe, who by then had recovered from his wounds, welcomed Schmitz back. The former company commander was now active in the division headquarters staff.

Oberleutnant Willrich once again assigned Schmitz to lead the company's medical section. Paul Raabe was gone. He had been shot two weeks earlier while attempting to recover members of a patrol. The German patrol had run into a Soviet force in no-man's-land.

Schmitz learned of the tragedy from Ralf Noll, the only man to escape from the operation with his life. The medical-corps Unteroffizier soon learned that the 95th Infantry Division was now part of the 9th Army and the XXVII Army Corps. Its neighbor on the left was the 72nd Infantry Division; to the right was the 2nd Panzer Division of the XXXIX Panzer Corps. The division's new commander was Generalleutnant Edgar Röhricht. General von Arnim had been given command of an army corps.

Schmitz spent Christmas outside in the field positions, the second time during the war he had done so. He and several litter bearers delivered the Christmas mail. Oberleutnant Willrich read from the Christmas gospel. It was a moving moment. An hour past midnight Unteroffizier Schmitz was called forward. A German patrol had stumbled onto a Russian mine. Calls for help had been heard from no-man's-land. Accompanied by Noll and Zünkley, he set out at once.

From the forward-most trench they saw that the Russians had fired several illumination flares. Schmitz and his two men were forced to wait ten minutes until the fireworks were over. Then they started forward, using the cover of a depression that traversed the snow-covered field. When even with the position of the wounded, they had to leave the depression and continue across absolutely level terrain. The three Germans were wearing snow capes and moved slowly. They were completely exposed for several minutes, but then they found the patrol.

Leutnant Herrmann, who had been leading the patrol, had stepped on a mine. He was dead. His severed leg lay a few meters away in the snow. Gefreiter Sichert and Gefreiter Boohmanns were still alive and had bandaged each other's wounds. Several meters further they found Helms. He had been caught in a burst of machine-gun fire and was also dead. Boohmanns' wounds were the more serious, so he was placed on the litter. Schmitz hoisted Gefreiter Sichert onto his back and carried him.

Schmitz and the others were forced to take cover three times, when Russian troops fired illumination flares and opened fire. Finally, however, they reached the depression and returned through it to the German trenches.

✠

One day passed like another. On 2 February 1943 they heard that Stalingrad had become the graveyard of the 6th Army. Hitler's resistance to any withdrawal of the extended German salient weakened after the fall of Stalingrad. He authorized Model's request for a withdrawal in stages.

Operation "Buffalo" was to see the 9th Army and those elements of the 4th Army still in the salient withdraw to a position which would shorten the front by 300 kilometers. Everything was kept secret. None of the men knew what was going on until mid-February, when a Russian propaganda loudspeaker blared out the following message to the men of the 95th Infantry Division: "German soldiers: Watch out! Your officers are already packing their bags. Take care that you return with them!"

A little later Oberleutnant Willrich returned from the regimental command post. He went to the individual squads and took the squad leaders aside. "Men, we're pulling back to a better position. We won't be caught in this mousetrap."

At last they knew what was being planned. A few days later, on 1 March, the withdrawal began. The weather was warm. The withdrawal lasted twenty-one days. More than once it looked as if it could never be done but, in the end, the gamble paid off.

Two Soviet army groups could not prevent twenty-nine German divisions from escaping the trap. Not once did the Russians interrupt the retreat. It was not until the large Volga bridge near Rzhev was blown did Soviet forces begin feeling their way forward.

The German withdrawal was a success. The divisions moved into well-built positions in the new defensive line before the onset of the muddy period. Known as the "Buffalo Position" to historians, the new German line extended from Spass Demensk through Dorogobush to Dukovchina.

The front was comparatively quiet. Schmitz was more disturbed by reports from home. In late May he received a telegram with news that his parents' home had been bombed. Fortunately, no one had been killed. Understandably, Schmitz wanted to go home to help with the rebuilding. He was immediately given a three-week "bombing leave". These three weeks were filled with hard work. Schmitz also experienced the apocalyptic days of the air battle over the Ruhr, which had begun on 3 July 1943 with an attack on Essen. Unteroffizier Schmitz also used this time to make wedding preparations. The ceremony took place on 3 July 1943. The next day he returned to the front.

Following his return, the division became involved in heavy fighting along the major road between Vyazma and Dorogobush. The early morning of 7 July 1943 had seen the beginning of Operation "Citadel," the German Army's last major offensive operation in the East. However, the Soviets had also prepared an offensive in the same sector. Army Group "Central Front" was ready to go to the offensive when it was struck by the German attack. Influenced significantly by the Allied invasion of Sicily, Hitler gave the order to call off "Citadel," even though it appeared that the southern group of forces was in position to bring the battle to a successful conclusion. STAVKA then committed three army groups to an assault on the German salient near Orel. Its objective was the destruction of Army Group

Middle. The Soviet attack tore a twenty-eight-kilometer breach in the German front the first day. When the front north of Bolkhov also crumbled, the 2nd Panzer Army found itself facing a crisis situation.

In this, the hour of greatest danger for Army Group Middle, the 95th Infantry Division was placed on alert and transported to the threatened area. The 279th Infantry Regiment was unloaded in the open steppe. Leading the way was the 1st Battalion under Major von Meden, who received the following order from the regimental commander: "Direction of march: Towards the enemy!"

The 1st Battalion took the lead. The company marched in a dispersed formation towards the village of Panoff. A reconnaissance patrol reported Mileyevo occupied by enemy forces. A patrol by Feldwebel Grenzel reported the enemy was also in Panoff and the woods to the south were "swarming with Russians". New orders were issued: "Companies deploy! When the Russians attack, the 3rd and 4th Companies will advance on the flanks and encircle the enemy."

Unteroffizier Schmitz instinctively felt that a decisive engagement was in the offing.

On the evening of 24 July 1943 the leading elements reached a vast cornfield. The corn was high and, suddenly, the squads came under fire from some woods on a ridge beyond the field.

"Take cover in the cornfield!" ordered the battalion commander.

They dug in. The ground was loose, which made the task easier. A half-hour later the soldiers in the cornfield began taking mortar fire from the direction of Panoff and Mileyevo. Soon Russian heavy artillery joined in and, five minutes later, rocket salvoes began falling on the cornfield. The earth seemed to sway. Schmitz saw a salvo of sixteen rockets fall on the positions of the 3rd Company. That company's 1st Platoon was wiped out. The grenadiers pressed themselves to the ground and listened to the sound of impacting rounds. The howling salvoes of the "Stalin Organs" smashed one position after another.

"Move forward! Take cover in the defile in front of the hill!"

The order was passed from man to man. It was the only possible way to escape this destructive blow by the Russians. The 3rd and 4th Companies got to their feet and moved forward. When the 1st and 2nd Companies followed, the men heard the hectic rattle of Russian automatic weapons ahead. They ran a few meters and threw themselves down again. They repeated the process until they reached the end of the cornfield.

"That's where the Third Battalion is!" yelled Oberleutnant Willrich to the medical-corps Unteroffizier. He was pointing to the right where heavy fire was falling on a wooded area. Suddenly, Russian tanks appeared between that patch of woods and the cornfield. Behind them were dense masses of infantry, clearly visible in the moonlight.

"First Platoon: Follow me! Bring explosive charges! We have to stop the tanks or they'll turn in behind us!"

Oberleutnant Willrich led them to the right. High-explosive rounds fell nearby. Several men were hit; they were left behind in the defile or in craters. A group of Russian soldiers appeared about fifty meters ahead and began to approach at a run. When they were about thirty meters away, the machine gunner opened fire. The others fired their submachine guns at the same time. The attackers had no chance.

"Get up! Move forward!"

Oberleutnant Willrich hurried from his hiding place. The others ran after him. They approached the enemy tanks in four groups. Meter-long flames spewed from the guns of the tanks as they fired at unseen targets. Schmitz ran along behind the Oberleutnant. As he watched, the officer leapt onto a tank and then jumped down again and dashed to one side. There was a loud explosion and the tank stopped. The turret had been dislodged from the tank's turret ring and the long gun barrel drooped towards the ground.

The party led by Feldwebel Klömmes reached three tanks moving in close formation. Two went up in flames immediately, but the third leapt forward. The Feldwebel tried to jump out of the way, but it was too late. The tank rolled over him and several of his men. Fifty meters farther, when it halted to fire its main gun, the tank was destroyed by a Teller mine placed by Stabsgefreiter Dickel. Schmitz ran through the fire to where he had seen Klömmes fall.

He found the Feldwebel, but what he saw caused a chill to run through him. A legless torso lay on the ground, bathed in moonlight. Blood poured from the severed thigh arteries. The severely injured man opened his mouth to scream, but no sound came out. The Unteroffizier threw himself down beside Klömmes. With shaking hands he began applying tourniquets above the two stumps. Klömmes tried to sit up. He gave one last, rattling groan and died. Schmitz looked to the left and right of the burning Russian tank. As he was about to move forward to join his companions, Schmitz noticed that there were Russian soldiers in numerous holes, and they were shooting at everything in sight.

"Back to the cornfield!"

The call passed from man to man. It reached Schmitz just as he was tending to an unconscious soldier. He hoisted the man onto his shoulder and ran back through the enemy fire. He felt the bullets as they whizzed past him. Once he was forced to take cover. As he lay gasping for breath,

Schmitz enjoys a warm reception at the headquarters of the German Red Cross in Berlin. He was the only combat medic in the German Armed Forces to have been awarded the Knight's Cross.

he thought about leaving the wounded man there; it might be his only chance of survival. But, as always, he decided otherwise.

"Franzie!" gasped the wounded man.

Schmitz heaved his burden onto his shoulder and staggered on. He received covering fire from the edge of the woods, which allowed him to reach safety. Then he heard Ralf Noll say: "There are at least ten wounded men near the knocked-out Russian tanks. I will go and get them, sir."

Oberleutnant Willrich stared at the seven burning tanks. The flames bathed the battlefield in flickering light. "No one could get through there, Noll!"

Two minutes later Schmitz was on his way. The Unteroffizier outdid himself that night. Constantly under fire, he and his friends Noll and Zünkley ran into no-man's-land. They brought eight men back one after another. Finally Schmitz found two men who had run ahead too far. They were lying in the forward Russian lines.

"I'll get them," he said. "Give me covering fire!"

Schmitz brought both men back. When he knew the last one was safe he collapsed from exhaustion.

The Soviets attacked in the early morning hours of 25 July 1943. The men of the 1st Battalion, reinforced by the arrival of antitank and antiaircraft guns and several mortar teams, held fast against the numerically superior Russians. As morning dawned the Soviets began pounding the huge cornfield with artillery. The leading German units had withdrawn into the field after the enemy infiltrated the heavily vegetated area. There were many fatal casualties. Schmitz and his medic section had been ordered back to the dressing station to help care for the large number of serious casualties. Suddenly, he saw a motorcycle come roaring up. The messenger reported to the senior medical officer. Schmitz walked over to see what was going on.

"Sir," said the messenger, "all of the First Battalion's litter bearers have been killed or wounded. I'm the only one left. We request you send Unteroffizier Schmitz up to the front."

"Schmitz has been assigned to the Fourth to help here, König!" replied the Stabsarzt.

Schmitz knew that he had been given a day of light duties to help him recover from the difficult night in no-man's-land. But after he learned of this catastrophic situation there was no holding him back in the comparative safety of the dressing station.

"I'm going to get our men out of there, sir!" he explained.

He went to the tent and got his submachine gun. Then he took leave of Noll and Zünkley, who had to stay behind. At the edge of the field he met Oberleutnant Willrich. But was this really the young officer they had come to know, their "Little Kurt"? Schmitz was shocked when he saw the lined face and sunken eyes. The strain of months of combat had left its mark.

"There are a lot of them out there, Schmitz," said Willrich hoarsely. After these words the medical-corps Unteroffizier ran off through the enemy fire until he found the first casualty. From that moment on Schmitz was constantly on the move, back and forth between the cornfield and the edge of the forest. Moved by his example, soldiers began crossing the open strip between the field and the woods to relieve him of his burden of wounded. Each time he delivered a casualty he shouted: "Back to the dressing station immediately!" And then he was gone again.

Schmitz kept this up for three hours. Just before midday he collapsed in the middle of the cornfield. He swallowed a Pervitine tablet (an amphetamine), took a drink from his canteen, got to his feet and evacuated the next wounded man. By 1530 hours Schmitz had rescued 98 soldiers from no-man's-land and had risked his life the same number of times. Finally, he could find no more wounded. He staggered back to the woods, where he sank to the ground, exhausted.

"Everyone get ready, we're attacking Panoff!"

This order, which arrived barely an hour later at 1640 hours, got the men on their feet again. Schmitz' endurance was incredible. When the company formed up he was ready to go again. The company advanced toward Panoff and stormed into the village. There was a brief engagement, during which one hut after another was taken. The soldiers pushed through and reached the woods on the far side of the village. Suddenly, heavy fire began coming in from the flank. Russian battle groups charged towards Panoff from the rear. The three German companies were virtually surrounded in the village.

Schmitz ran to the 3rd Company, the only one not yet outflanked. But before he could sound the warning, the company was caught in a hail of fire. The company commander was killed outright. Seconds later the two platoon leaders were hit and the now leaderless company streamed back.

"Halt!" roared Schmitz. He then spread both arms wide. "I'm taking command of the company!"

The seemingly impossible happened. The men rallied round him and took cover. Others came and soon all the survivors of the company were assembled around the Unteroffizier.

"We have to go through the woods and open the ring around the battalion from the flank!" he called to his men.

They nodded and prepared to move out. Schmitz and his small band of soldiers charged the thin Russian line of security and burst through into the forest. Groups of Russians emerged from the half-light of the woods and threw themselves against the Germans. A bitter firefight broke out. The Unteroffizier fired on the run. The company stayed with him, fighting desperately to force a breakthrough. It soon became apparent, however, that none of them would get out of the forest alive if they continued the battle in this fashion.

"Back to the western edge of the forest!" cried Schmitz.

The soldiers turned and, after breaking through a thin line of Russians, reached the forest's edge, where they took cover in foxholes. From there Schmitz saw that a powerful enemy force was preparing to attack the battalion's rear. If the battalion were caught in a crossfire, it would be lost for certain, and the enemy would be able to advance through the resulting gap and unhinge the entire regiment.

"We're going to take them from behind!" decided Schmitz.

He counted the soldiers. There were thirty-three men still on their feet and able to hold a rifle. Schmitz was about to lead this tiny group against two Russian battalions. First they backtracked about 100 meters, then Schmitz changed course. Soon they were behind the enemy unit that was preparing to attack the German battalion.

"Forward!" roared Schmitz.

He and his men charged toward the enemy, firing as they ran. The Red Army soldiers first became aware of the danger when bullets began whizzing about their ears. Unteroffizier Schmitz kept running. He could hear the others running beside him. They fired short bursts. A breach gaped before them. They used the opportunity for surprise. They went to ground, got up again, and then advanced, meter by meter. Confusion was spreading through the enemy's ranks. Concentrated defensive fire was impossible. They did not want to hit their own men.

In spite of this, several men were killed in the initial rush. But the rest got through. Finally Schmitz broke through to his surrounded comrades. He found Oberleutnant Willrich holding out in an abandoned brickworks. Finally, all of the 1st Battalion under Major von Meden managed to escape through the breach in the Russian ring made by Schmitz and his men.

The battalion dug in at the northeastern outskirts of Milejevo. Later, the remaining elements of the division arrived there and linked up with the 279th Infantry Regiment. The regiment's survival had largely been due to the efforts of the medical-corps Unteroffizier, Franz Schmitz.

Twice that day Franz Schmitz had performed outstanding feats of bravery. But it was not yet over. The grenadiers in Mileyevo were at the end of their strength as the Unteroffizier prepared to begin another rescue mission. It had been reported that there were nine men waiting for help in a small defile near the western patch of woods. Schmitz entered the defile, ran under enemy fire from the other end and brought out the first casualty. Several soldiers had hurried after him and these rescued several other wounded men. When the fifth had been saved, the Russians began firing into the defile with mortars. But even this could not prevent Schmitz from running back in to rescue the rest of the wounded.

It was beginning to get dark. While on his way into the defile for the eighth time, Schmitz sighted a Russian patrol. He allowed the Russians to pass, then evacuated the eighth man. Schmitz handed the casualty over to Noll and Zünkley. As he was about to go back in for the last man, Noll called to him: "You have to stay here! If you go in there again you've had it!"

"There's only one more, Ralf. I'm going in to get him!"

Once again Schmitz ran into the firing line. Mortar rounds hammered into the defile, blasting apart bushes and trees. Ducking and dodging, he reached the ninth wounded man and threw himself down next to him. The injured man extended his hand towards the medic and stammered: "Franz, get me out of here!"

Schmitz lifted the man up and hoisted him onto his shoulder. As he began to walk a group of four mortar rounds fell around him. He felt

sharp blows in both arms. The wounded man slipped to the ground and
Schmitz fell. Both arms were bleeding from fragment wounds. Suddenly
he noticed blood trickling from a wound in his thigh; the left side of his
tunic was red. In spite of his injuries, Schmitz crawled over to the man he
had been trying to evacuate and attempted to raise him up with his
injured arms. Stabbing pain shot through him. Nevertheless, he gritted his
teeth, lifted the man up and staggered off with him.

The others ran towards him and relieved him of his burden. By now
Schmitz was at the end of his strength. Oberleutnant Willrich took the
wounded medic to the dressing station in his own vehicle. Stabsarzt Dr.
Müller immediately began fighting to save the life of the Unteroffizier. For
more than an hour he worked on the unconscious man. Anxious faces
looked at him as he finished.

"He's going to pull through," the doctor promised. "He'll have to go
back to the field hospital on the next transport Junkers; they'll patch him
up."

✠

Schmitz was taken to the field hospital at Smolensk. For several days
he fought with death, but the Unteroffizier proved stronger on this occasion.

As soon as he was well enough to be moved, Schmitz was taken to a
hospital in East Prussia. While his division was carrying out a stubborn
fighting withdrawal, he was fighting equally hard to regain his health.
Slowly but surely his condition improved. After receiving the Close Combat Clasp in Silver in the field hospital, he was sent to Marien Hospital in
Bonn. There his wife could visit him daily. Soon Schmitz was making rapid
progress.

After spending one last day in Walenberg, near Bonn, where his par-
ent's house had been rebuilt, the Unteroffizier reported for duty. However,
instead of being sent back to his unit, he was sent to the 6th Medical
Replacement and Training Battalion at Hamm in Westphalia. The battalion wanted to keep Schmitz there to train young medics, but he had other
ideas: He wanted to see his comrades again.

Three weeks later Unteroffizier Schmitz took the first step on the road
back to his unit, when he was sent to Reserve Hospital II in Krakow.

By now it was September 1943 and Schmitz was feeling anything but
happy in the hospital. He was unaware, however, that a search for him had
been under way in every medical facility in Germany since the evening of

13 September. The chain of events had started during an interview between Major von Meden and the division commander. Von Meden described the events of 25 July 1943 and how the breakthrough by the battle group led by Unteroffizier Schmitz had saved the battalion—if not the regiment and the division—from certain destruction.

The division commander, Generalleutnant Röhricht, passed on another report by Oberst Hans Michaelis, the commander of Franz Schmitz' regiment, with a special recommendation. He closed his letter with the following notation:

> Medical-corps Unteroffizier Schmitz has demonstrated bravery and devotion to duty unmatched by any other soldier in his division. He averted a crisis situation by taking the initiative and made a decisive contribution in the Mileyevo combat zone. I recommend Unteroffizier Franz Schmitz for the Knight's Cross of the Iron Cross.

Schmitz was awarded the coveted decoration on 13 September 1943.

✠

It was 8 October 1943 and Schmitz had just turned on the radio in Ward II so that he and his companions could listen to the Wehrmacht Report. They listened to reports of heavy fighting in the east. At the end of the report the announcer paused briefly and then said: "On 13 September 1943 the Führer and Supreme Commander of the Wehrmacht awarded the Knight's Cross of the Iron Cross to Unteroffizier Franz Schmitz, the leader of a medic section in a grenadier regiment. The Unteroffizier is requested to report immediately."

The men in Ward II began to cheer wildly. The assistant doctor, who had heard the report in the watch room, came bursting in and gripped the hand of the Unteroffizier so hard that he nearly crushed it. Two days later Major von Meden arrived at Reserve Hospital II to present the Knight's Cross to Franz Schmitz.

Afterward, accompanied by his old battalion commander and two generals from the military facility, Unteroffizier Schmitz reviewed an honor guard that had been drawn up for the occasion.

On 11 October 1943 Schmitz left Krakow to begin seven weeks special leave. A day later, on his 25th birthday, he found himself standing in a train that had just stopped at Bonn station. When he appeared in the window he saw that a huge, jubilant crowd was waiting for him. His wife came into the compartment. On the platform a military band was playing. Schmitz was driven to city hall, where he signed his name in the Golden Book of the city of Bonn.

The following day saw a reception in his hometown of Walenberg. Schmitz' parents celebrated with him. The entire village was on its feet. Shortly before he was to return to his 95th Infantry Division, Schmitz received orders from the Army High Command to come to Berlin for fourteen days. He was to be featured in the headquarters of the German Red Cross, as he was the only medic to have received Germany's highest award for valor. Schmitz went to Berlin where he was feted.

He allowed all of this to pass over him, all the while thinking of the fastest way to get back to the front. For the time being, however, that was out of the question. To the Red Cross Schmitz was a soldier who had pulled nearly 2,000 fallen comrades out of the fire. Furthermore, he was a man who had translated the principles of the Red Cross into deeds in dramatic fashion. Unteroffizier Schmitz was now called upon to visit every replacement training battalion in Germany and give talks on the recovery of wounded.

✠

At the end of January 1945 Schmitz was in the Kevelaer area, where he was to deliver a talk to an infantry replacement training unit. There he learned that Oberstleutnant von Geldern was forming a battle group that was to be inserted between the paratroops and the home guard in the Reichswald. He gathered his things, reported to headquarters that he was leaving and went to the barracks where the battle group was being assembled.

Schmitz reported to the commander: "I'm at your disposal if you need another medic, sir."

"Excellent, Schmitz, you're in!" said the Oberstleutnant to the Unteroffizier with the Knight's Cross.

"What's the situation, sir?" asked Schmitz now that the formalities were over.

"Last night Oberstleutnant Herlin, the corps headquarters intelligence officer, interrogated a Canadian. He informed him that the Allies are preparing a new offensive. The Canadian First Army is to attack out of the north from the area between the Meuse and the Rhine together with the XXX Armoured Corps under General Horrocks. They plan to storm through the Reichswald and capture Kleve and Goch. The attack is to begin on 8 February."

Early on the morning of 6 February 1945 the battle group, which by then had grown to regiment size with several heavy weapons, moved out in the direction of Kranenburg. Von Geldern's forces took up defensive positions at the Nijmwegen-Kleve road, on the approaches to the "Siegfried Line." Schmitz and his medics moved into one of the bunkers. In position to the left and right were rifle squads. A dressing station had been set up in a fortified bunker farther in the rear.

The following day Stabsgefreiter Plümmer queried Schmitz: "What do you think, Franz? Will they really begin tomorrow? It's as quiet as a church around here."

"I have a damned uncomfortable feeling," interjected Obergefreiter Herbst. "They're coming, you can bet on it."

In fact "Veritable," as the British dubbed the operation, began the next morning. It was 0440 hours when Schmitz was awakened by a terrific din. 2,000 Allied guns had begun pounding a ten-kilometer section of front. More than a half-million rounds fell on the positions held by the German paratroops and Battle Group von Geldern.

This major Allied offensive toward the Reichswald marked the beginning of the decisive phase of the battle on the lower Rhine. After a twelve-hour bombardment, the five infantry divisions, three armored brigades and eleven special regiments of the British XXX Armoured Corps moved forward, accompanied by the Canadian units. This phalanx, with about 500 tanks, stormed towards the 7th Parachute Division under the command of Generalleutnant Erdmann. The mission of Battle Group von Geldern was to support the parachute division.

By midday Schmitz had carried nine casualties to the dressing station bunker and tended to their wounds. He worked as if indifferent to the terrible racket outside the bunker and the screaming sound of shrapnel whizzing through the air. He had just finished bandaging the last of the wounded when one of the messengers came running in and screamed: "The Canadians are coming!"

"Where are they?"

"They're already approaching the bunker!"

Schmitz turned to the Stabsgefreiter. "Well, Plümmer, what do you think?"

"What are we waiting for?" replied the Stabsgefreiter.

They reached for their submachine guns and ran outside. The sound of fighting rang out through the forest. Then they saw a group of Canadians. They were firing as they advanced toward one of the bunkers, which was still holding out. Schmitz and Plümmer fired several short bursts and ran towards the enemy. They reached the neighboring bunker and overcame the Canadians, who were about to force their way inside.

"Everyone listen to me!" cried Schmitz. "We're going to retake the two enemy-occupied bunkers. You two give the Stabsgefreiter covering fire. You over there with the assault rifle, come with me!"

Amid the rattle of enemy gunfire Schmitz ran toward the narrow trench that led around the bunker. He jumped in, approached the bunker's embrasure and fired a burst through the firing slit. Then he armed two hand grenades and tossed them inside. A few seconds after the explosions a number of wounded Canadians staggered outside and surrendered.

Several German soldiers who had fled when the bunker was taken now emerged from the bushes and the forest. Schmitz instructed them to man the bunker and its machine gun. Meanwhile, Plümmer had taken the second bunker. Schmitz then assembled sixteen men about him. With this small force he prepared to hold out in the three bunkers.

For three days and nights the Canadians tried to smoke out the German strongpoint. But they were unable to do so. By night Schmitz and Plümmer laid booby traps. Following their initial losses, the attackers halted their attacks. Enemy artillery then began pounding the area surrounding the three bunkers.

On the evening of 10 February Schmitz was forced to order a breakout. It had become clear to him that the counterattack by the 7th Parachute Division, which enjoyed the support of the XII Storm Parachute Brigade, was not going to get through.

"We break out at 0200," he said to the others.

Twenty-four hours earlier they had sent their nine wounded back through the dense woods in three groups. Led by Plümmer, who knew the forest like the back of his hand, they reached the German lines safely.

The breakout was a success. The same night Schmitz and fifteen men arrived at Gennep, on the Meuse. Oberstleutnant von Geldern had set up a new defensive line there, which also included elements of the 7th Parachute Division. In the days that followed the battle group was forced back, step by step, until the Goch-Siebengewaldt-Weeze-Kevelaer bunker line was reached. This, too, could only be held a short while before the retreat was resumed.

Near Sonsbeck the battle group was struck by a heavy air attack. Again there were dead and wounded. Schmitz and his loyal comrade Plümmer tended to the wounded during the brief pauses between attacks. A last defensive line was established between Veen and Wesel. From there Schmitz was able to evacuate the wounded to the hospital in Issum.

The objective of the Allied attack was Wesel. They wanted the city and the bridge over the Rhine. But first came the bombers, over and over again. On 14 February the Allied aviators destroyed the bridge near Wesel. Supplies for the German forces fighting west of the Rhine now crossed over the rail bridge, whose tracks had been repaired.

The bridgehead on the west bank of the Rhine near Wesel came under increasing pressure. By 6 March it had been reduced to an area fifteen kilometers wide and twelve kilometers deep. Enemy guns fired into the bridgehead without pause.

"Here they come, Franz!" warned Reinhard Plümmer.

But Schmitz had already spotted the approaching enemy in spite of the smoke rounds. Seconds later every available MG 42 opened fire on the attacking soldiers of the Canadian First Army. The first attack was halted about 100 meters from the trenches; the second bogged down in the barbed wire.

Calls for medics rang out to the left and right. Under fire, Schmitz and Plümmer ran toward the calls for help. They recovered the casualties and sent them to hospital in Issum in an ambulance that was waiting in the rear. The two medics returned at once to the scene of the fighting, where they recovered another twenty-three wounded comrades under fire. Finally, they went out for the Canadians still lying in the wire. Two officers and six soldiers were brought in and likewise taken to Issum.

Schmitz saw to it that the wounded Canadians were seen to immediately. Then he and Reinhard Plümmer headed back. They reached the battle group command post just as the Canadians were launching another attack. Again, hundreds of rounds hammered down on the men cowering in shell craters and foxholes. Shortly afterwards the enemy stormed and overran the positions. The grenadiers pulled back. Schmitz and Plümmer formed the rearguard, and managed to reach the second line in the rear.

Early on the morning of 8 March Schmitz was summoned by Oberstleutnant von Geldern. "Schmitz," he began, "there are seven wounded in the cellar of my former command post. They were taken there last night. If you can't get them out, they'll die in suffering there."

"I'll go, sir. And I'll go alone. Plümmer and Herbst can wait directly in front of the reception point where I'll deliver the wounded."

Soon afterwards Schmitz took leave of his comrades at an outpost in a small grove of birch trees. "Don't put one through my hide when I come back!" he said, and slapped Plümmer on the shoulder.

Schmitz ran through a patch of woods, came upon a Canadian forward outpost and skirted around it. Once he was challenged. He waved and said something unintelligible. Simply keep going was his plan, and it worked. He approached the bunker that had previously guarded the command post and then the house with the command post itself. It was empty.

He immediately raised a trapdoor hidden by a piece of linoleum and entered the cellar. Lying below were the seven wounded men. He poured some coffee into them, then placed the most severely wounded man across his shoulder and headed back.

Once again his luck held. Schmitz got through unscathed. For four hours he ran back and forth to the former command post.

During the night of 9-10 March 1945 Canadian assault groups once again attacked the bridgehead. Schmitz was wounded again. When the withdrawal towards the Wesel railroad bridge began, it was Plümmer who made sure that Schmitz was taken along. Pursued by enemy fire, they reached the bridge and crossed safely. The span was to have been blown at 0400 hours, but the pioneers of the 1st Parachute Army let it stand until 0710 hours since there were still thousands of German soldiers on the west bank.

Twenty-five minutes later four huge explosive charges were detonated. The collapsing bridge took a group of men to their deaths. In spite of warnings from the east bank, they had started to cross the bridge. Hundreds of German soldiers were now stranded on the west bank.

Schmitz was driven to Dorsten hospital the same day. There he saw the men he had rescued from the command post. The following day the Wehrmacht Report announced: "Our troops have carried out a planned and orderly evacuation of the Wesel bridgehead on the west bank of the Rhine in order to take advantage of better defensive lines on the west bank."

Schmitz was loaded aboard a hospital train with the wounded from Dorstner and moved to Melsungen. There he was awarded the Wound Badge in Gold.

The Americans came fourteen days later. The ambulatory wounded were immediately released. Unteroffizier Schmitz first made his way to Flensburg. When Flensburg—seat of the provisional Dönitz government—was occupied, he entered the customs school, which had been converted to a hospital. Schmitz was taken prisoner in this building. On 25 June 1945 he escaped and made his way home. A great surprise was awaiting him at his father's home, the likes of which he would not dared to have dreamed.

Standing at the fence was his youngest brother. Overjoyed, he shouted into the house: "Franz is coming! Franz is coming!"

People literally streamed out the door: His five brothers and four brothers-in-law! A kind fate had allowed them all to escape with their lives.

Alfred Schneidereit received the Knight's Cross as a SS-Rottenführer and the leader of the antitank section in the 8th Company of the 1st SS-Panzer Grenadier Regiment *"Leibstandarte SS Adolf Hitler."*

Alfred Schneidereit

SCHNEIDEREIT JOINS THE LEIBSTANDARTE
SS "ADOLF HITLER" (MOT.)

Alfred Schneidereit was born in Insterburg in East Prussia on 19 October 1919. On 15 November 1939 he joined the SS-*Verfügungstruppe* as a volunteer. Schneidereit received his basic training with the 18th Company of the *Leibstandarte SS "Adolf Hitler"* (mot.) and was assigned to the guard battalion in Berlin. Later, with its incorporation into the field force of Hitler's personal bodyguard, this company became the 13th Company. After thirteen months of service Schneidereit was promoted to the rank of SS-Sturmmann.

Following his basic training Schneidereit and his comrades were all sent to the Berlin guard battalion. This battalion saw no action in the French Campaign. Instead, as a member of the honor-guard company, Schneidereit had the opportunity to see all the state visitors to Berlin close up. On these occasions he also frequently saw Adolf Hitler.

Like his comrades and most of the German public, Schneidereit was fascinated by the personality of the "Führer" and was enthralled by Hitler's speeches, which were often made without notes and with great elan. Like so many others, this young man from Insterburg—located on the extreme fringe of the newly created Reich—became enchanted by this magical personality. His admiration for Hitler was great.

From Berlin Alfred Schneidereit went home on his first leave. Insterburg was a small city with great historical significance, but most of all it was his home. It was there that he had been confirmed in the fine, old Lutheran church. During his leave he took the opportunity to once again cross the bridge over the Angerapp and climb the three flights of steps leading up to the church.

From the church he could see the castle of the Teutonic Order, which had been built in 1336 to safeguard the important trade route of the old Prussian district of Nadrauen. As a student, but also later with friends, he had visited the museum in the castle several times, gazing at the artifacts from the history of the Order of the Teutonic Knights.

The Russians had temporarily occupied Insterburg in 1914. Not only did Schneidereit learn of this at school, but from the recollections of his father as well. During its brief occupation the city had become the head-quarters of the commander-in-chief of the northwest front, General Rennenkampf.

Then came the Battle of Tannenburg. Paul von Hindenburg and his Chief-of- Staff, General Ludendorff, turned a German retreat into a victory and the Russians were ejected from East Prussia. It was Adolf Hitler who returned Insterburg to the Reich after the Polish Campaign. Is it any wonder, therefore, that the young Schneidereit had a great deal of respect and admiration for these two men? Schneidereit could not have suspected that on 22 January 1945 the Russians would once again capture Insterburg and that the occupation would be permanent. But the horrors of the Red Army's march into East Prussia were still in the future, and he enjoyed the first leave of his soldier's life to the full.

OPERATIONS IN THE BALKANS

After the campaign in France, the regimentally sized *Leibstandarte SS "Adolf Hitler"* (mot.) was expanded to a motorized brigade. It was reorganized to include a reconnaissance battalion, an assault gun company, an antiaircraft battalion and two artillery battalions.

This time Alfred Schneidereit was on hand as a member of the 8th Company of SS-Infantry Regiment *"Leibstandarte SS Adolf Hitler."* Schneidereit's battalion—the regiment's 2nd—was commanded by SS-Sturmbannführer Theodor Wisch. Wisch was to become a great role model for Schneidereit and his comrades. Schneidereit was to see Wisch on numerous occasions as he led his troops out of dangerous situations.

In February 1941 the brigade, fully equipped and at full strength, set out through Strasbourg and Prague in the direction of Budapest. From there the formation moved through Hermannstadt and Kronstadt into the Campuling area in Rumania. There the brigade crossed over a pontoon bridge into Bulgaria. It was moving out for Operation Marita—the campaign against Yugoslavia—under its longtime commander, SS-Obergruppenführer Sepp Dietrich.

The attack against Yugoslavia, which had been seen as Germany's ally for a few days, began on 6 April. The SS brigade rolled through the Yugoslavian border positions at Kyustendil as part of the assault of the XXXX Army Corps toward southern Serbia. In addition to the SS brigade the corps included the 5th and 9th Panzer Divisions and the 73rd Infantry Division.

In command of XXXX Army Corps was General of Cavalry Stumme. The corps mission was to reach the Skoplje Basin and the Wardar River south of Veles with two powerful spearheads, thus cutting off the bulk of the Yugoslavian formations in the eastern frontier area. It was then to advance through the upper Wardar Valley to Albania and seek contact with the Italian front.

After reaching Skolpje on the evening of 7 April, the brigade's direction of advance was changed and it was sent toward the south. Advancing close behind the 9th Panzer Division, the brigade reached Prilep with its reconnaissance battalion leading the way,.

One of Schneidereit's friends recalled: "We advanced along narrow mountain roads, through the high passes and narrow gorges of the Macedonian mountains." Schneidereit had been assigned to the company headquarters section as a runner. With the advance guard he was one of the first to reach the Zrna, but it was unable to cross the river. The enemy had blown the bridge.

The Yugoslavian Third Army collapsed on 9 April. Among the leading elements of the XXXX Army Corps, the *Leibstandarte SS "Adolf Hitler"* (mot.) stormed ahead, with SS-Sturmbannführer Kurt Meyer and his men leading the way. As the 2nd Battalion made its way through Bitolje, it came under fire from several sides.

Schneidereit and his company provided cover as the battalion moved through the town. They shot up nests of resistance and silenced several machine guns. The Javat Pass was crossed and the city of Ohrig taken. The last Yugoslavian resistance had been extinguished.

At the same time the 9th Panzer Division had reached the Debar Pass. The division crawled over the 1,500-meter-high pass, negotiated sixty-six serpentine turns, crossed a forty-meter-long blown bridge and reached Debar ahead of the retreating Yugoslav units. Debar was taken in an engagement that lasted one hour. A battle group under the command of Major Walter Gorn—with the 1st Battalion of the 10th Motorized Rifle Regiment as its main striking force—captured the entire Yugoslavian Wardar Division. Among the personnel captured were with two generals, 150 officers and 2,500 men. In addition, several batteries of artillery and twelve antitank guns were captured. In recognition of this feat Gorn was awarded the Knight's Cross on 20 April 1941.

The *Leibstandarte SS "Adolf Hitler"* (mot.) then crossed the Klidi Pass, which was held by British troops and, on 12 April 1941, kicked open the door to Greece. Veering southwest, the brigade reached Lake Kastoria, negotiated the Klisura Pass and took the city of Koritzia, which housed the headquarters of the Greek III Army Corps. The surprise capture of Koritzia was the work of the advance guard under "Panzermeyer"—as its commander, Kurt Meyer, was already being called. Sepp Dietrich recommended Meyer for the Knight's Cross in recognition of this feat.

On 21 April the fighting continued. The brigade pushed through the Metsovon Pass. Once the pass had been cleared, the Greek Epirus-Macedonian Army sent emissaries wishing to negotiate a cease-fire. Escorted by several of his men, Sepp Dietrich went to Joanina. In the headquarters of the Epirus Army he and General Tsolakoglu signed the document of surrender. The Greek officers were allowed to keep their pistols. That evening Sepp Dietrich was the guest of the Greek archbishop, who expressed his personal gratitude to the German officer for ending the killing there. The entire Epirus Army went into captivity.

The advance in pursuit of the British troops was resumed from Joanina on 24 April. After another 250 kilometers, the Gulf of Patras was reached.

Alfred Schneidereit took part in this the last Blitz campaign by the Wehrmacht. He had already made a name for himself in the headquarters section as a runner who did not let obstacles or enemy fire prevent him from delivering his messages. It was in Greece that he earned his reputation for dependability. For Schneidereit the pursuit of the fleeing enemy south across the Peloponnese was an unforgettable experience.

On 29 April one last firefight with the enemy brought the Balkan Campaign to a close.

THE SS-DIVISION "LEIBSTANDARTE SS ADOLF HITLER" IN RUSSIA

Immediately before the beginning of the Eastern Campaign, the *Leibstandarte SS "Adolf Hitler"* (mot.) was redesignated and reorganized as the SS-Division *"Leibstandarte SS Adolf Hitler."* This measure did not increase the formation's size to that of a division, however. Its strength was only 10,796 men. It had only one full-strength motorized infantry regiment, whereas a motorized division usually had two. On the other hand, the SS-Infantry Regiment *"Leibstandarte SS Adolf Hitler"* did possess four battalions.

The division did not see action in the East until 30 June 1941, as it had to rest and refit after the Balkan Campaign. The division advanced through Klewan, Rovno and Kopylovo in the direction of Zhitomir. No one could suspect the significance that the city of Zhitomir would gain for them, especially Alfred Schneidereit, several years later.

On 31 July the division closed the Uman Pocket near Novo Arkhangelsk. Surrounded inside the pocket were the Soviet Sixth and Twelfth Armies. The division then attacked southeast as part of Panzer

Group 1. Near Kiryanovka it crossed the Ingul and cut off the line of retreat of Soviet units falling back before the 11th Army.

Kherson on the lower Dnieper was taken. It was there, while taking an important message from his company to the battalion, that Schneidereit had an encounter with Russian snipers. He was fired on each time he took a step. A bullet holed one of his boots and another pierced his left sleeve. Schneidereit crawled 100 meters to one side, crept along a deep trench and reached the battalion unhurt. He said nothing of his pursuit. Instead, after returning to his company, he set out with two well-known sharpshooters to where he had been fired on by the Russian snipers. As expected, they were fired on by the Russian snipers. The trio immediately took cover, then waited a few minutes. Schneidereit raised a homemade "head" that he had fashioned from a turnip. On it was perched a German steel helmet. Schneidereit felt a sharp blow as a bullet struck the helmet; they then heard the crack of the sniper's rifle.

"I saw the muzzle flash," one of the sharpshooters said softly. He carefully took aim at that exact spot.

Schneidereit raised the helmet again until it was just visible beyond cover. The Russian fired immediately. The muzzle flash gave the rifleman lying a few meters from Schneidereit his target. He made a slight correction and, a second after the enemy's shot, he fired. The Russian let out a piercing scream and rose up half a meter above his cover before falling backward. It was a dreadful sight, but Schneidereit knew that the first law of this struggle was "him or me".

They tried the ruse again, but there was no sign of the second sniper. Instead, the Russians opened fire on the trio with several mortars and forced them to withdraw.

The division crossed the Dniepr near Berislav and cleared the area south of Kherson. From there it resumed its advance toward Perekop. On 12 September the SS-Division *"Leibstandarte SS Adolf Hitler"* received orders from the 73rd Infantry Division, to which it was attached, to drive through the Isthmus of Perekop, which was only seven kilometers wide, and break through toward Ishun. The division carried out the attack but was halted by heavy defensive fire. The Russians had erected concrete strongpoints on both sides of the passable roads. These positions were linked by a deep trench system. A powerful armored train further strengthened the defenses.

The divisional commander, Sepp Dietrich, reported to the commander of the 73rd: "This breakthrough will not succeed without sufficient artillery and better armored troops." Nevertheless, it ordered a second attack, but Dietrich refused to execute it. He declared categorically that he would not sacrifice his troops senselessly. That was Sepp Dietrich, a man hard as iron and one who was unwilling to sacrifice even one man to further his own prestige or comply with a senseless order.

Finally, the 73rd attacked. Heavy artillery was moved up, but ten days of bitter fighting were required before it was able to force the isthmus. On 15 September the SS-Division *"Leibstandarte SS Adolf Hitler"* launched an attack near Salykov against the center of the three crossings over the Sivash. The Russian defensive ring north of the isthmus was smashed and a supply train heading for Sevastopol was taken. Eighty-six trucks, twenty-six tractors, two antitank guns and huge quantities of ammunition were captured.

The attack toward Genichesk, which lay to the east, turned out to be very difficult as the enemy had blown the bridge linking the mainland with the isthmus. The division's soldiers gained several hundred meters after crossing a footbridge erected by the pioneers, but then the attack was halted by heavy artillery fire.

The division was badly battered following these difficult engagements. Nevertheless, it took part in the great pursuit toward the Sea of Azov. Panzer Group had initiated the pursuit after its breakout from the Dniepr bridgeheads. Driving into the midst of the fleeing Russian units, the SS-Division *"Leibstandarte SS Adolf Hitler"* broke into the columns of the Soviet Ninth Army. The headquarters and units of the 30th Rifle Division were scattered and some elements captured.

The division crossed the river at Novo Spaskoye and set out toward Berdyansk on the Sea of Azov. The reconnaissance battalion under Kurt Meyer seized the city. The regiment's 8th Company under SS-Obersturm-führer Heinz Meier took part in much of the fighting. Alfred Schneidereit had to deal with several difficult situations, however, none of these stood out from the others. Schneidereit later explained: "There were several actions that were rather touch and go for us, but they did not stand out from the operations of the entire eastern army."

Nevertheless, the special Wehrmacht report of 8 October 1941 referred to the actions carried out by the entire division:

In a daring operation from the area east of Dniepropetrovsk, a German Panzer Army supported by Italian, Hungarian and Slovakian units has advanced to the Sea of Azov and forced the Soviet Ninth Army, which was attacked frontally near Melitopol, onto the retreat.

At the same time German and Romanian units have continued the pursuit from the west.

In the course of these actions, a motorized unit of the Waffen-SS has succeeded in breaking through along the coast of the Sea of Azov to Berdyansk and linking up there with armored forces coming from the north.

Tightly surrounded on all sides, six to seven enemy divisions found themselves facing destruction. Near Mariupol the SS unit has already set out after the weak remnants of the smashed enemy, which are trying to withdraw toward Rostov.

The SS-Division *"Leibstandarte SS Adolf Hitler"* set out in pursuit of the battered enemy with just 1,000 fighting men. The Russian field fortifications in front of Mariupol were pierced with the help of several assault guns of SS-Assault Battery *"Leibstandarte SS Adolf Hitler."* The division thus found itself with an opportunity to capture Mariupol.

The division's units pushed into the city. They took the Azov steel works and shipyards intact. On 12 October bitter fighting broke out for possession of the Mius bridges. A total of five officers and twenty-four men of the division became casualties. Four were killed.

Under the leadership of SS-Sturmbannführer Fritz Witt, the commander of the 1st Battalion of SS-Infantry Regiment *"Leibstandarte SS Adolf Hitler,*" the first bridgehead across the Mius was seized near Koselkin.

The regiment's 2nd Battalion, which was positioned north of the city under the command of SS-Sturmbannführer Theodor Wisch—known to all as "Teddy"—advanced into the midst of an enemy formation as it was beginning a counterattack. The enemy force included two armored trains and several waves of tanks. The men of the battalion suddenly found themselves fighting for their very lives. Alfred Schneidereit and the headquarters section of the 8th Company came under attack from a dense mass of Red Army troops.

"Open fire!" roared SS-Obersturmführer Kramer.

The SS troops fired at the onrushing enemy. Schneidereit and the others reached for the hand grenades they had prepared. They lobbed the grenades into the mass of shouting Russian troops, who were only fifty meters away at that point. They saw the last of the attackers fall.

"Teddy" Wisch appeared in their midst. "Hold on, Frey is coming!" he called to the men.

They held on, but the cost was high. Frey and his 3rd Battalion finally intervened and put the first armored train out of action, but the fighting was to go on for another five hours. The men of the 8th Company were attacked four times and each time the enemy assault was repulsed. Then the company commander was told that almost all of the men of the 5th Company had become casualties. The enemy had made that company's positions the focal point of his attack.

Albert Frey successfully put out of action the two remaining armored trains and all the enemy tanks in the field. The Soviets gave up and left the battlefield to the hard-fighting regiment. The 2nd Battalion alone had lost eighty men killed or wounded. It was a black day for Teddy Wisch and his men.

On 17 November Albert Frey was awarded the German Cross in Gold for his part in the attack, in which he had distinguished himself several times. Frey was one of the first members of the division to receive the recently created award. The German Cross in Gold was intended as an intermediate award between the Iron Cross, First Class, and the Knight's Cross.

On 19 October the Wehrmacht report declared: "The pursuit of the beaten enemy continues successfully between the Sea of Azov and the Donets. Units of the Waffen- SS have taken the port city of Taganrog in house and street fighting."

Not until 20 October did the division resume its march in the direction of Rostov. It was to participate in the capture of the city as part of General of Cavalry von Mackensen's III Panzer Corps.

Orders for the attack on Rostov were issued on 14 November. The SS-Division *"Leibstandarte SS Adolf Hitler"* was to be committed at the offensive concentration point. The tanks of the 13th Panzer Division were placed under the division's command and the attack began on 17 November. The fighting in front of the heavily fortified installations was very costly. Nevertheless, the division was able to fight its way through to Rostov. The 1st Battalion spearheaded the assault and reached the rail bridge south of the city after a dramatic charge through enemy positions.

The closely following companies of the 2nd Battalion fought their way through the rows of houses. Using the headquarters section's machine gun to good effect, Alfred Schneidereit was able to silence several enemy positions in houses. Nevertheless, groups of enemy soldiers continued to hold out at various points throughout the city, standing up fearlessly to the SS soldiers.

On 25 November the Red Army counterattacked. Artillery and mortar units as well as rocket battalions fired into the city. Red Army troops charged into the city across the ice that had formed on the river. The division was in danger of being cut off. General von Mackensen ordered Rostov abandoned. Sepp Dietrich was able to withdraw his division from the city without serious loss and lead it back to the Sambek position. The division held out there the entire winter against repeated Russian attacks.

On 31 December SS-Obergruppenführer Dietrich became the 41st German soldier to receive the Knight's Cross with Oak Leaves. It was in acknowledgement of his division's success and his qualities as a leader. To each member of the division, including Alfred Schneidereit, Sepp Dietrich was a father figure who was concerned about the welfare of every one of his soldiers.

In early 1942, Alfred Schneidereit and all the other members of the Eastern Army who had endured the dramatic winter campaign in temperatures as low as minus 50 degrees, received the Eastern Front Medal (*Ostmedaille*). The common soldiers referred to the new medal somewhat irreverently, but proudly, as the "order of the frozen flesh."

Schneidereit also received the Infantry Assault Badge in Bronze. He was supposed to receive the Iron Cross, Second Class, but the award did not come through and Schneidereit did not appeal the decision.

TRANSFER TO FRANCE—FORMATION OF
THE PANZER GRENADIER DIVISION

It was late May 1942 when the division was relieved in its winter position, where it had repulsed dozens of assaults. It was moved into the Stalino area. From there, the division was eventually sent to France. Sepp Dietrich had convinced Hitler to allow the division to be reorganized as a Panzer Grenadier Division. His long-term goal was to make it a Panzer Division.

The reorganization of the division was carried out in the Paris area. Dietrich had thus fulfilled a secret wish: The First World War tank commander had always wanted to command a large armored formation.

Command of the newly formed SS-Panzer Grenadier Regiment *"Leibstandarte SS Adolf Hitler"* was entrusted to SS-Standartenführer Fritz Witt. It was in this regiment that Alfred Schneidereit was to fight—initially as the leader of his company's headquarters section and, after Operation "Citadel," as leader of an antitank rifle squad. From France Schneidereit was able to go home on leave. There he met an old friend who was also on leave. Together they toured their homeland, until both had to return to their units.

ACTIONS IN THE KHARKOV AREA

With the beginning of the Russian winter offensive on 14 January 1943 the German front and that of its allies had been torn apart. The 2nd Army was badly battered. The Italian Alpine Corps fought its way back toward Oskol.

Its remnants and the XXIV Panzer Corps were incapable of further operations. Like Army Group Middle, which was holding the line Belgorod-Grayvoron-Lebedin, Army Group South was in danger of being overrun or encircled.

The hard-hit 320th Infantry Division was still holding east of Oskol. The shattered 298th Infantry Division had assembled near Kupyansk. Panzer Grenadier Division *"Großdeutschland"* was defending west of Valuiki. Between these scattered units were great gaps and it was only a question of time before the Soviet forces stormed through in a concentrated assault.

In January 1943 SS-Panzer Grenadier Division *"Leibstandarte SS Adolf Hitler"* was placed on alert. At the end of January it was transported back to Russia by train. With it came the 2nd SS-Panzer Grenadier Division *"Das Reich."* The division occupied a ninety-kilometer-wide defensive position on the Donets astride Chuguyev. SS-Obergruppenführer Dietrich's orders were: "Stop the attack by the Soviet Sixth Army and cover the retreat of the 298th Infantry Division, which is fighting its way out of the area east of Kupyansk."

The Red Army attacked the division at that point. The Soviets were trying to eliminate the German bridgehead beyond the Donets. The Soviets were beaten back with severe losses in front of the sector of SS-Panzer Grenadier Division *"Leibstandarte SS Adolf Hitler."* But, forty kilometers south of Merefa, the Red Army stormed through a forty-kilometer gap in the German defensive front and broke into the right flank of the forces defending Kharkov. This made the immediate withdrawal of the division from the Donets area imperative. Plans were drawn up to stem the Russian offensive with a German counterattack.

The newly formed SS-Panzer Corps was unable to launch a massed counterattack as planned by the Army High Command, however; the Red Army had already advanced too far. The primary objective at that point was to hold the line at Kharkov and relieve the encircled divisions. The SS-Panzer Corps faced encirclement in and around Kharkov until early February 1943. It received a direct order from the Führer: "Fight to the last round!"

When this order arrived the enemy had already begun to outflank and encircle Kharkov.

The situation left SS-Obergruppenführer Paul Hausser, the commanding general, two options. First: Immediate attack against the forces of the Red Army outflanking Kharkov to the south. Second: Pull back all forces for an all-round defense of Kharkov. This second option was not viable as it would have ended in encirclement and the inevitable destruction of his corps.

SS-Obergruppenführer Dietrich came up with a third solution, one forbidden by Hitler. He wanted to attack southwards with three battle groups, smash the threat on the right flank and thus prevent the encirclement of Kharkov.

On 9 February the newly formed SS-Panzer Corps established an attack group under the command of SS-Obergruppenführer Dietrich. SS-Panzer Grenadier Division *"Leibstandarte SS Adolf Hitler"* was sent in the direction of Kharkov, as was the 4th SS-Panzer Grenadier Regiment *"Der Führer"* of the 2nd SS-Panzer Grenadier Division *"Das Reich"* under SS-Obersturmbann-führer Otto Kumm.

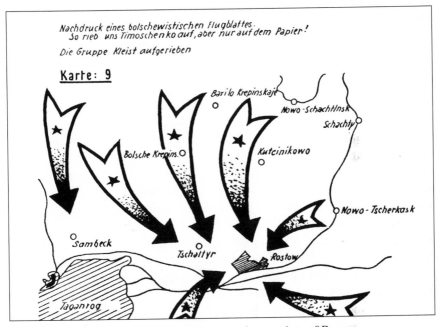

A Soviet leaflet detailing the destruction of Rostov.

The attack on the enemy's flank began in heavy blowing snow and bitter cold. Near Alexeyevka SS-Panzer Grenadier Division *"Leibstandarte SS Adolf Hitler"* ran into the Soviet 6th Guards Cavalry Corps and, in a dramatic struggle, smashed the enemy formation. On 14 February Sepp Dietrich received new instructions from General Lanz, the over-all commander. The first attack toward the south had to be halted. The captured territory was to be held, and an ad hoc battle group was to be formed and sent to Kharkov to strengthen the defenders there. An armored battle group was also to be sent toward Valki with the objective of recapturing Olchany.

The next day, while these movements were under way, orders were issued by SS-Obergruppenführer Hausser for the planned evacuation of Kharkov. He wanted to meet this crisis situation by withdrawing and keeping his corps and its fighting power intact. It was Hausser's intention to retake Kharkov at the first opportunity.

In the 8th Company of the 1st SS-Panzer Grenadier Regiment under SS-Obersturmführer Kramer, Alfred Schneidereit fought not only against the enemy, but against the deep snow and biting cold as well. As leader of the company headquarters section he was invaluable to Kramer. The strong East Prussian proved to be a cold-blooded runner and fighter. Schneidereit quietly went about his duties and only his closest comrades were aware of his feats as he "pulled their chestnuts out of the fire" time and time again.

The regiment was holding a sector of the front thirty-two kilometers wide at that point. But Witt, the regiment's commander, had no intention of defending. He was going to attack! He had always maintained: "The attack is the best defense!"

When the Soviets broke through the southern wing of the division in this critical situation, it was Witt who launched a bold thrust into the enemy's flank with his mechanized infrantry. Repeatedly attacking southward, he forced the Red Army to fight on his terms. The regiment's 2nd Battalion under SS-Sturmbannführer Max Hansen played a prominent role in the fighting. The 8th Company was always in the forefront. Alfred Schneidereit caught the battalion commander's attention on several occasions. On one occasion, he braved heavy fire to deliver a report to the battalion command post. Later, he led a hastily assembled squad against enemy forces that had broken into the German positions. His small force subsequently drove them out again.

The ice and snow-covered landscape was the second enemy. The same "General Winter" who had halted the German Army in 1941 struck again. But this time the troops were better equipped and able to withstand the onslaught.

Schneidereit's performance during the fighting around Kharkov warranted the Iron Cross, First Class, but no recommendation was submitted because his conduct could not be reported and he himself made little of it. The tireless efforts of Battle Group Witt enabled the division to establish a new front and a mobile main line of resistance. SS-Standartenführer Witt was always among his men. Alfred Schneidereit got to know and respect the brawny leader from the Westphalia district of Germany.

(On 1 March 1943 Fritz Witt received the long-overdue Knight's Cross with Oak Leaves—he was the 200th recipient in the entire Wehrmacht at that point—in recognition of his leadership and personal actions. But Witt himself insisted that the award was for his men as well: ". . . above all for the courageous actions of every one of my soldiers, who carried out every order no matter how difficult, because they knew that each of these orders had been dictated by necessity." When Fritz Witt was later called away to take charge of the formation of the newly forming 12th SS-Panzer Division *"Hitlerjugend,"* his place was taken by SS-Sturmbannführer Albert Frey, one of the division's most veteran fighters. On 28 March SS-Sturmbannführer Max Hansen, Schneidereit's battalion commander, received the Knight's Cross for his role in the seesaw fighting.)

In the operation to recapture Kharkov the 1st SS-Panzer Grenadier Regiment set out from Dergachi. Its 2nd Battalion under Max Hansen cleared the way for the division's attack on Kharkov, which took place the following day. When the mechanized infantry reached the city limits, they were met by fire from dug-in T-34s, which brought the advance to a halt.

The German artillery turned its fire on this enemy; one of the first Tiger tanks to reach the Eastern Front then appeared on the road from farther in the rear.

"Look at that monster!" called Schneidereit. "That should do the trick!"

The tank rolled forward and halted several hundred meters in front of the grenadiers, who had taken cover. It then opened fire. The first round blew the turret off one of the dug-in tanks. The Tiger picked up speed, halted again and once more destroyed a T-34 with a single round. Then, to everyone's surprise, it rolled back the way it had come. When the Tiger reached the troops, they learned that it had taken a hit on the mantlet, which had disabled the tank's main gun.

Suddenly, SS-Standartenführer Witt appeared. He raised his fist and the attack was resumed. The infantrymen made it into Kharkov, inspired by Witt's example.

For Alfred Schneidereit, the Battle of Kharkov became a nightmare. It was here that he experienced his first real close-quarters fighting, where one could see "the whites of the enemy's eyes". He fought with determination, took part in every assault and won the Close Combat Clasp in Bronze. For the soldiers it was a question of holding on and supporting one another; they also wanted to throw the Russians out of Kharkov.

It had been four days since the assault on Kharkov had started in Dergachi. When Sepp Dietrich arrived at the headquarters of Generalfeldmarschall von Manstein's Army Group South at Dergachi, he received a call from Hitler. Hitler inquired about the state of his bodyguard unit and ended his discussion with Dietrich with the following words: "If my *Leib-*

standarte attacks with its usual verve, then we will succeed in taking Kharkov back from the enemy."

This is exactly what happened, and Sepp Dietrich was able to report to Hitler that the division had carried out its orders. On 19 March 1943 Hitler released an order of the day in which he expressed his special appreciation to all the soldiers of the Army and Luftwaffe who had taken part in the operation. The order of the day ended with the words:

> Newly committed divisions of the Army and Waffen-SS saw action alongside the veteran soldiers of the Army and Waffen-SS. At the front's vital positions the Russians succumbed to their concerted, violent attack and the ongoing heroic actions of the Luftwaffe.
>
> Kharkov is once again in our hands!
> (signed) Adolf Hitler

THE BATTLE OF KURSK

On 1 July 1943 Albert Frey was promoted to the rank of SS-Obersturmbannführer. Beginning on 5 July 1943 he and his regiment saw action in Operation Citadel, the Battle of Kursk. The mission of the 1st SS-Panzer Grenadier Regiment: "Surprise and overcome the enemy combat outposts on the night of the attack. Take the forward antitank ditches, possession of which is vital to the division's advance."

It was here that Alfred Schneidereit first fought as the leader of an antitank squad. He had become acquainted with this "poor man's cannon" within a few days, learning how to use the sighting mechanism. He pushed his squad until it was able to field strip the *Panzerbüchse 41* down into four man-portable parts in a matter of minutes. When assembled, the antitank gun weighed nearly 500 pounds.

It was due to Schneidereit's reputation that he was assigned the antitank squad. When SS-Hauptsturmführer Kramer was asked to whom he could entrust the weapon, he replied immediately: "Schneidereit is the only man for the job!"

The *Panzerbüchse 41* was, in reality, a small cannon. Its caliber was 28 millimeters, which decreased to 20 millimeters at the end of the tapered barrel. The weapon's extremely high muzzle velocity of 1,402 meters per second enabled it to disable even heavy tanks, provided the round struck a vulnerable spot. The heavy antitank gun was able to deal with light tanks without a problem. Its overall barrel length was 1.714 meters. The weapon was mounted on a relatively tall, wheeled carriage which could be moved by the men of the squad. The gun's deflection capability was 90 degrees;

elevation went from minus 5 degrees to plus 45 degrees. The *Panzergranat-patrone 41* ammunition was light and allowed significant quantities to be carried by the squad. At the time of its introduction, this antitank gun was an excellent weapon with good penetration and a high rate of fire. A lightened version was also built for the parachute troops. Its greatest disadvantage was the limited life of its barrel, which had to be changed after about 500 rounds. During the Battle of Kursk Alfred Schneidereit achieved several successes that proved the worth of this particular weapon.

In spite of heavy defensive fire and bitter resistance, the regiment accomplished its mission. Assault squads cleared the antitank ditches. Schneidereit's antitank squad was able to demonstrate its effectiveness during the attack by eliminating two enemy machine-gun positions with only a few rounds. Following that, Schneidereit eliminated a number of heavy weapons emplaced in bunkers by putting armor-piercing rounds through the embrasures. He thus opened up the way through the first line of fortifications for his battalion.

The advance continued through barbed wire and minefields. Enemy artillery opened fire in an attempt to pin down the attackers and halt the advance at the anti tank ditches. When SS-Obersturmbannführer Albert Frey saw that the advance was in danger of bogging down, he assembled a pioneer platoon and advanced on the line of enemy positions. Behind the pioneers came a platoon of the 8th Company. Schneidereit's antitank squad was with them.

The pioneers blew up obstacles and cleared mines, allowing Schneidereit and his squad to move forward into a good firing position. From there he eliminated two antitank guns which were holding up the German advance.

In the meantime, the pioneers had blasted lanes through the antitank ditches, allowing the German tanks to roll through. The advance continued. Leading the way was SS-Obersturmbannführer Frey. His driver, SS-Rottenführer Balke, was at his side. The 8th Company surged forward after him. The men of the division were certain of victory, however, the overall outcome hung in the balance for days. Finally, on 12 July, the Kursk battle was called off on Hitler's order, even though Generalfeldmarschall von Manstein was thoroughly convinced that his southern pincer was gaining ground and could turn the tide of the fighting.

Hitler was rattled by the Allied landing in Sicily on the night of 10 July and ordered troops withdrawn from the Eastern Front to meet the threat in the south.

Following the cancellation of Operation Citadel, SS-Panzer Grenadier Division *"Leibstandarte SS Adolf Hitler"* was moved to Italy to meet an enemy assault on the mainland. (The Allies had, in fact, landed near Salerno during the night of 8–9 September 1943.)

Before the division could engage the Allied forces, an event took place which required the immediate action of the entire division. Italy withdrew from the Axis alliance on 8 September and the Germans feared that the approximately 500,000 Italian troops in Italy might take up arms against their former ally. Such a move had to be forestalled.

On the evening of 8 September Albert Frey and his driver drove into Milan, the site of an Italian corps headquarters. He reached the corps headquarters and began negotiations with its commanding general. Frey convinced the general of the hopelessness of a war against the Wehrmacht and succeeded in talking him into surrendering the troops under his command—in total, about 100,000 men. These were disarmed by the division over the next few days—without a shot being fired.

Following that, the Chief-of-Staff of the Italian Army, General Roatta, protested the presence of the Waffen-SS troops. However General Jodl and General Rommel, who discussed the situation with Roatta on 15 September in Bologna, both explained that the Waffen-SS division was an army division like the others. General Jodl commented on the critical situation in northern Italy, pointing out that instead of massing near Salerno in the south to fight the Allies, the Italian units were concentrated in the northern part of the country. He observed that it appeared that the Italians were preparing to join the Allies against their former ally if the occasion arose. It was in this situation that Erwin Rommel ran into his old comrade-in-arms, Sepp Dietrich. Rommel mentioned the meeting in his diary: "Dietrich is fully prepared to make things hot for the Italians should they revolt."

The disarming of all Italian troops on the mainland went smoothly, thanks in no small part to the energetic efforts of the Waffen-SS units. After completion of this operation, the division took part in anti-partisan efforts in Istria and Slovenia.

Also at the beginning of September 1943 the division was redesignated as the 1st SS-Panzer Division "Leibstandarte SS Adolf Hitler," the designation it carried until the end of the war.

Following its defensive success in the Kursk salient and subsequent successes near Belgorod and Orel, the Red Army pushed the hard-pressed units of the German Army back across the Dniepr. A crisis situation developed for the battered northern wing of Army Group South as a result. The army's 1st Panzer Division and the 1st SS-Panzer Division "Leibstandarte SS Adolf Hitler" were given the job of saving the situation. The SS division was withdrawn from northern Italy and, following a brief period of rest and refitting, was once again sent on its way to Russia.

The first member of the division to reach Russia was the division commander, SS-Oberführer Theodor Wisch. He arrived at the command post in Adshamka on 8 November 1943. A new chapter had opened in the life of the division, a chapter in which Alfred Schneidereit was to play a special role.

TEN DAYS IN A PITILESS STRUGGLE—THE 1ST SS-PANZER DIVISION *"LEIBSTANDARTE SS ADOLF HITLER"* ARRIVES

When the Red Army went over to the offensive following its defensive success in the Battle of Kursk, the 1st SS-Panzer Division *"Leibstandarte SS Adolf Hitler"* was placed on alert and sent east by fast train. By throwing in the last of its reserves, Army Group South under Generalfeldmarschall von Manstein had succeeded in halting the pursuing Red Army behind the Dniepr, thus preserving the cohesiveness of the entire front.

Heavy fighting continued at Nikopol, Zaporozhye and in the Kiev area. Heavy fighting had been going on since 7 October in the northern part of the Army Group South sector. The area was held by the 4th Panzer Army. At stake were the Kiev bridgehead and the city itself.

Generalfeldmarschall von Manstein urgently requested fresh forces to reinforce the defense of the Kiev area, including the city. The German High Command subsequently decided to send the bulk of the available mobile units to the southern front. These reinforcements consisted of one Panzer Division each from the commands of the Commander-in-Chief Southeast, the Commander-in-Chief West and the Commander-in-Chief Southwest. The units were sent to the threatened area by express rail transport.

First to head for the Russian Front was the 1st SS-Panzer Division *"Leibstandarte SS Adolf Hitler."* It was followed by the 1st Panzer-Division from Albania and the 25th Panzer Division from northern France and Norway. These divisions were later joined by the 7th, 8th and 19th Panzer Divisions and the 10th and 20th Panzer Grenadier Divisions.

As the elements of the divisions arrived in the area near the front they were thrown into the battle by the 4th Panzer Army to plug up or at least seal off the gaps in the front. The task at hand was to halt the divisions of the 1st Ukrainian Front, which had massed powerful mobile forces in the Kiev area before attacking with four powerful spearheads: They were heading toward Korosten in the northwest, Radomyshl in the west and—as the enemy's concentration point—along the highway to Zhitomir.

On 3 November 1943 General Vatutin, the Army group's commander, had attacked west from his Dniepr bridgehead with thirty infantry divisions, twenty-four tank brigades and ten mechanized brigades. In spite of the Soviets' great numerical superiority, the fighting for and on both sides of Kiev produced no decisive success. Kiev held on until 6 November when, bypassed on both sides by mobile forces, it had to be abandoned.

On 7 November the leading Russian units reached Fastov. In one final effort, the men and equipment of the 1st SS-Panzer Division *"Leibstandarte SS Adolf Hitler"* were sent to meet the threat. However, the rail line had been cut near Fastov and the division had to detrain in Berdichev, about fifty kilometers south of Zhitomir. The 1st Company of the 2nd SS-Panzer Grenadier Regiment detrained eighteen kilometers west of Fastov on 8 November. The remaining three battalions detrained at Popielna. All went straight into action from the loading ramps. The attached tank company and the regiment's small number of assault guns came under fire from T-34s while still detraining. The Soviet tanks rolled in from three directions, shooting up the tanks and assault guns that were scarcely in a position to return fire.

The tanks were followed by a regiment of Red Army troops. The 1st Company fought with everything it had, but it was unable to prevent the enemy from gaining the upper hand. The company was completely wiped out. Those of the company not killed in battle were dispatched with a bullet in the nape of the neck. The same fate was suffered by the company's wounded.

Following this grisly prelude, the main body of the 1st SS-Panzer Grenadier Regiment set out for Sokolov on 9 November. The regimental commander, SS-Obersturmbannführer Albert Frey, set up his headquarters there.

The battalion commanders were immediately summoned for a briefing. The commander of the 8th Company, SS-Hauptsturmführer Heinz Meier, represented the battalion commander, who was on leave. There he learned that the regiment was going to attack Fastovets the next morning. Albert Frey issued the orders in his straightforward manner: "First Battalion will set out to attack Fastovets. Second Battalion will follow closely and intervene at the crisis points. Both battalions will hold the village against any enemy attack and secure the area. Third Battalion will be deployed as required as soon as it arrives."

THE ATTACKS OF THE NEXT TWO DAYS

When the attack orders arrived the 8th Company began preparations for its next operation. SS-Obersturmführer Schuhknecht, who was leading the company while SS-Hauptsturmführer Meier was the acting battalion commander, took his place at the head of the company and rolled off after the 1st Battalion. The first enemy guns opened fire to the front; Schuhknecht informed the platoons. The two assault guns leading the attack opened fire. The first fires broke out among the low houses.

"Second Battalion: Deploy right and advance; move against Fastovets from the south flank and eliminate the positions at the edge of the village."

SS-Obersturmführer Schuhknecht acted immediately on receiving the battalion commander's order. He had his forces veer southeast and the panzer grenadiers rolled at high speed into the village's south flank. Alfred Schneidereit sat in the antitank squad's truck waiting for orders. They were not long in coming.

The column of vehicles halted. The panzer grenadiers were going to assault the village on foot. Two Russian heavy machine guns opened fire.

"Antitank gun forward!" ordered Schuhknecht.

The antitank gun was heaved out of the truck. Schneidereit's squad hauled the weapon along a line of vegetation that flanked a trench. Schneidereit spotted a good position for his "poor man's cannon" a few dozen meters ahead. He directed the antitank gun into position. His men brought the ammunition. To the left and right the panzer grenadiers had taken cover from the machine-gun fire and were returning fire with their rifles.

Schneidereit squatted behind his weapon. Ahead he could see the muzzle flashes of a machine gun. After a slight correction, the first *Panzergranate 41* left the barrel and raced toward the enemy position at 1,400 meters per second. The round was high and crashed into a wall above and behind the target. Schneidereit adjusted his aim. A few seconds later he fired again; less than three tenths of a second later there was a shattering impact. The machine gun abruptly fell silent. Schneidereit ordered his two men to swing the gun around. The muzzle of the long antitank gun was now pointing at the second machine gun. Schneidereit fired four rounds from the weapon he had learned to master and silenced the other machine gun. The panzer grenadiers made a determined dash forward. Behind them the men of the antitank squad struggled to keep pace.

In the meantime, the 1st Battalion had reached the town. Two green flares rose from the town center, the signal to everyone that the objective was in German hands. Schneidereit's squad reached Fastovets and took up position in the northeast part of the town in the first combat outpost line.

SS-Obersturmführer Schuhknecht came past the defensive line. "Well done, Alfred," he said. Schuhknecht was not a man who was lavish with his praise.

"A great weapon," added SS-Unterscharführer Willing, the leader of the headquarters section.

When the rations arrived Schneidereit sat down with the men of his squad; they had been assigned to him since June of that year. They spooned up the warm food silently.

"How do you think it will go from here, Alfred?" asked Siegfried Grigoleit, one of the loaders.

"The same thing happened in January when we were shipped from France to Kharkov. We'll soon bring Ivan to a halt."

"I have a feeling it's going to be tougher this time. This haste and rush seems fishy to me," interjected Hintze, a young trooper from Westphalia who had come to the unit after Kursk as a replacement.

"Thanks for the good news!" Wim Hummel exclaimed. He was known to everyone simply as "Bee" because of his name (*Hummel* is "bumblebee" in German).

SS-Hauptsturmführer Meier arrived at the front after dark. Together with Schuhknecht, he inspected the individual positions. Finally he announced: "We're moving up tomorrow. The objective is Snetinka."

"Wash up for a hero's death," called Hintze softly, which resulted in an outbreak of laughter.

The next morning the 2nd Battalion spearheaded the attack. The unit's vehicles rolled up to the town of Snetinka. Everyone was hoping that the enemy had already withdrawn, when enemy fire flared up from houses and behind shattered walls. The panzer grenadiers rolled through at high speed. The first Russian guns opened up but the vehicles were already beneath their fire. At the edge of the town the panzer grenadiers climbed down from their vehicles. Schneidereit and his men tried to keep pace with the others, but the antitank gun was too hard to handle for a fast attack. The gun never had a chance to fire. The town was in the battalion's hands within a half-hour.

The next day the 1st SS-Panzer Grenadier Regiment was relieved, which came as a surprise. It marched to Dunajka. The enemy had suddenly moved north and west of the regiment and was in the process of cutting the unit off. Wisch ordered his forces to regroup in order to prevent this from happening. It was vital that the enemy forces in and around Kornin be attacked and smashed.

Still without his 3rd Battalion, SS-Obersturmbannführer Frey attacked on the morning of 13 November 1943. The Russian forces were driven back and, the next day, a new security position was established at the Irpen Line, which was to be defended by the entire division.

The Red Army reached Zhitomir on 13 November and occupied the weakly defended city. This represented a deep penetration in the German southern front in the area held by the 4th Panzer Army.

Generalfeldmarschall von Manstein received the news in his headquarters at Vinnitsa and acted without delay. He assembled a powerful group of armored units along the line Fastov-Zhitomir and sent it to the attack under the command of Generaloberst Hermann Hoth, the commander of the 4th Panzer Army. The objective of this counterblow was to smash the dangerous Soviet armored thrust and regain the initiative.

The divisions for the attack to close the gaps in the front on both sides of Zhitomir were placed under the operational control of the XXXXVIII Panzer Corps, which was commanded by General of Armored Troops Hermann Balck. On the left flank were the 68th Infantry Division and the 7th Panzer Division (Generalleutnant Hasso von Manteuffel). In the center was the 1st Panzer Division (Generalleutnant Krüger) and, on the right, the 1st SS-Panzer Division *"Leibstandarte SS Adolf Hitler."* The 19th Panzer Division did not become available until 19 November. The 25th Panzer Division and the 2nd SS-Panzer Division *"Das Reich"* came later to join the right wing, while the 20th Panzer Grenadier Division and the reinforced 8th Panzer Division joined the left wing. The majority of the units moved out on 13 November and attacked from south to north.

THE NORTHWARD ASSAULT BY THE 1ST SS-PANZER DIVISION *"LEIBSTANDARTE SS ADOLF HITLER"*

On 15 November 1943 the 1st SS-Panzer Grenadier Regiment, reinforced by antitank units, tanks and assault guns, went on the attack with the other elements of the division. The objective of the attack was to penetrate the enemy positions north and northeast of Kornin. This attack was the beginning of a successful, but costly raid to the north highway and a prelude to the later all-round defense of Kocherova.

The regimental firepower had been significantly augmented. For the attack it had at its disposal two battalions of artillery and a separate battery, a tank battalion equipped with the potent Panther tank, two antitank companies and a pioneer company. However the regiment's 3rd Battalion had still not rejoined the regiment, as it had been deployed to protect the right flank. Not until 19 November did it return to the regiment.

Storming through the enemy positions, by midday the panzer grenadiers reached the village of Solovyevka. The village was taken after an hour of street fighting.

Alfred Schneidereit and the 8th Company hurried forward with the antitank units to the eastern edge of the Solovyevka. They arrived not a moment too soon, because the Soviets immediately launched a counterattack to recapture the village.

Schneidereit and his men destroyed three enemy vehicles. The Panthers engaged approaching T-34s, destroying several of them. Two of the German tanks were knocked out and another lost a track while fending off the enemy attack. When it was over nineteen Soviet tanks had been knocked out. During the engagement Schneidereit hit a light T-26 tank and saw it turn away smoking.

SS-Obersturmbannführer Frey assembled the battalion commanders. "The next objective is Vodoty. The 1st Panzer Division will be attacking on our left."

The attack got under way. Concealed antitank guns opened fire as soon as the vanguard came within firing range of Vodoty. T-34s that had taken cover behind houses and sheds joined in. The engagement lasted four and a half hours. Schneidereit and his company stormed through the streets. Where the Russians mounted resistance, they were smoked out by Schneidereit and his antitank gun and forced to surrender. Soon Vodoty was also in German hands.

A patrol under the command of SS-Oberscharführer Buhrke of the 8th Company discovered "powerful enemy formations preparing for a night attack on Vodoty." Buhrke was a first-rate fighter who was "decked out with decorations and medals like a tinsel-covered Christmas tree." With the consent of the divisional commander, SS-Obersturmbannführer Frey had the battle groups move out of Vodoty before midnight. It marched unopposed northwest in the direction of Romanovka.

The sentries were overpowered almost noiselessly and, when the German forces moved into the town, the Russian units there were taken by surprise as they slept. Following a brief firefight, which flared up again sporadically, the enemy forces in Romanovka were overcome. On receiving reports of the fighting, Albert Frey realized that his battle group had advanced directly into the headquarters of a Soviet rifle division.

The weather worsened day by day. It had even snowed several times, but most of the snow had melted. Only in the shadows and areas protected from the wind did it remain as a thick mat. The nights were already becoming very cold and, as Battle Group Frey often had to move by night, the men suffered terribly. Nevertheless, the night attack and the surprise capture of Romanovka brought a rich booty, as was discovered the next morning. The last resistance was extinguished as the fires from the burning houses were put out.

A large number of vehicles were captured. Those of American origin were incorporated into the regiment's vehicle columns. They were some of the thousands of such vehicles that had been sent from the USA and delivered to Russia by convoy from England to Murmansk.

Battle Group Frey moved out again at first light on 16 November. The point units came under fire as they approached the next village, Vishna. The resistance mounted by the Russian supply unit there was quickly bro-

All is made ready to repel an enemy counterattack, including ample supplies of both stick and egg grenades.

ken. The unit belonged to a cavalry unit that had crossed paths with Battle Group Frey the previous night.

When the battle group reached the village of Vilnya it became obvious straight away that it was facing more serious opposition. The panzer grenadiers attacked without stopping to form up. This time the 2nd Battalion led the attack. The assault gun battalion had provided a platoon of four vehicles to spearhead the assault. Together with the rest of the 8th Company Schneidereit's squad raced through the enemy fire. The assault guns cleared the way. The 5th and 6th Companies open the way on foot so that the 7th and 8th Companies could follow up quickly.

The village was cleared and the advance resumed. By the time darkness fell the Kampfgruppe had reached Voytachevka. The town was only two kilometers south of the objective, the north-south highway from Kiev to Zhitomir.

An attempt to cover the remaining 2,000 meters in one go proved too costly. After the first three vehicles had run over mines and one of the assault guns was disabled several hundred meters in front of the main body in a minefield, SS-Obersturmbannführer Frey decided to alter the direction of the assault. He would veer toward the northeast and seize the village of Kocherovo. None of the men of Battle Group Frey had ever heard of this village on the north-south highway, but it was to become something of an evil omen for all of them. The fate of a large part of the Kampfgruppe was to be decided there, and several soldiers of the division were to distinguish themselves in action.

In the early morning hours of 17 November a motorcycle reconnaissance platoon reported to the regiment's commander that Kocherovo was occupied by the enemy. After probing the town's defenses several times, SS-Obersturmbannführer Frey became convinced it was not that strongly defended. In any case, the enemy did not seem too eager to exchange fire.

Following a brief conference with his commanders, Frey issued his orders: "We will attack after brief preparations so as to exploit the element of surprise!" These preparations for the attack took place out of sight of the enemy behind a rise running about one kilometer south of the village. Frey issued his final order before the attack: "Second Battalion will carry out the attack. First Battalion stands by to follow up."

SS-Haupsturmführer Meier led the attack as SS-Obersturmbannführer Hansen was not yet back from leave.

The vehicles carrying the panzer grenadiers of the 2nd Battalion moved over the rise and rolled toward the village at high speed. The defenders were surprised by the speed of the attack and, before they could mount any major defensive effort, the assault guns had advanced into the village, crushing nests of resistance. The panzer grenadiers had not kept pace with the assault guns and resistance formed at various locations. Schneidereit and his antitank gun were sent forward after a Soviet antitank gun knocked out the first assault gun. The squad reached a favorable firing position and silenced the 76.2-mm antitank gun.

The planned flanking attack by the tanks of the 1st Battalion under SS-Sturmbannführer Herbert Kuhlmann, had failed to get through and the battalion's situation became increasingly critical as more antitank guns and tanks joined the engagement. The battalion got to within 200 meters of the village before it was halted, exhausted. A Russian truck appeared from the east, apparently intent on entering the village. Schneidereit hit it in the side. The vehicle stopped and brown-clad figures poured out. A second hit caused the truck's fuel tank to explode.

Looking to his left, Wim Hummel saw the first tanks with their long guns appear over the rise. "The tanks are coming!" he shouted.

The tanks opened fire. It all happened very quickly. Herbert Kuhlmann led his Panthers forward and the Russian resistance collapsed.

The tanks fired several salvoes after the enemy as they fled the village. The battalion settled into Kocherovo.

There was great joy when the news arrived that the 3rd Battalion had taken the village of Privorotye, only a few kilometers south of Kocherovo. When SS-Obersturmführer Schuhknecht and his men reached the center of the village they saw to their surprise a T-34 that had become bogged down in the muddy bank of a pond. The tank tried to turn and they saw that it had partially shed one of its tracks. The T-34 rolled around in a circle.

"We'll get him!" called one of the men of the company.

Three or four soldiers approached the T-34, but they came under fire from the tank's machine gun, which prevented them from getting close enough. Finally, an assault gun arrived and knocked out the enemy tank with two well-aimed rounds.

When the fighting was over there were indications that the enemy had once again been taken by surprise. The men of the 6th Company were especially surprised to find the crew of a T-34 sleeping in a hut. The Russians were captured along with their T-34.

Albert Frey arrived in his command vehicle and received the initial report of SS-Hauptsturmführer Meier.

"You must secure the village for all-round defense at once," Frey urged his comrade. "In all probability Ivan will want to retake this point. We have to continue to block the road."

"We'll do it, Albert. As always!" answered Meier coolly.

Kocherovo was located just south of the highway. Its northern road out of the town crossed the main road, making it one of the best positions from which to effectively block the thoroughfare, provided that fresh forces, especially heavy weapons, were sent quickly.

The 8th Company was assigned the northeast sector. The whole sector was about 300 meters wide and the hastily dug field positions were on both sides of the main road. Their primary orientation was east. It was there that the main attacks by Soviet forces coming from Kiev would probably strike. Deliveries of ammunition, fuel and food during the night enabled the Kampfgruppe to hold onto Kocherovo. This proved to be most important, because the Kampfgruppe was attacked during the course of 17 November. It was attacked not only from the north and east, but from the south as well and, finally, from the northwest. As a result, the Kampfgruppe under SS-Hauptsturmführer Meier was cut off and surrounded by the enemy.

The order to dig in was carried out as rapidly as possible, as a quick attack was expected. The Soviet assault began on the afternoon of 17 November. At first it was with weak forces, but then with company-sized elements. At the same time, a Russian supply column was still rolling toward Kocherovo. The first vehicles arrived as darkness was falling. They drove toward the town with shielded headlights.

August Korschowski, the burly East Prussian from Königsberg, called to Schneidereit: "We'll smash them to pieces!"

However, SS-Obersturmführer Schuhknecht, who had just appeared in the makeshift dugout housing the two flanking machine guns, ordered them to let the convoy drive into the village.

"Knock out the last vehicle as soon as it drives past your gun, Alfred! That will be the signal for everyone else to open fire."

The Soviet vehicles rolled past. The column included two T-26 light tanks and several personnel carriers, as well as trucks loaded with equipment, ammunition and fuel. Schneidereit took aim at the last vehicle as it approached. Then it showed the SS-Rottenführer its broadside. There was a crack as the antitank gun fired. Almost simultaneously the sound of the round striking the fuel truck could be heard. Seconds later the truck was in flames, illuminating a lurid scene.

The 8th Company opened fire on the column from all sides with every available weapon. The two flanking assault guns joined in. It was all over in a minute. The enemy abandoned his vehicles and fled in panic toward the north. Inspection of the booty turned up some worthwhile materiel and weapons, which were incorporated into the town's defenses.

That was the last Russian supply column to come that way. Word had obviously reached the enemy in the east that there was no getting through Kocherovo. During the night of 17–18 November the enemy tried to get through to Kocherovo from every direction with strong patrols and assault squads. The 8th Company repulsed a platoon-sized Soviet attack from the north in its field positions sited 200 to 300 meters east of the village.

Paul Raabe of the antitank squad began shoveling wet sand onto the breastworks of the squad's position and packing it down. "Too bad we can't spend the night in the houses," he said.

The squad was right beside the main road in a well-camouflaged dugout. The barrel of the antitank gun projected only about twenty-five centimeters above the breastworks; it was oriented east. Both flanking machine guns had been set up in positions forty meters left and right of the main road. The entire company was in trenches and holes on both sides of the guns.

SS-Hauptsturmführer Meier had ordered a second position set up behind them in the village. The soldiers of the battalion who were positioned further east could withdraw there should they find themselves in danger of being cut off. Running in front of the antitank squad and the two machine guns—at right angles to their direction of fire—was a rise that gave the enemy a good starting point for an assault on Kocherovo.

The few assault guns and two Panthers assumed responsibility for antitank defense. Schneidereit's weapon was not capable of knocking out a T-34, although several other antitank gunners had reported successes against the Soviet tank. In spite of its ineffectiveness against heavy tanks, the antitank gun was a useful weapon against light vehicles and machine-gun positions.

After barely a week back in Russia, Schneidereit and his comrades were struck by the Red Army's numerical superiority in men and weapons. The steadily worsening storms, snowfalls and cold nights wore down the soldiers' strength. In addition, casualties were heavy. Schneidereit learned that afternoon that the company had already lost forty of its 120 soldiers killed or wounded. The remaining companies of the battalion and regiment had suffered equally high casualties.

The company command post bunker was covered with stalks from a hop field. A SS-Rottenführer procured a saw from a resident of the village for this purpose. The man, a Russian of approximately fifty years, went along with the German to make sure he didn't lose his saw.

A war correspondent submitted a report on 17 November 1943 that described the lot of the civilians still living in Kocherovo:

> Here and there blaze the fires of war. Women wander about with water buckets and try to save their straw huts that are shrouded in sheets of flame, a hopeless undertaking. The few drops of water hiss away like nothing.
>
> Cattle bawl amid the wreckage of their destroyed stalls. A flock of hens with rumpled feathers has gathered on the still warm iron plates of one of the nine tanks destroyed in the first assault on the village.
>
> The broad road which, after days of rain, now looks more like a muddy field than a major thoroughfare, is once again in our hands. It leads from Kiev to Zhitomir and further to Lvov and from there to Germany.
>
> The 1st SS-Panzer Grenadier Regiment, with tank reinforcements, has pushed a powerful barricade across the road to the west. Now the night falls on this gray November day and brings a sleepless night for the SS soldiers exhausted by days and nights of assaults. (*Völkischer Beobachter*, 16 December 1943)

THE DEFENSIVE FIGHTING

The Soviet attack began on the morning of 18 November. At first a dense hail of rounds fell on the positions. The 2nd Battalion was showered by a succession of mortar rounds. A large number of these rounds fell near the positions of the 8th Company, but they failed to detonate!

At this time a large number of the rounds used by the Soviet rocket artillery were defective. Eventually there were several hundred rockets sticking out of the ground like asparagus in the gently sloping meadow in front of the company. Seeing the dud rockets, Grigoleit, the joker of the squad, observed: "But the effect is tremendous!"

Fortunately for the company this didn't apply to the explosive effect of the rockets. Even so, the howling of incoming rocket salvoes and their visual effect were enough to cause every member of the company to dig in.

In the meantime SS-Obersturmbannführer Max Hansen had returned from leave. He immediately made his way from the regimental command post to his battalion. SS-Hauptsturmführer Meier was about to hand command back to Hansen, but the latter declined.

"You have led here, Heinz, and you should continue to lead so there's no change in the command group during the battle. I'll go up front to the companies, encourage the men and help out if it should become necessary."

That morning Max Hansen turned up at the company command posts, where he was received with great jubilation. The Russians were making repeated assaults and he participated in the defensive effort wherever he happened to be when the attack began. SS-Obersturmführer Schuhknecht's driver described the morning of this eventful day as follows:

> I drove SS-Obersturmführer Schuhknecht together with the company headquarters section. I had to leave my Kfz 69 behind the first row of houses in Kocherovo. The remaining vehicles of the combat elements were driven back.
>
> From my position I had a good view to all sides and also of the company command post. Behind me, in the second row of houses, was the battalion command post and the dressing station.
>
> We had heavy losses. Everything that could still move was used to transport the wounded to the dressing station. There were no shelters. The wounded men all lay in slit trenches. As it was not possible to provide proper care, we were ordered to move them back under cover.
>
> For the first time during the war our field kitchen had driven up to the main line of resistance. It was damaged by enemy fire

and ordered back, but not before it had cooked and issued one last hot meal. The mess vehicle was driven by the "smart Alec" of the mess section, Jochen Lützke. An incoming rocket salvo caught Jochen as he was leaving the battalion command post, and he was killed on the spot. He had been looking forward to leaving that witch's cauldron with his field kitchen still in one piece.

Jochen was one of our best comrades and had been with us since Taganrog in 1941.

The way the Soviets employed their multiple rocket launchers was interesting. They drove out of the cover of the rise, halted in open terrain, fired their rockets and then disappeared behind the rise again. Why they did this was a mystery to the men of the 8th Company. At this range they could just as easily have fired from their protected positions beyond the rise and still reached the target.

When the "Stalin Organ" fire grew heavier, an unidentified SS-Sturmmann, who like all the others could clearly see the rockets being fired, just managed to reach cover in a crater. He narrowly missed jumping on top of a wounded soldier who had already taken cover there. He continues the story:

> I jumped into a hole in which there was a wounded Unterscharführer. When I saw him I knew who he was. It was the swine who had made my life Hell in France! But what did that matter at that point!
>
> He had been wounded in the hand and face and he had to be moved from there if he wasn't going to bleed to death.
>
> He held on to my neck with his bloody hands and I dragged him out of the shell hole and behind a house during a pause in the firing. There a medic looked after him.

SS-ROTTENFÜHRER SCHNEIDEREIT AND THE ENEMY TANKS

Nine more tanks approached on the left wing on the other side of the main road. They were followed closely by infantry. The alarm call reached the antitank squad. Alfred Schneidereit was already lying behind his weapon, but the tanks were still much too far away. Filled with rage, he saw how the T-34s moved around the German foxholes and crushed them with their grinding tracks.

"Just come closer," shouted Schneidereit furiously. "We'll blow you away!"

The chances of success were somewhat less than that, however. The T-34 was such a formidable tank that it seemed unimaginable that a mere antitank gun could stop one.

A group of Soviet infantry turned toward Schneidereit's position from off to the right. The flanking machine guns opened fire at once. The enemy infantry was caught in a hail of bullets that knocked some of them to the ground. The Soviets paused briefly then attacked again at 1000 hours on that eventful day. Once again, the tanks were there to clear a way through the thin German defensive line.

The tank destroyers rolled out to meet the Russian assault. One was hit and ground to a halt, pouring smoke. The crew was able to bail out and take cover. Seconds later, a second tank destroyer was hit. Damaged, it tried to escape. Two T-34s pursued the German vehicle and scored further hits which put the assault gun out of action. Finally, a third tank destroyer broke down with transmission trouble. This was a heavy blow for the 2nd Battalion. Its heavy weapons had been reduced to two assault guns, a 75-mm Pak and two tank destroyers.

The T-34s rolled on in the direction of the regiment's command post. When SS-Obersturmbannführer Frey heard the rattling of tank tracks he reached for the field telephone which linked him to the tank battalion's command post.

"Herbert, you must come with your tanks at once, otherwise Ivan will crack our line. Most of our heavy weapons are out of action."

It didn't take SS-Sturmbannführer Kuhlmann long to make up his mind: "I'll take the attacking enemy from behind by swinging out far to the north. Unfortunately, all I have available is a company."

"You can do it, Herbert," Frey said, relieved at this promise of help.

Albert Frey turned to the soldiers in the command post: "No need to worry! Kuhlmann's coming with his Panthers to get us out!" The officer exuded such confidence that the nervousness in the command post disappeared.

"Ammunition is running low," reported the man who had just compiled the periodic situation report.

"Keindl promised me ammunition. He keeps his word. The transport should be through soon."

No one said what they were all thinking: "If it hasn't been intercepted by Ivan."

Exactly ten minutes later the door of the command post burst open.

"A column of vehicles is approaching," the sentry shouted into the room. Seconds later a fast vehicle roared up and screeched to a halt in front of the command post. A SS-Untersturmführer climbed out.

"Where is the regimental commander?" he asked the sentry.

"In here, Untersturmführer!" answered the sentry.

The SS-Untersturnifiührer hurried into the room and informed Albert Frey that thirty-five ammunition vehicles were following and would be there soon. He wanted to know where to unload them so that he could leave again at once and deliver the next shipment to the division's other panzer grenadier regiment.

"You're heaven sent," declared Frey in relief.

He ordered his aides to help and these ran out after the SS-Untersturmführer to wave in the first arriving vehicles and begin the unloading and delivery of ammunition to the Kampfgruppen. The position had been saved at the last second. Barely thirty minutes later German tanks appeared far to the southeast and rolled into firing position behind the slow-moving T-34s. It became apparent to all that the threat of being overrun had been averted once again. The first T-34 had already been knocked out in the open terrain; dense clouds of black smoke were pouring from an open hatch. Then the second one was hit and knocked out. The enemy tanks turned north and reached the main road. Some headed back the way they had come.

The 8th Company had been badly shaken by the previous fighting. But now, as enemy tanks rolled towards the company, things became even more serious. SS-Rottenführer Schneidereit fired at the enemy tanks as they approached his position from off to the left. But the distance was too great. The squad saw the high-velocity rounds strike the frontal armor and bounce off in a shower of sparks.

"Wait, Alfred!" called SS-Obersturmführer Schuhknecht, who had worked his way over from the left machine-gun position. Schneidereit raised his arm briefly, a signal that he had understood.

"Penetration reported on the left by the outer sentry," reported one of the men of the 3rd Platoon.

SS-Obersturmführer Schuhknecht waved over the runner who accompanied him everywhere.

"Get to the battalion command post quickly, Wim. Tell them to seal off the penetration." The runner was about to leave when Schuhknecht called him back: "Tell them to send the pioneer company with enough explosives to stop the tanks."

The SS-Sturmmann nodded and ran off. When he ran past the field kitchen, the driver saw him and thought that the Russians must be coming to catch the "fleeing" Germans. However, the runner calmed him and continued on his way. On reaching the battalion command post the runner delivered his message, breathing heavily. The SS-Sturmmann recalled:

"I don't remember who took my report, but whoever it was told there was nothing that the battalion could do for 8th Company; all the reserves had been committed."

SS-Hauptsturmführer Meier: "I couldn't send the company any help even if the penetration meant the end of our blocking position. Only a miracle could help."

The runner made his way back to his company:

When I reached the company area I found neither the company nor the company commander. I ran from house to house and found many dead and wounded, but there was no sign of my platoon leader either.

During the search I was shot in the upper thigh. Sitting on my behind and pulling myself along with my hands, I was able to escape the ongoing enemy fire behind one of the houses. I called for a medic and one came. It was, as I found out later, SS-Rottenführer R. He tossed me a packet dressing and told me to stay where I was until it got dark. Then he would come and get me. He had to go to the field position where the men were in the midst of a firefight. I feared the worst, but I had not counted on my comrades. They abandoned no one. In the evening a tracked vehicle came rattling up to me. It was picking up the wounded and taking them to the dressing station. Because of my wound, I was unable to take part in the final engagement and the counterattack by our company.

The fighting had become a struggle for bare survival. Albert Frey picked up his submachine gun and, together with several men, prepared to defend the regimental command post. The acting battalion commander of the 2nd Battalion, SS-Sturmbannführer Hansen, had hurried up to the front line where he fought alongside his men.

The 1st Company had destroyed or driven back the enemy tanks. When the commander of the tank company rolled back in his badly damaged tank, he was followed by a T-34. On leaving the vehicle to take command of the 6th Company, which was supposed to hurry to the aid of the 8th Company, the tank was hit and the SS-Sturmführer was cut down by a burst of machine-gun fire.

By 1130 hours the situation had stabilized. The heavy losses inflicted on the enemy could not conceal the fact that the small Kampfgruppe would be shot to pieces in the next assault by Soviet tanks. The 75-mm antitank gun set up to the right of the 8th Company had also been knocked out. The destruction of fifteen enemy tanks was little consolation, even if friendly losses could be recovered and repaired in the maintenance facilities.

FINAL EFFORT

Alfred Schneidereit clenched his teeth when he saw the tanks rolling straight toward his sector. This was it. He looked around and saw the armor-piercing rounds that had been readied and the faces of his two men. He nodded to them.

The tanks came from all directions. Behind them, in dense clusters, ran the brown-clad infantry of the Red Army. The left wing of the 8th Company was overrun by the onrushing tanks. On the right wing, the 75-mm Pak, which had been repaired, was knocked out again after firing several rounds.

Four or five T-34s concentrated their fire on the antitank gun; two direct hits killed the gun crew. Both of the company's machine guns, which had been positioned to the left and right of the antitank gun, opened fire on the Russian infantry surging over the rise like a spring flood.

"There comes one, Alfred," called Hummel in warning.

Schneidereit turned the gun slightly, adjusted the traverse and acquired the enemy tank in his sight. The T-34 came closer and closer. Diesel fumes rolled into the position and the rattling of tracks rose to an ear-shattering roar. Then the T-34 stopped to search for a target. Schneidereit saw the long gun barrel swinging in his direction.

Then he took the gunner's vision block in his sight. The round shot out and there was an instantaneous shattering impact as the armor-piercing round struck the tank. The T-34 remained stationary. Suddenly the turret hatch flipped back, smoke poured out and the figure of the tank commander appeared, followed closely by the gunner. The machine gun to Schneidereit's right opened fire and mowed down both Russian tankers.

"Man, he's finished, Alfred," called a member of the squad enthusiastically.

The next round was already in the chamber. Russian infantry ran toward the antitank gun.

"Give Schneidereit cover," shouted the company commander.

Then he threw himself down behind the right machine gun to replace the leader of the machine-gun team who had been wounded and temporarily put out of action. Schuhknecht raked the small party of Russians who had turned toward Schneidereit's position. One of the next tanks was hit two or three times, causing it to veer off. Schneidereit fired one last round into the T-34. It began to smoke, but it kept going.

The shouts of "Urray!" died away, only to well up again seconds later as fresh waves of Russian troops appeared over the rise. The fire of the defenders grew weaker. A T-34 approached, heading almost straight toward the antitank gun. Schneidereit wanted to fire right away, but he forced himself to wait. He saw the red glow of muzzle flashes and felt the shock waves of tank rounds whizzing overhead.

The tank stopped, then rolled forward slowly. The target was right in front of Schneidereit, as big as a barn door, but he had to hit the narrow band of the turret ring. He took aim carefully. There was a loud crack as he fired and the tank halted abruptly. The next round was slipped into the chamber. Once again Schneidereit took aim at the turret ring. The report and the impact of the round merged into one sound. The tank began to swing its gun around but the turret would not move.

"He's finished, Alfred."

The men around Schneidereit were ecstatic. They had put two tanks out of action and forced another to flee.

Four minutes later the next tank approached the position. Schneidereit fired at the giant three times. The T-34 turned away, showing its flank. Another shot caused it to begin smoking. The Russian tank turned and rolled away at high speed.

More tanks appeared. Schuhknecht ordered his men to withdraw to the edge of the village. This move had been planned only in case of extreme emergency.

As they pulled back SS-Rottenführer Schneidereit was wounded by a shell fragment. He bandaged the wound himself in the cover of one of the village houses. The antitank gun was still in the forward position. The squad was unable to take it along as it withdrew.

The Russian infantry stormed the village without pause. In spite of losing the company commander, who had been wounded by machine-gun fire, and the only other company officer, the 8th Company was able to master the situation. The Russian artillery joined the fight and fired into the village. Fountains of dirt were thrown over the grenadiers. It was midday when the Soviets first broke into Kocherovo. Russian tanks rolled down the broad street.

"We must move up again," called Schneidereit to the men who had gathered round him.

"Here's another machine gun, Alfred," shouted one of the men.

"Give it to me!" answered Schneidereit.

When the enemy stopped briefly and the artillery fire shifted to the rear, Schneidereit waved the machine gun toward the front and began to run.

The immediate counterattack got under way. A group of Russian infantry appeared in front of them. Schneidereit aimed his weapon at them on the run and fired a long burst from the hip. The enemy fell to the ground. They stormed onward, ran past the Russians who had taken cover and jumped into their own foxholes. Hand grenades crashed and Schneidereit's machine gun roared. The other two members of the machine-gun team each carried a canister filled with belts of ammunition. They reached the antitank gun and found it undamaged. Schneidereit moved into position behind the gun and opened fire on the enemy, who had begun to storm the village again.

Stalin Organs and artillery fired at the forward German position. At the same time, Schneidereit had scored hits on two personnel carriers and forced a fifth T-34 to flee. The daring counterattack seemed pointless as casualties mounted. When Schneidereit's antitank gun was hit and damaged, the company lost its last "heavy weapon".

"We have to pull back, Alfred," warned Grigoleit. "Or the Russians will nab us in the darkness."

Schneidereit nodded. "We'll take the antitank gun with us and repair it," he ordered.

As he reached for the grip to turn the weapon around there was a howling noise. The antitank gun was hit again and flew apart. Schneidereit felt a stabbing pain in his left hand and when he looked down he saw that it was covered in blood. Several fingers had been torn off, one hung by a tendon. Several of his men came to his aid and applied a thick dressing to staunch the flow of blood.

"You must go back, Alfred," urged Hintze, but Schneidereit shook his head.

Seconds later a runner arrived from battalion: "The company must hold out until tomorrow morning!"

By now the company consisted of perhaps two full-strength squads, but the men stayed in the positions they had established at the outskirts of the village. The Russians attacked again and, when the next wave of infantry rolled toward the village, Schneidereit took a submachine gun that had been handed to him. He suddenly jumped from cover and took charge of the remaining members of the company. He led them forward and repulsed the enemy assault with perhaps twenty or thirty men, most of them wounded.

They stormed past holes and trenches, blasted the Russians from their makeshift positions and, once again, reached the road, where they dug in. Suddenly, a second machine gun was at hand, brought up by one of the men. In addition, August Korschowski found the machine gun that had

Schneidereit receives his Knight's Cross personally from Adolf Hitler on 16
1944.

been positioned to the left of the antitank gun. He dragged it up to the
road. Several belts of ammunition were found as well.

When a fresh Russian unit began feeling its way toward the German
positions, it was met by fire from the three machine guns. The enemy withdrew. Throughout the night Schneidereit had the three machine guns lay
down intermittent harassing fire to deceive the enemy as to the actual
"strength" of his small group. But the Soviets had suffered heavy losses and
had no desire to attack further. This occurred just in time for Alfred
Schneidereit, who was close to unconsciousness. Several members of the
company took him back to the dressing station, where he lost consciousness.

When Schneidereit woke up he saw the familiar face of SS-Brigadeführer "Teddy" Wisch looking down at him. He wanted to get up but the
officer gently pushed him back down on his cot.

"Stay where you are, Schneidereit! That's an order."

Then Wisch fumbled with his service jacket, took off his Iron Cross,
First Class and pinned it on Schneidereit's chest.

"Thank you, comrade Schneidereit!" was all the veteran officer said.
Then he turned away so as not to reveal the emotion that had seized him

on seeing the pale face of the wounded young man. "You have set an example for the entire division, Schneidereit. It was you who held the position."

Schneidereit said the following after the war:

Perhaps I was able to set an example for the tiny remnant of my company in that I overcame my fear and engaged the approaching T-34s against my better judgement. But they were firing into our ranks and had to be destroyed. With my antitank gun against that Russian heavy tank it became a very one-sided duel. This was primarily because once an enemy tank had spotted a German antitank gun it never let it out of its sights until it had turned it to a pile of junk. That was especially true in our position, since the enemy tanks had only this small weapon to deal with and had no tanks or antitank guns to worry about.

We didn't investigate why the two crews stopped their T-34s and bailed out. I think that one round penetrated the vision block, killed the gunner and wounded the others. The second round possibly damaged one of the elements of the turret drive.

But after fifty years I can only wonder at the things my comrades and fellow fighters can recall. I simply can't understand it. Perhaps everything happened to me in a sort of trance. How else would it have been possible to endure such hardships? It is therefore difficult for me to confirm details of the war correspondent's report.

The two dozen men who were still alive needed an example. In that great crisis that they and I experienced, I obviously gave them some inner courage through my defiant stand against the Russian tanks. It was not deliberate. Nevertheless, I know that my bitter fight against the Soviet tanks would never have been acknowledged had not the tiny remnant of our company recovered its former position and restored the cohesion of the defense.

Schneidereit neglected to mention that it was he who led the counterattack. Former SS-Hauptsturmführer Heinz Meier added: "Yes, that is Alfred Schneidereit's typical modesty. But it is a fact that he met all the requirements for the awarding of the Knight's Cross."

At the outset of the fighting at Kocherovo, which began on 9 November 1943 and ended on 18 November 1943, the 8th Company had 120 soldiers on its rolls instead of its authorized level of 178 soldiers. In the first six days of fighting outside Kocherovo, the company lost about forty men. Of the eighty soldiers who took part in the fighting in the village, fifty were killed. The unit's strength at the end of the fighting was thus about thirty men. The company suffered fifty casualties on 18 November alone.

On 20 December 1943 SS-Obersturmbannführer Albert Frey, commander of the reinforced the 1st SS-Panzer Grenadier Regiment, was awarded the Knight's Cross with Oak Leaves in recognition of the advance by his battle group during the fighting. During the night of 18 November 1943, SS-Hauptsturmführer Meier and SS-Obersturmbannführer Hansen recommended the awarding of the Knight's Cross to SS-Rottenführer Schneidereit. The same day the regimental commander decided to support the recommendation and submitted it to the division, where SS-Brigadeführer Wisch likewise recommended approval and passed it on. Schneidereit was unaware of this during the seven weeks he spent recovering from his wounds. The Iron Cross, First Class, was reward enough for him. Several days before the official presentation of the Knight's Cross to Alfred Schneidereit he learned that he and several other members of the division were to be personally decorated by the Führer.

On 16 January 1944 Alfred Schneidereit, who had been promoted to the rank of SS-Unterscharführer in December 1943 for bravery in the face of the enemy, found himself before the Führer, who presented him with the Knight's Cross and shook his hand. It was the high point of his career as a soldier and of his wartime service.

Schneidereit and his superiors were asked if the sacrifices in the fighting at Kocherovo had been justified. It was difficult to say, but one thing was certain: The daring deep flanking thrust by Battle Group Frey enabled Army Group South to retake Zhitomir and restore a shaky cohesion to the shattered German front. In this respect, the operations at and the defense of Kocherovo were of vital importance. Even though Kocherovo was only a minor episode that slowed but failed to halt the great German collapse in the east, it was a tremendous accomplishment for all those who had participated in and suffered through the attack.

IMPORTANT EVENTS IN THE LIFE OF ALFRED SCHNEIDEREIT

29 October 1919: Born at Insterburg in East Prussia.

15 November 1939: Joined the SS-Verfügungstruppe and received basic training in the 18th Company of *Leibstandarte SS "Adolf Hitler"* (mot.). Later transferred to the 13th Company, the field element of the bodyguard regiment.

December 1940: Joins the 8th Company of *Leibstandarte SS "Adolf Hitler"* (mot.) as an SS-Sturmmann. Participates in the Greek Campaign (attack on the Klidi Pass and the crossing of the Gulf of Patras).

June 1941: Participates in the invasion of Russia with the SS-Division *"Leibstandarte SS Adolf Hitler."* Fights in the battles of Luck, Kherson, Taganrog and Rostov.

1 December 1941: Promoted to SS-Rottenführer.

May 1942: Awarded the *Ostmedaille.*

6 August 1942: Awarded the Iron Cross, Second Class.

Late 1942–Early 1943: SS-Panzer Grenadier Division *"Leibstandarte SS Adolf Hitler"* formed in France. As part of reorganization, Schneidereit's company becomes the 8th Company of the 1st SS-Panzer Grenadier Regiment. Division returns to the Eastern Front, where it participates in the fighting for and recapture of Kharkov.

5 July 1943: Awarded the Infantry Assault Badge in Bronze. Participates in Operation Citadel as the leader of his company's antitank section. Later awarded the Close-Combat Clasp in Bronze as well as the Wound Badge in Black.

Fall 1943: Participates in the disarming of Italians in the Milan area. Engages in anti-partisan warfare in the Istria and Slovenia.

November 1943: Returns to the Eastern Front. Participates in the attack of Battle Group Frey in the southern sector. Wounded two more times. Receives the Iron Cross, First Class, from the hands of the divisional commander on 19 November 1943.

16 January 1944: Receives the Knight's Cross from Hitler. Subsequently promoted to SS-Scharführer for bravery in the face of the enemy. Attends officer training for disabled personnel.

October 1944: Graduated from the training course as a senior officer candidate (SS-Standartenoberjunker). Assigned duties as an instructor for the divisional replacement battalion at Spreenhagen.

January 1945: Promoted to SS-Untersturmführer.

April–May 1945: Participated in operations east of Berlin as a company commander within the replacement battalion. Wounded again by shrapnel.

12 May 1945: Disarmed by Soviet troops.

Feldwebel Josef Schreiber received the Knight's cross on 31 March 1943 as a platoon leader in the 4th Company of the 14th Assault Regiment. He was the 309th soldier to receive the Oak Leaves to the Knight's cross on 15 October 1943.

Josef Schreiber

Josef Schreiber hurried along the zigzag trench and reached his waiting squad.

"What's up, Unteroffizier, will the food be here soon?" asked Gefreiter Albert Maier.

"It will be here any minute," replied the squad leader.

"Hopefully," murmured one of the others.

Suddenly there was a hissing sound.

"Take cover!" shouted Schreiber, pressing himself against the wall of the trench.

Russian mortar rounds exploded in front of the trench, showering the men inside with muck and branches.

"They're coming again, Unteroffizier," observed Teutsch.

"There's nothing we can do about that," added Bölker, inspecting his machine gun after just installing a new firing pin. There were flashes from a Russian artillery position. The rounds fell farther to the left among the positions of the 14th Infantry Regiment's 1st Battalion.

"Hollerer, move forward!" ordered the Unteroffizier after glancing at his watch. Hollerer was the designated outpost.

Siegfried Hollerer grasped his rifle and disappeared through the shallow crawl trench to the sentry position that had been constructed three days earlier. Schreiber moved along the trench to Seiron's squad, where he was greeted by Unteroffizier Seiron.

"Listen to that, Josef!" he said, nodding his head in the direction of the enemy.

"It looks as if the Russians are going to come tonight and attack the village."

Schreiber confirmed his comrade's unspoken suspicion. Oberfeldwebel Kuntze, the platoon leader, came out of the platoon command post and approached the two men.

"Now then Schreiber, everything all right with you?" he asked.

"All clear, Oberfeldwebel!"

"Stay alert. I'm going to the 4th Platoon to see if the mortars and heavy machine guns can be moved up. It looks as if Ivan wants to take this village."

Suddenly, there was a roar behind them as the artillery fired a barrage.

The rounds hurtled over the forward infantry positions and hammered into the enemy positions on the slopes, in the gullies and at the forest's edge. Unteroffizier Schreiber took leave of his comrades: "I'll be going back now. See you later."

By the time he reached his own section the Russian fire had intensified. More and more rounds were bursting around the village as the rate of fire increased. The soldiers pressed themselves against the bottom of the trench to escape the whizzing round fragments. Schreiber's gaze fell involuntarily on the Infantry Assault Badge he wore on his tunic. He had received it on 16 August.

The 16th of August! That was already two weeks ago. His regiment had helped close the ring around Smolensk. In the pocket were three Russian armies seeking a way out at any cost. Near Mamayevka they had relieved the 900th Training Brigade—a training formation periodically sent to the field to keep the experience level of the personnel up to date with the latest combat developments.

They waited in the villages and the infantry positions in front of them to face the inevitable assault by Marshall Timoshenko's divisions. The 14th Infantry Regiment had seen extremely heavy fighting in the villages of Bakachevo, Asarinki, Isakova and Brakulina and near Shatuny and Ivaniki.

"There, Unteroffizier!" Hollerer's voice brought Schreiber back to reality.

He looked to his left and saw the two flares that had just burst over the battalion's sector. They were bathing the area in harsh light before extinguishing themselves. As if this had been a signal, machine guns began to rattle in the neighboring sector.

"Ivan's coming!" shouted Teutsch.

"I'm going to check on Hollerer," replied Schreiber and disappeared behind a bend in the trench. Hollerer held the binoculars in front of his eyes and stared into no-man's-land.

"See anything, Siegfried?" asked Schreiber.

The other nodded. But before he could answer, Schreiber spotted shadowy figures emerging from a small patch of woods whose treetops had been shredded by artillery fire.

"Alarm!"

Illumination flares rose into the night sky, lighting up the terrain in front of the trenches, dugouts and rifle pits. Red Army troops leapt up from the edge of the woods, from gullies and holes, and charged towards the German positions.

Schreiber called to the leader of the machine-gun team: "Don't shoot yet, Bölker!"

At the same time he slid his rifle over the parapet of the trench.

There was a roar in the night sky. Another artillery barrage rushed toward the enemy. The soldiers saw the rounds impact at the edge of the patch of woods. The whole area was lit by the flashes of impacting rounds and the earth trembled. The effect of the bombardment was devastating. Nevertheless, the Russians continued their attack. In their trenches the Germans could hear the shouts of the attacking Russians:

"Urray! Urray!"

"Open fire!" roared the platoon leader.

The two heavy machine guns in the flanking positions opened fire. The light machine guns joined in. Yellow tracers flashed through the darkness, striking the enemy from left and right and forcing them to take cover. In the meantime, the Russian artillery had concentrated its fire on the German artillery position.

The first wave of Russians was pinned down about 100 meters from the system of positions. It wasn't five minutes before the second wave appeared and stormed forward across no-man's-land. Again and again the Russians disappeared among the shattered trees and in craters. When they reappeared—ghostly shapes in the light of illumination flares and the harsh glare of exploding mortar rounds—they had gained another few dozen meters of ground.

"Enemy on the right!" called Hollerer from the listening post.

A short time later the Russians appeared from behind a low rise. They still had about one hundred meters to go. Schreiber fired. A burst from a Russian automatic rifle whistled over his head. From the right he heard the cry of a wounded man. About twelve Russians who had approached undetected suddenly got to their feet about thirty meters from the trench. Hand grenades flew toward the enemy troops. There were harsh flashes as the grenades exploded. Bölker's machine gun, which had jammed, was cleared just in time. Several bursts of fire halted the last of the enemy troops.

On the other hand the enemy had broken into the trench of the 1st Battalion. A pair of flares climbed into the night sky, a call for help. While the men of that battalion were engaged in close-quarters fighting, Schreiber's voice sounded above the noise of battle: "Squad, follow me!"

They immediately ran after the Unteroffizier. After about 100 meters the trench ended. In front of them were widely spaced foxholes. Machine-gun fire greeted them, but they soon reached the next section of trench and jumped in. A Russian appeared in front of Schreiber: The Unteroffizier fired and then threw a hand grenade. More Russians came running around a bend in the trench. There were shouts, curses and firing from the rear of the enemy group. Again, Schreiber raised his arm to throw a grenade. But, just in time, he realized that the firing was from members of the 3rd Platoon, who were clearing the trench from the other side. The two groups of Germans established contact by calling to one another. The surviving Russian soldiers surrendered and Schreiber and his squad returned to their own sector.

Nothing much happened throughout the remainder of the night. There was a burst of machine-gun fire occasionally as a forward sentry opened up on something he had seen.

Several days later Marshall Timoshenko achieved a breakthrough south of the 5th Infantry Division. His shock divisions had made deep penetrations into the positions of the German 161st Infantry Division. The 14th Infantry Regiment, which had just stood down as corps reserve, was sent south and was ordered to seal off the enemy penetrations at Shaklava and north of Asarinki.

The 2nd Battalion of the 14th Infantry Regiment was deployed in front of Asarinki and thus found itself at the focal point of the fighting. The platoon dug in and prepared to defend its positions in front of and north of Asarinki. The platoon command post was located in a small village. All of Kuntze's platoon was well dug-in and manned rifle pits and trenches.

Evening fell. Dark rain clouds filled the sky; there was not a star to be seen. Only the flashes of artillery fire lit the darkness. Schreiber peered through his binoculars in an effort to make out something. But the rolling, tree-covered terrain in front of the village appeared to be abandoned. Suddenly, artillery fire began to fall on the platoon's sector. The rounds howled in and burst in front of the village.

"Man, now we're going to get it," groaned Bölker.

The Gefreiter was correct in his assessment of the situation. The bursting rounds crept nearer and nearer. Then the first salvo howled down on the village itself. Seconds later, one of the straw-roofed houses was in flames.

"Get out of the hut!" shouted Schreiber to his now wide-awake men.

The four soldiers ran into the open and took cover in a trench that had been dug just behind a low hedge. It wasn't a minute too soon. After a few more distant explosions, a round from one of the enemy guns smashed into the gable wall of the house. The wall tumbled to the ground with a crash. Masonry and timbers showered four nearby fruit trees, causing apples and pears to rain down. A pall of stinking smoke spread over the site. An uninterrupted rain of artillery rounds was pouring down onto the village at that point.

In the battalion's sector there was an ear-splitting roar as a stockpile of artillery ammunition blew up. The large corn silo in the village also went up in flames. A messenger came running through the inferno.

"Unteroffizier Schreiber!" he gasped. "Unteroffizier Schreiber!"

"Here, here!" shouted Schreiber above the crackle of flames.

Bloody and out of breath, the messenger stammered something unintelligible. Schreiber pulled the man down into the trench. Then he took out his canteen and pressed it to the gasping man's lips. The messenger drank in large gulps.

"What's happened?"

"Hit on the platoon command post. Oberfeldwebel Kuntze is dead. The platoon is leaderless," blurted the man in broken sentences.

"Alarm! Ivan's coming!"

The call was passed from man to man and soon reached the Unteroffizier.

"I'm taking over the platoon. We're going to hold the position!" he shouted above the noise of battle.

The Soviets attacked from three sides over the level terrain. Machine-gun fire pinned them down for a few moments, but the first groups soon appeared at the outskirts of the village.

Schreiber and four men ran to the break-in point and opened fire with a machine gun he had received from the 4th Squad. A hail of bullets buzzed about him. He threw himself to the ground and crawled off to the side, pursued by the fountains of dust thrown up by the bullets striking the ground. Schreiber reached the cover of a house and rolled through the back door into the wooden building.

He ran through the dark room at a crouch. Pushing open the shutter, he found himself facing a group of Russians who had just crossed the street. At once he raised his weapon and fired. A few seconds later the gun jammed. He dropped the machine gun and reached for a hand grenade. It would have been too late for him had not the second machine gun opened fire. Bölker had followed the squad leader, and his burst of fire from point-blank range gave the Russians no chance.

The night was filled everywhere with the crack of rifle fire and the echoing explosions of hand grenades. There was the occasional roar of German machine guns and the tack-tack of Soviet Maxim heavy machine guns. Mounted on small carts, these fired without pause.

A half-hour later the Russians broke through the 3rd Squad, which was already badly weakened. They then entered the village. Unteroffizier

Schreiber led an immediate counterattack with a small force and drove them out again. One nest of resistance was blown up with high-explosives. Bursts of machine-gun fire sawed through the wooden walls of the shacks, leaving the enemy no possibility of escape.

As they were crossing the village street on their way to the flanking position, which had just fired a colored flare indicating that ammunition was running low, they were caught by a burst of fire from an automatic rifle. Siegfried Hollerer was hit and fell to the ground.

"Keep running!" shouted Schreiber to his two companions, who were carrying crates of ammunition.

He threw himself to the ground and crawled back to Hollerer. In spite of the darkness Schreiber knew at once that his friend was beyond help.

A pair of Russians came running. They ran into one of the cottages. Hand grenades were thrown into the wooden house from the fence. Hollerer tried to say something, but he was seized by a fit of coughing. The dying man's helmet lay close beside him. His dark hair hung down across his forehead.

"Siegfried," murmured Schreiber, "what is it?" He pushed back his hair, and watched as Hollerer took his final breath. As he knelt over his friend, exploding hand grenades, brief bursts of fire and scattered rifle fire transformed the night into an inferno of noise.

Unteroffizier Schreiber picked up one of the Russian automatic rifles, inserted a magazine and hurried across to his squad. He arrived just in time, because about twenty Russians were trying to break into the trenches.

"That was just about the end of us, Unteroffizier," croaked Mehnert. He passed the gunner a new bolt assembly. Schreiber felt his heart beating. His breathing fluttered. The clothing stuck to his sweat-soaked body.

The Russians attacked again. They were met by bursts of machine-gun fire. Ranks of Russian soldiers charged to their death. The platoon headquarters personnel came running. They had to make themselves understood with hand signals as the din made normal communication impossible. The men lay in their trench, breathing heavily, and waited for the next attack.

Where was the enemy? Were they already in the trench? Or there, behind the gray wall of the shed? Or on the other side of the burning house?

Increasing numbers of the defenders fell out—killed or wounded. In the meantime, at about 2200 hours, communications were established with the battalion by field telephone during a pause in the fighting. The word

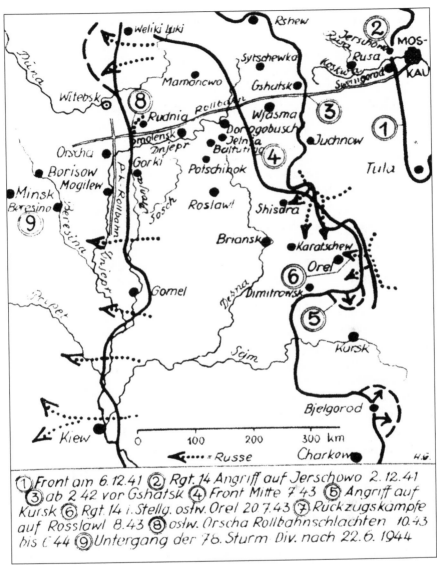

The battle trail of the 78th Assault Division.

from battalion was: "Hold out! Possession of the village is of decisive importance! Relief is on the way."

It was then 2300 hours. There was nothing to be seen of the relief elements. Instead, the Russians attacked again from the southeast. Teutsch and Maier had recovered the bodies of their dead comrades and laid them behind the trench at a low stone wall. They lay on the ground under a tarpaulin, rigid and unmoving.

Once again Russian attack groups stormed toward the German trenches with loud shouts of "Urray!"

Heavy machine guns fired into the village from atop a hill. In ones and twos Russian soldiers ran across the road, disappeared into a field of sunflowers and approached a sauna. A few mines exploded, scattering deadly shards of glowing metal into the night. Anyone within lethal range met a frightful end.

Schreiber crawled along the trench. Then he slid out and hurried along at a crouch, sweating profusely, until he could see the Maxim machine gun that was raking the 2nd Squad's positions. He took a few deep breaths and then raised his captured automatic rifle and fired. The enemy machine gun fell silent immediately. Several figures jumped up and tried to reach a cottage. A second burst of fire knocked them to the ground.

A second wave of attackers approached from off to the left. They crossed a harvested potato field. Not until they were about eighty meters from the German trench did the two machine guns positioned there open fire. The surviving Red Army soldiers surrendered. They emerged from the lighter background as outlines, their arms raised.

"Take them to the center of the village! Becker and Schober: Watch them!" ordered Schreiber.

Further Russian attacks were repulsed. Just as their ammunition was beginning to run low help arrived.

"Relief, Unteroffizier!" roared Teutsch.

Schreiber could also hear the approaching company above the rattle of automatic-weapons fire and the dull thud of bursting rounds.

"Go back to battalion with your platoon, Schreiber," decided Oberleutnant Krafft, who was commanding the relief company.

Some time later the remains of the platoon, led by Schreiber, reached the main German position. They had taken their badly wounded with them. Wordlessly, the battalion commander extended his hand to the Unteroffizier. The members of his platoon filed past, carrying their dead between them in shelter halves.

On 18 September Unteroffizier Schreiber received the Iron Cross, First Class in recognition for his defensive success. He intended to take over his squad again, but the company commander had other ideas:

"You've got the platoon, Schreiber. You've proven your ability to lead a platoon, even in the most difficult situations."

On 1 November Schreiber was promoted to Feldwebel. He had held the rank of Unteroffizier for exactly one year. During the months that followed Feldwebel Schreiber took part in his division's drive on Moscow. On 19 October the 14th Infantry Regiment was detached from the 5th Infantry Division and assigned to the 78th Infantry Division to replace the disbanded 238th Infantry Regiment.

The regiment was 200 kilometers from Moscow and. By 10 November it had reached Mozhaysk. Schreiber saw a sign there with the following inscription: "Moscow: 100 kilometers—Hanover: 2,267 kilometers."

The next day the regiment advanced another 25 kilometers toward the east. The regiment established contact with the 78th Infantry Division there. The division was bogged down in the mud.

The advance resumed on 19 November. The 14th Infantry Regiment's 2nd Battalion advanced along the Moskva River toward Ignatyevo and Porechye, guarding the regiment's flank. It began to snow. Siberian snipers picked off anyone who showed himself.

An icy east wind brought with it temperatures of zero degrees Fahrenheit. It was the beginning of the icy Russian winter of 1941–42. The first T-34 tanks also appeared. They were capable of negotiating the snow with ease and were invulnerable to the rounds of the standard 37-mm Pak. In addition, the deadly song of the "Stalin Organ"—the howling of hundreds of rocket projectiles—was heard for the first time. A hurricane of explosions, flames and glowing steel enveloped the battalion. Whole villages went up in flames under the fire of the Russian rocket launchers.

Svenigorod was taken. The battalion commander was wounded and Oberleutnant Reiser assumed command. The commander of the regiment's 7th Company, Oberleutnant Manner, knew that he could depend on Feldwebel Schreiber. When Reiser's battalion was placed under the command of another division near Tononino it repulsed a tank attack and several attacks by squadrons of Cossacks.

Russian tanks attacked again and again. The T-34s rolled over the horse-drawn wagons of the supply trains, crushing vehicles, horses and men. The regiment fought desperately against the numerically superior forces of the counterattacking Russians. German units tried to halt the advancing enemy in the Rusa Position.

Then it was Christmas. Schreiber and his men "celebrated" in their own way. Day after day they stood in their trenches and held off heavy attacks. Inspired by the example of Feldwebel Schreiber, the men of the platoon fought on to the edge of exhaustion.

Early on the morning of 31 December Obergefreiter Holm arrived in the platoon command post: "We're going to get a rest, Feldwebel!"

"I hope you're not just repeating a shithouse rumor, Holm," replied Schreiber.

The rumor proved true. A few days later the 2nd Battalion was withdrawn from the front and moved into a rest position in Novaya Deresnya, a few kilometers west of the Rusa.

The mood on New Year's Eve was one of relief. They had finally escaped the raging witches cauldron of Ogarkovo and had escaped the defensive fighting with their lives. Feldwebel Schreiber shook hands with each of his comrades-in-arms. Then Oberleutnant Reiser arrived unexpectedly. He had received orders. The battalion was to march to Wereja. The Soviets had broken through there in the sector of the 15th Infantry Division.

The battalion remained under the operational control of the 15th Infantry Division nearly three months. Oberleutnant Reiser was wounded. His place was taken by Major Dinglinger. Schreiber saw his platoon worn down until only a few of its original members were left.

✠

On 1 June 1942 Oberstleutnant Ernst Kaether assumed command of the 14th Infantry Regiment. Its 2nd Battalion fought in the battle of Rzhev under its new commander Hauptmann Kirstein, who was later to die a soldier's death near Prudy.

The division received a new commander, Generalleutnant Völckers and, on 29 December 1942, the 78th Infantry Division became the only one in the German Army to be awarded the designation Assault Division.

In mid-January 1943 the 78th Assault Division was transferred into the Smolensk area. Replacements arrived. Among the items of equipment were some of the new 75-mm Pak for the heavy companies. All of the companies were equipped with the new MG 42 machine gun.

By February 1943 the division was again ready for action. It was just in time, because the Soviet command then launched a number of major operations in the central sector. Stalin hoped to reduce the German salient by attacking south and west of Orel.

Among the forces defending the German line was the 78th Assault Division. The division entrained in Potshinok from 21 to 23 February and was transported to Orel via Roslavl. There it detrained and marched through Kromy into its new area of operations south of Dimitrovsk. The Soviets had massed 500,000 soldiers in this sector.

In the area of operations of the division, which was twenty-eight kilometers wide, there were 150,000 men with 400 T-34 tanks and numerous multiple rocket launchers. The number of identified enemy batteries stood at 150. The Soviet Air Force was very active over the front, especially the close-support units.

It was during late February, which saw the return of the Russian winter, that Schreiber produced his greatest achievements as a soldier.

An icy wind howled over the ridge south of Dimitrovsk. In the many holes in the snow and icy trenches were the men of the 78th. Among them were the assault grenadiers of the 7th Company of the 14th Assault Regiment—as the regiment had been redesignated—under Oberleutnant Schlenker. Once again "General Frost" was trying to regain mastery over events. And it looked as if he would be victorious.

Oberleutnant Schlenker hurried back to the company command post at a crouch. He had just inspected his company to see for himself that the men were ready for action.

The 78th Assault Division had been committed at that location to close a large gap in the front. The division had been forced to shovel a way clear to the ridge for its vehicles. Some of the positions had to be blasted out of the thick ice. The low-roofed hut that was the command post—located barely 600 meters behind the main line of resistance—appeared in front of the Oberleutnant. A gust of wind whipped against the officer before he reached the shelter of the hut and pulled open the door.

"Inside, quickly!" he said to his companion, the leader of the company headquarters section.

Oberfeldwebel Hockenjos mumbled something and slammed the door shut. Through the hall, where the field telephone sat in a corner, the two men went into the main room. Hauptfeldwebel Hauschild informed the Oberleutnant that he was to call battalion.

Schlenker nodded. Heels clicked in the anteroom. Hauptfeldwebel Hauschild spoke briefly. Seconds later the door was flung open. The brawny company first sergeant stood in the doorway.

"Sir: The division commander!"

Schlenker jumped to his feet. Hockenjos, one of the veteran frontline soldiers of the regiment, likewise came to attention. The imposing figure of Generalleutnant Paul Völckers pushed itself into the room. The light from an oil lamp fell on the glittering Knight's Cross at his throat, which he had received on 11 December 1942.

"Don't bother with a report!" he began. "Just tell me how the morale of your people is and whether your company is well prepared."

"Morale is good, sir. The men have been equipped with the best winter equipment one could imagine."

"We should have had that during the first Russian winter, Schlenker," said the General in agreement. "They'll be able to withstand the heaviest snowstorms with it."

"I've just come from the company, sir. All weapons have been positioned to lay down flanking fire. From the trenches and dugouts there is a good view of the approaches to the position to a depth of one kilometer. The only opportunity for an unobserved approach by the enemy is two gullies. I'm going to have listening posts set up in them."

"Good, Schlenker. Do that at once! We have learned from radio intercepts and statements by prisoners that the Russians are planning to attack tonight."

Oberfeldwebel Hockenjos' gaze involuntarily turned to the wall, where a large calendar was hung. It showed 28 February.

"I'll go out at once and see to everything," said the company commander.

"Good, let's go!" agreed the General.

The division liaison officer and the adjutant joined the other members of the small group as they trudged through the falling darkness toward the main line of resistance.

They hadn't gone far when a heavy barrage began. Rounds howled in from the Russian artillery positions. Shells burst all around, throwing up towering fountains of snow. Then there was a harsh flash in the southeast. A howling, wailing "Katushka" salvo streaked toward the ridge. There were multiple explosions as the rockets impacted among the German positions.

The night sky was suddenly filled with an eerie howling, which rapidly grew louder. A rocket salvo was headed their way.

"Take cover!" shouted Hockenjos.

The men threw themselves into a communications trench that zigzagged through the snow. Hockenjos landed almost on the back of the General. The crash of exploding rockets and the shrieking of fragments was deafening. The concussion pressed them against the ground.

"Move on!" ordered the General when the danger had passed.

They came to the first trench. One of the soldiers, a member of the machine-gun squad, recognized the General and disappeared into a side trench. Oberfeldwebel Arthur Klank, leader of the 2nd Platoon, came running and reported.

"Now then, Klepperle," said the General smiling, "how is everything?"

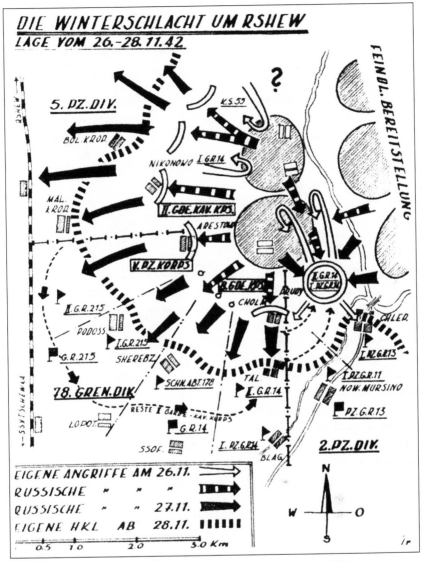

The Winter battle of Rzhev 26–28 November 1942.

"We could use some tobacco, sir," answered Klank. In spite of the near-darkness the division commander could see a grin on the face of the platoon leader.

Völckers turned and waved his liaison officer closer. The officer opened his bulging briefcase and produced a number of packs of cigarettes.

"Thank you, sir!" responded the Oberfeldwebel, who had been named "Klepperle" by his comrades.

"Now you owe me one, Klank," cautioned the General. The Oberfeldwebel nodded.

The division commander went from man to man, from dugout to dugout. The he said farewell to the four men of two listening posts as they went down the hill to the two ravines below. Finally, the General arrived at Josef Schreiber's platoon. The platoon messenger, Obergefreiter Albert Maier, had already informed the Feldwebel of the visit. The short, stocky platoon leader made his report.

✠

On the right flank, just visible through the blowing snow, was the rounded shape of Hill 266. Up there was the 1st Company under Leutnant Fischer. The remaining companies of the battalion were on either side. There was no doubt, however, that the concentration point of the coming fight was going to be on Hill 249.7. Somewhere, on one of the hills, was Oberst Kaether, the regiment's commander. He was up front with the troops, from where he could commit the reserves immediately if needed.

Gefreiter Waller, who was manning the new radio equipment, turned onto his other side with a groan. The trench was too small for him and his equipment, and he kept banging himself everywhere. Krause, who was with the platoon headquarters section as a medic, stared into the blowing snow, trying to see something. But in the howling and whistling of the worsening storm he could neither hear nor see anything.

At that point a signal flare hissed up out of the right ravine. It was followed seconds later by another.

"Alarm!" roared Sturmgrenadier Mauerhofen.

The two men from the forward outpost in the right ravine came running back up the hill. Behind them, almost invisible in the wall of snow in their white camouflage smocks, were Red Army troops of the NKVD Divisions.

"Open fire!" shouted Schreiber.

The two flanking machine guns began to rattle. Almost simultaneously they were joined by the two light machine guns. Yellow tracers flitted through the night. Lines of attackers fell into the snow. But behind the fallen others appeared—dozens, hundreds.

Skis swished over the snow. On them were Russian heavy machine guns. The weapons began to fire with their slow tack-tack-tack rhythm.

"Watch out: Incoming mortar fire!"

Small 50-mm mortars, which the Germans called "potato throwers," coughed. Soon after the first rounds fell on the hill and tore circular craters in the snow. A fragment hissed past Schreiber's head and stuck in the snow wall. With a crash, the German guns began laying down barrage fire. Fountains of snow spurted up in no-man's-land. Clumps of ice flew through the air.

Schreiber saw a Russian assault group appear from behind a shallow rise about seventy meters ahead. The Russians fired their submachine guns as they ran. The two MG 42s opened fire for the first time. Suddenly, the enemy had disappeared. There were no more to be seen. Then there was a loud racket farther to the left in front of Hill 266. Russian infantry in regiment strength were storming the German positions with loud shouts of "Urray!" Between the two positions, the 5th Company was also under attack.

"The Russians have broken into the Fifth's positions, Feldwebel!" reported Unteroffizier Gehr, who had come running over from the platoon's left dugout.

Schreiber deliberated. What was to be done? Was there anything he could do from there to drive the Red Army soldiers out of the trenches and save the German troops still alive? Should he try from the flank with a squad?

"There they are!" cried Maier.

Russian troops were storming up the hill. Their leading elements were already within hand-grenade range. All Hell broke loose. A hand grenade plopped down into the snow right in front of Schreiber. He dove for cover in the trench. The grenade went off with a blast. When Schreiber looked over the rim of the trench about twenty Russians were running straight toward him. He raised the barrel of his submachine gun and fired off a long burst.

Three bursts emptied the magazine. A press on the button and the empty magazine fell into the snow. Schreiber slipped in a fresh magazine. Bearded faces appeared. Red-yellow flames spurted from the muzzles of the Russian weapons; bullets whistled past on Schreiber's left. One of the men there fell without making a sound. One of the Russians was caught by a burst of fire right in front of the position. Carried forward by his momentum, the man stumbled on and fell on his face barely a meter in front of the Feldwebel.

There was a great racket coming from the right. Orders were shouted. Russian voices rang out from the machine-gun dugout, punctuated by exploding hand grenades.

"Headquarters section: Follow me!" ordered Schreiber.

He was already running along the trench. Russians appeared at the corner before the flanking position. They were cut down. Two others raised their hands in surrender. Schreiber reached the dugout. The three men of the machine-gun team were dead. One of the remaining men of Schneider's squad was still alive. He had escaped by feigning death.

"Krause, come here!" gasped Schreiber.

Gefreiter Krause bandaged the man's wounded arm. Haltingly, he described how the Russians had suddenly appeared from the right.

"But you must have seen them?" queried the Feldwebel.

The man shook his head. "Suddenly they were just there, and they opened fire before we knew where they were."

Only later did Schreiber learn how the enemy had approached undetected. It was almost unbelievable, but the evidence was there: The Soviets had burrowed sixty meters through the snow. In this way they had been able to approach to within three meters of the dugout without being seen.

"Bring me two Teller mines!" ordered Schreiber.

He then crawled into the narrow snow tunnel and placed the mines about twenty meters into them. The attack had been repulsed. All that had been left behind were the wounded lying on the approaches to the company positions. One of the wounded was not thirty meters from the trench of Schneider's squad. His voice rang through the night. Unteroffizier Krause crawled out and pulled the wounded man back into the positions. The Russian's wounds were dressed.

A short time later Schreiber walked through the trenches. He had lost three men killed. Five had been wounded, including Gefreiter Waller.

"You must go to the rear, Waller. If it turns cold, things won't look good for you," implored Schreiber. But the huge soldier only shook his head.

"I'm staying here," was his only answer.

Schreiber, who knew the man very well, said nothing more on the matter. The snowstorm abated and finally stopped. As dawn broke the reserve company attacked through the snow. They eliminated the penetration against the 5th Company and drove the enemy out of the trenches and foxholes.

When it was light Schreiber saw the crumpled forms of the dead Russian soldiers on the broad snow-covered field. Those who had been wounded during the night were rigid by then. The icy cold had completed its destructive work. The sun managed to find a gap in the low-hanging gray clouds. The first warming rays fell on the ice field, melting the upper layer of snow.

"Spring is coming, men!" called Oberfeldwebel Ott, who had just arrived to scout the positions for his heavy-weapons platoon. Some time later his 80-mm mortars and heavy machine guns went into position at the boundary with the 1st Battalion. The assault guns attached to the division had moved up to within firing range of the forward enemy positions behind the 3rd Battalion.

The assault guns opened fire on Russian antitank and field guns. While Soviet artillery and "Stalin Organs" pounded the entire width of the division's front—all twenty-eight kilometers of it—the individual companies were busy trying to restore their defensive positions.

Schreiber was deeply concerned about the coming night. The Russians would surely not rest until they had broken through. The rumors making the rounds suggested they had amassed a tremendous superiority in men and arms at this part of the front.

During the afternoon of 1 March two antitank guns and two assault guns went into position off to the right rear of Schreiber's platoon. From there they would be able to engage and destroy enemy tanks attacking Hill 249.7 or the neighboring hill.

Oberleutnant Schlenker called a meeting of his platoon leaders. He ended his brief talk: "You will have to hold the hill alone, Schreiber. All of Klank's Platoon is being moved to the neighboring hill, where it will take up position on the Fifth's right flank."

The men went back to their platoons. The sun had gone down. It was snowing lightly and, following a brief period of twilight, darkness spread over the land. Hot rations arrived soon after. There were roast potatoes with rissoles and pudding. The men ate quickly, while the food was still warm.

Schreiber ate with the men. When he was done he pulled his notebook from his pocket and jotted down the strength of the platoon and several other significant details. Schreiber's men were performing magnificently. Day and night they were in their trenches. They had no bunkers in which to get warm, no proper bivouac site. And then there was the cold, which refroze the upper surface of the snow that had melted during the day.

Russian mortars opened fire. There was an occasional crack from the Russian positions as a sniper fired a round. In most cases the bullets from these Russian sharpshooters found their targets.

Two antitank rifles had been moved up to the front line early the previous afternoon. Gefreiter Britz had taken charge of one and Kiengötter the other. When Schreiber returned to the platoon command post he felt reassured. Every man in his platoon was dependable. None of them gave up and that was worth a great deal in combat.

Ivan, as the Russian enemy was known to every German frontline soldier, was not long in coming. An entire ski battalion, virtually invisible in its white outfits, rushed forward. It moved under the cover of the clouds of swirling, white flakes. It seemed as if the wind were driving them toward the German positions.

Machine guns opened fire. Mortars coughed and the assault guns opened fire with high- explosive rounds. Streams of fire hissed through the dense curtain of snow, tearing it asunder and making the enemy visible for the next burst. Illumination flares hissed over the field, their ghostly light ripping away the twilight. The cries of "Urray!" and the sharp swish of the Russian skis were almost drowned out by the coughing mortars, the sawing sound of the German automatic weapons and the other sounds of battle. The attack collapsed 200 meters in front of the German main line of resistance.

✠

The next few days saw almost uninterrupted fighting. The Soviets attacked by day as well as by night. They also had tank support at that point. Numerically far superior, the four divisions of the NKVD 70th Army tried repeatedly to force a breakthrough against the 78th Assault Division. Each day demanded further sacrifices in the strongpoints. Schreiber saw his men fall, one after another. There were no replacements. The names of the dead, wounded and missing filled the pages of his notebook.

Schreiber made daily entries describing the close-quarters fighting. His main task was to preserve the defensive readiness of his platoon. Finally, it was 9 March. The soldiers of the 14th Assault Regiment had been in combat eight days without relief. The surviving members of Schreiber's platoon lay in their snow trenches. They were beyond exhaustion, their eyes red rimmed.

When Schreiber tallied his figures at noon on 9 March 1943 he found he had fourteen men. That was all that was left of his platoon. In the past eight days every one of his men had more than done his duty. Constantly on the threshold between life and death, they had held on, repelling attacks and helping their comrades in the neighboring sectors. Schreiber summoned Unteroffizier Schneider and Unteroffizier Gehr into the platoon command post.

"We're going to divide everything into two squads," he began. "All the machine guns are to be directed at the exits from the two ravines. That's where the Russians will come. Every one of us will fight to the end. If one fails, then we're all lost."

The first enemy attack began half an hour later. It was aimed at the 1st Company. Several tanks accompanying the infantry were knocked out by the antitank and assault guns. Immobilized, they sat smoking in front of the hill. Then it became dark. And with the darkness came the first attack on Hill 249.7.

For the last time the Soviets tried to crack the thin German front. They committed the last of their reserves. Infantry in battalion-sized formations charged the defensive positions held by Schreiber and his platoon. The four machine guns opened fire from the flanks. Nevertheless, hundreds of Red Army troops reached the gently sloping foot of the hill. From there the climb was much more difficult. Schreiber fired on the first wave with his submachine gun. The wall of men threw hand grenades up the hill.

Then the unlikely happened: The wave of attackers halted. The surviving Russians dug themselves into the snow and were soon invisible. A half-hour later the Soviets attacked again. Once again it was an entire battalion which attacked the positions of Schreiber's platoon. Maier, Waller and Krause, who were lying close to the platoon leader, fired on the enemy with their captured submachine guns and prevented them from getting out of the ravine. The two heavy machine guns fired long bursts in a steady tack-tack rhythm. The hectic bursts of fire from the "Hitler Saws"—the new MG 42s, so called on account of their very high rate of fire—gave the enemy no chance.

The division's artillery then used the last of its ammunition in an attempt to destroy identified Russian assembly areas. All of the company's heavy mortars joined the barrage. In spite of everything, the Russians attacked a third time. This time they managed to break into the German positions to the left of Hill 249.7.

"We've been outflanked on the left, Feldwebel!" cried Unteroffizier Gehr.

"We'll stay where we are," decided Schreiber.

The fourth attack, launched shortly before midnight, was carried out along the entire width of the regiment. The Russians committed four divisions to the attack. Once again, the enemy was halted in front of the trenches of Schreiber's platoon.

Farther left, however, all Hell appeared to have broken loose on Hill 266. There the bulk of two Russian regiments was charging the positions of

Schreiber and Fischer pose with their chain of command after the award ceremony (from right to left): Oberst Kaether, Feldwebel Schreiber, General Völk-
ers, Leutnant Fischer and Major Schneider.

the 1st Company. Looking through his binoculars, Schreiber saw the dense
masses of enemy troops storming up the hill. The bursts of fire flitting
back and forth were visible with the naked eye.

Finally, the defensive line was pushed back. The Russians appeared to
have overrun the entire top of the hill. Oberst Kaether assembled reserve
units from less-threatened sectors and personally led them to the endan-
gered part of the line. Leutnant Fischer and his company headquarters
personnel there had defended the command post. Then, when the enemy
pressure became too great, they pulled back about 100 meters and burrowed into the snow on the open terrain of the hill. They succeeded in
establishing a second line in front of the Russian break-in and halted the
enemy.

Schreiber and his men had little time to watch. The Russians soon
launched another attack. A short time later one of the enemy assault
groups pushed past the hill on the right. Schreiber and his platoon were
isolated.

"Stay alert!" Schreiber hissed, his bearded face turned toward the
enemy.

Hand grenades crashed, the barrels of the machine guns glowed and
the antitank rifles cracked. Suddenly, shadowy figures appeared in front of

the position—fire-spitting forms that jumped right into the trenches! Nobody knew where they had come from.

Schreiber emptied his magazine. Waller smashed the butt of his rifle against the steel helmet of a Russian as tall as he.

"Ammo!" roared Gefreiter Lemke through the dill of the battle.

One of the grenadiers ran toward Lemke with several belts of ammunition around his neck and carrying two boxes of ammunition. On the way he was hit in the hip. The man fell but managed to crawl the last thirty meters on all fours.

"Kiengötter has been killed!" reported Unteroffizier Schneider.

Schreiber knew he only had thirteen men left! Despite that, the Russian attack was repulsed. How they had done it, none of them knew, but the enemy had been driven out of the trenches and had disappeared into the snow. The thirteen survivors of Schreiber's platoon had been fighting nine hours. Gefreiter Breitz was wounded in the ninth Russian attack and was unable to fight any longer.

"Waller: Call for reinforcements!" Schreiber ordered for the third time.

Miraculously, the radio operator succeeded in establishing contact. But there were no reinforcements available from the battalion or regiment.

"Hold out!" ordered the battalion commander. "Hold out! We'll come as soon as we can!"

In the meantime several Russians had dug in directly in front of the hill. When a new attack began they jumped up and came running. The tenth attack succeeded in reaching the forward trench with the light machine gun.

"Back!" Schreiber ordered.

The men hurried back and set up in the main trench. When the attack was over they crawled forward through narrow communications trenches toward the enemy-occupied forward trench. Shortly afterward they attacked the positions from two sides, overwhelming the Russians.

The battle for Hill 249.7 had turned into a grim contest. There was no doubt that the Soviets were determined to break through there no matter what the cost. During pauses in the fighting the enemy turned his heavy weapons—the Stalin Organs, artillery and mortars—against the twelve surviving grenadiers. The eleventh attack began an hour before daybreak. It seemed as if this attack might succeed. The Russian battalions launched a ferocious charge in an effort to overwhelm the center of German resistance and smash an even wider breach in the enemy line.

The Soviets had already smashed gaps in the German main line of resistance to the left and right, but these could only be exploited if the strongpoint in the center fell as well. The Soviets again drove their way into the trenches. German machine-gun fire cut down the waves of attackers from point-blank range.

Schreiber had just emptied a magazine when he heard a submachine-gun fire a burst. The deadly bullets whistled past his face. He felt a sharp blow against his steel helmet and fell into the trench. Seconds later, however, he was back on his feet reaching for his weapon. He shoved in a fresh magazine and resumed firing.

The Russians were driven out of the platoon command post. Waller, Krause and Maier finished what their platoon leader had begun. A little later they attacked the Russians who had outflanked the heavy machine-gun position on the right. There was a brief but bloody hand-to-hand fight. Both flanking machine guns poured fire into the following Soviet battalion. The enemy was pinned down and those who had penetrated the position were killed or captured.

As Schreiber walked past an apparently dead Russian, the man jumped up and aimed his weapon at the Feldwebel. Schreiber would probably have been killed had not Grenadier Mauerhofer not recognized the danger. Mauerhofer fired a round that passed very close to his platoon leader. When Schreiber turned around he saw the Russian fall, who had only been playing dead.

Such scenes were repeated often during that desperate night. Twelve determined men, watching out for one another and depending on one another, were engaged in a desperate battle for survival.

The first light of the new day was just appearing when Waller called in a joyful voice: "They're coming, Feldwebel, they're coming! Help has arrived!"

"At last! Then prepare to counterattack!" said Schreiber.

The men stared at the Feldwebel in disbelief. A moment of hesitation went through the twelve men who had looked death in the eye countless times that one night during fourteen pitiless hours. But then they reached for their weapons, slung their reserve submachine guns, fed fresh belts of ammunition into the light machine guns and followed the small Feldwebel, who led the charge toward the Russian foxholes.

They reached the first enemy line. Hand grenades flew into the craters and submachine guns rattled. The first Russians pulled back. The Russians had apparently assumed that all life on the hill had been extinguished. They found out differently. In the pale light of dawn, Feldwebel Schreiber and his eleven men rolled up the Russian position in the break-in area. The twelve worked their way forward in stages.

What no one could have believed happened: The Russians began to run. The battalion then launched a counterattack on both sides. The Soviets, rattled by Schreiber's small group of men, withdrew. The 3rd Battalion eliminated both salients in the front. The battle was over. The Soviets had suffered a decisive defeat.

Oberst Ernst Kaether submitted a recommendation for the award of the Knight's Cross to Feldwebel Schreiber. In it he stated:

> In a fourteen-hour engagement Schreiber repulsed eleven enemy battalion-sized attacks. Although outflanked on the left and right, he held out until reinforcements arrived at daybreak. He then counterattacked, driving the enemy back so far that the 2nd Battalion was able to recover the positions on both sides of Schreiber's platoon.

On Hill 266 Leutnant Fischer likewise assembled all his remaining men around him before dawn. The acting battalion adjutant, a Stabsfeldwebel, rushed to his aid with fifteen men, mostly messengers, switchboard operators and radio operators. Fischer had been pushed back by the Russians during the night. He intended to win back the terrain that had been lost. As the small battle group prepared to attack at first light it was joined by two assault guns. With loud shouts of "Hurray!" the grenadiers stormed toward the surprised enemy. The counterattack gained ground. The former main line of resistance was reached and taken from the enemy in close-quarters fighting. The situation became stabilized. The desperate fighting of the 78th Assault Division received mention in the Wehrmacht Report of 11 March 1943:

> A Baden-Würtemberg infantry regiment has inflicted extremely heavy losses on the enemy in the fighting near Orel. After the enemy's massed attacks had been broken in fourteen hours of bitter close-quarters fighting, the regiment counterattacked on 10 March and drove back the Bolsheviks.

The great fight was over; the strength of the Russian divisions had been broken. Between Orel and Sevsk the weapons fell silent for a short time. Schreiber and the soldiers who had survived the battle bade their fallen comrades farewell as they were buried at the military cemetery in Solomino. Oberst Kaether called out the names of the fallen by company. The companies had been drawn up before the graves and stood in deep silence. The men, hardened by the daily fight for survival, saw the light of the March sun on the white birch crosses. None of those who were at Solomino Cemetery that day would ever forget the song sung that spring morning: *"Ich hatt' einen Kameraden"* ("I Had a Comrade"—the German equivalent of "Taps").

✠

The snow melted under the rays of the sun, which grew stronger day by day. The melting water streamed down the ravines toward the valley. Brooks became streams and roads muddy flatlands.

On 4 April 1943 there was hectic activity in the command post of the 14th Assault Regiment. Oberst Kaether was waiting in Solomino for Leutnant Fischer of the 1st Company and Feldwebel Schreiber of the 7th Company. The large square in front of the command post was decorated with flags when Schreiber arrived and reported. He already knew what was going on. A Teletype message had arrived a few days earlier notifying him that he had been awarded the Knight's Cross on 31 March.

The regimental personnel sergeant, Oberfeldwebel Hegner, greeted Schreiber. Soon Leutnant Fischer arrived, his young face beaming. The two men stepped outside and saw their many comrades drawn up in a rectangle. They took up position in front: The tall, thin Leutnant and the short, taciturn Feldwebel. A command rang out, and the honor guard snapped to attention. Generalleutnant Völckers reviewed the troops. Behind him and to his right was Oberst Kaether, who had led these men through the difficult fighting. Then the General stepped up to the two soldiers standing in front of the others.

"Leutnant Erich Fischer . . . Feldwebel Josef Schreiber: the supreme commander of the Wehrmacht has decorated you with the Knight's Cross of the Iron Cross. It is my pleasure and privilege to present it to you today."

✠

The 14th Assault Regiment of the 78th Assault Division spent Easter in the Solomino area. Schreiber had been sent on leave and was now back with his company, which was still led by Oberleutnant Schlenker. On his return Schreiber received an enthusiastic welcome from his comrades. In mid-April the division was relieved and transferred into the Glasunovka area. Feldwebel Schreiber knew something was up from the masses of supplies that were arriving. The division even received replacements and was brought back up to its authorized strength.

Operation "Citadel" was casting its shadow. Schreiber had never seen so many tanks, assault guns and tank destroyers as during the period of calm before the storm. Operation "Citadel" was the last great offensive in the east by the Wehrmacht following the disaster at Stalingrad.

The German command had mobilized all available forces for the attack. The objective was to cut off the Kursk salient. To this end the Armed Forces high Command deployed the 9th Army under Generaloberst Model in the north. Consisting of thirteen attack divisions, including the 78th Assault Division, two reserve divisions and six stationary divisions, the army stood ready to attack south of Orel. The 6th Air Fleet was assigned to provide air support.

Making up the southern spearhead were the 4th Panzer Army and Army Detachment Kempf. Fifteen divisions would form the southern attack spearhead, with four further divisions in a stationary role and two more in reserve. Responsible for securing the airspace over the Army and providing air sup-port was the 4th Air Fleet with 1,100 machines.

This was a greater concentration of forces than before any previous battle in the East. Feldmarschall von Manstein, who was in command of the southern group of forces, had more than 1,000 tanks and 400 assault guns at his disposal. A similar number of armored vehicles were available to the pincer in the north.

Hitler declared emphatically in the Wolf's Lair on 1 July: "Everything depends on preserving the element of surprise. The enemy must be kept in the dark as to the timing of the attack until the last moment!"

At the same time, they were celebrating Schreiber's promotion to Oberfeldwebel in the platoon command post.

The next four days were spent in preparations for the attack. Searing heat alternated with thunderstorms. As they rolled toward the front, the supply columns created huge dust clouds that settled only slowly. A few days before the attack Generaloberst Model, Commander-in-Chief of the 9th Army, arrived at the command post of the 14th Assault Regiment. He was visibly impressed by the level of training of the troops and the massing of heavy weapons, but could not refrain from some of the good-natured needling for which he was well known.

"Kaether," he said with a veiled grin, "your regiment has so many heavy weapons that it won't be able to run."

Kaether answered at once: "We'll see tomorrow, sir."

The grenadiers of the 14th Assault Regiment moved out of their positions in the early morning of 5 July 1943. On the regiment's left wing was its 7th Company. The division formed the left wing of the XXIII Army Corps under General Frießner. The division set out for Maloarkhangelsk train station. Whenever antitank guns tried to halt the advance, the huge Ferdinand tank destroyers of the 654th Heavy Panzer-Destroyer Battalion under Major Karl-Heinz Noak rolled forward.

Noak, who had been awarded the Oak Leaves to the Knight's Cross as a young Oberleutnant, accompanied the unit from a position at the front. With their terrific firepower, the Ferdinands were able to knock out any threat to come before their guns. Wherever the tank destroyers could not go, the small, remotely controlled demolition carriers—the Borgward B IV—were sent in.

Oberfeldwebel Schreiber saw the mighty clouds caused by their explosions. Eight of these vehicles cleared a broad lane through the minefields. The tank destroyers rolled through these gaps, followed by the assault grenadiers.

Schreiber and his platoon soon encountered the first enemy field positions. The enemy troops, members of the 410th Rifle Regiment (part of the 81st Rifle Division), were thrown back. Casualties were heavy. Nevertheless the assault grenadiers managed to reach Maloarkhangelsk Station. They had advanced four kilometers that day. During the next four days progress was slow for the soldiers. The Soviets had built their defensive belts to a depth of ten to fifteen kilometers, and the first breakthrough had failed to create the necessary gaps through which the northern group's armor elements could advance.

The attacking divisions were halted by a maze of rifle pits, minefields and underground bunkers. German tanks were knocked out by antitank guns. Artillery positions, including whole battalions with "Stalin Organs," showered the battlefield with a hurricane of fire and steel. Flamethrowers and innumerable machine-gun nests caused heavy casualties.

Receiving the Knight's Cross with Schreiber was Leutnant Erich Fischer, the commander of the 1st Company of the 14th Assault Regiment (left).

That Hill 249.7 was nonetheless reached on the first day was a testament to the bravery of the assault grenadiers. But the enemy was still in possession of the vital Hill 255.6. Capture of the hill would give the Germans a good view deep into the Soviet build-up area. The enemy was also still holding out in Trosna Valley, threatening the division's flank.

On 6 July the 14th Assault Regiment attacked an extended ridgeline with the 2nd Battalion as the spearhead. The fighting lasted two hours. When it was over the assault troops were atop the hill, having cleared the enemy's two-kilometer-long trench. Schreiber's platoon took dugout after dugout. Hand grenades, machine guns, submachine guns and spades were the weapons used in this bloody, pitiless fight. The Russian regiment defending the hill fought desperately but was thrown back with heavy losses.

From atop the hill the men could see a good fifteen kilometers to the east. Clearly visible were the Soviet approach roads. The capture of the hill also meant that the Soviet forces in the Trosna Valley were now surrounded. The division's artillery and mortars silenced the last resistance.

One thousand three-hundred Red Army troops seeking to break out to the south surrendered to the 14th Assault Regiment. The regiment had reached its second objective for the day.

At that point, however, the first enemy divisions of the second line appeared. The Russians employed every means in an attempt to drive into the flank of the northern pincer and threw several fresh divisions into the battle. The 7th Company defended a northward-facing front as far as the Trosna Valley, where the Soviets were still holding. This was to be the scene of further exploits by Schreiber and his platoon.

✠

The morning of 10 July began with a sudden enemy barrage. The heavy guns started firing even before the sun had climbed above the horizon. Rocket launchers joined in, blanketing the regiment with zone fire, especially the sector held by the 2nd Battalion. Oberfeldwebel Schreiber, whose unit had intercepted several powerful attack groups here in the past days, learned at the company command post that the regiment was about to attack again. On his return to the platoon he was asked how things looked.

"No comment!" was his curt reply. From the tone of his voice Albert Maier knew that they would learn nothing from the Oberfeldwebel.

A short time later Schreiber ordered: "Platoon headquarters section will accompany me through the platoon's positions."

The four men set out. Schreiber cast a critical eye everywhere.

"Move that heavy machine gun farther to the right. Over there...where it has a straight field of fire on the valley," he ordered. "Waller and Krause stay here."

Some time later the group came to the position from where it was possible for them to see the enemy positions about 300–400 meters away. Schreiber peered through his binoculars. Then he turned suddenly.

"Maier," he said in his quiet way, "the attack begins tomorrow, but keep it to yourself. Only a few platoon leaders know that."

"I thought so," replied the platoon messenger laconically.

Late that afternoon an order reached the platoon command post that Schreiber was to report to the company. Dusk was just falling when the Oberfeldwebel started on his way. Maier and several members of the platoon detailed to collect the hot rations went with him. Schreiber took his leave of the platoon messenger: "Good luck, Maier."

While the platoon messenger helped unload the ammunition that had just arrived Schreiber disappeared from the command post. As he worked, Maier saw artillery officers running about with map boards. Switchboard operators laid their cables. Tank officers and other ranks came and went.

"Something's up. I'll bet the attack goes today!" said a member of the 3rd Platoon.

A half-hour later Schreiber reappeared, accompanied by the other platoon leaders.

"Let's go, Maier," said the Oberfeldwebel curtly.

The hot rations had arrived in the meantime and Schreiber summoned the squad leaders. When Unteroffizier Schneider, Unteroffizier Gehr and Obergefreiter Möller were before him they heard the following: "Comrades, the attack on the Trosna Valley begins tomorrow. Our platoon will advance from here along the intersecting ravine. You can see it in this aerial photograph."

The three squad leaders studied the photograph then gave it back.

"Use caution," began Schreiber following a brief pause. "The 1st and 2nd Squads will advance to the left of the ravine. The 3rd Squad will work its way forward on the high slope on the right side."

"And the floor of the ravine, Oberfeldwebel?" asked Möller.

"I will advance along the floor of the ravine with the platoon headquarters section," Schreiber announced.

The squad leaders listened closely, because the floor of the ravine was the most dangerous place. Actually they had expected nothing different.

Nevertheless they were surprised by the disarming matter-of-factness with which their platoon leader reserved the most dangerous role for himself. "That's it. Now get same sleep, because tomorrow will be a hot day for us."

✠

"Get ready!" Schreiber ordered.

An artillery observation aircraft appeared overhead and began circling over the Trosna Valley. The men of the platoon formed up. The two squads that were to advance on the left side of the valley were ready. The machine gunners held their weapons, several belts of ammunition draped about their necks.

Suddenly, there was a droning in the air behind them. The noise grew louder and Stukas appeared in the morning sky. The Ju 87s roared over the company's position at low altitude. Soon they reached the valley, peeled off and dropped their bombs.

"Our fighters!" cried Sturmgrenadier Tausch. The fighters flashed over the front line at 3,000 meters. They were followed by bombers. Then more Stukas appeared and dove on their targets.

Suddenly, mortar fire began from both sides. The division's artillery and elements of the corps artillery fired into the Trosna Valley, while the Soviet artillery fired over the heads of the waiting assault troops. With a swift movement Schreiber slipped his helmet strap beneath his chin. Schreiber's platoon moved out. As he walked, Schreiber reached up to his throat, removed his Knight's Cross and put it in his breast packet. Albert Maier saw this, and he knew what it meant. The enemy favored such targets. The first fifty meters went by quickly.

Suddenly, there was a terrific howling above the heads of the advancing grenadiers. Swarms of rocket projectiles howled toward their former positions. A call went up from the squad on the right: "Medic!"

"Go, Krause!" ordered the Oberfeldwebel.

The Gefreiter medic ran off in the midst of the fountains of dirt from the next rocket salvo.

"Krause!" shouted Schreiber in alarm. But the Gefreiter emerged from the powder smoke and hurried on at a crouch toward the wounded man, who needed his help. A grain field appeared out of the mist at the eleven o'clock position.

"Into the cornfield!" called Schreiber.

Lungs burning, the men raced toward the field of corn. Schreiber could hear the whistle of bullets. Breathing heavily, he reached the far end of the cornfield and took cover. He raised his binoculars and scanned the brush-covered terrain that extended from the end of the ravine to the valley. Heavy machine-gun and mortar fire was being directed at the two squads on the left flank. The fire forced them to ground before they were even with the platoon leader's position.

"Maier, get over to the squads on the left!" Schreiber ordered. "Tell them to dig in and advance no farther!"

The Obergefreiter got up and started to run. He fell, then picked himself up. He had an order to deliver that might mean life or death for the 1st and 2nd Squads. In the meantime, the sun had climbed high in the sky and shone down brightly on the sweat-soaked grenadiers. Schreiber called over to his radio operator, who had followed him into the cornfield and had crawled some distance up the slope.

"Inform the company: Heavy enemy fire. We can't get through. Are digging in. Send Stukas and close-support aircraft!"

Waller began to call. He established contact and reported what was going on in the ravine. Russian close-support aircraft raced over the valley at low level. They dropped bombs and strafed. Schreiber ducked down in the depression he had scooped out of the ground. A round exploded about thirty meters in front of him and showered him with clumps of dirt. Maier came back and threw himself down beside the platoon leader.

"The platoon is digging in!" he gasped. Suddenly the artillery began to fire. The *Nebelwerfer* of the 51st *Werfer* Regiment and the mortars of the 5th Heavy Motorized Mortar Battalion added their weight to the barrage. A torrent of rounds of all calibers howled over the platoon and crashed into the Trosna Valley.

"Stukas, Oberfeldwebel!" cried Unteroffizier Schneider excitedly. He pointed skyward as the bent-winged aircraft flew over. This time they dove somewhat lower before releasing their bombs.

"I'm going to fire the signal to resume the attack, Schneider," said Schreiber, raising his flare pistol.

The men got up and ran into the devil's cauldron of the Trosna Valley. Leading the way was the figure of platoon leader Schreiber. Visibility had improved. Schreiber could make out the Russian trench system ahead. He leapt from crater to crater. As soon as a machine gun fired on him he dove for cover, then crawled on a distance before getting to his feet again and running, running, running.

The enemy was overwhelmed. A barbed-wire obstacle appeared in front of Schreiber and his men. They jumped through a gap torn in the wire by a round. There was the first trench!

A few more steps and Schreiber jumped in. He saw that everyone in the trench was dead. The German mortars had done their job well. It was a terrible sight.

Waller, Krause and Maier followed. Soon they were just about all in. Nevertheless, their leader gave them no rest. There were dead everywhere. Schreiber reached the first bunker. He tore open the door. The bunker was empty. The floor was covered with equipment, weapons and dead. From the left, where the first two squads were advancing, came the sounds of heavy fighting.

"Try to make contact with the 3rd Squad!" he ordered his three companions. He himself ran to the left to the other two squads.

"Position both machine guns here and clear the trenches on the far slope. The 3rd Squad can't get through there."

A burst of fire caused him to dive for cover. Then he was on his feet again, running through the fire back down to the floor of the valley to rejoin his men. They stopped to catch their breath in a shot-up communications trench. When they stood up to continue on their way, the men came under heavy mortar fire. A fragment knocked the submachine gun right out of the prone Waller's hand. The weapon had become useless.

"Take one of those!" ordered Schreiber, gesturing to the Russian submachine guns lying on the ground. Waller picked up one of the weapons and several magazines and ran after the others.

"Provide mutual covering fire. We'll attack the bunkers!" Schreiber gasped.

As Waller ran forward, he saw four Russians moving into position to bar the way. A short burst of fire cut down the four enemy soldiers. Suddenly, they saw a bunker that had been built into the slope. About fourteen steps led down to the installation.

"Hands up!" called Maier in Russian. About a dozen Russians came out of the bunker. They climbed up the steps and laid their weapons in a pile.

"Damn, that would have been trouble," observed Waller. But before one of the others could answer, a group of Russian close-support aircraft came roaring toward them. Friend and foe dove for cover in the Russian trench. Firing their cannon and machine guns, the aircraft raced past overhead and disappeared somewhere in the distance.

"Krause, take the prisoners into the bunker and watch them."

Schreiber and his men approached one nest of resistance and dugout after another. Those that resisted were overcome with hand grenades and bursts of machine-gun fire. The activities on the slope created some breathing room for the squad that was pinned down on the right. After taking ten bunkers and more than eighty prisoners, Schreiber and his men met up with the 3rd Squad.

"Thanks, Oberfeldwebel," called the squad leader. "We wouldn't have got through here without your help."

"Now we'll do it with our combined forces," observed Schreiber, a weak smile visible on his sweat-streaked face. Together they pushed on and reached their objective. The Trosna Valley was in their hands!

✠

"Get ready to defend!" Schreiber ordered.

While the exhausted grenadiers lay on the ground, Schreiber instructed the machine gunners where to put their weapons. Krause crawled through a thicket and, by chance, found the equipment of a Russian medic station, which he used to dress the wounds of the injured Russians.

The pitiless battle was over. The enemy soldiers, against whom they had fought so bitterly, had become men who needed his help. Some time later Waller and Maier found a Russian field kitchen. The burner was still lit and a pot of burned porridge bubbled away. Behind the kitchen were two trembling *panje* horses.

Russian aircraft and artillery then began to bombard the area captured by the assault troops. The men had already established themselves in the former Russian positions and bunkers, which offered a considerable degree of security.

"We're being pulled out of the line, men!" said the Oberfeldwebel on his return from the company.

The 7th Company had reached its objective for the day. Klank's and Hockenjos' platoons had veered off somewhat during the attack and, supported by tanks, had taken part in the attack on Hill 255.6. During the subsequent meeting of platoon leaders it was learned that Schreiber's platoon had suffered only one man killed. There were a number of wounded, but most of the wounds were minor and the men stayed with the company.

The platoon departed half an hour later. The grenadiers walked through the valley toward the East in long skirmishing lines. They climbed the right slope. Above, on the crest, Schreiber could see muzzle flashes on the horizon. The platoon went into position north of Hill 255.6 and on the north slope of the hill itself. Oberfeldwebel Klank was waiting for them and provided directions. His platoon was holding the neighboring position.

Soon after a messenger arrived to fetch the two platoon leaders for a briefing at the company command post, which had been set up about 150 meters behind the main line of resistance. Oberleutnant Schlenker opened the briefing with the following words:

"Men, I am happy to have the entire company together again, because in the next few days the Russians are probably going to attempt a breakthrough here aimed at dislocating the entire regiment."

"Are there indications that the Russians will be attacking soon, sir?" Klank asked.

The Oberleutnant nodded. "Our reconnaissance has spotted another enemy division moving into our sector. The enemy's advance guard may be here by tonight."

Referring to the map, Oberleutnant Schlenker issued instructions to each platoon. In a concise fashion he outlined what was to be done and where the machine guns were to be positioned. During the briefing Generalleutnant Hans Traut, the new division commander, arrived at the command post.

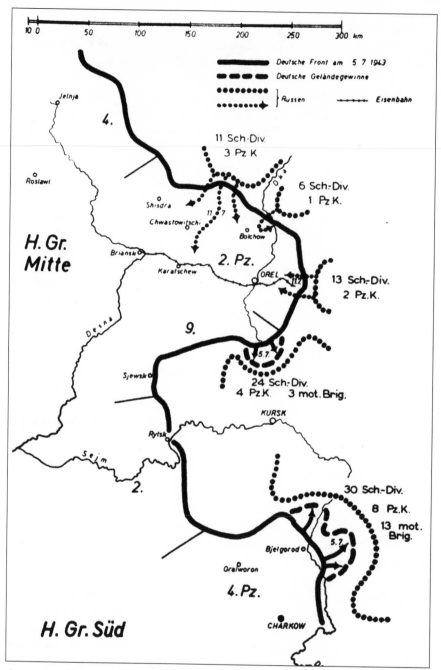

Operation Citadel, July 1943, showing the limit of the German forces' penetrations of the salient and the Russian counterattack aimed at encircling Orel and thereby trapping large numbers of German troops.

Oberleutnant Schlenker presented himself.

Following the salutes the General said: "Oberleutnant Schlenker, I would first like to present you with the Iron Cross, First Class. My congratulations! . . . and now describe what took place on 11 July, Schlenker."

The Oberleutnant gave a brief description. Then Generalleutnant Traut brought up the Trosna Valley. "Oberfeldwebel Schreiber will have to describe that for you, sir," said the company commander.

"Well, shoot then, Schreiber."

The Oberfeldwebel began to speak. When he finished there was a long silence.

Then the division commander observed: "On this 11 July, gentlemen, luck was with the brave. You, Schreiber, made a decisive contribution in the fighting for the Trosna Valley."

Next to describe his part was Oberfeldwebel Hockenjos, the leader of the company headquarters section. When he was finished, Generalleutnant Traut presented Oberfeldwebel Hockenjos and Oberfeldwebel Klank with the German Cross in Gold.

Before he left Generalleutnant Traut took the company commander aside. "Schlenker," he said softly, so that the platoon leaders could not hear, "in case of doubt depend fully on the opinions of these men. They know the war, and even if no one in the supreme command knows a way out, they will find one."

"*Jawohl*, sir, I'll do that," promised Schlenker.

The platoon leaders took their leave and returned to their positions.

During the two days that followed it became obvious in the divisional sector that the Soviets had not just made defensive preparations. They must have also planned a major offensive. Each successive day saw another enemy division moving up to the front. These Russian divisions had been assembled to surround and destroy the two German armies in the Orel salient. Day after day the Russians attacked the sector held by the 14th Assault Regiment in an effort to smash in the flank of the northern German spearhead and regain freedom of movement for their own forces.

On 13 July Adolf Hitler announced at his headquarters that Operation "Citadel" was being broken off. Allied invasion forces had landed in Sicily. Hitler was reinforced in his decision by a report from Feldmarschall von Kluge, which stated that the situation of the 9th Army was bad and that the army had not yet set out to break through at Teploye on 12 July. Model had called off his attack and had been forced to withdraw fast units from the front.

On 12 July the enemy had broken through the 2nd Panzer Army in the north of the Orel salient in the rear of the 9th Army. The Russians were now threatening Orel.

In contrast the German pincer operation was proceeding favorably in the south, and Feldmarschall von Manstein implored Hitler: "Victory on the southern front of the Kursk salient is within our grasp. The enemy has thrown almost all of his strategic reserve into the battle and has been badly battered. To break off the battle now would be to throw away victory!"

During the course of this dramatic meeting von Manstein went on to suggest that the northern pincer tie down the enemy, while the southern pincer under Hoth and Kempf should continue the fight and destroy the enemy forces south of Kursk. At least half of the "Citadel" plan would have succeeded. Feldmarschall von Kluge opposed this plan. He wanted a cessation of the attack and requested the battle be broken off. Hitler gave von Manstein permission to continue the battle in the south with his forces. The northern group was ordered to call off its attack. Further, it was not ordered to tie down enemy forces to support von Manstein's efforts.

✠

The 2nd Battalion withdrew during the night of 24–25 July as ordered. A situation briefing took place during a rest stop on the way to the new main line of resistance. At the same time, the battalion was given a new combat mission. The 7th Company was to be deployed on the regiment's right wing. Its right-hand neighbor would be the 195th Assault Regiment. Oberleutnant Schlenker gave Schreiber precise instructions and oriented him on the platoon's sector. In closing he said: "We won't be getting any visits from the other side tonight, Schreiber."

"I know, sir," replied the Oberfeldwebel. "The old main line of resistance won't be completely evacuated until after dark."

"Use the time to dig in, Schreiber! And if you need anything or have any suggestions, let me know."

Night fell. The noise of battle echoed from the east like a ceaseless, rolling thunderstorm. Schreiber assigned three sentries. While the remaining men of the platoon wrapped themselves in blankets and shelter halves and tried to sleep, he went over the defensive plan once more. Suddenly, a voice rang out from somewhere in the darkness:

"Oberfeldwebel Schreiber?" He recognized the voice as that of the company messenger, Pander.

"What's up?" he asked.

"I've brought a platoon from the pioneer battalion, Oberfeldwebel," answered the Gefreiter.

"Thanks, Pander. Now take off so we can get some rest."

The messenger disappeared into the night and Schreiber turned to the Feldwebel who was in charge of the group of pioneers. The latter gestured toward a vehicle.

"I've brought a few mines to mine the paths leading to your position."

"Good, you can get started right away. I'll inform the sentries so they don't take you for Russians."

While the pioneers dug, Unteroffizier Schneider led Schreiber's platoon into no-man's-land to take over the security role. Russian patrols might appear anywhere. A light strip of sky along the horizon heralded the beginning of a new day. The sounds of battle flared up quickly in the north and south, and swelled to a dull roaring and rumbling before receding slowly.

"Aircraft!" called one of the sentries in warning.

"Keep your heads down!" Unteroffizier Schneider warned.

The IL-2 close-support aircraft roared over the new German main line of resistance without firing their guns or dropping bombs. Apparently they hadn't discovered the new position yet. The Flak began to fire, first the "88s" and then the quad 20-mm weapons, which had gone into position near the division command post.

Peering through his binoculars Schreiber saw the gray Flak bursts. One of the close-support aircraft was hit as he watched. A round burst beneath the aircraft's fuselage. Seconds later it caught fire and fluttered to earth. Two parachutes hung in the sky like balls of cotton wool. They were driven off by the east wind and soon disappeared from his sight.

Things remained quiet in front of the company's position. The nervous sentries stared into the sun-bathed landscape. Despite several false alarms, there was no sign of the enemy. Relief arrived and the relieved men returned to the bivouac site. It was almost noon when Gefreiter Waller came crawling over to Schreiber and woke the sleeping platoon leader. Schreiber sat up.

"What is it, Waller?"

"The Russians, Oberfeldwebel. Looks like a patrol trying to feel its way forward."

Schreiber was wide awake at once. He scanned no-man's-land with his binoculars and discovered a group of Red Army soldiers. They were skillfully working their way through the scrub-covered terrain. Sometimes they were visible for a second before disappearing behind the bushes or into a fold in the earth. Each time Schreiber caught sight of them they were a few meters closer.

"Pass this on: No firing until I fire a red signal flare."

The order was passed down the line. Schreiber observed the area of terrain further. Suddenly, he froze. The supposed patrol was being followed by more infantry. It looked very much like an attack force. Schreiber raised his flare pistol. There was a dull thump and the flare arced into the clear sky.

"Attack in at least battalion strength, Waller!"

The radio operator transmitted the information. Contrary to their usual practice, this day the Russians attacked without artillery preparation and almost noiselessly. Obviously, they were trying to make use of the advantage offered by the broken terrain to unhinge the German position. The defenders opened fire abruptly. The Red Army troops disappeared into the cover offered by groups of bushes. But then the earth-brown figures began working their way toward the German positions.

"Watch out! Mortar fire!"

An entire enemy mortar battalion opened fire. The rounds smacked into the boggy soil. Most bored into the ground without exploding.

"The Russians are sending in reinforcements on the approach road, Oberfeldwebel!" shouted someone through the din.

Schreiber hurried up the hill behind the messenger until he could see the approach road. As he watched, Russian infantry leapt down from their trucks and disappeared into the bushes on both sides of the road. When these reinforcements reached the terrain in front of Schreiber's platoon, Oberfeldwebel Ott sent his mortars and heavy machine guns into action. Machine-gun fire raked the attackers from the flanks. The infantry guns fired high-explosive rounds. The Russian attack bogged down before it got anywhere near the German position.

The Russians undertook several more attacks during the course of the day. They no longer approached en masse, but in small groups. They tried to work their way up to the German positions unseen. When the sun sank beneath the western horizon, the Soviets changed their tactics. They turned away from the marshy ground and tried to approach the hill. But this attack also failed under the flanking fire of the heavy platoon.

At first light on 27 July the Soviets opened their new attack with barrage fire from their 76.2-mm field guns. Rounds smacked into the marshy ground, hurling black muck into the air. Mortars joined in. But like the day before, most of the mortar rounds fell in the mud and did little damage. A few machine guns opened fire and forced the men of Schreiber's platoon to take cover. There was also intermittent submachine-gun fire from the jungle-like growth in no-man's-land.

Suddenly, the Russian infantry attack began without any visible preparation from the left front. That attack also collapsed in front of the hill. Oberleutnant Schlenker and the battalion adjutant came forward to assess the situation. Wisely, they had brought with them several boxes of belted machine-gun ammunition.

"We have to hold out today, Schreiber," said Schlenker. "Tonight we'll pull out and withdraw as planned to the next blocking position."

"Back, sir?" asked Schreiber in amazement.

"Yes. The Russians have made deep penetrations in the regiment's neighboring sectors. If we don't pull back in time our company will be cut off. That's why the regimental commander has decided on a new blocking position."

The enemy attacks went on for hours. Each was repulsed. By the time evening was falling, the fury had gone out of the Soviet attacks. Cries for help from badly wounded soldiers rang out from the swampy thickets and the area in front of the German positions. The horrible crying and moaning went on all night. Under cover of darkness the company withdrew to the new position, relieved and happy that the two days of fighting had not cost the life of a single German soldier.

On 28 July 1943 the Army High Command ordered the evacuation of the entire Orel salient and the withdrawal of all German forces to the "Hagen Position." This move was forced by the overall situation on the Eastern Front. The withdrawal, which also affected the 78th Assault Division, began on 31 July.

Steady rain was falling as the 14th Assault Regiment withdrew on foot. All the men were soaked through. Deployed on the right wing of the 2nd Panzer Army, the 78th Assault Division evacuated the "Green Line" and occupied positions in the "Red Line" east of Orel during the night of 31 July-1 August. Rearguards remained in the "Green Line" to deceive the enemy. They were under instructions not to withdraw until the enemy pressure became heavy, thus allowing the "Red Line" to become established.

The Soviets appeared not to have noticed the withdrawal. On 1 August they pursued so vigorously that there was bitter close-quarters fighting in places. The 7th Company was also employed to man combat outposts. During the night of 2–3 August the company withdrew to the "Black Line." All of these moves were bringing the German front closer to Orel.

✠

It was pitch-black on 8 August when Oberfeldwebel Schreiber, who had just inspected his three squads, heard fighting going on in the sector to the platoon's right.

"It sounds bad over there, Oberfeldwebel," observed Waller excitedly. Within minutes the sound of fighting had intensified.

"The Russians are in the trench, and..."

"Oberfeldwebel, Oberfeldwebel!" Call for help from our right-hand neighbor. Enemy forces—two companies strong—have broken into the trench."

"If they break through there, Oberfeldwebel, our regiment will be in deep shit. They'll encircle us," Schneider called, who had just arrived at the platoon command post.

"Platoon prepare to counterattack."

The men assembled and Schreiber went from one squad to another.

"When we get to the enemy trench only one thing will help: Keep going and nothing but keep going!"

The platoon moved out. The first enemy troops to appear were cut down.

"Everyone follow me!" Schreiber ran on.

A bloody, pitiless close-quarters fight began. Meter-by-meter the platoon fought its way along the trench. Many Russian troops feigned death, hoping to let the Germans pass, then shoot them in the back. Five assault grenadiers followed 100 meters behind the platoon. It was their job to cover the platoon's rear.

The advance continued. Several attached dugouts came into view. The men were met by machine-gun fire from very close range.

"You're in charge here!" Schreiber shouted to Unteroffizier Schneider.

"But, Oberfeldwebel, what . . . ?"

But Schneider's last words did not reach Schreiber. Schreiber had already left the trench and was running at a crouch through the field of craters. In front of one of the dugouts he armed two grenades simultaneously and threw them into the enemy strongpoint. Then he jumped to his feet and ran through the communications trench to the second machine-gun position. He saw several Russians and opened fire. The two men behind the machine gun raised their arms. Schneider came running with his squad.

"Keep going, Schneider! Move quickly!"

They ran to the next bend in the trench. One of the assault troops lit a concentrated charge and threw it in the direction of the enemy. The platoon worked its way through the groups of enemy soldiers, whose resistance gradually lessened. The surviving Red Army troops threw their weapons away and surrendered. Schreiber and his platoon had overcome a far superior enemy force.

The captured Germans were freed and the wounded cared for. By the time Oberleutnant Schlenker appeared at the threatened area the danger had passed. Oberfeldwebel Schreiber had achieved a decisive defensive success.

The Soviets then counterattacked in an effort to recapture the trench. Schreiber and his men repulsed every counterattack. Finally, however, the Soviets forced their way to within striking distance of the trench.

Even the badly wounded shouldered a weapon and fired back. Every man who could raise a hand was part of the defense. Schreiber's Platoon was not going to be overcome.

Oberst Kaether, who learned of the action a short time later from Oberleutnant Schlenker, recommended Schreiber for the Oak Leaves. In part, the recommendation said: "This man has saved the front. He has averted the worst for our regiment, for our division. His contribution was decisive."

Schreiber knew nothing of this. He had other concerns, because the fighting was becoming increasingly bitter. At the present rate his platoon would soon be decimated. Despite all the tribulations, however, the withdrawal to the "Hagen Position" near Karachev was a success. When the battalion commander summoned the commanders of his companies for a meeting to discuss defensive measures, Oberleutnant Schlenker collapsed with a high fever.

This outstanding officer was loath to abandon his company. He had concealed his illness. At that point, however, he had to get to the main dressing station as quickly as possible. But Russian close-support aircraft were keeping the railway station under continuous attack, and it was impossible to evacuate even the severely ill and wounded. The division commander dispatched a quad 20-mm Flak to the station. The gun shot down two of the enemy machines. The rest disappeared, and the evacuation of the sick and wounded proceeded.

Delivery of rations to the front line of the Belgorod battle zone by an Sd.Kfz 251 armored personnel carrier.

Before leaving, Schlenker recommended Schreiber as his replacement. The Oberfeldwebel was designated the acting commander of the 7th Company. Schreiber directed the defense in the company's sector. He continued to lead his 1st Platoon. Oberfeldwebel Hockenjos took charge of 2nd Platoon, which consisted of three squads of assault grenadiers. Oberfeldwebel Ott was given the 4th Platoon. The latter platoon had only one heavy mortar and one heavy machine gun left. The 3rd Platoon had been disbanded due to heavy casualties. The survivors were distributed among the remaining platoons.

As the squads were fortifying their positions, a man from the 8th Company arrived with news that Oberfeldwebel Klank, who had been transferred to that company, had been killed. Stabsgefreiter Franz Auer had also been killed only a few hours earlier. He died as the result of a direct hit by an artillery round. It had been Auer who had hauled rations, ammunition and mail to the men at the front every day. Two of his drivers were wounded by the blast. Also wounded were six heavy draught horses.

Hauptfeldwebel Hauschild had just assembled all the company's staff personnel for a briefing, when the door opened. The wind blew in a deluge of rain, which was followed by a man draped in a shelter half. When the soldier threw off the shelter half Hauschild recognized the Hauptmann shoulder boards and stood up to report. The officer gestured for him to remain seated and stepped into the light of the oil lamp. It was Hauptmann Albert Brachat, who had won the Knight's Cross in France as a Feldwebel with the company.

"So," called Brachat after peeling off the shelter half, "I'm back. How are things with you?"

Before anyone answered the Hauptmann shook hands with each man present. Everyone was pleased that their old comrade had recovered from his wounds and had returned to the regiment.

Once again there was a reorganization within the regiment. Oberfeld-webel Schreiber returned to his former position of platoon leader. At that point, his platoon was up to four squads. Ott's Platoon was reinforced through the addition of a machine-gun squad.

As evening fell on 11 August Schreiber's Platoon was in a hastily con-structed defensive position. The enemy had not yet attacked, but the posi-tions were under continuous artillery and rocket fire. Just before midnight an advance party from another division arrived at the platoon command post.

"What's up, sir?" Schreiber asked the detachment's commander.

"We're to relieve you here prior to midnight," the Leutnant explained to the platoon leader.

"Really? Does the commander know?" asked Schreiber.

He was not particularly surprised. In the recent past they hadn't spent more than 24 hours in any one position.

"He was informed by telephone and should be here soon."

As if responding to his cue the Hauptmann arrived moments later.

"Schreiber, give them the information they need."

A thunderstorm had transformed the bottom of the trench into a muddy mess. The men inspected their weapons. By the time their relief finally arrived, the men of the 1st Platoon were soaked. Covered with mud, the assault troops waded toward the rear. They marched through the dark night toward their new position. After an hour they reached a village on the road. A guide was waiting for them there. The village teemed with motorized and horse-drawn vehicles.

"Is there a place for us here, Oberfeldwebel?" asked Maier.

Schreiber, who was accompanied by Hockenjos, answered: "I have arranged for a house in the center of the village for us, Maier."

When they stepped inside the troops were pleasantly surprised. Not only were there straw-filled mattresses, but the room was also heated.

Schreiber, who never missed a trick, ordered: "Cover the windows!"

The wet shelter halves were hung in front of the windows, so they could dry out. The food arrived. With it came hot tea, also arranged by Josef Schreiber. Morale improved perceptibly. The remnants of a few candles cast a dim light around the room. An hour was spent cleaning weapons and equipment, after which the men fell into their beds. But they got little sleep on account of the constant coming and going in the house. The door was opened repeatedly, each time flooding the large room with cold air. The heavy vehicles of the trains drove away. The sound of their engines roared through the night. Then only the light vehicles and their guards were left.

"Get ready! Departure in half an hour!"

This announcement by Oberfeldwebel Schreiber woke the exhausted men from their slumber. When they stepped outside they discovered it was broad daylight. The rain had stopped and the sun was now shining warmly. Mist rose from the muddy road in front of them. In the distance could be heard the rumble of artillery.

"Put all the equipment into the *panje* wagons!" the platoon leader ordered.

The men didn't have to be told twice. Having any kind of vehicle to haul their heavy gear was a luxury. The platoon moved out. The others followed. Leading the way were the *panje* wagons. They became stuck as soon as they reached the first low-lying area.

Schreiber instructed his men to help push the wagons free: "Form columns by squads. Each squad take a wagon."

"Shouldn't we carry the horses too, Oberfeldwebel?" asked Krüger sarcastically.

"It doesn't matter to me," replied Schreiber.

The temperature climbed quickly. By about 1000 hours the heat was so great that it was like being in a sauna. The canteens were already empty.

In the afternoon they came to a village. Bivouacked there were the trains elements that had moved out during the night. They met Hauptmann Brachat there. He ordered a two-hour rest. Once back on the move, the battalion adjutant informed them that the Soviets had been attacking with tank support in the Karachev area since daybreak and had made several deep penetrations. Shouting to make himself heard over the engine noise, Oberleutnant Lentjes explained:

"The enemy is already at the eastern and southern outskirts of Karachev. It's our job to stop up the holes."

Schreiber looked at his map; it was still thirty kilometers to Karachev. The nearer they came to the city, the heavier became the traffic on the road in both directions. The sound of Russian artillery and exploding bombs grew louder as well.

"They're beating the hell out of Karachev!" said one of the men.

"And perhaps us, too!" added another.

"Look at the fireworks!" called Oberfeldwebel Klimke of the 9th Company. Whole blocks of the heavily bombarded city were in flames.

"We're going to move around the city," explained the adjutant as the column changed direction. A look at his watch revealed to Schreiber that it was already 1600 hours. A halt was called on the east side of the city. The guide took cover behind a haystack on the level plain.

"Schreiber, come with me to establish contact," ordered the battalion adjutant.

The two men headed toward the main line of resistance to notify the battalion there that relief had arrived. They wanted to survey the positions. Those left behind watched as a stream of people fled the threatened city.

There were many refugees at the crossroads about 200 meters away. Military police struggled to get the German units streaming in from every direction through the intersection as quickly as possible. When a unit bound for the front arrived, everything else halted to allow it speedy passage through the bottleneck. Heavy artillery rolled in, followed by supply vehicles and ambulances. The latter came from the direction of the front, where the sounds of fighting had intensified to a continuous dull rumble. Finally, Schreiber returned to his men. With him were two trucks that the mechanized infantry battalion they were relieving had put at his disposal.

"Everyone climb aboard!" ordered the Oberfeldwebel.

They arrived at the battalion command post after a short drive. There was food there and even canteen items.

"They're happy that we're relieving them in this devil's cauldron," said Oberfeldwebel Jerzky, commenting on this astonishing generosity.

"For sure," agreed Schreiber. "But they would have been relieved anyway, even if they hadn't done this for us."

Schreiber and Maier went forward as darkness fell. The guides from the other companies followed. The 7th Company was assigned a position which was to the left and right of the Karachev-Orel road.

"We have to relieve two companies, Oberfeldwebel!" Maier called in surprise on being told that they would also have to take over a heavy mortar position and a heavy machine-gun position.

The positions for the heavy platoon were situated about 400–600 meters behind the main line of resistance. From there the heavy weapons could place effective fire on the enemy as soon as they attacked. The positions also provided a fallback position for the assault troops in case they were driven out of the main line of resistance.

The Russians were silent as the company arrived and Schreiber and Maier assigned the platoons their positions. Occasional harassing fire destined for Karachev passed overhead. The city was visible in spite of the darkness, as it was burning in several places. Karachev lay approximately three-and-a-half kilometers behind the German line. An artillery observer came forward to the platoon's positions. Schreiber greeted the man and handed him over to Maier for a briefing on the position.

"Bring us shovels and pick-axes," Schreiber reminded the messenger once again.

The relieved soldiers left their positions. A few words, the outlines of faces passing by, the tramping of feet, then the others had disappeared into the twilight. Schreiber's platoon dug in to the right of the road. On its left was Ott's Platoon, which had been reformed. Hauptmann Brachat arrived.

"How does it look, Schreiber?" he asked the platoon leader.

"Its coming along, sir. With a little work we'll soon have good positions."

"Good! If you need anything let me know. I have set up the command post directly behind the mortar position."

The men took turns at sentry duty. When not so engaged they dug.

By the time a dull gray in the east announced the arrival of a new day Schreiber's platoon had disappeared into the earth. All excess material—the loose earth and other telltale signs of digging in—had been removed. By 1500 hours Schreiber had sent everyone to get some sleep, except for the outposts, who maintained a watch on no-man's-land. Some time later the Oberfeldwebel was awakened by the sound of gunfire. He shook Maier by the shoulder.

"Maier, old buddy, wake up!"

The messenger sat up, yawned and rubbed his eyes. "It seems to be coming from the Eighth, or even perhaps the Sixth, Oberfeldwebel," he observed.

Hauptmann Brachat and Oberfeldwebel Hockenjos crawled up from behind.

"The situation would seem to indicate that the Russians are trying to break through here in order to cut off Orel. Regiment has ordered that we hold our positions until tonight no matter what. Reconnaissance has discovered strong concentrations of Russian tanks."

"We're in for it then," declared Schreiber.

Suddenly, they all ducked below the rim of the communications trench. Russian heavy artillery began firing into the main line of resistance to the left of the road. The exploding rounds produced towering clouds of smoke and dirt. Dust clouds rose high into the air. Flames lit the surrounding area with a flickering light. The first heavy round fell in the sector held by Schreiber's platoon. Fortunately, it didn't seem to be directed fire. The bursting rounds wandered toward the mortar positions before finally turning back toward the main line of resistance.

"You'll find me in the company command post in a group of bushes on the back side of the hill near the road," said Hauptmann Brachat, taking his leave. "If I'm not there one of the men will be able to tell you where I am. Good luck, Schreiber!"

The Hauptmann hadn't been gone three minutes when the enemy fire intensified and concentrated on Schreiber's sector.

"There, Oberfeldwebel!" called Waller, pointing to the left. A cluster of red flares rose into the sky, a sign that the Russians were attacking there. The assault troops could also hear the roar of engines. Krause listened intently to the roar of Russian tank engines.

"They're coming toward us!"

Schreiber scanned the area in front of him through his binoculars, but there were no enemy tanks in sight. The German artillery was now firing as well. Shells whistled over the front line on their way to their targets in enemy territory. The rounds struck the ground far ahead, spewing fountains of muck and columns of smoke into the air. The fighting had begun.

Soon afterward Schreiber heard shouts of "Urray!" from the left. The Russians were attacking!

Heavy shells were now falling on the road which led past Schreiber's positions about thirty meters away. The earth trembled. The stench of cordite burned the lungs of the soldiers and shock waves pressed them to the ground. Pieces of earth and stone were thrown as far as the company command post.

"Set up the scissors telescope!" ordered the Oberfeldwebel.

The scissors telescope was set up. It had been captured from the enemy in the Trosna Valley. Schreiber looked through it and saw them. The sight of several waves of enemy tanks attacking took his breath away. Would it be possible to stop this phalanx of steel giants? Schreiber hastily fired several violet signal flares. This was a signal to battalion that enemy tanks were approaching. One after another the Russian tanks and assault guns changed their general direction.

"They're driving almost parallel to the front now!" Schreiber called out.

The men in the trench listened breathlessly to his running account. Seconds later he shouted: "They've opened fire!"

Seconds later rounds howled in and smashed into the ground without, however, inflicting any damage. The tanks resumed their advance—somewhat hesitantly, it seemed. About 300 meters away a group of about twenty-five T-34s left the road and headed straight toward the 7th Company.

Someone shouted over the rattling and squeaking of tank tracks: "Friendly assault guns and self-propelled artillery behind us."

Schreiber breathed a sigh of relief on hearing the news. Without heavy weapons they would have been completely helpless. Perhaps they could have knocked out two or three of the Russian tanks, but the rest would have rolled right over the foxholes and trenches.

"Watch out!" Schreiber shouted, ducking his head.

Rounds fired by the German assault guns and artillery whistled toward the Russian tanks, passing only a few meters over the trenches and fox-

The infantry moves out once more.

holes. The assault troops cheered as the first T-34 belched black smoke and ground to a halt. The leading enemy tank was hit in the tracks. It turned on its axis several times before stopping. The Russian tank continued to fire. Then there was a direct hit on the tank's turret ring. Seconds later, there were three explosions that blew the T-34 apart. The sounds of battle had grown even louder to the left of the road. The artillery of both sides was firing without pause.

To the rear an assault gun took a direct hit and caught fire. The crew managed to escape the blazing wreck. The enemy tank group halted. Several T-34s turned and sought cover behind a rise.

A report came through from the 3rd Squad: "Have casualties!"

"Go on, Krause," Schreiber called to the medic.

The Gefreiter made his way to the squad and tended to two seriously wounded men. Several of their companions took the two to one of the assault guns, while two less-seriously wounded walked there under their own power.

Russian close-support aircraft then appeared on the scene. They flitted over the German positions, dropping fragmentation bombs and strafing. The surviving enemy tanks had soon regrouped and additional groups of tanks had arrived from the rear. They formed up for another attack. Schreiber saw that infantry accompanied the tanks rolling toward his sector. Several T-34s carried dense clusters of men. Sometimes he could see infantry advancing behind the tanks.

The T-34s without solders advanced too quickly, however. They left the following infantry far behind. The Soviet foot soldiers came within range of the German machine guns and were forced to take cover.

"Flanking fire to the left!" Schreiber ordered.

He had spotted a wave of Russian infantry approaching from that side. The two machine guns on the flank fired long bursts into the left wing of the advancing enemy. The T-34s came nearer and nearer. More tanks were knocked out or disabled. Nevertheless, a group of seven or eight managed to reach Schreiber's sector. The noise of the tank engines was deafening. The tracks whirred and, with an unnerving noise, the upper edges of the trenches and foxholes began to crumble.

"Take cover!" shouted Schreiber before disappearing into the deep hole he had dug for just such an eventuality.

One of the tanks crawled right over his hiding place, but the grinding tracks passed to either side of the hole. A stinking cloud of exhaust gas poured into the hole. Schreiber was paralyzed with fear. Just don't stop, he thought. If it did, the exhaust fumes would surely overcome him. The T-34 fired its main gun. Schreiber could hear the empty shell casings clatter to the floor of the tank. Then the T-34 moved off, and it was once again light above Schreiber.

Choking, his face blackened, he pushed himself up out of his hole. Red Army troops appeared behind the tanks. They were only fifty meters from the trench! Schreiber raised his submachine gun and fired. One of his machine guns began to fire, then another, and finally the heavy machine gun. One after another his men emerged from the ground. The narrow holes had provided effective protection. As a result of the effective machine-gun fire, the Russian troops advancing behind the tanks were forced to dig in or seek cover in one of the many craters. Behind them the assault troops could hear the crashing of tank cannon.

The German assault guns and Russian T-34s were engaged in a bitter duel. Once again the assault guns had lived up to their reputation as a mobile "fire brigade."

"There come the Russians!" shouted Unteroffizier Schneider.

In fact a large group of enemy soldiers was charging toward the platoon's position. The defenders opened up with everything they had. Not a single Russian soldier reached the position.

"What's wrong with the right machine gun?" Schreiber asked. The weapon had fallen silent.

"Go take a look, Maier."

Maier crawled off. He had to make a wide arc, as a large part of the trench had collapsed. At the same time, Schreiber crept over to the road to check the situation on the right. Maier reached a position behind the right squad. When he reached the position he found two members of the platoon. Both were dead. Their hole had taken a direct hit from an artillery round.

A little later he reached the right squad's machine-gun position. The members of the machine-gun team were on the ground—or at least what was left of them. Their machine gun was a twisted piece of metal, the result of a direct hit by another artillery round. Albert Maier later described the awful scene:

> Not far from the two dead machine gunners I found the squad leader, Unteroffizier Burghart. He was lying in a pool of blood. Burghart had been promoted to Unteroffizier only a few days earlier. The entire squad must have been wiped out. The thought filled me with horror. Quickly, I gathered as many dogtags and paybooks as I could find. I came to the next squad, where I found Krause. He was busy with a severely wounded man. I hurried on to tell the platoon leader what had happened.
>
> Schreiber had become nervous at my prolonged absence and was already on his way into the neighboring platoon's sector on the right. When I described what I had seen, his face, which was red from exertion, turned snow white. He looked at me in disbelief. Then he looked around in order to get a grasp of the situation. One could say that he was taking stock.

Just then Schneider reported: "New wave of enemy tanks, Oberfeldwebel!"

They ran back to the scissors telescope. Behind them it had become quiet. The assault guns had destroyed all the enemy tanks that had broken through.

"Maier, go to the company command post and report the platoon's situation. And don't forget to bring reinforcements!"

There was an imploring tone in the platoon leader's voice. Two entire squads had been put out of action. The platoon's position was now far too weakly manned. A fresh Soviet attack would lead to a breakthrough. After Maier had left, Schreiber reorganized his platoon. The Soviet tanks halted. Apparently, they were waiting for reinforcements as well. Secretly, Schreiber was praying for reinforcements and heavy weapons. When he heard the sound of the heavy tractors of an 88-mm Flak battery, he thought it was a hallucination. Then he saw that it was a reality.

"Men," he shouted with relief, "four 88s are moving into position behind us!"

Maier and Hauptmann Brachat arrived. They brought with them an infantry squad that had been in a reserve position.

"Schreiber, the 88s will do the job!" shouted the Hauptmann.

"I'll send you another squad. Now I have to go to Ott. The Russians have broken in there."

The commander's confidence encouraged the assault troops. They watched Brachat and Hockenjos run toward the positions of Ott's Platoon and disappear into the field of craters. Schreiber deployed the new squad. Finally, the Russian tanks rolled forward. They were accompanied by numerous infantry. The Flak opened fire when the first tank was within 1,500 meters. The four guns maintained a high rate of fire. The first T-34 was hit and ground to a halt.

Schreiber's voice rang out over the position: "Engage the escorting infantry!"

The platoon still had three machine guns and these fired long bursts. The mounted Russian infantry jumped down from the tanks and took cover. Schreiber called a warning to the men of the new squad: "Watch out! There are mortars in those trees!"

A few Russian machine guns fired from no-man's-land and the enemy's artillery opened up on the positions of Schreiber's Platoon once again. Soviet close-support aircraft appeared at brief intervals and dropped fragmentation bombs on the main line of resistance. The "88s" engaged the groups of Soviet aircraft. Five were shot down. A veritable curtain of Flak bursts filled the sky, forcing the enemy aircraft to turn away.

It had been an hour since Hauptmann Brachat left when Oberfeldwebel Hockenjos returned to Schreiber's platoon. Schreiber stared at his old comrade-in-arms in disbelief: There were tears in his eyes. Before the Oberfeldwebel could say anything, Hockenjos began to speak:

"Josef, you will have to take command of the company again—Hauptmann Brachat is dead."

"What happened? Hockenjos, tell me what happened!" pleaded Schreiber.

Speaking haltingly, the Unteroffizier told him how they had led a counterattack by Ott's platoon that had driven back the enemy. During the attack Brachat was shot in the chest.

"Two men brought him back. He was still alive at that point. But on the way they were caught by a surprise Russian artillery barrage. The two bearers were killed. Hauptmann Brachat sustained two more wounds that proved fatal."

"The company commander is dead!"

The word passed from mouth to mouth. Once again Oberfeldwebel Schreiber had halted an enemy attack, this time in the "Hagen Position". He and his soldiers again foiled every attempt by the enemy to break through during the Russian offensive that began on 26 August 1943. All of the regiment repeatedly distinguished itself during this phase of the fighting.

✠

"The men of the sole German assault division," wrote Karl Tress, "were especially hard pressed, as they were specialists in especially difficult offensive and defensive roles. As a result, their sacrifices were very high."

On 3 September the Wehrmacht Report announced the conclusion of the battle in the Orel bend. Five divisions were named in the report, among them the 78th Assault Division. Subsequently, the division was moved into the Orsha area. It was soon in action again. It fought east of the city, on the Baltutino-Yelnya road and west of Yelnya.

The division was sent to the "Panther Position," the line of positions on the Pronya, where the 4th Army (Generaloberst Henrici) had temporarily halted its withdrawal. It was there that the six legendary roadway battles were to take place during the fall and winter.

On 5 October 1943 Oberfeldwebel Schreiber was notified by Teletype message that he had become the 309th soldier of the German armed forces to be awarded the Knight's Cross with Oak Leaves. In doing so, he became the sixth noncommissioned officer in the Army and the first member of the 78th Assault Division to receive the high decoration.

✠

In early December 1943 Schreiber returned from leave and rejoined his unit. He was given command of the 7th Company, which he was to lead pending the arrival of a designated officer. A few days later the new company commander, Leutnant Schwarz, joined Oberfeldwebel Schreiber and Hauptfeldwebel Hauschild. On the evening of 9 December 1943 the 7th Company relieved the 6th Company of the 119th Mechanized Infantry Regiment (of the 25th Mechanized Infantry Division).

The following days saw heavy close-quarters fighting. On 20 December Oberfeldwebel Schreiber and Oberfeldwebel Ott received the Close-Combat Clasp in Silver (for thirty or more engagements). Schreiber became the first soldier of the entire corps to receive the decoration. After a relatively quiet few days over Christmas, the Soviets resumed their attacks on 27 December. Schreiber himself ran through the trench to the company command post to report: "The Russians are in the trench!"

He ran back together with Leutnant Schwarz. Once again the enemy was driven back. The company then advanced to the 14th Assault Regiment's 6th Company, reclaiming the sector that had been lost. During this period the regiment had been under the command of Oberstleutnant Gaden. Major Sellner was forced to assume command of the regiment when Gaden was transferred in early February.

At the end of February Oberleutnant Schlenker, the former commander of the 7th Company, returned to the regiment and assumed command of his old company. The 78th Assault Division was in the Lasirchiki area during the fifth roadway battle. Powerful Soviet forces attacked, fighting their way into the German main line of resistance—except in the sector held by the 7th Company. Generaloberst Henrici expressed his special appreciation to the company, and the 78th Assault Division was again named in the Wehrmacht Report.

At the end of 1944 Oberfeldwebel Schreiber was sent to Officer School V in Posen. When he arrived, Marshall Zhukov's divisions were already approaching the city. Schreiber initially joined the school's instructional staff. On 23 January all training activities ceased. Two days later, the Red Army surrounded Posen. The core of the defensive forces was made up of 2,000 young noncommissioned officers and officer cadets of the school. Oberfeldwebel Schreiber defended an important position with six men. After five of his comrades had been killed, he sent the sixth back with a situation report and a request for reinforcements.

That was 1 February 1945. Josef Schreiber was posted missing that day. No trace of him or information concerning his fate was ever found. Thus this brave soldier shared a fate suffered by hundreds of thousands of his fellow soldiers on every front.

BIOGRAPHICAL INFORMATION AND DECORATIONS

24 December 1919: Born in Mindersdorf.

14 August 1938: Joined the 14th Infantry Regiment as a volunteer. Advanced through the noncommissioned officer ranks and was finally commissioned a Leutnant.

16 August 1941: Infantry Assault Badge.

18 September 1941: Iron Cross, First Class.

31 March 1943: Knight's Cross of the Iron Cross.

5 October 1943: Oak Leaves to the Knight's Cross of the Iron Cross (309th recipient).

20 October 1943: Close-Combat Clasp in Silver (thirty or more engagements).

Oberfeldwebel Erich Vielwerth after receiving the Knight's Cross on 18 October 1941. At the time he was assigned to the 1st Company of the 87th Infantry Regiment.

Erich Vielwerth

Feldwebel Erich Vielwerth, the headquarters section leader of the 87th Infantry Regiment's 1st Company, was on home leave when he heard the call-up of soldiers of the Western Army on the radio on 10 May 1940.

At once he got in touch with his colleagues Stabsfeldwebel Koch and Oberfeldwebel Olff, who were likewise on leave. None of them had received the ominous telegram ordering the soldiers back to their units. Inquiries at the local base were not very productive. However, the three men did learn that there was a collection point for their division in Trier. Erich Vielwerth ended the speculation: "We'll go to Trier then. We'll be able to find out more there."

The three reached the cathedral city aboard an overloaded train. There they learned that a train would be leaving the following morning to take them and other soldiers back to their unit.

The next morning they listened for the call to assemble; the three were understandably nervous. Division after division was called out. Only the 36th Infantry Division was not named.

"Looks as if they've forgotten us," observed Stabsfeldwebel Koch.

Not until noon were they assigned a train; it was headed for the Luxembourg border. The last stop was ten kilometers from Bollendorf and the three noncommissioned officers struck out on foot.

In Bollendorf they made inquiries about their division, but learned nothing concrete. The mess sergeant promised to take them along to battalion the next morning. They were unable to find the sergeant again and there was nothing left for them to do but start hitchhiking and trust in their luck. Feldwebel Vielwerth's luck was, in fact, very good. He ran into their sister regiment's supply trains. The 118th Infantry Regiment took him along toward the front and the same day he found his brother, who was serving as a supply sergeant in the same battalion of the 36th Infantry Division.

Together with his brother, Erich Vielwerth went to Neu-Harbig, where he found his unit's combat trains. Finally, he was back with his own people. When he asked about his battalion, all they could tell him was that it had been there yesterday.

Oberfeldwebel Olff turned up on 13 May and the pair pedaled after their division along "Advance Route A" on Belgian military bicycles. It was a sunny day. The farther the two infantrymen went the greater became the throng on the roads. They pedaled past stopped armor columns. Their faces and uniforms were caked with dust. Along the way they picked up three signals men from the regimental headquarters. For the first time Erich Vielwerth saw large numbers of German tanks. Over their heads flew fighters, bombers and Stukas.

The five stragglers pedaled their way across Belgium all morning and into the afternoon. During a rest break a staff car of the 36th Infantry Division came by.

"Man, did you see that?" shouted Oberfeldwebel Olff. "That was Hauptmann Lindemann, the division commander's brother."

"Follow him!" said Vielwerth.

The five bicycles followed the staff car, which soon turned towards a chateau, where Generalleutnant Lindemann's command post was located.

"You can spend the night in the coachman's house," decided the division adjutant. Vielwerth slept for ten hours and, when he awoke, the sun was already high in the sky. He got himself ready and, an hour after leaving the chateau, he was receiving an enthusiastic welcome from his comrades of the 87th Infantry Regiment's 1st Company in the village of Escombre.

"You've come just in time, Vielwerth," said Hauptmann Schmitt in welcoming him. "Later on you and your company headquarters section will be coming with me to scout the terrain. The attack on the Maginot Line begins tomorrow."

"*Jawohl*, sir!" replied the Feldwebel.

That evening the company headquarters section went up with the company commander. The party scouted the battalion's assembly area. Early on 15 May the battalion moved forward and dug shallow rifle pits in the soft ground. There was still plenty of time before the attack began. The 1st Company was the battalion reserve and would not see action until the advance was under way. An 88-mm Flak went into position not far from the company. When the attack began, it would engage the enemy bunkers with direct fire.

"I'm eager to find out what the 88 can do, Feldwebel," whispered Obergefreiter Lamparter.

Before Vielwerth could answer, the German artillery opened fire. Light and heavy rounds howled over the assembly area and smashed into the enemy positions. The sound of the heavy rounds passing overhead was like heavy wagons rumbling over a distant road. The din of the preparatory artillery bombardment lasted an hour. During this time the French artillery fired not a round in reply. The cloud of powder smoke along the battlefield became thicker and thicker. Smoke rounds made the screen virtually impenetrable.

The firing ceased abruptly, and the battalion's other two companies moved out for the attack. They crossed the Chiers in inflatable boats. The troops stormed forward, reached the enemy position and were straddled by rifle and machine-gun fire.

An hour later Hauptmann Schmitt ordered: "Company: Form up!"

Feldwebel Vielwerth jumped up close on the heels of the company commander and ran toward the riverbank. All of a sudden, he caught sight of a tall figure with red general's stripes on his pants.

"Man, that's our General!" shouted Unteroffizier Holle in amazement.

They crossed the river barrier in assault boats and inflatable rafts. When they approached the first French position, they found it had been abandoned by the enemy, who had pulled back.

Three hours later the company had reached its objective for the day. The company headquarters section went into position in an abandoned farmhouse.

Security was posted. A few bundles of straw in the building's cellar served as beds.

The night passed quietly and, on the morning of 16 May, the 36th Infantry Division resumed its advance toward the Meuse, reaching the river valley near Mouzon. North of the city, Vielwerth crossed the river in an inflatable raft. His company had not yet seen anything of the enemy, except for a few prisoners on their way to the rear.

After crossing the Meuse, the company came upon a French battery position. This had also been abandoned. The farther they advanced, the more abandoned positions they found.

"If these had all been firing at us, Vielwerth, we wouldn't have got across the river quite so easily," observed Hauptmann Schmitt.

Several huge craters provided proof that the dive-bombers had been at work. But that alone couldn't have been the reason for the headlong flight by the French. It was also attributable to the fast German armor formations, which had outflanked the French positions as they stormed forward ahead of the infantry. The French had been forced to withdraw to avoid being cut off.

The division received orders to establish a bridgehead on the far side of the Meuse and secure to the west. A few hours later the regiment turned south and secured along the Mouzon-Antrecourt road. From there, it continued to orient south. Early on 17 May, the company was alerted and marched to Antrecourt.

During the advance Feldwebel Vielwerth wondered what this Friday was likely to bring him and the company. So far the enemy had not challenged the division. The divisions of Panzer Group Guderian and Panzer Group von Kleist had done most of the fighting. But their turn would come.

The bright sun climbed high in the sky. It was going to be a hot day. Above the men larks wheeled and sang. In this seemingly peaceful landscape it was difficult to think about war and death. But both were not far off.

Vielwerth occasionally chatted with the men of the company headquarters section. One of the company platoon leaders, Leutnant Klein, visited frequently. When they reached their assembly area there was still nothing to be seen of the enemy. The company continued its march. Vielwerth and the others were now moving due south, in the direction of Beaumont. The remaining companies had arrived, and all of the 1st Battalion moved out of a patch of woods and advanced across the fields and meadows in battle order. They were widely dispersed.

They crossed hills and valleys. The men had grown used to the quiet and the sunny day when, all of a sudden, they came under fire. The peaceful atmosphere was shattered by the hissing of bursts of machine-gun fire, exploding fountains of earth and the rattling echoes of salvoes of gunfire.

Someone shouted: "Machine-gun fire from the right."

Seconds later more machine guns opened fire from the right and directly ahead. The smoking trails made by their tracers revealed the locations of the enemy positions.

"Company: Bound your way forward!"

The first platoon ran forward while the other two platoons laid down covering fire. As he ran, Vielwerth found himself staring at the broad back of the company commander, who was leading the way. A burst of machine-gun fire came their way. The Feldwebel fell head over heels into a depression. Two of their own machine guns opened fire from the right flank and silenced the machine gun in front of the 1st Platoon.

"We're now taking fire from the village to our left, sir!" reported Vielwerth.

The enemy was now firing from all sides. The battalion's attack bogged down on the Beaumont high ground. The enemy fire intensified and French artillery began firing. Then, suddenly, tanks appeared. They rolled out of their camouflaged positions like sluggish beetles.

"They're going to try and crush our front!" Leutnant Klein called out.

"Green signal flare!" ordered Hauptmann Schmitt.

The flares hissed into the bright sky and exploded in a spray of color. The call was passed on from company to company:

"Move the Pak forward!"

Boom!—Boom!—Boom!

Three tank rounds struck the ground thirty meters in front of Erich Vielwerth, sending dirt and bushes spinning through the air. The Feldwebel pressed himself closer to the earth. Nearby was Unteroffizier Holle. He was breathing heavily. Vielwerth also felt the stress caused by this baptism of fire. This feeling was aggravated by the rumble of the advancing tanks and the crash of their guns. When were the 13th and 14th Companies of the 87th Infantry Regiment going to arrive with their antitank and infantry guns? If they didn't come soon the enemy tanks would roll through their positions.

Crash!

A high-explosive round struck the ground ten meters in front of the depression. Vielwerth felt clumps of dirt raining down onto his back. Where were the antitank guns?

There! Tracer flashed from a position off to the right rear of the battalion. It headed straight for the enemy tanks.

"The Pak are here!" shouted Obergefreiter Lamparter, relieved.

The Feldwebel smiled involuntarily. As he watched, two rounds whizzed over the turret of one of the steel giants, just missing. Then the third smashed into the armored front of the tank. Smoke curled upward and flames licked from the tank. The hatches flipped open and the crew bailed out. It was not a moment too soon. Seconds later the reserve ammunition went up, blowing the tank to pieces. It remained in front of the German lines, a blazing torch.

The infantry guns then joined in the duel between the tanks and Pak. A second tank was hit. A third spun around in a circle on its one intact track, while the other destroyed track remained piled up on the torn earth like a giant reptile.

"They're turning away!" shouted one of the soldiers.

The tanks had halted and opened fire on identified German positions, but then they apparently received orders to withdraw. Pursued by the last rounds from the Pak, the tanks disappeared behind a fold in the terrain, leaving those that had been knocked out burning and smoking on the rolling fields. But rifle and machine-gun fire continued to pour in from bushes and field positions. In spite of careful searching, the infantry could not pick out the well-camouflaged French positions.

The companies worked their way forward meter by meter. As evening approached, the French fire died down. Hauptmann Schmitt assembled two platoons, then stormed and took the important heights south of Beaumont. Many of Vielwerth's comrades were forced to pay for this success with their lives.

The sound of fighting, which had died down as dusk was falling, flared up again during the night. By midnight a pitched battle was under way. Schmitt's company remained covered and concealed in craters. None of the squads had contact with the others. The only indication Vielwerth had that friendly troops were nearby was the rattle of MG 34s. The Feldwebel saw the first enemy dead and prisoners. They were black colonial troops, stubborn fighters who knew every trick in the book.

An hour past midnight Vielwerth spotted a well-camouflaged group of enemy soldiers working their way toward the shell crater in which Obergefreiter Külker had set up his machine gun. Vielwerth called a warning to the leader of the machine-gun squad: "Külker, watch out! Three-hundred meters ahead. Beside the round bushes."

Külker scanned the area described by Vielwerth and he saw at once that the bushes were "moving" toward his position.

"Target identified!" he called back.

"Open fire!"

The machine gun began to rattle. The second member of the squad ensured that the belt fed smoothly so as to avoid a potentially disastrous stoppage. Discovered, the enemy troops stood up and charged the crater. Rifle bullets whistled. The machine gun rattled. The last attacker collapsed about twenty meters from the Feldwebel's position.

Vielwerth cautioned the men to stay alert. The French colonial troops made repeated attempts to infiltrate the German position and surprise the infantry in their holes. Some succeeded. However, none managed to get within striking distance of Vielwerth's men.

The entire night passed this way, a tense duel with the enemy. As the new day dawned in the east the Feldwebel breathed a sigh of relief.

"Thank God!" he said to Leutnant Klein, who had crawled over to him. "At least now we can see."

The men of the regiment had to hold their positions in that sector until night fell, when they were relieved. During the night, the regiment marched back a few kilometers and pitched its tents in a patch of woods. After forty-eight hours of continuous action without a break, Vielwerth fell into a deep sleep, not waking until the following noon.

For the first time in forty-eight hours the men could relax while they ate. As they looked around they saw empty places within their ranks. In the frontline newspaper, which showed up at noon on this first quiet day, the soldiers were able to read of the success of the armor units.

✠

It was early on the morning of 23 May when Feldwebel Vielwerth was rudely awakened by a runner.

"Alert, Feldwebel! Report to the company commander at once!"

When Vielwerth arrived, the platoon leaders were already there. Hauptmann Schmitt briefed the assembly: "Gentlemen, the advance is continuing. We have once again been made the regimental reserve."

One of the company officers cleared his throat: "That means marching along behind everyone else again, sir?"

"Perhaps with some artillery fire from the French," seconded another.

The Hauptmann shook his head doubtfully: "Possibly, possibly, gentlemen. But we must be ready for anything!"

A half-hour later the 1st Company moved into its assembly area. The march was completed without incident. Then the order was given to dig in. Mumbling, the men set about their work. It all seemed pointless to them. In all probability, they thought, they wouldn't be there long. Nevertheless, Feldwebel Vielwerth saw to it that the company headquarters section "went underground." In the event of a surprise artillery barrage the foxholes would be good "life insurance."

Once again Vielwerth and his section watched the artillery bombard the forward French positions. The barrage stopped and all was still for a second. It seemed to the Feldwebel as if his men were holding their breath. Then he heard the hectic rattle of a MG 34 and sporadic French rifle fire.

"Our assault companies have made contact, Feldwebel," offered Gefreiter Schindler, one of the runners.

Vielwerth nodded and listened. The noise of the fighting intensified, then moved away.

Hauptmann Schmitt ordered: "First Company: Move out!"

The company advanced with the 1st Platoon in the center and the 2nd and 3rd Platoons to the left and right, respectively. Slowly, they gained ground and reached the woods in which the initial fighting had taken place. The enemy was a master of the terrain. He was quite at home there, and the assault troops were met by fire from thickets, trees and bushes. The woods had to be combed meter by meter. The enemy troops fought with bitterness and determination.

Soon it was midday. The heat was oppressive. The men, some of whom had been pinned in their foxholes in the heat for hours, were dehydrated and at the end of their endurance. The company was moved up close behind the assault groups.

"Soon it will be our turn, Erich," said Feldwebel Zimmermann of the 2nd Platoon.

"Looks that way to me too," the leader of the company headquarters section agreed. Vielwerth looked around for any of his men who might be lagging behind. Schindler returned. He had been sent to the 3rd Platoon with orders for them to close ranks with the 1st Platoon. He came gasping over the rather flat terrain.

"Everything all right?" asked the Feldwebel, somewhat concerned.

Schindler nodded, but he couldn't speak. The Feldwebel observed the young man when he wasn't looking. Next time he would choose Lamparter, who was stronger. Soon afterward the word came back: "Reserves: Move forward!"

The order concerned the 1st Company as well. The objective was an extended valley, the floor of which was a meadow with forest on both flanks. Excellent cover for the enemy.

"Move forward quickly!" shouted the Feldwebel. "If we stay here too long the French will pin us down in the meadow."

The reserves ran through the valley as the crack of rifles and the rattle of machine guns echoed through the afternoon. The company commander ran at the head of the first platoon. Close behind were Feldwebel Vielwerth and his men. Behind him Vielwerth heard men cry out as they were hit and fell to the ground. As he ran he tried to locate the enemy, but there was no sign of them. Vielwerth plunged into an overgrown drainage ditch. As he fell, a burst of machine-gun fire hissed by, missing his head by a matter of millimeters. For a few seconds, the Feldwebel lay still. Four men of his unit were hit and tumbled into the fresh greenery. Then he jumped up and ran for his life. If only they could cross this piece of open terrain, they might have a chance of surviving.

Once again it was Hauptmann Schmitt, the veteran of the First World War, who got his company moving. The thought of simply staying in the cover of a trench or some low bushes had crossed Vielwerth's mind several times. But when the commander hurried forward, he also got to his feet and the others followed.

Obergefreiter Külker spotted the machine gun that was firing on the lead section; it was about eighty meters off to the right. He stopped in midstride and fired from the hip, silencing the French machine gun. The race with death went on. They suffered casualties but moved forward. The first enemy soldiers began surrendering. They emerged from field positions and behind bushes, first in small groups and then in greater numbers.

Infantry move through a burning village.

The assault groups stormed onwards, exploiting the confusion in the enemy's ranks. They reached their objective, a road leading out of Beaumont, and posted outposts. The remaining men took cover and waited. But nothing happened. The firing had ceased. The enemy appeared to have withdrawn.

Gradually, the excitement among the men died down. Lying next to Vielwerth, Unteroffizier Holle smoked a cigarette and inhaled deeply. The Feldwebel scanned the terrain as far as the forest. Nothing. No sign of the enemy. Gefreiter Schindler's voice broke the stillness:

"Have the French really cleared out, or are they just tricking us, Feldwebel?"

"No idea. If we . . ."

Vielwerth was interrupted by the rattle of machine-gun fire. Bullets whistled from bushes and hedges. To the right of the company headquarters section a burst of machine-gun fire sawed off the tops of the bushes.

"Take cover!" roared Vielwerth.

The next burst ripped at waist level through the bushes behind which the section had dug its shallow foxholes. Then there was a dull rumble from the road. Looking up, Vielwerth spotted the first enemy tank; it was rolling straight toward the battalion. There were more behind it.

"The enemy is forming up for a counterattack," said Leutnant Klein.

The Leutnant seemed quite undisturbed by the dangerous situation. Seconds later, heavy machine-gun fire began coming in from the flank. The tanks advanced quickly. They halted and fired at intervals, providing mutual support. But the Pak were ready and the first French tank was soon knocked out. The second one left the road and rolled through a patch of woods. Vielwerth saw it crash its way through the slender trees before reemerging on the near side of the trees.

A squad from the 1st Platoon was trying to work its way over to the right to silence the machine gun. As the men dashed across a clearing, they were caught by a long burst of machine-gun fire. Several of the squad lay dead; the rest were wounded. Vielwerth could hear them calling for help. He pressed his lips together. The Feldwebel felt fear, but anger and sadness as well.

"We're cut off, Feldwebel!" reported Unteroffizier Holle, who was lying to the far right.

But the German defensive fire soon halted the French armored attack and the threat to the 1st Company was averted. As darkness was falling, a runner arrived from the battalion with orders for Hauptmann Schmitt to leave the forward strongpoint for the night and pull back to the main line of resistance. There was a danger that the enemy might break through during the night and trap the entire company.

✠

The 1st Company remained in the main line of resistance until 25 May. The regiment provided proof of its ability to hold out, fending off repeated French counterattacks. As the regiment was being relieved, the enemy suddenly began laying down heavy harassing fire. Rounds burst along the entire length of the main line of resistance. The men of the 36th Infantry Division moved back in stages, frequently scrambling for cover as rounds whistled in. But the long march and the danger were soon over. The men occupied reserve positions; having seen an example of the enemy's firepower, they did so with greater care this time.

The deep foxholes soon proved their value when it was discovered that the new positions were still within range of the French guns. Even collecting rations was a dangerous undertaking. Vielwerth had to dive for cover more than once with his a mess kit full of chow.

The company was not relieved until 30 May. It marched into rest positions in the rear near Autrecourt. The 36th Infantry Division saw no more frontline action during the French Campaign. A period of quiet began for Feldwebel Vielwerth and his men. On 1 August he received the Infantry Assault Badge. Ten days later the division was transferred back to Germany, where it was reorganized as a motorized infantry division.

On 1 October 1940 Erich Vielwerth was promoted to Oberfeldwebel. He spent ten months at home before his unit was sent to eastern Germany on 2 June.

BUNKER SPECIALIST

In the early morning hours of 22 June 1941, Army Group North moved off on the extreme left wing of the German forces massed for the invasion of the Soviet Union. On the right was the LVI Panzer Corps under General von Manstein; on the left the XXXXI Panzer Corps under General of Armored Troops Reinhardt. The two corps made up Panzer Group 4 under the command of Generaloberst Hoeppner.

The objective given the Commander-in-Chief of Army Group North, Generalfeldmarschall Ritter von Leeb, was clear: Leningrad. Leningrad, with the Russian war port of Kronstadt, was the key to the north. This fortress on the Gulf of Finland was the cornerstone of the Russian defensive line. The German operational plans called for its capture.

The Chief-of-Staff of the XXXXI Panzer Corps was Oberst Röttinger, a member of the General Staff. The armored formation consisted of the 1st and 6th Panzer Divisions, the 36th Motorized Infantry Division and the 269th Infantry Division. The SS *Totenkopf* Division formed the reserve of the panzer group.

General of Armored Troops Reinhardt had received orders to break through the frontier fortifications near and east of Tauroggen and then advance as quickly as possible toward the Düna River. The objective was to establish bridgeheads across the river near and upstream from Jakobstadt in preparation for a further advance toward the northeast.

In addition, the corps was to advance rapidly toward Schaulen in order to support the advance of the 18th Army. The powerful enemy forces suspected to be there were to be destroyed.

Several army-level separate artillery battalions and one *Nebelwerfer* regiment, as well as Flak and pioneer battalions, were placed under the general's command to assist him in achieving his dual mission. The divisional artillery of the 36th Motorized Infantry Division was moved into the staging area of the 1st Panzer Division to reinforce the armored division.

Oberfeldwebel Vielwerth and his men experienced the eerie silence that hung over the front during the night of 21–22 June 1941. At 0305 hours the deceptive quiet in the corps' sector was shattered. With a sudden crash, 550 artillery pieces, rocket launchers and railway guns opened fire. The barrage rolled over the Baltic landscape for forty minutes. Even as the last salvoes were falling, the pioneers and infantry began moving forward. The first obstacles were cleared as German rounds fell on identified enemy positions just ahead of the advancing troops. Then the two panzer divisions, the spearhead of the attack, rolled forward. Behind them came the 36th Motorized Infantry Division.

German and Russian tanks met for the first time in the northern sector on 23 and 24 June near Rossienie. For the first time Oberfeldwebel Vielwerth witnessed the apparent invulnerability of the Soviet KV-I and KV-II tanks. These forty-six- and fifty-four-ton giants were not stopped until the artillery engaged them over open sights. After initially following the 1st Panzer Division, the 36th Motorized Infantry Division veered off to the right when it was even with the armored division. It then advanced to the northeast and parallel to the 1st Panzer Division.

During the tank fighting the 36th Motorized Infantry Division occupied a front oriented to the south between Saudininkai and Siaulenai. Enemy tanks that broke through had to be destroyed with explosive charges. They had simply driven through the ranks of the 1st Panzer Division and, in spite of being hit several times with special hollow-charge rounds, rolled through to the infantry before being stopped by a few determined men.

During the tank fighting Feldwebel Bunzel of the 1st Panzer Regiment's 6th Company destroyed three KV-Is from a range of only five meters.

The enemy unit involved was the well-trained 2nd Tank Division. Part of the Soviet 3rd Tank Corps, it put up stubborn resistance and lost a large number of its tanks. On closer examination it was found that the Soviet tanks were armored with 80-mm plates all round, with the armor protection increasing to 120 millimeters in the most vulnerable locations.

The huge tanks were armed with a 76-mm (KV-I) or 152-mm (KV-II) gun. Men of the 36th Motorized Infantry Division found a KV-II whose armor had been gouged by seventy hits. None had penetrated the armor of the Soviet tank. It had finally been stopped when a Teller mine blew off one of its tracks. A surviving divisional order issued by the 1st Panzer Division provides an insight into the problem presented by the heavily armored enemy tanks:

> Because our tanks and antitank guns are ineffective against these tanks, we must try to stop the enemy tanks by shooting at their tracks and immobilizing them so that artillery or Flak can engage them. Whenever possible, they are to be blown up with explosives . . .

The Soviet 48th Rifle Division was identified opposite the 36th Motorized Infantry Division. It was an elite unit that defended tenaciously. The Wehrmacht Report of 26 June 1941 reported on the armored fighting: "After two days of fighting, a tremendous tank battle north of Kovno was brought to a victorious conclusion. Several enemy divisions were surrounded and destroyed."

Even at this early stage of the campaign it had become obvious to Vielwerth that they were facing an enemy significantly more dangerous than the one they had met in France. He and his platoon—he had since become a platoon leader—were involved in numerous small engagements before they reached the Düna, the initial objective of the XXXXI Panzer Corps.

In the first seven days of the Russian campaign, the 36th Motorized Infantry Division covered three-hundred kilometers. Under the command of Oberst Walter Fries, the 87th Motorized Infantry Regiment pushed on as fast as it could go. Oberst Fries, who had taken command of the regiment in November 1940, had succeeded in completing the motorization of his new regiment prior to the beginning of the eastern campaign. The unit pressed on through Ostriv toward the Stalin Line.

The assault through the Stalin Line was a frightful experience for the infantry. They stormed forward through marshy terrain with well-camouflaged field positions and past blockhouses, some of which concealed fortified bunkers. Wiry and unbelievably tough, Oberst Walter Fries led his regiment from the front in spite of his forty-seven years.

In command of the division's other regiment—the 118th Motorized Infantry Regiment—was Oberst Carl Caspar. These were two men Generalleutnant Otto-Ernst Ottenbacher, the division commander, could depend on in any situation. The examples set by these two officers affected every soldier in the two formations. The leadership enjoyed by the division was the main reason for its great success in the field. Oberfeldwebel Vielwerth also distinguished himself among the bunkers of the Stalin Line. But his finest hour was yet to come.

The attack on Pskov began on 7 July. The assault was led by the armored units. The 36th Motorized Infantry Division followed the tanks off to the left. Swinging out to the east, the 1st Rifle Regiment, which was part of Battle Group Westhoven (of the 1st Panzer Division), reached the airfield. While Generalmajor Krüger's units were capturing an undamaged bridge across the Tserjoha, Generalleutnant Ottenbacher led the 36th in an assault on Pskov.

The motorized infantry rolled into the burning city, which was taken on 9 July following a twenty-four-hour fight. The three fast divisions of the XXXXI Panzer Corps stormed along the major road through Luga. It seemed as if the Russians were on the run, but they were only luring the corps into an area of marshy terrain unsuitable for tanks. On 12 July 1941 the attack bogged down along a line Sapolje-Pljussa.

The XXXXI Panzer Corps was then turned northward. The three divisions worked their way north through difficult terrain over a marshy road. The Luga River was reached. Near Gdov on Lake Peipus, the 36th Infantry Division was able to smash a large group of enemy forces. The divisions of the corps were then in a favorable position from which to launch the attack on Leningrad. Only 115 kilometers separated them from the city. However, Panzer Group 4 was held in its Luga bridgeheads on orders of the Armed Force High Command. The 87th Motorized Infantry Regiment relieved the elements of the 1st Panzer Division in the Ssabsk bridgehead.

Oberst Fries took command in the hotly contested Luga bridgehead on 19 July. The Soviets launched repeated attacks on the German positions in an attempt to break through. All were repulsed. A Russian attack against the sector held by the 1st Battalion of the 87th Infantry Regiment struck Vielwerth's platoon. The Oberfeldwebel had installed his machine guns in such a way that their fields of fire overlapped. The enemy attack collapsed under the fire of these guns.

The 2nd Platoon distinguished itself in the bridgehead battles and, on 1 August, Oberfeldwebel Vielwerth was awarded the Iron Cross, First Class. The attack on Leningrad resumed on 8 August. Elements of the 36th Motorized Infantry Division broke out of the Ssabsk bridgehead and advanced toward the northwest. The rest of the division remained to the right of the 1st Panzer Division, which was awaiting the arrival of the 8th Panzer Division. The attack then continued and the Kingisepp-Volosovo rail line was reached.

On 13 August Generalleutnant Ottenbacher received the Knight's Cross. In mid-August the LVI Panzer Corps was detached from Panzer Group 4 because of a crisis reported near Staraya Russa. For the second time Generaloberst Hoeppner was forced to halt the attack on Leningrad. The 36th Motorized Infantry Division was turned around to secure the long left flank. With every day that the German units were held up west and northwest of Krasnogvardeysk, the Soviet high command was able to send more forces to Leningrad.

In early September the 87th Motorized Infantry Regiment reached Mikino Forest, about fifteen kilometers west of Krasnogvardeysk. Oberst Fries had his regiment go into position in the forest. The order to attack could have come at any time. The regiment's vehicles were moved into well-camouflaged forest positions. The weather changed frequently. One day the sun would shine brightly, the next would bring rain showers. In their positions the men could hear the rumble of guns. The regiment's 1st Company sat in its tents as the rain poured down. In the forest, the regiment was invisible to the Russian aircraft that flew overhead to bomb the road over which German tanks and artillery were moving up.

The regiment's sister unit—the 118th Motorized Infantry Regiment—was nearby. It was also concealed in the forest.

Oberfeldwebel Vielwerth made yet another inspection of his platoon's tents. The attack was supposed to finally get under way on 7 September. Everyone hoped this was true, as the uncertainty frayed the nerves more than anything else. Vielwerth arrived to inspect the tents of one of his squads. He was greeted by the squad leader, Unteroffizier Mahr.

"Oberfeldwebel, when are going to do something?"

"If I only knew, Mahr," answered Vielwerth. "Not even the commander of the regiment knows that."

In fact Vielwerth had seen Oberst Fries in the company command post an hour earlier and had heard the company commander's talking with the "old man". When asked about the attack he had only shrugged his shoulders.

"But all that suggests that its about to begin," interjected Leutnant Klein, the platoon leader of the 1st Platoon.

"And today's assault tactics training has been called off," added Unteroffizier Weiser.

"Then I would like to think we'll soon hear something," said the Leutnant, closing the debate.

During the previous days the platoons had carried out assault training. The line of fortifications surrounding Leningrad was said to include large numbers of bunkers. This would mean plenty of work, but the regiment had learned in France how to deal with such fortifications.

By the time the Oberfeldwebel was summoned to the company command post an hour later, it had begun to drizzle. The air was damp. Soon afterward Vielwerth and Oberfeldwebel Maier, who was in charge of the 3rd Platoon, arrived. The company commander informed them that the attack was to begin that very day. An hour later the 1st Company moved into its assembly area. Dense undergrowth greeted the men. It was now raining heavily.

Obergefreiter Külker, leader of a machine-gun team since France, muttered: "Not exactly ideal attack weather."

"Never mind. The main thing is we're moving again," added another.

The company established contact with the companies to its left and right. The hour of the attack had arrived. Oberfeldwebel Vielwerth led his platoon through the thick undergrowth. To his right the neighboring platoon didn't have it so easy; it was forced to advance across open terrain. Initially, there was no resistance. Were the Soviets laying a trap for them?

The previous evening a patrol had reported that there were only weak enemy forces in the village in front of the platoon. However, a morning reconnaissance patrol found that the Russians had reinforced their forces in the village; the patrol came under heavy small-arms and even antitank-gun fire. Gefreiter Glöcke, the platoon runner was standing near his platoon leader. He whispered: "There go our tanks, Oberfeldwebel."

Vielwerth nodded and listened to the dull rumble of tank engines. Somehow the noise had a heartening effect on the men. Knowing that their tanks were attacking and would place direct fire on the bunkers was a great relief to the men and the platoon leader. Vielwerth repeatedly looked to the left, but his view of the tanks was blocked by the thick bushes.

The tanks moved around the last line of bushes and suddenly opened fire on the village from the left flank. The crash of tank cannon mixed with the softer crack of the enemy guns. The rattle of machine guns added to the din. Then Vielwerth reached the last line of bushes, about 150 meters from the village. So far his platoon had not been fired on and had seen nothing of the enemy. The Oberfeldwebel crawled to the edge of the row of bushes and scanned the ground in front of him. At the edge of the village he saw a field position. A look to the left revealed that the tanks were only 150 meters away.

"Second platoon: Rush the position! Move out!"

The men got to their feet behind the Oberfeldwebel and began running toward the village. Not a shot was directed at them. The platoon leader ordered his men to slow their pace to a walk. Soon they had passed the village.

Where were the Russians? Had they fled into the woods behind the village after the first exchange of fire with the tanks? The platoon had scarcely reached the first group of houses when the battalion commander appeared.

"Keep moving, Vielwerth! The Russians have pulled back. We're going to follow."

Then he disappeared in the direction of the 1st Platoon. Vielwerth ordered his men to advance. The battalion reached some woods approximately one kilometer from the main line of fortifications. The woods were the objective of the day for 7 September 1941.

The 1st Company had just formed up when an alarming shout was heard: "Russians in the rear."

The Oberfeldwebel ran in the direction of the shout. But no matter how hard he looked, he could find no sign of any Russians. It must have

Erich with his brother Helmut, a member of the maintenance section of the 87th Infantry Regiment's 1st Battalion.

been some of the Russian troops who had fled the village after the tanks opened fire.

"We have to be careful. Weiser's squad: Secure to the rear! Mahr's and Külker's squads: Move ahead to the forward edge of the wood line! Be careful, the terrain climbs somewhat in front of the woods."

Soon afterward the company's 1st Platoon under Leutnant Klein marched off toward another village, which was situated to the company's left. According to the map Vielwerth was studying, the few roofs directly in front of the 2nd Platoon had to belong to the village of Mutaküla. Just behind it began the bunkers of the Soviet defensive line. Aerial photographs showed that the defensive positions in front of them were very well done. The pictures revealed exact details: Field positions, large and small bunkers, communications trenches, and a mighty antitank ditch that zigzagged along the entire system of positions.

Statements made by prisoners and information from Latvian deserters had revealed that the terrain in front of the antitank ditch had been heavily mined. While searching for a good location for the platoon command post, Vielwerth came upon a hut that was half-concealed in the woods. When the platoon headquarters personnel moved in they found the floor was under water. The rain of the past few days had flooded the hut but, with the help of several layers of logs and beams, they had soon erected a good command post.

The platoon dug in. Soon afterward a company runner arrived. "Oberfeldwebel, the company commander has ordered the 2nd Platoon to form a patrol. You are to send a noncommissioned officer to the company command post for instructions."

"Very well, Engels."

Vielwerth looked inquiringly toward Unteroffizier Mahr. The cheerful young man nodded to him.

"I'll go, Oberfeldwebel," he offered without waiting to be asked.

"Fine, Mahr! Take off and make sure you come back in one piece!"

Mahr was the platoon's best and most dependable noncommissioned officer. The humorous soldier had already led more than a dozen patrols and always came home with good results.

An hour passed, during which most of Vielwerth's thoughts were on his friend, who was out there on his own. Perhaps he had run into the enemy. Finally, the door of the platoon command post opened and Mahr appeared in the doorway. The Oberfeldwebel sprang to his feet.

"Did everything go alright, Mahr?"

"The best, Oberfeldwebel! I was in Mutaküla."

A circle of dusty faces stared at the Unteroffizier. Mutaküla was in the Russian position. The bunker line began directly behind it.

"Mahr we'll have to go back in right away! We must make sketches and obtain further details of the position. But you must be dog-tired."

"You can say that again, but I'll go with you anyway!" Mahr said.

He had been on his feet since early morning and had not had time to eat. The pair set out with three other men. By then it was late in the afternoon. It was still broad daylight and the five soldiers had to exploit every bit of cover. Vielwerth and Mahr led the way, followed at a distance by the three soldiers. They followed the same path Mahr had taken and soon reached the spot where the noncommissioned officer had been.

"There are the bunkers, Oberfeldwebel."

Vielwerth couldn't believe his eyes. One bunker after another; there was an embrasure almost every five meters. Suddenly, a Russian sentry appeared. He came out from behind one of the dugouts and walked straight toward the two Germans.

"Cover!" hissed Vielwerth.

The two ducked close to the ground. The sentry came nearer and nearer. He whistled to himself and gazed in the direction of the German positions. The Russian stopped two meters in front of the depression. The he turned round and disappeared again behind the bunkers.

"Damn!" sighed Mahr, "that was close!"

The Oberfeldwebel secured his pistol and put it back into its holster. Then he began sketching. To the right, a huge bunker towered far above the others. The muzzle of a gun projected menacingly from the lower level. Its muzzle seemed to be aimed right at the two Germans.

A new barn caught the Oberfeldwebel's eye off to the left. He had seen before how the Russians used such structures to camouflage their large bunkers. In addition, deserters had reported that the Russians had camouflaged some of their strongest bunkers in this way.

After a pause the Unteroffizier whispered: "If these bunkers are well-manned we'll have Hell to pay!"

The same thoughts had been running through Vielwerth's mind.

"We'll have to get a closer look at that barn," he whispered into his comrade's ear. Unteroffizier Mahr nodded, indicating he had understood.

"We'll have to split up. You three men behind us will provide cover. Mahr: Come with me. We'll cross the road one at a time."

The Oberfeldwebel went first. Bent low, he hurried across the road. As he ran he noticed there were no foot prints or wheel marks in the soft ground; a sign that the Russians had not tried to scout the German positions. Mahr followed the Oberfeldwebel. Dusk was beginning to fall. Soon it would be dark. Vielwerth spotted a Russian walking back and forth in a trench about 150 meters ahead.

Just then a horse-drawn wagon rolled out from behind the new barn, probably a rations or munitions wagon. If that were so the barn would have to be concealing a mighty bunker. A lone rider followed the wagon. A commissar? Further right a pair of rifle shots shattered the stillness, but the patrol remained undisturbed. Soon it would be night. They had to get back before it was completely dark. The Oberfeldwebel memorized the terrain. He wanted another sketch as well, so he moved behind the nearest house, where the view was better.

There was another round fired as Mahr followed. "Keep a sharp lookout, Mahr!"

The Unteroffizier scanned the surrounding area as Vielwerth completed his sketch. When he had finished, Vielwerth whispered: "Let's go! The three others will precede us."

The soldiers started back the way they had come, covered by the Unteroffizier and the platoon leader. Not until they had crossed the approximately 50-meter-wide area of open terrain did Mahr and Vielwerth leave their positions. A few shots were fired in their direction but, in the growing darkness, all were wide of the target. The five reached cover untouched. Vielwerth took time to inspect some earthworks that had been marked on the reconnaissance photo with a question mark. It turned out they were harmless; there were no new bunkers behind them.

When the patrol reached the German lines the battalion commander was waiting. Oberfeldwebel Vielwerth made his report, referring to the sketches he had made of the enemy positions. When he finished, the battalion commander offered him his hand.

"Thank you, Vielwerth. An outstanding job. Did you know we were all standing around here worrying about you?"

"Why, sir?" was the Oberfeldwebel's response.

"There's a number of Russians in that house scarcely twenty-five meters away. If they had noticed your patrol, things could have become damned difficult."

But the Russians had apparently failed to notice the patrol. It would have been a rude awakening for them, had the patrol thrown a few hand grenades through a window.

"I want to go up there with you, Vielwerth," decided the battalion commander. "I have to get a look at what the battalion is facing."

The two men crept through the night. Their eyes had become used to the semi-darkness, and they caught sight of a patrol from the neighboring company. It, too, was working its way toward the Russian positions. The patrol crawled toward its objective. It turned out that the leader, a man with no experience at the front, was on his first patrol.

Finally, Vielwerth and the Major returned to the forward outpost. During the night Vielwerth and his men were awakened by firing from the houses occupied by the 1st Platoon. A Russian scouting party had been spotted reconnoitering the German positions; the entire enemy patrol was wiped out.

As 8 September dawned every man in the regiment was certain the attack was about to begin. But nothing happened. The only activity was Soviet harassing fire on the wooded sector manned by the 1st Company. The artillery fire occasionally became heavy, resulting in dead and wounded. The 2nd Platoon alone lost three men.

The Soviets were prepared to meet the German assault. The two defensive positions around Leningrad were manned by worker militias and active troops. Twenty divisions of Red militia—a total of 300,000 men—waited in the bunkers and field positions. General Sakharov, the commander of the city of Leningrad, had moved five brigades—each consisting of 10,000 men—into positions at the edge of the city. Leningrad had become one of the most heavily fortified centers in the Soviet Union.

On the evening of 8 September Oberfeldwebel Vielwerth accompanied his company commander into no-man's-land. The commanders of the battalion's remaining companies joined them. The foray was intended to familiarize the company commanders with the terrain over which their units were to attack.

The attack was to be spearheaded by the infantry. The corps' tanks would advance as the second wave as soon as the infantry had breached the Soviet defensive ring. With their hundreds of bunkers, emplaced guns and antitank ditches, the two defensive positions were an ideal battleground for well-trained infantry assault squads.

Led by Oberfeldwebel Vielwerth, the company commanders scouted the enemy positions. The small group then returned safely to the German lines. During the night *Nebelwerfer* were moved forward to support the pre-attack bombardment.

As the sun rose on the morning of 9 September, it heralded a bright, sunny day. There was hectic activity in the staging area of the 1st Battalion. The forward observers for the *Nebelwerfer* reported to their battery chiefs. The batteries had carried out adjustment fire on 7 and 8 September. Oberfeldwebel Vielwerth checked his platoon. The leaders of the machine-gun squads checked their guns one more time. Ammunition boxes were filled with belts of ammunition. Each member of the platoon was issued several hand grenades. The mood was one of subdued excitement.

Shortly before 0800 hours everything was ready. The men waited in their jumping-off positions for the bombardment to begin. Vielwerth looked at his watch. As the second hand made its last revolution and the minute hand jumped to the figure twelve, the German artillery opened up. Heavy rounds roared over the heads of the waiting soldiers for an hour. Salvoes of rockets roared into the sky on trails of fire and fell on the enemy positions. Within the company, the 2nd Platoon under Oberfeld-webel Vielwerth was on the right. To its left was the 1st Platoon, while the 3rd Platoon remained in the rear in reserve. To the right of Vielwerth's platoon was the 2nd Company. Each company was assigned a Russian deserter who knew the location of the enemy's minefields.

A flare rose into the sky.

"There's the signal, Oberfeldwebel!" called Obergefreiter Külker. "Move out!"

The Oberfeldwebel pushed his helmet strap under his chin and began to move. Together with his platoon he reached the place he had located while on patrol. Looking back, Vielwerth saw the battalion advancing in battle order. Moving forward with the troops were prime movers that were towing antitank and infantry guns. Farther to the rear the first tanks rumbled out of the forest.

As they advanced, the Oberfeldwebel shouted the objective to his squads. The squad leaders raised their arms, indicating they understood. As usual, the platoon leader had deployed two squads forward and one behind. German salvoes continued to roar over the heads of the advancing infantry. In the meantime, the Soviet batteries had begun to answer. There was a steady stream of incoming and outgoing rounds. The Russian rounds landed in the forest behind the advancing troops. The Soviets were obviously trying to knock out the *Nebelwerfer* batteries.

Finally, the 2nd Platoon reached the road. "Report to the company: Have reached the road!"

The runner went on his way. He had just disappeared when the enemy spotted the platoon. The Russians opened fire with their bunker guns. Two rounds hammered into the earth not far from the Oberfeldwebel. Dirt and lumps of clay rained down on the soldiers, who had quickly taken cover.

"Through that depression!" ordered Vielwerth, realizing that the right gun bunker was firing. As they reached the depression the fake barn let its mask drop. A gun barrel was visible. Flames spurted from the muzzle. An antitank gun commander moved up with 2nd Platoon to scout the area.

"There's your target, that barn over there!" instructed Vielwerth. "Check!" nodded the Unteroffizier.

He ran back to his gun under enemy rifle fire. The antitank gun was moved forward, while accompanying infantry answered the Russian rifle fire. Rifle fire crackled from the ditch in which Vielwerth's platoon was pinned down. Külker's machine gun poured bursts of fire into identified enemy targets. Shells crashed all around. Machine-gun fire chewed up the rims of the ditches; they were heavy Maxim machine guns, recognizable by their typical low rate of fire. The Russians answered every bullet fired by Vielwerth's platoon with accurate fire. Vielwerth stared at the terrain in front of his platoon. There was no way his men could get across without being cut down.

"There are mines there and there," warned the Russian deserter.

Before the platoon could attack, Vielwerth had to arrange supporting fire. He observed the line of bunkers carefully, noting the places from which most of the fire was coming. He gave the series of targets to the nearest machine gun, the one commanded by Külker. The machine gun rattled. The Soviets answered immediately, and the accurate burst silenced the German gun. Vielwerth crawled over to the machine gun.

"150 ahead, just to the right of the gun bunker, enemy machine gun." The gunner looked in the designated direction.

"Identified!" he reported.

The gunner had to move slightly to place the target under fire. At that instant there was the crack of a rifle shot and the leader of the machine-gun squad slumped over his gun. A litter bearer ran forward to administer first aid to the wounded man. The Russian defensive fire intensified. Vielwerth realized that an attack here was impossible. His platoon would be decimated if he sent it across the open area.

"Pass this on to the company commander: Unable to advance here!"

The report was passed from man to man. The noise of battle had become so loud in the meantime that the soldiers had to shout to make themselves heard by comrades only a few meters away. The situation was desperate.

Vielwerth racked his brains trying to think of what he could do to advance without suffering unbearable casualties. He knew every man in his platoon. He was responsible for each one. He would sacrifice none of their lives if there were any other possibility. He had to act. Waiting here until he was hit was not the right thing to do. Leutnant Zeller of the machine-gun platoon came over to the 2nd Platoon.

"I'm looking for a place for a heavy machine-gun squad. The company commander has sent me to give you support, Vielwerth."

"There to the right, sir. There should also be a good field of fire from that bend over there."

The men of the machine-gun squad moved forward laboriously with their heavy gun, utilizing every gully and ditch. Oberfeldwebel Vielwerth directed the platoon leader twenty meters farther to the right, where there was adequate cover to allow the heavy machine gun to be set up. Soon the men had assembled their heavy machine gun.

Vielwerth had meanwhile located the 1st Platoon in a group of bushes to his right. It might just be possible to sneak up on the enemy positions from there unseen. Vielwerth saw several wounded crawling toward the rear. Leutnant Klein's unit had also taken casualties. A look at his watch showed the Oberfeldwebel that they had been pinned down there for an hour.

Vielwerth signaled his reserve squad to work its way forward to the group of bushes. The squad's leader, Obergefreiter Külker, a veteran of the *Westwall* and France, knew what the signal meant. He and his squad began to work their way forward.

"Platoon: Move over to the left to that vegetation!" Vielwerth ordered.

He was the first to make the risky dash across the open space. After a few meters machine-gun fire forced him to take cover. Just then there was a terrific blast. An artillery round had struck the ditch where the heavy machine-gun squad had taken up position. The next man across, Unteroffizier Mahr, reported that the leader of the machine-gun platoon had been badly wounded. His own platoon's litter bearer had also been seriously wounded.

At that critical moment Vielwerth raised his head and listened. He heard the sound of aircraft engines. Looking up, he saw Stukas with their characteristic, bent gull-wings.

"Break out the air identification panels!" he ordered.

Then he began to count. There were thirty-seven machines, approaching in three groups. All along the width of the sector white signal flares hissed into the sky. They indicated the locations of the forward German troops to the Stukas. Hauptmann Cläsgen's company and a neighboring company were already so close to the bunker positions that the Stukas dared not attack there.

Somewhat farther to the rear the dive-bombers put their noses down and howled toward the positions of the Soviet heavy weapons. Oberfeldwebel Vielwerth's men watched the spectacle in fascination. The ear-splitting noise of the sirens, the thunder of engines and the high-pitched howl of falling bombs were all drowned out by the explosions of the heavy bombs. Vielwerth felt the earth tremble beneath him with each detonation. Huge, dense balls of smoke rolled upward, growing and expanding as they climbed higher into the sky.

"Now maybe we can get something done!" shouted Obergefreiter Külker during a pause between two bomb blasts.

As the last of the Stukas pulled up, the Soviets resumed firing. They had rightly deduced that the German infantry would launch its attack on the heels of the dive-bombers.

Vielwerth called to his men: "Farther to the left!—Farther to the left! Through the ditches!"

His orders were passed from man to man. The two squads followed him. They advanced slowly. A machine gun stayed back at the side of the road, pinning down the enemy with accurate bursts of fire. The leader of the machine-gun squad was already working his way forward, looking for a new position for his gun. Oberfeldwebel Vielwerth reached the few houses of the village. He came upon a tank positioned between the buildings.

The tank opened fire on the Soviet guns. There was a painful roar in Vielwerth's ears each time the 75-mm gun fired.

"Only another fifty meters and the platoon will be in the cover of the houses," he called to Unteroffizier Weiser, who had joined him.

The battalion mortars lay down a final protective fire during harsh winter fighting.

Vielwerth's men ran, crawled and burrowed their way into the village, until they had all reached safety. The platoon leader considered his next move very carefully. There was only one thing to do: Tackle the bunkers! The Russian guide urged him on. He had tied a bag on his back and had filled it with hand grenades taken from the wounded men. The deserter was Ukrainian. He was later severely wounded at the antitank ditch.

"Oberfeldwebel, it's the company commander."

Hauptmann Cläsgens appeared between the houses, having moved forward to the location of the 1st Platoon.

"How do you want to handle this, Vielwerth?" he asked.

The Oberfeldwebel gestured toward the bunker, which was spitting fire.

"The platoon will attack from here and take them out one at a time, sir."

"Good luck, Vielwerth!"

Before the Oberfeldwebel were the wounded of the 1st Platoon. Occasional cries were heard. Calls for the medic rang out above the noise of the fighting. If casualties continued to pile up, the attack would bog down among the bunkers before it had a chance to get going. Out of the corner of his eye Vielwerth saw two medics crawling forward to the wounded under heavy fire. He took a deep breath.

"First Squad: Follow me. We're going to make a dash for it. The other two squads will lay down covering fire."

The Oberfeldwebel jumped up and began to run. He had barely taken a few steps when fire began to come in from the farthest house on the left. A second later a machine gun began to fire from in front and to the right. A member of the 1st Platoon shouted to Vielwerth: "Watch out! There are Russians in the houses to the left!"

The Oberfeldwebel stifled a curse. This was bad. If he and his platoon continued to advance, these enemy soldiers would be in their rear. They would have to be eliminated. But they were in the neighboring sector and his mission was more important to the success of the attack. Farther right, where Obergefreiter Külker and his squad were in position, hectic machine-gun fire rang out. The Russians responded with several rounds fired in the direction of the machine gun. Two emplaced Russian machine guns joined in. Vielwerth heard a painful scream. At the same time the German machine gun stopped firing. Seconds later he heard a call:

"Our squad leader has been killed!"

That meant Külker! The old Obergefreiter, his comrade from France, a friend and reliable comrade-in-arms. More and more calls for the medics reached Vielwerth's ears. Casualties were inevitable in this terrible fire from the many dugouts and bunkers. And if they stayed there, things could only get worse. They had to move forward.

Vielwerth concentrated. Then he jumped to his feet and ran. One of his men followed. Bullets whistled past the two men. The Oberfeldwebel leapt into cover. Bursts of machine-gun fire whipped over the shallow trenches. Suddenly, the company commander ran past and threw himself to the ground as machine-gun fire turned its fire on him. Vielwerth got up and ran another half-dozen meters before taking cover again. They repeated this process several times, each time expecting to feel the impact of a bullet striking home.

Vielwerth hurried on. His training kicked in and everything became an almost instinctual response.

He came to a potato field. The furrows gave him cover. The tall plants made him invisible, but also blocked his view of the fire-spitting bunker. More men followed. Unknowingly, the pair had brought the whole platoon with them. Many men were dead or wounded.

"Let's rest here a minute, Oberfeldwebel!" gasped Oberschütze Heil. But there was no time. They had to take advantage of the opportunity they had been given.

"Let's go!" ordered the Oberfeldwebel.

Finally, they were far ahead of the other platoons, far ahead of the battalion and the regiment and right in the midst of the enemy.

"Where the fuck is that antitank ditch?" swore Vielwerth.

According to the aerial reconnaissance photo, it should have been right in front of him, yet it was nowhere to be seen.

"Take care that you don't fall in!" answered a voice not two meters in front of him.

Vielwerth crawled another meter and saw that the antitank ditch, which he had imagined had a high rim, actually fell away steeply to a depth of about five meters. He crawled forward and measured the distance to the bottom of the ditch. An excited voice behind him said, "at least five meters!"

"There's somebody down there," called one of the men behind him.

More soldiers jumped down into the antitank ditch. One moment they were there, the next they had disappeared. Someone waved to Vielwerth from down in the ditch. He recognized the company commander. Then the Oberfeldwebel jumped too, and landed with a painful thud on the bottom of the ditch. They were safe from the hail of bullets for a while.

Suddenly Leutnant Klein of the 1st Platoon appeared from the right. He and a few of his men had also worked their way to the antitank ditch. Ahead was a grassy valley. The nearest cover was behind some houses, about sixty meters away.

"Watch out!" called the Hauptmann. "It might be mined."

The rear wall of the antitank ditch was sloped, and the men had no difficulty scrambling up. Suddenly Unteroffizier Mahr appeared beside the platoon leader. Behind him someone stood up and ran toward the houses, straight through the valley. He was zigzagging to avoid the Russian rifle fire. Unteroffizier Weiser reached the nearest house and disappeared inside. Vielwerth had just stood up and was about to follow when he heard a curse behind him.

Looking around, he saw Oberschütze Heil hanging onto the wall of the antitank ditch, afraid to jump. The Russians were conducting target practice on him. Bullets chipped lumps of earth and clay from the vertical wall on either side of Heil. Vielwerth ran over and, grabbing him by the legs, hauled him down at the last second. A burst of machine-gun fire smacked into the wall where only a half-second before the Oberschütze had been hanging.

Heil landed hard and cursed loudly, but he had been saved. Vielwerth turned his attention to the front again. Where was Mahr? Had he disappeared? Then he spotted him striding through the grassy valley on his long legs.

"Follow him!" called the platoon leader, beginning to run.

But he stumbled after a few steps and fell to the ground. Bullets whistled past over his head. Stumbling had saved his life. A large piece of rock projected from the valley floor. In an instant the Oberfeldwebel was behind it. Bullets whistled all around him; some smacked into the rock, whistling and howling away in all directions.

He had to move on. If he stayed there he was finished. Again he took a deep breath and began to run toward the enemy. The air seemed to be made of steam. His lungs were on fire. Finally, he reached the protection of a house and threw himself to the ground. Two more men risked the dangerous obstacle course and joined him. Sixty meters across open ground under fire was an eternity!

"We'll stay to the right of the path. The 1st Platoon is supposed to advance to the left," Vielwerth ordered.

Slowly, the four men climbed up the slope toward the Russian positions. Luckily, the houses provided adequate cover. Gradually, their breathing returned to normal.

Suddenly there was firing behind them and to the left. The four men of the 2nd Platoon immediately pressed themselves into the earth. The bullets passed above them.

"We'll have to reach the trenches in the next dash or they'll wipe us out!" called Mahr.

Together they jumped up, ran toward the nearest Russian trench and slid inside. There were no Russians to be seen. But what would it be like beyond the bend in the trench? What was awaiting them there?

One of the platoon runners caught up with Vielwerth and his small group. The man was out of breath. "That was a bastard, Oberfeldwebel," he gasped.

Vielwerth clapped him on the shoulder. "The main thing is you're here."

"It looks better already," announced Gefreiter Biermann.

At that point they numbered eight. They had two machine guns. One of the gunners had been wounded, but the squad leader had brought the machine gun and another member of the gun crew with the ammunition boxes. A lively firefight was in progress behind them and to the left. That was where the 1st Platoon was supposed to advance. Then there was a crash as a hand grenade detonated.

"Russians from the left!" shouted the runner.

"Fire!" shouted Vielwerth.

But the Gefreiter did nothing. It was the first time the nineteen-year-old had to fire at a live target, and Vielwerth knew what was going through the young man's mind. But he also knew that the runner was finished if he didn't open fire on the Russians at once. Vielwerth urged him on. It was a grotesque and macabre situation, but it was the only chance of saving the young man's life. Finally, Gefreiter Göcke opened fire.

More Russians appeared from the left. Apparently the 1st Platoon had broken into the Russian positions. The Red Army troops were trying to withdraw and were firing in the direction of the 2nd Platoon, which was blocking their path.

"Get a machine gun up here!" the platoon leader called.

The machine gun went into position and, when another group of Russians appeared, it began to fire. Vielwerth glanced at his watch. It was 1330 hours. They had been fighting for four hours.

"Runner: report the following to the company commander!—The First is in the forward Russian trenches!"

Gefreiter Göcke started on his way. When he returned a few minutes later he brought with him three more members of the platoon he had picked up on his way back to the antitank ditch. The platoon was now eleven men strong. The Oberfeldwebel, his narrow face crusted with dust and mud, took only a few moments to decide on his next move. He and his ten men would expand their foothold in the enemy position. It proved fortunate that they had so many hand grenades with them, as rifles and machine guns were of little use against bunkers.

"The first machine gun will remain here to secure the point of penetration."

Vielwerth assigned each of his men a specific role. Then it was time. As Vielwerth reached the first bend in the trench line, he was met by rifle fire. It came from the left. But then there was firing from the right as well, which he had not expected.

"That must be one of ours, Oberfeldwebel!" called Unteroffizier Weiser.

"Break out the identification flag!"

The runner waved the flag and the firing stopped at once.

"That was close," observed Göcke as he rolled up the flag. Vielwerth determined that they were behind the new barn. He could see three Russian soldiers. The Oberfeldwebel gestured toward the barn.

"Mahr and Weiser: The three of us will throw hand grenades simultaneously."

He screwed off the cap and gripped the porcelain knob between the thumb and forefinger of his left hand.

"Throw!"

They ripped out the fuses, waited a few seconds and threw the hand grenades. There were three explosions from the barn, and the Russians left their cover and came out with raised hands.

"On to the bunker!" panted Vielwerth.

They stormed forward and reached the embrasures from which enemy machine guns were still firing, pinning down the German attackers. Vielwerth took out another hand grenade and stuck it through the embrasure. He heard it fall to the floor inside and ducked. There was a muffled boom as the grenade went off. Two further explosions followed. His two companions had pushed grenades through the other two embrasures.

The Russians in the bunker then came out with their hands above their heads. Vielwerth ran into the bunker and disabled the machine guns.

"That takes care of the first one. Move on!"

The next bunker was a small machine-gun post. More hand grenades were thrown and once again the Oberfeldwebel stormed into the bunker and took the surviving Russian troops prisoner. Vielwerth and his men hurried along the trench that linked the bunker line. In several places the trench had been collapsed by German artillery fire. There were dead Russian soldiers everywhere.

"Keep going! Keep going!" called the Oberfeldwebel.

"There's another machine-gun bunker!"

"Its no longer firing, probably empty," suggested Weiser.

But the Oberfeldwebel shook his head: "They're playing dead so they can catch us from behind. Get hand grenades and move forward!"

Hand grenades again flew through the embrasures and into the bunker. There were muffled explosions. Smoke rolled out. The roof of the bunker raised up, then collapsed.

The trench became ever narrower and the progress of Vielwerth and his men grew slower. But everything depended on a rapid advance. If the Soviets had a chance to reestablish themselves, it wouldn't be so easy to overcome the heavily fortified position. Oberfeldwebel Vielwerth climbed out of the trench and ran along its rim. He ran at a crouch, ready to jump back in at the first sound of gunfire.

From there he had a better view. There was one enemy position after another. The dugouts were overcome in rapid succession. Eleven men were storming the bunker line.

"There's another bunker to the rear. Unteroffizier Weiser: Take one man over there and smoke it out!"

The Unteroffizier ran the dozen meters to the bunker. The two men simultaneously stuck their hand grenades through the embrasure and waited for the explosions. But seconds later the grenades came flying back out through the embrasure. Reacting unbelievably quickly, the Russians had picked up the grenades and tossed them out of the bunker.

"Take cover!" screamed Weiser.

Both men threw themselves flat on the ground. The sound of the explosions deafened them and splinters struck their steel helmets. Schütze Lempke, who had accompanied the Unteroffizier, jumped up, pulled out his "08" pistol and ran toward the bunker entrance. Vielwerth heard the crack of pistol shots. Then all was still. It turned out that the crew of the bunker included a woman, who had been conscripted by the workers militia.

The small group of men took one bunker after another. Their appearance had obviously taken the Russians completely by surprise. The bunker crews came out with their hands up. There was some consternation when they realized how small the German force was but, by then, it was too late to offer resistance.

A short time later they stormed an artillery bunker. The Oberfeldwebel called a brief rest. All were on the threshold of total exhaustion. They had rolled up more than 400 meters of the main line of Russian positions and taken a total of fifty positions. Among these fifty positions were two artillery bunkers and six machine-gun bunkers. The new gun in the last bunker was fully intact. A large store of ammunition was piled nearby.

As they gasped for breath, the German troops realized that this gun could have inflicted heavy losses on the battalion and regiment. The Oberfeldwebel had just pulled off his boots to shake out the sand when a hand grenade exploded outside.

"Stay here! I'll check it out."

With these words Vielwerth ran into the open. Not thirty meters away was an enemy bunker. Heavy rifle fire was coming from it. The Oberfeldwebel took cover when a pair of bullets whizzed past overhead. Instinctively he reached into the hand grenade bag, but it was empty.

"Pass me a grenade!" he called back over his shoulder.

One was passed to him immediately. He pulled the fuse and tossed the grenade in the direction of the enemy bunker. But the grenade fell short and exploded in front of the bunker. Suddenly, Vielwerth noticed movement in the trench. It was a Russian soldier.

"*Stoy!*" shouted Vielwerth to him.

But the enemy soldier had already disappeared around a bend in the trench. Then a bayonet appeared, followed by a rifle and the pale face of the Russian. At the same instant there was a crack and a bullet whistled past the Oberfeldwebel's head.

Vielwerth reached for his rifle, which was fitted with a telescopic sight. He took aim and waited for the Russian to reappear. There! The bayonet! Vielwerth made a slight correction. Then the rifle reappeared, followed by the face. He squeezed the trigger. But the Russian fired at the same time. His bullet went wide. Vielwerth saw dirt fall from the wall of the trench close to the Russian's face. That must be where his bullet had struck.

Lying on their stomachs, the men of the platoon watched the cold-blooded duel between their platoon leader and the equally brave Russian. The act was repeated three times, then the Russian disappeared.

What had happened? Had Vielwerth hit the Russian? Was he dead? Before they moved on an assault squad met up with Vielwerth's Platoon. It was a squad from a neighboring company. The unit's commander had witnessed the daring attack by the small force and had sent reinforcements. Among the group were some pioneers, who were supposed to have facilitated the rolling up of this section of trench. However, like all the battalion's companies, they had been held up by the Russian fire.

"We're going to move on from here," explained the leader of the assault squad, a Leutnant.

"Good, then we'll set up a defensive position in the captured section of trench," replied the Oberfeldwebel.

Suddenly, someone called to Vielwerth from the artillery bunker, the one he had earlier missed with his hand grenade. His rifle at the ready,

Vielwerth ran over to the bunker. But there was no need. The Russians inside the bunker had convinced themselves that the Germans had taken the entire trench. They came out with hands raised. One after another they came out into the open. First ten, then twenty and finally twenty-five Russian soldiers. All surrendered to the Oberfeldwebel. Vielwerth delivered the prisoners to the platoon and returned to the bunker. To his surprise, he found that it had two levels.

A closer inspection of both parts of the bunker revealed that it had ten machine guns. A frontal attack against this position would have been doomed from the start. The assault squad went into action against the next bunker. Gunshots rang out and hand grenades exploded. Following that, the squad stormed into the bunker. Soon more prisoners joined those already in the hands of Vielwerth's Platoon. Erich Vielwerth looked at the prisoners. One of them, with a grazing head wound, looked familiar.

"Where did you get that wound?" asked one of the men who spoke some Russian. At first the man was reluctant to answer. Finally, however, he pointed to the Oberfeldwebel.

"It was that one there! He shot damned fast, and ruined my cap, too."

He hauled the torn cap from his pocket and showed it to the Oberfeldwebel. Vielwerth had one of his men give the Russian a cigarette. He had shown plenty of courage by even accepting combat after having the hat shot right off his head.

"Hard as iron, that fellow," observed Unteroffizier Weiser.

"Yes," agreed the Oberfeldwebel. "Good soldiers, damned good."

Vielwerth admired this man; he had fought extremely well. One after another the other members of the platoon turned up. The Oberfeldwebel posted outposts and sent a runner to establish contact with his company. When the runner failed to get through, he went himself. On the way to the company Vielwerth ran into the battalion commander, who had likewise moved up into the enemy position.

"Well done, Vielwerth! Without you and your brave men we would never have broken in. The Oberst has already been informed of your feat."

It turned out that Vielwerth's Platoon was the only one to have broken through the Russian main line of resistance and opened the gaps necessary for the assault into the enemy positions. With only a handful of men, Oberfeldwebel Vielwerth had rolled up the flank of a numerically far-superior enemy. In doing so he saved many lives which would have been lost in a frontal assault. At that point there was hectic activity in the captured sector. Everything the regiment could spare was poured into the gap.

Soon the word came down: "Make a passage for the tanks as quickly as possible!" Everyone pitched in to help knock down part of the vertical wall of the antitank ditch. Even the prisoners helped with the work without being ordered to do so. Harassing artillery fire flared up but was unable to halt the work. Soon the first tank rolled down the improvised ramp and rattled across the antitank ditch.

The men of Vielwerth's platoon were in the communication trenches—out of breath and with parched throats. Only the observers were active, scanning the approaches to the positions through their binoculars. Vielwerth ate some of the rations from his kit bag. Everything inside had caked together in the heat. At that point the reaction set in; the Oberfeldwebel felt totally exhausted. The past few hours, the heat, the running and the enemy fire had all frayed his nerves; more perhaps than his men suspected.

A runner appeared on the scene. "The 2nd Platoon is to form a patrol. Unteroffizier Mahr is to lead the patrol."

This time the company commander had specified Mahr. Not until then did Vielwerth realize that his friend had not yet spoken a word. Vielwerth tried to cheer up his comrade:

"What's up with you, Mahr? We've had great success."

"Yes, that's for sure, Oberfeldwebel," replied Mahr.

"You played a major role in the breakthrough, Mahr."

Erich Vielwerth poses for a propaganda photo with a comrade from Panzer Grenadier Division *"Großdeutschland."*

As he assembled the patrol, it seemed to the platoon leader that his normally so cheerful friend had been seized by an ominous premonition.

"Listen! Go through the trench until you reach that group of bushes there. From there you'll have a good chance of approaching the second Russian line unseen and . . ."

Vielwerth's instructions were interrupted by the crack of a rifle shot from the enemy lines. One of the men, an Obergefreiter who had been through the French campaign, tumbled from the edge of the trench. The Oberfeldwebel ran over and tried to sit him up, but the man was already dead.

"Did anyone see where the shot came from?" asked Vielwerth.

"It must have come from over there and to the right, Oberfeldwebel."

"Go and look there. It must have been a Russian who played dead before."

Three men stalked through the terrain, weapons at the ready.

Vielwerth bade farewell to the patrol: "Good luck Mahr, bring something back with you."

"Thank you, Oberfeldwebel!" replied Mahr.

Then he and his men disappeared into no-man's-land. A few moments later the battalion's heavy weapons began arriving. Now the attack could resume. The company commander deployed his forces. This time the 2nd Platoon was deployed behind the 1st and 3rd Platoons.

Russian machine guns soon began to rattle again. The crash of tank cannon was a sign that the German armor had reached the break-in area. Then the dry crack of Russian antitank guns joined in. The battle noises were coming from the forest in the battalion's line of attack. Apparently the Soviets had placed some of their reserves there. From the sound of the gunfire, there were tanks as well.

"At least fifteen of Ivan's tanks," observed Oberschütze Heil.

"Yes, there seems to be quite a few," confirmed the platoon leader.

The fighting became more bitter; the fire of both sides intensified into a rising and falling storm. For the second time the German attack became bogged down. The Soviets began using more mortars. The "potato throwers" hurled their 50-mm rounds into the advancing assault groups. As the rounds burst, they spread a fan of deadly shrapnel. Black, scorched circles marked the spots where the mortar rounds had gone off. Heavy and superheavy mortars participated in this devilish concert.

The plopping and howling, the bursting impacts and dull thump of enemy artillery merged into an infernal din. Oberfeldwebel Vielwerth pressed his lips together. Comrades were dying in front of him. Out there somewhere was Unteroffizier Mahr and his patrol. Vielwerth hoped that nothing had happened to him. Now mortar rounds began falling in the area where the 2nd Platoon was advancing.

"Take cover!"

The Oberfeldwebel threw himself into a pile of corn. Using both hands he quickly shoveled out a shallow depression for himself. An enemy machine gun swept the field with long bursts of fire. Every man of the platoon lay pressed to the earth, not daring to raise his head. Then the enemy tanks began firing on every bush, every raised feature—anything behind which German soldiers might be hiding.

The high-velocity rounds flitted low over the ground, cutting off the tops of bushes, striking the earth and raising fountains of dirt. German artillery rounds passed over the men on their way to the enemy-held woods. Treetops crashed to the ground. During a pause in the firing Vielwerth raised his head and saw a few men get up near the forest and run toward the trees.

Vielwerth turned to the runner: "Damn, where is our contact with the 1st Platoon?"

The Gefreiter looked up, bewildered.

"Move forward, we've got to reestablish contact!"

The platoon worked its way forward in stages. Just before the forest Vielwerth and his men met Mahr and his patrol. The Unteroffizier had brought back good results, but he still left Vielwerth with the same strange feeling. After Mahr had made his report Vielwerth said to him:

"You and your squad go to the rear of the platoon, Mahr."

After several more dashes the platoon reached the spot where men of the company had been caught in a mortar barrage. The Oberfeldwebel felt his mouth go dry as he saw some familiar faces among the dead. It was a horrible scene.

"Move on!" ordered Vielwerth hoarsely.

They came to the edge of the forest and found the company commander. Vielwerth made his report. The commander informed Vielwerth of his intentions, as he valued this man's opinions and suggestions. Again the Oberfeldwebel urged a further advance. As the advance continued, the Soviet mortars began firing again. The Oberfeldwebel ordered his men to zigzag as they ran. They dodged left and right to avoid the bursting rounds. Close behind him Vielwerth heard the panting breath of the runner, who had stayed close on his heels.

And so it went. After the first salvo the Oberfeldwebel's fear vanished. It was as if his continued survival removed the weight of his knowledge of the deadly danger. Suddenly, they came upon Leutnant Klein, the platoon leader of the 1st Platoon.

"Get down!" roared Klein. "We're under fire from antitank guns here!"

As he spoke there was a crack from the enemy positions, and a round struck the ground not five meters from Vielwerth, who had thrown himself down in a depression. For the first time he saw the foxholes of the men who had already dug in. The runner crawled forward to his platoon leader.

"Made it, Oberfeldwebel," he gasped between two deep breaths.

The Oberfeldwebel nodded. An Obergefreiter of Mahr's squad came running up. As he ran he called out: "Oberfeldwebel Vielwerth! Oberfeldwebel Vielwerth!"

"Here!" shouted Vielwerth.

An antitank round howled toward the man and struck the ground in front of him. But when the smoke cleared the Obergefreiter was unharmed. He crawled over to the platoon leader's hole and lay close to the runner.

"What is it, Wichkowski?"

"Unteroffizier Mahr has been wounded, Oberfeldwebel!" the man gasped. The news struck Vielwerth like a blow. Before him he saw his young, vital friend. All he could say in response was: "Badly?"

His eyes were fixed on the Obergefreiter's mouth. The latter shook his head: "The medic says he'll be alright."

"Thank God!"

Had his friend had a premonition that he would be wounded that day? Is that why he had been so quiet and withdrawn?

The firing from in front died down somewhat. By then the sun had sunk to the horizon, coloring the sky around it blood-red. Soon it would be dark.

"The Ivans have pulled back," Leutnant Klein reported to his opposite number. "We're to assemble and resume the advance."

"Thanks Herbert," replied the Oberfeldwebel.

Both men assembled their platoons. The advance resumed over muddy paths and roads.

Patrols ran forward to check out the situation. Suddenly, a gun roared in front of them. The harsh muzzle flash and the smoking trail of the round emptied the path in an instant. Everyone jumped into cover. Vielwerth leapt into a ditch at the side of the road. There was a second round fired and it hissed over the heads of the men.

"We can't stay here. We must get out of the danger zone.—Move left!"

The Oberfeldwebel jumped to his feet and started to run, but his foot had become entangled in some barbed wire. There was a third round fired. Summoning all his strength Vielwerth tore himself loose and raced toward a small hut. He reached the hut and, using hand and arm signals and shouts, assembled the men of his platoon in its cover. Amazingly, no one had been hit.

The enemy gun fired round after round in rapid succession. Between rounds there was the crackle of small-arms fire.

"You stay here; I'll look for the commander!" Vielwerth instructed his men. Finally, he found him.

"What's going on up front?" he asked the Hauptmann.

"The Russians have established a new position about 150 meters in front of us. Probably an artillery position with covering infantry."

"There! Do you hear that, sir?" asked Vielwerth. In the distance was the sound of engines and rattling tank tracks. What was in store for them tomorrow?

THE KNIGHT'S CROSS FOR ERICH VIELWERTH

The men were all awake when the first light of day appeared.

"I hope the field kitchen will get through, Oberfeldwebel," the runner said hopefully.

"That would be good," agreed Vielwerth.

He also longed for some warm food or coffee. But they were to be disappointed. The field kitchen didn't get through and they had to settle for the crusts of bread that one or another had stashed away in his knapsack. A short while later—the sun had just come up—the battalion moved out. The sounds of fighting rang out from farther to the left. The neighboring regiment must have begun its advance.

"The Ivans seem to have pulled back, Erich," observed Leutnant Klein.

"That would be nice, sir," replied Vielwerth with a smile. "Too nice to be true."

In the distance several bursts of machine-gun fire whipped through the early morning. The hectic bursts of German machine guns were easily distinguished from the slower rattling of the Soviet automatic weapons.

The 1st Battalion of the 87th Motorized Infantry Regiment met no resistance as it advanced. The dull drone of engines signaled the approach of German bombers, which were operating in support of the infantry attack on the powerful positions surrounding Leningrad. The He 111s passed over the battalion, their fuselages flashing silver in the morning sun. The bomber escort, fast Bf 109 fighters, circled round the bombers.

"They're on their way to Leningrad, Oberfeldwebel," said one of the men. "Perhaps to the Duderhofer Heights, if they haven't been stormed by Oberst Caspar's men."

"There, look at that!"

To the right front one of the fighters dove towards the earth, gray smoke trails snaking from its weapons.

"They're supporting people on the ground," commented one of the men.

"They're dropping bombs too," said another.

Small, glittering shapes were visible for a brief period before disappearing. As the soldiers watched breathlessly, columns of smoke rolled up from the ground as the bombs exploded.

Suddenly, a loud call rang out from in front of the column: "Antitank guns: Move forward!"

A light 37-mm Pak, the so-called "Army Door-knocker," and a medium 50-mm weapon were brought forward. Vielwerth tagged along behind them to see what was going on. The farther forward they went, the heavier the rifle fire became. Machine guns joined in. Finally, the antitank guns opened fire. The smoking paths of their armor-piercing rounds and the general alignment of their barrels showed Vielwerth where to look.

As he watched, he saw a Russian motorized column in the process of pulling back into the woods. One of the trucks was hit by the 37-mm Pak. Fire spurted from the back of the truck and it was soon enveloped in flames. To the right and left self-propelled antitank guns moved past the Oberfeldwebel and into position. Were they expecting tanks here? When the tank destroyers showed up there was always something up. The answer to Vielwerth's question was not long in coming.

A call rang out through the rattling and rumbling of tracked vehicles: "Tanks on the left!"

The Oberfeldwebel looked in the given direction. At first he saw nothing, but then he spotted a tank at a range of approximately three-hundred meters. It was so well camouflaged that he failed to notice it at first.

The antitank guns roared to life. The first round struck the ground close to the Russian tank. Earth flew into the air. The second round struck the steel giant with a shattering crash. Flames shot from the tank.

"Forward! Move forward!"

The Oberfeldwebel ran back to his platoon. They were advancing again. Passing the burning tank, they saw that it was partially dug in. Only its turret with the long-barreled gun projected above the earth and the surrounding bushes. Vielwerth and his men passed two more dug-in tanks.

These were unmanned. Their crews had apparently withdrawn. The advancing troops stopped to rest.

"We've already reached our objective for the day, Vielwerth," said Leutnant Klein.

"But will we continue to move forward? After all, we can't always advance this easily."

The Leutnant laughed. "Our Oberst knows that too and, if I know him, he'll have us moving again right away."

In front of the company was an open plain. It was bordered on the east by a patch of woods. Straight ahead—to the north, about five or six kilometers away—a distinctly formed ridge had become visible. Its slopes and crest were wooded. At the foot of the ridge was a large village. The white village church and its onion dome stood out clearly against the horizon. Bright, vertical cliffs were visible on the eastern part of the heights. Vielwerth took out his map to orient himself. Unteroffizier Weiser looked over his shoulder. He touched the map with a fingertip.

"We must be about here," he suggested.

The Oberfeldwebel looked up from the map and surveyed the countryside. Between the heights and their position were several villages; exactly as they were drawn in front of the Duderhofer Heights on the map. At that point he knew for sure. Only a few kilometers to the northwest was the city of Krasnoye Selo. In earlier times it had been the summer home of the czar of all the Russias. From there the Russian czars had watched summer maneuvers by the Guards Regiments from St. Petersburg, the old name for Leningrad.

The Defense Commissar of Leningrad, Stalin's friend Zhdanov, had deployed his guard at the same place. This guard—composed of active elite regiments expanded to brigade size through the addition of young communists and members of the workers militias—had occupied Hill 143 and the bald crest, which had been marked on the map as Point 167.

The Oberfeldwebel spoke to his squad leaders: "The Russians are sitting in their holes up there. Whoever tries to smoke them out will have a job on their hands. Now then, let's have a look."

The Oberfeldwebel raised his binoculars and peered in the direction of the road. The weather was clear with good visibility and the skies were filled with German aircraft. The men saw fighters, bombers and Stukas.

Soviet "Rata" fighters, short-bodied and plump looking, appeared and an air battle broke out. It ended with the crash of several Russian machines. More Russian fighters turned up, flying in groups of fifteen to twenty machines. As soon as a squadron of Bf 109s appeared, the enemy fighters broke away and fled at low level.

As the company watched, a formation of German bombers flew toward Krasnoye Selo. Their bomb doors opened. As he watched through his binoculars, Vielwerth could clearly see the falling bombs. The Ju 88s flew toward the center of Krasnoye Selo. They were met by antiaircraft fire. Dense clouds of smoke rose into the sky above the city. The waiting soldiers felt the ground tremble beneath their feet as the heavy bombs went off and felt the attendant shock waves.

Russian fighters dove on the bombers. An air battle broke out and soon one of the Ju 88s began trailing smoke. It turned away and dove toward the German lines.

"Hopefully, he'll come down behind our lines," said one of the infantrymen near Vielwerth.

The Soviet antiaircraft guns were firing from the direction of the brickworks. While the aerial combat was going on, the battalion commander had arrived at the 1st Company with an artillery officer. He told him to engage the antiaircraft battery. The Oberleutnant called his battalion and assigned the target. Moments later the first rounds roared over the forward area toward the enemy position. Flashes and smoke marked the locations of the impacting rounds. The Oberleutnant radioed corrections to his guns.

The next salvo hammered into the midst of the antiaircraft position. Soon afterward Vielwerth saw a staff car roar away and disappear to the northeast. It was not long before a heavily laden truck and then the guns followed the car. The German artillery increased its rate of fire. One of the trucks stopped. It was towing a limbered piece. Rounds dropped right in front of the truck. The Soviets ran away and abandoned the gun. The artillery then shifted its fire onto the fleeing vehicles.

Leutnant Klein turned to his companion: "When is the advance going to resume, Erich?"

"No idea!" replied Vielwerth. "Hopefully soon, before the Russians spot us and open up with their artillery."

"Look, sir! Over there!" one of the 1st Platoon's runners called out, pointing to the trees. Beyond the bushes five mounted Russian horsemen were trotting straight toward the neighboring sector.

"Cavalry patrol!" remarked Schütze Lempke. Concern for the five horses was obvious in the farmer's son's voice. The five horsemen disappeared from the company's sight. Two minutes later two of the riders came charging back through the bushes. They were heading straight towards the 1st Company.

"Don't fire!" ordered Hauptmann Cläsges.

When the two horsemen had come to within twenty meters, two soldiers stepped in front of them with raised rifles. The surprised Russians,

Vielwerth at his award ceremony. The Oberfeldwebel and his men knocked out innumerable enemy bunkers, thus allowing the division to advance against a heavily fortified Russian defensive system.

who had not expected to meet German troops there, raised their hands and surrendered.

"They're going to let us starve to death slowly out here," interjected Gefreiter Göcke. "Where's the field kitchen?"

"We've reached our objective for the day, so there's hope that the field kitchen will come soon," said Vielwerth, trying to console his men. Just then they began to take artillery fire.

"The firing came from the woods, Erich!" Klein said excitedly.

The platoon leader nodded and pointed his binoculars in that direction. The forward artillery observer had also seen where the round had come from. He called back to his battery and soon the first salvo howled into the woods. The enemy gun was silenced.

A German patrol in platoon strength disappeared into the woods. Minutes later hectic rifle and pistol fire rang out from the impenetrable tangle of tree trunks and undergrowth. Russian submachine guns and exploding hand grenades added to the din. A truck came racing out of the woods, rumbled on a few dozen meters and drove into a ditch. The Russian troops inside jumped out and ran away, pursued by gunfire from the patrol.

Oberst Fries had requested tanks to support the assault group, and these finally arrived. The six tanks rolled forward, firing on identified nests of resistance and opening the way for the following infantry.

A shout went through the position: "The field kitchen is here!"

The men sent to fetch the food had not yet returned when orders came to prepare to move out.

"They always order us to move when we're getting comfortable," grumbled Himmelmann.

The food arrived just in time. The platoons had just been drawn up when the men came running up with the food. The men ate the fatty soup as they advanced. The soup was no delight in the prevailing heat, and the men couldn't eat properly as they walked. Soon everyone was thirsting for water.

The next rest was in a village just before the second Russian line. The Russian inhabitants were still there, as no one had expected such a rapid advance by the Germans. The people remained calm and were not bothered by the German soldiers. Formations of bombers droned over the village in the direction of the second battle line. They dropped their bombs and, immediately afterward, the enemy positions were obscured by smoke and flame.

A number of tanks moved forward. The 87th Motorized Infantry Regiment had finally received the necessary support for the attack. The men had been busy digging foxholes. Several grumbled.

"Listen," Vielwerth cautioned his men, "it might be unnecessary to dig a hole ten times in a row. But the eleventh time you'll be happy that you have one and can crawl inside."

The battalion commander and the company commanders conducted a leaders' reconnaissance in order to assign attack sectors, boundaries and attack objectives. Oberst Fries joined the group; he had earlier visited his other two battalions. He also brought the first news from the neighboring regiment.

✠

The 118th Motorized Infantry Regiment's 1st Battalion, which had fought its way toward the Duderhofer Heights, was bogged down and had requested Stukas. Right away Generalleutnant Ottenbacher called the XXXXI Panzer Corps and requested air support. The corps chief-of-staff knew how vital this support was to the hard-fighting infantry, and he immediately called Panzer Group 4. The resident air liaison officer of the 1st Air Fleet passed on the request.

As complicated as the process may seem, the Stukas arrived a half-hour later. The aircraft were part of the VIII Air Corps. General von Richthofen had personally assigned the pilots their targets. The dive-bombers appeared over the attack sector of the 118th Motorized Infantry Regiment, where Oberst Carl Caspar awaited their arrival with the leading assault groups.

The Stukas dove on the enemy positions, howling toward the earth. They dropped their bombs on the Russian bunkers and dugouts, then pulled up sharply into the clear, cloudless sky. As the machines flew away Oberst Caspar jumped up and stormed into the enemy position at the head of his troops. Automatic weapons fire greeted the attackers. Hand grenades burst. The more stubborn bunkers were overcome by pioneers using flamethrowers. Thirty-meter-long streams of flame poured into the bunkers, burning everything in their path. It was a horrible weapon.

The German infantry rolled up the trenches between the dugouts and bunkers just as Vielwerth's platoon had done alone the day before. Although they defended desperately, were forced to withdraw in the end the Soviets. Many Russians fought to the last round.

The regiment broke into the first positions guarding Leningrad and stormed onward. The infantry reached Aropakosi and occupied this key position. News of the capture of Aropakosi by the regiment spread by word of mouth.

✠

Oberfeldwebel Vielwerth and his men didn't have long to wait for their next orders.

The company commander returned: "At 1800 hours we will attack the second Russian defensive line. The attack will be prepared by bombers and supported by close-support aircraft."

The company moved up into its attack sector and the men moved out across the open field that stretched to the Duderhofer Heights. Vielwerth and his platoon advanced at the rear of the company as the unit's reserves. The Oberfeldwebel could see the entire division.

The entire 36th Motorized Infantry Division advanced in open formation. All was quiet. It was an eerie silence, or so it seemed to Oberfeldwebel Vielwerth. Something didn't seem right. His fears were later to become bitter reality. When the leading elements of the division were within about 800 meters of the heights, they began taking heavy rifle fire from the Russian positions. Machine guns barked and the Soviets opened fire with field guns.

The rapid advance ground to a halt. Soon the companies were once again pinned down and had to dig in. Antitank guns were moved forward. They opened fire, but could achieve little against the hail of steel from the Russian positions.

"Move out! Work your way forward individually!" shouted Vielwerth to his squad leaders.

They reached a road running across the line of advance. Squatting in the ditches at the side of the road were many men of the 1st Platoon. As darkness fell the battle ebbed away. When Vielwerth had assembled his men he realized to his relief that no one was missing.

"We're going forward again! Mahr: Advance to those trees. Weiser: Go to the right with Külker's squad staggered to the rear."

After issuing instructions to his squads the Oberfeldwebel got up and, at a crouch, ran into a cabbage field, where he took cover. The two platoon runners followed him. Then someone called his name. It was Leutnant Heinrich, who was lying not ten meters from him. He crawled over to the leader of the 3rd Platoon. Then he saw that the Leutnant had been wounded.

"Where are you hurt, sir?"

"I've been shot in the thigh. It's well-bandaged, Vielwerth."

"Look after the Leutnant," Vielwerth instructed the two men who appeared at his side.

"Will do, Oberfeldwebel!"

"As soon as the enemy fire lets up, you take him back," said Vielwerth to the two soldiers, before he worked his way farther forward.

Gradually, the entire company arrived. The 3rd Platoon was split up. By then it was night. Flames from burning houses in no-man's-land cast a ghostly light over the area. The company commander arrived.

"The division is bogged down," he reported. "But the tanks of the 1st and 6th Panzer Divisions are rolling out.

"And us, sir?" asked Leutnant Klein.

"We're going to advance. You will take over the lead. You, Vielwerth, will follow with the rest."

The soldiers advanced through the night in skirmishing lines. They could hear the sound of fighting from the north crest of the Duderhofer Heights. Finally, Leutnant Klein reached the second antitank ditch.

"How does it look, Klein?" asked the company commander.

"At least four meters deep. The bottom is under almost a meter of water."

"We'll have to build steps then."

The men went to work and, half an hour later, they were able to cross the makeshift steps and the antitank ditch with dry feet. In the meantime, one of the battalion's companies had moved in between two platoons of the 1st Company. The soldiers helped each other across the antitank ditch. They would have to reach the railway line soon.

The advance continued with the troops widely dispersed. Vielwerth recognized the battalion commander in front of him. He was with the leading group. He wouldn't have been surprised if the regiment's commander had suddenly appeared. Oberst Fries was in the front line with one of the neighboring assault groups.

"The lead platoon has strayed too far to the right. Vielwerth take over the lead with your platoon. The new line of advance is between the houses of Duderhofer and toward the high ground behind!" the battalion commander ordered.

Once again Vielwerth was at the front of the company. The village houses appeared ahead. As they passed Vielwerth noticed several dugouts. They were filled with civilians, who had apparently taken cover there from the German artillery fire and bombing attacks. The Oberfeldwebel worked his way past them as noiselessly as possible, so as to give them no warning that the Germans were already there. He issued his orders in a whisper and they were passed on from man to man.

Farther to the right a pair of hand grenades exploded. Their neighbors on the right appeared to have met resistance. The 1st Company marched right into the Russian positions, but there was no sign of the Russian defenders. The Oberfeldwebel and his men crossed a road. When they had gone about another fifty meters, a truck appeared on the road they had just crossed. There was a brief flurry of gunfire as it was halted by the following troops. The advance continued. The company came to a steep slope.

"We're supposed to climb that!" grumbled one of the runners.

Wordlessly, the Oberfeldwebel approached the slope. They moved on, step by step, and occasionally on hands and feet. When he reached the top, Vielwerth determined that they had come out exactly where the company commander had instructed.

"We should let the others know we're up here, Oberfeldwebel," suggested Weiser.

"Yes, but not until my whole platoon is here."

When the last man had arrived and thrown himself down on the ground to rest, the Oberfeldwebel fired three white flares, which signified "we are here". Gefreiter Göcke held a dimmed flashlight as Vielwerth studied the map.

"We must move on. Through that valley there toward the large hill."

The platoon leader pointed in the direction. The men moved out. There seemed to be no end to this. How far had they marched today already? Their feet burned and exhaustion crept up their legs. Finally, they reached their objective and again three flares hissed into the night sky. The tired soldiers dropped where they stood. The ammunition bearers, each with his 400 rounds of ammunition, were at the end of their endurance. They had been relieved on the way, but had done the lion's share of the carrying themselves. The bunkers atop the hill were empty. The platoon took up positions and posted outposts.

When things had settled down, Weiser asked: "Are we through the second line?"

Vielwerth nodded: "It seems to me as if we are. I'd just like to know why the Russians have abandoned these bunkers?"

Within thirty-six hours Vielwerth's platoon had forced both major Soviet defensive lines. While they had assaulted the first line, they had simply sneaked through the second.

✠

The sounds of fighting still rang out from the neighboring hill. The assault companies of the sister regiment were fighting for possession of Hill 143. Generalleutnant Ottenbacher had sent the regiment into action at 2045 hours. The divisional artillery and the 73rd Artillery Regiment of the 1st Panzer Division had led off the attack with a massed bombardment. The 4th Company of the 118th Motorized Infantry Regiment stormed forward at the head of the attack groups. Twenty minutes later it successfully broke into the enemy positions. The remaining companies followed and turned Hill 143 into a support base for subsequent attacks.

At the same time the 6th Panzer Division, which was advancing to the right of the 36th Motorized Infantry Division, found itself in a crisis situation. This had resulted when the SS-Police Division on its right became bogged down in front of a powerful bunker line. Under the command of Generalmajor Landgraf, the 6th Panzer Division had rolled on, thinking its right flank secure. The Soviets quickly recognized the opportunity that had been presented them. They struck the armored division's open right flank with tanks, armored cars and antitank guns. The result was a bitter battle in which the 6th Panzer Division lost four tank commanders. The tank crews and motorized infantry finally managed to master the situation following heavy, close-quarters fighting.

When General Reinhardt learned of the situation he immediately ordered his forces to turn east to face the attacking Soviets. The 1st Panzer Division moved into the gap between the 6th Panzer Division and the 36th Motorized Infantry Division.

The tenth of September saw a resumption of the infantry attack by the 36th Motorized Infantry Division. The unit history called it "the most difficult day's fighting on the Northern Front." The men around Oberst Fries and Oberst Caspar fought their way toward the Duderhofer Heights, the commanding position in the second Soviet line, in which even heavy naval guns had been installed.

The 1st Panzer Division was also on the move. Elements of the division rolled along behind the 36th Motorized Infantry Division and took Novopurskova and Nishnyaya. After moving up beside the 36th Motorized Infantry Division, the tanks were attached to the 118th Motorized Infantry Regiment. They then led the way for the infantry into the northern part of the Duderhofer fortifications. As the morning of 11 September dawned, the strongly fortified "bald heights," whose central point was Hill 167, were directly in front of the 1st Panzer Division, positioned to the left of the 36th Motorized Infantry Division.

While moving up to the front, the operations staff of the 1st Panzer Division and the headquarters of the division's 1st Rifle Brigade came under air attack. Road demolitions further hindered their progress, leaving the forward units without orders. Faced with this situation, Oberst Westhoven, the commander of the 1st Rifle Regiment took command of a battle group consisting of his regiment, the 113th Rifle Regiment, the 1st Panzer Regiment, and elements of the 73rd Artillery Regiment. He ordered an attack on Hill 167.

This was the opening round. Battle Group Eckinger—the 1st Battalion of the 113th Rifle Regiment, reinforced by thirteen Panzer IIIs and two Panzer IVs of the 1st Panzer Regiment's 6th Company and the first platoon of the 37th Combat Engineer Battalion's 2nd Company—carried out what was later characterized as a "classic Eckinger tank raid" against the hill. The battle group was led by Major Dr. Eckinger. Pioneers leveled the antitank ditch west of the Taizy railway embankment, which had held up the 87th Motorized Infantry Regiment for a short time the previous night. The tanks rolled across.

Stukas plunged down on the Russian field positions in front of Battle Group Eckinger and bombed them. Eckinger's forces drove ahead and entered the southern portion of the town of Duderhofer. Russian infantry with antitank guns tried to stop the advance, but were overrun by the tanks. The battle group roared through Duderhofer and then turned into the bunker line. In the leading tanks and armored personnel carriers were the air liaison officers, who assigned targets to the ever-present Stukas. The dive-bombers attacked targets as close as fifty meters in front of the leading German attack groups, smashing nests of resistance.

The first bunkers appeared. A self-propelled gun moved up and destroyed a bunker housing a 180-mm gun. At 1200 hours Major Eckinger and Oberleutnant Darius stormed Point 167. Leading the tanks of the 1st Panzer Regiment's 6th Company, Darius shot up the bunkers. The pioneers overcame the last resistance. At 1230 hours Oberleutnant Darius sent a message up his chain of command, which reflected his understandable excitement: "I can see Leningrad and the sea!"

But what had happened in the meantime to the infantry, who had approached from the south through Apropakosi, Novopurskovo and Raskolovo, and found themselves at Hill 167's back door?

✠

When the morning of 11 September dawned the men of Vielwerth's platoon were surprised and amazed. What they saw in the early light of this clear day caused their hearts to beat faster. In the distance, illuminated by the first rays of the sun, were the domes of many churches and the roofs of large buildings.

"That's Leningrad!" said the Oberfeldwebel, as questioning voices grew louder.

"Leningrad!" echoed the men in disbelief. If that was Leningrad, they could be in the city by tomorrow or the day after. That was the legendary city on the Neva; the objective toward which everyone had been striving during the past weeks of heat, rain and mud. It seemed to be within their reach at that point.

Oberfeldwebel Vielwerth went up to the forward outposts. When he arrived he saw a number of trucks with limbered guns moving along the road from Krasnoye Selo to Duderhofer.

"Bring me a rifle!" Vielwerth shouted to the outposts.

"Here, Oberfeldwebel."

Vielwerth wanted to allow the trucks to approach to within 600 meters before firing. After that he would lose sight of them. The Oberfeldwebel fired three rounds in rapid succession. The first truck skidded to a halt. The men inside jumped out and took cover in the ditch.

"Quickly, go get two machine guns!" Vielwerth shouted.

One of the outposts ran back to the platoon. One of the trucks started to drive off and Vielwerth fired two more rounds. The truck stopped. Then the men arrived with the machine guns, which were quickly moved into position. Seconds later, bursts of fire rattled down the slope. Smoking tracers flitted into the ditches and trucks. The Russians fled toward Krasnoye Selo.

"I need three volunteers!" Vielwerth said.

Covered by the machine guns, the Oberfeldwebel led the three men toward the Russian column. It consisted of eight trucks and six 76.2-mm guns. The Russians hiding in the ditches were taken prisoner. Then a runner came running down the hill, waving his arms wildly. Vielwerth walked a few paces toward him.

"What's up Becker?" he asked the man.

"You're to return at once, Oberfeldwebel. The attack is about to begin."

Vielwerth and his men returned. When they reached the top of the hill the entire company had been assembled. There were plenty of artillery observers present, as the hill offered a good vantage point. The troops crossed a partially completed antitank ditch and entered the village. They were now in Duderhof. From the far side of the hill they could hear the noise generated by the tanks and armored personnel carriers of the 1st Panzer Division, which was likewise attacking.

There was one Russian position after another. The roads were littered with vehicles destroyed by the Stukas. The bodies of men and horses lay on the ground, killed by bombs and machine-gun fire. It was a terrible sight. The infantry attack on the hill positions on the north slope took place at about noon. The Russians withdrew following the first exchange of fire, apparently fearing encirclement. In spite of their retreat, almost half of the Russians were captured. Weak Soviet resistance was broken. In the distance

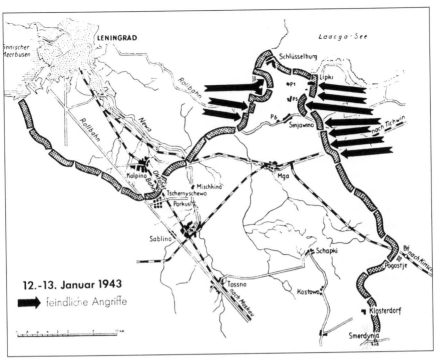

The First battle of Lake Ladoga, 12–13 January 1943.

Vielwerth recognized the main road to Leningrad, over which Russian columns were pouring back toward the city.

"Move a pair of machine guns into position—quickly!" he ordered.

Bursts of fire whipped down toward the road, but the range was too great. Not until a couple of antitank guns opened fire did the Russians take cover. Soon several trucks were burning. Then the 1st Company of the 87th Motorized Infantry Regiment stormed down the hill and reached the road. There it turned left, as the company had strayed too far to the right. An unsuspecting Russian sentry, going about his duties with rifle slung, was taken prisoner. Soon afterward the infantry reached its objective. According to the map it was only seven kilometers to the city limits of Leningrad. But the regiment had pushed ahead too far and was now isolated. It was forced to wait until its sister regiment and the tanks caught up.

It was exactly 2245 hours when the sirens began to howl in Leningrad. Air raid alarm! German bombers had appeared and dropped their deadly loads into the city in an effort to soften it up for the coming attack. On 12 September Oberfeldwebel Vielwerth could see a Russian battleship in drydock in the port of Kronstadt. Russian fighters tried to intercept the German Stukas and horizontal bombers. Many were shot down by German fighters and crashed before the eyes of the infantry.

Like the 87th Motorized Infantry Regiment on 9 September, the 118th Motorized Infantry Regiment spent 10 and 11 September engaging enemy bunkers. Oberst Carl Caspar, the regiment's commander, repeatedly led his men forward. Generalleutnant Ottenbacher acknowledged his outstanding leadership by recommending him for the Knight's Cross.

At the request of Oberst Fries and other officers of the 87th, the General submitted one other name for the Knight's Cross: Oberfeldwebel Erich Vielwerth. If it had not been for Vielwerth, the division might have still been held up in front of the first Russian defensive position.

Vielwerth knew nothing of this. He had merely tried to accomplish the missions assigned him and his platoon. Acting on his own initiative to crack the bunker line and destroy more than fifty bunkers and dugouts was simply doing his duty.

In the days that followed the soldiers of the 36th Motorized Infantry Division waited for the advance to resume. They waited until 17 September, when the contents of a letter from the Commander-in-Chief of Panzer Group 4 to the Commanding General of the XXXXI Panzer Corps were revealed to the divisions of the corps:

Effective today, the XXXXI Panzer Corps leaves Panzer Group 4. It is my special duty to express my thanks and recognition to you and your corps for your outstanding performance in command and battle. You have proved yourselves equal to every situation. With complete confidence in your leadership, the divisions of the XXXXI Panzer Corps have fulfilled the most difficult offensive and defensive roles with courage and endurance and endured every hardship and impediment of terrain and bad weather. The XXXXI Panzer Corps has played a significant part in the success of Panzer Group 4.

/signed/ Hoeppner

What the men had suspected when the rumor went through the divisions on 12 September had now become an unfathomable reality: Leningrad was not to be taken but only encircled. For weeks they had fought through dust, heat, rain, mud and dozens of bunker positions, only to be halted just short of their objective. They were being sent somewhere else. Was someone else perhaps going to achieve the victory for which so many of their comrades had fallen? None of the men around Vielwerth could suspect that Leningrad would hold out for more than 1,000 days in spite of being in a state of permanent siege.

On 17 September the 36th Motorized Infantry Division was withdrawn from the front and transferred to the central sector of the Eastern Front. The great victory in the battle of encirclement at Kiev had convinced Hitler that the Russians were on the verge of total collapse. He wanted to begin the final pursuit to Moscow. To do this he needed the XXXXI Panzer Corps. This miscalculation, one of the greatest in the Russian Campaign, was to cost Germany dear in the future.

The attack of Army Group Middle on Moscow began at 0615 hours on 2 October 1941 following a heavy bombardment by artillery and two *Nebelwerfer* regiments. The XXXXI Panzer Corps attacked between Lomonosovo and Novoselki. The attack was led by the 1st, 6th, and 7th Panzer Divisions. On the left flank was the Infantry Training Regiment. The two motorized divisions were part of the second wave. The 36th Motorized Infantry Division advanced behind and beside the 1st Panzer Division.

On 6 October Oberfeldwebel Vielwerth was wounded in action when a bullet pierced his hand.

"That's a lovely wound to get you sent home, Erich," suggested one of his friends. But the Oberfeldwebel shook his head.

"I'm not going back with this," he replied emphatically.

Vielwerth had his wound dressed at the main dressing station and rejoined his unit that evening. One of the men of the platoon had received an answer to a letter to the family of Unteroffizier Mahr. Two days after being wounded, the Unteroffizier had sent a note to the platoon from the dressing station. Vielwerth had kept the piece of paper among his things. He had read the sentences a dozen times already: "All is well, Erich. I'll be back with you all in a few days."

Eight days later the news had arrived that Unteroffizier Mahr had died of his wounds. It was simply inconceivable to Vielwerth how this could have happened. No one knew if his comrade had died of illness or succumbed to unrecognized complications resulting from his injuries.

In the days that followed the German advance seemed irresistible. The general direction was toward Kalinin. The 1st Panzer Division was setting such a pace that the 36th Motorized Infantry Division had difficulty keeping up.

On 14 October Kalinin was taken by assault groups of the 1st Panzer Division. The XXXXI Panzer Corps was now east of the Volga. On 15 October the 36th Motorcycle Battalion reached Kalinin and relieved the security forces of the 1st Panzer Division. At about 1400 hours on 17 October Major Eckinger was killed during the advance on Torshok. Advancing in his armored personnel carrier, the victor of Hill 167 ran into a Russian KV-II. A direct hit from this armored giant shattered the half-track, killing everyone inside.

Vielwerth's division relieved the 1st Panzer Division in the Volga bridgehead on 22 October. This marked the beginning of a period of extremely heavy fighting against repeated Soviet counterattacks. In the subsequent days Vielwerth and his platoon faced many dangerous situations.

On 18 October Vielwerth was awarded the Knight's Cross. However, he knew nothing of this when a courier from division headquarters arrived on the evening of 22 October. He brought an order from Generalmajor Hans Gollnick, who had assumed command of the division from Generalleutnant Ottenbacher, for the Oberfeldwebel to report to division headquarters in Kalinin the next morning.

The next morning Generalmajor Gollnick presented Oberfeldwebel Vielwerth the Knight's Cross in Republic Square in Kalinin. He then marched past an honor guard at the side of the Generalmajor. It was an unforgettable moment for Vielwerth. He was rightly filled with pride over the high decoration and over the fact that he had become the first noncommissioned officer of the division, indeed one of the first in the Russian Campaign, to receive it. At the same time he thought of the comrades of his platoon, of the brave Mahr, the tireless Kirchhoff and the many other men who had gone through fire with him. Vielwerth's platoon prepared a triumphant reception for him, but the war went on.

General of Armored Troops Model had been made Commanding General of the XXXXI Panzer Corps on 8 October, but was unable to join the corps until 28 October, as conditions prevented him from leaving his previous command, the 3rd Panzer Division, until then. The mission given the corps was to carry out an attack along the Volga reservoir north of Moscow toward the Soviet capital. The corps forces were inadequate for this task, however, and requests for reinforcements were denied. The day after assuming command General Model visited the 36th Motorized

Infantry Division. It was 29 October 1941. Generalleutnant Gollnick later recalled the visit:

> On 29 October he arrived at my headquarters and was briefed on the situation. I showed him the front from an observation post of the 87th Motorized Infantry Regiment. That satisfied him for the present, but he still wanted to visit the troops in the front lines. On 4 November I went with him to visit one of the battalions that was deployed north of the Upper Volga. The way there led across a high bridge that was under enemy observation. An enemy anti-tank gun was firing at anything that moved. However, this did not prevent General Model from running across the bridge.
>
> When we arrived at the command post the men were lying around in a large room on piles of straw. They were sleeping. Among them was the battalion commander. They had just repulsed a heavy Russian night attack. A company commander was still awake and was able to describe his company's situation.

When they returned, a sly wink from Model indicated he had seen enough.

On 6 November the muddy period was followed by a cold snap. Snow fell. And while the LVI Panzer Corps resumed its advance on 15 November, the XXXXI Panzer Corps was held in and around Kalinin by the 9th Army (Generaloberst Strauß). Not until 18 November was the 36th Motorized Infantry Division relieved by the 129th Infantry Division. The 1st Panzer Division was also freed for the attack. The situation around Kalinin had improved considerably. Every Soviet attack had been repulsed by the 36th.

The end of November brought renewed heavy fighting. Oberfeld-webel Vielwerth and his men were facing fresh Soviet formations brought in from the east. During the fighting near Rjabinki, about 30 kilometers north of Klin, the 87th Motorized Infantry Regiment's 1st Company achieved a great defensive success. It was once again in the center of the enemy attack. Generalmajor Gollnick described this operation in his morning report of 29 November. A little later General Model called the division commander and expressed the opinion that the division should not allow itself to be taken aback by the "bush war" or by several "cavalry patrols." At the same time he informed Generalmajor Gollnick that, effective immediately, the division was being placed under the command of the LVI Panzer Corps. It was to guard the corps' deep northern flank.

Once again Oberfeldwebel Vielwerth participated in a major offensive: The attack on Moscow. The German offensive soon bogged down, however, and the Soviets attacked at the boundary between the 14th Infantry Division and the 36th Motorized Infantry Division on 7 December. The infantry were unable to stop the advance, which had powerful armored support, and the Russians broke through. Completely on their own, the 36th and the 900th Training Brigade held out near Spas Saulok. On 10 December the division avoided disaster by preventing the enemy from advancing through the large gap north of Klin.

On 12 December the division was once again placed under General Model's command. At noon on 13 December the General appeared at the division command post in Koslovo. There, on the east shore of the Volga reservoir, the 87th Motorized Infantry Regiment under Oberst Fries had held off repeated enemy attacks. In this desperate situation men like Oberfeldwebel Vielwerth and the members of his platoon fought on and achieved the seemingly impossible. It had become bitterly cold. The men around Oberfeldwebel Vielwerth froze in their summer uniforms. No one could stay outside for more than an hour. Freezing was the order of the day. Vielwerth circulated among his men, warning them of the danger of frostbite.

With the cold came the Soviet counterattack. On 15 December General Model again showed up at the division command post in Kurjanovo. This time be came to present the Knight's Cross to Oberst Fries. A day later the entire division was engaged against pursuing Russian forces south of the Volga reservoir. The German forces were desperately trying to reestablish a cohesive front. Vielwerth experienced the grim union of the cold and the enemy offensive. General Model visited the division daily, as it had been given the key position.

On 18 December the enemy made another attempt to break through. Oberfeldwebel Vielwerth received shrapnel wounds in his right wrist and left shoulder. He was supposed to be sent to the rear, but he was back with his division several days later. He wanted to stay with his comrades in that time of crisis.

On 24 December the division occupied a new position on both sides of Latschino. Its neighbor on the right was the 2nd Panzer Division under Generalmajor Veil. During the fighting withdrawal the 87th was always in the thick of the fighting. It was a difficult time and Vielwerth saw many comrades fall. The unpretentious Oberfeldwebel, highly respected by his men, distinguished himself many times while leading patrols, assault groups and rearguard actions.

The fighting lasted into summer. But on 5 August 1942 fate caught up with Erich Vielwerth. During one of the heavy rounds of fighting he was shot in the back. The explosive bullet inflicted a dangerous wound. His first tour of duty in Russia was over. Vielwerth was sent from the main dressing station to Vienna and a hospital in Semmering, where be remained until 1 December 1942.

Following a period of home leave be was sent to Wiesbaden to join the 87th Infantry Replacement and Training Battalion, where be served as an instructor at the officer candidate school. On 1 May 1943 Vielwerth was promoted to Leutnant. He had previously been awarded the Wound Badge in Silver (1 September 1942) and the Eastern Front Medal (15 September 1942). He remained in contact with his former comrades and was able to keep track of his division, with which be maintained a close attachment. He was happy to learn that General Hans Gollnick had received the Knight's Cross on 21 November 1942. By the time Hans Gollnick, who had meanwhile been promoted to Generalleutnant, was awarded the Oak Leaves on 24 August 1943 Vielwerth was ready to return to his division. However, it was not until 1 November 1943 that be received orders transferring him back to Russia. By then the division had lost its motorized status and was referred to simply as the 36th Infantry Division again. The infantry regiments of the division were renamed as the 87th and 118th Grenadier Regiments.

BEHIND THE RUSSIAN LINES

When Leutnant Vielwerth rejoined his division it was one of the formations of the XXXXI Panzer Corps, which was fighting in the central sector as part of the 9th Army under General of Armored Troops Harpe.

The Leutnant received an enthusiastic welcome from the small number of his former comrades still left. He immediately assumed command of the depleted 3rd Company of the 87th Grenadier Regiment. A few days later he experienced his first Russian counterattack since becoming wounded. Vielwerth spent the entire winter in the front lines with his company. The Soviets failed to break through there. Where the enemy did manage to penetrate the German lines the Leutnant led his company in counterattacks. Each time he and his experienced grenadiers successfully threw back the enemy.

On 10 February 1944 the 36th Infantry Division was mentioned in the Wehrmacht Report. Vielwerth, who once again had been in the thick of things, was ordered to the army headquarters located in a forest north of Paritschi. As a guest of the Commander-in-Chief, General Harpe, he described the actions his company had been involved in.

On 1 March Vielwerth was promoted to Oberleutnant. His calmness and his ability to make quick decisions often spared his company from even heavier losses. On 1 May 1944 he received the Close Combat Clasp in

Erich Vielwerth poses for a group shot in 1944 with the commanding general of the 9th Army, Generaloberst Harpe (in greatcoat). Vielwerth, wearing his Knight's Cross, stands next to the Panzer officer (black uniform).

Bronze. Twenty-four days later he was awarded the same decoration in silver, an indication of the many actions the young officer had taken part in. While his unit was stationed in the central sector of the eastern Front Vielwerth participated in the climax of the dramatic struggle in the East. It was a time that is burned forever into the memory of this soldier.

Early on the morning of 26 June 1944 Oberleutnant Vielwerth received an order to leave his position and withdraw to a new sector to the rear. As one of the regiment's units he was to establish a bridgehead around the village of Paritschi. The Russians had launched a great offensive and had made several deep penetrations against the 2nd Panzer Army. Two Russian spearheads had outflanked Vitebsk and encircled the city. The Second White Russian Front also made several deep penetrations between the Dniepr and Beresina Rivers. On 24 June Panzer Grenadier Division *Feldherrnhalle* (the former 60th Infantry Division), which was in position behind Mogilev, received the following order from the XII Army Corps: "Unit is to break through to the west. The 12th Infantry Division is to defend Mogilev."

Thus all command had ceased in this most threatened sector. All the roads leading west were jammed. The Soviet Sixty-Fifth Army under General Batov rolled across marshland thought to have been impassable. Soviet engineers prepared log roads, permitting the tanks and other vehicles to cross. In this way the forward outposts of the 36th Infantry Division were overrun. The entire XXXXI Panzer Corps, under the command of General Hoffmann at that point, had been taken by surprise. This enemy breakthrough made necessary the withdrawal of the 36th Infantry Division.

Near Paritschi there was a bridge over the Beresina. The bridge was to be held so that every German unit in the sector might cross over to the west. The 3rd Company of the 87th Grenadier Regiment was still preparing its positions when a call came from the left that the Russians had already broken into Paritschi. The company's path to the bridge had been cut off. A runner arrived with an order from the battalion for the company to withdraw several hundred meters to the west. It was to attempt to reach the bridge from there. Leading his company, Vielwerth looked for a passable road. Machine-gun fire whipped toward them from the village. Only a narrow band of marshland between the village and the river appeared to be unoccupied. As they went on, Vielwerth saw hundreds of German soldiers trying to reach the bridge.

"Return fire!"

The grenadiers of the 3rd Company opened fire on the muzzle flashes from the houses. The men of Vielwerth's company worked their way through the marshes, often up to their waists in mud. Many were hit. There was virtually no cover. But the bridge was the only way to freedom. All of a sudden Oberleutnant Vielwerth felt a heavy blow against his left thigh and toppled into the ooze. Don't give up! He told himself. You can't stay here! He hauled himself to his feet and, stumbling more than walking, reached the bridge. There was a small German bridgehead there where the wounded were being cared for. Vielwerth was taken back in an armored personnel carrier. Rounds hammered into the river to the left and right of the bridge.

A doctor dressed Vielwerth's wounds at a first-aid station. The Oberleutnant was then to be taken to Bobruisk by ambulance. But the ambulance failed to get through and Vielwerth set out toward the city in another vehicle. There was another traffic jam at the second bridge. In spite of his leg wound the Oberleutnant continued on foot. Hobbling along the railway embankment he reached the bridge. A train was positioned in front of it and under steam. The bridge itself was under fire from enemy tanks. A few soldiers who ventured to swim the Beresina were being fired on by the Soviets.

Pioneers broke out their inflatable boats under enemy fire. German Flak moved forward from the city side of the river. Vielwerth watched all of this closely. There might yet be a chance to cross and, finally, he made it.

Bobruisk itself was full of soldiers. Harpe's headquarters had also moved there. A perfect target for Soviet bombers. Vielwerth had visited the headquarters in February and hoped to learn something of the situation by going there. To him, as an experienced Eastern Front soldier, it was already clear that the Russians had broken through in several places.

The city was surrounded. Rumors were rampant: The wounded were to be flown out! The aircraft were going to land on the citadel! Unfortunately, none of that held water when the landing strip and all hope for evacuation vanished. There was nothing left for the wounded to do but join one of the breakout groups.

Battle groups were formed. Unit leaders tried to track down their soldiers. At army headquarters Vielwerth learned that 100,000 men were going to attempt a breakout. The march into uncertainty began at dawn. During the early fighting Vielwerth encountered a driver from his company. The man hugged him in joy and relief. He gave the company commander some ammunition, chocolate and hardtack. The advance continued laboriously. Many of the escaping German troops fell to the heavy Russian fire. Suddenly, a familiar figure appeared near the Oberleutnant.

"Sir!" he cried.

During a pause Generalmajor Konradi shook hands with the Oberleutnant.

"We'll get through yet, Vielwerth," the General said to the Oberleutnant, his voice full of confidence.

A machine gun turned its fire on the group and Vielwerth dove into a trench. There were two men already inside. One of them, an officer of the 87th Grenadier Regiment, said laconically: "It's a silver mine in Siberia for us, Vielwerth. And that's if we're lucky."

"We'll see," replied Vielwerth.

He wanted to get through; that was his only goal. The fighting lasted into the night. The next morning the escaping troops resumed the attack. All was confusion. There were no longer any cohesive units. They stormed a Russian position and reached a patch of woods in which they could assemble. The sound of fighting died down. Had they done it?

"Relief is supposed to be coming from the west, Vielwerth," said Oberleutnant Dengler.

"The 12th Infantry Division is coming," offered another.

What these men could not know was that more than 5,000 German wounded had been left behind in Bobruisk. The fact that only 30,000 of the 100,000 men would reach the lines of the 9th Army, while the rest drowned in the Beresina, were mowed down by machine guns or died in the marshy forests, had not yet become a terrible reality.

Once Erich Vielwerth captured a Russian soldier, but he would tell them nothing. Later they came upon a Russian tank. It approached to within forty paces without firing. Then the Oberleutnant recognized a young woman sitting on the tank.

"Come here," the woman called out in rough German. "Nothing will happen to you!"

"Damn! We have to get past that tank!"

"I'll knock it out with a Panzerfaust!" offered an Oberfeldwebel.

He crept forward and fired, but the round missed its target. Nevertheless the tank—a heavy Josef Stalin—withdrew and opened the way for the continued breakout attempt. They reached a rally point on the evening of that eventful day. There were several tanks and armored personnel carriers from another battle group from Bobruisk there. The many wounded were tended to as best possible. Vielwerth's wound was looked at and another dressing was put on. Vielwerth was surprised that he had been able to keep up with his wounded thigh. The cold rations were good. The troops were confident. Soon several thousand men had gathered. Fuel was siphoned from the vehicles for the tanks.

They moved out during the night. The infantry clustered around the tanks like grapes. As morning was dawning they came to the edge of some woods. From there the battle group was to advance to the Bobruisk-Osipovichi rail line. Luckily Vielwerth found room in an armored personnel carrier. He would not have been able to keep up had he been forced to walk. The Oberleutnant was able to rest his leg. Reconnaissance discovered Russian tanks in front of the woods.

"We'll take them by surprise and break through en masse," the battle group commander decided. As the armored vehicles left the woods—the tanks in the lead—the Russians opened fire. Rounds hissed past the armored personnel carrier. As Oberleutnant Vielwerth watched, the tank driving beside his carrier took a direct hit. A fearful crash nearly deafened him. Parts of bodies whirled through the air before falling back to earth. It was a scene that encompassed all the horror of the war. Rounds fell in front of and behind the zigzagging carrier.

Then the carrier straightened out. "Keep zigzagging!" shouted Vielwerth to the driver. The man reacted immediately, and they managed to pass the first Russian tank. They drove toward a hedge, but suddenly it began to move. Behind it was a well-camouflaged T-34, and it was trying to ram the carrier. Vielwerth saw a road ahead; it was filled with Russian columns. Which way should they turn? The others had disappeared.

"Across the road!" he called to the driver. The driver stepped on the gas and the carrier rumbled across the road. The Russians fled, seeking cover. Infantry fire came from every haystack and bush. When they encountered groups of enemy soldiers Vielwerth threw hand grenades that he had found in the carrier. That helped clear a path.

Moving at high speed, the carrier came to a road. In the distance appeared the city limits of Osipovichi. They moved directly toward the city. The terrain on both sides of the road was marshy. To the right and ahead was a shallow rise. The carrier was forced to halt in front of the brush-covered hill. A small bridge over a brook had been destroyed.

"Hold on!" called the driver. "I'm going to drive down the bank next to the bridge."

Its engine roaring, the carrier nosed downward. A heavy blow shook the vehicle. It tipped over, spilling the occupants onto the ground. The first Russians were already running down the bank.

"Get out of here! Up the hill!"

Ignoring his wounded leg, the Oberleutnant leapt across the brook. He ran through the bushes up the rise, only to run into a group of Russians. In vain Vielwerth tried to work his way through. The entire hill was swarming with Russians. The Russians passed close by as he hid beneath some bushes. Sneaking back to the edge of the hill Vielwerth saw that the Red Army troops had captured the men from the carrier and were mistreating a wounded medical officer. The Oberleutnant was forced to watch. he wanted to help but was unable to do so.

Hours passed. The Russians combed the marshy area looking for other German soldiers who might be hiding there. Soon they would be right on top of Vielwerth's hiding place. The Oberleutnant was forced to move into the marshy area. Almost completely surrounded by water, he hoped to get away unseen. Vielwerth described his experience:

> I dared not move, I scarcely allowed myself to breathe. I didn't turn to look at the Russians, I could only hear their voices. Soon there was activity at the edge of the bushes. The Soviets appeared to have assembled there to rest. That meant they had passed my hiding place. After an hour the voices went away. I looked around carefully. All was quiet. I crept slowly back to my former location and organized my clothing, equipment and pistol. That's how I

passed the afternoon. When dusk came I tried to make my way through the bushes over the small hill in the direction of the main road. But the entire area was alive with Russians. I tried in other places, each time without success. I figured that the Russians were waiting for darkness before moving on, because everywhere I looked they were preparing to depart. During my attempts to reach the main road I encountered an Oberfeldwebel of the military police and three Gefreiters, all stragglers. All of us were happy we were no longer alone.

Darkness fell and we prepared to try to reach the main road again. But we had to wait until the Russians had left. It was almost midnight by the time we reached the road to Osipovichi. On the road were endless columns of Russian soldiers. Since the route we wanted was to the north, we had to cross the highway. I knew the terrain north of Osipovichi, as we had stayed there once after being taken out of the line and had combed the area for partisans. I also had a map and knew that we were already some distance beyond Osipovichi. Keeping the North Star to our right, we had marched westward and, by my calculations, had to be in the Marina Gorki area. Unfortunately, my map went no farther. There was still no sight or sound of the front. Our rations ran out. We frequently had to make detours to avoid the Russians. We slept by day and traveled by night. We frequently came across leaflets dropped by the Russians. They contained demands for German soldiers to come out of the woods. Some were signed with: "Committee for a Free Germany".

If one were at the end of his strength—suffering from hunger and the pain of unattended wounds and in doubt as to whether there was still a German front and whether he could really reach it—then one might give in to the lovely promises of the Soviets. But we had seen the "humanity" of the enemy all too often. For me there was only one thing: Get through or die!

The men trekked onward. The dense woods thinned out. The five soldiers were forced to hide by day. Once, after marching all night, they came upon a German sentry. Was this the front? No. It was a small battle group that had fought its way this far. It was led by the commander of a division, who had come from the Mogilev area with his staff. The group was roughly battalion-sized and Vielwerth found an Oberleutnant from his own division. The officer had been attached to a neighboring division several weeks earlier.

No one knew exactly where the German front was. At least the men could get attention for their wounds and the General informed Vielwerth that his group was welcome to join up with his force. But the Oberleutnant had doubts that such a large group would be able to get through. As a result, he and his small group left the apparent security of the larger circle of comrades and went on alone. When Vielwerth left that evening he had with him a new map, courtesy of the General.

The larger group was preparing to depart two hours later. Two days later Vielwerth and his four companions encountered another group of German soldiers, about 150 men strong. They still had about ten horses with them.

After a brief exchange of information Vielwerth continued on his way in the direction of Minsk. After crossing the Marina Gorka-Minsk road the five found themselves in marshy terrain again and were forced to travel during daylight. The men no longer knew how long they had been under way.

They were now walking through the Pripet Marshes. The five stalked through the unfamiliar terrain, taking cover at any sound. Once they came upon the body of a German soldier. Vielwerth looked for an identity disk, but there was none. Scarcely had they resumed their march when they came under rifle fire from some distance away to the left.

"They must be German, sir," suggested one of the Gefreiters.

Vielwerth waved his walking stick and the firing stopped.

As they walked on, the five saw a small haystack in the marsh. When they had approached to within fifty meters of the heap of grass, they suddenly came under submachine-gun fire. Vielwerth ran to the right and into the marsh. He was followed by his companions. They then came to a five-meter-wide brook. Three Russians burst forth from the haystack, firing their automatic weapons. When Vielwerth jumped into the stream he immediately went under. He swam several strokes and reached the far side. One of his companions, a non-swimmer, went under. Vielwerth swam back, grabbed him by a belt strap and dragged him to shore.

One of the pursuers reached the near bank, and raised his submachine gun. The fatal burst had to come at any second. Then the Russian yelled something—obviously a curse, because his gun had jammed. Vielwerth climbed up the bank and ran for his life. After fifty meters he collapsed, exhausted. His water-soaked clothing weighed twice as much as when dry. He lay among the birch trees and marsh grass, breathing heavily. Even Vielwerth doesn't know how much time went by until he got up again. Where were his companions? Where were his pursuers? He heard a soft call. One of his men called from nearby, then a second and a third. There was no sign of the fourth man.

"Stay put until darkness falls!" ordered the Oberleutnant. As he lay there, Vielwerth tried to strip off his clothing in order to dry it out. He fashioned a new bandage from a piece of his shirt. When it was dark the four men rejoined company. One was still missing. Where was he? One of the Gefreiters had seen him disappear into the bushes. They moved on during the night. The sole thought motivating them was to get out of these marshes. They stayed somewhat farther to the north and soon reached a wooded area, where they found some berries. Suddenly, they came under fire again. The crew of a Russian truck, who had likewise stopped to rest, were shooting at them. Once again the four Germans fled for their lives. Vielwerth's wound was scarcely bothering him at all by that point.

New problems soon developed. His groin became swollen and painful. Moreover, an abscess developed where the shank of his boot ended and his injured leg became swollen. To make matters worse, his food was gone. The outlook for Vielwerth was not good, but he did not give up.

Early the next morning the men knocked on the door of a cottage off to one side of a village. A woman answered the door. The men indicated that they were hungry and the woman gave them some bread and milk. Their first bread in weeks! The four also received salt, a few matches and a piece of striking paper. When Vielwerth made it clear to the old woman that he was in pain, she gave him a handful of caraway seeds. Then they left the house to avoid being discovered by the Russians. In a nearby forest the four found a hiding place in the undergrowth and slept for a few hours. The woman did not betray their presence.

The days passed. Cooking was done in the early morning. There were plenty of green potatoes and chickens. They encountered Russians almost daily. Occasionally, they knocked on the doors of isolated farmhouses. Vielwerth and his companions still had no idea what state the front was in or where it was. One day, they came upon a young man in an old suit. When he heard that they were really German soldiers and not Russians in German uniforms, he revealed his identity. The man was from Hamburg, an Unteroffizier with an artillery battery that had been in action east of Minsk.

The Russians had taken the position in a surprise night attack. He had played dead and thus escaped with his life. The only reminder of his life as a soldier was his 8-mm pistol, which he had retained in the event he was forced to defend himself.

"We'll take you with us, comrade. We'll get home, that I promise you."

Where Vielwerth got the strength to make this confident prediction, even he did not know. During the next few days they found nothing to eat. One of the villages they passed was abandoned, another was occupied by Russian troops. Morale sank.

The next evening Vielwerth left the forest and approached the nearest house in a village. All was quiet. Suddenly, he heard the click of a safety catch. And since Russian rifles were not equipped with safeties, it had to be a German rifle. He crept to the corner of the house and called softly. A German soldier emerged from his hiding place, rifle at the ready. Ten men followed him.

Vielwerth's surprise was indescribable; standing in front of him was Oberleutnant Reiter, an old comrade from his division. The men had already scoured the village for food. The group followed Vielwerth back into the forest. Oberleutnant Reiter described his odyssey. It was the story of the battle group led by the General from whom Vielwerth had received the map. The group had been surrounded in a village by the Russians one night and virtually wiped out. Only these few had escaped.

During the night Vielwerth sneaked back to his companions, having failed to find anything to eat. In the meantime, they had crossed the Minsk-Baranovichi road. The flight became ever more difficult. Finally, they reached a small farmhouse in an area concealed by trees and bushes. The men crawled into the hay-filled barn. Vielwerth awoke when a man began climbing the ladder to the hayloft. The Oberleutnant drew his pistol. The man answered his gestures that he was hungry with a nod. When he returned an hour later he brought with him a large pot filled with roast potatoes and bacon.

For a moment, the men forgot they were on the run. Not until evening, after darkness had fallen, did they resume their trek. Their confidence had been restored. That night German aircraft appeared overhead.

"Do you think they could get us out, sir?" asked one of the Gefreiters.

"We'd better not count on that," replied Vielwerth.

They marched on for days in the same rhythm. Then they came to the old border between Russia, Lithuania and Poland. They found refuge with a group of former partisans. They were Poles, who had fought against the Germans. However, they had been imprisoned by the Russians following the Soviet invasion. They suggested the four Germans join them. The five men and one woman told the Germans stories of terrible acts of cruelty of the Soviets.

The Germans stayed with the Poles two days, before going on their way. They reached the Wilna-Lida road. The Oberleutnant crawled up to the road in broad daylight. There he caught sight of Russian march columns. He immediately returned to his comrades. They would have to wait for darkness before crossing the road.

Their next goal was the Memel. Hopefully, there was still a bridge over the river, as there were two non-swimmers. Contact with local inhabitants

Winter in Russia: Vielwerth sits in a *panje* wagon

revealed that they were in Lithuania. The farmers understood some German, gave them food and drink and explained that there was only one bridge over the Memel. The bridge had been built by Russian engineers and was guarded. They marched on through the night and reached the east bank of the Memel early the next morning. The bank was very high, while that on the far side appeared to be flat. By day they had no chance of getting across the river.

Vielwerth and his men set about building a raft. But then fate stepped in to help out. That afternoon five Russians came to the river and went fishing with hand grenades. When they had finished they tied their boat up to a small pier on the far side and disappeared inland.

"Maybe they'll leave the boat there, sir," whispered one of the non-swimmers with hope in his voice.

"It's still there on the other bank."

"I'll go and fetch it!" offered the young Unteroffizier.

After dark the young man from Hamburg swam across and, a short time later, came paddling back. Everyone climbed in. The oars were slipped cautiously into the water. They reached the west bank of the river undisturbed. They let the boat float away and crept into the bushes. On the way they passed shot-up *panje* wagons and dead horses.

As the night wore on the sound of guns grew louder. The front was somewhere in this direction. The trek went on. One evening they came to an isolated house. A young man greeted them in good German. He was a teacher and invited them to have something to eat. He looked after the Germans well. Vielwerth wrote a long letter to his family, which the teacher promised to mail after the war.

Then the Germans moved on. Soon the five found themselves in open country. By day they were forced to split up and hide in the fields of tall corn. The sound of fighting grew nearer. They had to be close to the front. Russian artillery fired nearby. When morning dawned they once again took cover in a cornfield. They agreed to meet under a tree at the edge of the field at 2100 hours.

They all arrived at about the same time—except for the Unteroffizier from Hamburg. They searched his hiding place. It was empty. Had the Russians discovered him? They had used the cornfield as cover during an air-raid warning.

"We'll have to get through the Russian line together tonight," explained Vielwerth to his companions. "If we haven't made it by 0100 hours, we'll have to return here."

The men nodded. But they knew their chances of staying there without being found by the Russians were slim. The final dash for freedom began. Vielwerth again takes up the narrative:

We came to a road. Square holes had been dug a few meters apart. Beside them were Russian wooden box mines. I knew that the road led to Schaki. From the description given by the teacher, I knew that it must lead to the front. Suddenly, we saw the outline of a German prime mover in front of us, the type used by the Flak and the artillery. As we approached, we saw that it was a burnt-out wreck. We continued on our way. Suddenly, I found myself right behind an antitank gun. A Russian jumped to his feet. I stumbled over another. Before they could recover from their surprise, we had disappeared the way we came.

On the far side of the burnt-out prime mover we switched to the other side of the road. We tried to work our way across an open field. Cables and lines lay on the ground. We were in the midst of the Russians. We came to the first infantry trench. There was a bundle of cable there as well. The trench appeared to be unmanned. The night was coming to an end. Suddenly a MG 42 opened fire in front of us. One burst after another hissed overhead. The bullets were not meant for us. As day was breaking we had to conceal ourselves.

The group had lost the Oberfeldwebel in the encounter with the Russian antitank gun. The remaining men took cover under the rubble of a burnt-out farmhouse. They were forced to stay there until the next evening.

Vielwerth crawled over to the well. At the edge of a pool of water he came upon a Russian. The latter had not heard him, however, as a group of pigs was running loose, making a great deal of noise.

Vielwerth moved back to a nearby cornfield. While in hiding there he underwent a bombardment by German artillery. He tried to dig in with his spoon, but the ground was dried out and hard. The spoon broke off. Scratching with his hands and feet he managed to scoop out a shallow trough. He spent the day there. The sun beat down. Farther to the left light mortar rounds hammered into the field. Not until the afternoon did things quiet down. Vielwerth crept forward and came to a road. He crawled into a ditch and waited for darkness.

Night came and the men came together again. The Oberfeldwebel was still missing. They ran across the road, then crawled onward on all fours. Thistles scratched their hands and soon their knees were raw. This went on for about 300 meters. Then they lay still, exhausted.

"We'll have to walk," decided the Oberleutnant finally.

A light appeared briefly to the left. There was whispering in Russian. The men took cover. Suddenly the Oberleutnant became hung up on some barbed wire. He came under fire from thirty or forty meters away. That must be the German front. It was time to decide. It just had to be the German front.

"Don't shoot! Don't shoot!" shouted Vielwerth, but his calls seemed to be drowned out by gunfire.

There was a brief pause.

"Don't shoot! German officer!" he roared. The shooting stopped.

"Anyone could say that!" shouted one of the German soldiers from a trench. "We need proof!"

"If you want proof, you can kiss my ass free of charge," Vielwerth shouted back. Vielwerth believed that even the cleverest Russian would not have such a detailed knowledge of a reference to Goethe

"Come over one at a time! Keep your hands up!" ordered a voice.

Vielwerth went first. He handed over his pay book. He became suspicious when he saw an officer report with his right arm raised.

"Are you SS?" asked the Oberleutnant.

A little later Vielwerth heard of the assassination attempt on Hitler and the introduction of the new military salute. At the battalion command post the men were greeted and made welcome. There was food and drink. The battalion commander found it hard to believe that these men had reached their own lines after fifty-four days and a trek of more than 800 kilometers from the Russian hinterland.

Vielwerth weighed 118 pounds; his previous normal weight had been 164 pounds. At Schloßberg in East Prussia a recovery camp had been set up for the men who had made their way back from behind the lines. The next few days there were like a dream for Vielwerth. His joy was almost complete when the lost Oberfeldwebel turned up a few days later. Vielwerth's odyssey, which was possibly unique even in the eventful Russian Campaign, had ended.

On 1 September 1944 Vielwerth became commander of the 2nd Company of the 87th Infantry Replacement and Training Battalion in Wiesbaden. But his stay there was brief. On 26 November 1944 he returned to his company in the 87th Grenadier Regiment, which was staged along the Westwall fortifications. He became the company commander.

On 13 December 1944 he was forced to enter hospital. During a subsequent home leave he spent his first Christmas with his family since the beginning of the war. From there he went to Baumholder, where the regiment's 14th Company, the regiment's antitank company, was resting and refitting

On 1 March 1945 he went to the Vosges Mountains to become commander of the regiment's 1st Battalion. There he was awarded the German Cross in Gold four days later. Vielwerth saw action until 6 May 1945, when he entered American captivity near Traunstein. He was released on 12 August 1945.

The German Infantry
of World War II

INFANTRY TACTICS—GENERAL NOTES

Tactics—the art of employing troops at and below division level—have been known since the earliest days of warfare. Throughout the centuries they have changed as the weapons, equipment and means of transport of armies have changed. In the words of the Prussian general and philosopher Carl von Clausewitz, the former Chief of the General Staff of Gneisenau's army, they are "the doctrine of the use of armed forces in combat: The command of troops in battle." The discussion that follows concentrates on how German tactical doctrine evolved.

In contrast to tactics is operations and strategy, the doctrinal terminology for wide-ranging operations and the planning behind them, ranging from the employment of corps and field armies—usually considered an intermediate step between tactics and strategy called operations—to planning for the overall conduct of a campaign or war. Most books on World War Two concern themselves with operations or strategy: Campaigns such as Operation "Barbarossa", the great battles of encirclement of the first year of the war in the Soviet Union, the lightning campaigns of 1939 and 1940, the Soviet offensive against Army Group Center (*Heeresgruppe Mitte*) in 1944 or the Red Army's "Ten Blows" of 1944–45.

This book is about individual soldiers in whose actions tactics, not operations or strategy, played the decisive role. It is also the objective of this work to provide the reader with an understanding of tactics so as to allow him to develop his own assessment of the ongoing development of weaponry and the entire machinery of warfare. Tactics are more than the art of deploying of a division, they define everything about an engagement or a battle: Scouting of terrain, securing and camouflaging one's own positions, deception by means of feints, the approaches to and from the battlefield. Even though the tactics of all armies have undergone a profound change since the introduction of firearms, several basic rules remain which are as valid today as they were centuries ago. These include, for example, minimizing expenditure of resources, achieving freedom of action, the concentration of forces at key points and a series of other classical requirements.

In addition to prescriptive orders, mission-type orders—*Auftragstaktik*—were preeminent in the German Army were. These gave senior and junior commanders specific objectives while leaving them free to decide how best to achieve them. This meant that latitude of action was always guaranteed in the Wehrmacht and its predecessors. During the war this often led to outstanding military achievements. On the other hand, this latitude of action placed a high level of responsibility on the leaders of formations and units.

DECISIVE CHANGES

In describing the evolution of tactics, we shall go back to the period that saw the introduction of the machine gun. This period, which coincided with the beginning of motorization, saw the beginning of a rapid development in infantry tactics. The first attempts to develop multiple-shot weapons, which could reduce the laborious loading procedure and increase the rate of fire, appear early in the history of firearms. These resulted in the so-called "Organ Gun." Introduced in 1614, it was first used by the Saxon Army. Sixty-four barrels were arranged in rows of eight, one above the other. Each barrel was connected to the next by an igniting channel.

The organ gun used by Ferdinand von Schill at Stralsund in 1809 had eleven small-caliber barrels. The barrels of an organ gun were all fired more or less simultaneously, producing a grapeshot effect. In contrast, the next development, the "revolver", consisted of a number of barrels in a circular bundle that rotated around a central axis, firing one after another. Finally, a series of improvements led through the "Espagnols" and "Mitrailleusen" of the Franco-Prussian War to the first true machine gun. Hiram S. Maxim, an American engineer from Sangersville (Maine), developed it at the Vickers weapons firm in England in 1883. The Maxim was the prototype for many of the machine-gun designs that followed."

The soldiers of that time had been given a weapon that initially did not correspond to their fundamental role. Stopping to fire interrupted the soldier's advance on the battlefield and also impeded his rush to come to grips with the enemy which, at the time, was how battles were decided. The soldier of the nineteenth century saw the firing of weapons as a prelude to hand-to-hand combat and a means of weakening the enemy before beginning the same. The objective of every tactical move was always close combat.

It was not until the employment of massed armies—which reached its first high point during the First World War—that the regimented style of combat requiring long periods of training was discarded. For the first time the outcome of the fighting depended on masses of soldiers and not on highly trained close-in fighters. On the other hand, this gave impetus to improvements in firepower. Preparatory fire as practiced by the armies of Frederick the Great was not practical with armies of conscripts. This role was finally taken over by light field artillery, which showered the enemy with grape and canister shot.

New weapons developments, in particular the breach-loading rifle and its successor, the repeating rifle, which for the first time allowed soldiers to load and fire from a prone position, greatly increased the defensive power of the troops. The ability to fight from cover provided each defender with additional security. The term "possession of terrain" thus assumed a completely new tactical significance it had not had before. This presented the attacker with a new tactical problem: Destroying the enemy in his positions or driving him out of them.

What was required were additional tactical weapons that would enable attacking troops to do this. The solution to this new requirement was found in high-trajectory weapons, such as the mortar. The results of these developments saw two tactical possibilities markedly increase in capabilities: Now there were weapons which increased defensive firepower and others which increased offensive firepower. As weapons development continued, these differences became even more marked.

Frederick the Great summed up the principle in a simple maxim in his general principles: "Musket fire from the infantry serves the defensive. The bayonet is the offensive."

NEW LESSONS IN FIREPOWER AND TACTICS

The increase in range and rate of fire of rifles and the machine gun was not universally welcomed at first. The concept of achieving tactical success through fire was still not in the foreground of infantry thinking. The ultimate change from rifles to automatic weapons did not occur until the task of reloading was removed by weapons that functioned automatically. The Maxim machine gun and its descendants, which were tested in various colonial wars after 1871, revealed several new tactical lessons.

One of these was discovered and put into practice by the Boers in their war with England (1899–1902). The Boers understood how to make use of camouflage and the terrain. This rendered the British units—especially their machine guns, which went into open positions—ineffective. The Boers used very low carriages for their machine guns and employed their small number of automatic weapons in flanking positions in front of their lines. This tactical success by the Boers led Lord Kitchener to confess after his defeat at Paardenburg: "If I had known yesterday morning what I know today, I would not have attacked the Boers."

In this case, soldiers in well-camouflaged positions had been able to place accurate fire on the enemy without offering the latter a target. From the point of view of tactics, the Boers had discovered a new style of fighting.

In the Russo-Japanese War of 1904–5, on the other hand, both sides had been trained in the new principles and were organized and equipped with weapons suited to these principles. The results proved that the new tactics were more effective than anything seen in the past in increasing defensive capabilities. The Russian Army began the war with eighty-eight machine guns, a figure that eventually grew to 320. The Russians learned how effective their machine guns could be when the Japanese attacked near Wanshaopeng on 1 March 1905, when only two of these weapons halted the attackers just 200 meters from their objective. A Japanese battalion that ran into crossfire from Russian machine guns near Hatshenpu on 6 March 1905 lost more than 90 percent of its force within a few minutes.

Nevertheless, Russian troops made the same mistakes. During an assault by massed infantry near Salinpu, the 98th Infantry Regiment's 14th Company lost 149 of its 164 soldiers in five minutes. Such incidents demonstrated clearly that the machine gun had given armies a tremendous increase in defensive capability. Offensive tactics to counter that new threat lagged behind.

THE MACHINE GUN AS A TACTICAL WEAPON

In the years before the First World War the number of machine-gun companies in the German Army was increased. By the end of 1913 the Kaiser's army had 219 machine-gun companies, each with six machine guns. Each of the army's eleven cavalry divisions also possessed a machine-gun battalion. The total number of machine guns available was 3,500. Since the strategies of the European and other states at that time demanded a "vigorous offense" the question was whether tactical doctrine of the time would allow this objective to be reached given the quantitative increase in defensive capabilities. Army leaders were convinced that existing tactics would allow movement to be achieved and maintained. At the outset of the war one word was preeminent in both the German and French Armies: "Attack!" This produced the contradictory situation whereby the infantry, with its machine-gun companies, was powerfully armed for defense while its training was exclusively offensive in nature.

In the First World War the realities of the battlefield forced the decision. Tactics had to account for the ascendancy of firepower. The following example explains how this took place. In August 1914 the infantry of the opposing armies deployed in an effort to employ maximum battalion rifle power (the level at which such maneuver was measured). On average, there was one machine gun for every 500 men of an active regiment. By 1918 there was one machine gun for every twenty infantrymen. This constituted a twenty-five-fold increase in firepower. In four years of warfare, infantry tactics had become inextricably influenced by massed, automatic firepower. The machine gun had become the decisive infantry weapon, almost to the point of eliminating offensive warfare until new counteractive tactics could be developed.

The dramatic increase in the numbers of machine guns on both sides precluded the use of massed infantry on open battlefields as before. Commanders who failed to recognize this fact and continued to order attacks in dense formations were simply asking for terrible losses from the enemy. Just such a disaster befell a battalion of the French 42nd Division. On 25 September 1914 the French unit set out to attack the Ferme d'Algier and was completely wiped out by a small number of German machine guns. Colonel Gustav Döniker, a member of the Swiss General Staff and author of the instructive work, *Operation of Automatic Weapons within the Framework of Tactics*, observed that the "compact masses of troops were pulverized on the battlefield by the fire from the machine guns."

It was only natural that the tactics learned through experience at the front at a cost in blood were far in advance of theory. Not until all the experience gained on the battlefield had been evaluated could these practical lessons be integrated into the tactical manuals. Given adequate tactical preparation—dispositions, camouflage and fields of fire—the machine gun was a decisive weapon. The machine gun had demonstrated its advantages in a defensive role; all that remained was to find a way to use it in an offensive way.

Once the machine gun had replaced the rifle as the main weapon of the firefight, a way had to be found to employ it easily in the front line as well. The result was the light MG 08/15, which was nothing more than a lightened version of the Maxim machine gun. In spite of its low rate of fire—from three to eight rounds per burst—this light machine gun represented a significant advance. In the end, if not overnight, the light machine gun produced a revolution in infantry tactics. Now the machine gun could be carried into battle offensively and, for the first time, the two basic requirements for success—firepower and maneuver—were combined.

While the light machine-gun squads provided the firepower, the rifle squads embodied the maneuver element. Thus the union between infantry and machine guns that had long been missing had been achieved. From that point onwards the light machine gun would be considered the "foremost instrument of the firefight."

OTHER INFANTRY WEAPONS

During the First World War the infantryman was provided with another weapon, primarily for trench fighting: The machine pistol or submachine gun. Although its range was limited, the weapon was light and easy to use. If the light machine gun was the main firearm of the infantry, machine pistols and submachine guns were the favored weapons of squad and patrol leaders as well as trench fighters. Light machine guns were the primary source of firepower in platoons and companies, while machine pistols and pistols were weapons for close combat, especially trench fighting.

For fighting in areas where space was limited—in wooded areas or houses, for example—the submachine gun, pistol and hand grenade were indispensable. These three became the standard weapons of the junior officer and patrol member.

The first infantry manuals produced after the First World War placed great emphasis on battle tactics as they related to these weapons. One such manual stated: "The riflemen and light machine-gun squads advance under the covering fire of the heavy machine guns, then they open fire so that the heavy machine guns can follow and rejoin the firefight from closer range." As this manual was intended primarily for battalion commanders, the following instruction was included: "The function of the battalion commander goes beyond releasing weapons to subordinate units. He must lead himself, based on a base of created by him, which is to be moved forward step-by-step. He must ensure continuity of fire." More on the role of the battalion commander later.

It was soon realized that automatic weapons could not enable the attacker to cross the last 300 meters to an enemy trench or rifle pit. The infantry could not expect this of its machine-gun squads. The only weapon available to support the infantry during this final phase of the attack was at first the mine projector, later joined by the mortar. At first, however, these weapons were considered useful only for trench warfare.

Not until 1930 was there a change in philosophy, which assigned an offensive role to "high trajectory" weapons. It was decided that they possessed the necessary offensive power and could effectively support attacking infantry all the way. With this realization, which was incorporated into the service manuals, infantry weapons were organized as a cohesive whole according to a uniform fire plan and differentiated according to their various effects. High-trajectory weapons appeared at all levels of the infantry organization and overcame the machine-gun problem. The following was now considered tactically correct:

The machine-gun company provides the battalion commander with the ability to create a base of fire that can effectively support his unit in battle. With his machine guns the battalion commander commands the terrain in which his battalion's fight takes place. The covering fire of his machine guns creates the preconditions necessary for his riflemen.

A further innovation in battalion tactics resulted from the introduction of a weapon with which the commander of a rifle company could personally intervene in a battle. The weapon was the MG 34. Introduced by the German Army in 1934, it had been designed expressly for this purpose. The 7.9-mm weapon had a maximum range of 3,500 meters and was adopted as the standard machine gun. The MG 34 was assigned to every infantry unit and provided the company commander with a weapon with which he could eliminate minor pockets of resistance quickly. The MG 34 could also be used to engage low-flying enemy aircraft.

When the formation of machine-gun battalions began in 1934 the MG 34 was the weapon chosen; it was used in both the light and heavy roles. In 1939 the army reverted to machine-gun companies in an effort to simplify training. By the outbreak of war in 1939 automatic weapons—a 20-mm cannon had by now been added, primarily for antiaircraft purposes—had become integral elements of the army, and they were to play a major role in the fighting that followed. In order for any attacker to prevail, he first had to eliminate the enemy's machine-gun positions. For this reason, the training program placed great emphasis on engaging enemy machine guns.

To further increase its offensive power the infantry was provided with light artillery pieces—referred to as infantry guns—and light and heavy mortars. Developments in weapons technology dictated rapid changes in tactics, but there were other factors that necessitated doctrinal revision during World War Two. Among these were the rapidly increased speed of movement through motorization, the increase in the firepower of motorcycle units through the addition of armored personnel carriers and trucks and, finally, armored units.

These made a war of movement a necessity and thus dictated the tactics to be used. In addition, there was the dramatically increased speed with which information was transmitted resulting from the advent of radio and the teletype, the general use of motor vehicles and the special air transport of troops and supplies, right up to the transport of parachute troops—an army from the air. In the words of Major General Fuller these were "a revolution in tactics." All of this resulted in an increase in the caliber of automatic weapons to 40 mm, which once again resulted in new tactical possibilities for this class of weapon.

From a tactical standpoint there were three classes of infantry weapons at the beginning of the Second World War. One consisted of individual automatic and semiautomatic weapons wielded by individual soldiers. These were hand-fired weapons like the pistol, submachine gun, semiautomatic rifle and automatic rifle.

The second class of automatic weapons was referred to as crew-served weapons. These embodied the firepower of several rifles, but had to be served by several men. In this group it was the light machine gun that dominated the battle in the front lines. The infantry squads assembled around them as a "battle cell," whose role it was to move forward with its weapons and bring them to bear on the enemy. Farther back were the light and heavy machine guns mounted on carriages. By laying down preparatory fire these enabled the rifle squads to attack and then provide covering and supporting fire once the attack was underway.

The third class of infantry weaponry fell into a special-purpose category. These included such weapons as automatic cannon for defense against armored vehicles and aircraft, antitank rifles for antitank defense in the front lines within a rifle company, and super-heavy machine guns. Other weapons, such as flamethrowers and mines, were generally employed by the combat engineers and are not included here.

PISTOLS AND SUBMACHINE GUNS

The pistol is a close-combat weapon. All the requirements in its design flow from this. It must be able to engage human targets from close range to fifty meters. Its effect must be immediate, rendering the enemy unable to fight immediately after being hit. Thus it is not the severity of the wound that is important, rather the immediacy of the effects of a hit. The enemy must be rendered incapable of action at the moment the bullet strikes, no matter where he is hit.

This means that the bullet must strike the target with such force that he is knocked down straight away. This requirement eliminates small-caliber weapons. The minimum caliber to achieve the desired effect is 7.65 mm. Moreover, the weapon must be light and easy to handle and aim. Its dimensions must be such that it can be carried on the belt.

The 08/38 pistol, or *Parabellum*, with a caliber of 9-mm, was the standard pistol of the First and Second World Wars. The primary requirement, which outweighs all others, is that the weapon's safety can be released and the pistol fired quickly. Also important is a high rate of fire after the first round is fired.

The standard German pistol was designed as a self-loading weapon with a high rate of fire. It was equipped with a relatively large ammunition clip. Further developments in close-range weapons resulted in the fully automatic pistol. It was built for close combat and its caliber allowed it to fill this role. But there was still a requirement for a weapon with a high rate of fire that could fire in single-shot or automatic modes. The result was the submachine gun, a development of the pistol that used the same ammunition as the latter.

The submachine gun of the First World War, which used 7.9-mm ammunition, was generally superseded by the MP 40. This weapon fired 9-mm pistol ammunition, and its thirty-two-round magazine allowed for a high rate of fire.

THE MACHINE GUN IN ACTION

The nature of the terrain in which combat is to take place is of vital importance in the use of automatic weapons. The primary considerations in selecting a position are camouflage and cover and a location that provides a good field of fire. Other aspects of an optimal selection of positions include the possibility of catching the enemy with flanking fire, as well as laying down enfilade fire to support advancing infantry and eliminate enemy positions. The concept of enfilade fire is not connected with predetermined targets as is flanking fire. Rather it relates to a tactical situation as it exists at that moment. In enfilade fire the weapons are employed to fire to the sides rather than towards the front. Enfilade fire allows even wide fronts to be barricaded by a relatively small number of weapons. This means that weapons providing enfilade fire must be situated far to the front; they do not fire for themselves, but in support of an attacking neighbor.

THE FACE OF WARFARE TODAY

The face of warfare, as the introduction clearly showed, is subject to continuous change. It is determined by the advent of new weaponry and means of delivery, which means that it has no fixed form. This explains why every state in the world strives to keep pace with the latest developments in military technology, even when the major powers find themselves at peace.

The same requirement applies to everyone: To be able to meet any eventuality in the event of war. A nation that ignores this requirement will stand no chance in a future war which, in spite of the prevailing peace, might come at any time.

In German military circles it was recognized early on that there was no such thing as a limited war. The object was always the same: Victory! The means used to achieve it were almost irrelevant. Carl von Clausewitz made this clear: "War is an act of force. There are no limits in the use of the same. Everyone dictates to the other. This creates a reciprocal action which, according to its conception, must lead to the extreme."

The Second World War proved this clearly: The concept of "total war", the use of terror bombing on both sides, the demands for unconditional surrender and the dropping of atomic bombs on Hiroshima and Nagasaki, to cite just a few instances.

The means of self-preservation that every state in the world has are its armed forces and its weaponry. These should be operationally ready and capable if they are to deter aggression. Soldiers must be recruited and trained and provided with the best possible weapons and leaders so as to be ready to fight should their nation be attacked.

The objective of the national defense forces of every nation is to be successful in all types of combat against an attacking enemy. Second World War experience showed that massed armored forces have to be met by in-depth defenses of antitank weapons and tanks. Such a defense can prevent rapid breakthroughs and the battles of encirclement that follow.

The main element of a national defense is a home-defense force to protect the nation's borders from surprise attack. These illustrate the importance of the infantry and its weapons. Large infantry formations must be equal to the demands of any style of fighting. They must be able to master every type of weapon no matter what the conditions.

COMMAND PRINCIPLES: FROM LARGE FORMATIONS TO THE BATTALION

One of the main principles of command must be to retain or acquire free-dom of action. A commander must seize the initiative and never allow himself to be forced into the enemy's style of fighting. Strategic objectives set by the supreme command must be achieved tactically and operationally with the minimum possible losses. Superior speed in carrying out an assignment is vital in reaching an objective with minimum losses. Speed does not mean undue haste, however, but mobility in battle and rapid headway in terrain. Under the heading of mobility also falls the ability to change fighting styles quickly and safely, to concentrate all forces for the assault or to spread out for an advance into unfamiliar territory.

Periods of rest are absolutely necessary in order to preserve the strik-ing power of the troops at all times. Unnecessary heavy burdens placed on the troops result in a reduction in their fighting power in battle and are to be avoided. Reconnaissance is to be carried out at regular intervals so as to have a clear picture of the battlefield at all times and to be aware of the enemy's strength, disposition and positions. Reports and messages must be sent to the command post by radio or motorcycle dispatch rider for evaluation. Should a unit find itself pinned down it is vital to immediately take advantage of any available cover and dig in. "Sweat saves blood!" was the adage of the German forces in the Second World War. Fighting and marching by night offers better protection than by day. As the enemy also knows this, it is important to remain in contact with him or at least scout far in advance.

Terrain, the mission and the enemy situation determine command decisions in battle. The deployment of friendly forces must match these conditions. If it is to be successful, each firefight must be initiated as quickly as possible, based solely on information obtained through reconnaissance.

Each attack requires a point of main effort—a *Schwerpunkt*. The *Schwerpunkt* is created through the weighted use of firepower and maneuver forces, the timely employment of reserves, the allocation of necessary logistical support and the use of the combat-support elements, such as the air force. These elements were combined successfully by the Germans in the six great battles of encirclement during the first year of the eastern campaign.

All assigned missions must allow the lower levels of command room for freedom of action and responsibility and leave the manner in which the mission is carried out to the subordinate commander, whether the commander of a battalion or a company. Under this concept of the *Auftragstaktik*—mission-type orders—the responsible higher-level commander does not intervene unless the success of the mission he has assigned appears to be in jeopardy. In doing so he must be fully aware that every mission assigned by him must be capable of being accomplished. Any deviation from this unalterable requirement endangers the troops. Should a commander be put out of action in battle, every other available commander or leader must be prepared to act on his own initiative and assume command on the battlefield. The senior commander's intent must be known down all levels of the chain-of-command.

When the conditions under which a mission was assigned change, the responsible commander must modify or rescind the mission, even if he does not have the agreement of his superiors. In doing so the new commander bears the responsibility for his orders. It is a military prerequisite that every decision and directive should be based on an assessment of the situation. A commander must assess his own mission to determine what is required and how best to carry it out in the spirit of those who issued the orders. The officer who has been tasked requires an analytical mind and must know his business; he must attend the prerequisite professional-development courses and know how to translate military theory into practical results. He must assess his own situation as honestly as that of the enemy.

A commander must always assume that the enemy will select the course of action that is most disadvantageous to his own intentions. In this regard it is absolutely imperative that he know the enemy's command principles and never assume that the enemy will choose an incorrect course of action. Reconnoitering of terrain is part of an accurate assessment of the situation. The primary concerns are the terrain's suitability for the movement of men and vehicles and its potential for antitank defense and the creation of various ambush positions. Each leader's role in the battlefield reconnaissance plan must be clearly spelled out, should not be overly complicated and, above all, be practical.

It is a well-known fact that the situation can change rapidly prior to the beginning of an operation. For this reason a commander's assessment of the situation must be continually evaluated and expanded, allowing him to determine whether and when new decisions must be made. Only in this way can the battle plan be adapted to suit changing requirements. It is necessary that this reassessment of the situation be carried out by all leaders, right down to a patrol leader in the front lines. He must modify his decisions as the situation changes.

ASSESSMENT OF THE ENEMY SITUATION AND THE TERRAIN

The assessment of the enemy is made following the situation evaluation, which records all reports on the enemy. In estimating time, a value must always be used which is most favorable for the enemy. In addition to statements by prisoners, an assessment of the enemy's intentions is based on radio and telephone intercepts. Identified enemy units must be considered as fully operational, even when doubts exist. Each analyst must know the situation, fighting style and command principles of the enemy; this is absolutely necessary if an accurate assessment is to be made. In addition, there is the assessment of the options open to the enemy: His defensive strength and ability to counterattack, as well as the disposition of his defensive weapons. Also of importance are the enemy's suspected intentions—reinforced by statements from prisoners and communications intercepts.

Bearing in mind the options open to the enemy, it is vital to calculate the most probable action or reaction and to recognize diversionary measures as such. Further hints as to the way in which the enemy will proceed may be provided by the terrain, the weather and the enemy's style of fighting.

An assessment of the terrain, the importance of which has already been referred to, is also of significance to the decision-making process of one's own leaders. Evaluation of the terrain is a significant aspect of good tactical decision making. It is achieved through maps, information brought back by patrols and through the evaluation of photographs taken by army tactical reconnaissance aircraft. A personal inspection of the terrain is often of decisive importance. A leader's reconnaissance is the only sure way to determine current information on the terrain such as the state of the ground cover and conditions and the weather and its effects. A thorough personal reconnaissance of the terrain can also provide keys to the likely intentions of the enemy. Various types of terrain assessment are made. Terrain is analyzed for its effect on the movement of personnel and equipment; it is also analyzed to determine offensive and defensive courses of action.

Auftragstaktik was the means by which every leader translated into action the will of his superior. Its mastery was a must for all military leaders of the Reichswehr and the Wehrmacht. It was generally practiced as envisioned until 1942, before Hitler started micromanaging first operations and then even tactics. As in any bureaucracy, micro-management then tends to cascade downward.

Generaloberst Hans von Seeckt, Chief of Staff of the Reichswehr from March 1920 until October 1926, paraphrased the concept of *Auftragstaktik* as follows: "Mission-type orders means assigning the objective to be reached, providing the necessary means to do so but allowing complete freedom of action for the execution of the mission." This is based on the healthy notion that the one who bears the responsibility for its success must also choose the way in which it is achieved. Just as avoiding responsibility is the sign of a small mind, taking on a responsibility to which one is not equal is an overestimation of one's own capabilities.

The latter applies directly to Adolf Hitler who, in the decisive phase of the Second World War, cancelled the valid principle of the *Auftragstaktik* and variations on this theme and intervened personally in the control of individual units. As a result, flexibility of command was lost. Moreover, there were commanders who imitated this sad example and who intervened in the jurisdiction of subordinate leaders with the same negative results.

MARCH AND MARCH SPEED

In the march column, and in the movement of individual groups as well, the units moved forward with various intervals between vehicles. A march serial was a collection of several march groups. During offensive operations, another type of unit was employed—the advance guard. It was usually formed on an ad hoc basis from the available elements of a larger formation—a division or a brigade—and moved ahead of the main formation to ensure the main body was not surprised by the enemy or reach and secure important objectives far ahead of the main formation. Reaching a bridge and preventing it from being destroyed or establishing contact with encircled forces and relieving them are but two examples of missions assigned to an advance guard.

The sequence of forces within a march unit depended on its planned purpose. Establishing the direction of the march was the job of the leading march group, which was usually a company-sized element. In turn this group assigned forces to form the point. The larger formation was assigned an avenue of approach if contact was expected. It generally followed a main road or secondary roads as the situation demanded. The choice of the road within the avenue of approach was left up to the unit commander or march-unit leader. The order to deploy spread out the units and raised their combat readiness. This action was initiated by the battalion commander, while the type of deployment formation (wedge, inverted wedge, etc.) was determined by the company commanders.

If required, deployment could be made from a march formation, whereby the individual platoons of companies came to full battle readiness. The platoon leaders issued this command, so as to be able to initiate combat as quickly as possible in the specified formation.

During an extended motorized march technical halts were made to check the condition of the vehicles, refuel and repair minor damage. If a preliminary engagement had taken place it was also used to replenish ammunition stocks. There were also rest stops planned for the men, which were supposed to last at least two hours. No rest stops were planned for marches of less than six hours duration.

German Army Service Regulation 100/1 prescribed that "the situation must be assessed before a march" since "a chance engagement must be anticipated at any time." During the latter part of the Second World War the Russians emulated several characteristics of German doctrine. In particular they were able to improve their method of advance. In later years they advanced with open flanks, by day and night, especially after finding gaps in the German front or after breaching the same, resulting in penetrations they tried to expand into breakthroughs. For this purpose the Red Army sent fast, powerful reconnaissance units up to twenty-five kilometers ahead of their main forces. These consisted of reconnaissance and rifle units, supported by artillery and tanks and often by combat engineers and amphibious tanks as well.

THE ATTACK AND ITS MAIN CHARACTERISTICS

Attacks are generally divided into two categories: The immediate attack and the deliberate attack. An immediate attack is launched during a movement to contact and the enemy situation is unclear. A deliberate attack follows more deliberate planning measures and where the enemy situation is more defined. Both could be directed against the enemy's front, flank or rear.

In an outflanking operation the attacking forces strove to encircle the enemy forces in order to subsequently destroy them. The main attack was preceded by a diversionary attack or a secondary attack that served to divert attention from the main attack or establish more favorable conditions for the launching of the main attack. This fighting style was later also practiced by the Soviets, in particular during the Lake Ladoga battles and in the fighting in Courland.

On the German side the secondary attack often took the form of an attack with limited objectives. Examples of this were the preliminary attacks by the two German pincers of Operation "Citadel", whose purpose was to achieve favorable starting positions for the main attacks. Tying down and deceiving the enemy were the functions of the diversionary attack.

A multitude of basic requirements had to be considered in planning an attack. These included: the point of concentration (*Schwerpunkt*), the type and location of reserves, the disposition and deployment of forces, the attack groups, the combat sectors, and the areas of responsibility.

Preparatory fires before the beginning of an infantry or armored attack served to prevent the enemy from responding in an organized fashion, to pin him down or to destroy his forces. In this respect, the Red Army reached its height of proficiency in the final two years of the war, having improved its arms and tactics accordingly. Sometimes attacks are carried out without any preparatory fires in order to maximize the element of surprise, since the enemy generally expects to get shelled prior to being attacked.

The purpose of the attack was to eliminate the enemy as a threat, seize territory or force the enemy to fall back. Where the objective was to break through the enemy's front, forces were generally concentrated for a massed assault. In a battle of encirclement the enemy was pinned down frontally and outflanked on both sides.

When armored support was on hand, infantry or mechanized infantry (*Panzergrenadiere*) attacked in front of and between the tanks. The tanks provided supporting fire, with the interests and objectives of the grenadiers having priority. In the event that contact was lost during such an attack, the tanks called a halt until the troops had caught up and reassembled. In the case of a mounted attack, on the other hand, close battle order was maintained during the approach phase, which lasted until the attack force was close to the objective.

When a river or other body of water had to be crossed, the attack against the enemy-held shore was launched immediately after the completion of pre-attack preparations and was pursued with great speed and vigor. Armored forces provided support from the near shore whenever possible and were moved across as soon as the far bank had been secured by the assaulting infantry. Having crossed to the other side, the infantry had to engage the enemy forces straight away and without waiting to deploy fully. After the crossing by the first wave it was important to maintain the momentum of the attack and expand the bridgehead quickly. In the event of a counterattack, air and artillery forces began an immediate bombardment of the enemy's jumping-off positions.

An attack by night or in conditions of poor visibility increased the chances of success but also increased the chances of something going wrong due to command and control problems.

Contact with enemy forces was automatically expected when moving units through wooded terrain. The larger and more dense the forest, the greater the difficulties. Orientation was made more difficult and, in some cases, impossible, and the probability of ambush from well-concealed enemy positions was increased. In such cases the leading assault group was also responsible for battlefield reconnaissance.

The initiative of the junior officers became a decisive factor in attacks on towns and villages. An attack of this type was conducted in conjunction with forces positioned outside the town. Frontal attacks were avoided, and the presence of well-concealed snipers was anticipated. The tactics of envelopment and encirclement assured success with a minimum of casualties. Larger towns were encircled before the attack began. A quick strike by an advance unit with the support of armored units was one way of guaranteeing a rapid victory.

When the enemy had prepared defenses, pre-attack preparations had to be made. The following details had to be worked out: defeat/elimination of combat outposts, entering the outskirts of the built-up area, break-in into the town and the interior of same, clearing of houses and other buildings.

Such an attack was carried out sector by sector, block by block. Intermediate objectives included prominent buildings, intersections, railway installations and bridges. Attacks against such objectives were mostly carried out by assault groups. The advance of the latter was supported by the infiltration of small groups of soldiers over hills, through gardens, parks and narrow streets or alleys. Each of the forward groups was given heavy weapons. If needed, antitank, assault gun and tank platoons were attached as well. All entrances/exits from the town were to be engaged by tanks, which then moved into the town. Further tanks or antitank guns were kept ready to repel counterattacks.

Costly house-to-house fighting, which was often unavoidable, sometimes had to be conducted floor by floor and room by room. Other units guarded the flanks and rear of the forward assault groups.

The attack, which was regarded by the Reichswehr as the most important type of combat, led to the following directive to the units in the Soviet field regulations: "The attack is the Red Army's main battle tactic!" In fact, every decisive battle of the Second World War was won by the attack or counterattack. This tenet was also anchored in the basic principles of the German Army: "Only the attack can decide the battle!" (See German Army Regulation 101/1). The same regulation assigns equal importance to the counterattack: "The enemy's forces are to be smashed by counterattack!"

The experiences of the Second World War showed that attacks carried out with speed are the most successful and have the lowest casualty rates. The attack tempo of all large operations increased greatly between 1939 and 1945. The German concept of *Blitzkrieg* grew out of this demand for the quickest possible decision with minimum losses.

It is self-evident that the advances in motorization made a significant contribution to the increase in attack tempo. However, the fast movement of troops should never be allowed to become an end in itself. Its purpose is to create favorable conditions that allow the attacker to dictate the terms of engagement and employ the element of surprise. A surprise assault, conducted with speed, prevents the enemy from employing countermeasures in time to frustrate the attack.

This style of warfare demands several absolutely necessary prerequisites. First, the troops must be highly trained, so that they can maneuver and deploy quickly. They must have mastered the art of changing from mounted to dismounted combat, if they are mechanized infantry. The commander of the vehicle that is to carry the riflemen must be a tactically well-trained leader equipped with reliable communications with which to stay in contact with his superiors.

A fast attack also makes necessary fast reconnaissance. The skilled use of patrols is absolutely indispensable in finding gaps and holes in the enemy's front, which must be exploited in the course of the attack. Independent action by all leaders and the acceptance of open flanks played a decisive role in attacks and counterattacks. Standing opposite this main tactical maxim was the defense against enemy attacks, which was accorded equal importance. It was expected that the enemy would counterattack with all available forces, including local reserves, in an attempt to throw the attacker out of the positions he had won and halt his attack spearheads before a breakthrough was achieved.

It was thus of vital importance for the attack commander to know whether enemy movements involved an immediate counterattack, a local counterattack or an offensive. All relevant reports received by the commander had to be evaluated quickly but accurately. It was especially important that he prevent the attack from bogging down, which had the effect of hurting morale and making more difficult to get the attack rolling again. It was therefore imperative that enemy counterattacks be smashed immediately through concentrated fire. This was the quickest and most effective means of defending against the same.

Only when this fire proved ineffective did it become necessary to assign tank, mechanized infantry and antitank units the task of fighting off the enemy counterattack.

PURSUIT AND DEFENSE

The concept of pursuit envisaged the exploitation of the initial success gained by an attack. The attack turned into a pursuit whenever the enemy was incapable of putting up an organized defense. The pursuing forces remained close on the heels of the enemy and pursuit was maintained until they were destroyed. As a result, the pursuit was a very fluid form of battle.

The movements of the pursuing forces had to be coordinated in order to prevent the pursuit from bogging down, which would allow the enemy to regroup or flee. The object of the pursuit was to turn the enemy's retreat into a wild flight and bring about a total breakdown of order, which in itself made possible the total destruction of the enemy.

An energetic pursuit made it impossible for the enemy to stand his ground or organize a defense. Overtaking the enemy on both sides guaranteed his encirclement or capture. Any fresh resistance was to be broken as quickly as possible. Close air support was a valuable asset in that case. Deep advances were to be used for undertaking the pursuit; task-organized motorized units were preferred, as these were faster than standard units. Any resistance that flared up on the flanks or front was to be smashed by the artillery.

Commanders were taught to always accompany the forward units so as to be able to intervene personally. They could control the movement of the pursuing forces and direct operations better from the front. Once initiated, pursuit could only be halted on orders from the unit commander.

The defense had other requirements. In a fixed defense, it was vital to secure the defensive area to all sides and establish rear boundaries and blocking positions, before which the enemy could be engaged and halted.

The surest way to hold a defensive area was to defend from strongpoints. These strongpoints could be up to 150 meters wide and 80 meters in depth if fully manned. Each strongpoint was manned by a platoon of infantry or mechanized infantry. As antitank defense was of decisive significance to a successful defense, strongpoints had to be powerfully armed so as to be capable of dealing with armored attacks by the enemy.

Within the defensive area itself there were several methods of defense. These included defense through delaying tactics, the all-round defense and, the most difficult, fighting and holding at any cost, which carried the risk of the possible destruction of the entire strongpoint.

Unit or higher headquarters reserves were used to seal off breakthroughs or conduct immediate counterattacks. Immediate counterattacks were intended to destroy or drive back enemy forces that had penetrated the defender's main line of resistance before they could be reinforced. Counterattacks stood the best chance of success if they were carried out immediately after the enemy penetration, striking the enemy while he was at his weakest.

Ensuring that the artillery knew exactly how and where it was to fire was part of the defensive commander's job, which also included selecting suitable positions for the antitank weapons and field artillery.

The defense, whose purpose was to halt the enemy attack in the defensive area and destroy strong enemy forces in the process, was therefore a battle for territory. The defensive commander thus had to think in all-round terms, ensure that his flanks were secure and deploy his forces in depth. The most favorable defensive position was one where the enemy had to cross an obstacle, whether natural or manmade, in order to attack. This gave the defenders an excellent chance of halting the enemy, because is attacking momentum was inevitably slowed down by the obstacle. If the enemy succeeded in breaking through a point in the line, it was vital to seal off the penetration point and then destroy those forces that had broken through.

The Russian Campaign demonstrated that linear thinking in fixed fronts, as was practiced in the First World War, still had its place within the framework of the defense. The Maginot Line, the *Westwall*, the Atlantic Wall and the Stalin Line are all eloquent examples of this.

It was the infantry that bore the main burden in such positional warfare. A large number of the infantry "aces" distinguished themselves in such positions and sectors. One thing should not be forgotten, however:

Only the attack could ensure the destruction of the enemy's ground forces.

The attack remained the foremost battle tactic. It was, with few exceptions, carried out while on the move. Premature massing of forces could be spotted by the enemy's air force. That provided with the enemy with valuable intelligence information or allowed him to interdict and possibly destroy the massed forces. It was better to have forces mass at the last moment, even if infinitely more difficult from a command and control perspective, then to have them bunched together and an inviting target for the enemy. Despite that, there were numerous instances where offensives were launched with a prior and unmistakable massing for forces (e.g., Operation Citadel or the Soviet offensives at Orel and Kursk).

Defensive ideas were partly discarded in the face of the rapid pace of the motorization of armies during the Second World War and the total mechanization of divisions. Mobile forces had to fight on the move if they were to fulfil their purpose. Maneuver warfare was the product of World War Two; it has been employed ever since.

THE PLACE OF ARTILLERY ON THE BATTLEFIELD

Although not directly related to the theme of infantry "aces", a few lines will be devoted to the use of artillery. It was an integral part of an infantry division and played a vital role in relieving enemy pressure on units and formations and enabling them to advance.

The role of the artillery—the decisive player in the firefight—was to decimate the enemy's forces and to achieve and maintain fire superiority over the enemy in order to destroy his ability to resist. The artillery conducted the firefight over great distances. Organization, equipment and training, and the range and caliber of its weapons, enabled it to quickly change the focus of its fire. The artillery conducted the firefight in all situations and types of battle and was most effective when employed in mass. Forward observers provided the information necessary for accurate fire. The artillery commander controlled the fire of divisions, the senior artillery commander that of corps and armies.

The artillery's equipment ranged from light to super-heavy guns. Joining the various howitzers, cannon and field guns during the course of World War Two were the so-called *DO-Werfer* (a type of rocket launcher) and heavy howitzers or siege guns (such as the German *Thor* with a caliber of 600 mm).

In the German Army the commander of the artillery at division and higher level was called the *Artillerieführer*. In the case of a division, he was also the commanded of the division's artillery regiment.

The *Artillerieführer* advised the appropriate formation commander during the planning and actual conduct of the fight. He made suggestions as to how his batteries should be employed and directed fires after preparing his forces to carry out the missions given them by the divisional commander. The artillery was capable of fulfilling a broad range of roles. It might be called upon to lay down barrage fire to halt an enemy attack, eliminate enemy observation posts, engage enemy artillery, or bombard the enemy assembly areas.

Other possible missions were pinning down the enemy for a certain time and the destruction of installations of importance to the enemy, such as bridges, villages or bridgeheads. The primary concern of the artillery commander was to coordinate his fire with the movement of the unit. Artillery fire could not be permitted to interfere with the movement of friendly forces. On the other hand, troop movements could not be allowed to limit the artillery in its engagement of the enemy.

Achieving and maintaining fire superiority over the enemy was a primary objective. A fully functional telephone system was an absolutely vital requirement for effective fire control and a successful firefight. This was necessary not only for the transmission of reconnaissance and target information, but for control of the firefight as well. This placed great demands on the field telephone unit, which had to be prepared to go into the field at any time to repair severed lines.

The artillery commander had to carry out the missions given him by the divisional commander. His firing plan had to be tailored to the needs of the division. The commander specified when, where and for how long the artillery was to fire.

Munitions planning and deliveries were of vital importance to a sustained bombardment and were one of the main considerations of the artillery commander. Occasionally, the artillery was called upon to go into action while on the move, and thus had to be capable of moving into position and opening fire as rapidly as possible. This required proper positioning within the march column, and it was the job of the artillery commander to provide advice to the commander in that regard. Further, it was important to position part of the artillery far to the front and in the most important march group. Artillery observers or artillery liaison detachments were supposed to be installed at the head of every march group. Above all, observers for the long-range guns were supposed to move at the head of the march unit.

The need for fire and maneuver in the attack also applied to the artillery, and the artillery commander had to anticipate the most effective use of his assets at decisive locations. The artillery was of special significance when used in a defensive role, where strong artillery forces with a high rate of expenditure of ammunition were required. The aim of the artillery in a defensive role was to pin down the enemy and destroy his offensive power to the degree possible. That created the conditions necessary for his destruction by one's own ground forces. The artillery was to open fire at the earliest possible moment, so that the enemy was engaged and weakened at great range. This firefight had to be conducted actively and flexibly during the entire defensive battle in order to inflict maximum losses on the enemy in men, weapons and equipment and break his attacking strength. These principles applied to enemy penetrations and breakthroughs as well as delaying actions and during a pursuit.

ANTITANK DEFENSE BY ARMOR AND INFANTRY DIVISIONS

The success of the German Army in penetrating deep into Russia during the first months of the campaign against the Soviet Union in 1941 was due in large part to the tactical principles employed by the tank and mechanized infantry divisions.

In the first phase of the Eastern Campaign, German infantry in trucks and armored personnel carriers (*Schützenpanzerwagen,* or abbreviated SPW) quickly drove deep into the country and amassed worthwhile experience in battle. The discovery that infantry mounted in SPW could keep pace with the tanks in good terrain and thus roll up the front with them and achieve deep penetrations and breakthroughs while providing protection for the tanks provided the impetus for new operational possibilities. It resulted in the addition of a mechanized infantry battalion being reorganized from an existing truck-borne motorized infantry battalion in each tank division. The mechanized infantry battalions were used to protect the tank spearheads. Their task was to defend against enemy forces approaching to destroy the tanks.

On 5 July 1942 all motorized rifle regiments were redesignated as mechanized infantry regiments, even if they possessed no SPW or only one battalion with them. The effectiveness of the SPW-mounted mechanized infantry and their increased capabilities grew more obvious from month to month. Principles for the command of mechanized infantry formations were developed and tactical doctrine formulated. In the words of an influential tank expert, a mechanized infantry commander had to be "flexible and farsighted." (See Oskar Munzel in *Die deutschen gepanzerten Truppen, 1934 bis 1945.*)

During the Second World War the number of tanks was always disproportionately low compared to the number of available army divisions. As a result, each army division also had at its disposal an antitank battalion

(*Panzerabwehr-Abteilung* and later the *Panzerjäger-Abteilung*). Each infantry regiment also had an organic an antitank company. But these were not enough to deal with the vast numbers of tanks available to the Red Army, so separate army antitank battalions were formed and equipped with heavy tank destroyers.

In addition there were the assault-gun battalions (*Sturmgeschütz-Abteilungen*). They were later redesignated as brigades, although their effective end strength remained about the same, about forty assault guns. In addition to their primary role of providing the infantry with mobile artillery support, the assault guns came to be increasingly used in the antitank role, in which they achieved great success.

The most important German handheld antitank weapons were the *Panzerfaust* and the *Ofenrohr* (literally "stovepipe"). Both weapons fired a shaped high-explosive round about 100 meters; the latter resembled the American bazooka, from which it was reverse engineered. The squad or platoon leader assigned the *Panzerfaust* operator his target, ensuring that each fired at his tank. If tanks appeared without warning it was left to the initiative of the individual *Panzerfaust* operator to open fire when the prospects for success appeared certain.

Panzerfaust-equipped groups were capable of bringing massed armored attacks to a halt by themselves. Like the soldier armed with an *Ofenrohr* or an antitank rifle, a man with a *Panzerfaust* was a close-range fighter who exposed himself not only to the direct fire of the tanks he sought to engage but that of their escorting infantry as well. By war's end, the *Panzerfaust* had become ubiquitous and provided the Germans with an effective, close-in antitank weapon.

COMBAT ENGINEERS (PIONEERS) AND TACTICS

This section concerns the operations of the pioneers, whose ranks produced many winners of the Knight's Cross. Pioneers supported other units and arms in every engagement and in every type of fighting environment. They facilitated the forward progress of the combat forces by breaching and clearing obstacles and increased their combat power. They limited enemy movements and weakened the combat power of the enemy's forces.

Special combat-engineer roles included the laying of minefields and individual mines, the placing of explosive charges on bridges and other important objects, the clearing of enemy minefields and the laying of bridges. For any pioneer operation the presence of the necessary materials was a necessary precondition for the fulfillment of the assigned mission.

Other pioneer roles included helping infantry units negotiate difficult obstacles and augmenting natural obstacles against the enemy. The setting up of barricades and the destruction of road junctions and railway installations were also matters for the pioneers, as were the construction of forward airfields and the creation of camouflage and decoy installations. The restoration of logistical capacity was another important task.

In addition, the combat engineers conducted demolitions of all types and eliminated enemy barricades. They also cleared lanes through enemy minefields and barbed wire entanglements. It was the responsibility of combat engineers to prepare waterways for both contested and uncontested crossings.

It is obvious from this brief description of the roles of the pioneers that their employment was necessary at the company level. As dictated by their mission requirements, the pioneers were always employed at the front. The senior engineer of a division, corps or higher organization was also usually the commander of the respective engineer formation.

THE BATTALION AS THE FOCAL POINT OF THE INFANTRY BATTLE: AN OVERVIEW

The battalion was the focal point of the infantry battle. In their paper on tactics within the framework of the reinforced infantry battalion, Generalleutnant Heinrich Greiner (later director of the Regulations Section with the general in charge of infantry of the Army High Command) and his colleague Generalmajor Joachim Degener created a set of rules which were especially valid during the Second World War. Several extracts have been taken from this to illustrate to the reader the responsibilities of the various positions within the infantry battalion.

An early-war infantry battalion consisted of four infantry companies (with company headquarters sections), a battalion headquarters (with a headquarters section), the signals section, an antitank-rifle squad and a medical squad. Each battalion also included a machine-gun company, a heavy mortar platoon, an infantry combat-engineer platoon and the combat and field trains.

The battalion commander led the unit in battle, assisted by his adjutant. If the battalion commander was put out of action, the adjutant immediately notified the senior company commander, who took over command of the battalion. The commander of the signals section employed his communications equipment according to orders issued by the battalion commander and maintained contact with regiment and division. The battalion medical officer set up the forward dressing station on orders from the battalion commander. His orderlies and medics provided first aid to the sick and wounded and saw to it that they were evacuated to hospital.

Decisions by the battalion commander were made with the tactical employment of his unit in mind. Before he made these decisions he had to evaluate the situation and factor his mission into this evaluation. He also had to assess the enemy's situation and the terrain. The decisions made by him after weighing all these factors had to answer the questions: What do I want to achieve and how do I wish to achieve it?

The battalion commander had to ensure fire and movement were harmonized. The rifle companies were to be employed in the best possible way according to the nature of the terrain. The battalion commander never sent all his heavy machine guns forward; instead, he always held back some for special employment. Every opportunity for fire support by the machine-gun company was exploited. Elements of the machine-gun company followed close behind the rifle units. They supported the infantry but were not attached to it. Other elements of the machine-gun company followed the progress of the battle from positions in the rear.

The heavy mortar platoon was the battalion commander's own artillery asset. It enabled him to give the infantry supporting fire without endangering them, even when they were close to the objective. By employing mortar fire it was possible to drive the enemy from cover and effectively engage machine-gun positions so they could be taken by the infantry.

In each regiment was a light infantry-gun platoon. It supported the regiment's battalions and served as an organic artillery arm of the regiment.

It was the responsibility of the antitank platoon to protect the battalion against enemy tank attack. The antitank guns were used in platoon strength or singly according to the situation. The guns were either emplaced in concealed positions ready to fire or were kept limbered and ready to be moved elsewhere to meet a potential threat.

The signals section kept the battalion commander in contact with all the units in the battalion. Each senior command position was supposed to establish communication with lower level commanders, but this did not prevent the battalion commander from making contact with his superiors if communications were lost.

The unit dressing station had to be positioned far enough to the rear to place it beyond the range of the enemy's infantry weapons and, if possible, outside the range of his artillery. On the other hand, it had to be easily reached by the battalion, and a location on a passable road was advantageous for the rapid evacuation of the wounded.

The combat trains were also supposed to be set up beyond the range of enemy fire and out of sight. At the same time they needed to be close enough to the fighting units to ensure speedy delivery of ammunition and food to the troops.

The good battalion commander was always in the thick of things. He led from the front. By setting the example, he inspired his soldiers to do their duty and more. In some cases, a soldier rose to become an "infantry ace."

Index

Page numbers in italics indicates illustrations.